11/K

Martin Classical Lectures
Volume XXVI

The Martin Classical Lectures are delivered
annually at Oberlin College on a foundation
established by his many friends in honor of
Charles Beebe Martin, for forty-five
years a teacher of classical literature
and classical art in Oberlin.

Tragedy and Civilization
An Interpretation of Sophocles

Charles Segal

Published for Oberlin College by

Harvard University Press
Cambridge, Massachusetts, and London, England

1981

Library of Congress Cataloging in Publication Data

Segal, Charles, 1936–
    Tragedy and civilization.

    (Martin classical lectures; v. 26)
    Bibliography: p.
    Includes index.

    1. Sophocles—Criticism and interpretation.
I. Title. II. Series.
PA25.M3 vol. 26 [PA4417] 937s [882'.01]
80-19765   ISBN 0-674-90206-8

For Joshua and Thaddeus,
philois kai philomythois

Preface

To many critics of Greek tragedy, ideas and the poetry of ideas are the province of Euripides. Sophocles appears as a poet and dramatist of majestic power, extraordinary skill, distant, elusive, but not a thinker. Venturing to disagree, I try to deal with Sophocles here in terms of large, abstract concepts like civilization and savagery. What Sophoclean tragedy has to tell the twentieth, and soon the twenty-first, century, however, cannot be abstracted from the texture, verbal and dramatic, of his plays. These works are complex, difficult, and profound dramatic poems. However pleasant and reassuring generalization would be, only close attention to the text, I believe, can advance our understanding of them. To that end I have attempted to combine a broad view of the meaning of Sophoclean tragedy with a detailed reading of the text of each of the seven extant plays. The three introductory chapters set forth the large issues in the perspective of Greek tragedy and culture as a whole. The subsequent eight chapters focus these questions specifically upon each of the plays. My aim has been to define what one may call Sophocles' philosophical anthropology, in its characteristically tragic aspect. It is my hope that the book may be useful both as a unified discussion of Sophocles' interpretation of the human condition and as a series of literary commentaries on the separate plays.

These concerns were uppermost in the original series of four lectures, also entitled "Tragedy and Civilization," delivered under the auspices of the Martin Classical Lectures at Oberlin College in March 1974. I am deeply indebted to Professor Nathan Greenberg who, as chairman of the Martin Classical Lectures Committee, lent valuable support and encouragement to the project of expanding the initial lectures into a large-scale work on all of Sophocles.

I am painfully conscious of treating only a few aspects of Sophocles' many-faceted art. I have paid relatively little attention to plot construction, scenic action, or poetic language per se. Nor have I attempted to provide a scene-by-scene analysis of the text. Excellent studies of these topics are available in a number of recent works on Sophocles. My principal concern is with the implicit definitions of civilization in the plays and with the conflicts and contradictions inherent in the paradoxes of human nature, as explored in their tragic light.

In formulating these issues, I have profited from the structuralist approaches to culture pioneered by Claude Lévi-Strauss and applied to Greek and other cultures by scholars such as Victor Turner, Edmund Leach, Jean-Pierre Vernant, Marcel Detienne, Pierre Vidal-Naquet, and others. I will not repeat what I have written elsewhere about the utility and the limitations of this method for the study of early Greek literature, save to point out two of its important advantages: it enables us to correlate patterns in the text with larger patterns of thought and behavior in other areas of the culture, and it allows us to put new questions to the text and thereby see it in a fresh light.

The time is long past when we can delude ourselves with a false historicism and pretend that the complex poetry of the highly structured media of early Greece will be transparent to naively literal readings. Criticism is a continuous dialogue between whatever these works may have meant to their original audience and whatever they mean, or might mean, to us today. Each generation will bring different experiences and different conceptual tools to the great authors and thereby illuminate new facets of the old texts. Jakob Burckhardt put it very well a century ago in his *Weltgeschichtliche Betrachtungen*:

> Everyone must reread the books that have been a thousand times ransacked, for to every reader and to every century and even to every individual's different stage of life they present a particular countenance . . . The image which the art and poetry of the past awakens changes totally, ceaselessly. Sophocles could make an impression on those who are just now born radically different from his impression on us. Far from being a misfortune, this is only a consequence of an interchange that is steadily alive.

The contemporary reader is less likely than his predecessor of half a century ago to find in Sophocles what Paul Shorey called "the supreme embodiment in literature, as the Parthenon is in art, of the unique harmony of beauty and reason that is the note of the Greek genius in its prime," or, with A. C. Pearson, to extol "that flawless moderation which is truth to life itself." A case could be made for these qualities; the distinguished scholars who pronounced these judgments were responding to something real and important in the texts. But it is not the aspect of the text to which our age is most responsive. We are more sympathetic to the dissonances and disharmonies in the universe which it portrays. Sophocles obviously contains both the harmony, the proportion, the balanced grace *and* the violence, questioning, harshness. Critical judgment, in that "steadily alive interchange" of which Burckhardt speaks, will always veer between these poles because Sophocles' largeness of vision embraces both the unifying and disruptive phenomena of the human spirit.

Because I believe that these plays are important to more than a small circle of specialist readers, I have translated all the Greek. To the same end I have kept the use of Greek font to a minimum and transliterated wherever total unintelligibility would not result. I apologize for the occasional lack of elegance, but the alternative was a far more expensive volume. The translations do not aim at literary gracefulness; they are intended to render the literal meaning of the text. Sometimes I have sacrificed smooth English phrasing to the nuances of the Greek. I discuss the plays in their more or less accepted chronological order, except that I place the chapter on the *Trachiniae* first, for reasons which I explain at the beginning of that chapter. The *Philoctetes* is so central to the issues which this study addresses that I have had to devote two chapters to that play. Though I neither deny nor neglect Sophocles' development over the fifty or so years spanned by the surviving plays, my concern here is probably more with what is constant than with what changes.

The secondary literature on Sophocles is enormous. I have sampled a good deal of it and have indicated my indebtedness to the books and articles which I have found most helpful. I have not attempted anything like bibliographical completeness, nor did I deem it profitable to register agreement or disagreement with previous scholars on all the numerous points of controversy in Sophocles' text, language, characterization, dramatic structure, staging, and so forth. Further details on bibliography and on more specialized matters of style and subject matter may be found in a number of articles which I have published over the course of the past few years while I have been preparing this book. Citation of ancient works and authors follows standard usage; abbreviations for journals and reference works are also standard, but a list is included for the benefit of the nonspecialist. The Greek text is generally A. C. Pearson, *Sophoclis Fabulae*, OCT (Oxford 1924), with many (noted) departures in favor of Jebb or others.

Acknowledgments

As indicated in the Notes, a few pages of chapter 2 appeared in an earlier version in *Classical Journal* 69 (1973/4) 289–308. Parts of chapter 6, section xiv, and of chapter 7, sections viii and ix, appear, in an earlier form, in the *Miscellanea di Studi in memoria di Marino Barchiesi* (Edizioni dell' Ateneo e Bizzarri, Rome, 1980) and in *Contemporary Literary Hermeneutics and the Interpretation of Classical Texts,* ed. S. Kresic (University of Ottawa Press, Ottawa, Canada, forthcoming) respectively. I have borrowed a few paragraphs of chapter 8 from my earlier study of the *Electra, Transactions of the American Philological Association* 97 (1966) 473–545. I should point out that the focus and concerns of that essay, as of my earlier published essays on *Trachiniae, Antigone,* and *Philoctetes,* complement but do not entirely overlap those presented in this volume. I wish to thank the editors and publishers of the above works for kind permission to reuse some of that material here.

Work on this book was spread over some eight years and four countries. In the process I have incurred many obligations, very pleasant ones, to both individuals and institutions. In attempting to discharge some of those debts here, I realize afresh that the task of scholarship, though often solitary, is also very much a social and collaborative endeavor. Without the labors of my predecessors in this field and the support and assistance of friends and colleagues in America, Europe, and Australia, this book would not have been possible.

First of all, I wish to express my deep appreciation to the Martin Classical Lectures Committee of Oberlin College, and especially to Professors Nathan Greenberg, James Helm, and Charles Murphy, for inviting me to deliver the lectures from which this book developed and for the warm hospitality which, more than half a decade later, makes that week in Oberlin stand out in my memory with something like Pindaric *aglaia.*

A Fellowship from the American Council of Learned Societies in 1974–75 made possible that rare and indispensable continuity of "free" time for writing a large portion of the first draft. The American Academy in Rome, under successive Directors and Professors of the School of Classical Studies, particularly Henry Millon, Frank Brown, and John D'Arms, generously made its facilities and its lively community of scholars open to me in 1970–72, 1974–75, and 1977. I am extremely grateful to Jean-Pierre Vernant, Professor at the Collège de France, and to Marcel Detienne and Pierre Vidal-Naquet of the Ecole des Hautes Etudes in Paris for the opportunity to test out some of my ideas in a seminar at the Hautes Etudes in the fall and winter of 1975–76. To their cordial hospitality, friendship, and spirited sharing of ideas, both then and since, I owe more than I can say. A term as visiting professor at the University of Melbourne in 1978, made possible by a grant under the Fulbright-Hayes program of the United States government and the Australian-American Educational Exchange Foundation, enabled me to work in an atmosphere both congenial and critical. I especially thank Graeme Clarke, George Gellie, and Robin Jackson of Melbourne and A. J. Boyle and Gerald Fitzgerald of Monash University for the many courtesies and kindnesses shown me during my stay.

Brown University provided valuable support for this work with a sabbatical leave in 1974–75, a leave of absence in the fall term of 1975–76, and material aid in the preparation of the manuscript. Richard Damon and Craig Manning of Brown served faithfully and assiduously as research assistants, checking references and proofreading. Frances Eisenhauer of Brown University typed the entire book with a meticulousness and keenness of eye that often amounted to editorial collaboration. I am very deeply indebted to her for years of patient and devoted effort in this and in other projects.

I owe a special debt of thanks to Professor Froma Zeitlin of Princeton University, who read and commented on parts of the work in manuscript and offered invaluable advice on Greek myth, tragedy, and theoretical approaches to myth, ritual, and literature. Professor Bernard Knox, *il miglior fabbro* in matters Sophoclean, provided some characteristically wise and acute criticism. The limitation of space forbids listing the many other friends, colleagues, and students to whom I am indebted for discussion, comments, encouragement, and copies of publications. I wish particularly to thank the following: Geoffrey Arnott, Marylin Arthur, Charles Beye, Alan Boegehold, Albert Cook, Patricia Easterling, John Erwin, Charles Fornara, Bruno Gentili, Nicole Loraux, Gregory Nagy, Carlo Pavese, Pietro Pucci, Michael Putnam, Kenneth Reckford, Peter Rose, Luigi Rossi, Joseph Russo, Suzanne Saïd, Steven Scully, Eugene Vance, John Van Sickle, Paolo Vivante, and William Wyatt. To the many others whom I cannot list here I am no less grateful for sharing their time, knowledge, and good will:

χάρις χάριν γάρ ἐστιν ἡ τίκτουσ᾽ ἀεί.

One old friend and teacher is no longer alive to thank: Cedric Whitman, whose *Sophocles* is still a landmark for the literary study of the plays, died as I was putting my book into final form. To his literary sensitivity and humane counsel I owe a great deal. His premature death is both a personal sadness and a painful loss to students of Greek literature.

My debt to other teachers who introduced me to Greek literature and culture in my formative years at Harvard is no less strong: John H. Finley, Jr., Eric Havelock, Philip Levine, and the lamented Werner Jaeger and Arthur Darby Nock. All in their different ways, by learning, inspiration, and example, set my feet on the "myriad paths" and showed me how to understand and appreciate what I found along the way. That the present work is not worthier of them and of the many others who have helped is to be attributed solely to my own limitations; for its errors of fact, judgment, or interpretation I alone claim responsibility.

As the manuscript was put into final form in the spring of 1979, I could not take account of several recent and important publications on Sophoclean tragedy, particularly R. P. Winnington-Ingram's *Sophocles: An Interpretation* and R. W. B. Burton's *The Chorus in Sophocles' Tragedies*, nor could I cite Hazel and Francis Harvey's English translation of Karl Reinhardt's *Sophokles*. Clearly the dialectical, and dialogical, process of interpreting these great, fascinating, and elusive works is unending.

Contents

Life negates itself in literature only
so that it may survive better.
So that it may be better.
It does not negate itself
any more than it affirms itself.

—Jacques Derrida, *Writing and Difference*

1

Tragedy and the Civilizing Power

High on a mountainside in a rugged and lonely part of Arcadia stands a remote shrine to Zeus Lykaios, Wolf Zeus. Plato alludes to a legend that human sacrifice was regularly practiced there and the celebrant who partook of the flesh turned into a wolf. Across the valley from this grim precinct, in a spot of wild and desolate beauty, in a place known as the "glens," *Bassai,* a small Greek city erected an elaborate temple to the most civilized of its gods, Apollo Epikourios, the Helper.[1] Approaching this temple at Bassae from the city of Phigaleia, as the ancients did, the visitor experiences a striking visual confrontation of civilization and savagery. Before the ancient spectator stood the ordered geometry of columns and pediment outlined against the jagged mountaintops which stretch far into the distance. Freestanding and unexpected in that desolate setting, the temple seems as arbitrary an example of pure form and human design as an Attic amphora or the rhythms of a tragic chorus. But prominent just beyond the temple is the mountain where a grisly and primitive cult violated one of the first laws of human civilization as the Greeks defined it, the taboo against cannibalism.

What the Greek visitor would have thought of this spectacle we shall never know. The site itself stands as an architectural embodiment of the conflict between savage and civilized spaces, between nature and culture (*physis* and *nomos*), that pervades Greek thought, art, and religion. It attests to the inexhaustible power with which the Greeks were able to represent this basic antinomy to themselves and to us.

The Greek temple not only visually expresses the difference between man and nature but also forms a spiritual boundary between the safe, formed world of the polis and the dangerous, formless, territory outside, the *agros,* from which is derived the adjective *agrios,* "wild," "savage." Thus the temples that line the ridges at Acragas, now the outskirts of modern Agrigento, enlist the aid of the gods and the shaping intelligence of men to defend the city from the unknown beyond the frontiers.

The building which, more than any other, summed up the civilized achievement of fifth-century Athens presented on its great frieze the idealized citizens in a ritual procession celebrating the civic and religious order that made the city possible. The quiet, seated figures of the gods on the east frieze contrast sharply with the agitated movement of the human figures on the north and south. But the human figures in their stately advance contrast also with the unruly beasts

1

being led to the sacrifice. The metopes showed a harsh struggle between the bestial Centaurs and the Lapith youths who recall the young Athenians of the frieze. The metopes are a reminder that the realized order of the frieze was not achieved without struggle nor retained without effort. On the west pediment, facing toward the sea and the mountains of Salamis and Aegina, stood Athena, goddess of the city and its civilizing arts, involved in a magnificent contest with Poseidon, god of the unbridled strength of the sea in its stormy violence, deity of the earth in its deep destructive motions. The point of the contest is itself the issue of civilization, whether Athena's olive or Poseidon's gift is the truly civilizing possession.

In the previous generation the west pediment of the temple of Zeus at Olympia gave monumental expression to the struggle for the hierarchical order of god, man, and beast against the unruly beast-men and their lust. The human figures of the Lapiths, struggling to protect their women, confront the mixed forms of the Centaurs. Apollo, facing outward in his calm frontality, marks both divine distance and divine encouragement in the battle against violence.

In the celebrated Triptolemus relief, finally, roughly contemporary with the Parthenon, the mediating role of civilization between nature and the gods is beautifully expressed in the figure of the young hero, the human agent chosen to bring agriculture to men. This configuration, the mortal youth sheltered between the two goddesses, Kore the maiden and the maternal Demeter, evokes the other characteristic institution of human civilization, the house (*oikos*) or family. Triptolemus, we may recall, was the subject of the play with which Sophocles made his debut in the dramatic competition and won first prize.

II

By "civilization" I mean the totality of man's achievement in shaping his distinctively human life, his domination and exploitation of nature, his creation of familial, tribal, and civic organizations, his establishment of ethical and religious values, and that subordination of instinct to reason, of "nature" to "convention," which is the precondition of all these.[2] Until recently, Western man's view of civilization has been based on the modern idea of progress, a total confidence in the power of reason, and especially scientific reason, to master nature with ever-expanding control and increasingly beneficent results.

For the Greeks civilization (for which there is no single Greek word)[3] is something more basic and also more precarious. Within the structure of Greek thought, civilization—the totality of man's social organization and cultural attainments—occupies a mediate position between the "savage" life of the beasts on the one hand and the eternal happiness of the blessed gods on the other. Civilization is the fruit of man's struggle to discover and assert his humanness in the face of the impersonal forces of nature and his own potential violence on the one hand and the remote powers of the gods on the other.

The next chapter will explore more fully some of these implicit definitions of civilization relevant to tragedy. As a preliminary statement, Vico's "three human customs" come close to the essentials of the classical view: "All [nations] have some religion, all contract solemn marriages, all bury their dead. And in no nation, however savage and crude, are any human actions performed with more elaborate ceremonies and more sacred solemnity than the rites of religion, marriage, and burial . . . From these three institutions humanity began among them all, and therefore they must be most devoutly guarded by them all, so that the world should not again become a bestial wilderness."[4]

What is particularly characteristic of classical Athens, however, is the focus of definitions of civilization on the polis, the city-state. Aristotle's *Politics,* the culmination of this attitude, virtually hypostatizes the polis as the fundamental unit of civilization. Man is a being who by nature is political. He is lawful and amenable to law; political action—deliberation, decision, legislation, and, alas, litigation—is his most human activity. Civilized life for the fifth century is unthinkable without the polis, a bounded space dividing the human world from the wild. The polis shelters its citizens, grouped by interrelated families, within its walls; harbors its meeting places, assemblies, law courts, theater in its central area; is nourished by its tilled farmland in the *agros* beyond its walls; is in touch with other city-states through sea-borne commerce and travel; and is politically autonomous, safeguarding its territory through alliances and war.

In Sophoclean tragedy the city is also the focus for the hero's problematical relation to civilized values. This is especially true of the Theban plays but applies also to *Electra* and even to the three plays not actually set in a polis, *Ajax, Philoctetes, Trachiniae.* The first two merely project a polis society upon its extension, the Greek army at Troy. The *Trachiniae* is properly the tragedy of a house rather than a city, but even here the collapse of civilized values has the destruction of a polis in the background.

The Greeks view the human condition, as they view so much else, in terms of a set of spatial configurations, a structure whose spatial and moral coordinates coincide. Man is threatened by the beast world pushing up from below, but he is also illuminated by the radiance of the Olympian gods above. Myths of heroes attaining Olympus express the highest possible human achievement. Heroes like Tantalus and Ixion in Pindar, who betray the gods' trust in them, are sent from the radiance of Olympian feasts to the utter darkness of Hades. The vicissitudes endured by heroes like Pelops and Bellerophon take the form of upward and downward movement, which represents the task of achieving the proper mediation between earth and Olympus, lower and upper realms.

The human form, idealized in the images of the Olympian gods, is the culminating point on the scale of mortal being. The great civilizing heroes—Theseus, Heracles, Oedipus, Odysseus—defeat the savage hybrids of human and bestial shapes—the Minotaur, the centaurs, the Sphinx—or monstrous deformations of humanity like the Cyclops. They are paradigms of man's effort to impose human order on the chaos that threatens to engulf him.

I use the term "civilization" rather than "society" because I wish to consider not only the tragic hero's relation to other men, important as that is, but also his relation to the moral and intellectual capacities of man in general, his relation to the natural and divine order, his rationality and unreason, his capacity for autonomy as well as his dependence on society.

Not all of Sophocles' extant plays are equally concerned with civilization in this larger sense. *Oedipus Tyrannus, Trachiniae,* and *Philoctetes* deal most directly with these themes, man's power to control his world and himself and the quality and limitations of that control. *Ajax, Antigone, Electra,* and *Oedipus at Colonus* are more concerned with society in the narrow sense, the individual's relation to social and political organization. Yet such a distinction between the two sets of plays is arbitrary, for the more specific social issues also involve the larger questions of man's civilizing capacities. All of Sophocles' extant plays are concerned with the tension between man's autonomy and his dependence, between his power to transcend the physical and biological necessities that surround his life and his immanent position within those necessities. In this tension the institutions of society play a vital but ambiguous role. The polis, with its Olympian religion, its temples, gymnasia, theaters, and *agora,* its laws and its festivals, constitutes an area into which the (male) Athenian citizen operates with a freedom not vouchsafed him in the *oikos* (house), with its uncertainties of life and death, its demands of nurture (*trophē*), its overt or latent hostilities in the most intimate relations, its blood ties and the curses they can produce or transmit, and the underworld deities who enforce those curses.

III

Theories about the origins and development of human civilization fascinated Sophocles and his contemporaries.[5] It was a popular enough subject to appear on the comic stage, as we may infer from a comedy called *The Wild Men (Agrioi)* by the poet Pherecrates cited apropos of this topic in Plato's *Protagoras.* Sophocles himself wrote one of his most famous odes on man's conquest of nature, the first stasimon of the *Antigone.* The *Philoctetes* clearly owes much to contemporary theories of the origins of culture. In at least three of his lost plays—four if we include the *Daedalus*—he used myths relating to the creation of civilization. The *Triptolemus* concerns the mythical bringer of agriculture to men. A fragment of the *Palamedes* mentions the hero's "invention" of dice during the long days of the siege of Troy (frag. 438N = 479P). The *Nauplius'* catalogue of the protagonist's civilizing inventions (frag. 399N = 432P) invites comparison with that of Aeschylus' *Prometheus.*[6] At the other end of the spectrum, a few fragments of the *Rootcutters (Rhizotomoi),* like the *Trachiniae,* take us to the darker arts of civilization—magical, not medical drugs (*pharmaka*)—at the fringes of rational experience.

Interest in the origins of civilization reflects and reinforces the antinomy between culture and nature, *nomos* and *physis,* that pervades fifth-century literature.[7] The Periclean age is, basically, optimistic about reason, centered on man, and confident in his cultural achievements. The representations on the frieze and pediments of the Parthenon are counterparts to the political, social, and scientific theories of thinkers like Protagoras, Anaxagoras, Hippodamus of Miletus, Hippocrates, Democritus, as expressions of the new intellectual currents. Simultaneously the new emphasis on the *psychē*, the inner life and moral consciousness of the individual, in the tragedians and in philosophers like Socrates and Democritus deepened the appreciation of man's uniqueness and the disjunction between man and the rest of nature.[8]

This disjunction, however, does not remain absolute. Greek thought from Homer on was haunted by an awareness of the precarious division between man and beast. The boundary is an achievement to be guarded with care, not a possession fixed and static forever. The Peloponnesian War, with its shocking atrocities like the Corcyrean revolution and the Athenian treatment of the Mytileneans and the Melians, did its work as a "violent teacher" (Thucydides 3.82.2). It laid bare the paradox that civilization could hold within itself all the savagery of the beast world. Hence, toward the end of the century *nomos* and *physis*, law and nature, undergo a strange reversal: *nomos*, the norm of civilization, is seen as repressive and destructive, and nature, *physis*, as liberating. The fragments of the work called *Truth* by the Sophist Antiphon are the fullest fifth-century statement of this position, but the point of view persists, more aggressively, in the arguments of Plato's Callicles and Thrasymachus.

This development is a familiar part of the cultural history of the fifth century. It is worth recapitulating here as part of the intellectual background to the reversals of man and beast in Sophoclean (and also Euripidean) tragedy. The triumph over the beastlike life of savagery, so proudly celebrated by Sophocles in the *Antigone*, by Euripides in the *Suppliants*, by Critias in the *Peirithous*, rings hollow when set against the recrudescence of bestiality and savagery in man's own nature. To this paradox the tragic poets return again and again.

The enormous acceleration of cultural life in fifth-century Athens, combined with a new rapidity of social, economic, and moral change, produced a heightened awareness of conflicting values and an extraordinary expansion of consciousness. Individual and society appear to be in tension rather than in harmony. The year after the completion of the Parthenon, monument to Athenian confidence in rational humanism, the beauty of man and his creations, saw the outbreak of the Peloponnesian War and the production of the *Medea* of Euripides, with its unshrinking exposure of violent hatred and destructive passion. The Athens praised as the home of the arts (*Medea* 824–845) is also the refuge that enables the barbarian witch to execute with impunity her terrible revenge.

IV

When man became "the measure of all things," in Protagoras' phrase, he also became more exposed to the violent, irrational urges of his own nature. As creations of men, the institutions of civilization, the *nomoi,* lost their privileged sanctity as the work of gods. Like all human works, then, they are vulnerable and perishable. When they collapse, the relapse into savagery is swift and sudden. It is this process that grips the imagination of Euripides and Thucydides. In a different form it also permeates the structure and imagery of Sophoclean drama. Thucydides' description of the revolution at Corcyra (3.81–82) is perhaps the most relentless analysis of law disintegrating into lawlessness, civilization into savagery, with a consequent loss of the ethical discriminations of language on which civilization relies. Beside the scalpel of Thucydides' prose we may set the hammer blows of plays like Euripides' *Hecuba, Trojan Women, Electra, Orestes, Bacchae,* all of which show a dissolution of civilization and a regression to bestiality. Sophocles is subtler, more distant from the events themselves, more sensitive to the cruelly ironic juxtaposition of human greatness and human debasement. Yet in virtually all his plays, and most prominently in the *Trachiniae, Oedipus Tyrannus, Antigone,* and *Philoctetes,* nothing less than man's civilizing power is at stake.

Caught up in the currents of these disturbing theories and more disturbing events, the audience who watched the *Antigone* or the *Oedipus* were keenly sensitive to the violence latent in human society. "Classical serenity" is a label affixed to an age characterized by the most immense disruptions of spirit and of events. No contemporary of Sophocles would have much difficulty in understanding this modern thinker's memorable formulation of the reasons for the bloody history of our kind:

> Civilized society is perpetually menaced with disintegration through this primary hostility of men towards one another. Their interests in their common work would not hold them together; the passions of instinct are stronger than reasoned interests. Culture has to call up every possible reinforcement in order to erect barriers against the aggressive instincts of men and hold their manifestations in check . . . ; hence the restrictions on sexual life; and hence, too, its ideal command to love one's neighbour as oneself, which is really justified by the fact that nothing is so completely at variance with original human nature as this . . . Civilization expects to prevent the worst atrocities of brutal violence by taking upon itself the right to employ violence against criminals, but the law is not able to lay hands on the more discreet and subtle forms in which human aggressions are expressed. The time comes when every one of us has to abandon the illusory anticipations with which in our youth we regarded our fellow-men, and when we realize how much hardship and suffering we have been caused in life through their ill-will.[9]

The writer is, of course, Freud, but one can find close parallels to these ideas, mutatis mutandis, in Euripides, Thucydides, Antiphon the Sophist, and Plato's Callicles and Thrasymachus.

In a stimulating book René Girard has argued that violence and sacrificial ritual are the center of tragedy.[10] His point of view has its roots in Freud and particularly in the late Freudian emphasis on aggression. Greek tragedy, in Girard's view, makes sacred or numinous the aggressive force in man—the force that leads man to what I have been calling savagery. It thereby removes this violence from the human sphere and gives it to the gods. On such a view, the Greek solution to the problem of civilization, the ritualizing of violence and aggression, is almost the opposite of the solution proposed by Freud. Freud would have man accept his aggressiveness as a fundamental part of himself and deal with it through the integration of his ego, insofar as this is possible. Freud's solution has its analogue in the post-tragic period of fourth-century Athens, that is, in the period when the ritual and sacral solution to the problem of violence begins to break down, to be replaced by the Socratic notion of self-control (*enkrateia*) and the inward mastery of passion by reason described in the *Republic*. In this perspective one of the fifth century's great achievements would be the creation of a form that sublimates into the highest art man's harsh and painful confrontation with his own savagery. The ritual setting, with its ancient agonistic elements, dramatizes the importance of the struggle and provides some assurance of ultimate victory through the sense of continuity and tradition. At the same time the poetry, the complex dance movements, the splendid costumes surround the issue, be it distant victory or present defeat, with an aura of deep significance and great beauty. Distanced by the ritualized setting, the aesthetic frame, and the mythical subject, the conflicts which the highly competitive structure of Greek society concealed beneath its surface and sublimated into the workable fabric of everyday life could be brought out and expressed in drastic, if fictional, confrontations.[11]

The effect of sacralizing and ritualizing violence that tragedy promotes is a means of keeping man human and civilized. One may speculate whether the high civilization attained by Athens in its age of tragedy was not due, in part at least, to the cathartic agency of its dramatic festivals. A recent writer, stressing the "cathartic discharge" effected by ritual, speculates, "Thus it is ritual which avoids the catastrophe of society. In fact only the last decades have abolished nearly all the comparable rites in our world; so it is left to our generation to experience the truth that men cannot stand the uninterrupted steadiness even of the most prosperous life; it is an open question whether the resulting convulsions will lead to *katharsis* or catastrophe."[12]

In tragedy the violence that exists in our world is not only a divine power, a manifestation of Eros or Aphrodite or Zeus's will, as it is in archaic epic or lyric. It is a numinous power and simultaneously something within us; it is both a part of ourselves and a mysterious visitation of something beyond ourselves. We approach this force with awe, respect and dread; tragedy helps us to recognize, acknowledge, and expel it. Sophocles is the great master of commingling these two ways of accounting for the violence and suffering in human life, internal and external, psychological and religious. In Aeschylus the religious interpretation predominates; in Euripides, the psychological. The combination and balance of the two in Sophocles make him perhaps the hardest of the three Attic tragedians for the modern reader to understand.

V

Besides representing a human personality, the Sophoclean hero is also an element in a large symbolical design, a field for the clash and potential resolution of opposing forces. This is not to say that we do not *also* identify with him as a human being. If we did not, the dramatic fiction would lose its hold on us and become a cold, intellectual exercise, devoid of moral life and unable to perform that "purgation" of pity and fear which Aristotle regarded as fundamental to tragedy. But we must keep in mind those formal elements in Greek tragedy that distance the hero from his audience: the mask, the special boots or *kothornoi*, the stylized gestures, the artificial and often difficult poetic language.

"Character" in the modern sense, as has often been pointed out, is not to be expected from Greek tragedy. Even in the late fifth century the Greeks are concerned at least as much with the objective place of an act in the world, its relation to the human order of house and city or the divine order of the cosmos, as with the interior, mental processes of conflict and decision.[13]

The individuality of the Sophoclean hero appears not in small personal details but, as in Homer, in a few large essential gestures. It is revealed not so much through the free play of idiosyncratic personality as in the vision of an idealized heroic self and the realization and resolution of the conflict between that self and the restrictions imposed by the world of men and the world of the gods.[14]

To be an individual in Sophocles is to have a special destiny apart from other men and to suffer a potentially dangerous, indeed fatal, isolation from the community and its secure values. That destiny stamps his life with moral significance. Only if he fulfills that destiny can the hero realize himself, and not relinquish something essential to his nature. To have such a destiny also means to have a place within the larger order of the gods. The play of divine forces about the hero's life is the mark of such tragic individuality. Conversely, that individuality brings the gods, with the disturbance that their presence always involves, crashing into his life. The hero stands at the point where the divine and human spheres intersect, where the separation between them becomes difficult and mysterious, where the intelligible order of life meets with darker levels of existence.[15]

Tragic character in Sophocles exists in the tension between the isolation imposed by heroic individuality and the larger design which that destiny fulfills. The hero's task is to discover and accept his life as part of this larger design. In the discovery the external and the inward shape of his life come to coincide: his nature and the divinity of his "fate" or "lot" (*daimōn*) prove to be one and the same. "Character is fate for a man," as Heraclitus said (*ēthos anthrōpō(i) daimōn*). When Ajax learns that Tecmessa had hidden his son lest he kill him in his madness, his reply, "Yes, that would be the fitting act of my daimon" (*Ajax* 534),[16] takes in the full significance of his degradation and grasps it factually as the divinity or daimon that drives him, both from within and from without. Discerning his life as pattern, as destiny, the hero reaches not only forward into the future to fulfill that pattern, but also backward into the past to accept responsibility for what he has been and what he has done. Oedipus fulfills both movements when, on the one hand, he says, "Let my portion (*moira*) go wherever it will go" and on the other hand, "Only I could bear these sufferings" (*OT* 1458, 1414–15).

The ambiguities and paradoxes in the tragic hero's status, as I suggested above, reflect the experiences of a generation subjected to large-scale and sudden cultural and material changes. The situations of conflict and the antithetical debates, the *antilogiai* or *hamillai logōn*, of tragedy, reflect not only the intellectual tools being used by philosophers and practicing rhetoricians or Sophists, but also the sharp polarization of values that men were experiencing.[17] Though tragedy did not develop solely in response to such conflicts, it was especially well suited to depicting them. Its built-in structure of antitheses could give them a tough conceptual as well as poetic formulation.

Sophoclean tragedy's ample, yet austere, form could concentrate issues of enormous moment into remarkably small compass. Its climactic structure, building up from crisis to peripety to resolution, made it the ideal vehicle for exploring reversals and inversions in the situations and emotions of men, in language, in values. Sophocles especially made irony, paradox, and conscious ambiguity his stock-in-trade.

Tragedians tended to use those myths in which such reversals were especially prominent; tragic drama highlighted those myths or parts of myths which contained such patterns. Varying a limited range of plots and situations within a well-defined structure and employing a conventionalized, though rich, vocabulary of patterns, contrast, analogies, and reversals, it could point up and intensify such symmetries, transmutations, or inversions in events and make them elements in a significant moral pattern.[18] Its vivid images and bold metaphors fleshed out these structural relations with a gripping particularity that gave them a penetrating poetic and symbolic power. In Sophocles especially the ironies and paradoxes of man's self-knowledge and self-ignorance, the drive of the hero's life toward pattern and coherent meaning, the interlocking and divergence of divine and human intention are illuminated from multiple perspectives. As we situate ourselves in one or another of these perspectives, parallel or contrasting sets of relations emerge, shift, or overlap in different ways. Thus new structures are always emerging, new patterns always evolving. It is an extraordinary combination of what Jean-Pierre Vernant has called malleability and eternity.

In the chapters on the individual plays that follow, therefore, I view the tragic hero less in terms of psychological realism than in terms of the configurations of antitheses and boundary situations described above. The hero not only fulfills a pattern of attaining personal knowledge out of ignorance, reality out of illusion, but also enacts paradigmatically the place of man on the axis between god and beast, between the divine order and the threat of chaos or meaninglessness. The two axes intersect at the points of man's uniquely human creations: the city, the house, ritual, law, justice, language. It is just these creations and the structures on which they rest that the hero calls into question, threatens, and paradoxically affirms.

VI

In Homeric epic the limits between human and bestial, though threatened, are relatively stable. Homer's formulaic language confers a certain built-in continuity. In tragedy there are no such formulas to stabilize the norms; the norms themselves are called into question in the violent conflicts of values or the swing between community and isolation, grandeur and nothingness.

The interlocking system of formulas in epic implies the co-presence of all the parts of a coherent universe. "Wine-dark sea" or "eddying river" or "windy Ilion" evoke on each recurrence a steady, unchanging world, large unvarying forms, and the ever-present powers of nature in a clearly defined, if austerely circumscribed, reality.

In tragedy the clarity of the world, like the meaning of events, is hidden behind a foreground which none of the characters can penetrate with any degree of certainty. There is no objective, third-person voice defining the constant elements of the human and natural world in a crystallized language of metrically patterned repetitions. The will of Zeus is not manifest from the beginning, as it is in the proem of the *Iliad,* but is revealed only piecemeal, obscurely, or even absurdly. The magnificent continuous sweep of epic narrative gives way to a tortuous, discontinuous movement. We receive only fragments, muted hints, momentary glimpses of a larger whole, as in the silences or the omens at the beginning of the *Agamemnon* or the sinister oxymoron of night's death begetting the flaming sun in the parode of the *Trachiniae.* Choral lyric, to be sure, also breaks down the continuous narrative of epic into isolated, discontinuous images or vivid moments. Yet the paradigmatic function of myth in the single voice of the chorus or the poet gives this narrative a singleness and clarity of meaning not to be found in tragedy.[19]

In tragedy truth has many voices. The time that reveals truth moves in many different rhythms: the slow, relentless unfolding of a hidden past in its closer or more remote parts in the *Oedipus Tyrannus;* the sudden veiled moment of oracular vision in the Cassandra scene of the *Agamemnon;* the detailed reception of a crucial event of recent occurrence in the messenger speeches; the agonized moment of decision; the blinding flash of recognition at the peripety; the nightmarish fit of madness in the dark night of the *Ajax* or the unexpected paroxysm of the *Heracles.* But always the total meaning of events grows to fulfillment only slowly, partially, darkly. The complex language, shifting between dialogue and lyric and between straightforward narrative and imagistic figure, conspires with the obscurity and divided quality of truth until all the interconnected pieces of the pattern reach their terrible coherence in the tragic insight that stamps the hero's life with its hallmark of loneliness, suffering, death: Agamemnon's "Alas, I am struck"; Heracles' "Alas, I understand"; Jocasta's silence; Oedipus' rain of blows upon his eyes.

VII

Suspended between the upper and lower reaches of his nature, walking a perilous borderline between his civilized status and his capacity for bestial violence, the tragic hero is, as Cocteau suggests in his ironical version of a Greek tragedy, *déclassé* in more than one sense:

> Oedipus: Know that everything which falls into classes carries the taint of death. One has to declass oneself, Teiresias, go out of one's rank. That's the sign of masterpieces and of heroes. A déclassé—that's what astonishes, that's what rules.[20]

The hero's confrontation with the extreme polarities of the human condition springs the safe fastenings which hold together our logical, ordered world, the "inconclusive, compromised middle" where most human life is lived.[21]

The tragic hero occupies what Alfred Schlesinger has called "the moral frontier."[22] His sufferings comprise a metaphorical and sometimes a literal journey to the limits of human experience and beyond. In all the extant plays of Sophocles the hero's relation to *place* expresses his ambiguous status. Places that should give shelter or safety become destructive, savage. The domestic hearth of Aeschylus' *Agamemnon* or the domestic altar of Euripides' *Heracles* illustrates the pattern, and we shall observe it in detail in Sophocles' *Oedipus Tyrannus* and *Electra*. In *Trachiniae, Antigone,* and *Philoctetes* the tragic situation inverts or collapses the proper antithetical relation between civilization and the wild. Or the hero who embodies civilized values finds his closest affinities with isolated places and the elemental violence of nature.

In five of the seven plays the hero is explicitly called *apolis* or *apoptolis,* "citiless" or "cut off from city."[23] Ajax, pursued as an enemy by gods and men, separates himself from the Greek camp and kills himself by the lonely shore of a hostile land, cut off forever from his native Salamis. Antigone, whose devotion to the gods below calls into question Creon's polis as the locus of mediation between gods and beasts, Olympus and Hades, is expelled from the city to die in an underground cave in a deserted place. The *Trachiniae,* dominated by a landscape of mysterious mountains and dangerous rivers, utilizes the tension between the inner world of Deianeira's house and the beast world of Heracles' heroic exploits outside. Here the civilizing hero is himself an exile and becomes a destroyer of cities; the tamer of beasts is vanquished by a beast at a point of unsuccessful transition between the wild and the inner space of his house. In the *Oedipus Tyrannus* the king, whose place is at the very heart of the city, has his identity determined by an axis which runs between the royal palace at Thebes and the savage mountain, Cithaeron. The too intimate spaces of house and womb and the savage spaces of the mountain prove to be both opposites and the same. The most sheltered of places holds for Oedipus the secret that makes him simultaneously the legitimate heir to the palace and the child of the mountain, the king and the pollution.

In the *Electra,* as in Aeschylus' *Oresteia* from which so much of its imagery is drawn, city and palace become a dubious locus of civilization. A guilty usurper reigns in the palace. Both in the inner world which should offer security and in the larger realm of nature, life and death, light and darkness, are inverted. The legitimate heirs are threatened with burial in an underground, sunless chamber or must make their way back to their rightful place inside by undergoing themselves an inversion of life and death.

The hero of the *Philoctetes,* cruelly set apart from men to lead a lonely life on a deserted island, is in his ensavaged state a truer representative of heroic and civilized values than their official representatives, the leaders of the Greek host at Troy. The *Oedipus at Colonus* centers on the paradox that the accursed outcast and pollution confers benefits on the quintessentially civilized city of Athens. The play begins at a point of mysterious transition between the city and the wild, the mysterious grove of the Eumenides at the outskirts of Athens. Here the hero separates himself from his accursed past and from the strife-torn city of Thebes in which that past is localized. A basic symbol of mysterious transition, a "brazen-footed threshold" (57–58; cf. 1590–94), marks his passage not only between the wild and city, but also between human and divine worlds, visible and invisible space.

If the hero belongs in part to the "raw" world outside the polis, he also has, by virtue of his energy, intelligence, and capacity for loyalty and love, a place of honor within the polis.[24] Breaking the moral laws that give our lives order and security and bypassing the usual mediation between god and beast that constitutes civilization, the hero lacks that stability of place and identity which ordinary men, who do not have his capacity for greatness or proneness to excess, possess as a given of their humanness. The hero has to reconstruct his humanness on new terms.

The fifth-century polis is still not so secure that it can dispense with or fail to admire the heroic energy, the sheer physical strength, or the mental acumen that might be needed to defend it. Beside the graceful youths riding peacefully on the Parthenon frieze we may place the young Lapiths in mortal battle with Centaurs on the metopes. Pericles' vision of Athens' hegemony of culture includes also the need for physical and spiritual courage in the face of death.[25] The tragic hero, too, for all his dangerous potential, possesses some quality or qualities indispensable to civilization. Antigone and Electra champion honor and family bonds. Ajax, Oedipus, Heracles, Philoctetes—and in a sense Antigone and Electra—have been or will be saviors of the community which harbors them. Guilty, impure, cast beyond the pale, the hero is also needed, valued, and loved by those around him.

Homo sum: humani nihil a me alienum puto and *Homo homini lupus* ("I am a man; I consider nothing human foreign to me"; "Man a wolf to man"): these two extremes, as Albin Lesky remarks, circumscribe the whole course of man's history.[26] Between these two extremes Sophocles' tragic hero acts out the tensions and paradoxes of his—and our—existence.

2

A Structural Approach to Greek Myth and Tragedy

For the Greeks, to be civilized is to be human rather than bestial. Aristotle places the locus of civilization in the polis, the city. Man as a civilized being is a *zōon politikon*, a creature of the city. The city is the characteristic human space figuratively located between the polar extremes of beast and god. In his famous definition of man as a political animal at the beginning of the *Politics*, Aristotle insists that whoever cannot share in the polis must be either below it or above it, a beast or a god (*Pol.* 1.1253a2–7, 25–29).[1] One who so far excels other men as to be superior to them in every way could have no place in the polis and would have to be considered "as really a god among men" (*Pol.* 3.1284a 3–12). In the *Ethics*, too, man's capacity for moral virtue lies between bestiality (*thēriotēs*) and the divine or heroic excellence (*aretē*) that belongs to the gods, "so that if, as they say, men become gods on account of an excess of excellence (*aretē*), such clearly would be the moral condition (*hexis*) opposite to the bestial. For a beast has neither excellence nor vice, and neither does a god; but the latter is above excellence (*aretē*) in honor, while the former is another kind of vice (*kakia*)" (*EN* 7.1145a15ff.). Man's peculiar excellence or virtue, *aretē*, lies in his qualitative superiority to bestiality and his necessary inferiority to divinity.

Aristotle here reflects and generalizes the tendency in Greek culture as a whole to think in terms of antitheses.[2] Morality itself is a system of limits, a set of boundaries between deficiencies and excesses: "Nothing too much," "Seek not to become Zeus," "Measure is best." The apparently irreconcilable polarity between bestiality and divinity in defining moral and civic virtue, however, as several critics have recognized, is especially relevant to tragedy.[3] The present chapter seeks to explore some of the patterns of language and myth that express the double antithesis between man and god and between man and beast.

This concern with polarity and mediation obviously owes much to the work of Claude Lévi-Strauss and his followers. Lévi-Strauss's theories and methods are still controversial, their applicability to the study of literature no less so. Geoffrey Kirk, Brian Vickers, and others have made searching critiques of structuralist interpretations of Greek myth.[4] What can a method developed for "primitive" tales from the Amazonian rainforests or the Pacific Northwest tell us about the Greeks of the high classical period? Classicists and students of literature are likely to experience a reaction not unlike Jane Harrison's retrospectively defensive weariness and disgust at the "beastly devices of the heathen."[5] While it is not my intention to weary the reader with many of these heathen devices, I do wish to insist on the potential utility of some aspects of structuralist methodology for the study of Greek tragedy. Structuralism, despite limitations which need to be frankly avowed, remains a powerful conceptual tool. Its validity and utility are supported by impressive documentation. Thanks to the work of Jean-Pierre Vernant, Marcel Detienne, Pierre Vidal-Naquet, and a group of energetic researchers inspired by their results, it is being applied to a variety of classical and other literary texts. Properly used, it can offer new insights and allow us to pose new questions to the texts. Like any literary methodology, however, it must be used with an awareness of its assumptions and limitations.

The methodology of Lévi-Strauss—the interpretation of myth as a system of opposing values—is especially useful for Greek literature, which operates in terms of polarities, and for Greek tragedy, where the conflict of opposites is of fundamental importance. One hardly needs structuralism to recognize the significance of polarity in Greek thought. The techniques of structuralist analysis, however, enable us to clarify the logic that governs the relations among the various expressions of order in the human world and in the literary work that mirrors and transforms that world. Through a structuralist approach we seek to apprehend the system of relations in which a given symbol functions, not its absolute "meaning."

Myth itself, in the structuralist view, is a system of logical relations analogous to language. A narrative, whether of a myth or of a work of literature, is a system of signs, wherein there is no absolute signified, but rather a conventionally established set of relations between a signifier and a signified. Myth and literature, like man's other symbolic forms, project models of reality, each with its own coherence and each with an internal logic; myth uses a kind of syntax which structuralist analysis tries to make explicit. As Roland Barthes puts it, "Ultimately one might say that the object of structuralism is not man endowed with meanings, but man fabricating meanings, as if it could not be the *content* of meanings which exhausted the semantic goals of humanity, but only the act by which these meanings, historical and contingent variables, are produced. Homo significans: such would be the new man of structural inquiry."[6]

The anthropological structuralism of Lévi-Strauss, unlike the narratological structuralism of Vladimir Propp, A. J. Greimas, and Claude Bremond, is concerned not with the structure of the narrative alone, but rather with the syntax which myth and literature share with the other expressions of culture. The value systems of the culture are encoded in the myths and in their literary reformulation. The task of a structuralist analysis is, in part, to decode the system, to reveal the interlocking parallels, the homologies, among the various codes of the social order, familial, ritual, linguistic, sexual, biological, and others. Each of these areas functions not only as a part of the total life of the society but also as a symbolic expression of a system of values parallel with every other system of values, that is, as a "code."

The term "code," rather than "domain" or "area," emphasizes the system of logical relations that operates in the society's various means of expressing its values. It also implies a homology among the various expressions of such values both in the culture as a whole and in literary works. Thus the term "familial code" means not just the concrete values governing family life, but the parallels between those values as part of a cultural system and the values expressed in ritual or architecture or language. Each code is analogous to a single strand, and all the strands twisted together form the total fabric of the society's value systems, understood as a network of logical and semantic relations. A structuralist reading of literature attempts to take account of this network of codes as a preliminary step toward interpretation. Unlike the New Criticism, therefore, it does not isolate the literary work in the vacuum of its autonomous verbal structures but views it in the context of the interwoven "deep structures" which pervade the entire mental life of the community.

To return to the Greeks, the value system implicit in their recurrent antinomies between tame and wild, cooked and raw, functions across all areas of a society's activities. Myths, to recapitulate the structuralist view, encode that polarity into details of ritual, food, sexuality, family life, spatial relationships, and other areas. Each code is a patterned model of the whole, and each, in its own characteristic terms, expresses an analogous message. Uncoded, those particulars reveal the "deep structure" of the society's concern and its modes of organizing reality. Each code is homologous with every other code. Taken together all the codes constitute the value patterns and underlying mental structures of the society.

For literary study much a method holds the obvious risk of excessive schematization, abstraction, and rigidity. Lévi-Strauss's concept of the homology between the codes, however, has some fruitful applications for a particular aspect of Greek tragedy, its density of metaphor.

It is characteristic of the poetry of Greek tragedy that it consciously interweaves all the codes and thus calls attention to the fundamental value system which underlies them all. Thus the totality of the social and cosmic order becomes visible in its interlocking relations at just the moment when that order is deeply threatened or pushed to its furthest limits of intelligibility.

The densely woven texture of metaphors in tragedy emphasizes the interchangeability of corresponding terms within each code and thus makes it possible for the separate codes to interact. By twisting together many strands of relation and meaning, metaphor complicates our picture of reality and thus sharpens our encounter with its complexity and the interconnectedness of its separate elements. By showing the complexity of reality, however, literature functions in a way almost opposite to the Lévi-Straussian conception of myth.

The distortion of language implicit in metaphor calls attention to the linguistic code itself. The literary work thereby reflects on the way in which language interrelates with the other codes to structure our total perception of reality. Aeschylus is especially illuminating in this regard, and within Aeschylus the *Oresteia*. His boldness of metaphor and comprehensive range of subject allow the freest possible play to this interlocking of homologous codes. His juxtaposing and interweaving of metaphors drawn from different areas of experience forcibly run the codes together. Indeed, it is worth considering the possibility that Aeschylus, drawing upon the resources of late archaic lyric, developed this technique of interlocking imagery for tragedy and gradually trained audiences to understand it. For Sophocles and Euripides, in any case, the technique is well established.

The figurative language, the enacted rituals, and the staged events of the *Oresteia* repeatedly interlock the violations of the ritual, sexual, dietary, familial, and other codes of civilized behavior. Each code expresses this violation in its appropriate "language." A structuralist approach makes it possible to grasp this interrelation of image patterns and interlocking metaphors more comprehensively and synoptically than conventional methods permit.

When Clytaemnestra boasts that Cassandra's death will be "a dainty relish to my bed" (*Ag.* 1447), her metaphor is meant to shock, and part of the shock effect lies in the juxtaposition of the sexual with the dietary code. The latter recalls inevitably the violations in the sexual, dietary, and ritual codes in the history of this house. Her grim libation to Zeus violates the ritual order and the harmonious relation of *charis* ("favorable reciprocity") between god and man that ritual and prayer establish (cf. *euktaia charis*, 1387). When she goes on to compare her joy at the rain of blood from Agamemnon's body to the crops' joy in the fertilizing rain, she brackets that ritual violation with the larger violation of the cosmic order and the processes of nature. By using the word "childbirth," *locheumata* (1392), for the crops' burgeoning she also extends that violation of the natural order to the violation of the life-sustaining functions of the house and the family, for the word suggests human birth as well and hence recalls the perverted relation between parents and children in this house. Clytaemnestra herself is soon explicit about this last connection, for in her next speech she justifies her murder of Agamemnon by recalling how he sacrificed her daughter, literally her "birth-pang" (*ōdina*), like a beast (1415–18). The violation of the cosmic order is not only "overdetermined" in the redundant messages of the several codes, but also spelled out in a sequence of specific instances which are additive on the "syntagmatic" axis and parallel or homologous on the "paradigmatic" axis.

Analysis of this type is concerned not so much with the unfolding of the work in time, from its beginning to its end (its diachronic structure), but with the patterns that pervade all aspects of the work as a structure of logical relations in reversible time (the paradigmatic structure). It is the difference between following the meaning of a sentence from word to word and laying bare its syntax, the "deep structure" which establishes the relations of the parts. This deep structure belongs to the synchronic, as opposed to the diachronic aspect of the work, its underlying "syntax" viewed synoptically, without regard to its development in time. Lévi-Strauss's analogy with music is helpful:

> Below the level of sounds and rhythms, music acts upon a primitive terrain, which is the physiological time of the listener; this time is irreversible and therefore irredeemably diachronic, yet music trans-

mutes the segment devoted to listening to it into a synchronic totality, enclosed within itself . . .

We can say that music operates according to two grids. One is physiological—that is, natural: its existence arises from the fact that music exploits organic rhythms and thus gives relevance to phenomena of discontinuity that would otherwise remain latent and submerged, as it were, in time. The other grid is cultural: it consists of a scale of musical sounds, of which the number and the intervals vary from one culture to another. The system of intervals provides music with an initial level of articulation, which is a function . . . of the hierarchical relations among [the notes] on the scale.[7]

Attention to the synchronic design of the work, however, is also a serious limitation to the structuralist method as literary criticsm. In drama especially, the progressive unfolding and tightening of the conflicts is essential to the impact of the play on its audience. My approach will try to integrate some of the gains of structuralist interpretation with more traditional modes of reading. By shifting back and forth between the synchronic and diachronic structures, I hope to arrive at a more fully balanced view of the work, both as a semantic structure of signs and as the enacted sufferings of human characters.

Structuralist analysis proceeds by reducing narrative episodes to "basic constituent elements." This presents other problems. Though it is certainly illuminating to regard myth as a coded pattern of narrative functions, these basic units or "mythemes" are not just arbitrary counters, analogous to the arbitrary sounds of the phonemes that make up language. In addition to this relational function in a system or "code," they also have meaning in and for themselves. The yoking of Oedipus' ankles in infancy, for example, enters into a whole sequence of patterns having to do with unity and plurality, but also carries the violent emotional affect of parents mutilating their own helpless child.

Stripping the narrative down to its basic narrative kernel also divests it of that rich envelope of poetic language which, in Greek tragedy at least, is an essential part of the meaning. The "meaning" of a classical Greek tragedy is not merely what happens on the stage, but the rich texture of the language in which those events are embodied. Meaning here must be considered "resonant meaning," the words with their aura of ever expanding associations and connotations, not a reductive pattern of signs. In Greek tragedy especially there is a close, reciprocal interaction between language and myth. The myth may, and certainly does, influence language, suggesting nexuses of relationships often developed through metaphor. But language also operates upon myth, modifying and transforming it.[8]

This said, it is important to recognize that, although structuralism undervalues the transformative power of language upon myth, the language of Greek drama, traditional and stylized, is highly amenable to the kind of analysis developed by Lévi-Strauss and his followers. Homer's formulas, as Michael Nagler and Norman Austin have recently demonstrated afresh, form a web of interlocking relationships that express an implicit structuring of nature, geography, and social mores.[9] The transmission of cultural values through oral poetry, with its heavy reliance on conventional phraseology and normative types in both language and action, continues to operate through the mid-fifth century, as the poetry of Pindar and Bacchylides shows. In Sophocles' formative years, poetry is still felt to be not merely the personal creation of the individual artist, but the voice of tradition: cultural values are still crystallized into a small number of compelling instances—the myths of epic, lyric, and dramatic poetry—where the homology between linguistic structures and cultural patterns is especially close.[10]

Through its myths the society reaffirms again and again its underlying structures of kinship, ritual, familial and sexual mores, and so on. Precisely because these structures are informed by and help constitute the basic assumptions of social behavior, they operate below the level of full intellectual consciousness. They appear in symbolic actions (rituals) and symbolic narratives (myths). Myths, at least in part, revalidate the messages that make up social norms by encoding them repeatedly in richly varied forms. In the terminology of Roman Jakobson's linguistic theory, which strongly influenced Lévi-Strauss, myths are the allophones of a kind of super-phoneme, which is the totality of the social structure itself.[11] In Ferdinand de Saussure's terms, each myth constitutes the *parole*, the individualized embodiment of the total structure. That structure, the *langue*, itself exists only as an abstraction, a composite drawn from all the particular *paroles* realized in each myth. As in language, the relation between the elements of the system, especially distinctive contrast, is the determining factor in creating meaning. As long as the value system and the sign system flourish, the society will continue to generate myths to ratify, clarify, and explore these structures. As Lévi-Strauss himself puts it, "Myth grows spiral-wise until the intellectual impulse which has produced it is exhausted. Its *growth* is a continuous process, whereas its *structure* remains discontinuous. If this is the case, we should assume that it closely corresponds, in the realm of the spoken word, to a crystal in the realm of physical matter. This analogy may help us to better understand the relationship of myth both to *langue* on the one hand and *parole* on the other. Myth is an intermediary entity between a statistical aggregate of molecules and the molecular structure itself."[12]

Basic to this process of re-encoding is the effect of redundancy or overdetermination. Redundancy is probably necessary, and is certainly natural, to all human communications.[13] Because an important message needs emphatic assertion by restatement, its major points are presented in a superabundance of parallel terms. In the *Trachiniae*, for example, the monstrosity associated with the Centaur Nessus' sexual appetite is overdetermined by the plurality of the ingredients in the supposed love charm which he has given Deianeira: the blood of the beastman himself, the venom of the Hydra, and, in another version, his sperm. Or in Euripides' *Hippolytus* the destructive anger of the father Theseus is overdetermined by being doubled with the curses of another father, Poseidon. The son's manner of death is also overdetermined in another way: Theseus' sentence of exile in the human order, the curse of Poseidon in the supernatural order.[14]

Redundancy also establishes suggestive analogies among the different areas of the social system as well as analogies between those areas and the ordered structure of the universe. It thereby stretches the mind by inviting extrapolation of the system to new relations. It intensifies consciousness of the world as a place where the life of man is interwoven with the life of nature, from the plant world to the stars.

II

When we move from myth to literature, the question of intention inevitably arises. No question about a poet's intention can ever be answered with full satisfaction. Great mythic literature, and perhaps all great literature, operates at a level where that question is itself problematical.

The patterns of myth function below the level of full consciousness across all the codes of the social structure. One effect of the recasting of myth in tragedy is to call these implicit, unconscious structures into consciousness. This is a consciousness of emotionally experienced symbols rather than of abstractly perceived concepts. Myth and mythic literature are among the ways in which the members of a society can reach these structures. Myth presents them in tangible, concrete forms where they can be experienced as symbolic models of the actual conflicts or tensions of the society. Just because these models are arbitrary, fictitious, and remote, actual tensions can be projected upon them through a free interweaving of many areas of experience. In this way, too, connections between different categories of experience or areas of life which are half-consciously or unconsciously felt to be related can emerge into clearer analogical relations, like that between marriage and agriculture in classical Greece.[15]

Often the poet seems aware of the relations between the various codes united by the metaphors and symbols through which he reinterprets his myths. In the *Oresteia* Aeschylus is doubtless conscious of using sacrifice, language, sexuality, and agriculture as parallel and analogous manifestations of the violations of the social order. In a holistic society, like that of classical Greece, the order of nature, society, and family is felt as a coherent unity. The poet's skill lies in finding the terms which evoke that unity and touch it at points where it is visible, precarious, difficult, or mysterious. For him, as for his audience, this language of myth or mythicized language often operates in a penumbral region between intellectual clarity and emotional appeal. The myths he uses themselves consist of a vocabulary of symbols more or less familiar to the audience, symbols that mark certain privileged acts or characters or families with special significance, sometimes with a numinous aura, sometimes with an atmosphere of danger or dread. Modern man, in his largely de-ritualized and de-mythicized society, lacks such markers. For him, therefore, the interconnections between the various areas of experience—sacred and profane, public and private, work and home, society and nature—have given way to sharp divisions.

The poets of archaic and classical Greece draw upon the internal structure and coherence of myths or groups of myths. In this loose, symbolic system of analogies, all the parts of the social and cosmic order are virtually interchangeable, each implying the others. By analyzing the internal coherence of the literary work, we can establish some probabilities as to how much is the poet's secondarily imposed pattern and how much inheres in the myth itself. In practice, however, the overlap is great, particularly as the poet is often intensifying analogies already implicit in the myth, as Aeschylus probably does in the *Oresteia*. It is impossible to determine with certainty how many of such relations were present to the poet's conscious mind; we can only determine, by literary analysis, how these relations operate in the language and structure of the texts. That is our chief and proper concern.

By the very nature of symbolic thought, the totality of meanings which are generated by a text will always be more than the sum of the individual elements, for the individual elements in a symbolic system are continuously generating fresh analogies and polarities as we change or enlarge the frame of reference. That these meanings may be more than the poet himself could have consciously foreseen or logically distinguished is the condition of all signifiant symbolic forms. That our formulation of these meanings two and a half millennia after their creation differs radically from the terms in which the original audience would formulate them is the condition of understanding all great art produced in another place or time. It can be demonstrated, I believe, that these structures are important in the plays of Sophocles, but, because the system of relations discussed here is not our own inherited frame of reference, we have to make overt and explicit, by intellectual analysis, what was implicit and apprehended spontaneously and affectively by the original creators and their audiences.

III

Lévi-Strauss's antitheses between nature and culture, the raw and the cooked, are fruitful for approaching the Greeks' view of civilization, for they themselves often distinguish between nature and culture in just these terms.[16] This antinomy is only a subset of a much larger set of antinomies that includes man and beast, tame and wild, *nomos* and *physis* (law and nature). They can all be subsumed under a broader and more inclusive heading which I shall call savagery and civilization. The patterns and antitheses here discussed, it must be emphasized, are inherent in the Greek texts themselves and can be generated from the Greek texts themselves.

All literary works impose their own secondary, aesthetic structure—which is the structure of their artistic form, imagery, diction—upon the primary structure of their society, the cultural *donnée* of received ideas and underlying patterns of thought and of language. In the case of tragedy, that secondary, aesthetic structure is generally a deliberate distortion, inversion, or negation of conventional social and linguistic patterns.

"The purpose of myth," writes Lévi-Strauss in a celebrated essay, "is to provide a logical model capable of overcoming a contradiction (an impossible achievement if, as it happens, the contradiction is real)."[17] In Lévi-Strauss's analyses of myth, the contradiction is overcome by a process of mediation between opposing polarities. To take a simple example, in Pueblo myths hunting mediates between the irreconcilable extremes of life and death: akin to warfare, on the one hand, hunting brings death; as a source of nourishment, on the other hand, it supports and nurtures life. Myths dealing with the ambiguity of the hunter-warrior role work through this polarity in order to clarify and affirm a coherent, logical structure of reality. In tragedy, however, the stabilizing mediation that society seeks and expresses through its myths, or through some of its myths, is disrupted. Instead of reaching a resolution, polarities break apart into violent conflict or a dangerous preponderance of one side over the other.[18] Tragedy stresses less the unifying, synthesizing capacity of a mediator than the problematical and paradoxical status of the figure who stands at the point where opposites converge. Such a figure may assume contradictory attributes simultaneously. In the *Bacchae*, for instance, King Pentheus is both the antagonist and the subject of Dionysus, both ruler and beast-victim, while Dionysus is both the enemy and the hidden alter ego of the king.[19]

Even when the end of the tragedy resolves the conflict, the essence or mainspring of the tragic situation itself is in the questioning or destruction of this mediation. Tragedy recognizes the ultimate failure of the logical model, the elusiveness and ambiguity of reality even as we grasp it and *because* we grasp it. Tragedy is the form of myth which explores the ultimate impossibility of mediation by accepting the contradiction between the basic polarities that human existence confronts. Let us consider now some elements in the Greeks' primary linguistic and mythic structures in order better to appreciate the distortions and inversions that tragedy works on them.

IV

The playful satyrs and silenoi of Graeco-Roman art express an attitude to nature quite different from their pre-Praxitelean prototypes of the archaic and classical period. Then the animalism of these creatures is felt as a threat to man's humanness rather than a welcome release from its constraints. The exuberance of the centaurs and satyrs of the sixth century becomes ambiguous, lustful, and more overtly dangerous in the fifth.[20] Only in the Hellenistic age does the conviction of man's superiority to the beasts give way to an explicitly formulated attitude of wistful longing for the "natural" purity and uncorrupted simplicity of "lower" forms of nature.[21]

Unlike the Minoans, with their theriomorphic gods, the Greeks are hesitant and ambivalent about fusion or identification with the energies of animals or natural processes. Their concern is rather with delimiting those energies within fixed boundaries. The anthropomorphic beauty of the Olympian gods validates the moral and aesthetic superiority of the human form and the social superiority of the male-oriented city-state. Dionysus and his ecstatic female or bestial followers are allowed a place, but the rites of fusion with nature's energies and their god take place on the mountainside, far outside the walls of the polis. The rites are nocturnal, illuminated by torches, not by the full light of the sun. Euripides' *Bacchae* powerfully attests to the mixture of awe, fascination, and horror with which the Greeks of the classical age regard this god and his worshipers.

In early Greek poetry mythical narrative shows a concern with both binary opposition and the logical relations that effect mediation between the extremes of god and beast. The longer Homeric *Hymns* and many of the *Odes* of Pindar are in effect mythicized versions of mediation which operates across several different areas of the cosmic order. In Pindar's *First Pythian Ode*, for example, the "heavenly pillar," *kiōn ourania*, extending between Olympus and Hades, is a visual symbol of the cosmic order wherein the monstrous and bestial Typhos is kept at the furthest possible remove from the radiant beauty of the gods. In language, celebration, and ritual, a mediatory structure is set up wherein the song of the mortal poet reaches upward toward the golden lyre and the timeless harmony of Olympus to establish conjunction between man and god. That same song, however, is also contrasted with the volcanic roar of Aetna which keeps the monster, Typhos, beneath the earth, away from men and gods, in Tartarus, (*Pyth.* 1.19–26; cf. 15). The contrasting auditory phenomena emphasize the disjunction between man and beast, the human world and the chthonic realm. In Hesiod's account, Typhos' voice is a confused roar of many sounds, now resembling divine speech, now human (*Theog.* 830–835): that is, Typhos is as much an anomaly in the linguistic code as in the biological and spatial codes. His existence negates the mediate position between god and beast occupied by the human race. The opposite pole, in Pindar's ode, is defined by Olympus, Zeus, and Apollo's "golden lyre . . . beginning of radiance" (*archa aglaias, Pyth.* 1.1–2). The poem implicitly interweaves the codes in a manner which could be set forth diagrammatically:

Space		Biological status	Language
Olympus	*kiōn ourania* "heavenly pillar"	God	Immortal song of muses, golden lyre, radiance
Earth		Man	Song of the poet at the victory celebration
Tartarus		Beast, Monster	Confused roar, dissonance

The heavenly pillar crystallizes the structure with a definiteness and fixity characteristic of choral poetry, whose task is to celebrate rather than to call into question man's relation to gods, city, and the bestiality of the realms below.

The Homeric *Hymn to Aphrodite* operates with a similar but more complex structure of mediations.[22] Sex is here the mediatory link between gods, men, and beasts. Sexual union, in this case between Aphrodite and Anchises, goddess and mortal man, is the means by which divinity descends to man and man reaches up to incorporate the divine into human life (cf. 45–52). Sexuality, in its "raw" state, what we would call a fundamental life instinct, is the special province of Aphrodite (as distinguished from Hera, goddess of marriage). Hence Aphrodite is accompanied by wild beasts—lions, wolves, panthers—which lie by twos on the mountain. This elemental sex has no place in the realm of the city. Hence the union takes place on Mount Ida, "mother of beasts" (68), and involves a shepherd, inhabitant of marginal places and alone with his beasts (79–81), and a goddess disguised as a mortal girl. She tells, moreover, a false tale in which she has supposedly been carried off from a civilized place of dancing by Hermes, messenger between gods and men (117–125). Her alleged marginal status as a victim of rape sets her outside the social norms that protect and regularize the sexuality of her erstwhile companions, "maidens who will earn oxen for their parents" by their dowries (*parthenoi alphesiboiai*, 119).

The *Hymn* thus makes an implicit contrast between Hera and Aphrodite, sex within the legitimate bonds of marriage and the instant concupiscence that the love goddess inspires. Even when Aphrodite uses marriage to achieve her ends, it is part of deception and seduction. Hence when, in disguise, she claims to have been chosen as Anchises' lawfully wedded wife (*kouridiēn alochon*, 126–127), she is revealing her nature as the goddess of love and sex, which the Greeks closely associate with falsehood and deceit (*apatē*).[23] Anchises mentions this future marriage (148) but quickly brushes aside the sanctions due to a maiden in this position. Now under the spell of Aphrodite's seduction and fully in the orbit of the love goddess, he acts in a way consistent with her sphere of power: he insists on the irresistible force of sexual desire which overcomes him here (149–154) as it does Paris in *Iliad* 6 and Zeus in *Iliad* 14. The sex act over which Aphrodite presides is thus set deliberately outside the limits of house or city. Located on the wild mountain, it takes place, appropriately, on the skins of wild beasts which Anchises "himself had slain in the lofty mountains" (159–160). This detail is part of a set of homologies: Hera is to Aphrodite as marital sex is to elemental lust, as house is to mountain, as men are to beasts, as the civilized is to the wild.

Anchises' awakening brings a rapid, unmediated movement from the bestial accoutrements of the bed to the brilliance of the Olympian gods. At the goddess' epiphany the immortal radiance of her form and adornments stands at the opposite extreme from the furs of wild creatures (cf. 174–175). This abrupt shift from beast to god is one of the ways in which the poem demonstrates the normality of the barriers separating gods and men. Only in this marginal space between Troy and Olympus, with its strange proximity of beast and god, can these barriers be dissolved. The remote mountain in the wild, a shepherd, falsehood, Hermes in the background are all parallel manifestations of this breakdown of boundaries. The myth affirms the norm by denying its negative or by showing the marginal status of its infraction.

In the *Symposium*, Plato treats *eros* as a mediating power between mortality and divinity: it is the means by which a mortal creature achieves the (limited) equivalent of immortality, namely succession through offspring created by sexual reproduction. Sexuality has that function also in the *Hymn to Aphrodite*. Aeneas, the result of Anchises' union with the goddess, is defined as between man and god, Ida and Troy, mortal and immortal. He will have a place in the city, finally, but will not enter it immediately. Eventually, he will become the founder of a long line, whose succession brings the human equivalent of immortality to Anchises' race (cf. 196–201). The long-lived nymphs are the mythic correlative of that intermediate stage between death and immortality. Until "lovely youth takes him" (274), they will rear Aeneas in the forest, not in a human house or *oikos*. Not quite immortal, they yet live longer than men. Nurses of a mortal child, their life is in the forest, and their associations are with creatures that are half-men and half-beasts, the silenoi, and with the god of passage between men and gods, Hermes (259–272).

These mediations in the spatial, biological, and sexual codes have further analogues in the *Hymn* in the stories of Ganymede and Tithonus. These two additional paradigms for mortal-immortal unions illustrate the overdetermination or redundancy characteristic of mythic narration: they validate the original model (Anchises-Aphrodite) at still one more level. Repeating the initial pattern, the myth re-encodes it in dietary terms.

Tithonus himself is symmetrical to Ganymede: the boy is carried off to enjoy immortal youth, "deathless and ageless like the gods" (214). As divine cupbearer he himself pours out the gods' immortalizing "rosy nectar from golden jar" (206). Tithonus, however, gains immortality but not eternal youth (cf. 223). He still occupies a remote, marginal place, not on Olympus like the fully immortal Ganymede, but "by Ocean's streams at the limits of earth" (227). His food is not nectar and ambrosia, which belong only to the imperishable gods, but a mixture of grain and ambrosia (*sitos kai ambrosiē*, 232). In other words, his intermediary position between the privileges of divinity (immortal life) and the burdens of humanity (old age) is marked both spatially and dietarily. In the redundancy of the message, a "minus" in the spatial code is symmetrical with a "plus" in the dietary code. "By the streams of Ocean at the limits of earth" is equivalent to *neither* earth *nor* Olympus (hence "minus"). "*Both* grain *and* ambrosia" combines grain, men's proper food, with the otherwise mutually exclusive divine food (hence "plus").

Just beneath the gods' full immortality stands Tithonus' eternity of old age. Just above the mortals' bond to the changing cycles of the earth stand the nymphs of the forest who have a long life, not immortality, and consort with the silenoi or Hermes. Tithonus and the nymphs occupy complementary symmetrical positions, each filling a gap in a continuous scale from beast to god.

The Homeric *Hymn to Demeter* implies a similar narrative structure but focuses it on the Eleusinian cult. The ritual code effects the primary mediation between godhead and mortality.[24] The mortals who have had the benefit of initiation into these rites still descend to death and the "mouldy murkiness" of Hades (482); yet they enjoy a happiness (*olbios*, 480) which sets them apart from other "mortals dwelling on the earth" (*epichthonioi anthrōpoi*, 480). That mediation through ritual is revalidated in the dietary code through two symmetrical acts of eating: Demeter, in the grief and sterility-causing withdrawal at Persephone's loss, accepts reentrance into the mortal world and resumes a nurturing function when she agrees to break her fast with the *kykeōn* at Eleusis, a drink which consists of barley, water, and the herb pennyroyal (208–211). If Demeter consumes grain, food of mortals, to move from deathlike sterility to the rhythms of living things, Persephone, in accepting the honey-sweet pomegranate seed (372–412), relinquishes the perfect immortality which she might have enjoyed on Olympus. Connected with sexuality, the seed of this fruit involves her in reproduction, decay, death—the cycles of mortal life—so that she spends part of each year under the earth with her bridegroom Hades. The alternation of the seasons in mortal life is thus overdetermined in the myth of the Corn-Maiden: spatially, she moves from Olympus to Hades; in the dietary code, she moves from nectar and ambrosia to the pomegranate seed; biologically, she moves from flower to fruit, from the sterile narcissus (connected with death) to the sweet pomegranate.

As in the case of Tithonus in the Aphrodite Hymn, but on a larger scale, an enframed, secondary mythic paradigm encodes the message in complementary form. Demophon, infant son of Metaneira, queen of Eleusis, is nearly given immortality by the disguised goddess. At his mother's accidental intervention, Demeter puts him down on the ground, explains that now "there is no way for him to avoid death," but because he has lain in her arms he will receive not immortality but immortal honor in annual games at Eleusis (262–267). She thereupon reveals herself in her divine stature in an epiphany blazing with light and gives orders for the establishment of the Eleusinian cult and temple. At this point the daughters of Metaneira take up the crying infant, but he is not soothed, "for lesser nurses held him" (290–291).

The Demophon story establishes the symmetry of conjunction with the gods and disjunction from them. Demophon is separated from the promised immortality, put down from the arms of the immortal nurse, and then symbolically reborn into his mortal status by being taken up again from the ground by his mortal sisters. At the same time he remains in communication with divinity through the "honor imperishable" at the Eleusinian games: that is his share in the immortality which he has lost. The games, ordered by the goddess, are the intermediary between the unconditioned immortality of the gods and the tempered form of that immortality available to men. The games for Demophon, like the cult and the temple for the generality of men, mediate between man and god, mortal life and divine eternity.

This mediation in the ritual code parallels and supplements the mediation in the spatial and dietary codes; it is redundant, but it also expands some details and adds new ones. Significantly, the temple just ordered by Demeter at Eleusis is the place where she sits to receive the emissaries from the celestial regions who entreat her to send forth the grain again (302ff.). And it is "before the fragrant temple" that Hades finds her in his upward ascent from Hades to restore Persephone (385). Hence this temple, itself established as an act of mediation in the story of Demophon, is the point of conjunction between the downward journey of Olympian gods to do honor to Demeter and the upward ascent of the Underworld deity to restore her daughter. At that point of juncture on the spatial scale life and death can also cross: biologically in the transformation of barren fields to fertile grain (449–456); ritually in the establishment of a cult which mingles the darkness of death with a brighter vision (480–482); and sexually in the complementary transformations of Demeter from fruitless hag to mature and beautiful woman (cf. 101–102 and 275–280) and Persephone from maiden to bride.

As the *Hymn to Aphrodite* implies, sexuality has an ambiguous function as a mediator between immortality and death. Effecting upward movement toward the gods in the case of Aeneas, it is dangerous and potentially destructive for Tithonus and for Anchises. Essential to the continuity of house and city in the realm of culture, it also belongs to nature, to the "raw," as its association with Aphrodite's wild, "raw-eating" beasts in the *Hymn* makes clear (69ff., 123–124, 157–160).

The Homeric *Hymn to Pythian Apollo* illustrates how female sexuality forms another ambiguous mediation between culture and nature.[25] This Hymn operates within a scheme of contrasts wherein the birth of Athena, by male parthenogenesis from the head of Zeus, stands at the opposite extreme from the birth of Typhos, a dangerous monster created by female parthenogenesis from Hera, aided by Earth and a female serpent or *drakaina*. In the Greeks' malaise with the fully sexual female, total subjection to her reproductive sexuality is terrifying. In autochthonous monsters created solely by the female that fertility seems to run rampant. We may compare the role of Earth (Gaia) in Hesiod's account of Typhos at *Theogony* 821ff. At the opposite pole is the child sprung from Zeus alone, a virginal female, Athena, removed from sex and birth. Her loyalty is totally to her father and to the masculine arts of war and technology. The offspring of Hera's parthenogenesis is a hideous creature, "resembling neither gods nor mortals" (*h. Ap.* 351), who harms the works of men and destroys their flocks and the fields (302–304, 355).

The triumph of Apollo over these creatures asserts the possibility of mediation between the extremes of monstrosity and divinity. Born from a heterosexual union of god and goddess, Apollo is a beautiful being, less austere than Athena (hence perhaps the point of his sexual exploits briefly cited at the beginning of the narrative, 208–213) and more beautiful than Hera's immortal offspring, the lame Hephaestus, expelled from Olympus (316–321). Secure on Olympus, Apollo moves in a more positive way between divinity and mortality: spatially, through his journeys on earth; ritually, through his founding of oracle and temple at Delphi. Through his appearance in the form of a handsome mortal youth (449–450, 464), he increases the distance between hideous chthonic monstrosity and beautiful Olympian divinity. Putting monsters in their place by his godlike deeds, he ratifies and solidifies the Olympian order aesthetically when he takes on the most admired of human forms, that of the handsome *kouros* or youth. In this idealized human form, the form in which the gods are represented in art, he simultaneously narrows the distance between men and gods and increases that between gods and bestial monsters.

Apollo not only kills the monster, but he also leaves it to putrefy, and in Lévi-Straussian analysis putrefaction holds the lowest extreme of the culinary scale. Protecting the arable, grain-producing earth by this martial act, he also establishes the rite of sacrifice, with its implication of cooked food. In his role as cult founder he appears to his future temple servants in close association with their enjoyment of dietary normality: fire, sacrifice, grain (*sitos*) (490–492, 497–499; cf. 461). Ritual, biological, spatial, and sexual codes are closely correlated in a composite structure that can be represented as follows:

Olympus	God	Imperishable food (ambrosia, nectar)	Male partheno- genesis: Athena	Olympian order
Earth	Man	Cooked food, grain	Heterosexual birth	Apollo protects arable earth; founds temple and oracle; establishes sacrifice
Subterranean realm (Hades)	Monsters, beasts	Putrefaction	Female partheno- genesis: chaos	

In the sexual code of the *Hymn* the Olympians use heterosexual reproduction but are not dependent on it for the survival of identity in the way that mortals are. The two male Olympians who result from heterosexual union on Olympus stand in marked contrast: Apollo is called only son of Zeus, Hephaestus only son of Hera. The one is defined only by relation to his father, the other only by relation to his mother. Hephaestus is received by a female goddess in the depths of the sea (*h. Ap.* 318–320); Apollo defeats a female monster whose natural place is in the depths of the earth. When Apollo takes to the sea, he does so voluntarily, and he assumes the disguise of a dolphin who steers a ship at the surface of the sea in order to bring it to land at a place designated for a cult, a cult in fact named after the dolphin itself (493–496). When Hephaestus takes to the sea, he is expelled by force and, as noted, remains in dependent and passive relation to goddesses beneath the surface.

These comparisons suggest the equation, Athena is to Typhos and female serpent as Apollo is to Hephaestus. In fuller form, Athena, engendered by male parthenogenesis, is as superior to Typhos, engendered by female parthenogenesis, as Apollo, viewed as a son of Olympian Zeus, is superior to Hephaestus, viewed as a son of Olympian Hera. Apollo (positively) and Hephaestus (negatively) fill the gap between male parthenogenesis, at the one extreme (Athena) and female parthenogenesis (Typhos and the serpent) at the other. Apollo's beauty and security on Olympus contrast with Hephaestus' ugliness and instability there. Likewise on the sea, Hephaestus regresses to a quasi-infantile state of dependency to female goddesses in the depths, but Apollo has an active relation with adult males sailing a ship on the surface (a civilized activity) and soon takes the form of a handsome youth of godlike beauty (464–465).

A corollary of the preceding analysis of the *Hymn to Pythian Apollo* is the ambiguous place of the female in the structures which we have been describing. Even from this brief description of the role of Hera, it is clear that woman occupies a shifting position between the civilized and the wild, between interior and exterior space. Obviously part of the civilized world through her place at the center of the house, she is yet felt as akin to the mystery, otherness, and potential violence of the animal realm through her sexuality and closeness to the biological processes, particularly giving birth. Regarded also as less resistant than man to sexual passion, she has the function of a downward or negative mediation, from the orderliness of the human world of family, house, and city, to the threatening chaos of elemental nature, the cycles of coming to be and passing away, and recalcitrance to rational guidance.[26]

At the opposite extreme woman may have closer access to the supernatural, and especially the chthonic, although this aspect of the female is more important in Aeschylus than the extant Sophocles. Even so, this general ambiguity, as we shall see, is particularly important for the *Trachiniae, Antigone,* and *Electra.* Standing in a highly problematical relation to the dichotomies between man and beast, she is the "other," the stranger: a stranger in her husband's *oikos,* like Alcestis; a barbarian foreigner in a Greek city, like Medea; a figure who shifts dangerously between city and wild, like Agave in the *Bacchae.* Like the Amazon and the maenad, her status is both figuratively and literally liminal, at the boundary between civilization and savagery, in flux between the two extremes of protected virginity and dangerous promiscuity, golden-age freedom and wild cruelty, the yoked heifer and the untamed lioness. The *Oresteia* and especially the *Eumenides* are largely concerned with reconciling this liminal position of woman with her central, civilizing role inside the stable *oikos.*

While such an analysis does help us to understand the literary structure of the *Hymns* and to correlate those structures with other structures in the cultural norms of the society, at least two important limitations have to be noted.

First, there is an oversimplification in the analytical separation between synchronic and diachronic, that is, between the linear, nonreversible movement from beginning to end and the constant, reversible patterns present in every part of the whole. In the *Hymn to Aphrodite,* for instance, the diachronic (or syntagmatic) movement consists in the progression from the siring of Aeneas to his maturity as the founder of a line of heroes in the Troad. The synchronic (or paradigmatic) axis expresses the recurrent separation and conjunction of god and mortal in the various codes, sexual, dietary, spatial, and so forth. Yet at each crucial point on the diachronic axis the narrative also becomes transparent to the synchronic axis. The latter is an a-temporal cross-section which both stands apart from the linear, diachronic movement and also crystallizes that movement in repeated conflicts at successive points of crisis. It thus helps the diachronic movement progress to the next crisis, where the same process is repeated. Each intersection of synchronic and diachronic axes, therefore, is not only a microcosm of the whole work but also a microcosm within a dynamic structure which is continually going forward to new constellations of these elements and new encodings of them into fresh contradictions and fresh mediations. The process comes to an end only arbitrarily with the end of the poem, but obviously could be extrapolated further in an infinite series. What Jakobson wrote about synchrony and diachrony in language fifty years ago can also be applied to mythic narrative of the type studied here: "The history of a system is in turn a system. Pure synchronism now proves to be an illusion: every synchronic system has its past and its future as inseparable structural elements of the system . . . The opposition between synchrony and diachrony was an opposition between the concept of system and the concept of evolution: thus it loses its importance in principle as soon as we recognize that every system necessarily exists as an evolution, whereas on the other hand, evolution is inescapably of a systemic nature."[27]

The second limitation is especially important for the interpretation of tragedy: at nearly every point of the narrative other levels of analysis intrude. Recourse to other interpretative systems, even within the structural analysis, becomes necessary. This is true of the psychological patterns and psychodynamics within the society which were prominent in the three *Hymns* discussed above, particularly in the ambivalence about sexuality and reproduction.

V

The division between civilization and savagery, humanity and bestiality, has an additional counterpart in the distinction between Greek and barbarian.[28] In the emblematic text of Atossa's dream in the *Persians* of Aeschylus the anomalous situation of humans "yoked beneath the chariot," subjected to the reins and the bit (*Pers.* 181–196, especially 189–193), parallels the anomaly of barbarians ruling Greeks. In Euripides barbarians are particularly prone to savage acts: Colchian Medea kills her children; Egyptian Theoclymenus in the *Helen* tries to kill his sister; the Taurians perform human sacrifice. Beyond even the barbarian lands, however, at the extreme edges of the inhabited world, the *oikoumenē*, the two poles of savagery and civilization meet. The mountains of northern Greece, for example, contain both the "good" and "bad" centaurs, figures who conjoin the opposites of man and beast, golden-age mildness and bestial lust.[29]

Herodotus symmetrically pairs two peoples who lived beyond the eastern limits of the Persian Empire (Hdt. 3.101): one, "eaters of raw flesh" (*kreōn edestai ōmōn*), also practice cannibalism; the other, eating no living creature at all, subsist on grass which they cook (3.99–100). The two peoples, raw-eating and practicing cookery, embody the two extreme possibilities of human society in these remote, noncivilized regions. "Primitives" at this distance from the civilized centers will be either cannibals or vegetarians. The crop that the latter gather springs up "spontaneously from the earth" (*automaton ek tēs gēs*), as in the Golden Age, but they do not, in fact, eat it raw, but boil it (3.100). The cannibals kill and eat a man or woman who becomes sick, but the sick among the vegetarians "go to a deserted place and lie down, and no one concerns himself when one is dead or sick."[30] As in Euripides' account of his Maenads on the mountain in the *Bacchae*, the regions remote from civilization will contain either golden-age primitives or bestial savages. Both are equally removed from the normative human condition. Hellanicus resolves this ambiguity between savagery and bestiality at these outer fringes by shifting his idealized people, the just, kindly, vegetarian Hyperboreans, totally beyond the limits of geographical reality (*FGr Hist* 4F187b).

"Raw-eating," *ōmophagia*, characterizes a remote race of noseless people (*amyktēres*) described by the Hellenistic historian, Megasthenes, quoted by Strabo (15.1.57, 711C).[31] With the same symmetry as that of Herodotus' Indians, Megasthenes gives us a polar opposite to this unfortunate race, namely a people who lack mouths (*astomoi*). They are not savage, but tame (*hēmeroi*) and live on the smoke of roasted meat and the scent of fruit and flowers, that is, have nothing at all to do with the physical function of mastication and digestion which their "raw-eating" neighbors perform in its lowest and crudest form. If the wild Noseless Ones are like beasts, the tame Mouthless Ones are like gods, nourished by smoke of burnt offerings.

These ethnographical examples show the same kind of "deep structure" as the myths analyzed above, a pattern which imposes and reproduces itself, encoded into different forms, in endless detail and with remarkable tenacity. One appreciates the vehemence of Plato's struggle against myth and his insistence on the inexorable "ancient cleavage between poetry and philosophy" (*Rep.* 10.607b).

VI

Tragedy, I have suggested, deals with situations where the division between civilization and savagery no longer seems to apply. Where this division is disturbed, so is the very nature of man and his humanity. Tragedy no longer locates the boundary between the civilized and the savage on the frontiers of the society, at the limits of the inhabited world, but brings it within the polis itself, within the very hearts of its rulers and citizens. The seething rage of Heracles or the screams of the "ensavaged" Philoctetes are also within Athens and within each of the spectators. The god of the orgiastic rites of mountain and forest takes a place at the very center of the polis and in the *Bacchae* topples the palace which symbolizes its civic order.

In general, however, what is "raw" or "savage" (*agrion*) lies, by definition, outside the limits of the polis, in the fields (*agroi*) or on the mountains. The Centaurs, whom the Lapiths have to fight to protect their women—the sanctions of marriage and the house in a civilized community—are literally "mountain-dwelling beasts" in Homer's phrase, *phēres oresteroi* (*Il.* 1.268). In their remote mountains they negate both the physical form and the tempered sexuality of civilized beings. Their female equivalents are the Amazons who also dwell beyond the limits of the *oikoumenē*. As the centaurs embody a distorted form of the human male, they, like the maenads, embody a deformation of the female norm. By fighting and hunting they confuse the characteristic boundaries between male and female roles; by alternating between a virginal rejection of sexual union and promiscuity they destroy marriage. Like the centaurs, they affirm the normative value of the male, city-dwelling, hoplite, agriculturally supported warrior by enacting the nonviability of the opposite.[32]

Hunters and shepherds, though less immersed in the wild than centaurs or Amazons, are also felt as ambiguous throughout classical Greek literature, from Homer to Theocritus. Literally and metaphorically, they inhabit the borderland between savage and civilized realms: they journey between mountain and plain, country and city, and live in intimate contact with the wild. We may compare the mediating function of the herdsman Anchises in the *Hymn to Aphrodite* or the mysterious goatherd Lycidas in Theocritus' Seventh *Idyll*. Akin to the spirit of the wild in which he hunts, the hunter is often a virginal figure who remains unmarried (Hippolytus), or, if he marries, cannot channel his sexual energies into the creation of a stable house, but either dies or destroys his or her beloved (Adonis, Orion, Cephalus and Procris, Atalante).[33]

In the case of Atalante the refusal to marry parallels not only her status as a hunter, but also her flight into the wild: according to Theognis she flees "the house of her father and goes off into the lofty peaks of mountains, shunning lovely marriage, golden Aphrodite's gifts" (1290–94).[34] In Aeschylus' *Seven against Thebes* the violent and boastful Parthenopaeus, who will "sack the Cadmeans' city in despite of Zeus" (*Septem* 531) is born of a mother from the mountains (531). Though his name signifies "virginal" or "maidenly," he has a "raw spirit," shows a "Gorgon's eye," and bears on his shield the device of the "raw-eating Sphinx, the reproach of the city" (538–540). This sacker of cities has no settled place within a city, but is a *metoikos*, a resident alien, of the city to which he repays his "nurture" (*trophai*, 548). His ambiguous place between city and wild, tame and "raw," parallels his ambiguous sexual and generational status between "maidenly and virile" (see 536) and between boyhood and manhood (*andropais anēr*, "a man yet a boy," 533).

The wild quality of this unsocialized adolescence also applies to the child as well as the youth.[35] Democritus' aphorism, "It is the property of a child, not a man, to desire without measure" (*ametrōs epithymein*, 68B70DK), associates the child with the unlimited, generally an ominous trait. In the Nurse's speech in Aeschylus' *Choephoroe* (753–762) the child has affinities with the beast in his lack of thought (*to mē phronoun*, *Ch.* 753) and the autonomy of young bowels (757). This visceral unrestraint also characterizes the unruliness and irreverence of the infant Hermes (Homeric *Hymn to Hermes* 295–296), whose ambiguous relation to civilization is further defined by cave dwelling, stealing, nocturnal habits, and Promethean inventiveness.[36] In the Homeric *Hymn to Aphrodite*, Aeneas is entrusted to nymphs of the forest for the first five years of his life. This period of precivilized childhood, not yet quite appropriate to the settled *oikos*, has its spatial analogue in the wild forest of the nymphs who stand between gods and men. The very young child, defined as intermediate between bestial and human, is symmetrical with the nymphs, whose biological status is intermediary between human and divine.

The Nurse's speech, to return to the *Choephoroe*, brings together the codes of diet, language, and clothing (cleanliness). It is ironically appropriate that these codes of civilized behavior are invoked when Orestes, by killing his mother, violates that nurture (*trophē*) which makes a child into a civilized human being. In so doing he reverts again to the semibestial status of the exile, hunted down like a beast by the Furies, themselves the "angry dogs of the mother" (*Ch.* 1054ff.).

Childbirth itself, presided over at times by Artemis, goddess of the wild and its young creatures, is felt to draw new mothers closer to the wild, to the basic biological functions and instincts that transcend the boundary between man and beast. Thus the new mothers in Euripides' *Bacchae* can exchange their human infants for the savage wolfcubs (*skymnous lykōn agrious*) which they suckle on the mountainside (*Ba.* 699–702). The epithet "wild," *agrios*, in line 700 stresses the negation of this civilized division between the sheltered human house to which this value system assigns women, and the exposed natural world.[37]

VII

From Homer on, *agrios*, "wild," is a term of ethical judgment. It describes the literally wild beast, but it is also a value word, indicating uncivilized, savage behavior. Achilles is "savage like a lion" when he persists in mutilating Hector's corpse without "righteous thoughts and a mind that can be moved" (*Il.* 24.39–41). That treatment of the corpse sets him outside the pale of civilized men, among the raw-eating beasts which he in fact resembles when he desires to devour the body "raw" (*Il.* 22.347; cf. 23.21, 24.39–41, 24.207). He spurns Hector's entreaty in these terms (*Il.* 22.345–350):

> Dog, do not supplicate me by knees or by parents. If only my force and heart would let me cut you up and eat you as raw meat: such deeds have you done me. No, there is no one who would keep the dogs from your head, not even if they should place here ten times the ransoms and twenty times.

Rejection of supplication in the moral code is here homologous with the refusal of burial in the ritual code and also with "eating raw" in the dietary and biological codes. Standing at the extreme limits of human behavior at this moment, Achilles would treat a human body as a beast treats its prey. At the furthest extreme, too, of epic heroism and epic violence, he is the fullest example of the problematical status of war and the warrior in the *Iliad*, defined as between godlike *kleos aphthiton* ("immortal glory") and the beastlike life of removal from city and family.[38]

When the hero of the *Odyssey* is cast up on an unknown island, he puts to himself the two alternatives about its inhabitants: either they are "savage men who do outrage, men not just" (*agrioi hybristai oude dikaioi*) or they are "hospitable to strangers," possessed of "godlike spirit" (*Od.* 6.120–121). "Savage" here has an explicitly moral definition, the opposite of *dikaios*, "just." Later the Cyclops proves to be "a wild man (*agrios*) who knows not well the ways of justice (*dikai*) or lawful ordinances" (*Od.* 9.215).[39] *Agrios* is also the name of one of the first centaurs to attack Heracles in Pholus' cave, and he is driven back by fire. On this occasion, Apollodorus says, Pholus, the "good' centaur, "served Heracles roasted meat, but he himself ate it raw." Trouble ensues when Pholus reluctantly opens a vat of wine. The centaurs, despite Pholus' hospitality, veer toward the "raw" and cannot handle this characteristic, yet potentially dangerous, product of civilization.[40]

The connections of *agrios* with the antitheses of civilization and with savagery continue throughout the fifth and fourth centuries and can be amply documented from Thucydides, Plato, and Isocrates.[41] Sophistic writers on the origins of civilization extend the antithesis between savage and tame to the dietary and botanical as well as the ethical code (cf. Herodotus 8.115.2). "Tame fruit" is the generic term for the cultivated crops of a civilized diet (Plato, *Critias* 115a). Throughout antiquity this same expression recurs to describe the cultivation of cereals. Pausanias uses it of Demeter's gift of grain and agriculture to Triptolemus (Paus. 7.18.2 and 8.4.1). In the words of a postclassical writer, her gift enabled man to "change his nomadic diet for 'tame' (*hēmeros*) cereals" (Himerius, *Orat.* 25.3).

"Tameness" in food and in manners marks the decisive step in man's passage from a primitive to a civilized state. A fragment of the tragedian Moschion (frag. 6N) describes how man passes from a life "resembling the beasts' " (6) to the discovery of "holy Demeter's fruit of tame nourishment" (23–24). Upon this discovery follow the cultivation of the vine, plowing, the city, and the house (24–28), and so "men brought their savage life (*ēgriōmenos bios*) to a tame existence" (*hēmeros diaita*, 28–29). In Diodorus' account of the origins of civilization, possibly derived from Democritus, clothing, shelter, and fire go together with the tame nurture (*hēmeros trophē*) of a fully developed humanity (Diodorus 1.8.5 = Democritus 68B5DK). Pelasgus, who appears as a sort of remote culture hero and is credited with the invention of bread, is also said to have "changed men who were bestial (*thēriōdeis*) into a tamer state" (*eis to hēmerōteron*).

At the beginning of Aeschylus' *Eumenides*, the transference of oracular power from the chthonic and Titanic divinities to the Olympian order of Apollo is marked by the advent of "tameness." Apollo's triumphant procession to Delphi is accompanied by "Hephaestus' sons, builders of roads, who make the untamed earth to be tamed" (*chthona / an-hēmeron tithentes hēmerōmenēn, Eum.* 13–14). Here mantic utterance, Olympian cult, "tameness," and technology are all related aspects of the same civilized order. At the end of play the transformation of the Furies to benign deities and their incorporation into the civic order remove the threat of their "untamed shafts, devourers of seed" (*aichmas . . . an-hēmerous, Eum.* 803) and lead into images of agriculture. When they soften, Athena compares her love of just men to that of a gardener, literally a "shepherd of crops" (*phitypoimēn, Eum.* 911).[42] This rare word contrasts with the savagery of the Furies earlier in the play: Apollo says that they should inhabit "the cave of a blood-drinking lion" since caves and savagery go together, and he calls them "a flock without a shepherd," a "herd" whose members the gods detest (*Eum.* 193–197).

VIII

"Raw," *ōmos*, is an even stronger value word than "wild" or "untame."[43] The epithet "eating raw," *ōmophagos*, in Homer applies only to wolves, jackals, and lions. The word *ōmēstēs*, "raw-eater," describes lions or fish that devour human bodies. When applied to humans it marks a special intensity of hatred exceeding civilized limits (*Il.* 4.35, 24.207). Sophocles significantly uses this epithet in a situation of horrible outrage: Tydeus gnawing the head of his enemy Melanippus, a passage where the atavistic horror attaching to cannibalism lurks in the background (frag. 731N = 799P). Likewise he calls Thyestes, as we now know from a recently published scrap of papyrus, "raw-devouring," *ōmobōros*.[44]

The ethical values associated with "rawness" remain forceful even in late fifth-century prose. When Thucydides describes how "father killed son" at Corcyra and how the sacred precinct was desecrated with blood, he sums up, "To such a point of rawness (*ōmōs*) did the civil war progress" (3.82.1). One should note that "rawness" here characterizes the violation of fundamental sanctions of civilized society: the defilement of holy places and the shedding of kindred blood. Similarly, the Athenian decision to destroy the whole city of the Mytileneans, innocent and guilty together, seemed "raw" and ominously "big" (*ōmon . . . kai mega*, Th. 3.36.4). "Raw," like "savage," does not become merely a metaphor for cruelty; it retains its associations with the beast world and with the norms of civilization that keep it at bay.

Some of the ethical force of "raw" as a value term comes from its evocations of cannibalism. Homer's Cyclops is a shepherd who dwells in caves, eats no cooked food, and devours men, raw, when he has a chance. Euripides calls him a "raw-eating walker on the mountains" (*ōmobrōs oreibatēs*, *Troades* 436). Odysseus defeats him by wine, fire, and tool-making (note the simile of the drill for the extinction of his eye, *Od.* 9.384–388), all characteristics of developed human civilization.

In tragedy, as in Homer, the strongest value term in the antinomy of savagery and civilization is *ōmos*, "raw," and its compounds. It is reserved for the worst crimes and especially for the strong taboos pertaining to the sanctions of the family. In the *Choephoroe*, to take but one example, it is the "raw and bloody strife" which requires the children to slay their mother after her murder of their father (*Ch.* 470–474): this is a house where rawness has replaced civilized order, where the subject of food evokes memories of the outrage of that order.

A hero like Heracles literally defeats the beast and imposes civilized order upon the chaos of wild nature; society as a whole figuratively performs the same task. Thus in arguing for a war of Greeks against barbarians as an extension of civilization, Isocrates resorts to the analogy of "all men's most necessary and just war against the savagery of the beasts" (*tēn agriotēta tēn tōn thērōn*, *Panath.* 163). In gradually replacing the "mixed up and beastlike life" (*thēriōdēs bios*) of early times with a truly human existence, humanity becomes its own culture hero. Fifth-century speculation on this topic self-consciously replaces the mythical conquest of monsters in physical combat with intellectual attainments and the development of man's distinctive qualities of thought, language, law, and technology.[45] Yet it still uses the model of an antithesis of man and beast, tame and wild.

The Hippocratic treatise *On Ancient Medicine* phrases this struggle for civilized order in the terms of diet. Man replaces the strong and raw, unmixed foods of wild beasts with tame and cooked foods "invented and devised by art" (*heurēmena kai tetechnēmena*) over a long period of time (*Ancient Medicine* 3). It is the achievement of the doctor as "craftsman of the art" (*cheirotechnēs*) to have freed men from a diet which was savage and beastlike (*agriē kai thēriōdēs*, 7). Isocrates describes how Demeter's fruits and grain, often called tame, as we have noted, "became the cause of our not living in a bestial manner" (*thēriōdōs zēn*, *Paneg.* 28). Hippocrates in the *Ancient Medicine* goes on to suggest the proportion: the diet of the weak is to the diet of the healthy as the diet of wild beasts is to the diet of men (8).

We can summarize these parallel relationships in the following form:

	Civilization	*Savagery*
Ethical Code	Man and Hero	Beast
	Order and Law	*hybris, bia, anomia*
	Physical conquest of beasts	
History of mankind	Human development of thought, language, religion	Mixed up and bestial life; no development
Sexual code	Incest taboos	No restraints
Dietary code	Cooked food	Raw food
	Restriction on cannibalism	Eat one another
	Cereals (tame)	Meat (raw)

IX

Whoever puts himself beyond the pale of civilization by infringing one of its basic laws tears down the hard-won barrier between man and beast. In Euripides' *Orestes* the protagonist is ensavaged, *ēgriōmenos*, in the half-mad state consequent upon his matricide (*Or.* 226, 387). Similarly, Heracles, in the destructive and unholy (*anhosion*) madness in which he kills wife and sons, "had the raging spirit of a wild lion" (Eur., *HF* 1210–12). Because madness itself comes from the gods and is a sign of divine anger, even as early as Homer (cf. *Od.* 23.11–14), the madman is a living embodiment of a disruption in the civilized order. He must therefore be excluded from the rites which, in one way or another, affirm that order. Standing outside the limits of the social order, ritually impure, deprived of fully human thought and speech, the madman stands somewhere between man and beast.[46]

Bacchylides' *Eleventh Ode* provides a good illustration of how madness functions in poetic language and structure to implicate all the major codes in the civilized order.[47] The daughters of King Proetus of Tiryns utter a boastful remark in Hera's shrine, give forth a fearful cry, are then "yoked" as if beasts, by the goddess (46) in madness, and wander outside the walls, on the "slender-leafed mountain" (55) and the "thick-grown woodland" of Arcadia (93–95). Later their father's propitious sacrifice restores the ritual order that the girls' careless speech has disrupted (104–112, 47–54). Into that story Bacchylides also weaves the quarrel between their father and their uncle, Proetus and Acrisius. Proetus left Argos to avoid conflict with his brother, a positive variant on fratricidal strife and civil war familiar from the *Antigone*. He then founds Tiryns with its "god-built ways" and its massive Cyclopean wall (72–81). His daughters' madness, like that of Cadmus' daughters at Thebes and Minyas' daughters at Orchomenos, is a source of disorder to the entire city. "Unyoked" maidens, not fully civilized, have a precarious relation to civilization. Their foolish speech angers Hera, goddess of house and marriage; they are punished by being made to wander in the mountains, the negative space outside the polis. The narrative expresses this marginality of unmarried girls in the familial, spatial, biological, ritual, and linguistic codes. Their "unyoked" condition, unmarried state, shifting between city and wild, mental instability, improper ritual behavior, and inappropriate speech are all homologous manifestations of their marginality.

Decoded, the message of this myth is a redundant form of the statement that women at this transitional point between girlhood and sexual maturity are dangerous and need enclosure in domestic space. Only through the special help of gods and the patient efforts of their father can the "unyoked" females be brought from bestiality into the civilized space of house and polis. Their madness confuses the proper distinctions between man and beast, tame and wild, city and mountain, orderly and violated rituals, civic unity and civic chaos, family harmony and family strife. Bacchylides' epithets put particular emphasis on the disrupted geographical and agricultural codes: he associates the city with the domestication of animals (80, 114) and agriculture; he associates the mountains of the Proetides' mad wanderings with wild forest and pasture (55, 93–95).

Within this structure there is also a sharp polarity between male and female. Because the girls, "still with the spirit of maidenhood" (*partheniā(i) psychā(i)*, 47–48), boast that their father's wealth exceeds that of Zeus (47–52), Hera "yokes" them with "strong necessity" (46), a negative counterpart to their "yoking" in marriage over which this goddess would preside. For the male figures of the *Ode*, however, the brothers Proetus and Acrisius, Zeus who "yokes on high" (*hypsizygos*, 3) forestalls "harsh necessity" (72) and calms an incipient quarrel. The two brothers' story begins and ends with leaving Argos (60, 81). But this movement away from a city has a creative result, enframing the foundation of a new city, Tiryns, secure in the enclosure of its "most lovely wall" (76–79). For these two sons of old King Abas, the basic codes of civilization—city, agriculture (see "earth rich in barley," 70), ritual and hoplite warfare (see 62)—remain unthreatened. Zeus keeps strife between male rulers within limits, whereas the girls go off into the unlimited space of the wild. Proetus has a momentary impulse of suicidal violence (85–88), but his warriors, spear-bearing companions, restrain him with gentle words and force of hands (89–91).

The father's propitiatory sacrifice then brings the girls back within the pale of civilized life. His foundation of a precinct (*temenos*, 110) sacred to Artemis harks back to the very beginning of the myth (to 110–112, cf. 40–42) and answers the girls' disastrous folly in the precinct (*temenos*, 48) of another goddess, Hera. Just as the male's founding of a city contrasts with the girls' mad wandering outside a city, so the father's establishment of a sacred precinct makes good his daughters' impropriety in a sacred precinct.

When the poet then turns to the present occasion of the Ode, he asks the goddess, just now propitiated by the father in the myth, to accompany him to the victor's "horse-nurturing city" (114; cf. "horse-feeding Argos" in the myth, 80): "For thou dwellest with good fortune in Metapontion," he prays, addressing Artemis (116–117). Thus the structure of the Ode circumscribes a movement from the wild to settled urban places where men and gods dwell, *naiein*, a verb which recurs at crucial points of transition in the Ode (61, 80, 116).

Greek myths often stress the danger for the community if it does not expel the madman.[48] He receives the full force of the gods' violent blow;[49] but this special attention from the gods, as in the case of Agave, Ajax, or the Proetides here, confuses the distinction between man and beast. In other versions of the myth of the Proetides (to which Bacchylides probably alludes in 46 and 84), madness takes the form of the delusion that they actually are beasts, mooing like cows, so that the confusion between human and bestial is even greater. Physically and mentally the madman leaves the civilized space, wandering in body or mind. Like the bacchants or maenads ("mad women") who themselves occupy an ambiguous place between man and beast, city and wild, the madman goes off alone to forest or mountain.[50] The rituals which he or she performs, like dance or music, are askew, perverted, sinister. He or she is, or becomes, a hunter, is exposed to the elemental "storm" or "wave" of his madness, loses speech, status, honor (*timē*), or, in a further degradation, loses sexual identity or even human form (the Proetides; cf. Pentheus as "beast" in the *Bacchae*).[51]

These confusions of man and beast threaten civilization even more drastically when the maddened beast-man is the civilizing hero himself. This inversion is the motive force in the tragedy of Heracles in Sophocles' *Trachiniae* and in Euripides' *Heracles Mad*. In the *Heracles* the hero's madness is both the cause of the calamity in the house and the manifestation of an inward disorder of the soul. It is both the result of and the metaphor for the irrational in the universe, in gods and in men. It is the central node for a manifold disruption of civilization. It involves the shedding of kindred blood and the destruction of the family, indeed of the family's physical shelter, the house itself (996–1000).

The onset of Heracles' madness and its immediate aftermath dramatize in rapid succession the following violations of the civilized order:

The breakdown of the distinction between man and beast (869–870)

Perversion of communal dance and song (892, 897)

The hunting of men as if beasts (898; cf. 860)

Inversion of upper and lower worlds (872, 907–908; cf. 822, 834, 844, 883, 1110, 1119)

Destruction of the sanctity of hearth and altar (922ff.)

Destruction of speech (926, 930, 935)

Defilement of ritual purity (937, 940, 1145)

Corruption of sacrifice (995; cf. 453, 1023), combined with destruction of the house and murder of kin (the children as sacrificial victims).

The hero who had tamed the "wild sea" (851) now, in his madness, rolls his "wild-looking Gorgon's eye" (990; cf. 883–884). The tale of the Gorgon, a mythic paradigm of heroic victory over wild and monstrous forces, recurs to mark a hero who, in his madness, himself becomes a figure like the Gorgon, beyond the pale of the civilized world (see 867, 883, 990). His power to tame the wild sea and earth (20, 851–852) is swallowed up in the madness which itself floods over him with the violence of the sea (see 837, 1087, 1091), effacing that barrier between man and wild nature which his heroic labors have established (for examples, 359–430, especially 400–402). The hero who saved wife and children from being sacrificed as victims to Hades (451–453), grimly "yoked" in their death (454–455), now himself performs this very rite of perverted sacrifice and reduces his closest human ties to the level of beasts or birds (898, 974, 982). Euripides describes the act of killing in metaphors drawn from technology: the lathe and the forge (978, 992). The irony, once more, sharpens the paradox of the monster-killer turned monstrous. The purifying smoke of this inverted sacrifice in fact pollutes and leads downward to Hades and bestiality, not upward toward Olympus and the gods (936–937).

The following tabular summary shows how the madman is depicted in tragedy:

Beast	Madman	Man
The wild (*agrios*)	Outside pale of polis (exile)	Dweller in polis
Killing	Perverted sacrifice (Iphigeneia, Agamemnon, Cassandra, Ajax)	Duly performed sacrifice
Roars, grunts, etc.	Incoherent language	Speech
Hunted by man	The man who is hunted	The man who is hunter
No taboos	Kills blood kin ("raw strife," *Ch.* 474; cf. Eur., *HF*889)	Restraint on killing kin
No house (caves, mountains)	Destroys house	Inhabits and defends house
(Purity does not apply)	Ritually impure (outside civic order)	Purity (harmonious civic order)

X

For the Greeks the most horrible manifestation of savagery and "rawness" is cannibalism. We have already noted the connection between cannibalism and the "raw" in Homer's Cyclops and Herodotus' ethnography. The myth of Thyestes presented the most violent possible inversion of humanity and bestiality, weaving together cannibalism, adultery, fratricidal hatred, sacrifice, hospitality. The laws of table, bed, and altar are all violated together. No wonder that no fewer than eight dramatists—nine if we include the references to the legend in Aeschylus' *Oresteia*—wrote tragedies on Thyestes.[52]

Cannibalism breaks down the differentiation between man and beast and confounds *physis*, the state of nature, with *nomos*, the ordered structure of human society. The earliest formulation of this relation between civilization and cannibalism occurs in Hesiod's *Works and Days* (276–280):

> Zeus son of Kronos appointed this law (*nomos*) for men, that fishes and beasts and winged birds eat one another, since there is no justice (*dikē*) among them, but to men he gave justice, which is by far best.

Centuries later Plato uses essentially the same criterion for defining the state of civilization: the taboo against eating one another (*allēlophagia*) differentiates men from beasts (*Epinomis* 975a-b). In the *Republic* Lycaon's cannibalism on the mountain which bears his name is the negation of all civilized humanity.[53] Lycaon is the prototype of the tyrant, the figure whose outwardly human form conceals the terrible "many-figured beast" within. At the opposite extreme from Lycaon and the bestiality (*to thēriōdes*) of the tyrannical soul stands the near-divinity of the philosophical life, the highest and only proper goal for man, "to become like to God insofar as this is possible for a mortal" (*Rep.* 10. 613a–b; cf. 2.383c).

Within the code correlating diet with human values, cannibalism denotes the extreme polarity to the god's ambrosia: rawness, putrefaction, bestiality over against incorruptible purity, perfume, divinity. Lycaon, metamorphosed into a beast, is explicitly contrasted with heroes who become gods, Heracles, Britomartis, Amphiaraus, Castor and Pollux (Pausanias 8.2.3–6). In the story of Tydeus, too, a cannibalistic act marks the extreme terms of god and beast: according to Pherecydes, Tydeus lost the gift of immortality because he gnawed the head of his enemy, Melanippus, "like a beast" (*dikēn thēros*). Sophocles vividly described this scene in a lost play (frag. 731N = 799P).[54]

Lycaon's violation in the dietary code closely parallels that of another mythical evil-doer, Tantalus. The same message is encoded into slightly different but closely analogous terms. To mortal men Tantalus gives the divine food, nectar and ambrosia; to the gods he serves a cannibalistic feast of his own son, a meal thereby doubly marked (overdetermined) as outside the pale of humanity and close to the beasts. Instead of gaining the immortality which nectar and ambrosia would confer, therefore, he plunges from Olympus to Hades. There he is tormented with eternal hunger, the reverse of the plenitude and feasting which follow proper sacrifice. Lycaon, after tempting the gods with a banquet of human flesh, not only himself undergoes metamorphosis into a wolf, but jeopardizes the continued existence of the human race, as his act motivates Jupiter to destroy humanity. In both myths the perverted hierarchical order, god/man/beast, is homologous with ambrosia/cooked food or sacrifice/rawness or cannibalism in the dietary code and Olympus/earth/Hades in the spatial code.

Sacrifice sanctifies this order in an enacted ritual. In sacrifice man acknowledges his inferiority to the gods, to whom he offers the sacrificial victim, but he also asserts his superiority to the beast which he kills, but kills in an ordered structure of ritual, not "savagely," as beasts kill in the wild, in the realm of *physis*.[55] Sacrifice stands to cannibalism as civilization stands to savagery. In the Lycaon myth the participants in a perverted sacrifice lose their human status and experience in their own bodies the bestiality implicit in the cannibalistic act itself.

In Pindar's version of the Tantalus myth in his *First Olympian Ode*, the cannibalistic banquet offered the gods has a foil in Pelops' positive mediation between immortality and death through Poseidon's erotic "favor" or *charis* (see *Ol.* 1.38–40, 49–66, 77–78). Through the funeral games at his tomb, "an altar thronged by strangers" (*Ol.* 1.93), Pelops enjoys a valid equivalent of immortality, as opposed to his father's double abuse of immortality, feeding the gods the impure meal of human flesh and giving ambrosia to men (*Ol.* 1.63–66). Tantalus' attempt to offer ambrosia to mortal men stands to the proper food of men as his cannibalistic offering to the gods stands to the true food of the gods. Further, cannibalism is as remote from divinity as Hades is from Olympus. By stealing nectar to give it to his mortal companions in order to make them immortal, Tantalus echoes Prometheus' theft of fire. Prometheus' act, through Zeus's punitive intervention, results in the "separating" of god and men as solemnized by sacrifice;[56] Tantalus' act, punished by the gods, results in the reestablishment of proper order, since Tantalus is sent down to Hades and Pelops down to earth, from which he can again reach the realm of the gods through heroic action, divine favor, and cult.

Sacrifice is the ritual wherein the mediation of god and beast includes and symbolizes all other rituals. It is the mediating action par excellence. Plato, for example, has Diotima describe the *daimonion*, a highly intellectualized form of mediation between gods and men as follows (*Symposium* 202e): "The *daimonion* is that which interprets and conveys what is from men to the gods and what is from the gods to men, of the one requests and sacrifices (*thysiai*), of the other commands and return for sacrifices (*amoibas tōn thysiōn*); and, being in between both, it completes them so that the whole itself is bound together (*syndedesthai*) with itself." Facing both ways, the sacrificial act establishes both the upper and the lower limits of the human condition. It marks man's distance from the gods, but simultaneously establishes the possibility of man's drawing close to the gods in the relation established by the ritual: "Sacrifice creates a communication between man and god greater than the distance which it cannot fill."[57]

Given this ordering function of sacrifice, it is easy to see why its disruption should play so central a role in tragedy.[58] Tragedy elicits from the rites and myths of sacrifice not the stability but the ambiguity of the human condition. Man is set apart from the raw world of the beasts on the one hand, but lacks the incorruptible food of the gods on the other, though he looks up toward that immortal realm. He is neither above the processes of nature, as are the gods, nor a passive unquestioning participant in those processes, as are the beasts. The basic instrument of civilization, fire, is intimately linked with sacrifice, but that link, as Vernant has shown, also connects sacrifice with duplicity, trickery, guile.[59] Prometheus, mediator between gods and men and founder of sacrifice, is himself a highly ambiguous figure. Through Pandora, he is also connected with the parallel institution of marriage, which ratifies the position of men between divine and bestial in sexual terms. The complex of myths around Prometheus and Pandora which define the human condition in Hesiod shows civilization as compromised by those very activities of restless intelligence and guile that set it apart from the beasts and near the gods.

In tragedy sacrifice reveals its dark face, indicating not the stable position of man in a clearly delineated hierarchy, but rather his possible swing between godlike power and unruly violence. Again and again sacrifice is the backdrop for the most fearful crimes: Heracles' and Medea's slaughter of children; Clytaemnestra's and Deianeira's killing of husbands. Aeschylus' *Agamemnon* focuses on the swift convertibility of sacrifice into abomination. The king is slaughtered, sacrificed, like an animal at the altar, and therewith plummets from king to beast. This double violation (man/beast, man/god) converts the places of civilization—house, hearth, and city—into places of savagery and rawness, where even more fundamental sanctions will be violated. The rain of blood at Agamemnon's "sacrifice," we recall, soon becomes a grisly mockery of the rain that fertilizes the earth in the life-giving processes of nature (1388–93). A rite that ought to ensure the survival of city and house only sets the stage for darker crimes.

XI

To focus attention on structure rather than on the individual hero is at odds with the dominant tradition of Greek literary criticism. Yet the traditional approach may rest on assumptions about the centrality and strength of the self which tragedy seeks to question rather than support.

Structuralism itself arises out of the crisis about the assumptions of Western ego-centered subjectivity dominant since Descartes, but rooted in the Greek concern to separate subject and object and establish hierarchical categories of knowledge.[60] It is not clear that structuralism has as yet come to grips fully with this crisis of the self and of knowledge. But this crisis is at the center of Greek tragedy, perhaps of all tragedy. Rather than assuming an integrated self in control of a structured world, tragedy presents that self and the structures which surround it and emanate from it as threatened by dissolution. Viewed in structuralist terms, tragedy appears as concerned less with a coherent, well-ordered personality than with symbols of confrontation between structure and chaos, with the mental and verbal systems that individuals and societies have devised to keep chaos at bay.

An Ajax or an Oedipus becomes the focal point for the collapse of the polarities between culture and nature, civilization and savagery, order and disorder. The hero's tragic condition is the field in which these polarities reach their extreme tension and finally fly hopelessly apart rather than achieve mediation. Civilized and savage spaces become confused; inner and outer, city and wild, king and outlaw lose their distinctive identity and become dangerously ambiguous. The old, unquestioned norms and laws suddenly seem unfamiliar and inadequate to the new, nonnormative situation which tragedy presents. Terms like "raw," "tame," "wild," "savage" are not just metaphors but retain the enormous power which the Greeks felt to be present when man confronts the beast world outside and inside himself. Those antitheses and their ramifications are still meaningful in our own oscillation between civilization and savagery.

It is the paradox of tragedy that by exposing us to the chaos and violence of ourselves, it also saves us from ourselves. By destroying our structures, tragedy vouchsafes us a saving knowledge of the fragility and artificiality of those structures. Hence it keeps us from being trapped by them. It keeps us open to the otherness which comes through suffering and is apprehended only through suffering. Our cultural and linguistic structures seek perpetually to close the wound which the otherness of the world makes as it impinges upon us. Tragedy operates within civilization to keep civilization in touch with the complexity of its existence in a world that is not of its own making. "We have art," Nietzsche wrote, "that we may not perish of life." But we have tragic art that we may not forget the dimensions of life that our structures cannot encompass. Tragedy pushes back the structures and reopens the painful possibility of seeing life as chaos. Without that paradoxically pleasurable pain of tragedy, our order and our structures would become sterile, self-enclosed, solipsistic, arrogant with the hybris of their own intellectual power.

3

Kingship, Ritual, Language

 Greek tragedy, I have suggested, operates both within and beyond the limits of the polis, at the borders where polarities merge, definitions become unclear, the orderly composition of human institutions becomes ambiguous. Here, through the suffering of the tragic hero, man discovers and experiences anew the preciousness and the fragility of his most distinctively human, and therefore most ambiguous, attributes.

Like Hamlet, Western drama's other great paradigm of man's suspension between extreme and contradictory capacities ("in apprehension how like a God," and yet "this quintessence of dust"), Oedipus too stands at the precarious point where rationally comprehensible human order dissolves into mysteries. Both heroes, forced to delve beneath the surface appearance of the order of house and kingdom, unmask dark and horrible truths which negate that order. Hamlet's risks of damnation and madness in his initial step of following a ghost who might be a demon of Hell are the theological and psychological equivalents of the Sophoclean hero's literal and figurative journey beyond the pale of the civilized polis. Oedipus leaves his city for exile, the crossroads, the meeting with the Sphinx outside the walls of Thebes. Hamlet dares to follow the ghost to the most deserted parts of the battlements ("Whither wilt thou lead me? Speak. I'll go no further"), beyond the call or help of his friends, a place which, though part of the castle, is yet most exposed to supernatural beings who stand between grace and guilt. There is more than literal place involved in Horatio's talk of the "flood" and "dreadful summit" ("The very place puts toys of desperation / without more motive, into every brain"), or Lear's "dread summit of this chalkey bourne" that lies "within a foot of th' extreme verge."[1]

Both Hamlet and Oedipus, burdened with the duties and dangers of their kingly rank, act as mediators between the human and the supernatural. Hamlet bears the responsibility for "setting right" the "accursed time" and cleaning out the fetid "unweeded garden" that Denmark has become. To both figures falls the heavy task of avenging a slain king's blood. Oedipus himself bears the stain of that blood and its terrible pollution. In Sophocles, too, the citizens' supplication in the opening scene creates a vivid, visual representation of the sacral quality of Oedipus' kingship, his exposed position between human and superhuman forces. Charged with the responsibilities of this kingship, he must undertake to heal the ills which exist in its relation to the gods.

The hero-king symbolically concentrates in his own person the danger of man's position between natural and supernatural forces and between autonomous power and helplessness in the face of the unknown. His virtuous excesses, suffering, and death implicate the entire cosmos.

Oedipus is perhaps the most striking exemplar of this pattern, so striking that it remains stamped even on very un-Sophoclean adaptations of his tragedy centuries later. In Seneca, Oedipus' acceptance of his punishment stands in immediate relation to the cosmic powers. His exile at once affects sky and earth, cleanses the air and brings a "gentler condition of the heavens." "With myself I draw off the earth's death-bearing taints" is his exit line (*mortifera mecum vitia terrarum extraho*).[2] Even in the decorously trimmed versions of Corneille and Voltaire the ancient pattern, transmitted by Seneca, has a feeble survival. In Corneille's *Oedipe* one touch of the king's sacred blood on the earth ends the "Heavens' war."[3] Voltaire dispenses with the sacred blood, but even his rationalized and neoclassic form expands to admit mysterious offstage effects of thunder and lightning: thus does "the god of earth and sky" manifest the appeasement of his wrath as "the infectious fires are no longer kindled" and a "serener sun rises."[4]

More exposed than other men to the extremes of his existence and more intense in his reactions to those extremes, the Sophoclean hero is more likely to rush violently from one opposite to the other. For these same reasons his sufferings are paradigmatic of the precarious status of the entire human condition. His energies run at the highest voltages. A small event can short-circuit the whole system, suddenly reversing the charge, sending him to the opposite polarity.

Kingship, by its very power, is ambiguous. The ancients were fond of observing that the tallest trees and mountains were most likely to be struck by lightning. The lonely eagle-kings of the *Agamemnon's* first ode have their griefs in "pathless places" (*ekpatia algea*). A writer of late antiquity comments: "Wishing to show the king aloof (*idiazonta*) . . . they depict him as an eagle, for this creature has its rest in deserted places (*en erēmois topois*) and soars higher than all the birds."[5] The sad tales of the deaths of kings are as proverbial in classical Greece as in Elizabethan England. On finding interest in the Trojan War among the remote Taurians, Euripides' Pylades comments, "All who have any breadth of converse with the world know the sufferings of kings (*ta tōn basileōn pathēmata*)" (*Iphigeneia in Tauris* 670–671).

Royalty is bound especially closely to the wheel of fortune and is especially vulnerable to its sudden turns.[6] The point is a favorite one with Herodotus (e.g. 1.207). The king's (and hero's) special power, whether of body or of spirit, places him in a position to violate the taboos which ordinary men must respect. His special relation to the gods (marked, in the case of the Sophoclean hero, by oracles, omens, or other divine intervention) sets him at the limits of human strength and knowledge. Performing the dangerous function of interceding between the sacred and the profane for his people, he is, as the priest says of Oedipus in the *Tyrannus*, "the first of men . . . in the encounters with the gods" (33–34). The special irony of the fact that Oedipus suffers the sickness of his people more than all and feels the grief of the city more than if it were for his own life (59–64, 93–94) is only a tragic intensification of the king's exposed position between the social order and the numinous realm, between the secure institutions of civilization and the unknown.[7]

Like the sacrificial victim, the king-hero is the vehicle through whom sacred power courses; and this power is indifferent as to the direction in which it flows, whether upward to sanctify, or downward to render accursed, untouchable, *sacer*, *hieros*. One step and he moves beyond the pale, discharging the violence and disorder that the society tries to keep at bay.[8]

The mythological thinking of archaic peoples is especially concerned with these points where opposites intersect, the *coincidentia oppositorum* where the boundaries of opposing entities touch one another and "identity consists of two opposites."[9] Hence in ancient cosmology an especially rich body of myth attaches to places where East and West meet, where the sun dies and is reborn, where life and death cross.[10] The tragic hero occupies one such point, and his suffering is a symbolic locus of transition between opposing states: man and beast and man and god, upper and lower limits, light and darkness, and so on. The main female figures in the hero's life are drawn into a similar fusion of opposites: a Clytaemnestra, a Deianeira, a Gertrude are both "eternally traitorous wife" and "eternally fostering and protective mother."[11] In this crossing of polarities, psychology, with its concept of ambivalence, and structuralism complement one another.

This intersection of opposites passes into the language and imagery describing the tragic catastrophe. In Aeschylus' *Agamemnon*, as we have seen, the act which dooms the King appears in the context of a plunge from god to beast, from divine honor to bestial sacrifice. The opposing elements, fire and water, which open the trilogy in the beacon-fires crossing the seas, recur at points of crucial moral decision to create a cosmic frame for the inverted ritual slaughter of the king/victim.[12]

By calling the cosmic and social orders into question through his ambiguous position within and beyond established limits, the king-hero enacts in his doom the necessity for that order. The tragic pattern of his life is, in a sense, the photographic negative of the order that ordinary men live in the diurnal round. The tragic experience, therefore, in its gripping involvement of the audience in the suffering of an admired, but towering, more (and less) than human figure, creates a fresh sense of the cosmic order, a deeper perception of its interlocking "codes," and a renewed feeling of the place of the human condition within it.

The more shocking the king's violation of the order, the more fully the events which precede and result from the violation renew a "cosmological consciousness" in the spectators.[13] Oedipus' incest and patricide form the paradigm case. It is this "cosmological consciousness"—not necessarily the resolution of the conflicts between the extreme polarities—which the hero effects by following the dictates of his extraordinary nature and the destiny which that nature has established for him.

Only by overstepping the limits of civilization and suffering the consequences can the hero fulfill his role in the cosmic order. His task is the paradoxical one of enacting the necessity of that order by negating it. He "attracts magnetically all the contagious miasmas in order to convert them into stability and fecundity."[14] This is hardly to say that his tragic suffering frightens us back into the safety of firm limits by illustrating the dangers of exceeding them. It is the hero's curse and destiny to destroy the structures of "difference," to use Girard's term, the systems of distinctions that constitute civilization, but he does not necessarily return to the place where he began. His world cannot again contract into the secure frame of unquestioned normality.

It is tempting to compare this pattern of heroic suffering with the sacrificial rituals associated with the *pharmakos* or scapegoat, as Vernant, Girard, Jean-Pierre Guépin, and others have done.[15] Such rites often involve a loosening of normal constraints on behavior. The catharsis of tragedy results from the banishing of chaos by ritually and symbolically enacting chaos. The analogy, however, need not imply the origin of tragedy in such rites, nor the exclusively ritual function of tragedy in ancient society.

Ritual tends to be conservative and affirmative of the cosmic and social order. Tragedy is innovative, polysemous, and deeply questioning of that order. The myths embodied or reflected in ritual are basically unitary in their meaning. Those of tragedy are complex and problematical, open to new interpretations, focal points of conflicted points of view and divided values.

In tragedy the hero's selfhood loses its simplicity and becomes doubled with its own "chaotic adversary."[16] The same covering, the same mask, holds the greatest purity and the greatest corruption: one thinks of Oedipus or Hippolytus. Such a figure stands both at the center and at the confines of the civilized order. His ambiguous identity threatens the logical categories which civilization needs to safeguard against the engulfing sameness of nature. Many societies regard twins, pairs of doubles, as a dangerous occurrence, a curse to be expiated by elaborate rites or to be expunged even by destroying the pair.[17]

For this figure the unity of knowledge splits apart into a tragic knowledge of illusion and reality. To know reality in its oneness belongs to the gods; human knowledge is divided, ambiguous. "For the god," says Heraclitus, "all things are good and just, but men suppose some things just and other things unjust."[18] Sophoclean tragedy is often concerned with this difference in perspective between divine and human knowledge. The tragic oneness of reality, however, is very different from the philosophic oneness of Heraclitus' divine knowledge. For the tragic hero the oneness of his world is only the appearance of a concealed fearful duality. The violent shattering of this illusory oneness into duality, of surface order into conflict, is an essential part of the tragic experience.[19]

The tragic hero has the task of confronting the most violent divisions within himself, enduring his *Selbstentzweiung,* the experience of his self as contradiction and conflict. This experience is the riddle which he presents to himself. He becomes conscious of a self which is also his enemy.[20] Rather than evade or repress this vision, he suffers its full consequences. His life becomes an open existence with his evil double, his dark shadow. As the unity of the tragic polis divides to admit a potential savagery, so the king/hero (or queen/heroine), the guarantor of the civic or domestic order, divides and opens to reveal violence, destructive passion, blindness. But through the course of his suffering he compels this other self to stand apart and become visible in its separateness.

Hence in *Oedipus Tyrannus* the hero's initial fusion of king and pollution breaks apart into the doubleness which symbolizes the enigmatic and contradictory nature of man. When in the *Agamemnon* the two opposites, king and beast, stand clearly revealed in their terrible hidden union, the violations within the house of Atreus emerge into the light for their eventual purgation. In the *Bacchae* Euripides plays upon the strange fascination that links together the god and the human victim killed in his rites. In the *Medea* the heroine stands forth at the end revealed as something both greater and less than human, a quasi-goddess on her divinely given chariot, but yet a beast, a "lioness," in the murder of her own children.

The Sophoclean pattern, however, differs from the Euripidean. Pentheus in the *Bacchae* has only a moment, the last of his life, in which he recognizes that he, the king, has become the hunted beast, the sacrificial victim of the Maenads and their god whom he has persecuted and kept outside his city. Sophocles' Oedipus, having undergone the tragic experience of opening the breach between illusion and truth, will, like Teiresias, spend his old age living with this knowledge, its prophet and interpreter as well as its exemplar.

In passing between and confusing the basic polarities between god and beast, king and sacrificial victim, the Sophoclean hero powerfully enacts what anthropologists since Arnold Van Gennep have called "liminality," the boundary situations of human life, the experience of nothingness in moving between or beyond the familiar categories into the irregular, the interstitial, the ambiguous, the unique and unclassifiable. This experience, as we noted briefly in chapter 1, not only confuses the spatial divisions between inner and outer, city and wild, but also disturbs the fixed boundaries between nature and culture. As Victor Turner observes, it also forces culture to turn to nature and to relinquish its structures for the potentially fruitful denial of structure. In this liminal state, culture and nature cease to be necessary opposites. Here nature can hold up a mirror to culture's artifice and artificiality and thereby infuse fresh vigor into society's conventions and fictions: "Thus it is in liminality and also in those phases of ritual that abut on liminality that one finds profuse symbolic reference to beasts, birds, and vegetation. Animal masks, bird plumage, grass fibers, garments of leaves swathe and enshroud the human neophytes and priests. Thus, symbolically, their structural life is snuffed out by animality and nature, even as it is being regenerated by these very same forces. One dies *into* nature to be reborn *from* it. Structural custom, once broken, reveals two human traits. One is liberated intellect, whose liminal product is myth and proto-philosophical speculation; the other is bodily energy, represented by animal disguises and gestures. The two may then be combined in various ways."[21] Tragedy is surely one such combination of culture and nature at a point of fluid interchange. But all forms of art, to some extent, are liminal spaces, arbitrary models that can suspend old patterns, allow the familiar to be penetrated by the unknown and the alien, and experiment with other modes of grasping the world. The public, ritualized medium of tragedy in ancient Athens makes that liminal space visible in the center of the city.

Turner reminds us again that metaphors of bestiality are not just rhetorical or conventional motifs but have a deep significance for the structural relationships of the society. At the same time the dissolution of such structures in the experience of liminality has its creative side in that paradoxical enhancement of cosmological consciousness described earlier. This positive side has to do also with the fact that the experience of tragedy is not depressing, but somehow enhances our sense of life. Within the fictional framework itself the tragic hero who enters this liminal state and is stripped of his authority, strength, and the outward attributes of happiness or success gains in return a sacred power, a spiritual strength, a deeper knowledge, or a new depth of humanity. The figure of Oedipus in both the *Tyrannus* and the *Coloneus* is perhaps the clearest example, but the pattern holds to some extent for all other Sophoclean heroes.

This double function of liminality—the destruction of order and the creation of new sources of order and energy—is relevant not only to the tragic hero himself but also to the social context of the tragic performance in general. Standing at the border between social structure and the negation of structure, the dramatic performance, to some extent like all ritualized situations where works of art are realized, can reflect upon the system and its values in ways that other institutions—the assembly or the law courts, for example—cannot.[22] The paradoxical relation of the hero to the cosmic and social orders parallels the paradoxical relation of the tragic performance to the ritual structures of the society. Both tragic hero and tragic performance partake of the freedom of marginality. The tragic action, the *drōmenon* or *drama*, the "enacted thing," is part of a rite that affirms order and stability. The dramatic festivals come at a major boundary point in the year, the transition between winter and spring, and they honor the divinity who, next to Artemis, is most closely associated with the wild and the chaotic energies of the wild.

The privileged space of the orchestra is analogous to the privileged status of the hero-king. Kingship itself, viewed in spatial terms, is a kind of "politico-ritual space" which alone makes possible the high passions and the elemental violence wherein man strides to the extreme limits of his being.[23] In both the physically demarcated space of the orchestra and the metaphorically removed "space" of royal status is enacted the crossing of the fundamental barriers of the human condition.

And yet, in the imaginative experience of the pollution enacted in tragedy, there is, as Aristotle observes, something cleansing, a purification or catharsis.[24] In watching the negation of its order the community undergoes the deepest experience of its cosmological consciousness. In the logic of the paradoxes that we have been exploring, the tragic confrontation with the negation of civilization is a profoundly civilizing experience.[25]

The god of tragedy is the god in whose rites the barriers between man and beast and between man and god break down. Dionysus points to what is beyond the normal limits of civilization and occupies the space between city and wild, and between collective and individual devotion.[26] He opens the city to possibilities of latent or open contradiction to itself. Not only do his devotees in the great central speech of Euripides' *Bacchae* suckle the young of wild creatures (699–702), but the "mountain and the beasts join in the bacchic revel," *symbakcheuein*, with the human worshipers (726–727). In the imagery and illusionism of this play Dionysus is himself both beast and god, an anomalous union of the extreme polarities, just as his followers are both beasts and men.[27] Here human society no longer rests on the hierarchical division between gods, men, and beasts. As one commentator remarks, "When Aristotle said that the solitary man must be either a beast or a god, he forgot perhaps that there were social groups which could make a man both at once. To the *thiasos* of Dionysus everything is surrendered, including the intellect and the individuality; while it enables the individual to transcend his limitations, it is indifferent to the direction of that transcendence; it allows the lowest to set its easy and uncritical standard."[28] In this simultaneous coexistence of the lowest with the highest in the same soul, under the same mask, lie both Dionysus' fascination and his terror.

The mysterious foreigner arrived from distant lands, the giver of the ambiguous and dangerous blessings of wine and ecstasy, Dionysus has a place both within the polis and in the civic space of the theater, and outside the polis in the mountains and fields.[29] Even when he is accepted as part of the state religion he retains his dangerous aspect.[30] Later we shall see how the *Antigone* exploits this tension. In the cortège of this god follow creatures who mingle human and bestial shapes, satyrs and silenoi who themselves have a major role in the satyr play that accompanies each poet's three tragedies at the Dionysiac festival.

Under the protection of this god, the dramatic performances could express all that the disciplined life of the polis suppressed: release of emotion, the admission of the potential chaos of the universe, the loss of rational control over self and the world, the power of the female component both in society and in the individual personality.[31] The tragic universe, like its god, stands in some sense for an anti-world, a dimension coexistent with normal reality but usually invisible or denied. Here clear-cut boundaries and discrete forms give way to union and merger; duality surrenders to an ambiguous oneness, and apparent unity fractures into a dialectic of seeming and being, external and internal, accidental and essential.

Dionysus calls into question the clear separation of illusion and reality. The *Bacchae* again provides a powerful and frightening representation of his powers of illusion. He presides over the passage between the sober world of everyday reality and the ecstatic, corybantic, and hallucinatory madness that comes with his gifts of wine and the orgiastic dance.[32]

The mask, an essential element in the ancient tragic performance, is like the other formal constituents of tragedy, part of a rite and a theatrical convention. But the mask also points beyond itself to something mysterious: tangible, but not real; physical, but not substantial. It is an artifact, a creation of human hands, and, in addition, a visible symbol of the fragile surface of human life, of the masklike quality of existence itself, the potential emptiness of illusion beneath the forms of our daily, well-ordered lives.[33] The tragic performance at the Dionysia or Lenaea as a ritual and communal act affirms the solidity of those forms. But the mask reminds us of the emptiness and fictive quality of the mimesis which shapes human actions both on the stage and in "reality."

The mask momentarily denies the logical continuity of the functional in order to show us reality under the aspect of the alien playfulness of pure symbol. The mask may also function as a means of transcending the division between nature and culture.[34] The normal coherence of our practical, manipulative relation to reality is suspended, and with it the familiar utilitarian correspondence between signifier and signified. The "informational" function of the sign in the semantic system which governs all the codes of the civilized order is subordinated to an autonomous aesthetic-symbolic function.[35]

The spectator in the theater of Dionysus found himself confronted at once by another division. The individual characters, each distinctively costumed, are pushed to the limits of human understanding, whereas the collective personage of the chorus, twelve or fifteen figures, all dressed in the same way, represents in some sense the voice of the civic consciousness (which, of course, is not necessarily the voice of the poet). These visual details themselves repeat the tensions implicit in the situation of the performance: on the one hand the dissolution of the normative in the fiction, with its overreaching tragic hero; on the other hand the reassertion of the normative in the ritual dimension of the performance and in the grouped choristers who usually endorse accepted values: moderation, limits, traditional piety.

The tragic performance, its competitive structure, elaborate selection of plays and judges under the authority of one of the chief magistrates, the public celebration and commemoration of the poet's victory, and the architectural geometry of the theater itself all express the organizing power of the united polis and its aspiration toward harmony between man and god, city and nature. But the plays themselves show that order, social and cosmic both, torn or threatened.

The *content* of tragedy thus contradicts its social and ritual *context*. Greek tragedy's highly structured conventions of language, communal and ritual setting, and spectacle (including costume, staging, gesture, and the ordered space of the theater) sharpen that confrontation between security in the collective and the dangerous venture into loneliness and the unknown. Even more than Sophocles, Euripides self-consciously mirrors that tension within the play itself, opposing the continuity of future ritual to the finality of present suffering. The *Hippolytus*, for example, contrasts the death of the hero who denies the power of sexuality with his future role in the rites of girls about to be married (*Hipp.* 1423–30). At the end of the *Medea* the passionate Colchian witch, possessing the attributes of both goddess and beast (lioness; see 1342–43, 1358), announces the ritual commemoration of her slaughtered children. This rite will take place in the precinct of Hera, goddess of the sanctity of marriage, which Medea has both savagely defended and savagely outraged. In these situations, as in some analogous cases in Sophocles' *Ajax* and *Trachiniae*, the ritual functions both as the resolution and as the sharper crystallization of a contradiction.[36]

This tension between content and context is perhaps latent in all tragedy insofar as tragedy presupposes a social context, the ritual (however diluted and secularized) of performance. In the ancient plays the most sacred laws of human civilization are desecrated. The acts committed in these plays, if done intentionally, bring, as Aristotle emphasizes, *to miaron*, that which pollutes with its indelible stain, the uncleanness of terrible crimes.[37] Sons kill fathers and fathers kill sons. Children slay their mothers. Gods are defied. Shrine, altar, and hearth are violated. Incest, lust, the transgressive language of boast or insult are the rule.[38] Innocent men scream with the agony of torments or diseases which they have not deserved. The spectators of these plays come into contact with the "uncleanness" which must be excluded from their ritual context itself.

In the magic circle of the orchestra, ritual itself is perverted. Sacrifice is violated; kings are ritually impure; the hierarchical order embracing god, man, and beast that ritual helps affirm is overturned.

What is true of tragedy's relation to ritual in its social functions is also true of tragedy's relation to myth and to language. Whereas the myth that provided the material of tragedy moves toward the resolution of oppositions, tragedy itself recasts the myth so as to complicate, distort, or deny the mediations. "The myth," as Roland Barthes remarks, "starts from contradictions and tends progressively toward their mediation; tragedy, on the contrary, refuses the mediation, keeps the conflict open."[39]

The comedies and satyr plays at these festivals present similar violations of social and ritual order, but move in an opposite and complementary direction. The animal choruses of old comedy break down the barriers between man and beast. Plots like those of Aristophanes' *Peace* or *Birds* blur or reverse the distinction between man and god. The exchange of roles between the generations in the *Wasps* or between the sexes in the *Lysistrata* reverses terms in the familial and social codes, but without the nightmarish consequences that befall Pentheus in the *Bacchae*. The sacred processions of the *Acharnians* or *Frogs* distort and parody the ritual order. Plays like the *Wasps* or *Knights* reduce the lawcourts and the democracy itself to the status of laughable bungling, ignorance, stupidity. But these inversions turn out to be affirmative rather than dangerous: they express the limitless plasticity of existence rather than ominous violations of a closely knit hierarchical order.

The world of comedy is open to infinite possibility; that of tragedy hedged about by a mysterious cosmic order that must be respected. Hence the fusion of opposites in comedy is part of a utopian confidence in life. The Dionysiac merging of antitheses is not resisted; joyful exuberance can spring the usual limits without the reflex action of a retributive justice or *dikē*. Sexual appetite can have full play without the threat of crossing over into a negative, bestial violence. The

51

inept, lecherous satyrs of the satyr plays resemble a comic inversion of the tragic hero. The discrepancy between god and beast in them is grotesque and amusing, not tragic.

The comic hero too may exceed the limits of divine and social order; his motivation and ultimate fate, however, are a return to or a restoration of that order, not the exploration of infinities beyond it. His error or bungling is no irreparable *hamartia*. The flexible limits of the comic universe will always stretch to accommodate him and receive him back bigger and better than before.[41] In Aristophanes' *Peace* the hero reaches Olympus on his grotesquely earthy variant of Pegasus and there attains the divine prerogatives of Zeus. His analogue in "serious" literature and myth is hurled down to enfeeblement and disaster (*Iliad* 6.200–202, *Isthmian* 7.44–46).

With a few exceptions, the gods of comedy are completely intelligible. Their all-too-human appetites are transparent foibles, not dark symbols of the unknowable and uncontrollable in a mysterious universe. Comedy's violation or ambiguity of language is merely another reflection of the elasticity of limits in a world where everything is possible. Animals speak and men insult gods but without the risk of terrible reprisal. Grotesque compounds and outrageous puns can deform speech, but the confusion threatens no ultimate unintelligibility or failure of communication. For all its fantastic exaggerations the fictional frame of comedy reaffirms the present ritual context by reflecting back into it the joyful rites of feast or marriage which unite rather than divide the community.

Just as the hero's perverted sacrifices disrupt the ritually affirmed order of society, its ritual code, so the medium through which he communicates disrupts the linguistic order. Language is not just the medium of tragedy; it is itself an element in the tragic situation. The metaphors of Greek tragic poetry bend the cosmological, social, and linguistic order together in a common suffering. The tortured *logos*, like the violated cosmos and the disrupted polis, has its own agony.

In the dense imagistic language of tragedy, the ritual, verbal, familial, and political codes are all threaded together in a common, complex message. Tragedy, like all literature, performs the special function of calling attention to the code itself. As the ritual within the orchestral space mirrors back, distorted or perverted, the ritual context of the performance itself, so the complex language of the play renders back to the audience its familiar medium of communication, but with the accustomed harmonies jarred in the echo. The language of tragedy, magnified by the tragic mask and stylized by well-established traditions, raises the problem of all human communication which is, in turn, the basis of all society. On the one hand the elevation of tragic language affirms the order-imposing power of the human *logos*. On the other hand the ambiguity, density, syntactical and lexical ambiguity, and irony of language in tragedy threaten the *logos* even as they enrich and exploit its resources to the fullest.

The *logos*, like every other element in the tragic structure, becomes divided against itself. It enters into the tragic division between illusion and reality. The conflicts which themselves constitute the tragic situation wrench language into paradoxes and oxymora like Antigone's "holy impiety," Oedipus' "wedless wedlock," Ajax's "darkness my light, dimness most brilliant."[42]

In the *Frogs* Aeschylus accuses Euripides of introducing women "who say that life is not life" (1082). Aristophanes here dramatizes comedy's criticism of the divided reality with which tragedy deals. The comic *logos*, like the comic ritual, restores unity and affirms simplicity in the face of chaos. In tragedy simplicity is the first victim. It is worth lingering a moment longer on this passage in the *Frogs*, for the objection to the language of tragedy soon ramifies into objections to other violations. These Euripidean heroines, says Aeschylus, also give birth in temples (a violation of ritual purity), commit incest (disruption of the familial code), and ultimately render life in the city unlivable because of bureaucracy and deceiving demagogues (*Frogs* 1080–86). The comic effect lies, in part, in the amusing and illogical rapidity with which the poet leaps from one code to another: ritual, kinship, language, civic order. Yet that leap has its own intuitive logic which rests upon an insight into the equivalence of all the codes.

As the action of tragedy represents the negation of the religious norms such as the violation of taboos against incest and murder, so the language of tragedy presents the violation of the linguistic norms: ambiguity, confusion, screams of agony, roars of pain, the incoherence of terror or madness. Logical argument fails. The words of friends or loved ones (*philoi*) are unable to persuade. Civilized discourse gives way suddenly to curse or bellow, to horrendous cries or ominous silences.

As the unity of the world cracks to reveal its duality of seeming and being, so the unity of the *logos* dissolves into dichotomy and ambiguity. Instead of mediating between mind and world, language becomes entangled in a series of conflicts which confuse and obscure perception of reality. Key words like justice (*dikē*), law (*nomos*), love (*philia*), wisdom (*sophia*), nobility (*gennaios*), fair and noble (*kalos*) become focal points for clashes of will and attitudes that have enormous and destructive dimensions.[43] Rather than a medium of communication, language becomes a source of blockage. Rather than opening the contiguous thought worlds of men to one another, it locks men more disastrously into their own world of isolated values and passions. In the *Antigone*, *Electra* and *Philoctetes*, claims of "law," "justice," and "piety" divide and confuse; in Euripides' *Hippolytus* ideals of "good name" (*eukleia*), purity, reverence (*aidōs*) become the spurs to destructive reversals of moral values.[44] In the rampant irony of the *Oedipus Tyrannus* words have one meaning for the character who speaks them and another for the spectator.

As the hero is suspended between god and beast, so is his discourse suspended between clarity and ambiguity, sense and silence. Ajax' loss of language or bull-like roar, like Cassandra's *otototoi* or Lear's "Howl, Howl, Howl," expresses the deepest level of his suffering.[45] It is akin to the madness that marks his total isolation from society. To have lost the ability to communicate by language is itself to be an outcast, an exile even in the midst of the most populous city.

The hero's relation to language reflects the same precariousness as his relation to myth, society, and the gods. The *logoi* of the oracles lift a Heracles or an Oedipus to seemingly divine stature, only to drop him to the level of the beasts, made as inarticulate as they.[46] In Aeschylus the wildly speaking cow maiden, Io, longs to hear the *logos* that belongs to a wisdom more ancient than Zeus, the tale of how she is to become the mother of a godlike offspring, founder of a great people (*PV* 593ff.). The resolution of her present suffering is this civilizing act of foundation which will eventually redress the fusion of man and beast in her present form. Euripides' Medea, at the point where she passes beyond the limits of civilized behavior and would destroy her own children, also passes beyond the limits of civilized language. Rejecting the arguments of the chorus who would dissuade her from her crime, she utters a striking oxymoron which itself expresses the destruction of the mediatory function of language:

περισσοὶ πάντες οὖν μέσῳ λόγοι.
All the words in the middle are excessive (*Med.* 819)

Here the "middle ground," the *meson*, has disappeared; only "excess," the "extraordinary," is left, *perissos*.[47] Elsewhere in Sophocles this word describes the "outsized," immoderate nature of the tragic hero. In Euripides' *Bacchae* the same word describes the strange and terrible inversions of man and beast, ritual and frenzy, that attend Agave's "extraordinary" or "excessive" hunting down and sacrifice of her son/beast/victim (1197).[48]

In one sense the action of the *Oedipus Tyrannus* is quite literally a matter of language, the solving of a riddle and the interpretations or oracles. The meaning of the play is the question of hermeneutics on a grand scale. The riddle of language is here the riddle of existence; language, like existence itself, becomes riddling. It signifies both too much and not enough at the same time. In a modern adaptation of Greek tragedy the German dramatist Gerhart Hauptmann exploits this double significance of the riddle when, amid the rising horror of his *Atridentetralogie*, the riddle emerges as a fundamental quality of life in "this strange world":

> Thestor: Quäl mich mit Rätseln nicht!
> Peitho: Ein frommer Wunsch, in dieser fremden Welt, die ganz nur Rätsel
>   ist.

> —Torture me not with riddles.
> —A pious wish, in this strange world, which is all riddle, nothing else.[49]

Or, to return once more to *Hamlet*, where the rottenness of Denmark shows man as less, at times, than "a beast that wants discourse of reason,"[50] the hero's words are twisted into riddles and the crazily true hints of his "madness." Ophelia, he says,

> speaks things in doubt,
> That carry but half sense. Her speech is nothing,
> Yet the unshaped use of it doth move
> The hearers to collection; they yawn at it,

And botch the words up to fit their own thoughts;
Which, as her winks and nods and gestures yield them,
Indeed would make one think there might be thought,
Though nothing sure, yet much unhappily.   (IV.v.6–14)

The fate of Sophocles' Oedipus, like Cassandra's in Aeschylus, poses the question of a world too anomalous for the regularizing norms of human language. As Oedipus' life eliminates the "difference" which makes civilization possible, blending son and husband, father and brother into a horrible precivilized oneness or "equality" (cf. *OT* 425, 1403–1408), so all the language which describes him begins in seeming unity and clarity, but it is the task of his life to break it down into its hidden "difference." Beneath *tyrannos* lurks *basileus* (Oedipus being simultaneously the legitimate king and usurper);[51] beneath "husband" lurks "son"; beneath "wife," "mother"; beneath "know," the first syllable of man's primary *logos*, his own name, lurks his existential ignorance of who and what he is. Traversing the space between the two poles of the "difference," Oedipus calls into question both the limits on which civilization rests and the *logoi* which define those limits. Cassandra's dreadful and misunderstood prophecies in the *Agamemnon*, like Teiresias' uncomprehended revelations in the *Oedipus Tyrannus*, place the disruption of language at the very center of the tragic significance. Only the frantic cries of desperation or the ferocity of angered prophecy can speak these horrors.

The *Oresteia* as a whole circumscribes a large-scale destruction and recreation of language. Language here has physical reality, a density of texture and concreteness that intertwines word and object, speech and scenic action in a new imagistic unity, something between incantation, magic, rite, and poetry.[52]

The famous tapestry scene of the *Agamemnon* brings together ritual, familial, and sexual codes in the King's destructive bypassing of mediation between god and beast through an inverted sacrifice and simultaneously enacts a destruction of language. The tapestry itself is a visual emanation and a tangible symbol of Clytaemnestra's cloying, seductive rhetoric. It is itself the emblem and the instrument of disruption in the sign system on which all civilized order rests. Waste, pride, and luxury are as dangerous in speech as in the house and in the kingdom. As a red stream emerging from the house, the tapestry discloses a truth about the interior of that house which the King cannot read. When he steps into it, never again to emerge into the light of day, he is lost, confused by the hidden contradictions of the message as much as he is entrapped in the visible, physical involutions of the net/robe in Clytaemnestra's inner chambers, his manhood negated by the massive reversal of hierarchies acted and prefigured in his defeat over the tapestry. The violence done through the tapestry within the house parallels the violence which Clytaemnestra's speech wreaks on language in both house and city, in both sacred and profane space. At a time of crisis for the city there is no clear means of communication between man and man and between man and God. Messages of the king and queen, as of the poet himself, can be conveyed only in dense, contorted, difficult speech. The simple word no longer has direct access to truth. As Democritus will say a generation or so later, "Truth lies in the deep" (68B117DK).

Agamemnon's first words of direct address to Clytaemnestra, as he struggles to avoid walking on her proferred tapestry, make this concern with language explicit (*Ag.* 914–925):

> Offspring of Leda, guardian of my house,
> You *have spoken* in a way appropriate to my absence;
> For you stretched (speech) to great length.
> But as to *rightly praising*, this honor should come from others.
> And, as to the rest, do not, in the manner of a woman,
> Pamper me, nor like a barbarian
> *Gape forth* for me a salute that falls to the ground,
> Nor strewing my path with tapestries make it
> Subject to envy. Gods should one honor with such things,
> But on such richly beauteous stuffs for me, a mortal,
> To tread can in no way be without terror.
> As a man, not a god, I ask, do reverence to me

Appropriate speech is here closely correlated with the appropriate relation between male and female, man and god, Greek and barbarian, excessive and moderate wealth. The metaphors here link the several codes in a characteristically Aeschylean node of intersecting human activities.

Lines 919–920 deserve particular attention:

> μηδὲ βαρβάρου φωτὸς δίκην
> χαμαιπετὲς βόαμα προσχάνῃς ἐμοί·
>   In the manner of a barbarian
> Do not gape forth for me a shout that falls to the ground.

Coming just before Agamemnon's first explicit reference to the tapestry, the extraordinary phrasing calls attention both to itself and to the gesture of the strewn carpet as modes of communication which exceed limits. The reference to the "barbarian manner" in the first half of the sentence (919) suggests not only the dangerous pomp of an oriental potentate but also the incomprehensibility of barbarian speech. This exaggerated "shout" accompanying the Eastern *salaam* down to the ground is metaphorically identified with the carpet strewn on the ground. An exaggerated mark of respect, it also suggests Clytaemnestra's thoughts of something else that will "fall to the ground" later in a red stream.

The improper salute of the "shout" (*boama*) is also the speechless open mouth, empty of sound, "agape" (cf. *pros-chanē(i)s*). The bold oxymoron intensifies the outrage of the deception which underlies this speech and reflects the contradiction whereby the very excess of language leads to its devaluation or cancellation. The enacted gesture of the strewn tapestry works together with the language that accompanies it to create a symbol of failed communication. The "gaped" salute of the "shout which falls to the ground" verbally reinforces the visual meaning of the tapestry itself as a destruction of communication: the tapestry enacts the paradoxical negation of language by exaggeration. The excess in the exchange of signs only reveals the deceptiveness inherent in those signs. The speech act and the gestural act pull in opposite directions. The hyperbole in both, rather than reinforcing the communicative power of the semantic system, only reveals its hollowness when the sender exploits the ambiguity of the message rather than its unitary, truth-conveying power.

So regarded, Clytaemnestra's victory through the tapestry scene is the victory of pure rhetoric. Speech separated from content or intent luxuriates in its own capacity for increment as phrase leads to phrase, ornament to further ornament, until the receiver is as deeply enmeshed in the endlessly proliferating embellishments of words as in the innumerable tangles of the net. The dangerous fertility of the female can generate enfolding superfluities of words that are as deadly as the excessive growths of her monstrous lust or monstrous offspring (cf. *Choephoroe* 585–638). This scene has a crucial place in the trilogy because it is the most powerful enactment of the linguistic code at the point where the disturbances in all the codes converge.

Viewed in this perspective, the trilogy is concerned as much with the evolution of language as of law and ritual. The ominously suppressed speech and misplaced song or dirge in the *Agamemnon*, where only Cassandra's shrieks of scarcely intelligible prophecy break through falsehood and hypocrisy, give way to the legitimate, but still primitive, ritualized chants for blood vengeance in the *Choephoroe*, until finally in the *Eumenides* speech can resolve primeval conflict. The Furies' inarticulate moans as they hunt their man (see *Eum.* 131–133) change to paeans of blessings.[53] Their savage refusal of Persuasion, Peitho (972), is balanced by Zeus Agoraios (973), Zeus of the Market Place, the god whose spirit of civilizing community makes the polis possible (968–975). When Olympian persuasion prevails over the unreasoning recalcitrance of the chthonic deities and their stubborn, instinctive pursuit of blood vengeance, the city has at least the means for grasping and maintaining its place between the opposing forces of the universe. The establishment of valid civic discourse and the establishment of a firm judiciary obviously go together. When these are created, or recreated, the city achieves the basis for its mediating position between cosmic opposites. Tensions still remain: Apollo is harsh in dismissing the mother's title to blood kinship with her child; the Areopagus' verdict would pronounce with the Furies. Yet what we see in the closing scenes of the play is an attempt to construct symbolically that mediation between men and gods on which the polis rests.

Cassandra's language sums up the paradox of the tragic situation: the attempt to communicate that which is incommunicable. In her speech we see the civilized forms of human discourse both resisting and becoming their own negation, trying to mediate the hopelessly remote polarity and the fearful conflation of god and beast which together destroy both communication and the social fabric. Her very act of speaking is one of the most electrifying moments on the Greek stage. Her staccato shriek bursts from the anticipated silence of the mute character as she unexpectedly assumes the speaking part of the third actor, said to have been a Sophoclean innovation. The sounds which pour out are themselves scarcely speech: *otototototoi popoi da* / *ōpollon ōpollon* (*Ag.* 1072). The stream of unintelligible syllables is, as Bernard Knox says, "a formulaic cry of grief and terror, one of those cries ancient Greek is so rich in, not words at all but merely syllables, which express emotion no words could adequately convey."[54] This inarticulate cry of almost animal pain links her to the dumb beasts, like Io in the *Prometheus*; and yet it is also the prelude to a mysterious revelation of divine knowledge, a knowledge that transcends speech because the insight and the horror cannot be circumscribed by the logical structure of language. Her cry is simultaneously visionary and demonic, divine and bestial, as her Apollo is both the Olympian god of prophecy and a cruel, powerful male inflamed with lust (1202ff.). The only intelligible sound in her opening cry is the name of the god through whom the future becomes knowable and communicable in language, Apollo. But the sound she utters signifies "destroyer" as well as "Apollo," her lover and her curse (*ōpollon*). In this threatening inversion of the god's role in maintaining order and clarity, the confusion in the linguistic code runs parallel to that in the ritual and sexual codes.

Because tragic knowledge eludes the boundaries of ordinary language, it needs visual dramatization. Words are not enough for it, for it is in latent conflict with the coded, regularized structuring of experience that language itself implies. "The tragic," writes Emil Staiger, "never comes clearly and immediately to verbal expression in poetry. He who could express it is already removed beyond the sphere of an existence intelligible to other men. Understanding rests on the community of a limited world. But in tragic despair it is just those limits that are burst asunder."[55]

With its capacity and need for symmetry and limit, the Greek mind is prophetic and paradigmatic of the whole course of Western civilization. In the tragedies the Greeks' triumphant achievement of limit and conceptual order so decisive for the history of the West makes way for a darker consciousness. Doubt and self-questioning surface from other strata of the mind. The ordered framework of differences and degrees cracks apart to reveal something like the primal magma of existence. This is the realm of Hades and Dionysus, Eros and Thanatos. The self no longer stands apart from the world in calm mastery, but loses control, becomes confused, falls prey to dark impulses and passions. The self defined by social position, noble birth, competence, intelligence, dies and gives birth to a new unknown self, alone, in pain, exposed to the vastness of an inscrutable universe. The lucid present, set off and protected within its rationally defined coordinates of specific time and space, is engulfed by the all-encompassing darkness of death and of the past, the infinite void of nonbeing, the irrationality of inherited evil.

Here the savior-king is the despised outcast and pollution (*Oedipus Tyrannus*); the unmovable, stalwart warrior of the Greek battle line is the treacherous night killer and the hated enemy (*Ajax*); the civilizing beast tamer is the bestial destroyer (*Trachiniae*); the daughter of the royal house is the criminal (*Antigone*, *Electra*); the future hero of the Trojan war is savage like a beast (*Philoctetes*); or, in the reverse direction, the unclean pariah holds mysterious blessings for the city (*Oedipus at Colonus*). The world itself, divided by polarities that no longer find mediation, breaks through human differentiation and threatens to revert to a prelogical oneness, absolutely Other, unknown and momentarily unknowable, the face of chaos, and yet the face of God.

4

Trachiniae

 Love charms, magic, primitive battles between fantastic creatures, sexual violence and desire, bull-shaped river gods, centaurs, the invisible poison of the Hydra's blood: all these make the *Trachiniae* unique in Sophocles' extant work.[1] The antithesis between man's civilizing power and the brutish violence that he both opposes and admits, between his ordered creations of house and city and the primordial forces both within and without, is sharper here than in any other Sophoclean play.

Not only does the play fall into two unequal parts, divided between Deianeira and Heracles respectively, but it is also divided between domestic realism and highly symbolic myth. We glimpse the woman's realm of house and hearth with an intimacy which Sophocles rarely affords us. Yet the bestial figure of the Centaur Nessus, invisible but ever-present throughout the action, conveys into the human foreground an archaic, phantasmagoric world of monstrous shapes.

The long narrative speeches, together with the elaborate poetical language and the tendency to compound adjectives, have led some scholars to assign an early date to the play, for it seems to exhibit the "weight" or *onkos* of Sophocles' so-called Aeschylean period.[2] Yet these stylistic qualities may also be the result of the poet's attempt to render a mythic vision, to find poetic equivalents for forces and drives hidden deep within us, as the Centaur's poisonous love charm is hidden deep within the house. It may be that the long recitatives detract from the success of the work as dramatic performance. Yet its power derives precisely from the close interaction between the violence of the surface emotions and the compelling force of its universal symbols. I discuss it first not because I believe it to be the earliest extant play (with many scholars, I would date it somewhere in the 430s, between the *Antigone* and the *Oedipus Tyrannus*),[3] but because it contains the starkest formulation of the polarities with which this study is concerned.

In defining the hypothetical "citiless man," the *apolis*, Aristotle says that he must be either above or below the level of humanity. "The man who cannot enter into association [with his fellow man] or has no need to do so because of his self-sufficiency (*autarkeia*) is no part of the polis, so that he is either beast or god." For Aristotle nature itself validates the role of the polis as the mediator between the extreme limits of bestiality and divinity. But in tragedy, as we have seen, man's place on the scale between beast and god is not fixed with such assurance. Here human nature is problematical, and the focus is upon the ambiguities of a figure who cannot or will not stay within the limits, whether of human nature or the polis. Man "perfected," Aristotle continues, is the best of animals, whereas man who lacks law and justice (*nomos* and *dikē*) is the worst. When he misuses his characteristic virtues of intelligence and excellence, he becomes "the most unholy and savage (*agriōtaton*) of creatures and worst with respect to sex and food."[4]

Greek mythology contains one figure who exemplifies par excellence the ambiguity of the human condition of which Aristotle speaks: Heracles. With his bow and his club he has purified the world of its savagery (*agriotēs*) and made it safe for civilized life. Earlier in the fifth century Pindar had celebrated this civilizing achievement in a number of brilliant odes.[5] Heracles has his reward of immortality on Olympus, where he dwells in eternal bliss with Hebe, praising "Zeus's solemn law" (*Nem.* 1.72b). On the other hand Heracles is also insatiable and excessive in just those appetites that Aristotle singles out. He can be, as he is called in this play, "the best of men," but he is also, to repeat Aristotle's phrase, "worst of creatures with respect to sex and food." This is the Heracles ridiculed in the comic tradition (the *Frogs* and *Alcestis* will be the most familiar examples). This figure is not the "hero god," as Pindar calls him (*Nem.* 3.22) or the "divine man" of the Stoics, but the hero-beast. For Virgil he is both a conqueror of monsters and a destroyer of great cities (*Aen.* 8.290–291). He is, as Philip Slater suggests, a civilizing force but not a civilized man. His enormous energies are, for the most part, channeled into constructive endeavors but some portion of his animal vitality escapes or resists sublimation.[6] Hence these violent acts, depicted here and in Euripides' *Heracles Mad*, which overturn civic, religious, and familial order.

"Worst with respect to sex and food": it is precisely in these areas that Greek culture draws the clearest line between civilization and savagery. Over against the promiscuous sexuality of the beasts stands the human institution of marriage. Over against the violent killing and raw eating of the animal world stands the human institution of sacrifice, where the animal is killed in a prescribed, stylized manner and the flesh is cooked and consumed as part of a holy ritual. These distinctions, as we have seen, pervade Greek literature from Homer and Hesiod on. A figure like Circe in the *Odyssey* combines both the sexual and the dietary violations. She turns men into beasts by exploiting their own gluttony, but she is also a powerful sexual enchantress whose seduction threatens and then considerably delays the hero on his homeward course. These Odyssean themes, as we shall see, have their special relevance to the *Trachiniae*.

City, house, marriage, fire and cooked food and therefore also sacrifice, the settled pursuit of agriculture are all woven together in the fabric which constitutes civilization. In the homology of the "codes" of the social structure, as Vernant and Detienne suggest, "marriage is to the sexual act what sacrifice is to the consumption of animal food."[7] Hesiod's myth of Prometheus connects sacrifice with fire, woman, marriage, self-perpetuation through legitimate offspring in a family (*Theogony* 535–616; cf. *Works and Days* 42–105). Of Hesiod's three races of men who precede human life as it is now, the men of the Golden Race do not need agriculture (*Works and Days* 116–117); those of the Silver Race "were not willing to worship the immortals nor do sacrifice upon the holy altars of the Blessed Ones, as is lawful for men (*Works and Days* 135–137); and those of the Bronze Age do not eat grain (146). On the other hand the formula, "men who toil for livelihood," *andres alphēstai*, with its implication of agriculture, introduces the aetiology of sacrifice in the *Theogony* (512) and occurs nowhere else in Hesiod.

The *Trachiniae* is the only extant play of Sophocles in which a human community, the polis or the heroic society of warriors, does not exert strong pressure on the protagonists. Trachis is the vaguest of political entities (cf. 39–40). This is a play not of cities, but of wild landscapes. Cities here are either hopelessly distant, like Heracles' Tiryns, or objects of plunder, like Eurytus' Oechalia.

Returning in triumph from fifteen months of battles and adventures, Heracles leads from the ruined Oechalia the beautiful young Iole and her cortege of maidens. Prior to his return he prepares to offer a sacrifice of bulls at Cape Cenaeum across the water. Bacchylides had already developed some of the details of the sacrifice (16.17ff.), but Sophocles gives it a far more important role. The act of sacrifice becomes the focal point in a movement from outer world to inner, from the unsheltered wild to the safety of house and city. This spatial pattern may be compared with the *Odyssey* and also with Sophocles' last play, the *Oedipus at Colonus*. But unlike the heroes of both these works, Heracles fails to make a successful transition between outer and inner realms. He never enters the house which is his goal. For him, unlike the aged Oedipus, there is no ritual mediation between city and wild. The sacrificial act which should perform that function operates in just the opposite way. Heracles' last movement in the play is once more a journey outward, to the lonely crag of Mount Oeta beyond the city. Here, fulfilling a mysterious command that he must burn his body on a funeral pyre, he does establish a ritual communication with the gods, but, unlike Oedipus, he still bypasses the polis.

Marriage and sacrifice function in the play as complementary expressions of civilization. It is to preserve her marriage that Deianeira anoints Heracles' sacrificial robe with what she believes to be a love charm. The fire of the sacrificial altars will kindle the destructive power of the ointment, composed of the blood of the Centaur mingled with the venom of the Hydra with which Heracles' arrow was tipped. The active ingredient in the charm is the Hydra's blood. As in the *Oedipus Tyrannus*, then, the forward movement of the play simultaneously brings with it a retrograde motion. Behind the human institutions of house and marriage there gradually unfolds the archaic beast world of Heracles' remoter triumphs. The sacrifice which celebrates the last of these triumphs delivers the hero up to the primitive beasts he has supposedly conquered. The Centaur's poison makes its first appearance as "the old gift of the ancient beast" (556). "Beast" or "beast Centaur" is the term used for Nessus throughout the play.[8]

Though operating in separate realms, Heracles and Deianeira perform complementary and symmetrical actions. Both are drawn back to a savage and archaic

realm which they have ostensibly left behind in their past. Deianeira, twice res-
cued from a suitor of bestial form, would preserve her house by recourse to the
blood of the beast which she has kept hidden deep within the house. Heracles,
protector of civilization, has destroyed the city and house of King Eurytus to
possess Iole. A "sacker of cities" (244, 364–365, 750), he becomes an opponent
of civilization, like one of those threatening beasts he has subdued. He is punished by being "sacked," like a town, himself (1104). His wooing of Iole closely
parallels the monstrous Achelous' wooing of Deianeira. Achelous "asked for
(Deianeira) from her father" (10), and she was saved by Heracles' violent intervention (18–27, 497–530). Ironically, Heracles' later wooing is both less honorable and less considerate of the girl's father than his monstrous rival had been.
Heracles' wooing ·of Iole contains no request and brooks no refusal (359–365):

> But when he did not persuade the father who begot her to give him the
> child to have in secret union [literally, bed], preparing a small charge and
> pretext, he marches against the country and sacked the city.

The phrase "secret bed" (rather than "secret concubine") stresses the raw sexuality
of Heracles' motives. Iole is only a sexual object, a *kryphion lechos*. Deianeira, by
contrast, regarded her chaste marital bed as chosen, not secret (*lechos kriton*, 27).

The description of King Eurytus as the begetter of his child, Iole, in
359–360 (*ton phytosporon / tēn paida dounai*) suggests also the protective nurturing function of the house which this "suitor" would destroy. The word for
"begetter" here is *phytosporos*, literally "he who sows the seed," and it connects
the settled house with the stability and regular care of agriculture, just as
Deianeira does in the prologue (31ff.). This parallel between the begetting of
legitimate children in the house and agriculture is even written into the ancient
betrothal ceremony (the bride is bestowed "for the sowing—*arotos*—of legitimate
children").[9] But Heracles' lustful wooing of this secret bed insults the "bride,"
outrages the father, and leads to no new *oikos* with its conferral of honorific status
on the girl. Lichas supposedly does not even know Iole's name and has not
sought out her lineage (314ff.; cf. 380–382), one of the most fundamental pieces
of information for a Greek marriage.[10] She enters as a nameless female, without
identity, sought only for her sexuality as a beast would seek a mate. Given the
parallelism between all the areas of civilized life, the destruction of this "bride's"
fatherland (*patris*, 363) and city (*polis*, 364) is the logical progression. Achelous,
in retrospect, might appear almost a gentle swain. The monstrous figures of the
remote mythical past return as the inward monstrousness of present lust.

II

From his adventures outside, Heracles brings back a possession (*ktēma*,
245) that would normally become part of the treasure accumulated within the
house. But his possession is a cruel reward for the wife's faithful care of the house

(*oikouria*, 542). She replies with a treasure from the recesses of the house, one of those household *keimēlia* or stored up goods which lie under her supervision.[11] Instead of protecting the interiority of house and hearth, the space assigned to women and free of the elemental forces of Eros and Aphrodite, she admits into it the savagery of the wild and the violence of sexual passion.[12] Instead of the woven gift, product of her domestic arts, to welcome her husband within, she bestows a garment whose associations with secure inner space are negated by the venom of a primordial monster which covers it. Instead of an article of household use, she gives a "woven net" (*hyphanton amphiblēstron*, 1052), an instrument for hunting in the wild. In this reversal the man is now the hunted victim, for that net/robe becomes the savage beast itself, "devouring" the flesh and "drinking the blood" of its human victim (1053–57; cf. 769–771).

The wool with which the robe is anointed comes from the *ktēsion boton* (690), the flock which is also part of the property of the house. This application of the love charm/poison, however, destroys the distinction between inner and outer. Deianeira reaches from the secrecy (689) of the interior space of the house to the domain outside, the flocks which, strictly speaking, lie under the man's rather than the woman's care.[13] According to a famous passage in Demosthenes (*Against Neaera* 122), the wife's role was "to bear legitimate children and to be a faithful guardian of the property inside." Both the goods fixed and stored up inside the house, the *keimēlia*, and the mobile property on its outer limits are pressed into service to destroy the owner of this wealth (a parallel with the rich carpet of the *Agamemnon* comes to mind). And in the case of both robe and flock, the ordered, sheltered life of the *oikos* is brought into contact with a poisonous, chaotic element from the savage realm outside that breaks in and overwhelms it.

This symmetry of inward and outward movement, instead of being a complementary relation of husband and wife, cancels out their point of union, the house and the bed. The bed, the object of Heracles' violent struggle against Achelous (514), becomes the place of the couple's definitive separation. Heracles is carried in, and later carried out, on a bed taken from the house. It is, significantly, when Deianeira sees Hyllus preparing that bed in the courtyard, not within the house, that she makes ready for death (900–903).

Deianeira speaks of the violence of *eros* (441ff.) but fails to recognize its terrible power in herself. Hence she is unable to give an account of the savage contest of which she is the prize (21–25). When the chorus depicts the scene in lyrical form, they depict her as a helpless onlooker, like a heifer without its mother (526–530). And yet in her prologue and her two long speeches in the center of the play she has more to say about the bestial monsters than any one else. The guardian of house and hearth, she yet speaks the language of primordial myth, which is also the language of the sexual instinct's uncompromising power, the language of her own latent sexual violence. Heracles needs her fixity and stability, but she can give him back only his own raw sexuality, and so destroys them both. The house must, after all, accommodate those drives and desires which the Centaur acts out without inhibition. Yet their place in that house involves contradictions which are at the heart of Deianeira's tragedy.

Deianeira harbors the Centaur's envenomed blood in the recesses of her household domain. She would keep safe its interiority by a remedy which harks back to rape in a wild setting. In the only explicit statement of sexual jealousy that she allows herself, she says that she finds it impossible to "share house with," *syn-oikein*, the mistress of Heracles (545). Yet that same word, "share house with," recurs to describe the savage and bestial force of the Centaur's poison: the robe is a beast which "shares its house with" Heracles (1055), devouring his flesh and drinking his blood. This metaphor reveals the house as its total opposite: the inner space becomes the place where the beast once more attacks marriage.

Our first news of Heracles combines victory and preparations for a sacrifice. The Messenger reports him "alive and victorious and from the battle bringing the first fruits to the gods of the place" (182–183). But what are these first fruits (*aparchai*)? We learn soon enough: they include the maidens of the sacked Oechalia. This sacrifice celebrates the destruction of a city and the enslavement of its inhabitants. The ritual term, *aparchē,* returns later when the sacrifice is actually performed and its destructive implications are fulfilled (760–761).[14]

The Messenger is succeeded by Lichas, who calls the sacrifice "full-fruited offerings," *telē enkarpa* (238). This term, also part of the technical language of ritual, suggests offerings of fruit and cereals, that is, offerings from tilling the soil.[15] But Deianeira's comparison of Heracles to the husbandmen in the prologue has already established his ambiguous relationship to agriculture and the settled life associated with it. These full-fruited offerings will be a sacrifice of flesh and blood in more than one sense.

Deianeira asks Lichas whether the sacrifice at Cenaeum is directed by an oracle or the result of a vow. Lichas answers that it is the result of a vow which he was to fulfill "when he overthrew and took with his spear the country of these women whom you see before your eyes" (240–241). The detail at once links the sacrifice with the sack of Oechalia. The corruption of the rite is already implicit in the motivation which lies behind it.

Heracles, Lichas says, is laying out the limits of the sacred precinct (237–238). The verb here is *horizein*, used in a rather unusual sense. It does not mean "consecrate," but rather "to set out the boundaries." It implies the defining of limits to separate the sacred from the profane, the civilizing act of establishing order fundamental to religious rituals.[16] To set boundaries is to create a human space for the special act that sets men apart from the beasts. Where Sophocles used the verb elsewhere, it connotes the creation of order within the city and the family. It is the word which Antigone uses to describe the laws which Justice "established" among men (*Antig.* 451–452). Aegeus, in an unknown play, uses it to describe a father's distribution of his lands among his sons (frag. 872N = 24P). In Plato *horizein* refers to the basic founding act of the city (*Republic* 4.423b). But in our play it is part of the celebration of the destruction of a city and the prelude to the destruction of a house. Lichas' assertion here that Heracles is "alive and blooming and heavy with no disease" (235) will soon be undercut by the sacrifice which will bring the "savage disease" (975, 1030) and the "heaviness immeasurable" of disaster (746, 982).

Lichas' answer to Deianeira's urgent question about the captive women deepens the ambiguities of the ritual motifs (242–245):

Deian.: These women, in the name of the gods, whose are they and who are they? For they are pitiable if their circumstances mislead me not.

Lichas: When he sacked Eurytus' city he took them apart, for himself and the god a select possession (*exeileth' autō(i) ktēma kai theois kriton*, 245).

The syntactical ambiguity of the last line raises doubts about the dedication of these first fruits.[17] They are as much the possession of Heracles as of the gods. The detail of sacking the city also calls into question the suitability of such a dedication.

Deianeira is naturally curious about how Heracles spent the rest of his fifteen-month absence. Lichas supplies a detailed account, complicated and rather unclear,[18] at the end of which he returns to the girls. The language once more entwines corrupted marriage and corrupted sacrifice in one of those dense Sophoclean passages where every word is important (283–290):

τάσδε δ' ἄσπερ εἰσορᾷς
ἐξ ὀλβίων ἄζηλον εὑροῦσαι βίον
χωροῦσι πρὸς σέ· ταῦτα γὰρ πόσις τε σὸς
ἐφεῖτ', ἐγὼ δέ, πιστὸς ὢν κείνῳ, τελῶ·
αὐτὸν δ' ἐκεῖνον, εὖτ'ἂν ἁγνὰ θύματα
ῥέξῃ πατρῴῳ Ζηνὶ τῆς ἁλώσεως,
φρόνει νιν ὡς ἥξοντα· τοῦτο γὰρ λόγου
πολλοῦ καλῶς λεχθέντος ἥδιστον κλύειν

These women whom you see, once happy, have found a life unenvied and come to you. Such orders did your husband (*posis*) lay upon me; and I am accomplishing them, faithful to him (*pistos*). He himself, know it well, will arrive here as soon as he has performed pure sacrifices (*hagna thymata*) to Zeus, his family god. Of the ample tale, now spoken well and happily (*kalōs*), this is the sweetest thing to hear.

Lichas' closing generalization on the "well-spoken tale" underlines how ill-spoken it has been. Word and act are sharply at variance. The sweetest news of his coming sacrifice will soon turn into Hyllus' hideous description of the actual event. The emphasis on speaking well ironically foreshadows the play's massive perversion of language, of which Lichas' report is itself the first instance. Lichas boasts of his fidelity to Heracles, but her doubts soon after about his "fidelity to the truth" (398) ramify to more bitter doubts about the fidelity of Heracles, "our so-called faithful (*pistos*) and noble husband" (541). "Your spouse," Lichas had said (285), but Deianeira soon enough sees that the title will be empty, when "Heracles is called my spouse (*posis*), but that young girl's man" (*anēr*, 550–551).

Heracles will come, Lichas says, "as soon as he performs the pure sacrifices at Cenaeum" (287–288). The sacrifice is a kind of pre-condition of the reunion in the house. But instead the sacrifice will make the union impossible.

The victims, like the circumstances of the whole celebration, will be far from pure, *hagna* (287). The word "capture," emphatic at the end of the clause, recalls the violence behind this sacrifice, the sack of the city in Lichas' initial description (244). Heracles himself has just recovered from impurity: he had to wait, Lichas had explained, until he was "pure" (*hagnos*) after his enslavement to Omphale before he could return to Greece and attack Oechalia (258–259). The impurity of that enslavement parallels the impurity of his sacrifice, and like that is a focal point for a multiple disruption of heroic values: a free man enslaved, a man serving a woman, a Greek subordinate to a barbarian, a strong man made weak.

Heracles' rite at Cenaeum is basically a sacrifice of desacralization, a ritual familiar in the ancient world. It serves to discharge the enormous impurity accumulated by the killing and violence perpetrated in his adventures. Lichas' grim line about the Oechalians, "They are all inhabitants of Hades" (282), like the brief allusions to the death of the shepherds in the *Ajax*, is enough to suggest how much impurity Heracles has in fact accumulated. The ritual discharge of this violence is an essential step in enabling Heracles to return to the peaceful world of house and city.[19] But here too the ritual backfires. Instead of dispelling that impurity, it intensifies it. Instead of desacralizing Heracles, it makes him *sacer*—as the victim, not the celebrant. Instead of returning him to the human order, it sets him once more apart from that order as the consecrated beast victim. Only at the end does the sacrificial ritual take on another meaning, as a rite of expiation which frees him, finally, from the violence let loose by his fusion with his bestial double. Here in the rite at Cenaeum, however, the hero-king who should mediate between sacred and profane by offering the sacrifice effects that mediation by becoming the victim: the victim "penetrates into the perilous domain of sacrifice, it dies there, and indeed it is there in order to die."[20]

The sacrifice is also the point of juncture between Deianeira, yearning for Heracles, and the hero returning to her and to his house. In offering the robe she reaches out from the house to his sacrificial ritual (604–615):

> Give him this robe and tell him that no mortal is to put it on his skin before him, and let not the light of the sun look upon it, nor the sacred enclosure nor the altar's hearth-fire until he stands there conspicuous and shows it conspicuously to the gods on this day for slaying bulls. For so I vowed, that if I should ever see or hear of him (come) saved within the house, I would clothe him in this robe with full justice and show him to the gods a new sacrificer in a garment new. And of this you will bear a token which he will know with ease, set upon this enclosure of my seal (that is, the bezel of my ring).[21]

The sacred enclosure (*herkos*, 607) recalls the ordering act of *horizein*, setting out the limits of the precinct in 237–238. But the same word, *herkos*, also describes the wife's signet (615), the proof of her fidelity as the guardian of the house. The tokens of order, one outside, the other within, fit together only for the destruction of what they symbolize. The token that assures the safekeeping of the wife's interior realm—and perhaps also by extension of the wife's sexuality, that other aspect of the "property" of the house—is in fact the seal which insures that the Centaur's lustful, envenomed blood will arrive intact from the recesses of the house to Heracles.

The description of the altar's fire marks a similar confusion of outer and inner realms. It is called *ephestion selas*, literally "the flash of fire at the hearth" (607); the same word has twice before described the hearth of a house (206, 262). In the latter two passages also the interior safety of hearth and home is destroyed. In 206 the joyful cry of the house at the hearth (*ephestiois alalagais*, if the text is correct) will soon turn to cries of horror as the house is ruined (see 805, 863–867, 904, 947–1017) and the promised union of male and female in the common voice of choral celebration (207–216) becomes mutual slaughter. In 262 Lichas' fabrication about Eurytus, the reception of Heracles as an "ancient guest at the hearth" (*ephestion xenon palaion*), turns at once to the dissonant clash of inner and outer space as Heracles, allegedly cast outside (269), obliterates this house (256–257), and also commits murder in a setting of rocks and hills associated with pasturage and hunting (271–273).

To return to 607, the phrase *ephestion selas*, "flash of fire at the hearth," suggests an identification between the interior domestic fire, which Heracles will in fact never see, and the fire at the open-air altars.[22] This fire of the hearth/altar kindles the poison of the beast. The result is to confound celebrant and victim, man and beast, the civilizing hero and his savage adversary.[23] Nessus' ambiguous status between beast and man finds resonances in the status of Heracles between house and wild, civilizing order and animal instincts. We may recall the hearth fire of Euripides' *Heracles Mad* where the victorious hero turns the security of the house, which he has just now successfully protected, into a bloody shambles of children slaughtered as if they were his enemies outside.[24]

From the other side of the hearth/altar equation, the hearth, functioning as an altar, can serve as the point of communication not only between inner and outer space, but also between upper and lower realms, Olympian and chthonic divinities.[25] Here both systems of exchange collapse simultaneously. The success of this interiorized venom from the wild confuses living and dead and revives, with new power, an inhabitant of Hades (1159–63):

> It was foretold to me of old from my father (Zeus) that death would come from no one with the breath of life, but rather from one who was an inhabitant of Hades, dead. This Centaur beast, then, just as the divine prophecy foretold, killed me, alive, though himself dead.

The celebration of a triumph by the slaying of bulls (609) recalls Heracles' earlier victory over a "bull" in winning Deianeira. Shape or apparition of a bull was Achelous' guise in the battle vividly described in the first stasimon (*phasma taurou*, 509; cf. 11, 518). As the lawful wooing of Deianeira against a bull-like rival was subverted by the illicit wooing of Iole's secret bed (360, 514), so the present sacrifice of bulls turns into a kind of posthumous victory for that taurine monster. The victor, a new sacrificer in a new robe (611–612), will roar (805) like the bulls he immolates; the devouring disease (*diaboros nosos*, 1084) turns the celebrant into the animal which is eaten after the sacrifice (770–771, 987, 1053–55). The disease itself becomes an almost living being: the violence of the bestial Nessus lives again in the body of his slayer and feasts on his flesh and blood (1053–55).

The ritual character of the new robe for the new sacrificer is emphasized by the expression *peplos endytēr* which Deianeira uses later, a robe put on for festal occasions. In her initial instructions to Lichas she uses the related verb, *amphidyō*: "let no mortal before him put it on around his flesh" (*amphidysetai chroï*, 605). The phrase looks like a harmless periphrasis until we realize what effect this robe will have on his flesh or skin. When he puts it on (*endys*, 759), the sweat comes out upon his skin and the robe clings and eats into it (766–770).[26] Now the festal robe is the robe of death (758). Heracles' initial joy in the decorative beauty of the garment (*kosmos*, 763–764) changes to horror as the celebrant appears as the victim decked out for the slaughter just as the ox in Nestor's sacrifice is decked out to be an object of beauty, *agalma*, to the god who receives the sacrifice (*Odyssey* 3.432–438).

As Lichas departs with the robe, the chorus sings an ode which juxtaposes civilized habitation with the ruggedness of Trachis (633–639). Harbors for ships, the assemblies of the Amphictyonic council, and the evocation of a happy world of benign and brilliant mythical beings (cf. Artemis of the Golden Shafts in 637) express the chorus' anticipation of a happy return, as if the rite of the previous scene will indeed restore Heracles to house and hearth. But they speak also of the mysterious warm springs of the rocks—warmth and water are ominous in this play—and of Oeta's crags. In the antistrophe they look forward to the joyful flute music welcoming Heracles home (640ff.; cf. 216ff.), but the sounds of his return will be far from musical, and the songs of ensuing odes will be the dirge of lamentation (846–870, 947–949, 962–970).[27] Heracles will reach the house, they sing, with the spoils of all his *aretē* (646), but those spoils, as we know, have no place in the house. Heracles in the next line is *apoptolis*, removed from the city, but the word also reminds us of his ambiguous relation to cities. Deianeira here is his "dear consort" (650), but we may recall her ironical "faithful husband" a hundred lines earlier and the other contorted marital terms of the play. "But now," the chorus continues, "Ares stung to madness has loosed the day of toil" (653–654). But releasing or loosing in this play is ambiguous too (see 21, 554), and Deianeira's supposed release from fear and suffering proves as illusory and empty as Heracles' (see 1171). Ares stung to madness, *oistrētheis*, is hardly a propitious deity. The participle suggests the violence of war and sexuality (a frequent connotation of *oistros*) from which there will be no easy release. Elsewhere in Sophocles, Ares, "a god without honor among the gods"

(*OT* 215), brings destruction not peace.[28] This day of bull slaying (609) will prove to be the very day of suffering from which the chorus expects release. One lesson drawn from the catastrophe will be that one cannot reckon on two or more days, "for tomorrow has no existence until one has his experience of the present day" (943–946).

In the very last lines of the ode the chorus returns to the sacrificial language of the previous scene (657–662):

> May he come, may he come. Let not the many-oared vehicle of his ship rest until he makes his journey to this city, leaving his island hearth, where he is called sacrificer. From there may he come all tame, melted with the all-anointed beguiling by the beast's persuading.

Ship and hearth mark the opposite poles of man's civilized achievements, the imposition of order in both outer and inner realms. But what transpires at the "island hearth," that is, the altar at Cenaeum, will only separate Heracles farther from the house and city that are here welcoming him.

The word "sacrificer," *thytēr*, in 659, brings back all the ambiguities of that perverted sacrifice. The erotic meanings latent in almost every word of these last three lines are meant to point to the resolidification of the family but instead signify its dissolution, as the violence of the beast makes its power felt in the *oikos*. The "melting" (if that is the right reading) will be no melting in love, as between Heracles and Iole (463), but the melting of the poison into Heracles' flesh, as the next ode in fact makes clear (836). "All-tame" (keeping the reading of the manuscripts) points to the ironical inversion of beast and man through Nessus' poison. The chorus, like Deianeira, is hideously wrong in believing that the erotic "melting" and "persuasion" here can lead to hearth and home. As Hyllus explains later, "Nessus *persuaded* her long ago to madden your desire for her with some such philter" (1141–42). Rational persuasion has its "bestial double," as it were, in the erotic "persuasion" (Peitho is a helper of Aphrodite) through which, ultimately, the Centaur works upon Deianeira. Persuasion, the logical power of speech to direct action, here serves beast rather than man, passion rather than reason.[29]

The joyous anticipation of the sacrifice earlier is now drastically reversed. There are close parallels both of language and of situation.[30] In each case Deianeira makes a long speech (141–177; 672–722), the chorus advises prudent silence (178–179; 731–733), and a messenger enters with the news (180ff., 734ff.). Once more Lichas performs the task of herald (189 and 757), but the expected gratitude (*charis*, 179, 191, 471; cf. 201, 228, 485) is far different from what he receives. Deianeira had urged him to hasten back with the robe "so that (Heracles') gratitude (*charis*) and mine, coming together for you, may appear twofold from single" (*ex haplēs diplē*, 618–619). But this double *charis* "comes together" upon Lichas as its total opposite, the negation of all human sympathy and communication in the bestial imagery attending Heracles' pain and Lichas' death.

With the killing of Lichas the violence released by the impure sacrifice shows itself for what it is and expands to new corruption.[31] Instead of absorbing and dissipating that accumulated violence in Heracles, the sacrifice at Cenaeum only turns it back more powerfully upon the celebrant, and detonates even greater explosions, as it moves from the rocky mountainside of Lichas' (and Iphitus') death toward the house and the city.

The fire at these altars is a "bloody flame," *phlox haimatēra* (766). "Bloody" refers not only to the actual circumstances of the rite, but recalls also the poisonous robe of the beast which will turn sanctity into sacrilege; a hallowing fire releases the beast's savagery in more than one sense. The robe, its poison released by the heat of these flames, clings to Heracles like the work of a joiner (767–768): the arts of civilization ironically collaborate with the vengeance of the monstrous beast-man. Violent images of biting and devouring in the next lines (769–771) at once engulf this fleeting glimmer of civilized pursuits. The celebrant now in truth becomes the sacrificial beast as the pain "eats" him (*adagmos*, 769–770) and the Hydra's poison "feasts" on him (*edainuto*, 771). The pure victims promised by Lichas (*hagna thymata*, 287) now become Heracles and, later, Lichas himself.

In a proper sacrifice the smoke of the burning fat should mingle with the incense and carry the sweet savor to the gods as a harmonious communion between higher and lower orders.[32] Pindar, describing one such joyous sacrifice, speaks of the "rising flame (*phlox anatellomena*) that kicks the aether with the fragrant savor of its smoke," (*Isth.* 4.71–72). But here that smoke clings to the earth: it is a *prosedros lignys*, a murky, low-lying cloud, out of which Heracles, in his confusion and agony, can barely discern his son (794–795). This impure fire, kindling the flame-like poison of archaic monsters, effects an inverse mediation, not upward from man to god, but downward, from man to beast.[33] There is a close parallel here with the disturbed sacrifices of the *Antigone*, which also reflect a disharmony between upper and lower realms and a "disease" or "distemper" in the city (*Antig.* 1015). There the fire refuses "to flash forth from the sacrificial victims, but on the ashes an oozing stain drips from the thighs and smoked and sputtered; and the gall was flung upwards and scattered, and the thighs, dripping, were laid bare of the covering fat" (*Antig.* 1005–10). Seneca may have had such passages in mind for his *Thyestes*, where the fire of an outrageous sacrifice of human victims sends forth pitchy smoke (*piceos fumos*) that hangs over the images of the household gods in an ugly cloud (772–775).

Twice before the chorus cried out for the flute to accompany their premature joy (217, 641), but the flute and the echoes of the "divine muse" (643–644) which should accompany the sacrifice give way to subhuman roars of pain (787, 805).[34] In its ode of happy expectation, the chorus uttered the *ololygmos* (205), the shout of joy that accompanies the actual killing at the sacrifice.[35] At the first sign of news about Heracles they invoked the holy *euphēmia* of ritual silence (178). But at the sacrifice which should fulfill their joy there are only shrieks of agony. The *euphēmia* becomes the ill-omened groan of the crowd at the defilement of Lichas' brutal death (*aneuphēmēsen oimōgē(i)*, 783).[36] At the news of

Heracles' arrival all the people pressed eagerly around the herald to listen with delight (194–197); now all the people utter the inverted *euphēmia* of their groan (783). The Messenger had described how Lichas told his news to an eager throng (188)[37]; this crowd now backs away in fear (785) as they hear Heracles shouting, shrieking (786). No human voice, only the wild mountains, echo the sound (787–788), the rocks against which Heracles smashes the innocent Lichas.[38]

When the Messenger appeared with his joyful news he wore a garland on his head (178). Participants in sacrifice also wear garlands.[39] But the rite at Cenaeum tells us something else about the hair: hurling Lichas against the rocks Heracles "drenched his hair in the white marrow of the brain as the skull's crown shattered spattering blood at the same time" (781–782). The poet of "classic serenity" does not spare us the gruesome details. The shedding of human, not animal, blood is itself a pollution of the sacrifice. But the details of the shattered skull and brain cause a particular shiver of horror. Lichas becomes a second human victim, even more sacrilegiously, for the skull of the sacrificed animal was to be kept intact, and the sight of the brain was a horrible desecration.[40]

The inversion of civilization and savagery here works at still another level: Heracles' act recalls the Cyclops of the *Odyssey*, a paradigm of subhuman savagery. Heracles' "snatching (Lichas) by the foot" (779) is in fact a verbal echo of the Cyclops' grisly murder (*Od.* 9.289). Heracles' sacrifice thus becomes a nightmarish reenactment of a brutal killing by a half-bestial monster, one who has no reverence for the gods, practices cannibalism, and eats raw flesh.

Lichas' death is only the reenactment of Heracles' earlier brutality. The herald himself had accounted for Iole's presence with an elaborate tale of revenge which included hurling Iphitus from the citadel of Tiryns (269–273; cf. 357, 780). Though the Trachinian Messenger denies that Iphitus' "death by hurling" (357) was the cause of Oechalia's ruin, that earlier murder not only signals Heracles' homicidal violence but also reveals the false basis for the joyful sacrifice at Cenaeum. Like lies in Sophocles generally, Lichas' misrepresentation contains a certain truth, a truth which rebounds upon the speaker.

At the sacrifice the power of the beast, both in Nessus and in Heracles himself, did its work. Now the figurative disease (*nosos*) of love (445, 544) for the first time becomes the literal disease ravaging the hero's body (784). And yet this disease remains, in part, the elusive, inward disease of soul that medicine cannot treat.[41] Indeed, the medicine is itself the source of the sickness, the maddening *pharmakon* or drug of the beast who is both its source and its ministrant (*pharmakeus*, 1140).

The pattern repeats itself again and again in this scene. The wife's robe becomes the "woven net" of the Furies which traps her husband (1052). The collocation of net and loom here parallels the play's destructive collocation of male and female, exterior and interior space. The gift from the house is combined with the implement of perverted hunting by hateful goddesses who punish crimes against the house. Sophocles' phrase also echoes the description of the net which entrapped Agamemnon in another perverted sacrifice (*Ag.* 1580–81; cf. 1382).[42] Thus the loving, feminine Deianeira is viewed against the image of her opposite, the murderous, male-hearted Clytaemnestra of Aeschylus. Here and again thirty lines later, Heracles is the beastlike victim, devoured and feasted upon (1054–56, 1084, 1087) even as he enumerates his conquests over the savage monsters of his labors (1088–1102).[43]

This fusion of humanity and bestiality, rite and desecration, also becomes a nightmarish reenactment of the lust through which Heracles and Deianeira have played into the hands of their beast enemy. The heat, the sweating, the clinging embrace of the robe both reflect and parody the latent destructiveness of sexuality. The catastrophe is acted out both in metaphor and in physical reality.[44]

With that innocence which is the source of both her strength and her doom, Deianeira strangely prefers to ignore the power of this heat of lust. The grove of maidenhood to which she looks back in escapist nostalgia is sheltered, she says, from the "sun-god's heat" (*thalpos*, 145). Hence, although the Messenger warned her about lust's inflammatory effects (368), she dismisses the lovers' "melting" as something she could tolerate (463). But the heat, like the disease, moves from metaphor to reality until its terrible consequences stand before her and us in their massive concreteness.

Heated inwardly by desire when he sacked Oechalia (368),[45] Heracles is now heated by flames which celebrate that victory and becomes vulnerable to the heat of the beast's poison. Kept away from the sun's warm beam (*aktis thermē*, 685–686), the drug is innocuous; when it is heated, (*ethalpeto*, 697), the poison can do its work.[46] As a result Heracles is heated in a different way, by the maddening spasms of pain (*ethalpse*, 1082), a retributive manifestation of his own inner lustful heat. The two forms of heat, literal and metaphorical, together negate Heracles' conquest of beasts through the many warm toils of his labors (1046–47), a striking use of the adjective "warm" in this bitter outcry.[47]

There is an associative bond between bestiality, the Centaur, the charm formed from his blood, and the darkness of night. The Centaur and his acts have a natural affinity for darkness; his use of the light, whether of fire or sun, is destructive. He and his blood are repeatedly called black (573, 717, 837; cf. 856). In applying the philter, Deianeira speaks of "shameful things done in darkness" (596–597). The paradoxes of light and dark are part of the inversions resulting from the beast's victory over the civilizing hero. The philter properly belongs in some dark and secret place. Uncovered to light and to fire (685), it transforms the civilizing fire of altar and hearth into a destructive force. Darkness seems to win out over light; the sacrificial fire blends with the impure fire of lust and of the devouring disease.

It is characteristic of this play's concern with the elemental forces of nature that it enframes these inversions in a cosmic perspective. The chorus begins its first ode with a disturbing invocation of the Sun (94–96):

ὃν αἰόλα νὺξ ἐναριζομένα
τίκτει κατευνάζει τε φλογιζόμενον,
Ἅλιον, Ἅλιον αἰτῶ.

Helios, Helios, I call upon you, you whom the shimmering night, as it is slain, brings to birth and then lays to rest, set ablaze with fire.

In some Indo-European myths the birth of the king kindles the fire of the sun, or the king's sacrifices kindle the new dawn light.[48] Here the blazing sun seems rather to foreshadow the king's flaming death on his pyre, just as his altar fires bring destruction and bestialization rather than renewal of cosmic energies and exaltation to the divine.

The lines play upon the paradoxes of life coming forth from violent death. The dense poetical language mingles together dying and giving birth. The two verbs of gentler action, *tiktei* and *kateunazei*, "bring to birth" and "lay to rest," are framed by the two middle or passive participles which convey destructive action, *enarizomena* and *phlogizomenon*, "being slain" and "set ablaze." It is as if all of the natural world beats with the pulses of a destructive sexuality. Relentless time, an important theme,[49] is here experienced in its most direct, visual form, the setting of the sun each day. Time adds its urgency to the struggle between life and death and to the force of sexual desire. Deianeira discerns its pitiless rhythm in her own diminishing attraction for Heracles as he turns to younger women. "For I see her youth advancing onward, while my own wanes." Then, with a sudden change to the plural, she generalizes, and develops the sexual imagery: "Such (women's) bloom the eye loves to seize, but from the others to turn aside" (547–549).

With such ominous interrelations of sunlight, birth, and death, it is not surprising that the "rising sun," literally "rising eye," of the news of Heracles' return (203–204) should fill us with foreboding. Deianeira would "pluck" this bright news (*karpoumetha*, 204); but flowers here are not happy in their associations (see 549, 999, 1089; *enkarpa*, 238). Iole, "exceeding bright in eye and form" (379), renders Heracles vulnerable to the complex of dangerous fires within and without, and to the destructive implications of the sun in the opening ode (94–96). Its beam can bring only death (cf. 685–686, 1085).

Showing things to the light remains dangerous throughout. The verb *phainō*, "show, reveal," from its occurrence in the very first line, has sinister connotations.[50] Deianeira uncovers the poison to the light, and Heracles, as a consequence, uncovers his hideously wracked body as he urges all the onlookers to behold his pitiable state (1078–80). From the first news of his arrival, as we have seen, vision and light come together in disaster (203–204). There is also the distracted eye of the murdered Iphitus (272), Heracles' eye rolling in pain (794–795), his eyes' vision of the flower of madness (997–999), and the blind infatuation which ravages him (1104).

III

Corrupted sacrifice points inward to the distempered heat of Heracles' lusts and outward to a disrupted relation between man and the natural order. The full-fruited offerings (238) bring only death to the celebrant's world.

Trachiniae

Homer had told how Deianeira's father, Oeneus, failed to make the proper harvest sacrifice, or *thalysia*, to Artemis, whereupon the goddess sent a savage boar to ravage the fields (*Iliad* 9.533–542). The corruption of sacrifice which Deianeira causes in this play has a similar effect. The motif of the corrupted sacrifice, the act which should promote fertility turning to its opposite, had been richly developed by Aeschylus.[51] Iole, who is among the first fruits of a specious offering, is repeatedly described in terms of growth, seed, bloom,[52] but she destroys the generative pair of the house she enters.

Images of birth and nurture consistently describe fear, anxiety, separation and death.[53] In the prologue Deianeira uses an agricultural simile to describe her marriage (31–33), but her image, Heracles as the farmer of an outlying field which he visits at the time of sowing and reaping only, suggests neither the nurturing quality nor the stability of agriculture. At the same time it foreshadows Deianeira's own ambiguous relation to the life-giving and nurturant aspects of the house, for if she, as wife and mother, is, in the conventional image, a plowed field, she is a field that stands at the edge of the cultivated and domesticated land, at the point of contact with the wild (*aroura ektopos*, 32).

From the very beginning the ambiguities of this marriage reflect the precariousness of human control over the violence that is both within and without the house. Deianeira had "the most painful fear of marriage rites" of any girl of Aetolia (7–8), and with good reason as she unfolds the picture of her suitor (9ff.). The joy of the house in the coming "marriage," the reunion between Heracles and Deianeira (*domos . . . mellonymphos*, 205–207), turns to grief when she meets Heracles' actual "bride" (843, 894; cf. 460). Deianeira is repeatedly called the wife of Heracles (*damar*, 406, 650), but Heracles has brought Iole home as a second *damar* (428–429). *Damar* might also mean "concubine," but Sophocles exploits the ambiguity of the marital terms to suggest the confusion wrought upon the house by this new bride and new marriage (842–843, 893–895). Deianeira is the mistress of the house (*despoina*, 430, 472), but the reward for her service (542) is a young and beautiful rival (551).

When Deianeira speaks of her husband's "marrying" (*gamein*) other women (460–461), the verb may be a polite euphemism by a dignified wife generous enough to pardon his infidelities. Near the end, Hyllus, explaining her motives, says that she anointed the robe with what she took to be a love charm (*stergēma*), "when she saw the marriage within" (*tous endon gamous*, 1139). Heracles has brought within the house a kind of sexuality which could have a place only outside. Although *gamos* need not mean "lawful wedlock,"[54] these two places, 460 and 1139, are the only passages in Sophocles where *gamos* or *gamein* means "sexual union" and not "marriage proper" (cf. 504, 546, 792). Where *gamein* is used in this purely sexual sense, it generally refers to illicit or violent union, e.g. Aegisthus' "marrying Agamemnon's wedded wife" (*Odyssey* 1.36), or Agamemnon's "forced, dark wedding" of Cassandra (Euripides, *Troades* 44), or Apollo's rape of Creusa (Euripides, *Ion* 10–11). Even in the two passages in the *Trachiniae*, the context makes clear the special sense given to the word. The forcing of language corresponds to the forcing of the institution itself. Heracles' lust imposes on the house two *gamoi* and two *damartes*; the result is its destruction by the poison of the beast who himself attacked the marriage. When Deianeira prepares to take the steps that will destroy her house in protecting it, she confronts the contradictions which this new "marriage" presents to the "house" and uses the two words in close conjunction. With the vivid sense of the rights of that bed for which and on which she will later die, she pictures to herself "two women in embrace under one coverlet" (539–540; cf. 916, 922). Then, after reviewing her conflicting emotions about Heracles' "disease," she says that she is not angry (545–546), "But as for sharing a house (*synoikein*) together with her, what woman could do it, sharing the same marriage (*koinōnousa tōn autōn gamōn*)." The *gamoi* here might mean merely the physical union of 460, like the embrace of 540. But the juxtaposition with "sharing the house" suggests rather that Deianeira is thinking of marriage in its most exclusive sense, her rights as the *damar* within the house.

Finally facing the necessity to act, she brings the issue down to the physical and biological question of natural selection: looks, youth, physique (547–549). When she calls Iole, a few lines before, "no maiden, but already yoked" (536), the metaphor lays bare the harsh sexual competition beneath the now empty title, "husband" versus "man" (550–551). This new *damar*, "yoked" like a domesticated beast, reduces Heracles' house to the savage bestiality that in fact destroys it.

Deianeira's near-wedding with Achelous reminds us throughout of the gulf between order and passion which marriage spans. The play began with the wooing of a bride (9–27), but this suit is itself an elemental contest between man and nature's brute forces that is later reenacted, in less flamboyant form and with less happy outcome, within Heracles' house. Smitten out of her mind long ago by the fear of this monstrous lover (24), Deianeira is again smitten with dismay, but now from the defection rather than the importunity of a mate, when she hears the truth about Iole (386). Her reply, the robe, leaves Lichas smitten in his heart with joy (629) as apparently lawful desire (*pothos*, 630–632) answers the illicit and destructive desire of Heracles for Iole (368).

The second stasimon leads us from the restrained sexuality of marriage to the violence it may actually contain. Despite the Olympian mythology of the opening strophe, its nervous dochmiac rhythms take us back to the elemental beast world which Deianeira in the prologue was so relieved to escape. Achelous appears in all his phantasmagoric brutality, "the force of river, form of four-legged high-horned bull" (507–509). He and Heracles meet amid the fearful clash of "fist and bow and taurine horns all mingled together" (518–520). Deianeira sits apart, "like a heifer, abandoned" (530), an anticipation of that bestial level of emotion and action which appears in the surge of jealousy about the "yoked" Iole a few lines later (536).

The ode begins as a celebration of the triumphs of Kypris, but Kypris, however necessary to marriage, is not the goddess to preside over its stable, settled aspect. Here she deceives (another erotic term; cf. 662) Zeus himself, disrupting the basic pattern of marital union on Olympus. In the next ode, when the new marriage has brought its harm to the house (842), Kypris, though unheard, is "made visible as the clear agent of these things" (861–862). The new bride, in the inverted fertility of this destructive marriage, only "gives birth to an Erinys for the house" (893–895). The union of husband and wife in their longing (631–632) takes place through the close embrace and melting of the robe in a grim parody of the sexual act (767–768, 833, 836). Deianeira's suicide complements Heracles' pain: she prepares herself for death in a reenactment of her wedding night.[55] After elaborately preparing their bed (916ff.), she looses her robe and bares her side to drive the dagger home (924–926, 930–931). As in the case of Haemon and of course Virgil's Dido, sexual consummation is replaced by consummation in death.

Whereas Heracles openly acts out his lustful violence in paradoxical resemblance to his bestial opposite, Deianeira is forced to acknowledge the elemental sexuality in the midst of which she has lived with a curious innocence and unawareness. Though sexual metaphors pervade her language, she seems only dimly conscious of their power. She cannot give a clear account of the savage contest of which she was the prize (22), for she sat by thunderstruck with fear (24; cf. 523ff.). She looks back nostalgically upon the "meadow" of maidenhood (144ff.), which she describes in beautiful lines recalling Ajax' pathetic evocation of the happy innocence of his son's infancy (*Ajax* 552ff.). Yet that uncut meadow of her girlhood contains its violent side too: it was as a girl, *pais et' ousa* (557), that she met the shaggy-chested ancient beast in the deep-flowing river. Sexuality appears to her in monstrous shapes which she cannot fully comprehend. Even marriage is colored by the anxiety and fear which weigh her down (5, 152; cf. 8–9, 148–152). Not fully aware of the depths of her own sexual instincts, sheltered from the bestial realm where Heracles does his work, she has no defenses against the passions with which she must now deal. For all her horror of the Centaur and his attack with lustful hands, she is disastrously credulous of his love charm. She could see herself, in a sort of helpless terror, as some one for whom Heracles would fight. But not until it is too late does she confront the implications of her fighting for him. Her tragedy is indeed a tragedy of late learning, as it has often been called; what she has to learn, among other things, is the deadly force of the love charms which she rashly uses (cf. 584–597) and the dark power of the realm from which they come.

In her tragedy of "late learning" the audience sees, even if she does not, a growing rift between her emotional sensitivity and the male view of her as sexual object or means of producing legitimate children. We can discern three main stages. In the first, she is a gentle, forgiving wife, anxious, but free of jealousy. In the second stage, as the power of her own sexuality begins to work in her, she resolves to use the Centaur's love charm. She yields only for a moment to bitterness (540–542), but her decision is taken without malice or hatred. It is her own naiveté about the forces with which she is dealing that leads to the double entendres and tragic ironies of her presentation of Lichas with the robe (600–632). Finally in the third movement, having witnessed the effects of her unguent, she realizes what she has been working with, and she takes her life. The act of carrying the poison from the darkness of the house into the bright sunlight where she can recognize its baleful power corresponds to an inward movement also, as she passes from the darkness of ignorance to a clarity which is lucid, but, like all light in this play, destructive.

The gradual realization of the elemental sexual forces around her brings a change in Deianeira's language. Erotic words that are initially innocent become steadily more ominous.[56] When Deianeira does finally speak of Eros, she refuses to face his hold on her own mind. "No one," she says, "stands up against Eros with his fists, like a boxer, for he rules over all the gods, and me too" (444). "How, then," she asks, "does he not rule the other women as well as me?" "I should be mad" (*mainomai*), she concludes, "if I should blame either my husband, now that he is seized by this disease, or this woman here, who is responsible for nothing shameful or bad towards me" (445–448). The logic is extraordinary. She merely glances quickly at love's power over her in a brief phrase (*kamou ge*, 444); this power serves only to excuse Iole and Heracles.[57] But love's rule over her too will soon become the motive force in the tragedy. In the next two odes, as we have seen, love's power becomes increasingly visible until Kypris is finally revealed as the "soundless agent" behind it all (861–862).

Deianeira's comparison of Eros to an invincible boxer becomes real and concrete in the clash of hand and fist in the battle between Heracles and Achelous (517ff.). The madness to which Deianeira alludes figuratively in 446 becomes the terrible madness of love with which she tried to inflame Heracles' desire (1142) and the flowering madness of the pain caused by the love poison (999). "Seized by the disease" becomes more than a figure of speech. Her exoneration of Iole as not responsible (*metaitia*) for anything shameful or bad toward her (447) is echoed by Hyllus in his denunciation of Deianeira; she caused the death of Lichas who was "responsible (*aitios*) for nothing bad toward you" (773). At the very end he blames Iole as the "only one responsible (*metaitios*) for my mother's death" (1233–34).

The first stasimon marks the transitional point between the two stages of Deianeira's awareness. The ode describes the brutal contest between Heracles and Achelous which attended Deianeira's passage from virginity to marriage. That latent sexual violence of her past is now active in the present. After the ode she speaks of Iole not as "melting in love," but as a "yoked" heifer (536). Immediately after this she mentions the "ancient gift of the old beast," as if the description of the violent battle which ended in legitimate union recalls also the still more elemental sexuality of her remote past.

When, in the third stage, she recognizes, to her horror, the malevolence of the beast whose power she has tried to enlist in her own cause (705–718), she sees that his charm has been operative on her as well as on her intended victim: "He charmed me," *m'ethelge*, she says, taking up the word which the messenger had used to describe Heracles' lust: "It was for this girl that he took Eurytus and high-towered Oechalia, and it was Eros alone of the gods who *charmed* him (*thelgein*) to fight these battles" (352–355). The Centaur's charm working in her is her own unleashed sexuality from which Heracles' strength and her own domesticity had sheltered her earlier. She has gained her knowledge late, as she says (710–711). Hyllus enters with the lurid details of fire, blood, screams, and pain which the charm has released; Deianeira, like Jocasta in the *Oedipus Tyrannus*, slips out in silence to die (813–821).

In this encounter with her bestial past Deianeira reaches outside the safe limits of the house back into that wild setting of dangerous rivers in her youth. Achelous, himself actually "the strength of rivers" (507), belongs to a preanthropomorphic mythology of primordial images which run together the elements of nature and human forms: "From the thickets of his beard break forth runnels of water, as from springs" (13–14).[58] "Such was the suitor I received," Deianeira comments bitterly (15). Nessus not only plies his trade in the deep-flowing river Evenus (559), a setting quite different from Bacchylides' rose-covered banks (16.34), but meets his end in the very middle of those streams (*en mesōi porōi*, 564), a detail which Sophocles perhaps added to the myth without troubling himself too much about how Nessus, to say nothing of Deianeira, made it to the other side.[59]

IV

Heracles' defeat by the female sexuality unleashed by Deianeira is prefigured in the story of his enslavement to Omphale (69–70, 248–250, 356–357). As an embodiment of the power of female sexuality, Omphale is a doublet of Iole and also a hidden aspect of Deianeira herself, that quality in Heracles' faithful spouse which emerges into prominence under the effect of the Centaur's poison. Heracles' own extreme, physical masculinity is defenseless against this distillation of feminine sexuality.[60] The encounters with Achelous and Nessus, however, remind us that the power of female sexuality, though overshadowed by the roles of stable housewife and nurturing mother, still lives in Deianeira. Greek social norms dictate the separation of erotic sexuality and the house, the sexually seductive and the maternal woman, but Heracles' introduction of Iole into his house breaks down these firm barriers and thus produces chaos and destruction.

If Omphale suggests a hidden side of Deianeira's femininity, she also reveals another aspect of Heracles' masculinity. A heroic conqueror through the strength of his body, Heracles is also vulnerable through his body, the force of his physical impulses. In opposition to the hero of Dorian endurance stands the sensual, gluttonous Heracles of Old Comedy and the satyr plays, the Heracles who could be enslaved to a barbarian mistress, ruler of soft Lydia (70, 248; cf. 236, 252).[61] The Omphale story, therefore, suggests the paradoxical permutation of opposites in both protagonists. The devoted housewife seeks the irresistible allure of the kept woman; the stern, tough warrior, like Odysseus with Circe and Aeneas with Dido, bides a whole year (69, 248) in servitude to an Oriental queen.

This champion of the values of the free, male polis is not only enslaved himself, but when freed from his enslavement to Omphale (248–250) will enslave a Greek city (257, 283, 467). His alleged motive is that Eurytus addressed him, a free man, as a slave (267). Here, as in the story of Iphitus' murder which follows it, the lie holds a kind of truth: his enslavement by a licentious Lydian queen prefigures the truth of his emotional enslavement to his own lusts.[62] The metaphor of lust as enslavement is not uncommon. Sophocles himself, according to Plato, used a vivid form of it in conversation, calling eros "a raging and savage master" (*Rep.* 1.329c).

For all his wandering and adventures, Heracles needs a settled house and the continuity it provides for his line and his deeds. We first see him, through Deianeira's eyes, as a protector against the violent forces of nature and as a farmer of sorts (30–33). It is a human touch that even this great figure feels the need for family ties when his own extinction seems close. Early in the play Deianeira told how he arranged for the division of his patrimony as he set off for his new adventures (161–165). At the end he cries to Hyllus to summon his clan "that you may all learn the tale (*phēmē*) of my end from such oracles as I know" (1147–50). He appears for a moment as a patriarchal figure concerned that his tale be handed down within the house as the preserver of his memory. Yet Heracles himself has destroyed the settledness which would make such a reunion possible: his family, Hyllus points out, is scattered (1151–56).[63] His killing of Iphitus has caused them to be uprooted, *anastatoi* (39), a word evocative of the age of migrations in early Greece.[64] He dwells a stranger in a strange city (40), and he soon appears as the uprooter (*anastaton*, 240) of another city. When he does finally set foot in his adoptive land, he does not know "where in the earth" he is (984) or among what people (1010–11), another grim inversion of the returning Odysseus (cf. *Od.* 13.187ff.).

Deianeira's compassion for the homeless, fatherless, wandering condition of Iole and her companions (299–300) foreshadows the uprooted, desolate state of her own house (cf. 911 and 300). Vowing to enslave Eurytus with wife and child (257), Heracles ruins both another house and his own. The violence rebounds on his own wife and child. Looking upon Iole, Deianeira prays for her own house (303–305): "O Zeus the Turner, may I never see you thus advancing against my seed, but if you do so, may it be while I no longer live." Ironically, this prayer, like the prayer about the robe (609ff.), is fulfilled but not in the way she hopes. Zeus's care for his own seed is ambiguous (see 139–140, 824ff., 1268ff.), and it is hard to distinguish between the ordering will of Zeus and the violent forces of Eros or Kypris (cf. 250–251 and 860–862; 354–365 and 1086, 1022).

The destruction of the house by the house is Deianeira's tragedy. Celebrating Heracles "saved within the house" (610–611) is the alleged motive for sending the robe. Lichas brings it, Hyllus explains in the next scene, "his own house's servant from the house" (*ap'oikōn . . . oikeios*, 757). Bringing Iole within "to share his house," Heracles "shares house with" a grimmer inhabitant, the disease which ravages his body (*synoikein*, 545 and 1055). The fair body he hoped to have beside him within his house (539–546) turns into the horrible disease, the monstrous form of that disease of love which centers on Iole.

Heracles' house, however, is no ordinary human family. It comes from Zeus and has its destiny under the will of Zeus. Hence this house is also a focal point for the question of the divine order. The problem of suffering is phrased in terms of the father's care of his children. In their first ode the chorus reassures Deianeira by asking, "For who ever saw Zeus without concern in such a way for his children?" (139–140). But this confident rhetorical question implies a different answer when they see the appalling fulfillment of the oracle for Zeus' own son (824–826). Their question brushes the tragic reality, but, as is often the case with the Sophoclean chorus, remains at a safe distance behind the screen of misapprehension. Their initial confidence is answered by the puzzlement and pain of Hyllus at the end when he accuses the "unfeelingness" (*agnōmosynē*) of the gods "who, begetting children and being called their fathers, look upon such sufferings" (1266–69). We may recall too that the ode celebrating Kypris begins with her power over Zeus, that is, her disturbance of the paradigmatic divine *oikos* on Olympus (497–500).

The play suggests the possibility of viewing the moral order as a whole in terms of *oikos* relationships: Heracles' failure toward his own house is only a lesser reflection of Zeus's failure toward his. At the same time both the human and divine fathers show some measure of responsibility, problematical though it is. Heracles arranges for the marriage that will continue this line, and Zeus, whose plan includes Heracles' apotheosis, may not, ultimately, have been so remiss in his care for his son as that other afflicted son, Hyllus, believes.

Hyllus, therefore, is not only necessary to indicate the fullness of relationships within the house; like Heracles, he is also the suffering son, the chief survivor, who bears the brunt of the collapsed order of house and of universe. The two father-son relationships interlock in his question at the end about the irresponsibility of Zeus's paternity.

Like Telemachus in the *Odyssey*, Hyllus' identity is initially framed by the *oikos*. But also like Telemachus he can move outside of it as his mother cannot (67ff.). Both in spatial and familial terms, he mediates between Heracles and Deianeira. Unlike Deianeira, he can enter Heracles' world. Unlike Heracles, he still has his root in the house. He combines his mother's emotional tenderness, revealed in his intense grief for both parents, with his father's capacity for action and decision. His initial response to Deianeira's guilt also shows something of his father's violent temper.

The action creates a pathetic counterpoint between the destruction of the house on the one hand and the maturation of its youngest visible member on the other hand. It compresses into a single moment of crisis his passage from adolescence to the conflicts and responsibilities of adulthood and, in prospect, marriage. In his opening words he appears almost as a child, asking his mother to "teach him what may be taught" (64). But he undergoes a process of tragic learning as he is taught too late the truth of her error (934). Young and capable of learning, he is open to change as Heracles is not. Hence his bitter denunciation of his mother in 734–821 is balanced by his noble defence of her to Heracles in 1114–42. Placed in an impossible position between opposites who cannot be mediated, forced to an Orestean choice with no Apollo to guide him (1065,

1067–69, 1125, 1137), he experiences the anguish of seeing the house torn apart and finding himself orphaned of father and mother both at one stroke (940–942).

The confusion which Heracles has wrought in the house involves Hyllus in some potentially incestuous situations.[65] He lies side to side near Deianeira in her death (938–939), like Haemon beside Antigone (*Antig.* 1235ff.). He is forced to marry a woman who has lain at Heracles' side (1225–26). These suggestions should not be pushed too far; Hyllus is not a candidate for psychoanalysis. But the incestuous themes suggest once again the libidinal forces working beneath the surface of the house, even when its surviving member, through Heracles' command about Iole, agrees to preserve its property (245) and continuity.

Hyllus' recovery from deluded hatred of his mother and his compassionate love for her still come up against his father's blind, rigid hatred. The continuity of the house assured by Hyllus' marriage to Iole is still clouded by the unreasoning violence and archaic possessiveness of the father for what has once been "his." Heracles' apotheosis and the founding of the Dorian race through his descendants remain inextricable from the destructive passions and blind heroic code of a rude figure who seems closer to the monstrous world he has subdued than to the civilized order which he protects. Such are the flawed vessels of the will of Zeus.

V

For Greek culture the *Odyssey* is the great archetype of the house that successfully resists its enemies and reestablishes its vigor and unity. Like Penelope, Deianeira holds out alone in the house during her husband's long absence. Hyllus, like Telemachus, goes in quest of his father; and Heracles, like Odysseus, returns from his wanderings by a passage over water, asleep.[66] Each of these parallels is inverted. The play's Penelope takes the role of Clytaemnestra; Telemachus-Hyllus resembles the Orestes who kills his mother. Odysseus-Heracles finds no fruitful, familiar earth to salute, but only the vengeance of the beast in a country not his own (39–40; cf. 983–986). There are no orchards and plowlands which are his by inheritance from his father, no bed of living olive wood, but only separate beds of pain and death in a ruined house where birth is of death and curses (834, 842, 893–895). The faithful wife loses her right to the title of mother (817–818); and the fertility of the house is inverted in its fearful, savage "nurslings" (*thremmata*) from the wild, the Hydra, Cerberus, the Nemean lion (574, 1099, 1094).[67] Veering between the extremes of Penelope and Clytaemnestra, between passivity and aggressiveness, Deianeira stands outside the stable norms of a settled house. She moves as far from the role of loving wife as Heracles from the role of civilizing benefactor of men.

The poetry of the parode, as we have seen, lifts the conflicts between husband and wife within the house to the level of a cosmic conflict between powers of nature. The ensuing action is not merely a domestic tragedy, but a disaster in which all of nature participates. The destructive associations of sun and light point ahead to the sacrifice itself which binds together in a single node the corruption of the relations between man and God in the ritual, man and man in the house, and man and beast in the inversion of Heracles' civilizing triumphs in the outside world. Possibly too, the sun's figurative death in a blaze of fire (*phlogizomenon*, 95) foreshadows Heracles' suffering in the "bloody fire" (*phlox*) of the sacrifice (766) and later his flaming death on the pyre of Oeta.[68] The Centaur is associated with darkness and night, but it is the light as well as the darkness which kills Heracles (609, 740, 944–946). The female night, who "begets and lays to rest" the sun (94ff.), suggests Deianeira who will seek her final rest, and also kill her husband through the agency of sun and fire. The alternating rhythms of nature have a unity which leads only to destruction.

The earth that is distributed as property by the father (162–163), the earth divided off by boundaries in the ritual order of the sacrificial ceremony (235–238), the ancestral earth of the city (466; cf. 478) all come to reflect this negation of man's fruitful relation to the larger world around him. Kypris' victims include Poseidon, "shaker of the earth" (502), along with Zeus and Hades—the three gods whose spheres of power include the whole world in its ordered Olympian aspect. "From the earth to the earth" bubbles up the foam which reveals the effect of the poison (701–704): "From the earth where it lay there seethe up clots of foam as when the rich drink of Bacchus' vine is poured upon the earth." Given the symbolic significance of the poison which Sophocles has established, this parody of agriculture charges fertility with a corrosive sexual violence. In the next ode the chorus' realization of the meaning of the oracle takes the form of a metaphor of plowing as the twelve-month plowing season (*arotos*) brings forth death, not release from toil (824–825). Heracles has cleansed the earth (1061) of its "earth-born" monsters like the Giants (1058–59), but the impurities which still exist within himself and within Deianeira send up this monstrous apparition from the earth (701).

The tragic catstrophe collapses basic oppositions in a deadly cancellation of difference between night and day, darkness and sunlight, celebrant and victim, man and beast, sheltered inner world and the raw savagery outside, human agriculture and a crop of venomous monsters.

VI

The presence of the monster's poison in the very recesses of the house reverses the usual relation between inner and outer realms, the woman inside tending the house, the man outside. The early scenes of the play present an extreme form of that contrast: Deianeira the plowed field, Heracles the farmer who comes and goes (32–33), she having only the vaguest idea of his whereabouts (cf. 52–60), he spanning continents,[69] wandering over broad tracts of the stormy sea (100–101, 112–119), and battling monsters in Hades and the remotest places (1097–1100). With that contrast of spatial relations goes also a double standard of sexuality: she weighed down by all the cares of the house, he engaged in his dubious service to Omphale in Lydia and his taking of Iole in Euboea. Deianeira's recourse to the gift of the beast creates an even more extreme reassertion of the original dichotomy between inside and outside, but it transforms that dichotomy into destructive separation: Heracles moves outward from the house to "the highest crag of Zeus's Oeta" (1191) escorted by his son and servants; Deianeira ends as she began, "alone within the house" (*dōmatōn eisō monē*, 900).

After describing Achelous' wild river world of her prologue, Deianeira, in her second long speech, looks back to another vision of youth (*to neazon*). She compares girlhood to an enclosed, virginal meadow which "no heat of the sky god, no rain, no blasts of wind shake, but it has a life of joy apart, free of toil, until a girl is called a woman" (144–149). These lines in their pathos and beauty depict a woman caught, as she knows, within the onward-moving cycle of life looking back longingly toward a protected inner world which, like the Homeric Olympus, is free of generation, time, and change.[70] Yet the unreality of this world for her has already been confirmed by the landscape which she sketches in the prologue. That dreamy serene meadow rudely gives way to the actuality of the ox-pasturing meadow of Lichas and Heracles, with its noisy crowds (188). In joy and relief at the news of Heracles' arrival, Deianeira invokes "Zeus who holds Oeta's uncut meadow" (200). But Zeus's meadow, though uncut, is the very antithesis of her sheltered meadow of virginity. Zeus and Oeta will bring her no joy. To try to assimilate Oeta to her sheltered world ("uncut meadow" suggests a virginal place)[71] only involves her in contradictions that cancel one another out. When she learns the painful truth about Heracles' return she invokes another aspect of Zeus and Oeta (436–437): "Do not deceive me, I beg you, in the name of Zeus who flashes his lightning down Mount Oeta's glens." The violent poetry of the lines is surprising in the gentle Deianeira. The virginal innocence of the meadow of girlhood retreats farther into the distance. It seems to be touched, after all, by the dangerous heat (*thalpos*) of the sky god (145, 437), with the associations of destructive lust that heat carries in this play (cf. 368, 697).

The contrasts between the sheltered meadow and the exposed world of Heracles, Oeta, Zeus, and the heat and storms of lust create a gulf not easily bridged, and the house that might mediate the polarities experiences their destructive and confused union. "Things in the house" (624–625) do not stand quite as she would later have Lichas believe.

In both seeking the sheltered meadow and in using the love charm locked up in the recesses of the house (579, 686), Deianeira falls back upon interiority. The first retreat is misguided, the second disastrous. The first conceals the dangerous consequences of the second. The two movements are in opposite directions; yet in the fusion of opposites they complement one another. The first is a denial of mature sexuality; the second is an excessive release of sexuality. An element of evasion lies at the root of both. In the first case Deianeira longs for a stage of life to which she cannot return; in the second she falls prey to an unrealistic naiveté about a lustful Centaur's helpfulness in preserving a marriage that he once attempted to violate. Although it evokes both the "unshakable seat" of Olympus and the fertile garden of Alcinous,[72] her meadow in fact comes to point downward to the beasts rather than upward to the gods, away from the fruitfulness of a settled life of house and farm to a wild realm where birth and nurture are deadly. The meadow fantasy thus reflects that imbalance between hope and reality, innocence and maturity, which she evinces in her initial helplessness about sending someone out of the house to inquire after Heracles (54ff.) and more disastrously in her trust of Nessus. Hence the meadow, too, comes to reflect its opposites: shelter from heat turns into the full force of the heat of lust; protection from time in Olympian serenity becomes the total subjection to human transitoriness which Deianeira knows and fears (cf. 1–5, 943–946).

The two protagonists are as the asymptotes of two lines which bend toward one another but can never meet.[73] Hermes, the god who effects passage and communication between distant places or persons, is here invoked only to convey the gift that seals the failure of communication between the two parties (620). Even at the long-awaited news of Heracles' arrival, there is an invisible barrier between inner and outer realms. Deianeira asks, "How then can he be absent if indeed he fares well?" (192): absent, yet not absent; faring well, yet doomed. The language itself reflects confusions that are soon to become more than verbal. Even when Heracles is so close, the public world of his deeds and renown forms an obstacle: "All the people of Malis stand around him in a circle," the messenger explains, "and do not let him advance, for each one would not give up his desire to learn" (194–197). This public desire (*pothein*) will soon echo ominously in Heracles' and Deianeira's ambiguous desires (368, 431, 630–632, 755). "All the people" too will soon groan at a public event of a very different character (783). Elated by the messenger's news, however, Deianeira cries that the women should shout for joy both within the house and outside the courtyard (202–203). But the conjunction of inner and outer, like the places Deianeira mentions here, *stegē*, *aulē*, can only bring disaster: Iole, she cries out, is a "secret grief brought under the roof" (*pēmonē hypostegos*, 376), and she begins her funereal lamentation preliminary to suicide when she sees Hyllus preparing Heracles' bed in the courtyard (*en aulais*, 901).[74]

As the faithful guardian of the house has admitted the destructive power of the savage beast to its center, so the returning hero is both an "outsider" (*ektopos*) and an "out-citied man" (*apoptolis*). At Deianeira's death the sheltered world of hearth and house seem overwhelmed by the motifs of journey and distance associated with Heracles. The chorus prays for a "windy gust at the hearth" to "send them away from the house, out of these places" (*apoikizein ek topōn*, 954–955). We may recall the destructive winds which Heracles let loose on Iole's city (327). "Windy gust at the hearth," *anemoessa . . . hestiōtis aura*, is itself an oxymoron which suggests the destructive fusion of outer and inner realms in the "hearth/altar" of Heracles' sacrifice (607).[75] Eurytus' alleged mistreatment of his old hearth guest (262–263) figured in the destruction of his (and then Heracles') house.

Shouts of happiness at the hearth (206) and the joyful prayer for Heracles' arrival from the island hearth (658), which, incidentally, he has destroyed, all ironically foreshadow a conflation of inner and outer in the total collapse of the house.

Heracles' "last journey," Deianeira had said early in the play, was "out of the house" (155–156). Her own "last journey" (almost the identical phrase) is taken "with unmoved foot" (874–875) and gets her no farther than the marriage bed.[76] She died, Hyllus explains to Heracles near the end, not killed by anyone outside of the place (*ektopos*, 1132), the word she used in lamenting Heracles' rare visits to the "out-of-the-way plowland" of the marriage bed in the prologue (32). The clash between centripetal and centrifugal movements divides them to the last.

These spatial divisions form the following configuration:

Deianeira as destroyer from within	Complementation of inner and outer	Heracles as destroyer from without
Female reticence and fear	House as mediation	Nature and external world; male violence
Sheltered meadow of virginity	Tilled plowland	Wind, storm, heat
Fear of sexuality	Marriage	Violent sexuality; untrammeled instincts (beasts, rivers)
Woman who keeps the beast's poison in recesses of house (misguided protection of house)	Woman as guardian of house (cf. 542)	Heracles' neglect of his house
Fire as heat of lust; altar/hearth as destructive	Stable hearth and civilizing fire	Heracles' absence from the hearth

The middle column represents society's accommodation of feminine and masculine impulses in the institutions of house and marriage. The two end columns contain the polarities which, in this play, fly apart in hostility and mutual destruction instead of reaching accord and mediation.

If Deianeira's inner world reaches out in perverted communication to destroy the adventurous husband outside, he would now send within the house, to deliver Deianeira into his hand from the house (1066), the son whom Deianeira once sent outside to search for him (64–93). In the total collapse of the balance between inner and outer realms, this destructive use of the living mediator between husband and wife would be the truest proof of the son's paternity: "Prove yourself born truly my son and give into my hand the woman who gave you birth" (*tēn tekousan*). In this disintegration Hyllus can find no forgetting of pain "either within or without" (*oute endothen oute thyrathen*, 1020–22). At the news of Heracles' approach the chorus uttered a joyful shout (*klanga*) to Apollo *prostatēs*, Apollo who "stands before" the door (208–209) and protects the house. But at Deianeira's death there is only her cacophonous

"roaring" at the altars of the domestic shrines inside the house (*brychato . .
.bōmoisi*, 904), as she reenacts emotionally and inside those roars of physical pain
that wracked Heracles at his altars outside (805).

VII

The good Centaur, Chiron, combining the best of god, man, and beast,
could serve as a positive mediator between nature and culture.[77] Thus Machiavelli
could cite the Centaur as an emblem of the efficient ruler.[78] But generally the
Centaur's mixture of half-divine ancestry (the result of Ixion's attempt to rape
Hera) and human and bestial form reflects an unmediated clash between the
extreme terms.[79] The sculptures and paintings of Centaurs and Lapiths which
Sophocles' fellow citizens saw in temples like the Parthenon and Theseion seem
to have conveyed "the difference between civilization and savagery . . . , the
contrast between self-control and self-indulgence, responsible guardianship and
irresponsible passion, lawful marriage and lawless rape."[80] "A two-natured un-
approachable, horse-marching band of beasts, destructive, lawless, outstanding
for violence" is Heracles' characterization of these now defeated monsters
(1095–96).

In one of the play's major inversions of man and beast the Centaur appears
as a kind of bestial doctor who "anoints" his patient with a salve that changes
him into a wild creature, managed by the "curbs" of the disease (831–840):

> For if the deceit-fashioning necessity of the Centaur anoints him with its
> deadly cloud[81] as the poison melts into his sides, the poison begotten by
> death, nourished by the shimmering snake, how would he see a sun other
> than today's, melted with the most terrible form of the Hydra? The deadly
> guile-speaking spurs of the black-maned one in their mingling outrage him
> as they seethe upon his flesh.

The equine beast-man, with the help of snake and Hydra, uses human speech to
"deceive" (*doliomytha*, 839; cf. *dolopoios*, 832). The erstwhile conqueror, Heracles, metaphorically becomes a horse, controlled by the "seething goad" or spur
of the poison itself (840). The fruitfulness of the house in birth and nurture
(*teketo, etrephe*) means its ruinous dissolution (834; 893). At the same time the
repeated verb "melt" traces the inversion of beast and man to the hero's inner
surrender of civilized restraint when he was melted by the heat of his own lust
(463; cf. 662).

The Centaur's short-circuiting of the biological, sexual, familial, and ritual
codes, all interwoven in the passage we have just examined, applies also to man's
proudest superiority over beasts, the area of intellect and technology celebrated
in the great Ode on Man in the *Antigone*.[82] The *Trachiniae's* major symbol of
emotional violence and loss of rational control is the poison/love charm, the
thelktron. It not only emanates from the Centaur, but in fact consists of a part of

his body, his blood. Deianeira's reliance on a love charm parallels Heracles' defeat by bestial lust. She too abandons reason and surrenders to the dark powers of the beast. Recourse to this magic weakens both her logical powers and her moral judgment and fuses her with her monstrous double, the husband-destroying Clytaemnestra or the sorceress, Medea.

Under the influence of the irrational power emanating from the Centaur, she involves herself in logical and emotional contradictions. "I detest acts of evil daring," she says, "and the women who dare them. But if I can overreach this girl, somehow, with philters and with the charm against Heracles, the deed has been devised, unless I seem to be doing something rash (*mataion*); but, if not, I shall stop" (582–587). The shifting accumulation of "if" clauses, the abrupt change from a future action ("if I can overreach . . . ") to the finished act ("the deed has been devised"), the ambiguous "if not, I shall stop" when it is too late to stop betray rampant logical and emotional confusion. She hates evil-doing and rash action but in the next lines thinks only of "surpassing" or "overreaching" (*hyperballesthai*) the "girl" (*paida*, 585), another reminder of that youth which Deianeira finds so threatening (547ff.). She wonders if she is doing something *mataion*, "rash," "violent": it was the word she used twenty lines before to describe the Centaur's lustful attack "with violent (*mataiais*) hands" (565). She admits that she relies only on appearances and has no tested knowledge (590–591), but she seems oblivious to the danger of the very position which she is describing. She ends this part of her reflection with the extraordinarily ingenuous, "If you do shameful things in darkness you will not fall into shame" (596–597), a statement which recalls some of the dubious morality of Phaedra in Euripides' *Hippolytus*.[83] This darkness of her deed is, in fact, quite literal (see 685–692). As the sequel tells us, it is also the destructive darkness of the black beast and the black poison (606ff.; cf. 573, 717, 837).

In another way too her case resembles Phaedra's: the very fact of using the magical philter symbolizes the sapping of her ratiocinative powers by passion and blind hope. When that passion leaps forth in the single thought of victory over her rival, "overreaching this girl," the words "philter" and "magical charms" literally frame her utterance (*philtra, thelktra*, 584–585). With these *philtra* and *thelktra* she enters the dark mythic world of the Centaur and the Hydra which entraps her in the irrational, subliminal violence of her own mind.

With Lichas' departure and the choral ode of anticipation (which ends, however, with ambiguous melting, persuasion, anointing, beguiling, 660–662), Deianeira begins to confront reality in a different way. As she describes the marvel of the tuft of wool dissolving in the sunlight (673–679), she relives her act in the darkness (685–692), goes over the wool's disintegration again, "a tale incomprehensible" (693–694), in even greater detail (695–704), and concludes with a new realization of her mental confusion (705): "And so, alas, I know not to what resolve (*gnōmē*) to turn." Gone is the specious daring and the confident-looking, but actually hollow, reasoning of the preceding scene (582–595). Reckoning with cold accuracy from probability (707–708) and past experience

(714–716), she reaches the inevitable conclusion that she is about to cause Heracles' death (713). Now she "refuses to be deceived in thought" (*gnōmē*, 713; cf. 705). She frames sharp questions (707–708, 716–718) and draws her inferences with lucid, certain judgment (cf. *doxēi goun emēi*, "in my judgment, at least," 718). At once she echoes the word *doxa* in her "resolved judgment" (*dedoktai*, 719) to die along with Heracles. She closes her long and painful self-scrutiny with a clearly reasoned basis for her action, a general moral principle introduced by *gar*, "for" (721–722): "For it is unendurable that one who esteems being not of base nature should live with the reputation of baseness." We are in a different world from that evasive expediency and moral ambiguity of the previous scene. She recognizes that she has been under a spell of irrational power as great as the spell she hoped to cast: the Centaur charmed her (*thelgein*, 710), just as she hoped to charm Heracles (*thelktroisi tois eph' Hēraklei*, 585; cf. 575). Too late does she learn (710–711; cf. 934) and get better sense (*phrenes*, 736).

The great ode of the *Antigone* sums up its praise of man with his cleverness (*sophia*) and power of artful device (*to machanoen technas*, *Antig.* 365–366). In the *Trachiniae's* inversions of civilization, "art" and "device" have sinister connotations. "Device," *mēchanē*, twice describes Deianeira's anointing of the robe (586, 774). Twice also the verb *technasthai*, "to devise by art," describes her application of the Centaur's blood to the sacrificial robe (534, 928).

Deianeira's recognition, or anagnorisis, of how she has played into the power of the beast takes the form of images of inverted technology: woodcutting (699–701), agriculture (703–704), carpentry (767–768). The sawdust-like powder of the disintegrated wool is literally the "devourings," *ekbrōmata* (700, only here in Sophocles), which foreshadows the "devouring" of Heracles by the savage disease and with it the reversal of beast and sacrificer. The image was developed even more explicitly in her first description of the tuft as being devoured or eaten (*diaboron, edeston*, 676–677). The crumbled remains lie there, fallen on the ground, *propetes* (701), as Heracles is to lie limply on the ground (*propetēs*, 976, the only two occurrences of the word in Sophocles), a prey to his savage pain.[84]

When the poisoned robe clings to Heracles like the "tightly fitted work of a carpenter" (767–768), we are reminded of Deianeira's metaphorical "fitting" of "gifts in return for gifts" (494 and cf. 623, 687).[85]

The disruption of language combines with an ominous "joining" again as Hyllus approaches with the evil tidings from Cenaeum. Deianeira fears something heavy for the house (730), but the chorus advises caution (731): "Silence about the greater part of this tale would fit you best" (*harmozoi*). This is the third occurrence of the verb in a hundred lines. All the instances of "joining" then culminate in that deadly vicarious "embrace" of the "close-fit robe" (767–768) which in fact disjoins this house.

After intelligence or mind (*phrenes, gnōmē*), perhaps nothing else is so basic to man's civilizing skills as the hand. But in this play the hero who "excels everywhere by force of hands" (488) is defeated by Eros (489) and the beast.

He calls out for a craftsman of skilled hand (*cheirotechnēs*, 1000) in healing at the moment when he seems completely under the power of this baleful drug. Yet Heracles' victory over monsters has been by the physical force rather than the skill of hands. The crashing of hand defeated Achelous (518). He laments his hand's strength in the conquest of other monsters (1047, 1089, 1102) when that conquest is at least partially overturned by an act that appears as skilled handiwork: Deianeira describes her anointing of the robe as an act "devised by craft of hands" (*chersin ha technēsamēn*, 534). Later the robe is a "net" which subdues Heracles as by the force of hand (*cheirōtheis*, 1057). The inversion of this basic sign of man's power over the beasts is perhaps most terrible at the end when Heracles' hand are bent only on murderous physical violence. The human hand that protected her from the Centaur's wanton hands (565; cf. 517) would do her a greater violence than the beast's. "Give me your mother with your hands into my hand," he commands Hyllus in what one scholar calls "perhaps the most savage passage in Greek tragedy."[86] Deianeira, to be sure, achieved a noble death with vigorous hand (923), but Heracles still regrets that she "did not die at my hand" (1133).

The deed of greatest tragic heroism in the play is, ironically, that of a woman's hand, described, significantly, in a metaphor of the arts, the "building" of a solid structure as of a temple or a house: "Did a woman's hand dare to build (*ktisai*) such deeds?" (898). Given the inversions of technology, this union of human heroism with technological skill is anomalous: it appears only in the speech of a minor character and a woman, the Nurse. There is something equivalent on Heracles' side, undercut though it is by his preceding violence about "hands," when the pledge of a right hand affirms the authority of a father in the house (1181, 1184). Even so, this unifying touch of hands is attended by the horror of pollution which Hyllus might contract by lighting his father's bier with his own hands (1194, 1214).

Fire in the play, too, functions as the very reverse of a civilizing tool.[87] In its literal aspect it destroys the ritual order (see 766): it serves the Beast's designs (685, 696) and releases the monstrous poisons of Heracles' past. In its figurative aspect it forms a symbolic amalgam with the threat to civilized order from within, the heat of poisonous lust which the house contains (see 145, 368, 697). It thus forms part of the contrast between inner and outer space, for the sheltered, interior fire of the hearth gives way to the destructive fire associated with bestial lust at Cenaeum and the dangerous celestial fire of Zeus (436–437).[88]

From the beginning of the play agriculture separates civilization and savagery, the wild river world of Achelous and a human marriage. Heracles' house appears under the metaphor of farmland, but Heracles is as ambiguous a farmer as he is a husband (31–33). When Deianeira knows that the Centaur's charm will destroy, not save, her house, it reveals its sinister power to her in the form of a perverted cultivation of the vine. "Clotted foam seethes up from the ground, as if the rich drink of Bacchus' fruit . . . were poured upon the earth" (701–704). Wine, like cereal grains, is a mark of civilization. The Cyclopes of Euripides neither sow the earth nor enjoy wine (*Cyclops*, 120–124). Philoctetes, in his "savage" life, is deprived both of the fruits of the earth and of the vine (*Phil.* 707–715). Deianeira's "wine" underlines the grim intertwining of the two codes of civilization, house and agriculture, for their destruction.

In this simile too Deianeira, who saw herself initially in the conventional image of the passively plowed field (31–33), now transmits the destructive, not the creative power of "earth" (*gē*, 701): the "field," as it were, destroys the "farmer," just as birth and nurture in the house change to death (834, 893–895). The ritual code is also involved, for the foaming poison functions as a perverted libation of a wine which appears as a wild and destructive, not a cultivated and life-giving product. This "clotted" wine-like foam (*thrombōdeis*, 702) grimly recalls the other evil effects of blood in this play. The horror is poetically transfigured and transferred to Heracles himself in the next ode, where the poison has now become the "deadly, guile-speaking spurs" (*kentra*) of the black-maned beast, spurs that "seethe upon" (*epizesanta*) the skin of the victim (838–840). The fatal effects of this "seething" now work directly upon the "farmer" himself. They are correlated with further inversions in language and man-beast definition. Mastered by these "seething spurs" and by a sinister "wine" that "seethes up from the ground," Heracles is also overcome by an inward distemper, for "seething" is a common metaphor in authors of the period, including Sophocles himself, for the working of violent passions.[89]

Wine and centaurs do not mix. The poured wine describing the effects of Nessus' charm is emblematic of the perversions of civilization which these mythic creatures embody. Drunken centaurs attempted to carry off a bride at her wedding; Nessus follows in his compeers' footsteps (or hoofsteps): he would rape a new bride in her husband's presence. Heracles came "from Bacchic Thebes" to defeat a monster and win Deianeira in legitimate marriage (511). But when he himself changes places with the Centaur and becomes subject to the poison of his blood, the Bacchic fruit (704) for him too points not to the city, but to the wild. The Bacchic joy of revelry for Heracles' return to the house (219) will soon change to wails of grief (947ff.).

Wine has another association with the destruction of a house. In Lichas' false explanation for the sack of Oechalia, Heracles' anger derives from an insult at dinner, when he was well plied with wine (268). Once more a lie conceals truth, for it gives us a momentary glimpse of the drunken, brawling Heracles, an *Hēraklēs ō(i)nōmenos* (268) whose appetites bring him perilously near the centaurs he has destroyed.

Nessus practices the trade of ferryman across the "deep-flowing stream of the Evenos" (559), and even gains a wage (*misthos*, 560), like a respectable member of society.[90] Yet he does this ferrying "not rowing with propelling oars or with a ship's sails" (560–561). One might compare the maenads' hunting without nets or assaulting Pentheus' tree "with levers not of iron" in Euripides' *Bacchae* (1206, 1104). Even Nessus' approximation to a civilized function lacks its basic quality, the use of tools. His work as ferryman, like his physical form, is a kind of parody of civilization. Once he has Deianeira on his back in midstream (564), he abandons this quasi-civilized activity for the bestial proclivities it overlays.

Heracles has his "ferrying," too (802; cf. 571); like Nessus', it also expresses an ambiguous relation to civilization. Transported to Trachis by "the conveyance of a ship" (*ochēma naos*, 657), he will arrive defeated by the beast (660–662). It is hard to bring him ashore, roaring and writhing in his pain (803–805). Though he has defeated an "ox-prowed" monster (13; cf. 223) and has cleansed both sea and earth of dangerous creatures (1012), he is still caught in the "sea's valleys" (99–100) and the stormy "sea of travail" (112–119), from which he never escapes (see 1170ff.). The sea breeze (*ouros*) which should attend the propitious voyage reuniting the civilizing hero with his house in this play recurs to mark its collapse (468, 815, 827, 953–955).

The sea in this play is not the element controlled by the art of sailing, the first achievement listed in the *Antigone*'s Ode on Man. It is associated, rather, with uncontrolled passion and savagery, notably in the case of Lichas' death (780).[91] In the ode which precedes that event the chorus sings of harbors (*naulocha*), but Heracles is still "at sea . . . far from the city" (*apoptolin pelagion*, 647–649). His dear spouse awaits him in the city (650, 657), but the "island hearth" (that is, the altar) which the ship is leaving will destroy the whole nexus of civilized order connected with the hearth on the other side of the water.

Closely connected with the sea is commerce, fundamental to the polis (see Plato, *Rep.* 2.371a–e) and especially to Athens with its maritime empire. In the most striking inversion of this civilized activity, Deianeira, who initially hopes for success (*eu prattein*) and a purchase of gain (*kerdos empolāi*, 92–93), discovers that she has taken in Iole "as a shipmaster receives freight, a piece of goods for traffic, a merchandise of insult to my heart" (537–538). "Success" and "profit" (*eu prattein, kerdos*) come together as part of Lichas' lie (230–231), and the former word has ominous reverberations throughout the play.[92] Lichas tells how Heracles himself was bought and sold in his service to Omphale (250–252, 276). As Deianeira's interior realm is freighted with an inappropriate import from the outside and she, the housekeeper (542), turned into a merchant, Heracles, when he reaches his supposedly safe house, has his "profit" only in the coma that dulls his pain (988–991).

The inversions of civilization are especially marked in the case of medicine. Sophocles had a rich field of myth and metaphor to draw on. From Homer on, drugs, *pharmaka*, are ambiguous:[93] they are both healing and noxious. The stories of Circe and Medea not only associated such *pharmaka* with sexual desire, the beast world, and the destruction of the house, but also helped suggest that these drugs operated in part through the lusts and desires of the victim himself.[94]

A nightmarish inversion of a real medicine, the Centaur's *pharmakon* only feeds the "disease" it treats (685, 1142). The melting of the ointment signifies both the physical and spiritual sickness of the patient; it both causes and manifests disorder of body as of soul.[95] In some legends, like those of Achilles and Demophon, a hero is "anointed" by a god and thereby made immortal[96]; here a hero is "anointed" by a beast (661, 832) and reduced to a near bestiality of pain. Heracles calls for a doctor skilled in healing to charm away (*katakēlein*) his pain and madness (*atē*, 1000–1002), not knowing that the source of this madness is a charm (*kēlētērion*, 575) applied by a bestial ministrant (1140, *pharmakeus*).[97]

From a metaphor of lust (445, 544), the disease becomes a physical ailment (first at 784). But even as it becomes tangible, it remains elusive, a disease that medicine cannot treat, both because the medicine is itself the source of the malady and because the disease is one with the diseased. Hence the disease becomes alive, a kind of wild beast (*agria*, 1030), devouring, drinking, leaping, and rushing forth, blooming, grasping, creeping (769ff., 987, 1010, 1026, 1053–56, 1083–84, 1089).[98] Becoming itself a kind of "beast," the disease is the bestial violence of Nessus, "the ancient beast," but has a new life in the body of Heracles released by the bestiality of his own lust. Lichas joyfully announced the arrival of Heracles "blooming and not weighed down by any disease" (235). But Heracles in fact nourishes a "flowering disease" (999, 1089) far more sinister than any Lichas has in mind. By linking cause with effect, physical with spiritual distemper, this disease reveals inner and outer perspectives simultaneously. Opposites coalesce as the blood and venom of the old monsters seep into the hero's own blood. The poison which kills all the beasts (716) now kills Heracles himself.

VIII

The intrusion of the beast, literal and figurative, into the human world wrenches language too out of its human shape. Roars, shrieks, screams, the thud of blows are the dominant sounds. We have already seen how the ritual silence or *euphēmia* becomes the groan of the crowd at Lichas' death (194 and 783). Milton found in this passage inspiration for a simile to describe Hell's "wild uproar."[99] The joyful flutes, harmoniously echoing the divine muse (639–642; cf. 217–218), make way for the cacophony of Lichas' screams and Heracles' roars. Describing the effect of the Centaur's unguent on the woollen applicator, Deianeira says that she has "*seen* a tale not to be told, incomprehensible to man's understanding" (693–694), a striking synaesthesia which stresses the uncanny nature of these events: they are beyond the usual limits of human speech.[100]

All three main characters are at some point reduced to inarticulate cries of pain or lamentation (see 805, 904, 909, 936–942, 1004ff.). Crucial words like "fare well" (*eu prattein*) become ambiguous, and basic terms of kinship are emptied of meaning (see 541–542, 736, 817–818). Heracles, weeping like a girl (1071ff.), loses the control over his tongue that is part of heroic restraint.

The *Trachiniae* is unusual among Sophocles' extant plays in treating the perversion of communication through the written as well as the spoken word.[101] Deianeira twice mentioned a tablet left her by Heracles on his departure (47, 156ff.). This written tablet (*deltos engegrammenē*, 157) shows us a Heracles responsibly concerned for the division of his patrimony and the future of his house (see 161ff.). But there is another "tablet" in the house, the metaphorical "bronze tablet's indelible writing" to which Deianeira compares her faithful memory of Nessus' instructions (683). Deianeira even calls these instructions "laws" or "ordinances," *thesmoi*, giving this solemn term to the guileful speech that in fact negates the well-founded order of law.

The other vehicle of communication between Heracles and Deianeira is also nonverbal: the protagonists exchange no words in the play, only the robe, with its seal (614–615), token of good faith (623). The failure of both tablet and sealed missive reveals the deep rupture in communication between the house and the outside. Heracles and Deianeira speak virtually different languages.[102] What Deianeira understands as a gift of love, Heracles receives as a gift of death. In their interchange of go-betweens she will use a messenger to awaken mutual desire (631–632); but later, if Heracles had his way, he would make her a "messenger" to all men of his power of just and brutal vengeance (1110–11).

Persuasion, the drug, magic, and poisonous *eros* work together to undercut language as rational communication. The Centaur's "persuasion" is both his speech and his drug. Both work on Deianeira (710), as they work on Heracles (661–662), through the victim's own latent violent sexuality and irrationality. Having failed by force, Nessus resorts to language. His magic charm seduces ("persuades") Deianeira and accomplishes verbally what his licentious hands (565) could not effect.[103]

As his charm of words "persuades" Deianeira, the literal charm of his drug "persuades" Heracles and, in a complex tissue of literal and metaphorical meanings, "melts" him, both erotically and in fusion with "the most terrible shape of the Hydra" (836–837),[104] one of the symbols of the released bestiality within Heracles himself. Under the compulsion of *eros*, the hero of straight speech and straight action is implicated in lies and trickery (cf. *dolos*, 277).

The choral passages on either side of the catastrophe emphasize the ambiguities of this persuasive power. In both 660–662 and 831–840, it is the beast, not the man who speaks and speaks seductively (*peithein, parphasis*, 660–662) and falsely (*dolo*-compounds, 832, 839).[105] The beast does the "taming" (cf.[Heracles] . . . *panameros*, 660) and applies the "spurs" (840).

Everything that should express rational human behavior does the reverse. Speech, like the drug, works at the most primitive levels: both are ultimately the envenomed blood of the beast (572, 717), working through the blood of the victim (1054), heating the poisonous lusts that are already there, destroying articulate speech. The Centaur's persuasion and charming of Deianeira are verbally ambiguous: Nessus promised so to affect Heracles' mind "that he would never look upon another woman rather than you" (575–577). Beguilement and drug, persuasion and ointment are virtually interchangeable; both are the language of the ancient beast and bring a common destruction of civilized order and reason.

The action of the Centaur's drug reveals itself for what it is, the dark enchantment (*thelxis*) of violent passion. In the symbolism of the play erotic desire is a black poison that clouds the mind and brutalizes the soul. This symbolism unites the internal self-deception which takes place under love's "persuasion" and the deception and trickery, which are here the concomitants of love (*peithō, apatē, dolos*). The Centaur, his poisoned blood, and the use he and Deianeira make of it crystallize into visual images the complex of acts and behavior that forms the extremes and dangerous illusions of eros: deceit, persuasion, seduction, the quasi-magical power of the beloved, the oscillation between reason and unreason in the violence of emotions, and the sweeping away of inhibitions before the force of animal instincts.

Heracles, impatient when he fails to persuade Eurytus to give him Iole as his concubine (359–360), behaves like the *misologos* and *amousos* of Plato's *Republic*, the *logos*-hating, uneducated man who "makes no use of persuasion by words, but like a beast (*thērion*) does everything by force and savagery" (*bia, agriotēs*, 3.411d–e). Language undergoes a similar reversal in Deianeira. The lies and secrecy about the union with Iole (recall *kryphion lechos*, 360) lead eventually to the "secrecy" of her obedience to the Centaur (556, 689) and finally the "secrecy" of her death (903).[106]

The first contact of husband and wife through the false and complicated reports of Lichas, prefigures the more deadly distortions of communication to come. Lichas tries to gloss over his lies with the simple joy of Heracles' arrival (289–290): "Know well that he will come. Of the full account that has been spoken well (*logou kalōs lechthentos*) this is the sweetest thing to hear." Like a clever speaker, he wants to convey pleasure in the hearing. We may recall the warnings against such "pleasurable speaking" (*kath' hēdonēn legein*) in Thucydides.[107] He is corrected by the Trachinian Messenger who has no pleasure in speaking unpleasant things (*ouch hēdomai*), but at least gives a straight account (*orthon*, 373–374).

Deianeira replies with her own ambiguity of communication. The doubleness of verbal signification (600–632) parallels the doubleness of signification in the narrative movement, the gift of a robe which both is and is not what she claims it to be. Actually, the robe at this point has three different meanings: to Lichas it signifies Deianeira's thank-offering; to Deianeira, a love charm; to the dead Nessus and to the audience, a deadly poison.

The destruction of communication is especially important for the theme of trust. Words like *pistis, pistos, pisteuō* refer both to belief in the truth of a message and trust in the fidelity of husband or wife. The linguistic and familial codes are homologous. When the credulity of *logos* is destroyed, the trust between the members of the house also perishes. Thucydides' famous description of the revolt at Corcyra presents a similar situation from the perspective of the city rather than the house. The breakdown of values coincides with the breakdown of language as a tool of reason and communication. In Thucydides' analysis (3.82–83), as in Sophocles' play, language comes to subserve passion. The result is the disintegration of *pistis*, the trust that must exist between the members of a polis, as between the members of an *oikos*, if they are not to destroy one another.[108]

Lichas' lie, the initial source of infection in the realm of *logos*, introduces also the infection in the realm of trust, *pistis*.[109] He declares himself faithful (*pistos*) to Heracles in reporting his commands (285–286). Giving Heracles the title, "your husband," *posis sos* (285), foreshadows the disruption of the familial relationship. Deianeira soon has cause to question his faithfulness about truth (*to piston tēs alētheias*, 398). Lichas' way of maintaining faithfulness soon leads to Deianeira's irony about her faithful husband (541) and that title of *posis* (541, 550–551).

By giving the robe, visible sign of the trust that should exist between members of a house, Deianeira in fact puts her trust in the beast rather than her husband. Hence she is made to reflect with the chorus on *pistis* in her deliberations about the robe (588–591). Lichas, the herald who is to bring a message of words and gifts in return for gifts (493–496), will be the recipient of ambiguous words, and will transmit the "old gift of the ancient beast" (555–556). Communication by gifts to be "fastened on" (*prosharmosai*, 494) becomes the destructive "persuasion" of the robe's poison, kept in darkness until the time of fastening it on (*harmozein*, 687).[110] The word "gift" echoes ominously through the next scenes (603, 668, 691–692, 758, 776), until finally Deianeira's hesitations about that gift are confirmed in Hyllus' pronouncement that the gift is one of death; the robe is a *thanasimos peplos* (758).

The climax of the ambiguities of both language and robe, both forms of exchange, comes in Deianeira's speech of bestowal and Lichas' reply (600–632). Lichas praises the art (*technē*) of civilized communication which he practices: "If I perform this secure art of the messenger that belongs to Hermes, I shall never fail in your service, conveying and showing to Heracles this container, fastening on him (*eph-harmosai*) the trust of words which you pronounce" (620–623). Never has a supposed expert in the art of communication been more deceitful or deceived. This art secretly becomes the tool of the beast. Verbal ambiguity subverts real communication: the "joining of the good faith of words" (623) becomes the physical "joining" of the deceitful and baleful love charm (687; cf. 767–768). The god who presides over this art of communication, Hermes the messenger (*pompos*; cf. 620, 617), had also the office of leading the dead to Hades. As messenger, Lichas performs virtually this task as well.[111]

The destruction of language involves the contrast not only between clear and untrustworthy speech, but also between speech and no speech at all. The almost Aeschylean silence of Iole at the beginning poses the first threat both to the house and to communication. Treated as a piece of captured property, Iole seems to have lost the power of speech. Ever since the catastrophe to her house and city she has only wept (322–327). The destruction of the civilized framework which gave her a human identity has made her a "yoked heifer" (536) and left her silent.

The silence around Iole breaks down the house of Deianeira, too. Evading her questions about his beautiful captive, Lichas claims ignorance, "for I made no lengthy inquiries" (317). A true companion of Heracles he "did (his) work in silence" (319). When the truth comes out, Lichas admits that Heracles "did not tell me to conceal it" (480). The deception was all his own idea, since he "feared to wound (her) breast with these words" (481–482). For Heracles, as we learn later, words are mere "embroidery" (*poikillein*, 1121); Lichas at least has some sense of their power, whether spoken or not.

After the exchange of words Lichas takes the gift which he is to convey to Heracles. The chorus tries to gloss over with silence Deianeira's newly discovered truth of what she has sent (731–732): "Silence in the rest of the *logos* would be fitting, unless you will say something to your son." But Hyllus has his own *logos* to tell, and his words deny her the name of mother (736, 817–819). Her reply is—nothing, one of the great dramatic silences in this play of violent sound. "Why do you creep off in silence?" the chorus asks (813). But her silence only convicts her more deeply in her son's eyes. "Don't you know that by keeping silent you speak in accord with your accuser?" (814). The son who denied Deianeira's right to the title of mother has now moved to an extra-familial kind of exchange with her in becoming her "accuser" (*katēgoros*). When her silence is broken, it is by the off-stage cry of her death, answering the "soundless agent," Kypris (861–862) with a sound "not uncertain," an "ill-starred groan" (866–867). When Heracles finally appears, Hyllus' cries and broken phrases are answered by a call for silence, lest speech "awaken the savage disease of (his) raw-minded father" (971–977). Now the only profit lies in silence (988–991).

Only toward the end of the play does human speech begin to reestablish itself, falteringly, against frightened silence or bestial roaring. Hyllus' firm demand for silence so that Heracles can learn the truth about Deianeira (1114–21, 1126) redeems his incriminatory interpretation of her parting silence. Then silence "spoke in agreement with" the accuser (*synēgorein*, 814); now a new and higher form of *logos*, the divinely given new oracles, "speak in agreement" (*synēgora*, 1165) with the old prophecies and enable Heracles to grasp the meaning of his death. Here, too, the old (*palai*, 1165) loses some of its sinister hold over the new: something other than chaos begins to emerge from the Centaur's evil persuasion of old (1141; cf. 555–556, 1159).

The "persuasion of the beast" (660–662; cf. 1141) had effected a downward mediation from man to animal; this oracular *logos* reveals to man his destiny in the perspective of the gods.[112] Now, instead of human speech doubling with bestial roar, the inarticulate natural world gives tongue to messages that speak to the hero's nobility and heroism and afford at least a glimpse of that Heracles, "best of men," whom we expected to encounter. The "Doves" (presumably priestesses and not actual birds),[113] beech tree, and "much-talking oak" (*polyglōssos drys*) at Dodona (172–173, 1168ff.) have spoken to Heracles words whose full import he now understands. As in the myths of the Golden Age, the barriers between man and nature are effaced for benign, not destructive, ends; through the beasts man comes into contact with the gods, not his own latent bestiality. So far in the play, it has been just the reverse.

Heracles kept these prophecies written down (1167) as Deianeira kept Nessus' instructions "like the indelible writing of bronze tablet" (683). But this time the writing serves its true function and preserves the words of the gods, not the speech-destroying message of a dark monster.

No *logos*, however, spans the gulf between Heracles and Deianeira. For all

Hyllus' effort in obtaining the calm silence to explain her situation (1114–39), she gets no more than silence from Heracles.[114] Odysseus and Penelope, together once more in a reunited house, converse in the intimacy of their bed of living olive wood, the appropriate emblem of the thriving, fruitful house. Heracles and Deianeira perish on their separate beds of pain, never having spoken to one another, their exchanges enmeshed in falsehoods, ambiguities, curses, and mis-used tokens of fidelity to an empty house (see 614–615, 542).

IX

Yet not everything is swept away in the tide of the Centaur's "persuasion." As Dodona is a reminder of happier relations between man and the lower orders of nature, so at one of the bleakest moments of the play, a different image of the centaur appears, Chiron. When Deianeira recognizes Nessus' drug for what it is, she tells how the Hydra's blood wounded Chiron too (714–715). This Cen-taur is not a beast, like Nessus, but a god, "the god Chiron," she calls him (*theos Cheirōn*).[115] He is no *pharmakeus* with a deadly poison, but as Pindar says, the teacher of Asclepius, "tame craftsman of limb-helping anodyne" (*Pyth.* 3.6). Deianeira cites Chiron's case as another decisive instance of the venom's potency. Chiron, the good Centaur, points to a more benign series of mediations between beast and god. Deianeira, however, is excluded from these. Her centaur, Nessus, would in fact have palmed himself off as a benevolent centaur, teaching (681), helping (570), persuading (570), when actually he has just enacted the part of the archetypally malevolent centaur, attempting to rape a new bride.

Like sacrifice, oracles are a vehicle of communication between man and God, but, unlike sacrifice, these oracles cannot be corrupted, only misunder-stood. Early in the play oracles and sacrifices are closely linked: Deianeira asks Lichas if Heracles' sacrifice is motivated by a vow or "some prophecy" (239). An oracle told her that Heracles' expedition against Oechalia will bring either the end of his life or happiness ever after (76–81). Heracles reaches a new knowl-edge of what his suffering means when he connects the dead Nessus with the prophecy that nothing alive could kill him (1157–72). The two oracles, Deian-eira's and Heracles', express from two different angles the disastrous conse-quences of Heracles' savagery: willful destruction of a civilized city and defeat by the beast Centaur.

The oracle that only the dead can kill Heracles reveals its hidden meaning. It is indeed something in Heracles' dead and remote past which kills him. The Centaur's gift is old, the beast himself ancient (555). "Of old," *palai*, is an im-portant word at the moment of recognition (1141). The Centaur and his gift belong to an earlier, more primitive world that still survives. Nessus lives in buried, remote strata of our being but can still return, symbolically as we would say, with unexpected virulence. Heracles has subdued this archaic world of bestial powers, but he has not entirely subdued the archaic bestiality within himself. The Centaur's poison, acting in concert with the heat of his own lust and his own anarchic impulses, brings it to life again. By confronting this more primitive self with a more developed human self, by suffering and then overcoming the "ancient gift of the beast of old," as by fitting the old oracles with the new (1165), Heracles wins again his old victories over the beasts and can become the truly civilizing hero, worthy to be Zeus's son and "best of men." We witness Heracles' loss and then recovery of his humanity, and, as in the case of Oedipus, the process requires the confrontation with and the integration of the old and the new (cf. *Trach.* 1165 and *OT* 916). Here, as in *Oedipus Tyrannus, Ajax,* and *Philoctetes,* the oracles are wise and tell us truths that we resist or are reluctant to uncover.[116]

Within the structure of the civilized codes that we have been studying, prophecy is symmetrical with sacrifice. The perverted sacrifice fuses the victorious hero with his bestial double. Yet the burning of the hero on his pyre also appears as a kind of sacrifice (see 1192), and, as in a sacrifice, a person other than the victim must serve as celebrant and light the fire.[117] This fire on Oeta, ordered by the gods, answers the impure, "bloody fire" at Cenaeum, which served the stratagem of the beast. There the sacrificial flames caused the disease and sent the hero on a downward path toward his bestial opposite; here on Oeta the flames are a mysterious cure (1208–10), part of a secret knowledge that Heracles possesses because of his special relation to the gods.

"This is the only healing that I have, the only doctor of my sufferings," Heracles says mysteriously in 1208–1209. Hyllus does not understand. "How," he asks, "would I cure your body by burning it?" (1210). Heracles replies with an unexpected reasonableness (1211): "But if you are afraid in this matter, at least do the rest." The calm tone in itself intimates the cure, for the old disease, as we have seen, was as much of the spirit as of the body.

As the mysterious knowledge of 1208–1209 intimates, Heracles has found the healing that he called for so desperately in his throes of agony (1000–1003). His first word for "cure" here is not the ambiguous *pharmakon*, but *paiōnion* (1208), the healing power of the Olympian Paian or Apollo Paian.[118] There is a world of difference between this calm certainty about the healing fire which awaits him and his wild shouting for fire at his first appearance on the stage (1013–14): "I perish, alas. Will no one turn upon this wretched ailing man fire or a sword in aid?" There he was subject to the beast and to the bestial in himself; here he is in touch with the gods and with his own divinity.

Sophocles never says explicitly that Heracles will become a god after his immolation on Oeta. Heracles' apotheosis is one of the most controversial issues in the criticism of the play.[119] Though it is always dangerous to use material *exō tou dramatos* ("outside the drama") to interpret a work, several considerations strongly suggest that Sophocles means us to view Heracles' sufferings against the larger framework of the legend. The apotheosis does not mitigate those sufferings or transform the bitterness of the conclusion into anything approaching a happy ending. Nor does it make Heracles any gentler: heroes in tragedy, as in cult, remain harsh and remote. But it does suggest a symmetrical design which includes an upward as well as a downward mediation.

Leaving aside the fairly clear reference to apotheosis in 1206–10, we may cite four points in its favor. First, this version of the legend is the accepted one in Sophocles' time, and Sophocles himself uses it in the *Philoctetes*.[120] Sophocles' fellow citizens saw the divinized Heracles on the main facade of the city's chief sanctuary, the east pediment of the Parthenon.[121] Second, the emphasis on the oracles throughout the play and on the pyre at the end presents the outcome as part of a divinely appointed plan that must include the divinization of Heracles. It is hard to see how Sophocles could lay such emphasis on the pyre if he had not intended us to think of its purpose, the apotheosis. Without that apotheosis in the background the careful details about the pyre would make no sense.[122] Third, Heracles' kinship with Zeus is stressed throughout, and this too leads in the direction of the hero's adoption among the Olympians. Fourth and last, two of the other six extant plays refer beyond the dramatic framework to the worship of the hero after death, namely the *Ajax* and the *Oedipus at Colonus*. Three of the other six plays close with some reference to events which occur after the time of the dramatic action, but are part of the myth: *Electra*, *Philoctetes*, *Oedipus at Colonus*. Reference to Heracles' apotheosis in the *Trachiniae*, therefore, would not be inconsistent with Sophocles' treatment of his mythical material in his *oeuvre* as we have it.

Heracles' apotheosis is little comfort to the dead Deianeira, the uprooted Iole, the orphaned, mourning Hyllus. Heracles has oracles from the gods, but for the other characters the designs of the gods are still dark, and the hero's kinship with Zeus only sets off the gods' apparent neglect of those closest to them. Yet the discontinuity on the personal level is balanced by the reestablishment of continuities within the disrupted order of civilization.

In the mythology of sacrifice the victim and the god can be interchanged. Thanks to this "mythological doubling of the divine being and the victim . . . the god appears to escape death."[123] The function of the victim is mediation, and the victim itself "remains indifferent to the direction of the current that passes through it."[124] In the *Trachiniae*, however, the identification between victim and god (or, in this case, the divinely born hero) initially confuses the distinction between divinity and bestiality. The god seems to be vanquished by the beast. The godlike hero becomes one with the bestial victim at Cenaeum only to separate himself from that victim, and from his own bestiality, on Oeta. On that lofty mountain top, "Zeus's highest crag" (1191), the purging fire will finally enable his divinity to appear. The sacrificial rite of the pyre (1192) finally separates Heracles from his monstrous double, Nessus, and restores the differentiation that had collapsed earlier.

We must remember, however, that for Sophocles divinity does not mean anything like our sainthood. His gods are not kindly, beneficent beings. To become a god is not to become suddenly gentle and benign. It means rather to enter that mysterious, remote realm of power and eternity that the gods inhabit. A divinized Heracles does not put off his harshness any more than a divinized Oedipus.

Heracles' last utterances show the hero inwardly ready for apotheosis. His command that there be no lamentation (1200) and his own sternly enforced silence (1259ff.) anticipate the sacred silence (*euphēmia*) that was so brutally violated in the perverted sacrifice at Cenaeum (783). The rite at Oeta will reenact the Cenaean rite, but in exactly the opposite spirit and with exactly the opposite outcome. As Heracles performs the ritual function of the scapegoat, his own end, with its heroic stifling of the cry of pain, absorbs the violence which he has let loose.[125] This last act of muffled violence, Heracles' death, is itself enclosed within an established ritual frame, the victim a willingly sacrificed man become god, not a struggling man become beast.

The end of the play can also be read as a reflection on the civilizing power of tragedy itself. It represents the cathartic process by which unleashed violence is once again absorbed into an ordered structure shown elastic enough to contain it. The tragedy lets loose chaos in a fearful destruction of the boundaries between man and beast, but at the same time its aesthetic form asserts the framework which can contain and neutralize that violence. Yet within the fictional frame itself, innocent and guilty pay with their lives for the restoration of the civilized limits, and Heracles contains the violence only by purging himself in his fiery death on Oeta.

It is with a return to Nessus and the magical philter that Heracles begins the last, upward movement of the action. When he hears the name "Nessus," he understands that the oracles are coming to fulfillment. Now this hero of brute strength utters a crucial and unexpected word of intellectual perception: *oimoi, phronō*, "Alas, I understand" (1145); "the oracles that I *know*" (*oida*), he says a few lines later (1150).

Heracles' "intelligence" about the disaster in which he stands (1145) contrasts with Deianeira's earlier confusion about where her situation lies (375). In her sensitive and empathetic appreciation of another woman's suffering, understanding (*phronein*) appears as an intensifier of pain: she pities Iole, she says, "in proportion as she alone knows how to understand" (*phronein oiden*, 313). For the two women, helpless victims, understanding gives no way out; it is truly tragic knowledge. Yet Heracles' understanding of his fate in 1145 and his new knowledge of the meaning of the oracles' "release from toil" ("For to the dead no suffering comes," 1173) are at least partially qualified by his murderous blind hatred just a few moments before. Here what he would teach Deianeira is the heavy vengeance of his death-dealing hands (1107–11), an aspect of himself which should be directed against the monsters "outside," not the wife of his own house.

"I am gone, gone," Heracles cries; "My light is no longer" (1144). Out of the pervasive darkness of the play, however, comes a light of another kind: "since these things come together in clarity" (*lampra*), he begins, as he unfolds his mysterious knowledge of what his end must be (1174). The light that characterized Iole's destructive beauty (*lampra*, 379) and kindled the poison (685–686, 691, 697) now denotes an inward illumination that points toward the gods. Heracles' sufferings began with the altar's flash (607) in a corrupted sacrifice celebrating an egoistic triumph of bestial lust. They are to end with the torch's flash commanded by the gods (*lampados selas*, 1198; *ephestion selas*, 607). The restoration of intelligence at last seems to overcome the beast's destruction of mind (*phrēn*) through the dark magic of his philter. As at the unmasking of Iago in Shakespeare's *Othello*, a play whose themes of love charms, monsters, poison, darkness, and devils have some interesting parallels with the *Trachiniae*, we emerge with the hero from the beclouded violence of the beast's enchantment into the light of sanity.

X

Along with his newly achieved intellectual clarity and place within the ritual order, Heracles also regains his place within the familial order. At this point he again appears as the founder of a civilized house with its continuities in the past and the future. He speaks of "son" and "father" and calls for the gathering of his clan (1146–50): "Come, my son, your father is no longer. Call all the seed of your brothers, call wretched Alcmene, Zeus's bride, in vain, that all of you may learn the report of the oracles that I know." The once brutalized hero regains his status as the son of Zeus (1148), bitter though he is at Zeus's apparent neglect (1149–50).

Heracles will now found a new *oikos* to replace the *oikoi* he destroyed. This new union between Hyllus and Iole will come about as part of the son's *charis* toward the father (1129, 1252). Now the bestial "persuasion" of the Centaur gives way to the father's "persuasion" of an obedient son (see 1179, 1224, 1229). The *nomos* of filial obedience answers the Centaur's *anomia* (1096, 1177).

Early in the play, through the tablet entrusted to Deianeira (157), we saw Heracles, as yet untarnished, concerned with the future order of his house and the due succession of property. That domestic order, effaced by Deianeira's obedience to another (figurative) tablet, one that brought the destruction rather than the ordering of the house (683), is reestablished, in part, when Heracles understands the oracles which he wrote down at Dodona (1167).

Yet despite this pattern of destruction and recreation, the most fundamental wound in the *oikos* is left unhealed. Heracles, first of all, had not a word to say about Deianeira. That division still remains, gaping. Second, the corruption of trust (*pistis*) in the exchange between husband and wife is not entirely made good in the exchange between father and son. Though Heracles persuades Hyllus, the boy is taken aback by the need for a formal oath (1181–83):

Her.: First lay your right hand upon mine.
Hyll.: With what end do you so vehemently [*agan*, literally, "too much"] urge this mark of trust (*pistis*)?
Her.: Won't you then give me (your hand) and not show lack of trust [*apistein*, also "disobedience"]?

The reason for this disquietude about "trust" is precisely the distasteful nature of the union which Heracles is enjoining upon his son: the new house is too closely linked to the destruction of the old (1233–37).

Third, Heracles' desire for this union of Iole and Hyllus is not free of the selfish possessiveness which characterized his earlier behavior.[126] "Let no one except you take her who once lay at my side," he tells Hyllus (1225–26). Heracles cannot transcend the egotism and possessiveness of his past. He is still, as one interpreter suggests, "a typical heroic warrior who regards the preservation of his property . . . as an integral and necessary component of his honourable status."[127] With this archaic male possessiveness there seems to flare up a momentary flame of his lust as he remembers her "lying by my side."

It is not easy to judge Heracles. Some have seen a new tenderness and concern, a desire at least to limit the havoc he has brought to human lives.[128] Here, as often in Sophocles, divine and human perspectives interpenetrate. Heracles, almost reluctantly, acts as the instrument of larger continuities, of an order beyond his own life. On the one hand he speaks as the possessive, lustful warrior who wants to hand on to his own flesh and blood the "property" (*ktēma*, 245) which he won in the heat and dust of battle. On the other hand his action fulfills the will of the gods, the necessary pattern of historical events. Hyllus and Iole, albeit against their will, are to be the founders of a great race of warriors and heroes. Heracles' act sees to it that this foundation is secure, even though he has to use threats and curses to enforce it (1238–40). Hyllus, who views the events with the raw emotions of suffering and loss, finds the command repugnant, and we sympathize with his feelings and his scruples. But the gods, remote and impenetrable as ever in Sophocles, are with Heracles. The gulf between human happiness, even human justice, and the divine will, remains deep and dark; here at the end father and son, harsh warrior and sensitive youth, stand on opposite sides of the divide.

Sophocles does not excuse Heracles' violence or his brutal unconcern for Deianeira. These traits are part of the larger destiny that the gods require of him. Yet the qualities of excess and power that lift him to Oeta and eventually to Olympus also destroy him. Everything about him, as about Ajax, is outsized, shocking, ambiguous.[129] His disposal of Iole is shocking. So is, perhaps, the way in which he redefines "piety" in terms of what "gives pleasure to [his] heart" (1246).[130] Yet this statement, for all its egocentric confidence, also reflects Heracles' recognition of an order beyond the limits of most mortals. The oracles were given to him; only he understands them and can fulfill them. Amid the dark passions in Heracles flash glimmers of the heroism which justifies his title as "best of men."

Linking the two poles of this divided house, Hyllus endures the pain on both sides. He accuses his mother in the name of his father's sufferings (807–820), and he grieves at her death and suffers the pain of her loss with the most piercing acuteness (936–946). He goes from the *oikos* to search for his father (64ff.) and carries from the *oikos* the bed on which Heracles will make the last journey from outer to inner worlds, from Cenaeum to Trachis (901–903), the bed which he will also die. Heracles' savagery forces on him a divisive choice between mother and father (1107ff.). Yet his defense of Deianeira in 1114–39 is a partial restoration of the collapsed order of the house, at least in the memory of its one surviving member important in the play (of Deianeira's other children we hear nothing, save that they exist: 31, 54). In terms of the Odyssean archetypes in the background of the action, he is a Telemachus who comes to maturity at the cost of losing both parents. Like Telemachus he leaves the *oikos*, finds his father, and aids him in his final heroic labor or *ponos*. For Hyllus, unlike Telemachus, the continuity of the *oikos* which the son embodies is founded on the ruin of the *oikos* from which he comes.

With the intimations of a restored, though still painful, domestic order, however, come also intimations of a restored balance between civilization and savagery. The arts of civilization, the *technai*, regain something of their proper standing: Deianeira "devises" her noble death (928; cf. 898); Heracles foresees a mysterious Olympian "healing" that conquers the poison of the bestial *pharmakeus* (1208ff. cf. 1140).

XI

Heracles' speaking role might have ended at 1255–56, a highly suitable exit line: "Lift me up, this is my rest from ills, the final end of this man." Instead, Sophocles gives him a closing speech of five anapaests (1259–63). The passage is an important pendant to earlier passages where the beast's triumph confuses all the various codes of the civilized order (659–662, 695–704, 831–840).

> ἄγε νυν, πρὶν τήνδ' ἀνακινῆσαι
> νόσον, ὦ ψυχὴ σκληρά, χάλυβος
> λιθοκόλλητον στόμιον παρέχουσ',
> ἀνάπαυε βοήν, ὡς ἐπίχαρτον
> τελέουσ' ἀεκούσιον ἔργον.   (1259-63)

Come, my hard soul, before this disease stirs again, fit on a bit of steel set with stones and cease your cry that you may fulfill as an act of joy this deed done by constraint.[131]

This bit "fixed with stones" recalls the effect of the poisoned robe, fixed to Heracles' flesh like finely joined carpentry (*artikollos*, 768: in Greek the same word describes the setting of both stone and wood). This image of domination over beasts (the bit) sets right the beast's prior conquest of the man with his "curbs" or "spurs" (*kentra*, 840).

With this reestablishment of order in the technological code comes also the restoration of order in the biological and linguistic codes. The hierarchy of man over beast is reestablished, and the hero who once roared like a bull and wept like a girl (805, 1070–75) now enjoins a heroic silence on his *psychē*, his soul, which, though harsh (*sklēra*) is still the organ of his human consciousness. He fulfills in advance that spirit of silent, heroic enduring to which he had exhorted Hyllus shortly before (see *astenaktos*, 1200; cf. 1177). The hard-won joy of this "deed done by constraint" answers the premature joy of the perverted sacrifice at Cenaeum with a sacrifice of a very different sort.

At Heracles' entrance onstage the old man warned Hyllus to "bite his mouth (*stoma*) closed" in silence (977–978) lest he waken the cries of his "raw-minded father's savage pain" (*agrian odynēn patros ōmophronos*, 975). Now Heracles, no longer savage, wields the curb of silence himself. Instead of being gadfly-driven, like a horse or bull (*oistrētheis*, 1254, previously used as an epithet of the chaotic war god, Ares, in 653), Heracles is, at last, a tamer of wild beasts, but in a deeper sense than before: he becomes a tamer of inner beasts by defeating the bestial in himself. The bit that he possesses at the end of the play makes him the conqueror of the horse-man Nessus in a far more significant way than the arrow at the Evenus. His defense against the bestial is now not a poison which itself comes from the realm of primitive monsters, but a carefully wrought human artifact, a tool which does not kill, but turns animal force to human purposes. As a traditional metaphor for civic order and regal power, the bit also carries associations of both self-control and the restored authority of kingship and thus suggests a larger dimension of Heracles' new spirit.[132]

Heracles' soul is "hard," "firm," *sklēra*, like the steel of the bit itself. But the address to his soul has its special significance. It is, perhaps, an echo of epic heroism; but, like the flash of understanding of the oracles (1145), it also marks a sudden glow of spirit in this hero of physical strength. His address to his *psychē* points to that inner world which is man's most distinctive possession and his sharpest point of differentiation from the beasts.[133] Heracles' painful journey from Euboea to Cenaeum traversed a horizontal axis; he will now take a vertical direction upward to the summit of Oeta as he moves from bestiality toward divinity.[134] Simultaneously he enacts a difficult and necessary transition from an archaic heroism of lust, physical strength, and bloodshed, the heroism of the old epic world, to a heroism that is truly tragic. This is a heroism which, for all its kinship with the "raw" violence "outside," might find a place of honor within the polis.

XII

Deianeira's suffering, of course, still remains closed within the house. Her death continues the circularity which, as the chorus says, characterizes the flux and change in all mortal life, the wheel of fortune.[135] This circularity reaches deeply within the nature of Deianeira's tragedy and expresses its essential quality as distinct from Heracles'. It reflects also the circularity and interiority of feminine experience, in contrast to the goal-directed linear certainty of Heracles.[136] Her very language is stamped with the circular rhythm of nature's eternal return and thus looks toward the chorus' lyrical generalizations on the circular rhythms of day and night and of human fortunes (94ff., 129–135). Expressions like "I nourish fear from fear," "Night brings in and night leads out my suffering," "into the house and then from the house" (28–29, 34) express her total involvement in life's circular rhythms.[137] For her there is no transcendence, no upward, linear movement to a divinely granted destiny. Hers is a tragedy of immanence. She remains caught within the house. Her escapist visions of serene interior spaces in the natural world (144ff.) are grimly cancelled by the reality of the chamber which has been her principal concern and by the reality of the violence which the natural world reveals.

This spatial divergence between the two protagonists, circle and line, inward and outward movement, constitutes their tragedy of separation. It runs from the first scene of the play to the last: Deianeira's body lies within the house, but Hyllus' last lines point ahead to the journey to Oeta's summit, the play's ultimate symbol of the god's mysterious, harsh transcendence. Each figure is destroyed in his or her essential values, values which, in an untragic world, would complement and strengthen one another. Heracles weeps like a girl and is defeated by the beast world he has subdued. Hero of physical strength, he sees his massive body ruined and helpless, an envelope of pain. Deianeira, guardian of the house, nurturer of life, kills her husband, obliterates her house, and gains her son's curse. Each becomes his bestial double: Heracles, the protector of civilization, destroys cities; Deianeira, instrument of the beast's vengeance, destroys her husband. In the disruption of language, both roar in pain around the altars that represent their principal concerns, Heracles at the altar celebrating his victories, Deianeira at the altars of the house (805, 904).

The play confronts us with the paradox that the beast killer becomes the beast in himself while the woman who has killed her husband, "best of men," is a deeply sympathetic and tragic figure. Like Heracles, Deianeira has her noble silence in death (813). In what are virtually her last words onstage she too expresses her determination to meet her end nobly and with honor (719–722): "And yet it is my resolve that if he is caught I too shall die with him in the same impulse. For a woman who values above all not being base it is not endurable to live with the reputation of baseness." Her death, then, is no bestial death, but follows the civilized and heroic norms of nobility and reputation (*timē, eukleia*). Like Heracles she has her heroic endurance, for all the weakness of sex (898): "Did a woman's hand have the daring (*etlē*, "endurance") to lay such a foundation of deeds?" She does voluntarily what Heracles asked Hyllus to be ready to do, *synthanein*, "join him in death" (720 and 798).[138]

For all her reliance on the Centaur's civilization-negating "arts," she proves at the end, like Heracles, a civilizing figure. As Heracles on the road to Oeta becomes a true conqueror of the beast world, Deianeira dying in her house liberates herself finally from the power of the beast that she has kept ready, enclosed in the recesses of that house all these years. For Heracles the sacrificial ritual and all that it involves, for Deianeira the preservation of her house and marriage form the decisive testing ground where they fail or succeed in this necessary task of defining again and again the boundaries between civilization and savagery, the boundaries on which our order and our humanity depend.

Deianeira refuses, finally, to be used by the sexual drives that have played the major role in her life.[139] But the only way in which she can escape nature's cycle of desire and procreation is either to deny it in escapist dream (144ff.) or to fulfill the final movement of those cycles in death. As in the *Ajax*, it is only in death that both figures achieve their freedom from the elemental forces that have played such havoc with their lives. Like Ajax, Deianeira, victim of time and change, escapes time and change only in death, the last freedom permitted to man. That is the darkest side of this tragedy, as of the *Ajax*. But over against it stand her refusal, as ultimately also Heracles', to be victimized by the sexual drives which have directed the course of her life, and her determination, as his, to rise above the triumphant design of the beast through a noble death.

XIII

In the case of both Deianeira and Heracles, however, Sophocles leaves us with something not yet fully closed, an equilibrium not yet fully established. Deianeira, though exonerated, gets no explicit vindication in the eyes of the one person whose judgment most mattered to her. Heracles, though triumphant and heroic in his final speech, exits to a fate which, like that of the aged Oedipus, is dark and mysterious. The new *oikos* is established, but at a dreadful price. Hyllus suffers not only the loss of both parents—both, in a sense, at his own hand—but also the violation of his personal will in an enforced and distasteful union.

The principals of this new *oikos* experience the destruction of their respective *oikoi*, the house which each of them loved. When Hyllus protests that he would rather die than "dwell with (*synnaiein*) those most hateful to him" (1236–37), he not only expresses the extreme violence done to his emotions by his founding of the new *oikos*, but also recalls the lust and destruction which have brought events to this pass. His dwelling with Iole echoes Deianeira's bitter words about "living with" Heracles' latest mistress (*synoikein*, 545). It recalls too the effects of that jealousy, the "net of Furies," which like a wild beast or demonic parasite lives with (*synoikoun*, 1055) and devours Heracles. Correspondingly, his previous line, "Who, unless he is *diseased* (*nosei*) because of avenging spirits (*alastores*), would choose such a fate?" (1235–36), keeps alive the demonic, supernatural dimension of the action[140] and holds still before us the results of that metaphorical disease of lust in the real, physical disease inflicted by the robe. Thus Hyllus' words call up once more the grim metaphors that throughout the play have accompanied destructive violence and inner disorder. The raw wounds refuse to close.

Sophocles does nothing to temper the clash between the brutal insouciance of Heracles and divine will on the one hand and the vulnerable, fragile lives of men and women like Deianeira, Iole, and Hyllus on the other. Although the "maiden" addressed in Hyllus' closing words at 1275 is probably the chorus collectively and not Iole,[141] Heracles' command fifty lines before, "Take her as wife and do not disobey your father" (1224), indicates that Iole is not forgotten. Heracles' words, like his deeds, define her as totally subject to an absolute patriarchal authority, her selfhood and maidenhood violated as she is forcibly shifted from one *oikos* to another.[142] For these "lesser" figures the equilibrium established on the divine plane seems only a vast and cruel confusion.

Thus Sophocles gives the last words not to Heracles, who is passing beyond the mortal suffering, but to Hyllus who is still fully immersed in it: "You have seen fresh deaths, great deaths, and many sufferings freshly made fast, and nothing of this that is not Zeus" (1276–78).[143] Over against this bitterly accused Zeus of Hyllus' speech, however, there is another Zeus, the Zeus who has called Heracles to Oeta and given the oracles that enable him to meet his final sufferings with strength and heroism.

On the divine level, then, there is equilibrium, for the gods are themselves equilibrium, the point where violently expended energies come to rest. But Deianeira's death and Hyllus' closing words destroy the equilibrium on the human level.

The play creates a dialectical tension between a structure that transcends human life and the unstructured and unstructurable grief of those to whom "Zeus" is only indifference, an arbitrary and remote force, and pain. This tension is part of a perpetual dialectic in tragedy between chaos and order, suffering and meaning, the intense concreteness of the individual's grief and the promise of some larger, supra-individual coherence. Sophoclean tragedy reveals the inevitability of that structure, while at the same time protesting against its harshness and the suffering by which it comes to pass. Exactly this penetration of a larger divine order by human suffering, which is also the penetration of transcendence by immanence, constitutes the fundamental element of Sophoclean—and other—tragedy.

The oracles and the closing speech of Heracles intimate that some chord in the invisible harmonies of the universe may be responsive to man's need for meaning and man's capacity to achieve greatness. But Sophocles has so constructed his play that even such a possibility is not enough. The cost on the human level, to Deianeira and to Hyllus, has been too great. We are thrown back, ultimately, on the purely human solace that civilized men and women can give one another through human speech and human institutions. Hyllus' defence of Deianeira's innocence, though it matters not a jot to Heracles, falls on the more receptive ears of the listening chorus. It is to them that Hyllus can address his last words, his final lament on the deaths and sufferings he has witnessed (1275–78). He and the house which he will found provide the measure of human continuity that balances the divinely appointed destiny of Heracles. For those whose sufferings form part of no divinely foreseen plan, there can be no solace, only the continuity of memory among survivors who, like Hamlet's Horatio, "in this harsh world draw their breath in pain." It is, then, to the maidens of the house that Hyllus speaks at the end; and he is thinking as much of Deianeira as of Heracles when, in his last lines, he laments "the great deaths."

5

Ajax

The hero's perilous place between godhead and bestiality in the *Trachiniae* is tested in the areas of physical strength and sexuality. In the *Ajax* the areas are time and change. In Greek thought freedom from change is the primary attribute of divinity. In the *Ajax* change defines the basic condition of mortal life: change from honor to dishonor, from strength to weakness, from friendship to enmity. Against these changes in the human world stand the cycles of ever-repeated, inexhaustible change in nature. That Ajax takes these cycles of eternal flux, changeless change, as the model for his apparent yielding to time is one of the central ironies of his great speech on vicissitude (646–692).

Like Heracles in *Trachiniae*, Ajax is caught between transcendence and the immanence of kin ties, relation to society, responsibility to those who depend on him. Like Heracles, too, he has a female foil for his heroic independence. Tecmessa, like Deianeira, does not break free of the relationships which the hero rejects. For her and for Deianeira, as for Jocasta also in the *Oedipus Tyrannus*, the woman's tragedy of immanence has its own heroic side; this reaches its fullest scope in Antigone and Electra, figures who fuse the male hero's defiant commitment to an ideal with the heroine's devotion to personal ties, to *philia*.

Even more than the *Trachiniae*, however, the *Ajax* presents a man's world. Tecmessa may move the hero to pity, but her role is to be a helpless, though not entirely passive, victim of his heroic drive. The hero who stalks off to the deserted shore, alone, with his sword embodies the essence of male heroic pride. His suicide affirms the Dorian warrior's aristocratic firmness against the alleged softness of Ionian civilization. "Softness," *malakia*, is Pericles' word in the Funeral Speech in Thucydides as he seeks to defend the Ionian strand of Athenian culture against the harsh Dorian ethic of Spartan militarism. The "hardness" of Ajax, like the "rawness" of Heracles in *Trachiniae*, belongs to an older and fiercer set of heroic values, glorious, but rude by the standards of civility toward which Athens had been steadily moving from Peisistratus to Pericles.[1] Sophocles' contemporaries, unlike the imagined contemporaries of his character, Ajax, would also esteem the emotional fullness of a Deianeira or a Tecmessa, with her explicit plea for softness (594). How highly Sophocles himself valued such qualities is clear from his sympathetic portrayal of these women.

If Tecmessa, valuing this softer way of being, embodies the more developed emotional sensibilities of civilized communities, Odysseus embodies their capacity for reasonableness, flexibility, and intelligence. His civilized qualities complement hers. He too opposes the rigidity of the old heroism, hardness of spirit (1361). Like the reasonable and moderate man he is, however, he is free of her tragic suffering. Yet unlike Deianeira, Tecmessa is not forced to a heroic decision parallel to that of the male protagonist. For the tragic dimension of the *Ajax* what is important is not so much the emergence of civilized values per se as the clash between those values and the unbending epic heroism doomed to a glorious end in its unyielding hardness.

Change involves this unbending hero in a series of contradictions with what he has conceived his essential nature to be.[2] Instead of fighting by day, he makes a night attack on the leaders of his own army. Instead of firmness and steadiness of discipline, he exhibits uncontrolled violence and desperation. Instead of generosity, he displays cruelty and egotism. Read psychologically, his leap upon his rigid, upright sword, symbol of his heroic way of life, reflects a phallic narcissism, a self-centered and self-aggrandizing distortion of vision in response to the symbolic castration implied in the loss of Achilles' arms.[3] To possess these arms would be to validate his own self-image as the greatest of Achaean warriors. To lose them is to be robbed of external proof of his heroic greatness, his *aretē*.

Having lost this means of self-validation, the hero who has deemed himself the noblest and worthiest of warriors performs an act that points back to the opposite end of the spectrum of heroic values, the craft and guile of Odysseus as he performed the bloody nocturnal exploit of the Doloneia in the *Iliad*. More important, we witness this solid bulwark of the hoplite battle line in the process of becoming the citiless outcast, the *apolis*.

The deeds of his "greatest excellence," the chorus of his Salaminian followers laments, "fell friendless among the Atreids who are no friends" (618–620). The hero whose great deed in the *Iliad* is the defense and rescue of a companion's body (*Iliad* 17.626–655, 717–753) nearly suffers the traitor's punishment of having his own body exposed by his erstwhile "friends," and he receives burial only through the intervention of his bitterest foe.

Ajax thus fulfills the characteristically Sophoclean pattern: by apparently losing everything that defines "himself," the hero becomes "himself" in a profounder and truer way. Oedipus, becoming identical with the pollution and murderer, becomes a more essential heroic self. So Ajax, by fusion with his bestial opposite in the isolated madness that slaughters beasts as men, draws close to something in himself that is also eternal and therefore divine. Becoming a user of words like Odysseus—and yet, as we shall see, not like Odysseus—he moves to the pole which is the very opposite of his *aretē*; yet he thereby realizes his peculiarly Aiantean form of heroism in its most radical, absolute form.

This process calls into question all the traditional categories of experience and hierarchies of values. The space surrounding the hero's tragic suffering becomes paradigmatic of the ambiguous, ever-shifting reality in which men must live. Just as the lustful and murderous Heracles of the *Trachiniae* is "the best of men," so Ajax, accused of treason, shamed before the whole army, exposed to view in all the helpless violence of his delirium, can be proclaimed at the end as "noble in all respects, inferior to no one while he lived" (1415–17).

II

The civilized community is a buffer between nothing and eternity. As the member of a society that extends far beyond the temporal limits of a single life, civilized man is protected from endless, meaningless change on the one hand and offered permanence without the torment of a desperate longing for infinity and eternity on the other. Yet to be a member of society and enjoy its benefit of mediated time, the individual must also accept some measure of change. The human ties that bind together the polis involve him in the succession and continuity of generations and in the contingencies to which human relationships are liable. It is no accident that Tecmessa describes the *charis*, gratitude or reciprocity, of her bond with Ajax under the metaphor of birth (522). She follows this up at once with a metaphor of flowing as of a river. Near the end of the play Teucer echoes these lines as he laments the flux that governs human relations (1266–67): "Alas, how swiftly does gratitude (*charis*) toward the dead flow away, caught in betrayal (*prodous' halisketai*)." The juxtaposition of nature's movement of flowing with the juridical figure "caught in betrayal" links change in human affairs with change in the natural world. Ajax refuses both aspects of change.[4]

Civilization resists all-effacing time through "memorials," means of remembering (*mnēmeia*). These enable the individual to survive the effects of time through communal memory. When Ajax rejects the contingency of changeful human ties and measures himself against the endless cycles of nature, he not only oversteps human limits in a movement toward godlike permanence, but also runs the risk of falling into the diametrical opposite of divinity, total exposure to the lawless, value-neutral cycles of nature. Without the commemoration of the "always-remembering tomb" (1166–67), he confronts the full force of time, the utter effacement of his existence and identity.

The structure of the *Ajax*, far from being an awkwardly joined "diptych,"[5] effectively expresses this interplay between time as the absolute measure of existence and time as mediated by the human constructs of society. In the first half of the play Ajax weighs human effort and achievement, his own included, against time in the absolute, nothingness or eternity, permanence or flux. He concludes by rejecting both humanity and nature to seek his own kind of fixity and permanence. The second half of the play narrows this perspective. It moves us back to human limits. The lonely outcast is redefined in terms of those very ties which he rejected. Reaccepted into society, he forces upon society a redefinition of its nature and its stance toward time: gratitude, memory, honor. With Ajax' death the issue is no longer the relation between nature and society or between cosmic and human time, but the relation between different views of society and different parts of the social order. The figure of Ajax in the first half of the play creates a continuous tension between what is inside and what is outside society, between man and God and between man and beast. The purview of the second half is almost wholly intrasocietal: definitions of law and justice, forms of authority, punishments, rewards. Yet Ajax' presence, dead though he is, is still forceful enough to retain that tension to the end.

Odysseus is the perfect embodiment of the social view of time: time accommodated to the flux and movements of the mortal condition, to the jarring of circumstances. Like Creon in the *Oedipus Tyrannus*, Odysseus is man bounded by the safe limits of his social framework, adapted and adaptable to changeful time. We see him in the prologue twice deferring to Athena's sense of the *kairos*, the "right time" or "proper moment" (34, 38). He uses the limits of time past and time future, experience and expectation, to frame an attitude of submissiveness totally antithetical to Ajax' defiance: "For in all things, both those before and those to come, I am governed by your hand" (34–35). Ajax, Athena says, after showing him in his madness to Odysseus, was once the most foresighted of men, best at doing what the proper moment demanded, *ta kairia* (119–120). But Ajax' respect for *kairos* belongs to the past, and Athena cites it only as a foil to his present derangement, the sign of the power of the gods (118). When Ajax with time regains sanity (306), it is only to see his tent full of disaster and then to remain silent for the greatest time (311). This "greatest time," far from being something calculable or measurable, like Odysseus' *kairos*, is the endless field of his great sufferings.

In a single day Ajax, like Oedipus, goes from honor to disgrace. "A single day," "a single night:" the words echo throughout the play.[6] They become dramatically operative as plot in Calchas' prophecy that Ajax is saved if he can survive "this one day" (753, 756, 778). Measured by this basic unit of time, Ajax, again like Oedipus, becomes the paradigm of man's subjection to the vicissitudes of a single day, man as *ephēmeros*, "creature of a day."[7] Even as Ajax strives to break out of his ephemerality to a permanence beyond the mortal condition, he enacts its most basic limitation. A man who would rather die than tolerate a single day of disgrace is grandly and heroically *ephēmeros*, defiant of time, but also a victim of time.[8]

Although interpreters generally stress Ajax' isolation, what makes Ajax tragic is not that isolation per se, but the contrast between that isolation and the personal ties which have hitherto defined his being. "Bulwark of the Achaeans," he is no lonely Achilles, but a warrior who fights in and for the whole army.

In his speech to Achilles in *Iliad* 9 Ajax blames the savage spirit (*agrion thymon*) which had led Achilles to set himself apart from his comrades (9.629). He appeals to the friendship of his companions and to the singular honor which the army is willing to bestow on the angry hero (9.630–642). At the end of the Sophoclean play Teucer, in a vivid address to the dead Ajax, rehearses his services to the army as a whole (1269–70). True, he stresses Ajax' exploits in single combat (1283), but even those are part of his devotion to the collective cause. He alone saved the ships of the Achaeans from Hector's onslaught (1274–79) and dared to meet Hector alone in behalf of the whole army (1283–87).

In his first appearance on the field of battle in the *Iliad*, Helen singles him out with the monumental line (*Il.* 3.229):

Οὗτος δ᾽ Αἴας ἐστὶ πελώριος, ἕρκος Ἀχαιῶν.

That is Ajax, gigantic, bulwark of Achaeans.

"Great," *megas*, is his frequent epithet in Homer. Sophocles takes pains that we recognize this serviceable, loyal fighter beneath the despairing, alienated tragic hero. Athena herself, as we have seen, praises his foresight and capacity for timely action (119–120); later the kindly manner of Calchas' advice to Teucer attests to the army's esteem (749–755). In the anapaests of their opening song the chorus defend "the great" against the slanders of "the small," with an unmistakable glance at the Homeric warrior, unmoved and unmovable behind his "tower-like" shield (158–159): "And yet, without the great, small men / Are but the faulty bulwark of a tower." Even Odysseus, in that silent meeting in the Underworld, praised him as a "tower" to the Greeks (*Od.* 11.556). In applying the tower metaphor not to Ajax, but to his enemies, Sophocles indicates the disruptions in Ajax' relation to his society and his heroic values.

This reversal is the source of Ajax' greatest suffering: "You behold me, the bold, the brave-hearted, the man fearless in every hostile encounter, now fearsome (*deinos*) in strength against beasts that cause no fear: alas for the laughter, for the insult" (364–367). And Tecmessa cries out "that this good and serviceable man (*chrēsimos*) should say things such as he would never have been able to utter before" (410–411). Yet even as he considers ending his life, he considers doing something good and serviceable (*chrēston*, 468), attacking Troy and fighting "alone with them alone" (467) as once, in his moment of glory, he fought Hector "alone with him alone" (1283). The hero of honor par excellence (*timē*) will die in dishonor (*atimia*, 426, 440). The hero who has been the bulwark of the Achaeans, protecting them with his great shield, will be without the protective barrier of friends, *apharktos philōn* (910). Man cannot live in so unsheltered a state. To that degree of isolation, death on the open beach corresponds both as emblem and as answer. This protector who is something "cast before" his friends (cf. *probola*, 1212) has to fear being "cast forth" (*problētos*) as a prey to dogs and birds (830). Echoing here the proem to the *Iliad*, Ajax can envisage as his own the grimmest fate that could befall an epic hero.

III

The most subtle and yet most critical of the reversals that Ajax undergoes takes place in the great speech on time (646–692). Although there is nothing like a consensus on this difficult problem, the majority of scholars seem to agree that the speech really is a *Trugrede*, a speech of deception.[9] Ajax has no intention of yielding but must deceive his friends in order to complete his heroic death. At the least he must allow them to deceive themselves by hearing in his words what they want to hear. Yet even his lie, if such it is, speaks truth. He utters not a single word of actual falsehood.[10] To assert his heroic greatness, he must momentarily assume the traditional role of his enemy and opposite (cf. 187–189): he plays Odysseus to be more deeply Ajax.[11] He lies not as an Odysseus would lie: "he cannot use a deception without having it grow majestic in his mouth."[12] In fact he cannot fully deceive the person who understands him best. The joy in the subsequent ode is the chorus' (693ff.).[13] When the Messenger appears and addresses Tecmessa, she is ready for the worst (787, 791).

The mighty opposites of the physical world are both the subject and the analogue of the speech itself. These contraries of our physical world are brought into forcible union in nature just as dissembling and truth are forcibly drawn together in the ambiguity of Ajax' utterance and intention. This ambiguity, in fact, may be more important than any certainty (remote in any case) about Ajax' actual aims here. Ajax' tragic heroism and the isolation and independence that are part of it create an impassable barrier between him and those who surround him. The imperfect communication which results from that barrier fuses and confuses reality and appearance, yielding and firmness, truth and falsehood, openness to nature's rhythms and enclosure in self-imposed boundaries. Ironically, as Reinhardt points out, the full truth of his tragic isolation comes only with the illusion of accommodation and reintegration.[14] Through this ambiguity of language Ajax' straightforward heroism is divided against itself; its simplicity is rendered problematical.

Even if Ajax is pursuing his path to death with unswerving determination, undistracted by concern for his friends, those who love and respect him are caught in falsehood. To this falsehood Ajax, whether willingly or not, contributes by the very isolation and uncommunicativeness of his heroic stance. The failure of communication and the resultant deception mark in fact a double failure of language. First, Ajax speaks without seeming to address anyone; until 684 his speech is essentially a monologue.[15] Second, the others bend Ajax' meaning to the limited understanding of their own untragic view of life.[16] Where Ajax sees finality, they see hope in time's change and forgetting (710–718).

As in the *Tyrannus*, an initial (and illusory) unity splits into tragic dichotomy; unity is restored only through the hero's painful suffering. The dramatic and verbal action confirms on the public space of the stage the private, unseen experience of the dark night of madness before. For the first time the warrior of simple ways experiences the clouding of the clear and rigid norms of heroic behavior.[17] Whether intentionally or not, he, the man of straight speech and straight deeds, profits from the deceptive potential inherent in words.

If Ajax uses his *Trugrede* to deceive, even if he does not utter a word of literal falsehood, his motive can be only to spare those close to him: he misleads them because he pities them.[18] In that case the ambiguous language of this powerful speech does perform a valid act of communication but in a contorted and oblique manner. His love for his *philoi*, like all his social bonds, takes this complicated, indirect form. Only by an ambiguously false (or paradoxically true) *logos*, which hides as much as it shows, can he express his feeling for those closest to him. Even this most basic communication hovers between concealing and revealing.

Deceptiveness of language, so inconsistent with Ajax' martial code, helps him find his way back to heroic simplicity. The warrior's laconic, "The well-born man must live well or die well: you have heard all I have to say" (479–480), is simultaneously undercut and vindicated by the elusive potential of language itself. Or, to put it differently, the hero himself suffers as part of his tragedy the contradiction between his nature and the verbal medium he must use to express that nature, until, about to die, he is able to bring together word and deed in a speech where medium and intention are again one. At that point, really alone, he addresses not men who may mistake the import of his words but the gods and the enduring, mute powers of nature (831–865). Here his heroic deed will finally break through the double-edged power of verbal representation and reach an absolute reality.

IV

To complete the tragic dimension of Ajax' suffering Sophocles shows him rooted not only in the more or less public bonds of martial comradeship, but also in the personal bonds of a house, an *oikos*. If Teucer champions the former, Tecmessa is the center of the latter. With her is bound up whatever capacity he has to reach beyond himself to others in the closest human relationships. Her long and moving plea is closely modelled on the scene between Hector and Andromache in *Iliad* 6. Yet none of the Homeric joy and grief (*Il.* 6.484) illuminates this dark scene, nor do lord and slave woman fully share the tenderness that Homer depicted between husband and wife. Yet the very fact that Ajax can be compared with Hector at all is significant. In this loneliest hour, Ajax can be paired with that hero whose tragedy is, above all, one of involvement in human ties, family responsibilities, civic duty.[19]

Ajax' tragic isolation is defined against the coordinates of human time and human space. The isolated shore where he goes to die brings the two together. It is his point of contact with the timeless absolutes of his heroic world and the point of greatest removal from the shelter of human habitation. In his last speech, immediately before the leap upon the sword, the solidity of the sacred plain (*pedon*) of his native Salamis and the seat (*bathron*) of his ancestral hearth (859–860), however appropriate to his own yearning for permanence, contrast with his exposure to all that is outside the human world. His last words, in fact, call up the human world of time and time-conditioned bonds, a world touched by memories, affection, a feeling for sacredness of place (859–861): "O light, O sacred plain of Salamis, my native earth, O ancestral seat of my hearth, and glorious Athens and the race akin to mine in nurture."[20] Even so, the rivers and springs and earth of Troy are his "nurturers" (*trophēs*, 863), just as Athens is a "race of kindred nurture" in 861 (*syntrophon genos*). This word, "nurture," evokes his own place in the cycle of human life. The chorus had used it three times in their lament for his resolve of suicide, twice in connection with his mother and his family (624, 644), once of his alienation from the temper with which he was nurtured (639–640): "No longer does he converse firmly with the nature he was nurtured with, but has his converse (*homilei*) outside."[21] Ironically, this "converse" describes Ajax' removal from the human ties that it, like "nurture," implies.

Ajax has given his son nurture, and the boy, he hopes, will one day "show among his enemies what sort of nurture he has had and from whom" (557). Yet Ajax' nurture is of a peculiar kind. Shortly before, he had described his son's education as the breaking in of a colt and the experience of his father's "raw ways" (*ōmoi nomoi*, 548–549). As Ajax the educator refuses to be educated (594–595), so his training of his son reflects the "rawness" of his own ambiguous relation to society. This great bulwark will not be there to protect his son with his tower shield, but will need Teucer to "stand guard at the gates of (his son's) nurture" (*pylōron phylaka . . . leipsō trophēs*, 562–563). Yet just those kindred ties of nurture that Ajax has repudiated are to vindicate the honor that he had died to preserve. Tecmessa, cheated of her man and "cast out of long-earned gratitude" (807–808), speaks only half the truth in what is nearly her last speech (970): "Not for the Atreids did he die, no, but for the gods," for at once Teucer enters and addresses Ajax in terms of the deep bond of *philia* between blood kin (977): "Dearest Ajax, kindred in blood to me."

V

The tensions between Ajax the outcast and Ajax the stalwart, "serviceable" warrior, "bulwark of the Achaeans" (1212; cf. 159), receive emblematic representation in the contrast between sword and shield. Ajax' great tower shield is the instrument of his "cooperative" virtues, to use Adkin's term, the token of his security and respect in the warrior society at Troy. "Ajax the shield-bearer," *Aias sakesphoros*, Odysseus calls him early in the play (19), recalling the defensive prowess of the hero of the *Iliad*.[22] In the passage in which Ajax speaks of kin ties, nurture, and personal obligations, he calls his companions "shield men," *andres aspistēres* (565–566) and bequeaths to his son, himself named "Broad Shield" (cf. *epōnymon*, 574), the great "seven-fold unbreakable shield" (575–576). The shield is the only part of the armor which is not to follow him to the grave (577). At the end of the play, when Ajax is received back into society through the rite of burial, the body armor which accompanies the corpse in honor to the tomb is defined in terms of the shield (*hypaspidion kosmon*, 1408, "the fine equipment that his shield protected").[23] The phrase reminds us of his lonely dispensation of the armor but also recalls the one piece of equipment which will remain above ground as his link with the changeful human world and the succession from father to son that binds even Ajax to the rhythms of life and death.

The sword, on the other hand, "the killer," *sphageus*, belongs to the destructive, and self-destructive, side of Ajax. "Dripping from sword-slaughtering

116

hands" and "leaping over the plain with freshly reeking sword": these are our first visual impressions of Ajax (10, 30). Dwelling on the details later, the chorus comes back to the sword (229–232): "This glorious man is sure to die, he who killed the cattle and the horse-riding shepherds along with them, with hand gone amuck, with black sword." It is with the deadly double-edged sword (*amphēkes enchos*) that he goes out in the late night on his lonely quest for revenge (286–287).

As the play continues, the sword becomes increasingly associated with his solitary doom and his determination to defy change and time by setting himself apart, forever, in death. Metaphors of cutting and the blade's whetted edge describe his resolute distance from those who would pull him back into life (see 581–584, 651, 815, 820). Ajax will hide the sword in the "untrodden place" deep in the earth, out of human sight (657–659). Dedicated to "Night and Hades below" (660), the sword belongs to the dark night of his isolating, murderous frenzy. It embodies the destructive side of his *arete*, the curse of his own fate and of his own unyielding character. Whereas the shield wins him his place in the public world of cooperative *arete* and in the bright light of praise and glory, the sword belongs to the dark, private realm of his own demons and the mysterious powers of a fearful supernatural world. The forger of the sword, Teucer cries, was the Erinys; its craftsman was Hades (1034–35).

The firmly fastened, unmoved sword works with the "swift leap" of death (833), with the "swift-footed" Erinyes (837; cf. 843), and the "swiftness" (853) of Ajax himself to challenge movement and change. In making the sword the fixed point around which all else revolves (815), Ajax, like Achilles, asserts his will to permanence, but it is the permanence of death, of Night and Hades (680).[24]

Unlike the shield, the sword will not be bequeathed to his living kin. Both literally and metaphorically the sword separates him from Tecmessa and the more tender emotions toward which she draws him. Her two closely related statements on the discovery of the body are revealing:

> Here lies our Ajax, newly slain, wrapped in the embrace (*periptychēs*) of the hidden sword. (898–899)

> He is not to be looked upon. But I shall cover him all around with this embracing cloak (*periptychei pharei*) since no one who holds him dear could stand to look upon this sight. (915–917)

The deadly "embrace" by the "hidden sword" contrasts with the lovingly spread "embracing cloak" with which Tecmessa would "cover" the grim sight. On the one hand stands the soft, enfolding woman's garment, on the other the rigid male weapon. Tecmessa's concealing is the loving act of *philia* (cf. 917), whereas Ajax' concealing (658, 899) is an act which rejects *philoi*.

The collocation of sword and cloak condenses Ajax' tragic situation into a powerful visual symbol on the stage. It is the kind of sharp juxtaposition of large, essential forms dear to the artists of the Severe Style in early classical art; in fact the painter Brygos illustrated the scene on a celebrated red-figure vase of about 470 B.C.[25] The gesture that binds the two actors together expresses both the closeness and the infinite distance between them.

Tecmessa's enveloping of Ajax by her soft cloak—a very different embrace from Deianeira's tunic of flame around Heracles—anticipates that firmer protection of his body by his fellow warriors. Teucer's strength and Odysseus' diplomacy will carry through what Tecmessa intends with her cloak. The spontaneous emotional gesture of the woman points the way, and the male companions in battle complete the deed. Though lacking the physical force or personal authority that could provide a permanent covering for the corpse, Tecmessa's gentle act is nevertheless vital to the burial of Ajax. It shows the hero even in death as deserving the loyalty of his *philoi*. First by a symbolic, visually prominent gesture, then by verbal battle and the promise of strong action, they gather around him and shelter him from the last ravages of time and decay.

The reciprocity in the exchange of the sword, however, is restricted to the narrow heroic code of male warriors who may kill one another when next they meet. Ajax received the sword, he says, as a gift from his deadly enemy, Hector, "a gift which is no gift" (662, 665). Twice more we hear of this gift, again from Ajax (817–818) and later from Teucer (1026–33). The apparent shift from enmity to friendship in the exchange is deceptive. Hector remains his bitterest foe, as Ajax points out (818), and the transaction proved fatal to Hector too (1029–31). The *charis* of such an exchange is purely negative; it does not reach the life-giving continuity of Tecmessa's *charis* (520–524). This exchange draws on a brief episode in the *Iliad* (7.299–305). It has behind it also the more elaborate exchange of armor between Glaucus and Diomedes in *Iliad* 6, a brilliant moment of chivalric glory, indeed one of the few moments in the *Iliad* when a notion of chivalry is really appropriate. But even in Homer this exchange on the battlefield stands in sharp contrast to the deeper human tragedy enacted immediately afterward within the walls of Troy, the interview between Hector and Andromache (cf. *Iliad* 6.369–375 and 7.307–310). Possessing Hector's sword, Ajax gains only that warrior's destructive, death-bent devotion to the code of honor, not the tenderness of Hector's meeting with Andromache, so similar to and yet so different from Ajax' with Tecmessa.

VI

Space as well as time measures Ajax' distance from other men. Ajax' heroism evokes images of the city, the tower, the bulwark. A whole series of images of violent, destructive phenomena, however, describes his madness: storms, fire, darkness. Yet in his tragic assertion of honor and freedom from change, Ajax also sets himself outside nature. He rejects its cycles for the inflexible permanence of his own determination. Words for "circling" describe what is outside himself: hostile men or hostile nature.[26] As Odysseus, Tecmessa, and the chorus all "circle" and "wander" to discover what Ajax has done or where he is, the hero himself, like Heracles at the end of the *Trachiniae*, travels a straight path or road (*hodos, exodos*) to his goal: "I shall go there where I must go" (690).[27] Nature moves in ever-changing cycles about the great hero, but through the defiance of his firmly fixed sword Ajax would become more than man, perfected in the clarity and dark logic of his heroic will. That same sword, however, has also made him something less than man: "Look at me," he shouted early in the play, "the man fearless in hostile encounter, terrible in my hands against—beasts that inspire no fear" (365–366).

When Ajax describes the alternation of the seasons (646ff., 670ff.), he makes no reference to the changing appearance of the earth as Pindar, for example, does in similar contexts.[28] The earth is only a hostile place (819) in which he can conceal or fasten his sword (658, 820, 906–907). When he does invoke earth in a kindlier relation (859), it is only to bid it farewell for the journey "beneath the earth" (832, 865).

The tension between the otherness of nature and Ajax' striving for heroic autonomy reaches its highest point in the great speech on time. The splendid poetry which describes the rhythms of the natural world conveys Ajax' own largeness of vision as he moves beyond the dark, enclosed tent to the whole phenomenal world. His language like Achilles' in the *Iliad*, rings with the authority of this tragic knowledge.[29] His death is no blind defiance but the result of bitter understanding. Yet his movement from the narrow self-enclosure of the tent to the extreme limits of the human world only removes him further from that world. His understanding of its processes and his vivid awareness of its beauty—an aspect of his two last long speeches that adds considerably to the pathos—are the foil to his new understanding of himself, which in turn brings a more resolute understanding of his removal from this world.[30] His distinctive quality is that of the *perissos*, "outsized," "gigantic," "extraordinary,"[31] a man for whom the mediations of civilization appear as the compromised middle of small and cowardly spirits or as the Odyssean "good sense" which maintains safe limits (cf. 677).

Ajax' speech on time rejects the three fundamental terms of human existence: the order of the gods, the order of society, and the order of nature. As in the other plays, each implies the others and each functions metaphorically for the others. Ajax, for example, uses the verb *sebein*, "to revere," for his supposed acceptance of the social order ("We shall learn how to yield to the gods and *revere* the Atreids," 666–667). But the collocation of the political with the divine order deliberately confounds them both: Ajax will have neither.[32]

For these reasons too the prophet Calchas' report of Ajax' *hybris* against the gods, whatever its validity as a motive force in the action, contains a paradigmatic truth. Ajax' very nature flouts the limits set by the human condition, limits that the gods both symbolize and enforce. Like Teiresias in both *Antigone* and *Oedipus Tyrannus*, Calchas is an important reminder of these limits. By the process of "double determination" frequent in Greek poetry, his prophecy, that Ajax must remain in his tent this one day or die, only confirms the inevitability of Ajax' doom.[33] There is nothing cruel in the oracle; in the divine perspective its helpful intent is not ironical. Like Athena in the prologue it merely speaks truth: it asserts the limits of the human condition and expresses the larger terms of Ajax' rejection of those limits. Unlike the characters in the other oracle plays of Sophocles, however, Ajax himself never hears the prophecy. He acts entirely from within himself, but at the same time fulfills a larger pattern, deny it though he will, of which that self is a part.

Ajax' tragedy follows a model that runs throughout Greek literature from Homer's Achilles to Theocritus' Daphnis. His heroic aspirations are in contradiction with life itself. His striving toward the fulfillment of his autonomous will constitutes a rejection not only of mortality but of existence. "Ajax may be the purest form of tragic hero in that his very instincts elect death."[34] The impulse toward self-realization is both glorious ennoblement and a union with dark, self-destructive forces.

In the shifting balance between these two extremes lies the complexity of Sophoclean tragedy. Does the spectator take his stand on the side of life or on the side of heroic autonomy? The difficulty of choosing is responsible for a good part of the divergence in the interpretation of the plays. Like Antigone, Electra, and Philoctetes, Ajax would rather die than submit to the infringement of his heroic will. For a being defined by time, death is the ultimate and, in the tragic perspective, the only act of freedom. The irreducible uniqueness of the tragic hero's individuality is itself a disruption of the leveling, regularizing order of nature; the hero pays the penalty for this disruption, much as the cosmic forces, in Anaximander's famous fragment, "pay the penalty and recompense to one another" for their disruption of the equilibrium in the universe (12 B1 DK). In Sophocles, however, the "justice and compensation" are enacted inwardly. The "necessity" or "necessary fortune" (*anagkaia tychē*) of this and other plays is not so much the all-ruling Fate of a deterministic system as it is the inward necessity of the hero's character.

The natural processes in Ajax' speech on time come to reflect only the destructive half of the cycle. Amid nature's rhythms of concealment and emergence, night and day (646–647, 670–673), Ajax' "concealment" will be permanent (see 658 and 647). The dark night of his madness will see no bright day. Hades' eternal darkness follows his "light" of life (856–865). What Ajax "sows," cries Teucer over the corpse, is the grief which he has left behind by "perishing" (1005). Tecmessa, the mother of his son, can use a metaphor of birth to urge compliance with life's demands (522). But Ajax' metaphors, when he talks of yielding, implicitly contrast steel's hardness with womanhood, the rigid male sword with Tecmessa's feminine softness (650–652).

Like tragic heroes from Prometheus to Philoctetes, Ajax marshalls the whole of the natural world as the frame for his suffering.[35] He sweeps the horizon from East to West and in his final farewell takes in sky and earth, plains and rivers (845–847, 856–865). The search for his body involves sky and earth and the opposite quadrants of the heavens, "the hollows toward the West . . . and those which face the sun," and the terms are repeated later (805–806, 874, 877–878).

Ajax' own movements, however, are the opposite of those of the processes which he cites. Like Philoctetes addressing the rocky landscape of Lemnos, Ajax sees in nature only the reflection of his own isolation and heroic defiance.[36] The sea, snow, and light of day in which the chorus, echoing Ajax' words, finds an exultant beauty (695–696, 708–714) are for Ajax marks of a bondage to change and flux (670–673). The "circle of night" is grim (*aianēs*, 672),[37] and even the light of day which succeeds it blazes violently, as with fire (*phlegein*, 673). His sea is tossed by storm and wind and "groans" as in pain (674–675). The storms, like men, will find release in sleep (*ekoimise*, 674; *hypnos*, 675), but we may wonder if Ajax is thinking already of that eternal sleep which is free of all change (cf. *koimisai*, 832). His friends, left behind in this world of flux, search for his body with the "sleepless hunt" of fishermen by the sea (879–880).

Time and change are nature's means of moving between extremes, but Ajax permits no mediation of opposites.[38] When he says "the terrible and mighty things yield to prerogatives" (669–670), it is against the background of his own mighty enduring of terrible things shortly before, as he spoke of tempering steel (650–653).[39] He is himself almost one of those "terrible" (*deinos*) phenomena of nature, flawed and violent like them (we may recall his affinities with violent storms, 206, 257ff.); yet his "prerogatives" (*timai*), unlike theirs, can admit no yielding.

Ajax confronts from the beginning what Electra finds only at the end of her tragedy, the empty face of endless, meaningless time: "What joy is there in day following day, now pushing us forward toward dying, now drawing us back?" (475–476, Jebb's translation, modified). One may compare Electra's "Since mortal lives are mingled with woes, what profit of time would he gain who is about to die" (*El.* 1485–86). Athena ends the prologue of the *Ajax* with the pronouncement: "Day inclines and brings up again all things human" (131–132). She deduces from this process of cyclical time the need for men to practice moderation and good sense, *sōphronein* (132). Ajax draws a different conclusion. Time, says Athena, restores ("leads back") as well as destroys (131).[40] Great time withers all things, the chorus conclude in their ode of joy, and nothing must be declared impossible since Ajax has changed in an unexpected, unhoped for way (714ff.; *ex aelptōn*, 716). For Ajax, too, nothing was unexpected, unhoped for (*aelpton ouden*, 648) in the changeful field of time. But hopeful change in the chorus' illusion signifies fixity in Ajax' tragic reality, where things are timeless and changeless.

VII

Sea and shore dominate Ajax' landscape. Like the rest of the phenomenal world, they appear both as a harshly indifferent, value-neutral background and as a setting defined by human feelings and human forms. The sea can serve as a vast mirror for the violence within Ajax or as the means of excape to a more secure, intimate past.

To the chorus the sea is a place of human associations (134–135) or a means of escape from a hopeless situation (see 246ff.). But Ajax' first despairing address to the natural world stresses the bleak line of the deserted shore, the paths of the sea in their inhuman roaring, the caves and groves (412–415). The only gentle feature in the landscape, the Scamander's streams, are kindly to the Greeks, now his enemies (417–420). His last address to nature, however, will take in not only sun, earth, and his native Salamis but even the rivers, springs, and plain of Troy (856–863). Every part of his world holds the warmth of life, now renounced with full consciousness of the loss.

The opening lines of the play set us at the border between the sea and the inhabited, formed space of men, "at the tents of Ajax by the ships, where he holds the last place." This last place, *taxis eschatē* (4), marks the ambiguity of Ajax' position between human and natural worlds, defined and undefined space, and also connects his exposed spatial position with the problem of authority, since *taxis* refers to one's station in the line of battle (cf. *tachthen*, 528). The very location of Ajax' ships implies his ambiguous relation to the power structure of the Greek armada. When Teucer defends him at the end, that "stationing at the limits" signifies just the opposite of his marginality, for it was here that Ajax warded off Hector's attack (1276ff.). As "bulwark of the Achaeans" in his martial prowess, he can be counted on to secure this exposed "last post."

Ajax' place by the sea is defined initially in terms of the arrangement of tents and ships by the sea (*skēnai nautikai*, 3; *ephaloi klisiai*, 190). But whereas the chorus, though doubtful, hopes that he will not lose honor by staying in those tents by the sea (190–191), he will vindicate that honor at the "untrodden place," at the "meadows by the shore" (654–659). For him, as for his heroic prototype, Achilles in the *Iliad*, the vast, unlimited sea is the appropriate setting for communion with the permanence that the human world cannot give. In these bleak meadows by the shore, an extension of the open, undefined sea, Ajax will escape the "horse-maddened meadow" of his deed of shame (143–144) or the "glens of lovely breezes" where the army will mock him (197).

As these last two passages indicate, the chorus views the natural world in a very different way from Ajax, for though these descriptions reflect a hostile land world, they occur as part of the chorus' sympathetic attempts to rouse Ajax from his suicidal stupor in the dark enclosure of his tent. The marine settings of the odes that surround Ajax' speech on time, with its isolated seascape of projected suicide, reach back to a human world of kin ties and festal celebration (597, 695, 701–706). The meadows and snowy mountains which they cite abound in shared human experiences, be they the companionship of suffering in war (600–605; cf. 1185–91) or the choral dance (695–700).[41] Just as the happier sea world of these odes contrasts with the turbulent sea of Ajax' madness (see 206–207, 257ff., 351–353), so the comparison of the grief of Ajax' mother to the nightingale's lament (627–632) implies a natural world resonant with human grief, in contrast to the violent bird of prey, eagle or vulture in the chorus' description of Ajax in 167–171 (cf. 139–140). For a moment, in his first words of fully articulate communication, Ajax addresses his sailors in terms of their helpful mastery of the sea (349–360), only to end with the harsh plea, "Slaughter me" (361).

"You who hold the firm seat of ocean-washed Salamis by the sea": these first words addressed to Ajax by a fellow mortal (134–135) give him a secure place in the human world. When Ajax echoes them in his farewell to this earth (859–860) in the shore meadows of that untrodden place, the plain or "firm seat" (*bathron*, 860; cf. 139) cannot give him the permanence which he seeks. Shortly before, Ajax addresses other aspects of nature (845–848): "You, Sun, who drive your chariot across the steep heavens, when you see my native earth, pull in your reins of gold and tell my father and poor mother of my infatuation and my doom." The beloved earth of his ancestral land contrasts with the Homeric remoteness of the "steep heavens." In his final line of the play (865), the solid plain and firm seat of homeland and house momentarily fill his mind before their negation in the Underworld.

Ajax' last farewell is for what has nourished him, the earth he has walked on, the water he has drunk. In his early lyrics he saw himself as cut off both from the Greek army and the Trojan plains (457–459; cf. 413–420, 460ff.); now, the Trojan setting, once kindly to the Greeks (418–420) but not to him, is among his nurturers (*trophēs emoi*, 863), included in the same fostering relation as the people of his homeland (*syntrophon genos*, "race that shared my nurture," 861). The Trojan earth in which he fastens his sword is as hostile to him as ever (cf. 819, 1208–1209), but his present perspective outside the boundaries of spatial differences dwarfs the distinction between Troy and Salamis.

For one moment, addressing his son, Ajax seems to conceive of a gentler natural order (558–559): "Till then [that is, while still a child] be raised and grow in soft and gentle breezes, taking pleasure in your young life, to your mother here a joy."[42] But this happy childhood, with its "gentle breezes," is but a short interlude before the "blasts of terrible breezes" in Ajax' next speech (674). These terrible (*deina*) breezes are akin to that quality of "the terrible" in the world which it has been Ajax' heroic fate to endure ("I who braved the terrible," 650). The peaceful childhood of his son can be a temporary shelter from the elemental violence of this universe, but for Ajax himself the "harbor of companionship" which seems to protect "the many" from the meaningless flux of reality is "untrustworthy" (682–683).

The chorus, seeking to reclaim the hero who has gone alone to the "untrodden place" by the sea, themselves "tread" all the western shore (cf. *astibē chōron*, 657; *estibētai*, 874). Their search comprehends a happy sea world, toilsome but full of joy (879–887), in contrast to the fruitless toil of this doomed effort (*ponos*, 866; cf. *philoponos*, 879). The fishermen practice their "sleepless hunt" in their toil to sustain life (879–880), whereas Ajax, in his rejection of life and its compromises, also rejects that succession of night and sleep which forms its rhythms (cf. 675). In like manner this normal, productive hunting to sustain life contrasts with the murderous hunting of Ajax (64, 93), as a consequence of which he himself becomes the hunted quarry (5, 20, 32, 59f., 997, and others).[43] In their last ode the chorus then turns away from their loss of Ajax with a wishful image of a place sheltered from the sea: the sacred, glorious civilized places of Sounion and Athens (1219–22).

Ajax' anomalous relation to the world around him stems from his rejection of the fundamental condition of his mortal nature, his status as *ephēmeros*, "creature of a day." His invocation to the Sun and its chariot as he stands on the verge of death (845–847, 856–859) confirms his refusal to yield to the rhythms of life as night yields to "white-horsed day" (672–673). Turning away from the parent who is "nurtured with the day of age" (622), he has plunged through the night-like darkness of his madness (85, 216–217, 301) to the remote and brilliant sun that he addresses in his last speech, when his path is to death and Hades (854, 865).[44]

Such light as appears in the midst of this unnatural darkness is strange and violent. Ajax' madness in the night is a cosmic fire, a blaze of disaster reaching to the sky (*atan ouranian phlegōn*, 195), and he himself is a "man ablaze" (*aithōn*, 221, 1088).[45] His wild enterprise is itself a kind of fire which, according to Menelaus, the god has "quenched" (1057). His madness is a storm from whose clouds flashes of bright lightning break forth (257–258). His frenzy fell upon him, Tecmessa says, "at the steep edge of night, when the evening lights (in the sky) no longer blazed" (285–286). As sanity returns, his strange cries join light and darkness not in the rhythmic succession of the heavens' regularity but in violent oxymora. Flashes of luminescence rip through the blackness of his doom like the jagged light tearing an El Greco sky: "O darkness my light, dimness most brilliant, take me to dwell with you, take me. For I am no longer worthy to look for help either to the race of the gods or to any one of mortals, creatures of a day." (393–400). The last phrase foreshadows Ajax' isolation from his fellow men, "creatures of a day," *hamerioi anthrōpoi*, who passively accept the rhythms of mortal life.[46]

For all its horror and violence, Ajax' dark night of madness and brilliant darkness (393–395) expresses something of his contact with the divine forces that play about him as one both above and below the human condition.[47] Odysseus, encountering the invisible Athena in the prologue, is uneasy about not "seeing" (14–17, 21, 23) and falls back upon the visual "clarity" of a witness, the scout who saw and "made clearly known" Ajax' deed (29–31).[48] Odysseus' *sōphrosynē* allows no running together of light and dark, even though he can take in a vision both of the gods' strength and men's "shadow" lives (125–126).

Oxymoron is the rhetorical figure appropriate for a hero in whom opposites coalesce (393–395). The hero who grandly called for light out of darkness in Homer, even at the cost of his death (*Iliad* 17.645–647), becomes both the perpetrator and the victim of nocturnal wiles, *ennychioi mēchanai* (180–181). "Alone, at night, in stealth": these three words in Athena's description of Ajax' attack (47) set forth the total negation of heroism as Ajax has understood it in the past.

Ajax the hero is *periphantos* (229), a man who stands out visible beyond all others. But the chorus gives him this epithet in an ode which sings of the atrocity committed by his "black sword" and of his certain disgrace and death. His value system, like that of all Greek heroes, is predicated on being regarded with honor and on regarding others with pride in his face.[49] But now he wonders, "What *eye* shall I *show* to my father Telamon when I *appear* before him? How will he bear to *look upon* me when I *appear* without the prize of glory?" (462–464). It is important for him to *see* his son there clearly before him (538) and important that the boy show no fear when he looks upon the carnage of the night before (545–547). But after that deed Ajax has kept his "eye" hidden in the dark tent (190–191). The chorus hopes that he may feel shame, *aidōs*, a strong term in the heroic value system, when he looks on them (345). Tecmessa then reveals him to their eyes with the words, "See, I open [the tent]. You can look at his deeds and his own plight" (346–347). "Look at what a wave of disaster whirls around me" is Ajax' reply (350–352).

In such a total inversion of his world, the return of day, light, and vision can only mean his death. In this sense, too, his darkness is light (393–395), for it protects him, temporarily, from the vision that will destroy him as a hero. Hence his concern with the sun and its brilliance when he determines the only course he can imagine for recovering his right to be looked on as a hero (673, 847, 857). When he "hides" his sword in a place where no one will see (658–659) and by his resolute and grim death has made himself "a sight [literally, eye] hard to look upon for others (*omma dystheaton*, 1004), he has regained his stature as *periphantos* in the eyes of men.[50] His concealment of his sword for Night and Hades to keep below 658–660), like his coupling of Helios and Hades in his final speech (854–865), returns him to the only light which matters to him: not the natural succession of light and dark (647, 672–673), but the inward light of heroism, the foil to that dark light and luminous darkness of his spiritual annihilation in madness. That an act of hiding should make him conspicuous in valor (*periphantos*), however, is another instance of his paradoxical interpretation of the heroic code.

Commenting on his suicide, the chorus combines his fusion of light and darkness with a criticism of his unyielding "hardness" and "rawness" of spirit (925–932):

Piteous man, hard of mind (*stereophrōn*), in time were you bound to accomplish an evil destiny of limitless sufferings. Raw of mind (*ōmophrōn*), such sayings of hate against the Atreids with destructive suffering did you cry out all night and in the blaze of day (*pannycha kai phaethonta*).

Yet at the end, as the human world which he rejected musters around him to defend his body and his name, his relation to darkness and light moves back within the frame of human civilization. Though far from the "night joy" of festive companionship (cf. 1203), Ajax is no "blazing doer of insult" as Menelaus charges (1088), but a "bulwark against the fear of the night" (1211–12), a hero who protected his companions against the destructive fire of Hector's onslaught (1278).

VIII

Ajax' tent, the locus of his human relations, stands, as we have seen, at the edge of the space that sets off the Greek encampment from the hostile sea and plain of the Troad (3–4). That tent is also the locus of his madness and "savagery." Through that madness, the inner space, befouled by the blood and gore of beasts, becomes the place of carnage where no civilized man could dwell. The protected interior doubles with the dark inner world of nocturnal delusion and hatred.

The prologue stresses the gruesome things inside that tent. Odysseus feels horror at the thought of calling Ajax outside (7, 9, 11, 73–74, 76, 80, 88). Our first vision of Ajax as he emerges from the tent, holding a dripping sword and stained with blood himself, is an impressive indication of what lies within. "Hand-slaughtered, blood-dripping killings, the 'sacrifices' performed by this man: such are the things you would see within the tent," laments Tecmessa (218–221). Later she adds more grim details about what is inside (*eisō*, 235, 296). As the fit of madness recedes, Ajax dashed out through the doors (301), and then after muttering some unintelligible words, rushed back inside the dwelling once more (305). As he becomes lucid, he beholds his dwelling full of madness and disaster (307). The tent, full of disaster (*atē*), is no longer a human dwelling place, but a nightmarish slaughterhouse of beasts confused with men. The symbol as well as the scene of Ajax' madness, it is the fitting shelter of that bestial, monstrous self that he has momentarily become, the place of his utter despair, the negation of everything that he has valued.

To leave his tent is also to leave the enclosed space of his inner turbulence, his *atē*, to return from delusion to reality. Once outside, he ceases to battle false enemies; he abandons the dark night of insanity to confront the real alternation of light and darkness in the natural order. From the destructive forces within, Ajax moves to the destructive forces of time and change without.

Athena, hostile as she is, assists that movement from inside to outside. Like the Athena who checks Achilles in the first book of the *Iliad*, she is a principle of reality. Calling him outside the tent, she initiates, both literally and symbolically, the process of restoring him to the conditions of mortal life. Although Ajax finally rejects this upper world of the Olympian-governed order for the darkness of Hades, that darkness is no longer the delusion of madness but the ultimate, if grim, reality of death. When the mad Ajax leaves his tent to execute his demented revenge, his act is a false exit, a "senseless" or "empty" going forth (*exodoi kenai*), not a true escape from what the tent contains. In his last journey, however, Ajax clearly distinguishes between light and dark, life and death.

The announcement of the prophecy that Ajax must be kept inside his tent and not permitted to go outside (741–742) introduces the final stage of his isolation. He is now an outsider, exiled from both the human and the divine order. The fact that he is not within (735) seals his doom (793–794). Not only could Ajax in such a state not be kept within his tent, but there is no possibility of his remaining there: the interior of that tent is a shambles of revolting carnage, the wreckage of the awful night before. He is as incapable of remaining in that tent, reeking with the gore of his terrible deed, as he is of yielding, revering the Atreids, or practicing "good sense."

The oracle, then, like other oracles in Sophocles, is not only a prediction, but also a clear vision of the realities of character and situation that comprise the necessity of the action. The news that Ajax has made a destructive outside journey (*exodos olethria*, 798–799) wrings from Tecmessa, as it earlier wrung from the chorus, a cry of tragic foreboding (798–800; cf. 735–739), and she repeats the phrase a few lines later: the man's evil road outside (*exodos kakē*, 806). From Tecmessa's point of view, the journey outside is evil, *kakē* (806), but it enables Ajax to leave behind the charge of *kakia*, baseness (see 486, 551) and reach its opposite, the nobility (*kalos*) that is his only standard (479–480).

The sheltering tent ironically becomes the lonely place of a beastlike savage. It contains an inversion of beast and man, ritual impurity, incoherent speech. Here Ajax "shares his dwelling with divine madness" (*theia(i) mania(i) xynaulos*, 611), reduced to the status of a beast which is driven or hunted (see infra). Here too he is a "lone shepherd of his thoughts" (*phrenos oiobōtas*, 614–615), and his deeds are "friendless among those who are no friends" (619–620). In a verbal echo of his "dwelling with madness" (611), the death-cry which culminates his unmediated position between divinity and savagery has a kind of shelter (892): "What cry that has its dwelling near at hand (*paraulos*) came forth from the grove?"[51] Insofar as this man, deprived of the protection of friends (910), has any shelter it is in the wild grove, not the enclosure of a tent (cf. 796).

Once the action leaves the setting by the tents, it never returns there. Friends and foe alike leave the camp for the desolate place of Ajax' suicide.[52] But, in another inversion of civilized and savage space, that body on the barren shore, threatened with exposure to wild beasts (830, 1065), becomes a new locus of social action, a crucial point for the definition of civilization. Here, as more strikingly in the *Oedipus at Colonus*, the desolate spot constitutes a virtually sacred space where our sense of civilized values is both questioned and intensified. The body becomes a focal point for a rite of supplication (1173), a juridical debate, and in the gathering of child, mother, and brother about the body a renewal of family ties (1168–81).

Just as Ajax' tent, filled with the results of that madness, places the hero in an ambiguous relation to a human dwelling, so the madness itself sets him beyond the pale of normal society and makes him an object of horror and fear (82–83). The madness that confuses beast and man comes from the gods but has a special affinity with the gods of the wild, here Artemis Tauropolos (172–179), but elsewhere Pan, Dictynna, and the Mountain Mother.[53]

For us madness arises from the complexities of civilization; for the Greeks it is the negation of civilization. Thus when Ajax gives vent to his murderous desires in the dark night of his passion, he sweeps away the barrier that separates man from beast.[54] Ritually impure, akin to the wild where he often wanders, outside the bonds of kin and city, the madman lacks the protection from the violence of nature that civilization affords.[55] The mad Ajax, like the mad Heracles, Io, or Orestes, tosses in a "storm" (206–207, 257, 274) and lacks the "shelter" of the camp or of friends (910).[56]

Ajax' madness also has a special relation to his status as a warrior. As Dumézil has demonstrated, the prowess of the great warrior often takes the form of a beastlike *furor*, an access of furious energy, like that of the "berserker," which actually identifies him with the beasts.[57] Dumézil quotes from a Swedish saga, "As to his men, they went without cuirass, wild like dogs and wolves. They bit their bucklers and were as strong as bears and bulls. They massacred men and neither iron nor steel could prevail against them. This was called 'beserkr furor.' "[58] He comments, "The connection that Odinn's *berserkir* had with wolves, bears, etc., was not only a resemblance in matters of force and ferocity; in a certain sense they were these animals themselves. Their furor exteriorized a second being which lived within them." In Ajax' tragic situation, however, this excess of furor is directed not against the common enemy but against his own army. The madness of tragedy does not affirm the warrior's strength, like the raging of Achilles' wolflike Myrmidons (*Il.* 16.156ff.), but rather overwhelms the warrior's dignity with helplessness, shame, the loss of *timē* or honor.[59]

At the same time the madness that makes the hero the opposite of himself has its roots within Ajax. Athena only adds a secondary degree of madness. In turning his wrath against the animals, she helps Ajax in one way while degrading him in another.[60] His madness is debasing and magnificent at the same time; it is a pathetic "disease" which leaves him weak and helpless but also a desperate vindication of injustice and outraged honor. The chorus tries to distinguish Ajax' heroism from his madness (cf. 612–613): that is the common-sense, untragic view. For Ajax himself the two are dangerously akin.[61] His paradox of the darkness that is his light (393–395) has both pathos and grandeur and expresses an agony of spirit that places him both below and above normal reality.[62] Deep springs of his nature, connected with that warrior's fury discussed by Dumézil, have an affinity with the madness and take pleasure in it (see 271–272). When he is fully sane, he regrets not the attack itself but its failure (447–448). Even in his normal state, Calchas warns, he was one of those excessive, huge figures (*perissa sōmata*) that fall afoul of the gods (758–759). Calchas judges Ajax, who boasted that he did not need the gods' help, to be "senseless," *anous* (763).[63]

The double significance of Ajax' madness, both heroic and degrading, noble and ridiculous, parallels the double significance of Athena. On the one hand her appearance brings an intensification of Ajax' heroic aspirations, fixing him as well as his opponent, as Whitman suggests, in timeless perspective.[64] Only Ajax can see her (15); indeed he even ventures to give her orders (116). But on the other hand Athena embodies the impersonal limits of the cosmic order that not even an Ajax can defy with impunity.

Ajax can regard Athena as the spiteful goddess who "does him destructive outrage" (*aikizei olethrion*, 402; cf. 450–453).[65] But his own violence outrages others (*aikizein*, 65, 300), despite Athena's attempt at restraint (111). If she reflects, in some measure, the quasi-divinity of his heroic self, she also reflects the destructive power of its search for absolutes, the demonic energy which, when allowed an unchecked course, drains a human life.

As in the *Philoctetes*, the natural and supernatural sources of the affliction come together: the hero's greatness of spirit becomes one with the helplessness of his emotional vehemence. The madness is both proximity to the divine and a disease.[66] The hero is godlike and childlike at the same time. He aspires toward godlike autonomy in a magnificent rejection of the conditioned being of mortal life but smoulders with a bitterness that makes him "hard," "raw," unfeeling.

When Athena withdraws and Ajax' madness ebbs, he is left to face the turbulent emotions of his own nature and the gap between his aspirations and reality. The madness is both the natural psychological reaction to the discrepancy between his sense of honor and the injustices of his society, and the symbol of that discrepancy.[67] As a form of removal from all civilized life, the madness protected him from the full truth of this discrepancy, as it protected the chiefs from his murderous hatred.[68] When the madness falls away there is, at first, nothing to close the gap between his heroic vision of himself and the corrupted, belittling judgment of his peers: he can only look upon his own sufferings (260) until he draws from his despair a new and boldly paradoxical relation to the reality that he has defied, the oxymoron, "darkness my light, dimness most brilliant."

Aspiring, as Calchas says, to "thought beyond man's estate," *mē kat' anthrōpon phronē(i)* (761, 777), Ajax becomes less than human in his loss of sane thought (*phronein*, 82; *sōphronein*, 132; cf. 677). Plato, we may recall, represented Ajax in Hades as "choosing the life of a lion, for he shunned being human (*anthrōpos*), recollecting the judgment of the arms" (*Rep.* 10.620b).

In his madness Ajax not only confuses beasts with men but also enters the beast world. In his night of delirium he traverses the "horse-mad meadow," or "meadow where the horses run mad" (*hippomanēs leimōn*, 143). The ambiguity of his human status has deep roots in the "rawness" of his character (*ōmos*: see 205, 548, 885, 930).[69] "Rawness," as we have seen, denotes the subhuman violence appropriate to beasts of prey. The "raw laws," *ōmoi nomoi*, in which Ajax would educate his son (548), are a contradiction in terms. Immediately after, Ajax uses another animal metaphor when he speaks of this education as *pōlodamnein*, "breaking in a colt" (549). In terms of Ajax' character, his "rawness" consists in his lack of flexibility, another fundamental attribute of a civilized man (cf. *Antigone* 1023–30). Others may change, but not Ajax (note the two *meta-* compounds in 717 and 750).

IX

"In no other tragedy by Sophocles," Jan Kott remarks, "are the opposites of human and inhuman so sharply contrasted."[70] Yet the opposites of this play do not merely contrast; they also fuse together. Here the metaphors of hunting and herding play a special role. Ajax is a hunter who is simultaneously a hunted beast, a herdsman who is also the herded animal.[71] The first twenty lines of dialogue contain no less than seven metaphors of hunting or tracking.[72] This scene, which centers on defining the limits of the human condition (cf. 118ff.), establishes three basic points: the goddess at the upper limit, the moderate and sensible mortal in between, and the maddened hero, bestialized in his overreaching, at the lower extreme. When Odysseus, the first mortal to speak, compares Athena's voice to a "brazen-mouthed trumpet" (17), he further increases the distance between the bestialized Ajax and the brilliant heroic world of men.[73]

In his madness Ajax is a herdsman who "roars like a bull" (322), "yoked" and "driven" like the beasts he herds (53–54, 60, 123, 275, 756, 771).[74] He has also killed other herdsmen (27, 53–54, 231–232) and used upon men (as he thinks) a strap intended to control beasts (241). In his isolation he "pastures his thought alone, a great grief to his friends" (614–616).[75] The fact that the expression *phrenos oiobōtas* in 614 can refer either to a herdsman or to the herded animal reflects the hero's ambiguous place between human and bestial. The grimmest inversion of Ajax' herding comes at the end of the play in the *syrinx* of his gaping wound which "blows forth" the black blood (1412–14; cf. 918–919). The syrinx or flute is the regular instrument of the shepherd, but here its tune is death.[76]

Ajax' madness also destructively conflates the more primitive and the more civilized use of animals, hunting and herding. His "hunted prey" is horned or well-fleeced (*eukerōn agran*, 64; *eueron agran*, 297), epithets regularly used of tame cattle, beasts which should not be hunted. When he comes to his senses Ajax himself feels the ridicule of having turned his mighty hands against beasts that give no fear, *aphoboi thēres* (366). Artemis Tauropola, the chorus conjectures, has "driven him against cattle of the herds" (174–175), and because he has gained spoils from this foolish hunt (407) he would offer a golden trophy to Athena (93). The latter image contains a grotesque collocation of the bestial and the divine, the beauty of gold and the bloody hunt. When Athena describes how she "drove him into evil enclosures," *herkē kaka* (60), Ajax appears simultaneously as the hunted beast driven to the nets (*herkos*) and the herded animal penned in the stalls (cf. his *herkeios stegē* of penning the "cattle" in 108).

As a man made beast, Ajax appears as a helpless victim of the divine wrath. Yet there is grandeur as well as pathos in this alienation from his own humanity. Just before describing him as a victim of Artemis Tauropola, the chorus suddenly break out of their threnodic mood and rise in indignation to an Homeric image of Ajax, a great eagle before whom "the flocks of birds would cower in silence, voiceless" (167–172).[77] We should note the contrast with the chorus' comparison of themselves to trembling doves thirty lines before (139–140).

The metaphor of the yoke likewise expresses not only the helplessness of Ajax in his beastlike madness (275) but also the concern which his plight causes others (24 and 944). Though driven or yoked as a helpless victim, when he returns to sanity he walks in decisive, determined stride to the place "where he must go" (654–655, 690).[78] He himself imposes a "yoke of new counsels upon new ways" (736): the metaphor now refers to distinctively human qualities (see also 24, 944).

The most revealing reversal of this beast imagery comes in Teucer's instructions to bring Eurysaces from the tent just after he finds Ajax' body (985–987): "Won't you at once bring him here, lest some enemy carry him off like the cub of a lioness robbed of her young." In the terms of the simile it is now a man who protects the beast, the protector who is in need of protection, and the lone male warrior who is the helpless mother of an exposed young one. As Ajax begins to be restored to human society, even the wild is viewed with tenderness and compassion.[79] Near the end of the play, too, when it is a man and not a god who defines Ajax as a huge ox controlled by the small whip (1253–54), we feel keenly the injustice of this inversion and side with Teucer in his fierce opposition. Now that Ajax has regained his heroic stature, the beast simile is no longer apposite.

X

As Ajax' madness violates the normal relation between man and beast, his relation to society takes on the form of an anomalous technology. In the prologue Odysseus, as the user of tools, stands squarely in the center of civilization, over against Ajax' figurative bestiality. While Ajax rages, Odysseus has been "of old hunting and measuring," *palai kynēgetounta kai metroumenon* (5). The two verbs grandly fill the single verse. Ajax' hunting, unlike Odysseus, belongs outside the framework of civilization.

Odysseus hears Athena's voice "like the bronze-mouthed Etruscan trumpet," (17), an allusion to the metallurgical craft for which the Etruscans were famous. But Ajax, whose power of communication, never great, was virtually destroyed by his madness (cf. 292), left his tent called by no messenger, hearing no trumpet (289–290). Ajax, "driven" by the goddess, is like a beast of the fields (53–54, 59–60); Odysseus is "steered" by the goddess' hand (*kybernōmai*, 35), a figure which suggests a more complex intellectual control and points to a more developed art of civilization. Ajax, by contrast, is tossed in the storm of his madness (206–209, 351–353). True, Odysseus too is "yoked" (24), but it is a yoke which he takes upon himself willingly (24), and it is he, not Ajax, who speaks of Ajax' "yoke" in 123. Finally, he sees Athena's display of her power not just as a show of brute strength, even though that is Athena's own way of presenting it in 118, but as the exercise of a craft or skill, *technē* (86).

When Ajax emerges from the storm and wave of his madness, he addresses his sailors in terms of their art (357): "Helpful companions of skill (*technē*) in sailing." But soon after, he laments that he is beyond all help (*onasis*) of men or gods (398–400), and, when his heroic resolve is firm, he looks again on a violent sea (674–675), where friendship is no safe harbor (682–683).

Metallurgy plays an especially significant role in Ajax' ambiguous relation to civilization. Iron, repeatedly associated with his destructive fury and emotional "hardness" (147, 325, 651, 820),[80] has an important place in the central speech on time. After speaking of softening the hardest hearts (649), he goes on (650–652):

κἀγὼ γάρ, ὃς τὰ δείν᾽ ἐκαρτέρουν τότε,
βαφῇ σίδηρος ὥς, ἐθηλύνθην στόμα
πρὸς τῆσδε τῆς γυναικός·

And I who once endured things terrible, like iron in the dipping, am made womanish in my speech [mouth] by this woman here.

These lines exploit a series of implicit contrasts: water and fire, maleness and womanhood, hardness and softness, fixity and change.[81] Yet here the opposites converge. Ajax cites the civilized image, as he uses the orderly processes of change in nature (669ff.), to reject them and affirm his own autonomy. The phrase "like iron in the dipping," is so placed that for a moment it seems to go with "am made womanish" and thus to refer to the softening or tempering, not the hardening, of iron. The ambiguity parallels the ambiguity of Ajax' own speech here, which masks firm resolution with apparent yielding.[82] The "mouth" (*stoma*) which is softened can refer also to the sword's "edge" which, as we soon learn, has kept its fierce hardness for that last uncompromising gesture (cf. 815). The sword which asserts that final independence from the constraints of men and gods is "newly sharpened with iron-eating whetstone," a line of near-Aeschylean grandeur (820). When Ajax talks of dipping the sword (651), he recalls a dipping of another kind, the raging "blood-dipped" slaughter (*haimobaphēs*, 219) of his madness. "Did you dip your sword well in the Argive army?" Athena asked him in the prologue (95). It is only by being dipped again, this time in Ajax' own blood (cf. 828), that the sword can finally wipe out the shame of that earlier dipping.

Iron-whetting and another skill, medicine, paradoxically reflect Ajax's removal from society just before the speech on time (581–582): "It is not a wise doctor who wails an incantation over a hurt that wants cutting." Tecmessa replies that his tongue is "whetted sharp" (*tethēgmenē*, 584). But it is the whetted sword, not the tongue, that will give Ajax' final answer (820); that weapon, not the doctor's scalpel, will do the "cutting" (cf. *tomōtatos*, "most cutting," 815, and *tomōnti*, "in need of cutting," 582). When the medical image recurs later in the play, it not only interchanges beast and men but suggests an unviable social order: the small whip with which the great ox is controlled is the harsh "medicine" with which Menelaus crudely threatens Teucer (1253–56).

Hector's sword, fatal for Ajax, was forged, says Teucer, by the Erinyes, while "Hades, savage craftsman" (*dēmiourgos agrios*), made Hector's equally disastrous belt (1034–35).[83] Rather than reflecting man's power over his world, technology here illustrates his subjection to demonic forces. Teucer's next lines about the gods' "devising" (*mēchanan*) such things now give an even grimmer turn to Odysseus' more acquiescent view of the gods' power of "artful design" (*technōmenos*, 86).

In the last ode of the play human inventiveness appears as a curse. The chorus turn the praise of the culture hero or inventor, familiar from Aeschylus' *Prometheus* or the first stasimon of the *Antigone*, into an execration of the man who invented weapons of war.[84] As in the metallurgical images of Ajax in 650–652 and Teucer in 1034–35, so here technology is seen as primarily destructive. In this respect the ode is an appropriate prelude to the entrance of Agamemnon and the limited view of human society which he embodies (1226ff.).

XI

In the *Ajax*, as in the other plays, the hero's relation to society is deeply involved with language.[85] Ajax is silent and uncommunicative; Odysseus, the social man par excellence, is an adept manipulator of language, not for the deceitful and vicious ends for which Ajax and his friends stigmatize him (148–153, 187–191), but, as the end of the play shows, for the maintenance of humane and lawful institutions. The silence of Ajax and the persuasive fluency of Odysseus are the two poles of language. Sophocles exploits the polarity already established in Homer, whose depiction of Ajax' silence before Odysseus in the Underworld is one of the most telling pieces of characterization in the epic tradition. Closer to Sophocles' time is Pindar's vivid representation of the defeat of Ajax' steadfast action by Odysseus' verbal dexterity.[86] In Sophocles this silence has an even more deeply tragic significance, linked as it is with Ajax' madness and his precarious place between men and beasts. Even the name by which he, "ill-named Ajax," is called (914) is an inarticulate cry of pain, *aiai*, a grim pun that recurs again and again (370, 430–431, 904, 914).

Ajax is isolated in the silence of his grief as he is in the delusions of his madness. Each of the major characters speaks from his own concern or values, but none can break through to him.[87] When Ajax addresses others, it is to issue curt commands for obedience or silence, to terminate rather than invite speech. The chorus proves mistaken in thinking that Ajax is one of those who can be won over by the speech of friends (330). Everyone speaks to Ajax but no one really makes an impression. He has to work out his decision in his own terms, through his own essentially private, uncommunicative meditations. We have already noted the ambiguity of the central speech in which that decision is taken. The others may hear, or overhear, these words, but they are, in some sense, addressed to Ajax' own soul.

Ajax' incapacity for fluent speech is basic to his inflexibility. For Odysseus, in whom we can recognize the adaptability and the communicative skills of the new democratic society, speech is an instrument for change. Ajax, with his stern fixity of purpose, looks back to an older, more static aristocratic world.[88] The calm, rapid speech of Odysseus' line-by-line argumentation (*stichomythia*) at the end is foreign to him (1318–69). When he engages in stichomythia it is not to persuade but to reinforce his commands or express impatience with talk (530–545, 585–595).

With Ajax, speech is always suspended, precarious, in crisis. The first words addressed to him when he finally appears on the stage are, "You have spoken well" (94). But in his deluded joy at seeing Athena he has not spoken well at all. His reply is a defiant boast about the bloody deed (96). Here and elsewhere Ajax talks big and even gives orders to Athena.[89] It is with a warning about talking big to the gods that Athena leaves the stage (127–130).

In a shame culture language is at least as important for its honorific, status-conferring as for its communicative function. It is with this aspect of language, its power to praise or blame, to confer honor or dishonor, that Ajax is most concerned.[90] The hostile speech of mockery or insult that he will receive from the army torments him and his comrades. Were Ajax well, the chorus says, he would make his enemies cower in silence (171), but now the horror of his crime has itself imposed speechlessness (214), and the madness itself brings total incoherence of speech (292). Later, as Tecmessa tries to recall Ajax to his human responsibilities, she invokes the Homeric values of shaming speech, what "someone will say" (500ff.). Yet even this appeal fails, and the scene ends in a harsh rupture of communication (589–595), which reenacts the old saw enjoining women to silence that Ajax muttered in his madness (293).

The madness itself "teaches" a language of violence that comes from the cruel daimon, not from men (243–244). Ajax can only "drag out" his curses against his enemies as he mutilates the cattle (303). His cracked, demented laughter dominates the early scenes of the play.[91] But later Ajax and his friends are haunted by the mocking laughter of his enemies (454, 957, 961, 969, 989, 1011, 1043). His utterances are all groans, threats, shouts, with intermittent long silences (308, 311, 312, 317). He vacillates between the extremes of talking big and utter silence. When he does return to himself, his old language will not fit: he will say what he never said before (410–411).

Ajax' struggle for sanity is also a struggle for speech. Haltingly he reacquires the use of his tongue. When he learns what happened "he broke forth at once in baleful groans which I never heard before from him, for he always held that such lamentations belong to mean and base-souled men" (317–320). Then he reverts to inarticulate cries, roaring like a bull (322) and uttering monosyllables or groans (333, 336, 339). Painfully he manages to articulate, "Teucer I call. Where (is) Teucer" (342), before the connected sentence which the chorus takes to be the mark of his return to sanity (*phronein*, 344).

Whatever is healing and conciliatory in language in these early scenes belongs to Tecmessa. It is she who urges the chorus to patience and understanding with the hope that "such men are won by the words of friends" (330). But Ajax' terms for speech in their long scene together, as we have seen, show only harshness (581–582, 586ff.; cf. 650–651). Homer's Hector and Andromache, the prototypes of that scene, can hear and move one another; Ajax and Tecmessa, like Heracles and Deianeira, speak different languages.[92] Speech cannot penetrate the barrier between their separate worlds. His next speech is, for forty lines, virtually a monologue (646–684). The man of straight speech "deceives" (Tecmessa's word, 807) this woman of gentle words. Enclosed in his own shame, he is deaf to the "painful words," "bitter name," and "ugly sayings" which she will receive from the army if he dies (494–495, 500–505). That death reduces her to monosyllabic moans and staccato questions that closely echo his earlier cries (cf. 891 and 333, 385; 921 and 342; 810 and 690).

In the *Ajax*, as in the *Trachiniae*, we can distinguish a hierarchy of forms of speech which can be correlated with the violated hierarchy of god, man, and beast. Calchas' oracle stands at the highest level. At the opposite end of the scale stands the inarticulate, bull-like groaning of Ajax, the dumb lamentation of his mother (624–634), or the bitter curses and invocations to deities of the lower world (see 835–844, 1034, 1387ff.).

Ajax' madness, in its simultaneous short-circuiting of ritual, linguistic, and biological order confuses the language of beasts and the language of gods. "A god, no man, taught him" the evil words with which he reviles the "cattle" as he strikes them (242–244). The oracular speech which might have brought salvation (779; cf. 692), in fact confirms his doom.[93]

Addressing only remote gods or powers of nature at his death, Ajax is cut off from the gentler uses of speech. He had asked the gods to send a messenger to bring the "evil report" of his death to Teucer (826–827), but Tecmessa's first reaction when she finds the body is that the sword itself has announced the death (906–907). Yet later Teucer can speak of the "swift report, as of some god" that brought the news to the Achaean host (998–999). As Ajax has denied the softness of private speech, so he can see only the harshness of public speech. True, the public voice in the play is largely sinister, made up of whispers, rumors, insults, accusations (150–151, 186, 188, 723ff.). Yet the elders are capable of conciliating speech (*synallagē logou*, 732), and Calchas separates himself from the rest of the army with words that are intended to be friendly and helpful (748ff.).

The struggle to reestablish normal discourse after its disintegration in Ajax' solitary emotions takes a different form with the hero's disappearance from the stage. Discourse in the latter half of the play is more regular. Teucer, the Atreids, Odysseus all accept the basic public, forensic framework of communication, however much they may differ in their styles and modes of argumentation.[94]

Here too, however, communication threatens to break down but for reasons different from those which produced Ajax' silences, oxymora, or monologues. Both Atreids regard language as an extension of authority, a matter of "hearing" and "obeying" (1069–70, 1352). Hence the debate with Teucer soon degenerates from logical argument to insult, boasting, big talk (1122ff.), accusations of a violent mouth and empty words (1148, 1162, 1223–28).[95] The chorus' warning that such hard words "bite" (*daknein*, 1118–19) reverts to the collapse of language into bestiality early in the play. Menelaus subverts the rational basis of discussion in preferring force (*biazesthai*) to words (1159–60; cf. *bia* 1327, 1334–35), his parting shot at Teucer.[96]

Like his brother, Agamemnon ends his first tirade with a threatened breakdown of communication. He accuses Teucer of being a barbarian whom he cannot and will not understand (1259–62): "Why don't you bring another man, not a slave, to state your case. From your speech I could not learn it. I have no comprehension of a barbarian tongue." Agamemnon literally denies that he and Teucer speak the same language.

Odysseus, man of moderation and good sense, prevents the utter disintegration of speech to force. He restores the rational communication that makes civilized society possible. He not only introduces conciliating speech but also understands and thereby transcends the mechanism of quarrelling by which insult leads to insult (1322–23): "I pardon a man who, when he hears mean words, rejoins with harsh speech." He is here echoing Teucer's sharp rejoinder to Menelaus at the end of their encounter (1162, 1323), but his calm reasonableness stands apart from Menelaus' overbearing and Teucer's emotional indignation. Just the opposite of the aloof, inward, partisan speech of Ajax, Odysseus' fair and flexible speech can reach both sides. Odysseus insists on the friendliness of truly spoken advice (1328–29, 1351). His speech is the proper vehicle for the laws and justice of men and gods that the Atreids would violate.[97] It is the language of arbitration in the civilized community. Ajax' speech is the more magnificent, but also the more precarious.

Closely connected with language in Ajax' problematical relation to civilized communication is *charis*. The word, which denotes the bond of affection between men, spans both the closest human relations and remoter social obligations. As we have seen, the closing lines of Tecmessa's plea connect *charis* with a man's vulnerability to time and change through those time-bound relationships (520–523):

> But consider and remember me. If a man has had the benefit of pleasure (*terpnon*), there should be remembering, for kindness (*charis*) begets kindness always (*charis charin gar estin hē tiktous' aei*, 522). But the man from whose mind the recollection of the good that he has experienced flows away, that man would not be noble.

The very form of line 522, with its polyptoton, expresses the mutual giving and taking embodied in *charis*. Tecmessa's metaphor of "begetting" belongs to the erotic connotations of *charis*. She thereby seeks to reinvolve Ajax in the cycles of procreation and birth with which she, like Deianeira, is especially concerned.[98] Her solution to the problem of change, however, cannot satisfy Ajax, as his long speech on time shows. The military imagery of his brusque, third-person reply here (527–528), "She'll get her praise from me if she can execute her orders well," reduces the rich emotional tonality of her *charis* to the severity of the soldier's camp.

His rejection of change in death-bound heroism appears as the reverse of Tecmessa's regenerative energy. When she realizes that his departure may mean his death, she suffers the negative "birth-pangs" of anxiety (*ōdinein*, 794) and sees herself as cast out of old gratitude (*charis*, 808), an expression which recalls Ajax' risk of being cast out from men.[99] The metaphor of birth recurs with bitter irony when she finds his body, final witness of her own destruction and deception (791, 807), and cries (952–953): "Such pain does Athena, terrible daughter of Zeus, bring to birth (*phyteuei*) as a favor (*charis*) to Odysseus." It is for his son alone that Ajax requests *charis* as he enjoins the Salaminians and Teucer to protect his safety as a "favor shared between you" (*koinēn . . . charin*, 566). But his closing instruction, to bury the arms "in common with me," "sharing the grave with me" (*koin' emoi*, 577), makes a paradoxical use of *koinos* and reflects a very different view of sharing.[100]

Just the opposite of Odysseus (cf. *Odyssey* 24.515), Ajax deletes himself as a link between the generations, his son and his parents. When he requests *charis* in this scene, Ajax explains that Eurysaces, the small grandson—not himself, the grown father—will go to his house to care for his parents in their old age (570–571) "that he may be their nurturer in old age, forever, until they reach the chambers of the nether god." The word "forever," *esaei*, hangs heavy at the end of 570.[101] The next line, with its reference to the nether god of death, seems almost an afterthought, but the sharp juxtaposition repeats that swing between total annihilation and eternity that for Ajax makes the mediate position of human *charis* tragically impossible. The absolutes of death and the timeless, never far from his thoughts, are in constant counterpoint with the continuities of family and society.

Like Tecmessa, Teucer connects *charis* with memory and the flowing change of time (1266–70):

O Ajax, dead, how swiftly gratitude (*charis*) flows away [*diarrhei*; cf. *aporrhei mnēstis*, 523] and is caught, betrayed, if this man here, making no small boast, has no recollection (*mnēstis*) of you—he for whom you toiled with your spear and risked your life.[102]

Teucer broadens the range of *charis* from private affection to the heroic community.

For the Atreid rulers, however, memory is a negative quality, retentive of old grudges and old hatreds rather than of the old gratitude that Tecmessa so valued and lost (808). When Odysseus takes Ajax' part, Agamemnon exclaims, indignantly, "Remember to what sort of man you are giving gratitude" (*charis*, 1354). Agamemnon's *charis* is narrow and selfish. Even when he accedes to Odysseus' arguments, he does so only as a limited, personal favor to Odysseus (1371); his hatred for Ajax is unchanged (1370–73). Agamemnon's stubborn vengefulness prevents him from grasping the real nature of *charis*. His *charis* is in hatred what Tecmessa's is in love. He bestows this *charis* not on Ajax but on Odysseus. He thereby reenacts the situation which initially robbed Ajax of the *charis* that he deserved, the judgment of the arms. This society failed to discern where lay its true *charis*, its true bonds of obligation toward its great and extraordinary men.

Now, however, Teucer's emotional force and just indignation carry the intimate *charis* of Tecmessa into the wider social world. Odysseus' calm persuasiveness cements Ajax' rightful claim to gratitude. As in the judgment of the arms, Odysseus wins a victory by words before the tribunal of Atreid authority, but this time it is a victory for, not against, Ajax.

XII

Rituals are the analogue in the divine realm to *charis* in the human. Ajax' madness, as we have seen, constitutes a violation of the ritual order as well as the social order. The act that definitively refuses the *charis* for which Tecmessa asked is presented as a rite of purification (see 654–660). But the hero's return to sanity does not bring an immediate reintegration to the social order. Blood, not water, will be his means of cleansing his impurity. The blood-dipped sword (219) will be cleansed by a dipping no less violent and no less lonely than that which stained it.

The second half of the play is concerned with rites of burial, but the eventual performance of that rite still stands in tension with the hero's own self-chosen isolation. That tension remains through the very last scene, for Odysseus who has made possible Ajax' burial rites is excluded from them.

In his first appearance on the stage Ajax appears amidst distorted rituals. He greets Athena and then offers "to crown [her] with all-gold spoils in gratitude for this hunt" (92–93):

καί σε παγχρύσοις ἐγὼ
στέψω λαφύροις τῆσδε τῆς ἄγρας χάριν·

In this grisly offering man and beast are confused, propriety of speech is disrupted by the boast of Ajax' next line, and the relation between civilized and wild spaces is confounded by a "hunt" within protected boundaries. Ajax has in fact destroyed the spoils of which a portion would naturally be set apart for the gods (cf. *Trach.* 244–245) and has thereby committed an outrage (*aikizein*, 65, 111, 300) which returns upon himself through the god's intervention (*aikizein*, 402).

These "sacrificed" beasts and the blood-dipped sword (95), contrasting with the "all-gold spoils" of the promised votive, endow this offering with the grotesque, macabre quality appropriate to Ajax' insanity. The madman's offering can only pervert the ritual process. Soon after, the chorus attributes this madness to the wrath of Artemis Tauropolos because of the "gratitude of a victory offering which lacked its fruit" (*tinos nikas akarpōton charin*, 176). In both cases the *charis*, or favorable reciprocity, between gods and men is destroyed (cf. 93),[103] and this destruction takes the form of the madman's ritual impurity. The gods next cited as authors of the madness, Ares and Enyalius, likewise stand on the fringes of civilization (179–181).[104]

Later, when the chorus mistakenly believes that Ajax has renounced his earlier plan of suicide, they picture him performing proper sacrifices (*panthyta thesmia*) with "the reverence of greatest lawfulness" (713–714). But this description occurs in an ode to Pan, god of mountains and lonely places (693ff.), who is more appropriate to Ajax' real intentions than they know. We may compare the not dissimilar situation of the chorus' celebration of Mount Cithaeron in the *Tyrannus* at the point when they too are deluded about the hero's movement from pollution to purity. Here Ares recurs, having released them, they say, from their grief (706); yet in their final ode the chorus will curse Ares' destructiveness (1196).

Dedication, sacrifice, purification, and burial are the rituals with which the *Ajax* is primarily concerned. The votive dedications to Athena and Artemis reflect a violated *charis*; when Ajax himself "dedicates" his sword to the lower world, purification and reconciliation are ambiguous (658–660). This dedication also completes the pattern of inverted light and darkness in the play: rather than allowing Ajax to look upon the light of the sun, the dedication initiates his movement downward to the dark realms where that sword has its origins, fashioned as it is by the Erinys (1034–35; cf. 854–865). The final offering to the lower gods is Ajax himself, described in the last ode as "dedicated to the hateful daimon" (*aneitai stygerō(i) daimoni*, 1214).[105]

In his madness Ajax not only confuses beasts with men, but virtually sacrifices these beasts in a perverted ritual. The slaughtered cattle are *sphagia* (219), the regular word for sacrificial victims. *Sphazein* and its compounds, the verb for killing in the sacrificial act, occur more frequently in *Ajax* than in any other Sophoclean play.[106] The "freshly slaughtered carnage," *neo-sphagēs phonos* (546), of the cattle is no joyful sight but something to school Eurysaces in those "raw ways" of his father (545–549). These cattle are also called *chrēstēria* (220), a striking usage of a word which usually indicates the victims offered before approaching an oracle.[107] Ajax cuts out their tongues (238), also a regular part of the sacrificial act.

The irony of *chrēstēria* in 220 matches the irony of the "saving" oracle itself. It is of a piece with the irony of the chorus' image of Ajax reverently performing sacrificial rites when he is in fact meditating his own lonely death (711–713).

Ajax' "sacrifice" of himself with his sword as *sphageus*, "the sacrificer" as well as the "sacrificing knife," answers his perverted "sacrifice" of the beasts. The burial of this sacrificial implement (658–659) both grimly parodies sacrificial ritual[108] and links the deadly "sacrifice" to the motifs of impurity and expulsion to be discussed later. In a sense the chorus' image in 711–713 is correct: Ajax is performing a sacrifice; he is making peace with the gods and the cosmic order but on his own terms. His is a private sacrifice, the celebrant fused with the victim; the rest of the community, the normal beneficiary of such a sacrifice, is excluded.

As in the *Trachiniae*, the sacrificer doubles with the bestial victim. Here the bestial imagery which describes Ajax—hunted, driven, yoked, roaring—has a further significance in his removal from the order of men and gods. He is, as we have seen, virtually "dedicated" to the god (1214). Having treated beasts as if they were men in the dark night of his madness, he becomes himself the beast victim in an unhallowed sacrifice outside the spatial and moral limits of civilized society.

In this isolation Ajax' death enacts another ritual: threatened with death by stoning, he is the scapegoat or *pharmakos*, laden with all the pollutions of the city and driven out by the community as a whole.[109] Similarly, the exposure of his corpse was the punishment for one who had forfeited his rights to membership in the polis. Yet when he occupies the lowest point among men as *pharmakos*, Ajax at the end of the play, like Heracles in the *Trachiniae*, is hailed as "best of men" (1416), "noble in all respects," *ho pant' agathos* (1415). Standing between the polluted scapegoat and the pure victim, Ajax confounds the polarity between beast and god. "Dedicated to the hateful daimon" and connected with the powers of the lower world through his sword fashioned by the Erinys, he can still address Helios and ask Zeus to protect his body (829–831). As the polluted scapegoat, he is hateful in the sight of gods and men; as the sacrificial victim, self-immolated, he stands apart as *sacer*, numinous with his heroic autonomy or *autarkeia*, in touch with the divine timelessness. It is this special relationship to the gods that Tecmessa grasps when she describes his triumph in death: he has died as he wished (966), free of the mockery and insults of his enemies (969–973). As she puts it in her great commemorative line (970),

θεοῖς τέθνηκεν οὗτος, οὐ κείνοισιν, οὔ·

For the gods he died, for them not at all.[110]

Ajax' relation to pollution and purification shows a similar ambiguity.[111] Having polluted his hand (*cheira chrainesthai phonō(i)*, 43) by the dreadful dipping of his sword (95, 219), he will seek cleanliness not by a ritual dipping in water (cf. 651) but by a violent act of blood appropriate to his "raw ways." The most polluted of all men in the camp, he cannot be cleansed by a normal human ritual. The washing places (654) to which he goes for purification (cf. *hagnizein*, 655) are places of his total isolation; from these, unlike the participant in a normal rite of purification, he will not return. He will not accept the cleansing properties of the sea's water any more than he will accept the natural alternation of the seasonal cycles. Blood, not water, will wash off his stain. At the end he will receive the holy ablutions (*hosia loutra*, 1405; cf. *loutra*, 654) which restore him to society, but now it is only his corpse that is washed clean. His own means of cleansing (*lymath' hagnisas ema*, 655) bypass the ritual forms and put him into unmediated relation with the divine powers, his own celebrant and his own victim (*sphageus*, 815).

A study by C. W. Eckert suggests another way of viewing the motif of pollution and purification in the *Ajax*.[112] Eckert has pointed out that the madness of the hero who kills cattle and men and tyrannizes over women is related to festivals of purification and renewal, especially those connected with the New Year, the obvious point of crisis between waning life and new energy. These rites create a momentary return to chaos from which a fresh and more vigorous order is reborn.

In these rites the victims are also *sphagia*, as in *Ajax*; the sacrifice takes place at night, not by day; and the celebrant is himself polluted and stands in need of purification.[113] The ritual pattern has parallels in Germanic legend. In Greece it is exemplified in Heracles' killing of his children and Orestes' slaughter of sheep (Euripides, *Iphigeneia in Tauris*, 285–300). The madness is part of the chaos of the endangered house or kingdom. The hero himself acts as a sort of purgative daimon *malgré lui*, cleansing the community of its evil and restoring it to vitality. His passage from madness, bloodshed, and disorder to sanity, health, and heroic status enacts in microcosm the regeneration of house and city. Understood psychologically, as the work of Burkert suggests, this madness, when incorporated into ritual, helps channel and control aggression, purging the society of its repressed violence.[114]

In its relation to ritual forms that deliberately dissolve order to reaffirm order and to the personal life of the character, the warrior's madness also has a positive side. It is the expression of the potential chaos in the hero and the heroic world,[115] but its dissolution of existing forms also contains the potential for a new vision of order. As a response to a hopeless conflict in heroic values, Ajax' madness was perhaps inevitable, a necessary, even creative solution. Here he achieves a realization of his heroism no longer dependent on the externalized, material recognition of the old heroic code, as embodied in the award of Achilles' arms. That code works as long as the hero's peers are fair and honorable. When they are corrupt, it breaks down. Ajax thereupon, like Homer's Achilles before him, must take the lonely path of self-affirmation, apart from or in conflict with society. His heroism becomes internal and self-determined.[116]

In this breakthrough to a more interior and independent valuation of self, madness plays an indispensable role. A powerful purgative agent, it violently sweeps the soul clean of past attachments and prepares for a radical review and redirection of action. After passing through this liminal state of madness and its beastlike destructiveness, Ajax reaffirms his heroic status with clearer, and harsher, resolution. His noble death, though still ambiguous in terms of the norms represented by the Atreids, makes possible a rite of reintegration, in the form of proper burial for the body, and a clarification of values, in the form of the defeat of the authoritarian Atreids by archer-warriors who represent some of the qualities of Athenian democracy.

The play, of course, is far more than the enactment or illustration of a liminal rite of cathartic madness. Both play and rite reflect common, though independent, concerns and follow similar logic.[117] Such parallelism is to be expected in a society where analogy is a major mode of thought.

Great literature, however much it may use inherited mythical or ritual structures, operates in a manner quite distinct from them. Tragedy especially does not merely reflect such structures but deforms them, renders them problematical, distant, complex, and ambiguous, in accordance with the tragic hero's own ambiguous place between the highest and lowest levels of the social order. Hence the underlying ritual pattern of *Ajax* has to be seen against the particularized fullness of the tragic protagonist whose death, despite all his faults, still engages our sympathies.

"Renewal" and "rebirth" take on paradoxical meanings when the dominant presence in the closing scenes is the huge, bloody corpse. Here, as in all Sophoclean tragedy, patterns of renewal are played off against something darker and deeper. In this case the reaffirmation of social and cosmic order contrasts with the tragic and heroic refusal to be part of the normal rhythms of life. Other paradoxes attend Ajax' reintegration into the social and ritual order. This most silent of heroes owes his burial to the persuasive speech of his enemy and opposite, Odysseus. The warrior who prided himself on taking his stand unmoved has to appoint someone else to guard his son (*phylax*, 562) and then is himself guarded (*phylasse*, 1180) by this child, who is told, "Let no one move you" (1180–81).[118] This "bulwark of the Achaeans" is protected by a woman and a child, the feeblest members of his house, the figures who link him with those rhythms of time and change which he rejected.

XIII

The restoration of Ajax to full honor and ritual purity (cf. 1405) at the end surely owes something to the hero cult of Ajax at Athens and the intense veneration which local heroes could inspire.[119] Sophocles repeatedly stresses Ajax' special connection with Athens (860–861, 1217ff.). He and his men are sprung of the autochthonous Erechtheids, (201–202), that is, of the purest blood of Attica. The question of burial will naturally be important for a hero whose cult centers about his tomb. Like other heroes (in both the general and the technical cult sense), he is one whose life and death call forth the operation of divine forces. For all his madness, even Athena commends his good sense in prior behavior (119–120; cf. 182), and Calchas shows a friendly attitude (749–755). The oracle, though it in fact foreshadows the certainty of his doom, also demonstrates the gods' concern.

Ajax, however, is not remade into a communal hero of the polis in any simple sense. His last gesture confirms him in that isolated, archaic self-centered heroism of the Homeric warrior. He still remains an anomaly, a remote, gigantic figure, "the last of the heroes," as Bernard Knox says.[120]

"How could a warrior so stubborn, manic, and self-willed," Herbert Musurillo asks, "become a hero worthy of cult?"[121] The question is not the central issue of the play, cult heroes not being renowned for reasonableness or modesty, but it does touch the play insofar as one of the effects of Greek tragedy is to bring the city into contact with the polarities inherent in its culture. In Ajax' violence of suffering and action reverberate some of the major clashes of values in midfifth-century Athens. The most recalcitrant and individualistic of heroes commands respect from those who must reject his attitudes if their institutions are to survive. The polluted madman and would-be murderer still receives a special place in the divine order and is acknowledged as "the best of mortals while he lived" (1416–17). His greatness is recognized even by his opposite, Odysseus, the man skilled in those forensic, civic arts which Ajax rejects. The play dramatizes not merely the clash between aristocratic and democratic ideals or between the

Pindaric and the Athenian hero but also the conflict between two kinds of *aretai*, the competitive and the cooperative. What is more, these clash not merely in the basic contrast between Ajax and Odysseus, but also in the conflict within Ajax himself (cf. 457–470).[122]

Teucer's instructions about Ajax in 1168–79 are especially important for the hero cult in the background. As Peter Burian has recently shown, three ritual elements are conjoined in an unusual combination: supplication and the power of the hero's body to protect suppliants, offerings to the dead, and the power to curse.[123] The scene exhibits the "final vindication of the hero" in his "heroic power to extend his curse on his enemies and his blessings on his loved ones from the world below." The vivid and characteristically Sophoclean tableau on the stage—the big body and the woman and child bent over it—also creates a sacred setting in itself.[124] It is as if the resting place of the hero's body is being reconstituted as a holy place before our eyes. Ajax receives the permanence he strove for by being taken into the community which he abandoned, protected by those whom he left behind. His heroic status involves a kind of posthumous participation in human time and birth. The continuity of family, all that *charis* by which Tecmessa entreated him in vain (521ff.), surrounds him and protects him in that part of himself which is still vulnerable and in need of shelter.

Ajax, who supplicated Zeus to receive proper burial (*prostrepō*, 831), now protects suppliants. His bitter curse on the Atreids, at this point of his sharpest isolation (835ff.), is answered by a power to curse which can protect suppliants at his body (1175–78). That curse of 835ff. recurs, but it is uttered now by Ajax' champion, Teucer, when his enemies are defeated in their intended outrage of his corpse (1388–92). Ajax' curse of 835ff., like the implicit curse of the sword (1034–35), could only destroy. Teucer's two curses at the end have a more positive, reintegrative function (1175ff., 1387ff.; cf. 1177 and 1391). They confirm Ajax' place within the ritual framework of proper burial.

Ajax' heroization contains a tension of another kind. In Pindar the heroes celebrated by the poet are closely linked with the eternizing power of song. Solidly established within the community, the heroes' poetic and cultic immortality through fame overcomes individual death. Ajax, however, achieves his heroic status only through the terrible loneliness of his end. This loneliness creates a tension between the ritual context of the cult and the tragic content of myth, as Sophocles interprets it. He has rejected the society which will heroize him; he has set himself outside the ritual and social forms that could provide some palliative for his death. These are recurrent tensions in Sophocles and become especially prominent in his last two plays.

Ajax had deliberately chosen as his last place on earth a wild locale, outside the social and ritual order. When his friends reincorporate him into that order, it is only in the face of a threatened re-expulsion. Now the ritual lament over the corpse in the whole city (851–852), which seemed only a distant and impossible wish at the time of utterance, is fulfilled in the most impressive way. "Hapless Ajax, such a man in such a fate, how worthy to receive lamentation (*thrēnoi*), even among your enemies," Tecmessa cried out over the newly-found corpse

(923–924). The claim is not mere rhetoric: Ajax' "enemy," Odysseus, does request to share in the honor and the grief of burial (1378–79). Earlier, at Menelaus' approach and then at his discomfiture, the chorus hoped for a hasty burial at best (1040, 1164–65). Instead Ajax receives full honors, symbolically enacted in Teucer's closing anapaests with their tone of ritual solemnity (1402–17). As part of this return to ritual order, the ambiguous and violent purificatory ablutions of Ajax now bring a peaceful cleansing (654–655 and 1404–1405). The fires of the night that flared in the midst of Ajax' madness are now the fires of ritual. In the armor carried in the funeral procession the shield has the most prominent role (*hypaspidion*, 1408). The focal point of commemorating Ajax' warrior prowess, in other words, is the part which embodied his cooperative virtues and the *charis* they inspired (see 1266–70).

Even here, however, Ajax remains in touch with the savage immensity of his passion. We are reminded forcefully of the suicide (1411–13):

> ἔτι γὰρ θερμαὶ
> σύριγγες ἄνω φυσῶσι μέλαν
> μένος·

Still the warm veins [literally, pipes] blow upward their black force.

The "black force," *melan menos*, of his blood recalls both the violence of the deed and the violence of emotion, *menos*, which impelled it. These *syrinxes* of his wound recall the god of the wild whom the chorus invoked in their misplaced joy at the hero's ostensible "purification" (693ff.).

The rites of burial and concern for the dead keep the deceased alive through memory.[125] Through memory civilization mediates between the value-neutral change of nature and the timelessness of the gods. Ajax will gain a grave always remembered by mortals (*aeimnēstos*, 1166). As a creation of time-bound mortals, however, memory too is subject to transitoriness. This same grave is a place of corruption and "mouldering" (*euröeis*, 1167). Tecmessa had complained of the flux to which memory is subject (523), and Teucer invoked the "remembering Fury" (1390) against the Atreids for their failure to remember the *charis* which they owe Ajax (cf. 1266–69).

To possess whatever eternity memory can confer (1166), Ajax has to reoccupy a place within the changeful cycle of birth and death and the human ties of which *charis*, like memory, is a part. Even the commemoration of Teucer's closing words sets Ajax within the perspective in time (1417):

> Αἴαντος, ὅτ' ἦν, τότε φωνῶ·

I speak of Ajax when he was.[126]

The temporal clause and imperfect tense of "when he was" keep us aware of the human limits of Ajax' life even as he takes his place in a long-remembered heroic past. The chorus, as they close the play, again underscore human mutability (1418–20): "Many are the things for mortals to behold and to learn. But in respect to the things to come, no one, before he sees them, is prophet of how we will fare." Just as eternal memory is juxtaposed with the mould of the grave in the first attempt to bury Ajax (1166–67), so here at the end even Ajax' fame remains enshrined against the unreclaimable transitoriness of greatness and man's helplessness before an unseen future.

The reacceptance of Ajax into the ritual framework of society is further defined in the last stasimon (1185–1222). This ode follows directly upon the implicit heroization of Ajax and the quasi-sacred status given his body in Teucer's speech of 1168–83. After the initial strophe calling up the long sufferings at Troy and execrating the inventor of war, the chorus turns to the pleasures of life that war destroys. These are primarily the joys of the most social of all institutions, the symposium. Counted among the losses of war are the delights of garlands, flute music, drinking, love (1199–1208). They contrast with the pain suffered in the open air at Troy, where, however, Ajax was a protector (1199–1216). Then, with another shift between friendly and hostile space (the first being from banquet hall to Troy), the sailors wish that they were back in their native land, near Sunion and holy Athens (1217–22).

Besides juxtaposing peace and war, shelter and exposure, pleasure and toil, the ode also evokes images of civilized life that contrast with Ajax' savagery. The festal garlands of the symposium (1199) recall the garland of spoils that Ajax, in his madness, would present to Athena (93). "The joy of converse (*homilein*) in the deep cups" (1200–1201) contrasts with Ajax' isolation when he refused to eat or drink (*asitos, apotos*, 324). Love, *erōtes* (1205–1206) contrasts with Ajax' grim love for death at the end of his central speech (684–686), fulfilled when Tecmessa pronounces over the body, "The aim with which he was in love (*erasthē*) he won for himself, the death he wished for" (967)[127] "He died bitter to me, as sweet to his enemies, but to himself joyful" (*terpnos*): these words, just before the remark about love (966–967) point to a joy very different from that of this ode (*terpsis*, 1201, 1205, 1215). Throughout the play Ajax has stood apart from the joy of normal life (114, 475, 521). In the prologue Athena blocked the grim incurable pleasure of his bloody revenge (*anēkestos chara*, 52). In this ode the shared joys of civilized pursuits are part of a threatened order of civilization. The hero's death stirs up all of our anxieties at its precariousness, the fragility of the barrier between order and chaos. The pleasures of civilized pursuits, the "joy of night," *ennychia terpsis* (1203–1204) stand at the opposite pole from the solitary night of Ajax' madness. Yet as the second stasimon soon reminds us, Ajax was a "bulwark against the night's fear" (1211–12): his nights were spent not in symposiac joy, but in guarding the army against night attack.[128]

By thus reminding us of Ajax' cooperative virtues, the ode helps prepare for Teucer's defense in the next scene (1266ff.). But it also presents a microcosm of the tensions between civilization and savagery that cross in Ajax. The outcast and suicide is now both sheltered (1168ff.) and sheltering (1211–13). The hero who rejected all joy is now addressed as the lost joy of his companions (1215–16). The sea which symbolized the wild turbulence of his madness is now associated with home, friends, sacred places, Athens itself. But all of these positive aspects of Ajax and his world are threatened. Ajax' burial is still uncertain. The debased survivors and exultant victors, proposing a "bulwark of fear" (*problēma phobou*, 1076) of a very different sort from that which Ajax provided to the chorus (1211–13), threaten the erstwhile "bulwark" (*probola*) of the army with being "cast forth" (*problētos*, 830) to dogs and birds. The chorus' return to the civilized, inhabited places of holy Athens at the end, even though in fantasy (1221–22), contrasts with Ajax' lonely farewell to the holy plain of native Salamis and glorious Athens (859–861). Later the contrast between the harsh "blowing" of those "warm pipes" of Ajax' wound (1411–12) and the sweet sound of flutes at the banquet (1202) keep Ajax fixed to the end in the savage realm "outside," far from the happy interior of festive music.

By contrasting different forms of love and pleasure, interior and exterior scenes, present and distant landscapes, protection and exposure, funeral and symposium, the ode projects upon a larger screen the question of Ajax' isolation and relation to the life-affirming values of civilization. Beneath these contrasts runs the deeper contrast of Ajax' status as suicide and esteemed hero, criminal and protector, polluted outcast and cult hero.

XIV

In the first half of the play, these tensions appear primarily in terms of the singleness of Ajax' will. In the second half, with the news of Teucer's arrival, the oracle of Calchas, and the great debates, the focus shifts to the social and political framework against which that isolation is asserted. The second half of the play itself falls into two approximately equal sections. The first (719–1039) views the isolated hero primarily from the point of view of his intimate personal ties, his blood kin and the reciprocity of *charis* given and exacted by the family (807–808). The second section, from the entrance of Menelaus to the end (1040–1420), expands this personal focus to the community as a whole. It develops contrasting visions of a social order which has to confront both the savage greatness of uncompromising heroism and the nothingness of death. There is something artificial about so neat a division, as there is about the alleged "diptych" structure as a whole. In the prologue the figure of Odysseus already embodies the larger social concerns; conversely Teucer, the representative of Ajax' ties of blood, remains on stage to the very end.

The contest between Teucer and the Atreids frames conflicting views of how society deals with death. The Atreids lay claim to the external form of civilized humanity, but in fact their veneer of piety thinly covers high-handed authoritarianism (see 1062ff., 1159–60, 1326–27, 1334). They pervert valid principles of conduct, like good sense (*sōphrosynē*), into oligarchic catchwords.[129] Though their intransigence superficially resembles Ajax', it is in fact only a narrow personal vindictiveness, totally without Ajax' greatness of spirit.[130] When Menelaus "thinks big" (1087–88) he does not, like Ajax, assert a tragic autonomy against an unacceptable world order but only gloats over a helpless enemy. Their world has no place for such greatness. They would reduce Ajax to their own narrow limits, trying to control the great by the small (1253–55). In such a society the great hero would have to become an *apolis*, the citiless outcast. In defending their position they can only make a specious appeal to the corrupt institutions that have already condemned Ajax: the jury that awarded the arms to Odysseus (1239ff.), with its biased vote and judges (cf. *psēphos*, 1135; *dikastai*, 1136; *kritai*, 1243).

The conflicts at the end, therefore, only continue those of the early part of the play. With the exception of Odysseus, all the participants are prisoners of the same values that have caused the murderous rift between the great man and the rest of the community. The Atreids defend the narrow, formal discipline of the army. Teucer defends the rights of the *genos* or family, charged with the burial of its members and still possessed by a clannish exclusiveness that bars Odysseus from those rites of burial at the end. Only Odysseus is able to span both sides. He transcends the Atreids' partisan rigidity through his compassionate grasp of the mortal condition, and he balances the narrow loyalties of family with his enlightened generosity and fairness to greatness even in enemies.

If Ajax sees the gods only as a hostile, alien power, the Atreids view them only in terms of their own purposes. They identify the will of the gods with the good of the army which they command (1057, 1060–61, 1129–32). In this respect they anticipate not only the authoritarian legalism of Creon in the *Antigone* but also the success-minded opportunism of Odysseus in the *Philoctetes*.[131] Menelaus echoes Athena's precepts on the need for authority in Aeschylus' *Eumenides* but uses them only to defend his own autocratic conception of authority (1071–86).[132]

In the second encounter Teucer bypasses the religious violations in favor of some sharp ad hominem arguments. He rattles the skeletons of "impiety" in the Atreid closet (1291–98) and concludes with a fierce assertion of family loyalties (1310–15). But Odysseus goes to the heart of the matter. He echoes Menelaus' hypocritical invocation of the laws of the gods only to demolish totally the moral basis of the Atreid position (1334–45; cf. 1130 and 1343–44). Even when Agamemnon finally yields, however, he shows no respect for Odysseus' ethical and religious arguments. Egotism, personal commitment, narrow prejudice govern him to the end (1370–73).

We have already seen how images of inverted technology in the early part of the play reflect Ajax' ambiguous relation to civilized values. Similar inversions apply to the Atreids, too. Menelaus uses an image of a ship lost in the waves (1083) or out of control as all effective communication has broken down (1142–46):

> Once I saw a man bold in tongue urging his sailors to sail during a storm, but when he found himself caught in the thick of the storm you couldn't find any voice (*phthegma*) in him. Instead he hid under the rigging and let any sailor who wanted trample him.

The parable form itself reflects Menelaus' disdain. It is to Teucer's credit that he scorns such cheap "riddles" (1158) and uses forthright speech (1154): "Do not, my friend, do wrong to the dead."[133]

Agamemnon's comparison of Ajax to a big ox kept on a straight course by a small whip (1253–55) asserts human control over beasts and might seem to contrast favorably with Ajax' confusion of man and beast and his own destructive use of a whip (110, 242). But Agamemnon's unfeeling discipline stands as far from civilized humanity as Ajax' madness. Ironically the "bigness" or "greatness" of Ajax (*megas* in 1253 means both) was precisely what eluded the Atreids' control.[134] The comparison recalls a famous passage in the *Iliad* which illustrated Ajax' heroic combination of stubbornness and bigness: steadfast against the enemy, he is like a donkey in a grain field which even the blows of boys cannot drive out until he is ready to move in his own good time (*Il.* 11.558ff.). Within the framework of the play itself, the authoritarian point of view expressed by Agamemnon's simile clashes with a very different and far more plausible relation between "small" and "great," one which acknowledged the heroic role of Ajax as "bulwark of the Achaeans" (158–161): "And yet, without the great, the small are but the faulty bulwark of a tower. The small, in company with the great, and the great, helped by the small, would keep a straight course best of all."[135]

Over against the passions and private loyalties of Teucer and the Atreids stand the calm humanity and self-control of Odysseus. He commands the good sense or *sōphrosynē* that the characters of this play so often desire but so rarely possess.[136] He can appreciate Ajax' virtues as well as his faults, his greatness as well as his savagery. Combining clarity of mind with reverence, persuasiveness with morality, flexibility with respect for heroic fixity, he comes as close as any figure in Sophocles to representing human civilization at its best.[137] He is held in esteem by both sides: the chorus and Agamemnon address him as "Lord Odysseus (*anax Odysseus*) (1316, 1321); Teucer calls him *aristos*, "best," "noblest," (1381).

Odysseus' untragic humanity is the foil for Ajax' doomed greatness. He contrasts with but does not cancel out Ajax' dark heroism, even though he makes possible the recognition of honor in the world which Ajax left behind (1339–42; cf. 98, 426, 440). Seeing beyond the division that separates Ajax from the rest of the army, he can himself pronounce Ajax "next to Achilles best of all of us who came to Troy" (1340–41), anticipating Teucer's closing eulogy (1415–17). His first-person verb in 1340 ranks Ajax above himself, thereby reversing the judgment of the arms. Yet the very qualities that enable Odysseus to sympathize with Ajax and secure his burial also place him worlds away from Ajax' heroism. If it is appropriate, from Ajax' point of view, that Odysseus be excluded from the burial, it is also appropriate, from the point of view of Odysseus' character, that he should so reasonably acquiesce in that rejection. They are the last lines he speaks on stage (1400–1401): "I wished (to share in the burial). But if it is not dear (*philon*) to you that I do these things, I shall depart, assenting to your words." Even his use of the word *philon*, "dear," "friendly," in an impersonal construction reflects a patience and tolerance quite different from the exclusive spirit of *philia* in which Teucer performs the burial (*philos*, 1413).

Some of these differences of attitude are reflected in the changes rung on the verb *ponein*, "suffer," "toil," in the closing scene. Teucer uses the verb to assert the claims of family over those of the army (1310–12): "It is honorable for me to die before all men's eyes toiling in his [Ajax'] behalf (*hyperponein*) rather than for your wife, or should I say your brother's?" Odysseus, on the other hand, fights on behalf of Ajax (*hypermachein*) on the grounds of general moral principles: appreciation of greatness and the injustice of perpetuating narrow hatred (*misos*) beyond the grave (1344–49). Agamemnon, however, can see in Odysseus' behavior only a kind of egotistic individualism (1366–67):

> Ag.: Everything is the same; every man toils (*ponei*) for himself.
> Od.: For whom is it likely that I should toil (*ponein*) more than for myself?

Odysseus here echoes Teucer's *hyperponein* in 1310, but his attitude is quite different. With characteristic flexibility, informed by humane understanding, Odysseus shifts from his early "toil" against Ajax (*ponein*, 24 and 38) to "toil" on his behalf (1366). His "enlightened self-interest" or "higher selfishness," as it has been called,[138] rests on that appreciation of human ephemerality which he expressed in the prologue (121–126): "I pity him (Ajax), enemy though he is . . . In this I consider his lot no more than my own. For I see that all of us who are alive are images or weightless shadows, nothing more." For the Atreids the nothingness and shadowiness of Ajax (1231, 1257; cf. 126) offer an opportunity for revenge: "If we could not conquer him while he was alive," Menelaus crudely tells Teucer, "we shall rule him in death" (1067–68). Agamemnon echoes his sentiments and is surprised that Odysseus opposes taking such "unseemly advantage" (1346–49).

When Agamemnon departs, Odysseus tells Teucer that he would like to "share in the burial" and "share in the toil" (*synthaptein, symponein*, 1378–79) and "omit nothing of those things in which mortals should toil for the best of men" (1379–80):

καὶ ξυμπονεῖν καὶ μηδὲν ἐλλείπειν ὅσων
χρὴ τοῖς ἀρίστοις ἀνδράσιν πονεῖν βροτούς·

This sharing of toil, then, rests on the respect which mortal men in general (*brotoi*) owe to great men (*aristoi*). Teucer's horizons are less large. His closing words, *tō(i) d' andri ponōn tō(i) pant' agathō(i)*, "toiling for this man who was in all respects noble" (1415), though echoing Odysseus' precept of "toiling for great men," are addressed only to *philoi* (1413), by which he means those linked to Ajax by ties of blood or homeland.

XV

The change from life to the shadowy nothingness of death of which Odysseus spoke in the prologue (125–126) is the harshest form of change which man has to undergo. This prospect leads Odysseus not to the stern fixity of Ajax, rejecting time and change for heroic absolutes but to its opposite, a humane flexibility rooted in the mind's grasp of the human condition. Ajax' prowess and value lay in being "unmovable." The virtue of his erstwhile enemy lies in being "moved" by the valor (*arete*) of a great man: "His valor moves me (*kinei*)[139] much more than his enmity," he tells Agamemnon, who is indignant that he should show respect for an enemy's corpse (1356–57).

Adapting the bitter wisdom of the old sage, Bias, Ajax had reflected that in this world one had to expect friends to become enemies and enemies friends (678–680). Ajax' "friends," the Greeks, have become his "enemies." His old enemy, Hector, had exchanged weapons with him as a friend (661–665). Odysseus, appropriately, exemplifies the complete cycle of change: he declares that he is now as great a friend as once he was an enemy (1377).[140] But this change, unlike Hector's, has a quality of Ajax' own permanence about it. Hector's gift was a single gallant gesture, an impulse of the moment, and even Ajax realizes that the underlying hatred remains unchanged (665, 817–818; cf. 1024–35). Odysseus' change involves deep, inward attitudes, not external tokens or conventions on the field of battle.

The refusal to accept change can be heroic or tragic, but it is not the mark of a civilized man.[141] Measured by that standard, both Ajax and the Atreids, and to some extent Teucer too, fall short. Agamemnon is as inflexible as Ajax. "There as well as here Ajax will be most hateful to me," he says in his last lines (1372–73), thereby grimly refuting Ajax' own theory of change (678–680).

Ajax had assumed that Teucer, a warrior like himself, would be able to secure his burial (826–830). But in this world in which Ajax could not live, loyalty, passion, and courage are not enough. For the commemoration of the greatness which Ajax' honor demands, the reasonableness, efficiency, persuasiveness, and compassion of an Odysseus are also necessary. Even in his quest for autonomy the tragic *apolis* needs the cooperative virtues of a *politikos*, a man with the skills of the city.

The humane flexibility of Odysseus represents the consolation that secular humanism can offer to the threats of the ultimate nothingness of our existence that Ajax confronts. But at the end the universalism of Odysseus gives way, after all, to family-centered ritual and kin ties. The *Ajax'* last tension is played out between the two poles of Odysseus and Teucer: the tolerant reasonableness of a man who can turn calmly away from a ritual which excludes him although he has made it possible, and the rootedness, intimacy, and security of a group defined by unchanging and unchangeable facts of blood and birth.

The funerary ritual at the end implies a civilized community that can enclose and affirm the lonely heroism of Ajax, just as the orderly ritual "context" of the tragic performance can enclose and enframe the sufferings and negations of order that it contains. Even as a corpse, however, Ajax seems to challenge the ritual framework with the massiveness of his death. Gentle Tecmessa's cloak had enfolded and concealed the horribly pierced body of the "raw-spirited" outcast (898–899, 915). Yet, as the body is about to be uncovered once more for its final purification, the "pipes" which blow their "black force" from Ajax' breast seem to play in harsh counterpoint against the flutes of the performers in the theater of Dionysus.

6

Antigone: Death and Love, Hades and Dionysus

Like other Sophoclean heroes, Antigone stands in an ambiguous relation to civilized values. She does so, however, not so much to assert a highly personalized individual honor, like Ajax, as to defend a valid and necessary aspect of civilization, the rights of the family and the proper treatment of the dead. By challenging one principle of civilization in the name of another, she generates a tragic division that calls the nature of social order itself into question. Her opponent is no Odysseus, spokesman of a moderate and humane society, but a rigid king who, like the Atreids of the *Ajax*, actually subverts the civilized principles that he should be defending.[1] Whereas Odysseus can lead the society out of its deadlocked conflict of values, no human figure can release Creon and Antigone from theirs. Teiresias comes closest to this function, but his intervention comes too late to save Antigone. In any case he is effective through his authority as the mouthpiece of the gods not through his human qualities per se.

The most famous lyrics in the *Antigone*, and one of the most famous passages in all Greek poetry, sing the praises of man and civilizer (332–375): "Many are the things of wonder (terror, *deina*) but nothing more wonderful (terrible) than man." This choral ode, the first stasimon of the play, draws on Sophistic speculation about the origin of human culture and invites us to consider the action of the play in this broad perspective of the achievement of civilization.

The ode extols man's invention of sailing, agriculture, domestication of animals, shelter, medicine, and law. It seems therefore to support the position of Creon, who begins as the embodiment of the secular rationalism of the Sophistic Enlightenment.[2] Nothing could be further from the truth. The subsequent action negates or qualifies nearly all the achievements which the ode celebrates. Sophocles' dramatic irony holds up to this radiant image of human intelligence a mirror that reflects a darker picture. This song of man's triumph is, as Linforth suggests, "a long concessive clause."[3]

At the point in the action at which the ode occurs, both city and family, ruler and private citizen have shown their most violent and most irrational side. The quarrel between the two sons of Oedipus, Polyneices and Eteocles, over the inheritance of the royal power, simultaneously uproots both city and family. The parode has described the violence of Polyneices' attack in the vivid bestial imagery of an eagle screeching over the roofs of the city or a beast thirsting for blood

(112–127). Creon himself soon echoes this language (201–202), but the ruler's very next lines themselves efface man's protection from the beasts (205–206). Images of men reduced to beasts recur soon after to describe Antigone's grief (423–425) and Creon's anger (473–479). Her defiance has already presented limits opposing Creon's civic control, and Creon's anger, both here and in the previous scene (241–331) has raised the question of whether this controller can control himself.

The ode praises man as the most *deinon* of all creatures (332–333). The epithet means "fearful" as well as "wonderful." The apartness of man as the most wonderful/terrible of all creatures is also the source of his tragic status.[4] This *deinotēs* points to the problematical part of his civilizing power: it denotes something elemental, gigantic, beyond the norms of ethical considerations. If his astonishing power frees man from the constraints that nature imposes on other creatures, it also makes him capable of greater extremes of violence. It thus makes him even "more terrible" (*deinoteron*) than the most terrible phenomena in nature.

In the ode in Aeschylus' *Libation Bearers* which Sophocles here echoes, the "terrible" monsters of sea, earth, and sky are a foil to the violent daring and passions of men and women (585–601). For Aeschylus man's uniqueness in nature is a negative rather than a positive quality: he stands alone in the vehemence and boldness of his lusts. In Sophocles' ode this boldness or daring, *tolma*, puts man outside the limits of civilization, makes him *apolis*, "citiless" (370–371). It is a quality which Creon imputes to Antigone: "Did you dare (*etolmas*) to transgress these laws?" he asks her (449). "To Creon," she explains in a later defense, "I seemed to be committing this wrong and daring terrible things" (*deina tolman*, 915). This "terrible daring" is already present in her readiness to follow what Ismene regards as her "ill counsel" and suffer her "terrible fate" (95–96).

The metaphors embedded in Creon's language echo the themes of the Ode on Man; sailing, yoking, trading. But these metaphors come to reflect not control and rationality but the unmasterable violence within man or man's helplessness before the gods.[5] The birds and the horse, which illustrate man's power to tame the beasts for his own ends (342, 343–344, 351) consistently describe passion and violence within the city. The struggle for the throne of Thebes is a battle between eagle and serpent (125–27).[6]

The ode boasts that man "has taught himself language and thought swift as the wind and the temper of lawfulness that creates the town" (354–356). But language, law, and thought all become precarious elements in this play which ends with a warning about "teaching thought" through disaster (1354). The chorus' word for "temper" here, *orgai* (356) also refers to the anger of the three main characters—Creon's (280), Antigone's (875), Haemon's (766). Anger also leads to the punishment of another imperious king, Lycurgus, who undergoes a metaphorical change to bestial status, "yoked" because of his "insulting anger" (*kertomioi orgai*, 956–957) toward Dionysus. In Lycurgus and Creon rational language disintegrates into insult.[7] Not thought, but madness, *mania*, and especially the madness of Eros or Dionysus, increasingly characterizes human action.[8]

Man possesses "the wise craft of device beyond expectation" (or, "beyond hope," *hyper elpida*, 365–366). But when the guard leads in Antigone for the scene which will challenge Creon's supposed rationality, he congratulates himself on his "joy outside of and beyond hope" (392). The unpredictability of human events ("Nothing is to be sworn impossible for mortals," 388) soon reverses the optimism of the guard, Creon, and the chorus. In the next ode hope can be a "help" (*onasis*) but can also be "the deception of light-minded loves" (615–617): through hope man seems as vulnerable to passion and deception as those "light-minded" birds which he traps (343). Creon's entrance line in this scene, just before the guard's pronouncement on hope, combines one of his favorite intellect words (*symmetros*, connoting quantitative measurement) with the ominous irrationality of chance, *tychē* (387): "What is it? In measure with what chance (*symmetros tychē(i)*) have I come forth?"[9] Chance later reveals its characteristic tragic destructiveness as Creon stands on that "razor's edge of chance" (996) which brings happiness or bad luck (1158–59; cf. also 328, 1182).

The cleverness of "device" (*machanoen*, 365), which Creon has incorporated into his state-centered ethic (cf. 175–177), has been implicitly challenged by "love for the impossible," where "device" seems of no avail (*amēchana*, 90, 92). Just before, the chorus praised man's intelligent "escape from overmaster diseases," "diseases without device" (*nosoi amēchanoi*, 363–364); but "diseases" are less easily evaded by technology (cf. 421). The one apparently in health proves to be the source of the disease (732, 1014, 1052, 1142). Man the "all-resourceful," (*pantoporos*) "comes to nothing in the future without resource" (*aporos*, 360–361); but this triumphant "resource" is also the "path" (another meaning of *poros*) which leads to the dark "roads" which Creon has to traverse at the end (1212–13 and 1274).[10] The future, *to mellon*, reflects not man's security in a benignly controlled world but his utter helplessness and ruin in a universe capable of strange and sudden reversals (cf. *to mellon*, 611; *mellonta tauta*, 1334). The annihilation of Creon's present world (1344–46) leaves him, finally, with no future at all: he has no wish to see another day (1331).

A very different view of nature emerges later in the play. Trying to persuade his father to relent, Haemon cites the natural world as a paradigm for yielding to change and time (712–718):

> You see how the trees which yield (*hypeikein*) by the streams' rushing torrents save their branches, but those which strain against the current perish root and all. And so whoever strains too much the ship's controlling rudder and does not yield at all (*hypeikei*) overturns and makes the rest of his voyage on a capsized hull. So do you yield (*eike*) in your anger and give way to change (*metastasis*).

This relation of harmony with nature correlates Creon's rigidity with the conquest of nature praised in the Ode on Man. Sailing plays a prominent part in both passages. The less easily controllable aspects of the world finally force Creon to yield, in a line that echoes the lead word of the Ode: "To yield is fearful" (*deinon*, 1096; contrast 690). His disaster is, finally, a kind of grotesque sailing to "Hades' harbor" (1284).

Whereas Creon's language and attitudes associate him with the aggressive, manipulative rationalism of the Ode on Man, Antigone appears as part of the human-dominated natural world. In her grief she is the mother bird lamenting her empty nest (423–425), the hunted animal (433). She herself compares her fate to that of Niobe, fused with the organic processes of nature, "she whom the growth of rock (*petraia blasta*) like close-winding ivy subdued" (826–827). The image inverts the conquest of nature reflected in the Ode on Man, for it is the rock, itself virtually instinct with vegetative life (*blasta*), that "subdues" (*damasen*) man.

In the great fifth-century debate between nature and convention, *physis* and *nomos*, Antigone stands on the side of nature. She defends those relations and aspects of life that man possesses by the given conditions of his birth against those which he creates by strength and force. Yet nature's rhythms do not teach her to yield any more than they do Creon. Her simile of Niobe connects her not with the yielding growth of the living trees of which Haemon spoke but with the "petrified growth" of rock. The entwining ivy in that passage is part of a simile which sets off the hardness of the rock itself (826). The Niobe passage focuses the tension between Antigone's responsiveness to life and her rejection of life.[11] While pointing downward to the natural world and its changeful life, it also points upward toward eternal, unchanging forms, the timeless world of myth, and death, in which Antigone sees herself "laid to rest" by divine powers, her daimon (832–833).[12] Like Ajax, but more poignantly because more closely bound to the personal bonds of blood, she has an ambiguous place between the rhythms of nature and the fixity of what is touched by the gods. Unmarried, she is the mother bird who has lost her fledglings (423) but also the human mother petrified in unchanging grief.

In the *Antigone*, as in the *Ajax* and much of early Greek poetry, time and man's ephemerality define man's nature.[13] Celebrating the power of Eros the chorus calls mortals *hamerioi*, "ephemerids," creatures subject to the changes of the day (789; cf. *Ajax* 399). A "creature of the day" should know how to allow for change. "Change," *metastasis*, is Haemon's word when he urges Creon to yield (718). It is also the word which Simonides used to characterize the swift passage to which human life is subject (521 Page): "Being a man never declare what will be tomorrow, nor seeing a man happy affirm for how long he will be so. For not even a long-winged fly's change (*metastasis*) is so swift."

Even in his conquest of nature man must follow the seasonal rhythms of the year, while nature herself is immortal. Hence Earth, Ge, is imperishable and unwearied (*aphthitos, akamata* (339), while the plow follows its toilsome movements as it "passes to and fro year in, year out" (340). "Unwearied Earth," after all, exhausts her human conqueror. At the end of the antistrophe the bull too, though subject to the human yoke, is likewise unwearied (*akmēs*, 353).

Like Ajax, Antigone's heroic determination reaches beyond time to the eternal. "Always," *aiei*, is her measure of time in two of her strongest statements of her principles (76, 456). Like Creon, she makes a quantitative calculation, but the "more time" (*pleiōn chronos*, 74) of her reckoning is the "always" of the dead (75–76). Her "profit" (*kerdos*) of time is radically different from the "profit" Creon envisages (461–464; cf. 312, 1037, 1047, 1055–56, 1061).[14] Yet the timelessness toward which she reaches in these two passages is not that of Zeus above, who "ageless in time holds the flashing brilliance of Olympus" (609–611) but rather the dark emptiness of the chthonic Zeus (452) and "the dead below" (75).

For the guard "long time" means the restless hours of his uneasy night vigil (422), for Creon the waiting period of his human justice ("to pay the penalty in time," 303), for the chorus and Haemon a sign of the weakness of human judgment, the age or youth which leads to error (681, 728). Only Antigone takes in a perspective beyond the tangible limits of man's powers or the anxieties and hesitations of those who must yield to human authority. In his first speech Creon uses "always" confidently of his power in the state (166; cf. 184), but he is bent by the sufferings which recall him to his ephemeral, transitory condition (718). Teiresias warns that he will not look on many circlings of the sun before disaster strikes (1064–66), and he himself, arrived at the final day (1330), asks never to look upon another day (1332). Yet Antigone too, for all her movements toward eternity, is still, like Ajax in his last speech, caught between time and the timeless. She may compare herself to the rock that Niobe became but the very comparison reminds us of the unfulfillment of her womanhood as she becomes "Hades' bride" (423–425, 569, 905ff., 1240–41).

A being so subject to time and its changes for the fulfillment or destruction of his life must be ready not only to yield, but also to learn. Learning or being taught (*manthanein, didaskesthai*) are among the most pervasive themes in the play.[15] The play closes with "learning sense in old age," which reminds us that learning takes place in time. It is a function not just of intellect but also of flexibility and openness to experience.

To learn, in this sense, is just what Creon, for all his rationalism, cannot do. Teiresias' plea, like Haemon's, that he yield and not be unmoved (*akinētos*, 1027), calls forth a torrent of abuse (1033ff.). His relation to time, therefore, acts out and resolves disastrously the tension between human control and time in the Ode on Man. Man's subjugation of the "imperishable" and "tireless' earth echoes against the "power" (*dynasis*) of the "ageless" and "tireless" gods in the ensuing ode (606–608), a statement of an almost antithetical attitude about man's control of his world. And in a still later ode the power that is *deinos*, "terrible," is not human at all but the mysterious power of destiny, given by the gods (*moiridia tis dynasis deina*, 951–952). Finally, the proud achievements and power of thought (*phronēma*) which man has taught himself (*edidaxato*, 354–356) are as nothing to the hard teaching of thought (*phronein*) that Creon will undergo in his old age (*gēra(i) to phronein edidaxan*, 1353; cf. *agērōs*, "ageless," in 608).

At quite the opposite extreme from Antigone's tragic movement into the timeless, Creon is caught in a bitter conflict between age and youth (719–720). The older man who bristled at being "taught sense" (*didaxomestha phronein*) by his young son (726–729) has to learn the hard lesson of yielding from both youth and age, from the young son and from the old prophet who tells him, "My child, be sensible (*teknon phronēson*) . . . Yield to the dead" (1023, 1029). Here, too, his violent refusal of this "good sense" inverts the proud achievements of the Ode on Man. Teiresias urges him to "heal" the hurt he has done (1027) and not to "goad" (*kentei*, 1030) the dead. The first metaphor recalls the Ode's victory over disease (364–365); the second applies to man the degrading treatment appropriate only to beasts.

II

Creon's treatment of the corpse destroys the distinction which human civilization draws between the death of men and the death of animals. He negates that division in an especially offensive way, for he reduces the human corpse to the status of carrion. The play which contains one of the most stunning exaltations of human achievement in Greek poetry has the desecration of a human being at the center of its plot.[16]

Early in the prologue Antigone reports the terms of Creon's decree (28–30): "No one should cover [Polyneices] in burial, not lament over him, but he must be left unwept, unburied, a sweet treasury for the birds looking upon him for the pleasure of their feeding." She grasps the meaning of the decree in the most immediate, physical terms. Her sense of civilized values is personal, specific, visceral. She pictures the corpse, exposed in wild places, the vultures circling over it eagerly in increasing numbers.[17] Her word for "feeding," *bora*, is generally used of animals;[18] "treasury," *thēsauros*, has its religious associations.[19] The juxtaposition harshly conveys both her bitterness and the violence done to man and to civilized values. The irony in the contrast of "feeding" and "treasury" powerfully conveys the degradation.

In the next scene, Creon's "intention" to expose the corpse is *phronēma* (207), the word which in the Ode on Man describes the "intelligence" that gives man his superiority over the beasts (355). Now to Antigone's birds Creon adds dogs and gives the "feeding" an even more graphic verbal form (*edeston*, 206). He is also more explicit about the visual impact: the citizens are "to look upon (*idein*) the body eaten by birds and dogs and outraged" (205–206). This last word, "outrage," *aikisthen*, from Homer on, carries a strong negative charge. It is to prevent further "outrage" of the corpse of Hector that the gods finally intervene against Achilles in the last book of the *Iliad*. The legalistic language of "decree" (203) clashes with the religious violation of the "outrage" that it licenses. The undermining of civilized values already implicit in a "treasury" which consists of human carrion is all the greater because the king himself speaks these words and is not even aware of the contradiction.

Haemon carries the horror of the exposed corpse a stage further when he describes how the city "laments this girl who refused to permit her own brother, fallen in the slaughter of battle, to lie unburied and be destroyed by raw-eating dogs and birds. Is not she worthy to receive golden honor?" (696–699). The effect here is analogous to the contrast between Ajax' "all-gold offerings" of garlands and the bloody victims of his "well-dipped" sword (*Ajax*, 91–95). The addition of "raw-eating," *ōmestai*, in 697 evokes the furious violence attaching to the mutilation of the corpse in Homer.[20] "Eating raw" also marks another basic violation of a fundamental division between civilization and bestiality. Over against that destruction of civilization stands the respect for family ties expressed in the previous line, "her own brother," *autadelphon* (696), which echoes Antigone's address to Ismene in her first line (*autadelphon*, 1). Sophocles uses that term for "brother" in only one other place in the extant plays, and that is in the preceding scene, where Antigone defends her action against Creon (502–503): "And yet how would I have won a fame more glorious (*eukleesteron*; cf. *erga eukleestata*, 695) than by laying my own brother (*autadelphon*) in the grave?" Haemon's speech, coming at the midpoint of the play, is not just a personal opinion but the judgment of the whole polis. Echoing the earlier descriptions of the outraged corpse, it both justifies Antigone's claims to honor (*kleos*, *timē*) and also shows us civilization reaffirming itself against this affront to its basic values.

When next we meet dogs and birds, the outrage which Creon's decree has committed expands to the cosmic order as a whole. "The altars and hearths," Teiresias says, "are full in their entirety with the carrion meat (*bora*) of the unfortunate fallen son of Oedipus thanks to birds and dogs" (1016–18). This speech, which describes the collapse of a basic civilized mediation between gods, men, and beasts, begins with intellect words which recall the noble achievements celebrated in the Ode on Man, "teach," "know," "art" (992, 996, 998). There is also sailing (994) and medicine (1015). The disruption of civilization expressed in the violated ritual of burial now spreads to the other forms of god-man mediation, sacrifice and prophecy (1003ff., 1019–22).

Prophecy, curiously enough, was omitted from the catalogue of man's civilizing arts in the Ode on Man, though it appears in analogous contemporary passages (Aeschylus, *Prometheus* 484–500 and 484–492 on augury specifically; Euripides, *Suppliants*, 211–213). The omission is all the more striking as Teiresias calls his knowledge a *technē* (998; cf. 366). Later in the play Creon's scorn for prophecy recoils on his own head (see 631, 988ff., 1034ff., 1055, 1059). The messenger begins his recital of his sudden calamity with gnomic utterances about fortune (*tychē*) of which "no one is a prophet" (1160). Creon himself, at the point of fateful approach to the cave, cried out, "Alas for me! Am I then a prophet?" (1211–12).

Creon's attitudes toward burial and prophecy represent analogous excesses of confidence in man's power to control his world. These reach their furthest extreme when Creon angrily retorts, "You will not cover him in burial, no, not even if the eagles of Zeus snatch him up and bear the carrion flesh (*bora*) to Zeus's throne" (1039–41). The sacrilege of this imagined upward movement, an act in which a man's body treated as an animal's, parallels Creon's inversion of the proper upward movement of the sacrificial smoke (1006ff.).[21] The repetition of "Zeus" (*Zēnos, Dios*) and the conversion of his eagles into birds of carrion make the sacrilege even more flagrant. Creon violates the two ritual acts which establish the boundaries between man, beast, and god: sacrifice, effecting an upward mediation between man and god; burial, distinguishing between man and beast. Zeus's eagle, guardian of the hierarchy separating beast, man, and god (cf. Pindar's *First Pythian*), becomes a bird of prey. Teiresias' details about the altars establish the parallel between burial and sacrifice, and Creon's violation of the division between man and beast appears as symmetrical with that between man and god. Prophecy, another form of mediation between man and god, is also disrupted, for the birds, having battened on human flesh, do not give their accustomed signs of augury (1021–22).[22]

The reply of the gods turns these inversions against Creon himself. When he finally attempts to perform the ritual ablutions for the corpse, he suffers a terrifying irruption of bestiality into his own life. The corpse, at this point called "torn by dogs," *kynosparakton* (1198), a word which occurs only here in the extant Sophocles, recalls that reduction of man to beast effected by the decree. Then the son attacks the father, a form of aggression which fifth-century authors regard as belonging in the world of animals, of wild nature or *physis*.[23] In this attack, moreover, Haemon occupies the quasi-bestial status of the madman, advancing against his father murderously "with wild eyes" (*agria ossa*, 1231–32).

Antigone's action, like Creon's, juxtaposes the human world with the two realms, inferior and superior, on either side. The burial of Polyneices has three possible perpetrators: beast, man, god. Creon, with his typically man-centered (and male-centered) point of view, asks at once, "who *of men* (*andrōn*) had the effrontery to do the deed?" (248). Given the details, he rules out beasts (257–258): "There appeared no trace of any beast or dog that had come up and torn the body." The chorus suggests that it may have been the gods (278–279). Their tone is reverent and tentative, and they use the solemn, evocative word, *theēlaton*, "god-sent," the word used of the curse and prophecy in the *Oedipus Tyrannus* (255, 992).[24] Creon thunders back, insulting their intelligence (281), that the gods would not bury a traitor (280–288). He falls back on "men," "men of the city" (289–290) who are trying to shake off his "yoke" (289–292). This last image includes his treatment of the corpse in his characteristic view of his subjects as animals, controlled and subjugated.

The scene ends with Creon's threats to the guard. Then, after the Ode on Man, Antigone, absent since the prologue, returns to the stage. She has been captured in the act of burying the corpse a second time. Why she returned for this second burial is one of the most puzzling details of the plot.[25] Presumably the first sprinkling of dust, as the guard said, would have averted the pollution (256). The difficulty is not a pseudo-problem, a minor detail which the audience would not observe. Sophocles emphatically calls attention to the two burials (434–435): "We charge her with the *previous* and the *present* deeds. She denied nothing." Antigone, of course, may have performed both burials out of a purely emotional desire to protect the corpse, even though she had already performed the requisite ritual sprinkling. Yet she never says in so many words, "I performed both acts"; nor does Sophocles ever *exclude* the possibility of burial by the gods. The chorus may have been right. This very possibility of divine intervention, vague as it is, introduces a dimension beyond the confident rationalism of Creon.

Creon had made the gods' nonparticipation a test case for his view of the moral order (280–303). The indefiniteness of the evidence, the kind of evidence which Creon's legalism could judge valid, qualifies his conception of the civic order and introduces the first major split between the world of the polis and a larger reality. Antigone's eagerness to accept the guilt for both burials might then be viewed as a part of the gods' plan, part of that mysterious game which they sometimes play with men.[26] The very violence of the reaction which the deed and the chorus' hesitant interpretation provoke in Creon creates the paradox, not unlike that of the *Tyrannus*, of intelligence blinded by its own confidence.

The evidence, in fact, had Creon listened to it, inclines in the chorus' favor. The indications of time, as Marsh McCall has suggested, point to, though do not definitely prove, the gods' agency in the first burial.[27] When Antigone is led forth as the perpetrator of the deed, the language of supernatural miracle resonates in strong counterpoint to the praise of human reason in the ode just preceding: "With respect to this divine prodigy (*daimonion teras*) I am of two minds" (376–377).[28] The circumstances of the second burial are mysterious: the strange dust storm and the "divine disease" which it brings (421). Its "outrage" (*aikizein*) to the watchers' bodies seems to answer the "outrage" of the corpse. So later the "rotting" stench of the corpse reappears as the "rotting" stain on the polluted altars (*mydōn*, 410, 1008). Such details do not justify reading back divine intervention into the first burial, but they do show that there are "more things in heaven and earth than are dreamt of" in Creon's philosophy. The clash of values in this first meeting of the two protagonists involves far more than individual personalities.

If the burial eludes Creon's much-vaunted power of intellectual calculation, it also negates another basic human achievement, the use of tools. There are no marks of axe, shovel, or wheel (249–252). The absence of tools might suggest beasts (see 257–258); it might also suggest the beings at the other end of the spectrum: gods. In the second burial Antigone's lack of implements as she carries the dust in her bare hands (429) has the pathos of heroic isolation.[29] When Creon finally moves to bury the corpse, he orders his men to take up tools (1109–10) but cannot of course avert the disasters which the violated rituals have set into motion. Antigone's bare hands, along with the bird simile of 423–425 and the hunting metaphor of 433, underline the irony that the one who performs this basic civilizing act is reduced by the decree of the city to less than human status. But this inversion only parallels the ambiguity of values created by Antigone's deed: piety is impiety (74, 924); decree clashes with law, and the laws of the city clash with the "unwritten laws" of the gods below (450ff.). In the failure of Creon's polis to mediate between beast and god, the one who performs this most basic act of civilization is cast outside the pale of humanity and enters the beast world. And yet the deed done in this beastlike way may be the work of gods.

In defining the polis in terms of its man-made, rational structures, Creon in fact exposes their fragility. He is then constrained to travel the tragic road of discovering his own humanness through the limits of his strength and weakness. Moral and civic order in Greek thought, though closely linked with the divine order, does not have that link given as an absolute certitude. There is a large area of autonomy to be tested and discovered, and that is the field for tragic suffering. Within the limits of strict legalism Creon's exposure of Polyneices' corpse may be justified but the relation to the larger divine order remains to be resolved.[30] The city's laws have no clearly revealed divine authority. The Greek king, unlike the Biblical King David, cannot safely boast,

> This day will the Lord deliver thee into my hand; and I will smite thee; and I will give the carcasses of the host of the Philistines this day unto the fowls of the air, and to the wild beasts of the earth, that all the earth may know that there is a God in Israel . . . ; for the battle is the Lord's, and he will give you into our hand. (1 *Sam.* 17:46)

III

"Speech he has taught himself and windlike thought": "speech," *phthegma*, opens the second half of the Ode on Man (354). Recognized as a vital step in the development of civilization by contemporaries of Sophocles, language is here closely associated with "the temper that creates the laws of the town" (355).[31] The *Antigone*, concerned especially with this communal and civilizing function of language, also shows language divided between its private and public, familial and civic functions. The conflict between state and family rights polarizes language as well.

In the very first scene public speech, the decree, appears as part of an anonymous, ill-defined public voice (7–8): "What is this decree," Antigone asks, "which they say (*phasi*) that the general has just established for the city's whole populace?" (*pandēmō(i) polei*). Over against this rumored public decree stands the personal anxiety of the two sisters. The lack of any tale about their loved ones, *mythos philōn* (11), is part of Ismene's uneasiness. Antigone sharpens this contrast between public and private *logos* (speech) in her next lines. Mentioning Creon by name for the first time (he was only "the general" in 8), she reports the details of the decree which, "they say" (*phasi*, 27), keeps the body unburied and unlamented. Then for the third time, Antigone repeats "they say . . . decree" (31–32): "Such are the things *they say* (*phasi*) that the good Creon has *decreed* for you and me, yes, *I say* (*legō*) for me" (cf. *phasi . . . kērygma*, 7–8; *phasin ekkekērychthai*, 27). The contrast is not merely between a public voice of rumor or decree and a private tale of friends (*mythos philōn*) but between "they say" and an assertive "I say" (*legō*) in the first person. That polarization deepens as greater emphasis is placed on the negative side of the public *logos*, what the city and its ruler have "forbidden" (44, 47).

The parode takes the division of the *logos* back in time. Here the contentiousness of the brothers transforms speech into "strife-riven disputes" (*neikea amphiloga*, 111) and the cry of beasts of prey as Polyneices, "man of many disputes" (*neikea*), appears in the image of a "shrill-screaming eagle" (113–114). That quarrel of brothers in the parode has a parallel, just before, in the degeneration of the intimate conversation of sisters into quarrel (84–87):

> Ism.: But at least do not inform any one of this deed. Rather hide it in secret, and I will do likewise.
> Antig.: Alas, cry it out. You will be much more hateful in keeping silence if you do not announce it (*kēryxē(i)s*) to all.

Antigone's "announce," *kēryttein* (87), is the verb used consistently for Creon's decree. Usurping his word, she mounts a total challenge to the civic *logos*. Ismene had replied to Antigone's opening speech with concern that they had no tale of dear ones, *mythos philōn* (11). As kinship becomes hatred for the brothers, so for the sisters a private tale of dear ones moves to a bitter *logos* that is to be "announced" in public and "decreed to all" (87). The parallel inversions of language between the sisters in the prologue and the brothers in the parode throw both private and public communication into crisis.

If Antigone's private world usurps public words like "decree" and "law" (cf. 450ff.), Creon's speech belongs entirely to the civic realm. For him speech consists in giving orders, and we may contrast her angry "I would not order you to do this" as she flares up against Ismene's hesitation to defy the decree. How different from Creon's authoritarian mode is Antigone's way of broaching her plan to Ismene (41):

εἰ ξυμπονήσεις καὶ ξυνεργάσει σκόπει·

Consider if you would share the toil and share the deed with me.

No direct command, but verbs of "joining," compounded with *syn-*, "together with," begin her plea. Yet thirty lines later she rejects any such common action (69–70): "I would not order you; nor even, should you be willing to do this, would I have any pleasure in your sharing (*meta*) that act with me." By the end of that first scene neither intimate conversation nor logical persuasion nor authoritarian orders can carry the messages that Antigone has to convey. But, even as both protagonists become progressively less able to communicate with those closest to them, they paradoxically draw together into a common pattern.

Creon's opening words are characteristic of his speech, which is marked by gnomic statements full of weighty, commonplace generalization. On his scale of values the lowest point (*kakistos*) is the man who withholds *logos* for the city (180–181) or keeps silent when he sees disaster approaching for his fellow citizens (185–186). We may contrast Antigone's very different remarks about speech and silence a hundred lines earlier (86–87).

Creon's *logos* is an instrument of rule. For him, as for the Atreids in the *Ajax*, communication is one-way: the leader speaks and the subjects "hear" or "obey" (*klyein*, 666). His encounter with the guard in the first episode is marked by impatience and violence about speech (241–244, 283, 315) and ends with an exchange of insults about speaking and hearing (316–320). The scenes with Haemon and Teiresias follow similar patterns (731ff., 1053ff.). Language also reflects his suspiciousness about the "profit" that motivates men (cf. 1045–47, 1061, 1077–78). Antigone's utterances are not proverbial generalizations but the forbidden wails of lamentation (423). Compared to the cry of a bereaved mother bird, these thus have a kinship with the subdued natural world in the Ode on Man. The word which she "darkly forms" in the first scene (*kalchainous' epos*, 20) associates her language both with the conquered sea of the first stasimon, and also with the mysterious forces which both sea and darkness symbolize in the play.[32]

For Antigone, words take second place to feelings. "I do not love a friend who loves in words," she says rather cruelly of Ismene (543). Creon, of course, has no sympathy with these emotional *logoi* and cuts off speech, as he often does, with insult: "Don't you know that, if it would avail, no one would ever stop saying his chants and lamentation (*aoidas kai goous*) before dying," he says, as he commands Antigone to be taken away "as quickly as possible" to her underground tomb "as I have spoken" (883–886).

For Creon Antigone's *hybris* or outrage of public order lies not only in having done the deed but in her manner of communicating it, "boasting and laughing at what she has done" (482–483; cf. 435). She openly rejects his *logoi* (499–500) and in fact challenges one of his central principles. He had labelled *kakistos*, "basest," the man who out of fear kept his mouth closed (180–181). Antigone says that the others would speak in sympathy with her "if fear did not close their mouths" (505). One of the privileges of tyranny, she goes on, is that it can do and say what it wants (506–507). "They see the truth," she continues, "but make their tongues cower to you" (509). The verb translated "cower," *hypillein*, is used of animals putting their tails between their legs in fear. It is also the word used of the plow's movement in the conquest of the earth in the first stasimon (340). In conjunction with Creon's metaphors of the bit and bridle shortly before (477), it reflects the collapse of the distinction between man and beast wherein civilization consists. One is reminded of the tyrannical city of Plato's *Republic*, where the relations are between beasts, not men.[33]

In the scene with Haemon, a sharp stichomythia shows Creon's perverted concept of *logos*. (733–735, 752–758). When Haemon tries to break through his father's authoritarian *logos* of total obedience (733–734, 748), Creon calls his speech a whining and slavish entreaty for a woman (756).[34] Haemon's rejoinder hits the exposed nerve of the truth (757): "Do you then want to speak and speaking get back no answer to hear?" The considered speech of the old king is, as his son points out, full of youthful violence (735; cf. 719–720, 726–727). Confusion in the hierarchies of language parallels confusion in the hierarchies of the generations. Language and family are interwoven with politics in the increasingly questionable order of Creon's city.

Over against the rational *logos* praised in the Ode on Man, therefore, stand utterances of a different sort: the "dark" saying of Antigone in 20; the quarrels of the two brothers, where the effect is strengthened by the etymological play on Polyneices' name (110–111); threats (128–129, 480–483, 756ff.); the "dark rumor" of the city that creeps up in silence and stealth to dispute Creon's decree (700); the shrill lamentation over the dead which, despite his prohibition of lamentation over the corpse (29, 204), spreads to his own house as he wails over his own corpses (1207, 1210–11, 1226–27, 1302, 1316);[35] the ominous prophecies; the terrible curses (427, 1296, 1304–1305). The "heavy silence" and the "multitude of shouts in vain" shortly after Eurydice enters the house (1250–51) are a grim reduction of glorious speech in the Ode on Man. Finally, the big words (*megaloi logoi*) of overboastful men (*hyperauchōn*) in the chorus' closing remarks, exact their punishment and, in a vivid personification, "teach wisdom in old age" (1350–53).

The inversions in language, ritual, and family are all bound together. Creon's scornful "Let her sing her hymn to Zeus who looks after kindred blood" (*Dia syn-haimon*, 658–659) brings together in a shocking way ritual forms relating to the dead and the religious practices centering on the family.[36] The Zeus whom he cites ironically here is *Zeus Herkeios*, Protector of the Family, whose altar stood in the courtyard of the house. Creon had in fact mentioned this god of the sanctities of house and kinship in another demeaning remark about kindred blood (*syn-haimōn*, 486–489). But that scorned inner space of house and family will prove not so easily dismissed as Creon finds there "sorrow of his own house" (*penthos oikeion*, 1249; cf. *oikeion kakon*, 1187), where silence or cries of grief in that interior space of "shelter," "house," or "inmost recesses" (*hypo stegēs*, 1248; *en domois*, 1279; *en mychois*, 1293) wipe out the king's confident decrees and gnomic speeches in the public spaces of his city. In Creon's own house the roles of father, son, and mother undergo a series of grim reversals: Eurydice, whose ritual lamentation for her son recalls Antigone's for her brother (*kōkysasa*, 1302; cf. *anakōkyei*, 423), stands by the altar (*bōmia*, 1301) and "hymns" curses upon Creon as "killer of sons" (1304–1305): we recall Creon's mocking of Antigone's "hymns to Zeus who looks after kindred blood" (*eph-hymneitō*, 658; cf. *eph-hymnēsasa*, 1305). Now Creon's proud, imperious commands and assured commonplaces change to the staccato lyrics of acute grief.[37]

The birds in Teiresias' warnings not only echo the passions that destroy human communication but also disrupt the voices that tell man of the purposes of the gods. Language that differentiated between man and beast in the Ode on Man now breaks down as mediation between man and god. "Taking my place in the ancient seat of my bird-watching," says Teiresias, "where I had a harbor of refuge for every bird, I heard the birds' unfamiliar cry, shrieking with the dire gadfly sting of madness made barbarous" (999–1002).[38] The last line is dense and powerful: *klazontas oistrō(i) kai bebarbarōmenō(i)*. The parode's harmonious choral song joyously celebrated the defeat of the "shrieking eagle" (*oxea klazōn*, 112) as a metaphor for the jarring quarrels of the two brothers (cf. *Polyneikēs . . . neikeōn ex amphilogōn*, "Man of Many Quarrels . . . quarrels of divided words," 110–111). The shrieking (*klazontas*, 1002) of angry birds returns when the threats to the order of the polis are neither entirely outside the walls nor even entirely human. The diction of line 1002 correlates the frenzy of animalistic madness with the loss of intelligible speech (*bebarbarōmenos*).[39]

Along with this loss of speech, the birds, like their human counterparts, lose the capacity to form a peaceful society and, like the eagle of the parode (112–113), tear at each other with death-dealing claws (1003). This combination of unintelligibility, madness, violence, bestialization, and social disintegration is soon transferred to the human world when the voice of the maddened son "fawns" on the father and king (1214). Then the son, attacking his father, looks on him with savage eyes (1231),[40] utters no word in reply (*ouden anteipōn*, 1232), and spits in animal fashion (1231–32), an ironical answer to Creon's demand that he "spit out" Antigone to Hades (653–654). "The voice of woe" of Creon's own house (*phthongos oikeiou kakou*, 1187–88) which "smites through" his ears and the "voice of a son" which "fawns" give language an ominous autonomy, as if this instrument of man's control of his world has escaped human direction.[41]

The contrast between the wondrous achievement of language in the Ode on Man and the eaglelike scream of Polyneices' attack continues as a leitmotif throughout the choral odes. The curse on the house of Oedipus in the second stasimon holds "madness of speech, Fury of the mind" (*logou anoia kai phrenōn Erinys*, 603–604), a combination which Teiresias' warnings later apply to Creon himself (1089–90). Eros in the third stasimon returns to the quarrel (*neikos*) among those of kindred blood of the parode (793; cf. 111). Madness, insulting speech, and anger come together again in the story of King Lycurgus in the fourth stasimon (955–965): he not only uses an insulting tongue (*kertomioi glōssai*, 962–963; cf. *kertomiois orgais*, 956–957) but also destroys the harmonious sounds of the Muses (965). The last ode seems to restore this musical side of Dionysus, invoked as the "chorus-leader of . . . stars, overseer of the night's voices" (1146–48); but his dance of the constellations beckons us to a large and calm harmony only when it is hopelessly remote from the shattered and discordant human world of the closing scenes.

Logos informs the conflicts of the *Antigone* in another way, too, namely in a contrast between *mythos* and *logos*, between a "mythical" and "rational" mode of apprehending reality, a dichotomy much discussed among Sophocles' contemporaries. The Ode on Man, with its rationalistic confidence, is the only ode in the play without mythical allusions. It is as if the spirit of reason, extolling itself, displaces myth as the principal mode of understanding and structuring reality.

Rejection of the mythical and the sacred informs Creon's scornful, irreverent way of speaking of Zeus or Hades (see 486–487, 658–659, 1039–40; 575, 580–581, 776–780). His cold line, "There are other fields for Haemon to plow"

(569), subsumes Eros too into his secular rationalism. The lyric expression of grief in song and lamentation (*aoidai, gooi*, 883) only excites his anger and impatience. He never speaks in a lyric meter himself until the disintegration of his rational world at the end of the play. Coherent rational discourse now collapses into inarticulate cries: *io io, aiai, aiai; oimoi; pheu pheu* (1283–84, 1290, 1294, 1300, 1306).

For Antigone, on the other hand, the world of myth is a living reality. To the chorus' discomfort (823–838) she identifies herself with Niobe. Between the present moment and the timeless realm of myth the chorus erects a barrier that for Antigone does not exist. For her the gods of the lower world, the chthonic Zeus, Hades, Acheron, exist with an intense reality that no one else in the play feels (cf. 451–452, 542, 810–816). And along with this feeling for what we may broadly call *mythos* go a deep feeling for and an identification with the ancestral past and its ancient curse, of which she speaks repeatedly, from her first words to her last (2, 857–866). The dead in Hades are virtually present to her (898–904, 913–915). For Creon, on the other hand, though we are twice told of the suffering of his house in the past (626–627, 1303), life centers upon a static, gnomically comprehensible present or a future rationally calculable in terms of gain (*kerdos*).

IV

Of all the achievements of human civilization in the Ode on Man, one item is conspicuous by its absence: fire, the source of all technology in the Hesiodic and Aeschylean anthropologies, is not mentioned at all. It has an important role, however, in the language and imagery of the play: it denotes not man's control over his environment but either the savagery within man that threatens civilization or the forces beyond man that transcend it. In the first category belong the fires which Polyneices brought against his native city (122, 131, 135, 200–201); in the second, at the opposite extreme, are the remote "fire-breathing stars" of Dionysus' "chorus" in the night sky (1126–30).[42] King Lycurgus, similar in some ways to the present king of Thebes, is "yoked," that is, afflicted with a bestial punishment, for "trying to stop . . . the Bacchantic fire" (965). In describing the sacrificial fire, Teiresias calls it "Hephaestus" (1007), not merely a "Homeric" metonymy[43] but an indication of fire as something sacred and divine, more than a human invention or convenience.

The Guard's willingness "to walk through fire" (265) to prove his veracity makes no impression on Creon. The passage finds an echo in the second stasimon, where it is connected with the irrational force of unexpected disasters (617–619).[44] Creon uses fire in a metallurgical simile which also implicitly treats men as beasts, the spirited horse (477–478) controlled by the bridle (473–476): "Know that thoughts (*phronēmata*) that are too harsh do most fall low, and the firmest iron, baked too hard in the fire, you would most often see shattered and broken." Even here the image of technology is negative: the artifact breaks; the tempering fire fails.[45]

Shelter, according to the Ode on Man, distinguishes human life from bestial. The beast walks on the mountains and inhabits his wild lair, while men have "taught themselves the temper of lawful towns and flight from the open-air stormy missiles of frost that make hard lodging" (354–360; cf. *agrauloi*, 349 and *dysauloi*, 356). But this image of human shelter has already been challenged by Polyneices' animal-like attack upon Thebes (112–113, 120–121) which makes that "temper of lawful towns" look precarious. The gates and walls which have protected Thebes (101, 141–143) can keep out an enemy but also exclude a friend with legitimate claim to its shelter. Creon's edict exposes men of the polis to the violence of the open air (411, 416, 418 with 357). "Thought like the wind," in the Ode on Man echoes ironically against the exposure of the guards "beneath the winds" (411) as they try to escape the stench of the rotting corpse. The dust storm which enables Antigone to spread the dust due to the dead and the gods below the earth is "a trouble in the sky" or, as the phrase might also mean, "a celestial grief" (*ouranion achos*, 418).[46]

The place where the corpse is exposed is the utter negation of the sheltered space of the polis. Again and again Sophocles reminds us of its desolation (see also 1110, 1197–98).[47] Antigone, first seen against the background of house and palace ("outside the gates of the courtyard," 18), is immured in a place "where the path is deserted of mortals" (773), a cave where no human being should dwell, a terrible "caverned dwelling" (*oikēsis*, 892) which offers no shelter to a living person. The deserted (*erēmos*) quality of this cave (773, 887, 919) parallels the remote and exposed place of Polyneices' exposure. Haemon points out to his father that his authoritarian rule would leave him with a deserted city (739), cancelling out the shelter of a civilized habitation. Teiresias' birds, at the borders of city and wild, indicate with their maddened cries (998ff.) that the king has brought disease and disturbance within the city (1015, 1080). Then Creon will himself enter the dark cave, meet its "savagery" (1231–32) and walk on wild roads (1274). The metaphor of walking or advancing accompanies the full "resourcefulness" of man in the great ode (360–361). But the outlaw who goes beyond the limits of Creon's *nomoi* (*hyperbainein*, 449, 481, 663; cf. 59–60, 1351) and "strides to the furthest extreme of boldness," in the chorus' criticism of Antigone (852), may have the more justified place within the civilized polis.[48]

The spatial limits of vertical movement are as ambiguous as those of horizontal: the one who is "high in the city" and the one "without city" (*hypsipolis*, *apolis*, 370) may be one and the same or may exchange places.[49] Here again opposites fuse. The absolute division between *apolis* and *hypsipolis* blurs. The ruler clashes with the united opinion of his people (*homoptolis leōs*, 733; cf. 739). The girl buried in the deserted cave has a valid place at the center of the polis and its values. Creon, if not made actually *apolis*, "citiless," is left virtually without hearth through the curses and suicide of the wife of his house and its altars or hearth (cf. 374 and 1301).

The "blasts of wind" which buffet Antigone's soul in the chorus' description of her passion (929–930) recall the violence of Polyneices' attack (135–137) and the irrationality of the family curse, symbolized in the wind-tossed seas of Thrace of the second stasimon (588–593). Burial in the isolated cave is also in part (but only in part) a symbolic fulfillment of her devotion to death and her violent rejection of living kin. Her ambiguously "reverent irreverence" or "pious wrong-doing" (924 and 74), her harshness toward Ismene, her enormous concern with honor (see *kleos*, 502), her devotion to death and to Hades reveal a heroism as problematical as that of any Sophoclean protagonist.[50] The fact that she has much of the right on her side does not mean that she has all of the right. In her last lines she, like Ajax, addresses her ancestral city (937) and calls herself the last of its ruling line. Yet the heroic exemplar that she chooses for herself is the remote queen in the mountains of Asia Minor, exposed forever in her rocky metamorphosis to the rain and snow from which man's great achievements have devised shelter (828–30; cf. 356–359).

V

> Possessing the clever skill of craft beyond all hope, he creeps now to woe, now to noble life, honoring (?) the laws of the earth (*nomous chthonos*) and the oath-bound justice of the gods (*theōn enorkon dikan*), high in his city; citiless is he to whom baseness clings because of his rash daring (*tolma*). May he have no place at my hearth nor share my counsels, he who does such things. (365–375)

"The laws of the earth" and the "oath-bound justice of the gods": both Antigone and Creon claim to honor these sanctions, and both Antigone and Creon refuse to do so. Each one, therefore, is *hypsipolis* and *apolis*, though in contrasting ways: Creon's limited view of civilization makes him "citiless" when he seems "high in his city"; Antigone's heroic defense of one set of "laws of the earth," far more literally than the chorus means here, makes her "high in her city" (see 692ff., 733) at a moment when she is legally and literally *apolis* (see 508, 656, "alone of all the city"). Creon is subsequently revealed as a bane to the city (1015, 1080). As leader after civil war, he seems to have restored a divided unity of the polis. That unity now shatters about him, again through a member of the house of Oedipus, who, ironically, has the voice of the people in their civic harmony (*homoptolis*, 733; cf. 692–700).[51]

Nomos (*nomoi*, pl.) carries a wide range of meanings: "institution," "custom," "universal norm," "law of a state." Most of its meanings have to do with the values which make civilization possible, with "the temper that governs the towns with law" (*astynomoi orgai*, 355–356) that man has taught himself. The ode hesitates between law as humanly created (by and large the Sophistic position) and law as divinely sanctioned ("the oath-bound justice of the gods," 369). This hesitation, along with the wide range of meanings in *nomos* itself,[52] leaves a broad field for the inversions in the two protagonists' relation to civilization.

For Antigone *nomos* is personal, familial, emanating from the gods, eternal, (450ff., 519, 905–908, 913–914)[53]; for Creon *nomos* is secular and civic: above all, it demands obedience and discipline (see 175–191). He identifies the *nomoi* with his decrees and indeed with his own personal voice. The whole of his little speech on his political philosophy begins and ends with "I" (184 and 191; cf. also 173, 178). His civic order subsumes the divine. As his lines on Polyneices' attack make clear, shrines, temples, earth, and *nomoi* all stand on the same footing. "Did the gods bury him," he asks indignantly after the chorus' suggestion of divine intervention, "the man who came to burn their columned temples and their dedications and their earth and to disperse their laws?" (284–287). The phrasing of line 287 is important:

> ὅστις ἀμφικίονας
> ναοὺς πυρώσων ἦλθε κἀναθήματα
> καὶ γῆν ἐκείνων καὶ νόμους διασκεδῶν· (285–287)

We may also translate, "the man who came to burn their columned temples and dedications and disperse their earth and laws."[54] In that case Creon views earth not as part of nature but as an extension of the laws of the state. His stress on the "earth of the fatherland," *patrōa gē* in 199 (cf. also 110 and 113), makes the same assumption. In the Ode on Man, however, earth, though subdued, is still a god, Ga, "imperishable, timeless, highest of gods" (338–339). The earth Antigone snatches at with her hands in the remote place where her brother lies is hard, dry ground, *styphlos gē* (250), uncultivated, "unbroken, untraversed by wagons' wheels" (251–252).

Creon's *dikē*, like his "laws" of earth, though it seems at first to be the impartial "justice" that holds the city together, becomes increasingly personal and emotional (cf. 400, 1059), increasingly distant from the "oath-bound justice of the gods" praised in the Ode on Man (369). He can even go so far as to require obedience to the city "in what is just and *the opposite*" (666–667). Antigone's *dikē* is the justice due the dead and the gods below (94, 451, 459–460). It is private, exclusive, jealously guarded (cf. 538).

Both Creon and Antigone, however, encounter another kind of *dikē* and *nomos*. Antigone "stumbles against the lofty throne of Dike" (853–855). This justice belongs with the Olympian gods, in contrast to her *dikē* ("Justice who dwells with the gods below," 451). Creon encounters the "law" of the gods connected with *atē* and the powers of the lower world (the Erinys, 613–614).[55] He has to yield, in fear, to "the established laws" (1113–14) and thereby seeks to restore to *nomoi* their civilizing function as "the norms of a well-ordered society"[56] but too late to avert his own doom. As much as Antigone he experiences the power of Eros which is indifferent to justice (791). He too is touched by the law about the curse and infatuation (613–614) which is less submissive or rational than the laws he enforces. "Alas, you see justice (*dikē*) late, it seems"

(1270), the chorus tells him, near the end. Neither figure embodies a "law" or a "justice" which is fully satisfactory as a civilizing principle; each encounters "laws" and "justice" that destroy his or her own cherished and exclusive view. Creon's doom also shows that merely "keeping the established laws" is not enough. Antigone's tragic heroism has set another "law" and another "justice" into motion (613–614, 791).

VI

Unlike other fifth-century culture histories—notably those of Aeschylus, Protagoras, and Democritus—the Ode on Man makes no reference to the development of religion and worship as a creation of human civilization.[57] Yet, as we have already seen, piety and reverence prove major issues in the clash of values between the two protagonists. Polyneices, if we can believe the chorus of Creon, committed impious acts against the gods and their shrines (110–127, 134–137, 285–287). But this makes not a jot of difference to Antigone, whose reverence is all for the principle of blood kinship, *homosplanchnous sebein*, "to revere those of the same womb" (511). The charge of sacrilege against her brother is simply irrelevant, for, as she says defiantly to her accusers, "Hades demands equal laws" (519).

Creon has no grasp at all of her ambiguous "pious wrongdoing" or "impious piety" (74, 924). With the former expression one should compare his tirade against the corruptions of money (300–301): "This has shown to men wrongdoing (*panourgias*) and the knowledge of impiety (*dyssebeia*) in every deed." His rationalistic mentality dissolves the complexity of Antigone's oxymoron. "Wrongdoing" and "impiety" are independent entities, and both are defined in terms of the polis (cf. 296). His "reverence" and "oath" (*horkios*, 305; cf. 369) in the next lines are in fact for the force of his own authority, even though he mentions Zeus (304). Later he plays loose and free even with reverence for Zeus (487, 1040–41). His main demand is "reverence always for the power of the throne" (166). Later he asks Haemon, "Do I err then in revering (*sebōn*) my own power?" (*tas emas archas*). Infuriated by the honest reply, he asserts, self-righteously, "You have no reverence (*ou sebeis*), at least when you trample down the prerogatives of the gods" (744–745). Haemon makes no impression on his father, whose last words in the scene are a twice-repeated mockery of Antigone's "reverence for Hades" (777, 780).[58]

In the Ode on Man earth appears both as part of subjugated nature—the source of man's food as he plows it year by year with his equally subjugated "race of horses" (338–341)—and at the same time as a goddess, "Ga, highest of the gods (*hypertatan Gan*), imperishable, unwearying" (337–339). The basic civilized art of tilling the earth, then, appears both as a possible affront to a divine power and a petty, insignificant scratching at something eternal and invulnerable (339).[59] The chorus soon praises the "high-citied man" for "honoring" [reading *gerairōn* with Jebb] "laws of the land" (*nomoi chthonos*, 368–370; cf. 187). But *nomoi chthonos* can also mean "laws of earth" which point away from that "highest earth" of 337 to the dark lower world for which and in which Antigone dies.[60] This tension between earth as passive nature and earth as goddess, earth as "highest" and as "lowest," then expands to a very different view of agriculture in the nether god's destructive "mowing" (601–603), where "earth's" subterranean associations are a dark foil to the confident "speech" and "wind-like thought and temper of lawful governance of towns" in the Ode on Man (354–356). The adjective "wind-like," *anemoen*, connects the civilizing intelligence with the upper air. But the hostile "missiles of storm beneath the sky" in the next lines, like "highest earth" in the first strophe, make that upper realm ambiguous, too. In withholding burial, Creon in effect dishonors Zeus's throne later in a blasphemous upward movement from beast to god, earth to heavens (1040ff.).

The offerings that should mount upward to establish the *charis* or favorable mediation between gods and men sputter and ooze downward like the clinging smoke of Heracles' sacrifice in the *Trachiniae* (794). What should go up goes down, and vice versa (1008–1011). As Teiresias tells him soon after (1068–73):

> You have put below one of those from the realm above and made a living soul to have his house (*katoikizein*) in a tomb, and in turn you have kept here, in this realm, one of those who belongs to the gods below, deprived of his due portion, deprived of burial rites, deprived of sanctity. In these neither you nor the gods above have a rightful share, but thus are they [the lower gods] violated by you.

The dust storm prefigures the consequences of this perverted relation between highest and lowest. Here the dust of the earth (*chthōn*) rises anomalously and destructively upward to the sky (*ouranion*, 417–418) at the time when "the bright orb of the sun stands in the midpoint of the aether" (416–417). This storm, moreover, enables Antigone to give the corpse that covering of dust which is due to "one of those below" and to the gods below the earth. That storm itself is "a trouble in the sky," *ouranion achos*, a suggestive phrase which can also mean "a trouble sent from (or by) the sky" or "a celestial grief." In these latter two meanings it suggests the cooperation of the Olympian gods above with the outraged gods below. A few lines later the guard calls it a "divine disease" (*theia nosos*, 421), and this too spreads to the whole city in a movement which complements the storm as "a celestial grief": as the birds bring their carrion down from the sky to the altars on the earth (116–117, 1082–83), they disrupt the normal upward mediation of the sacrificial rite (1005ff.).

Caught between the Olympian order of the polis and the earth deities of family, human and natural fertility, and death, the house becomes the turbulent center for these tensions between upper and lower realms.[61] In the family curse of the second stasimon, upper and lower, earth and light, undergo reciprocally destructive inversions (600–603):

νῦν γὰρ ἐσχάτας ὑπὲρ
ῥίζας ὃ τέτατο φάος ἐν Οἰδίπου δόμοις,

κατ᾽ αὖ νιν φοινία θεῶν τῶν νερτέρων
ἀμᾷ κόνις . . .

The light had been stretched *above the last root* of the house of Oedipus; now in turn the bloody dust of the nether gods mows it down.

In the first sentence the "light" stands anomalously "above" the "root." In the second, the earth ("dust," *konis*) itself, like the uplifted dust of the storm in the second episode (415–421), arises for its deadly downward harvesting of the living.[62] Light over the root is answered by the sinister inversion of dust below (cf. *nerterōn*) which mows "down" (*kat-*) light.[63]

In the following scene Haemon begins his important speech to Creon with the words, "Father, the gods plant (*phyousi*) intelligence in man as the highest (*hypertaton*) of all things that exist" (683–684) The "height" of this intelligence (*hypertaton* emphatically at the end of the line) contrasts with the "growth" or "planting" (*phyousi*) that still binds man to earth. In the Ode on Man intelligence (*phronēma*) was man's own creation (354–356); here intelligence (*phrenes*) is the gift of the gods. There agriculture was defined as man's subjugation of earth, "highest of the gods" (337–338); here it is the gods who do the "planting" in a very different notion of man's relationship to the natural world (cf. 710ff.). To put the relation between these two passages into other terms, man's creation of intelligence is to intelligence "planted" by the gods as his subjugation of earth beneath his plow is to earth's status as "highest of the gods." "Terrible" in mastering by reason what is on the surface of the earth, man's intelligence proves inadequate to deal with the dark secrets below, including Death (361), and the mysterious operations of the gods above.[64]

Later in the same speech Haemon accuses his father of "trampling" the laws of the gods (745); but when Thebes is "honored as the highest of cities" later (*hypertatan poleōn*, 1137–39), it is by a god whose ritual fire flashes "above (*hyper*) the twin-peaked rock" (1126; cf. *hyper klityn*, 1145). Even Dionysus' birth from a mortal mother, destroyed by the sky god's lightning (1139), and his place in the "folds of Eleusinian Demeter" (1120–21) link him with the earth. Immediately after, Creon himself will literally enter the earth and the first stage of his figurative plunge to the "harbor of Hades" below (1284), until the chorus, in their last lines, views his fate as a warning against those whose speech exceeds the upper limit (*hyperauchoi*, 1351). The paradoxes of "highest Earth" in the Ode on Man, then, reveal multiple meanings only gradually: they span the tensions between supremacy and debasement, power and helplessness, Olympian and chthonic divinity, civic Zeus and the irrational Fury of the house, reason and irrationality, fostering of life and devotion to death.

This double meaning of "earth" strikes to the heart of the tragic conflict. For Creon "earth" is a matter of political boundaries, a territory to be fought over, protected, and ruled. Belonging to the "earth" of Thebes means adhering to the "laws of the earth" (368) in the political sense.[65] But for Antigone "earth" is her "ancestral land," *patria gē*, her bond in blood with the inhabitants of Thebes

(806, 937), an inalienable right transmitted through the family. Creon at the end is finally compelled to give Polyneices his share in this "native earth" (*oikeia chthōn*, 1203).

In challenging Creon's view of "earth" and its "laws," Antigone is also challenging the fundamental assumptions of Creon's political ethics. In a series of sharp antithetical *men . . . de* clauses, Creon establishes the distinction of total observance of burial for the one brother (*ta pant' aphagnisai*, "to hallow with all due rites," 196) and total neglect for the other. But for Antigone, blood, like earth, is an absolute which has nothing to do with such distinctions: "Hades desires equal laws" (519). Her verb, "desires," *pothei*, simultaneously links her *nomoi* with private and emotional rather than impersonal and rationalistic attitudes. For Creon the fact that those of the same blood killed one another with a "double fate" pertains to the law of succession, according to which he holds the throne of Thebes (170–174).[66] But this tragic confusion of sameness and difference in the family, that is, in the mutual slaughter of two brothers "born of one father and one mother,"[67] though observed with a mixture of sympathy and horror by the chorus (143–146), has no effect on Antigone. On the basis of his civic laws Creon can separate one blood brother from another (*ton d'au synaimon*, 198). Antigone, however, struggles to restore the primordial unity of that "one womb" (cf. *homosplanchnoi*, 511) in the face of the double-striking blow which has divided the two brothers in their civic status even as it unites them in the reciprocity of their death. Her enclosure in the cave then fuses the oneness of the womb with the mysterious oneness of death. For her, earth is like blood, a vehicle for the powers of life and death that transcend whatever secondary, "conventional" distinctions society may impose.[68] This earth, giver of life and receiver of the dead, is akin to the Persephone who "receives the dead" (894) and to her mother, Demeter, whose folds or bosom (*kolpoi*), of earth as of body, are "common to all" (1120–21).

In like fashion Creon treats the dust (*konis*) as he treats death itself: it is something which he can deny or dispense at will (246–247, 256, 429).[69] The dust too proves not entirely under his control. It arose in a mysteriously swirling storm from earth to heaven to aid Antigone in circumventing his decree (415–421). In the second stasimon the "bloody dust" of the family curse arises to "mow down" the living (601–602). Later, in a related figure, again in contrast to the rational mastery of the plow celebrated in the Ode on Man and alluded to by Creon in his harsh metaphor, "There are other fields for him to plow" (569), Antigone calls her family curse "the thrice-plowed doom of our whole fate" (858–860).

VII

The violation of the rites of burial soon involves all aspects and areas of ritual. The first ode of the play creates a civic frame for a ritual act, a dance of public rejoicing in which the chorus invokes Victory and Dionysus, patron god of Thebes, and then calls for a procession of all the citizens "to the temples of the gods in all-night dances" (147–154). Over against this public and civic rite of joyful thanksgiving stands the conflicted, private, and furtive rite of Antigone, burial of her brother on the desolate hills.

The new direction of the plot at the peripety links together rituals of purification, burial, and sacrifice. In all of them the city's mediate position in the hierarchy of god, man, and beast is overturned. Because of the exposure of the corpse the altars of both house and city (*bōmoi, escharai*) do not hold acceptable offerings but are "full of the carrion of the ill-fated son of Oedipus, brought by dogs and birds" (1016–18).[70] The city, therefore, is polluted, "diseased" (1015). Sacrifice is interrupted (1019–20). The victims do not burn properly on the altars (1005–11). The sweet savor which should mount up to the heavens is replaced by a "rotting stain" which recalls the corpse that Creon has left to "rot" (*mydaō*, 410, 1008). An "unholy smell" comes from the beasts' carrion into the cities and their "hearths" (*hestiouchon es polin*, 1083, "to each city that contains the hearths of the dead," Jebb). That movement effaces the barrier between inner, sheltered, sanctified space and the savage realm outside. The violation, in turn, harks back to the evil smell to which Creon's decree had exposed the guards, made to watch over an "unhallowed corpse" (1071, 1081) in an exposed, savage place (410–412 and cf. *osmē*, "smell," in 412 and 1083). Similarly, the ironical "hallowing" of the body by beasts undoes the "hallowing" which it receives at human hands (cf. 196, 247 with 1081).

Creon behaves toward rites averting pollution as he behaves toward piety and reverence in general. Like Oedipus, he is a ruler charged with removing a pollution of which he is in fact the cause. But he has only the most limited notion of what constitutes pollution and what constitutes purity. Not only does he discount the possibility that the unburied corpse may spread pollution, but he uses a legalistic expedient to avoid the pollution of killing Antigone. He would immure her with just enough food so that "the whole city may escape pollution" (*miasma*, 776), a procedure which may be compared to the treatment of Philoctetes in a later play (*Phil.* 274–275).[71] "With respect to this girl we are pure" (*hagnoi*, 889), he proclaims with Pilate-like righteousness.

This same rationalism finds its most violent and confident expression when he angrily defies the one man who should know about pollutions, Teiresias. "Never," he tells the prophet, "will I trembling with fear of a pollution (*miasma*) allow him to be buried. For well I know that no man can pollute the gods" (1042–44). The generalization is the sort of rationalistic principle that one might find in Protagoras or Prodicus. It is certainly, as Wilhelm Nestle observed, in the spirit of the Hippocratic treatise *On the Sacred Disease*.[72] But any rationality is undercut by the emotional vehemence, by the scornful phrase, "trembling in fear of a *miasma*," and especially by the staggering hybris of the sentence which precedes (1039–40): "You will not conceal him in burial, no, not even if Zeus's eagles wish to carry him as food up to the throne of Zeus." This assertion is of a piece with his violent oath earlier to punish Antigone "even if she is closer in blood than the whole altar of Zeus Guardian of Households" (486–487) and his insulting invocation of "Zeus who watches over kindred blood" in 658. The public pollution (see 1015) works with the family curse to destroy him, and it is at the altar of the household gods, perhaps the altar of Zeus Herkeios, that Eurydice sits (*bōmia*, 1301) when she recalls the sufferings of Creon's house and calls down her curses on its lord.

The *pharmakos* or scapegoating pattern operative in the *Ajax* informs the action of the *Antigone*. The perpetrator of the burial is threatened with death by stoning (36), as in *Ajax* the punishment of the polluted outcast. Antigone serves, in part, as a human sacrifice that would cleanse the city of its polluted past.[73]

Further back in the action lies another myth of human sacrifice, the death of Creon's own son, whom Sophocles here calls Megareus (1303). Eurydice's last lament probably refers to a legend in which this son threw himself into the dragon's den in order to save Thebes (1301–1305).[74] Only one of the Spartoi, the original "dragon-sown" race of Thebes, could make this sacrifice.

Be this as it may, the city's attempt to perform the purificatory ritual which would end the violence released by the brothers' strife and self-slaughter fails disastrously with Antigone's death. Burying her with just enough food "that the whole city may avoid a pollution," Creon in fact brings a far larger pollution upon the whole city (998ff.) and indeed on the whole of the human world which it touches (1080ff.). The expelled scapegoat becomes the source of a new and more dangerous pollution. Having denied one form of ritual in the city, the proper burial of a corpse, Creon confronts a harsher inversion of ritual in his own house. His wife becomes the "victim" of a perverted sacrifice (*sphagion*, 1291).[75] By calling down curses on Creon as "killer of his son" by the altar, presumably of Zeus Herkeios, within the house (1301–1305), she leaves that house a polluted "harbor" of the dead (1284).

Creon chooses Antigone as the *miasma*, the source of the pollution, the "disease" of the city (732; cf. 421). But the final choice of the *miasma* is made by the gods, not by men, and it is Creon himself. He proves to be the real source of the disease (1015, 1052, 1142). He is reviled and spit upon by his son, accursed by his wife, left alone in a house now polluted by a perverted sacrifice (1291) and a stain of kindred blood which clings to him, "slayer of his son" (1305). Finally he accuses himself as the unintentional killer of both son and wife, the remaining members of his house (1339–41). He, rather than Antigone, resembles the *pharmakos* laden with the city's pollutions. As he says in his last lines, he is virtually an exile; he has no place to go, no one to turn to; his world reduced to chaos (1341–45). On his head, as on Oedipus' in the *Tyrannus*, an "unbearable portion" of suffering has suddenly "leapt forth" (*potmos . . . eisēlato*, 1345–46). These are his last lines in the play. The chorus' closing act is to point him out as the example of irreverent behavior to the gods ("Against the gods one must commit no impiety," 1349–50), the moral scapegoat whose separation by suffering teaches the lesson by which the rest may survive.

Even as Creon accepts the judgment of the gods conveyed in the prophet's warnings, he acts in a way which effectively continues the old pattern. Convinced, finally, by the chorus' advice, he gives orders for the burial of Polyneices and then says (1111–12): "And I, since my decision (*doxa*) has turned this way, as I imprisoned her myself, so will I set her free (*eklysomai*)." He speaks as one still in full command of his civic authority. His release has the same confident first-person future form as his condemnation (cf. 658, 774). The change of mind is a matter of political decision or judgment, *doxa*, and he goes on to speak of "observing the established laws" (*nomoi*, 1113). But the "setting free" (*eklyein*) that results is not one which Creon can control: this same verb describes the deaths of Haemon (1268) and Eurydice (1302, 1314), thus "loosed" with an irrational, emotional violence unforeseen by Creon (cf. 40, 597).

With characteristic energy Creon acts on his new decision (1111) but follows its letter rather than the spirit. He attends to the polluting corpse before he frees the girl who might still be living (1196–1205). The fact that the chorus, a hundred lines earlier, had reversed this order (1100–1101) makes his inversion all the more striking.[76] Whether he might have saved Antigone is not the question. In his decisive warning about the death of Creon's son, Teiresias had closely coupled the imprisonment of Antigone and the pollution of the corpse. He had, in fact, even placed Antigone first (1066–71). But now, Creon, placing the city and the civic pollution above the life of the individual, destroys his own house and himself. Ironically, in attending to the dead before the living he is acting exactly as Antigone did. But she acted out of wholehearted, if narrow, devotion to her loved ones (*philoi*), Creon out of insensitivity to human priorities.

The manner in which Creon actually revokes his outrage of Polyneices' corpse is significant (1199–1205):

> Asking Hecate, goddess of the roads, and Pluto to check their wrath in mercy, we washed him with holy washing amid fresh-plucked branches, burned what there was left, and then piling up a high-headed mound of native earth, entered the rock-strewn hollow marriage chamber of the girl.

Burning the body, Creon still refuses to give it to the gods of the lower world in the way that Antigone had wished (cf. 23ff.). Hitherto only burial or the sprinkling of dust have been mentioned. Just as Creon's initial reaction to Teiresias' warnings about the sacrificial fires and carrion on the Olympians' altars showed his lack of deep reverence for the gods of the upper air, so his ritual act here rests on no deep acknowledgment of those powers below the earth that he would appease, even though Hecate and Pluto are named (1199–1200).[77] "What was left we burned" (1202):

ὃ δὴ 'λέλειπτο συγκατῇθομεν·

Sophocles' restraint effectively conveys the gruesome state of that "dog-worried body" (*kynosparakton sōma*, 1198) "still lying there," an outrage to the lower gods and a pollution to those above which Creon would, too late, set right.[78]

VIII

Abandoning her loyalties and love for the living in favor of those below, Antigone upsets the balance between upper and lower worlds. Hence her relation to that very center of civilized values which she champions, the house, becomes ambiguous. Devoted to "the Justice housed (*synoikos*) with the gods below" (451), she risks her life for her house but comes to have no "common house" with either the living or the dead (*metoikos*, 850–852). Instead she has a sub-human "dwelling" of the dead underground (*kataskaphēs oikēsis*, 891–892; cf. also 868, 885, 888, 890).

Caught between an accursed house pursued by its infernal deity, the Erinys of the second stasimon, and a new, living house to which she is united only in death (1235–41), she destroys the mediation between past and future, which the house should effect, and simultaneously, in the clash between this aspect of the house and the city, destroys the mediation between upper and lower worlds. As the chorus tells her in another passage, "Advancing to the extreme of boldness [*thrasos*, like the "reckless daring" of *tolma*], you fell against the lofty throne of Justice" (853–854). This "lofty throne of Justice" complements the "Justice housed with the gods below" in Antigone's great speech on the unwritten laws. It is to this lower Justice that Antigone sacrifices everything. She will discount the Olympian Justice that presides over the civic order and over the laws that make civilization possible.

If Antigone fails to acknowledge the Olympian Justice, Creon fails to respect the sanctities of both realms. "Hades" and "the gods below" are for him subjects of threats or taunts (308ff., 580–581, 654, 777–780). Not only do the omens reported by Teiresias reveal his inversions of upper and lower worlds, but Teiresias' description of the unhallowed corpse also echoes Antigone's lament over herself as she is to "wed" Acheron:

aklautos, aphilos, anhymenaios . . . agomai (876)
 Unlamented, unfriended, unwed

amoiron, akteriston, anosion nekyn (1071)
 A corpse unburied, unhonored, all unhallowed (Jebb)

The parallel forges another link between Creon's two inversions of upper and lower realms, life and death.

As a result of Creon's interference in the balance between upper and lower worlds, the gods of Hades arise to punish him. "The late-destroying avengers of Hades and the gods, the Furies, lie in wait for you," warns Teiresias (1075), recalling that dangerous Fury of the accursed house in the second stasimon (603). The chorus, too, hesitant to suggest divine intervention earlier (278–279), is now quick to warn Creon against "the gods' swift-footed Destroyers," the Erinyes (1103–1104).[79]

The Fury's vengeance is appropriate, for Creon's dishonor to Polyneices' corpse doubly violates the rights of the house. First, those same laws of kinship which Creon respects with regard to his civic power (173–174) he neglects with regard to his house. By these laws, Antigone, orphaned of parents and brothers, is his to dispose of in marriage.[80] He had, in fact, already incorporated her into his house for her "nurture" (533; cf. *esō*, "within," 491). Marriage to his son, her cousin, Haemon, would be almost obligatory and certainly familiar procedure to an Athenian audience. But instead of giving her to Haemon, he gives her to Hades. Acting as the authoritarian chief of the limited family, he violates the claims and sanctities of that larger *oikos* of which Antigone is a part.

Second, the fusion of the rites of marriage with the rites of death, of the nuptial with the funeral procession, and of the bridal chamber with the tomb creates a sinister and destructive fusion of two opposites, the one solemnizing the condition for the creation of life, the other solemnizing its passing away. It is part of the symmetrical justice or *dikē* in the moral and ritual structures of the play that Creon then experiences in his own person and in his own marriage that confusion of life and death which he inflicted on Antigone. Instead of "blooming in the noble seed of children" (1164), he comes to occupy, like Antigone, an ambiguous place between life and death: he becomes a "living corpse," (*empsychos nekros*, 1167), the "shadow of smoke" (1170). Still living, he yearns to see the light for the last time (cf. 808ff. and 1330ff.).

Although Creon's attendants invoked the neglected gods of the lower world, Hecate and Pluto, as they performed "the holy ablution" (*lousantes . . . hagnon loutron*),[81] the unholiness and impurity of that "unpitied dog-torn body" (1197–98) have done their work. The infernal deities are not so easily appeased. Creon's discriminatory cleansing ritual (*aphagnisai*, 196) and his attempt to declare himself "pure" (*hagnos*) of the pollution of Antigone's death (775–776, 889) become in effect a source of infection. "Dogs or beasts" do another kind of "cleansing" (*kath-hagnizein*, 1081–82).

"Hades is the only thing that man cannot escape," said the chorus in the Ode on Man (361–362). This sentence haunts the tragic action of the play. Like Antigone, Creon enters the dark and mysterious hollows of the earth. Quite literally he descends into the cave or the cavern-like tomb where he has immured Antigone. There he encounters both love and death in their most extreme, most savage form. "We went," says the Messenger, "to the girl's rock-piled hollow bridal chamber of Hades" (1204–1205). Hearing a voice that chills his blood, Creon calls on his followers "to descend to the cavern's very mouth" (*dyntes pros auto stomion*, 1217). It is then that Creon discovers what that dark hollow contains.[82] He finds his son, though alive, joined with the dead, below, lamenting "the destruction of his union there below" (1224).[83] Reduced for the first time in the play to suppliant posture, he asks his son to come out (*exelthe*, 1230). But it is too late, and Haemon's "savage eyes" answer Creon's plea (1231ff.). Creon rushes out of the cave, escaping his son's murderous attack, but Haemon plunges back into the cave: "He dies a corpse upon a corpse . . . fulfilling the full marriage rites in Hades' house" (1240–41). Hades is no longer an instrument of Creon's authority but a power in its own right which destroys him (1284–85). When soon afterward he "flies upward," it is the flutter of fear soon to be confirmed (*aneptan phobō(i)*, 1307); the metaphor also recalls the helplessness of Antigone in her grief for the unburied dead (423–425).

This "marriage" by Creon's last remaining son is the final blow to the house. Far from affirming and continuing the house, this marriage-in-death is the first major stage in its ruin. With the house, basic unit of civilization, the orderly structures of the polis are also thrown into question. A union that might have perpetuated the royal line and royal house of Thebes is in fact its destruction.

Creon began as ruler and general, "King of the country" (155), ruler of "all the city" (178), defender of its boundaries between man and nature (cf. 100, 117ff.), the confident pilot of the ship of state (162ff., 178, 189–190). He ends with his private grief in the unformed cavity of the earth outside the walls, on "wild roads" (1274), the negation of that man-made shelter of which he has been the champion. Then he moves toward the desolate interior of his house, whose recesses (*mychoi*, 1293) hold the culminating disaster and complete the identification of his house with the "harbor of Hades" (1284). The image of the harbor in 1284 implies safe enclosure from the destructive sea that symbolizes the irrationality, mystery, and violence in the world in the second and fourth stasima.[84] Here it images the total destruction of man-made shelter.

Creon's world is, literally, turned upside down. The "straight," *orthos*, one of his favorite words, becomes the "crooked": "Everything in my hands is awry" (*lechria*, 1344–45).[85] The ruler who so confidently declared that he will lead Antigone to her rocky tomb (774) gives himself over limply to his servants to be led (1324) after he has himself experienced the darkness of that tomb. The man who prided himself on his intelligence and resolution (*phronein*, 169, 176, 207) and impatiently charged others with folly (cf. *anous*, 281) becomes irresolute before the chorus' advice (cf. 1098–1104) and finally proves the example of the man who needs to be taught "intelligence" (*phronein*, 1348–52).

If Creon is destroyed in his central values of authority and rationality, Antigone, devoted to love and the family, receives the Underworld as her house and Hades as her bridegroom. Each figure suffers the negation of the central values of his or her life; each, in the diametrical opposition of their values, becomes the instrument of the other's doom. But whereas Creon's unexpected disaster is merely a destruction, Antigone's self-chosen death is also an affirmation.

IX

Antigone's lonely journey to the cave and Hades follows an ancient heroic pattern, the dangerous quest into the unknown, which pervades ancient literature from the Gilgamesh Epic through the *Odyssey*, *Aeneid*, and beyond. Her heroic journey, however, also has a distinctly feminine character. She defies the city in the name of the house, and she takes on the role of Kore the Maiden, carried off to marry Death in the Underworld and then returned, after a period of barrenness and mourning on earth, with the joyful new vegetative life of the spring. Antigone's cave is a place of contact between worlds: between life and death, between Olympian and chthonic divinity, between gods and men. In moving into the darkness of the cave Antigone effects a passage between life and death, the familiar and the unknown, vitality and sterility. This experience is in part modeled on that of Kore-Persephone in her descent to become the bride of Hades.

Antigone, however, is a Kore who does not rise again to new life. She refers to herself repeatedly as "bride of Hades," a term that makes the analogy with Persephone unmistakable, particularly as the association with Persephone was a regular feature of funerary practices and funerary epigrams for girls who died young.[86] Yet although the Eleusinian Demeter plays a prominent role in the fifth stasimon, there is no clear allusion to the return of her daughter. When Antigone invokes Persephone by name in the context of her imminent descent to Hades as her "underground bridal chamber" (*nympheion*, 891, 1205), it is to Persephone as queen of the dead, "she who has received the greatest number of my perished (kinsmen) among the dead" (893–894).

The mythic paradigm of Persephone enlarges the reversal of upper and lower realms predicted by Teiresias. Not only are rites of burial and sacrifice inverted but the Kore's cycle of descent and ascent as well. This Kore remains in the lower world and draws her living spouse down after her. We may recall again Antigone's special devotion to the cult of the dead and to "the Justice who shares her house with the gods below" (451).

In the Kore myth the maternal figure, Demeter, remains a constant source of hope for the return to life and light. In this play that figure is Eurydice, whose name, "the wide-ruling one," signifies the Queen of the Dead. At the end, more like Antigone's Niobe than the chorus' Demeter (cf. 1120ff.), she mourns the hopeless death of her children and then returns to the death-filled interior recesses of the doomed house. A *mater dolorosa*, she too is drawn into the dark, Hades-like hollows of enclosure. There is no Demeter-like mother left alive to call the Kore back to life. The maternal figures of the fourth stasimon, Danae, Cleopatra, Eidothea, either suffer or inflict imprisonment and in the last example destroy rather than nurture children.

Antigone herself doubles with the grieving figure of the Great Mother. In comparing herself to the petrified Niobe, she projects an image of herself as the *mater dolorosa* as well as the maiden wedded to Hades. Logically, Antigone cannot be Kore and Demeter at the same time. Yet mythic imagery often operates with exactly this fruitfully illogical union of opposites. Here a mythic archetype is split into two contradictory and yet simultaneously coexisting aspects of the self. The Kore is also the mother at an earlier stage. So here Antigone, who takes on herself the task of burying and mourning the dead son, often the role of mother or wife, is the Earth Mother who grieves over her children. The maiden claimed by Death, who ought to be resurrected with the new life of the year, will instead remain in the Underworld with her dead (893–894).

Sophocles' dramatic structure makes clear the discrepancy between the reality of Antigone's life and the mythic patterns to which she assimilates herself.

She is a virgin girl, neither mythical *mater dolorosa* nor a maiden wedded to a god in the Underworld. Her union with death, though figuratively a marriage, is in fact a cruel, desolate end. Her future husband, a living mortal not the awesome god below, chooses the same cavernous hollow and the same doom but with no hope of any future union. The pattern of universal renewal of vitality implicit in the Kore myth contrasts also with the bleak reality facing Creon's city. It, too, has lost touch with those cosmic processes that involve passage between Olympian and chthonic realms, the interchange between life and death, renewal and destruction.

No longer a principle of continued life, this Kore-figure appropriates a *mater dolorosa*, ever-weeping Niobe, image of her own crystallized grief. No new life after a sojourn in darkness awaits her, but perpetual sadness and loss. Haemon, plunging into the cave, claims his bride-of-death as an inaccessible Kore, whom he can embrace only in a grimly funereal version of a sexual union (1236–41). In the Kore myth the grieving Demeter's withdrawal threatens to extinguish life on earth, but she relinquishes grief when Zeus "leads holy Persephone forth from the murky darkness into the light" (Homeric *Hymn to Demeter*, 337–338; cf. 302–309). Thereupon Demeter again "sends the grain upward from the fertile plowlands, and all the wide earth is heavy with leafage, heavy with flowers" (471–473). In this play, however, the divinely sanctioned command, "Send up the maiden (*korē*) from the dwelling dug beneath (the earth)," is not fulfilled (1100–1101). The phrasing of these lines, literally "send the *korē* upward," uses the same verb of ascent (*an-hiēmi*) as the Eleusinian text, where Demeter, mourning her daughter underground, refuses to "send upward" the rising grain (*Hymn to Demeter* 307, 332, 471). Sophocles' Kore-figure, however, leaves house and kingdom plunged in darkness and sterility, both literally and metaphorically.

Each of the male characters discovers that aspect of the female appropriate to his experience and attitude. Haemon, a victim of Eros, is united with Antigone as the bride of Death. Creon will find in the female figure who dwells in the recesses of his house neither Kore nor Demeter but their complement, the grieving mother and "wide-ruling" (Eury-Dike) Queen of the Dead, whose desolation has now spread over his entire realm. Having denied the basic ties of kinship and the sanctity of family bonds, he finds his wife a corpse, herself the "all-mother of the corpse" (1282). As a manifestation of chthonic female power and maternal vengeance, she makes the interior spaces of his own house (*mychoi*, 1293) a dark place of corpses (1298–1300).

It is not by accident, therefore, that the tale of the disasters of his house centers on Eurydice. The full, grim account is addressed not to the chorus but to Eurydice as she emerges from the house (1181–82, 1184) to address Pallas Athena in prayer (1184). These prayers to Olympian Athena, goddess of the city in all its glory, are answered, in a sense, by Creon's belated, failed prayers to the chthonic Hecate and Pluto (1199–1200) as catastrophe inside the gates of house and city (*oikeion kakon*, 1187; *penthos oikeion*, 1249) overwhelms victories outside the gates. Creon had defended the gates and ramparts of "seven-gated Thebes" from invaders outside, as the chorus joyfully sang in the parode (101, 122, 141).

When Eurydice crosses the gate (*pylē*, 1186) of her house to the outside, it is only for a moment. Then she returns within (1255), to draw Creon with her into the dark spaces of that Hades-house, as she draws him after her into the dark, passionate grief which she "secretly hides held down in her angered heart" (*katascheton / kryphē(i) kalyptei kardia(i) thymoumenē(i)*, 1253–54; note the powerful alliteration).

These reversals and their spatial analogues of ascent or descent find other mythical correlates in the last two odes of the play. The three myths of the fourth stasimon, Danae, Lycurgus, and the blinding of Phineus' sons, all have to do with imprisonment and deprivation of light. The first myth, that of Danae, has the closest analogies to Antigone's situation. Danae, like Antigone, "changes the light of the sky" for a confining chamber's vault (944–946) and is "hidden in a tomb-like chamber" (946–947; cf. 886–887). Yet this downward movement of a mortal into darkness is balanced by a happier descent on the part of Zeus, whose "gold-flowing seed" (*gonai*, 950) accomplishes a sexual union and a reunion with life which are denied Antigone.[87] The implicit comparison, like Antigone's own comparison of herself to Niobe, has its pathos: Antigone will be the bride of Hades, not of Olympian Zeus. Like the Niobe simile, it suggests the frustrated rhythms of fertility and renewal (cf. 827–832). For King Lycurgus, however, who corresponds much more closely to Creon, imprisonment in a cave is a punishment only, and this is appropriate to Creon's "descent."

In the grim third myth, the tale of the blinding of Cleopatra's two sons by their stepmother in Thrace, the motif of the cave veers between savagery and divine ancestry. Daughter of the wind god Boreas and the Athenian Oreithyia, Cleopatra "received her nurture in distant caves, amid the winds of her father" (983–985). Yet her kinship with Boreas in the far North also connects her with the violence of nature (*thyellai*, "winds," usually indicates destructive storms). At the opposite extreme from the subjugated nature of Creon's city and close to Niobe in her identification with the forces of the wild, she is nevertheless deprived of the civilized city par excellence, the Athens of her mother, "seed of the Erechtheids of ancient birth" (*sperma archaiogonōn antas' Erechtheidân*, 981–982). "Seed" and "birth" here take up the theme of marriage and fertility from the previous strophe.

Cleopatra's blinded sons "have their origin from an unhappily married mother" (so Jebb for *matros echontes anympheuton gonan*, 980). *Anympheutos gona*, however, means literally "wedless birth." Not only does it contrast to the "ancient birth" of her Erechtheid ancestry in the next line, but in moving from the sky god's "birth seed" (*gonai*, 950) to the dark, cavernous spaces of dangerous stepmother it cancels out Danae's Zeus-sent, fruitful "births" (950) and recalls the unfulfilled "birth" of Antigone, the "brideless bride" of Hades (*nympheusō*, 816; *an-hymenaios*, 876; *nympheion*, 891). The grim "bride rites" (*nymphika*) of Hades in the cave will then definitively cancel "births" (1240; cf. *nympheion Haidou*, 1205). In the same semantic field as "birth," "the dragon's seed" (*spora drakontos*, 1125) is connected with the death of Creon's sons in present and in past (cf. 1302–1305). Thus Danae and Cleopatra interlock with Niobe as multivalent paradigms for the hopes of fertile marriage and their destruction in the house of Antigone and Creon. They also bring the deeper mythic pattern of Kore and Demeter closer into the foreground. The struggle between Creon and Antigone expands to include a dialectic between house and cave, city and wild nature, central Greece (Argos, Athens) and the remote periphery (Thrace) in these myths of royal women encountering divinity.

The fifth stasimon, the Ode to Dionysus, returns us again to nature's fertility (1131ff.) and to astral imagery (1126ff., 1146ff.). The starlit night sky of the purifying Dionysus (1144, 1146–47) sets off by contrast Creon's figurative descent from happiness to misery (1155ff.) and the literal details of his descent to the cave (1204ff.).

This cave and the dark forces which it contains prove to be the final test of Creon's conception of human power and of Antigone's tragic heroism. For her it is a place of tragic isolation and tragic fulfillment, ambiguous locus of the tension between her devotion to loved ones and death-bent, stony heroism.[88] For Creon the cave symbolizes all that he has repressed. It is the subterranean reservoir of dark passions and the place of lonely encounter with love and death, Eros and Hades. The Eros which Creon denied in a crude image drawn from the arts of civilization ("There are other fields for him to plow," 569) returns in the cave to defeat him: Eros takes his son from him and gives him to Antigone for an inverted union in the realm of the dead (1240–41).

X

The conflict between Creon and Antigone is not only between city and house, but also between man and woman.[89] Creon identifies his political authority and his sexual identity. "If this victory (*kratē*) rests with her without punishment, then I am not the man, but she's the man" (484–485). The word *kratē*, "victory," "power," repeatedly describes his sovereign power in the state (166, 173, for example).[90] He sees Antigone, then, as a challenge to his most important values and his self-image. "A woman will not rule me (*arxei*) while I live, " he says a little later, again linking the conflict of the sexes with political power.

In this same speech Creon confronts an opposing principle of an especially feminine kind, Antigone's "reverence for those of the same womb," *homosplanch-nous sebein* (511). On this basis Antigone defends herself against the male-oriented, civic ethic of the polis. She makes kinship a function of the female procreative power: she defines kinship in terms of the womb (*splanchna*). Thus at the end of her great speech on the unwritten laws she calls Polyneices "the one (born) from my mother, dead" (*ton ex emēs / mētros thanonta*) whom she, for that reason, will not leave "a corpse unburied" (*athapton . . . nekyn*, 466–467). As her defiance of Creon continues into the stichomythy, her word *homosplanch-nos* some fifty lines later etymologically defines "brother" as "one of the same womb" (511). *Homosplanchnos* calls attention to the root meaning of the familiar word for "brother," *adelphos*, from *a*- ("same," equivalent to *homo*-) and *delphys* ("womb," equivalent to *splanchna*).[91] In this view of kinship she reopens, on a personal level, the debate between Apollo and the Erinyes in Aeschylus' *Oresteia*;[92] however, she gives the decisive tie of blood not to the father's seed, as Olympian Apollo and Olympian Athena do (*Eumenides* 657–666, 734–741), but to the mother's womb.

Antigone's definition of kinship as *homosplanchnous sebein* reaches deep into the conflicts of values in the fifth-century polis. The establishment of Cleisthenian democracy at the beginning of the century rested, in part, on breaking down the power of the clan and blood ties; instead, allegiance to the polis was to subsume and transcend the ties of blood. Benveniste's study of kinship terminology in Greece takes this conflict back a stage further.[93] The Greek vocabulary of kinship sharply distinguishes between male and female lineage. The old Indo-European term for "brother," *phratēr* (I.E. **bhratēr*, Latin *frater*) survives in the Greek term for the members of a phratry (*phratēr*; cf. *phratra*). The phratry consists of men united as members of the male band through the masculine, patriarchal line and "issued mystically from the same father."[94] Though based on kinship, it is kinship extending beyond the *oikos* into the polis, where it has political power.[95] An old term for "brother," *kasis*, *kasignētos*, which may originally have denoted maternal lineage, becomes assimilated to the strictly paternal line, and the original Indo-European word for "sister" (equivalent to Latin *soror*) is then lost.[96] For brothers related by blood Greek then develops a new term, *adelphos*, "of the same womb" (*a-delphys*), which denotes kinship through the mother.[97] Symmetrical to *adelphos* is *homogastrios*, or the doublet, *ogastōr*, literally 'co-uterine," from *gastēr*, "belly," "womb." Antigone's *homosplanchnos* is the exact equivalent of *homogastrios*. Whether or not *homogastrios* and *homosplanchnos* are historical survivals of a pre-Indo-European matrilinear system of kinship in Greece does not concern us here. What is important for the *Antigone* is that the distinction between paternal and maternal lineage is a live issue for audiences of mid-fifth century Athens.

Antigone does not phrase her conflict with Creon strictly in terms of maternal versus paternal kinship, but that division is relevant since Cleisthenes' reforms involved cutting across the exclusive blood ties of the clan or *genos*, where ties through the mother are more obvious.[98] As Freud long ago pointed out, paternity is only an inferential relation, whereas maternity is immediate and visual. There can be no doubt about the mother who has given birth to the child, but there is no equivalent certainty about the father who sired it.[99] It is in keeping with Creon's fierce adherence to the polis and his inferential, abstractive mentality that he leans heavily on patriarchal lineage and authority (639–647; cf. 635). His stress on patriarchy, though illogical in one sense (see 182–183), is congruent with his antifeminine, antimaternal attitude (see, e.g., 569).[100] The conflict between him and Antigone, then, is not just between family and city, but between fundamentally different concepts of life.

That conflict necessarily involves Creon's son, the extension of his power in the male line both in the city and in the house. As the victory of Orestes in the *Eumenides* reflects a successful separation of the male adolescent from his ties to the mother and an initiation into the male society of phratry and polis,[101] the death of Haemon reflects just the opposite: the failure of the political tie of the male band to pull the youth away from the mother to the city and a return to the womb as the underground cavern, the mysterious seat of life-and-death, the elemental procreative power which remains under the control of the woman, the "All-Mother," whom Creon will soon encounter in her destructive and vengeful aspect. Haemon thereby rejects not only his father but also his adult male role of political responsibility in the city, succeeding his father to the throne of Thebes. In both literal and symbolical action he fulfills Creon's worst fear, "alliance" with the woman (740; cf. 648–651).

The tie through blood alone, through the womb, Antigone makes the basis of her *philia*. *Philia*, which includes notions of "love," "loyalty," "friendship," and "kinship," is another fundamental point of division between Creon and Antigone. An exchange a few lines after her "reverence for the *homosplanchnoi*" (511) sharpens the clash between the two views (522–523):

> Creon: The enemy (*echthros*) is not a loved one (*philos*), not even when he is dead.
>
> Antig.: It is my nature to share not in enmity, but in loving (*synechthein, symphilein*).

Creon here repeats his political definition of *philos* from his first speech (182–183), but now it is opposed by Antigone's fierce personal loyalties. Once more the "sameness" of the womb cuts through that principle of differentiation that separates *philos* from *echthros*. Creon's "politicization of burial" distinguishes between the two brothers as hostile political forces: "The one he promotes in honor; the other he dishonors" (22).[102] To Antigone, however, those "of the same womb" are worthy of the same degree of honor (*timē*) and love (*philia*). The *homo-splanchnoi* are to be joined in the sister's *sym-philein*.

Antigone's claim of sameness, however, overlooks a critical difference. As the first ode points out, origin from that one womb is a source of horror and pollution: the two brothers are the "miserable wretches who, born from one father and one mother, leveled double-conquering spears against one another and so won, both of them, a common share of death" (143–146):

> τοῖν στυγεροῖν, ὦ πατρὸς ἑνὸς
> μητρός τε μιᾶς φύντε καθ' αὐτοῖν
> δικρατεῖς λόγχας στήσαντ' ἔχετον
> κοινοῦ θανάτου μέρος ἄμφω·

The contrast of "one" and "two," the use of the dual forms, the interplay between "common" and "both" in the last line all stress the pollution: "They destroyed one another in double portion on one day, smiting and being smitten with pollution of the same hand" (*autocheir miasma*), says Creon soon after (170–172). That those so intimately linked in "oneness" should suffer such violent "difference" is itself the expression of an infectious division in the house.

It is Antigone's tragic task to insist on the ultimate "oneness" or "sameness" and thereby close over this difference.

The struggle is marked in her opening words. Her striking phrase of address to Ismene, "common self-(wombed) sister" (*koinon autadelphon*, 1), attempts to reaffirm family unity in blood against the harsh reality of Ismene's picture of the "two" brothers who on "one day" died with "double hand" (13–14). Antigone's "common" sister contrasts also with the chorus' "common death" (146) of the two brothers. That phrasing of kinship in the first line of the play intensifies the blood tie and points back, in turn, to the deeper horrors of sameness in the house of Oedipus, the incestuous marriage and the patricide.[103] "The woes that come from Oedipus" occur in her second line. Even her dual form when speaking of herself and Ismene in the third line has its significance, for it repeatedly denotes the polluted fratricides (recall 143–146, above) and comes to mark a shift of allegiance on Antigone's part as she leaves the living kin for her bond to the dead. Creon's path is, of course, just the opposite: he insists on "difference" and carries it to its logical conclusion in the face of those bonds of "sameness" which the gods finally vindicate. The list below will recapitulate:

Creon	Antigone
Philoi as those devoted to city	*Philoi* as kin ties
Differentiation by political loyalties	Oneness of "same womb"

Separation from mother
    Patriarchal kinship (phratry)
	Return to womb and mother (earth)
	    Matrilinear kinship (*homosplanchnoi*)

Earth as political territory	Earth as locus of blood kinship
Earth as plowed terrain	Earth as receiver of the dead
World above (Olympian religion)	World below (chthonic gods)
Control over nature	Fusion and sympathy with nature
Use of death	Acceptance of death
Rejection of *eros* (cf. 569)	Tragic death as "Hades' bride"
Logos (mutually exclusive alternatives)	*Mythos* (paradox)

Future or gnomic present
    Calculations of time
	Past (the dead, inherited curse)
	    Timeless

Manipulative rationality	Emotionality

XI

Parallel to the loss of the unrestored Kore in the house of Oedipus is the premature death of the unmarried son in the house of Creon. Here Creon's strength crumbles at its weakest point, that is, at the point of his own link with the cycle of generation. In the two encounters with Haemon in the middle and at the end of the play Creon has his sharpest confrontation with forces beyond his control. Haemon is Creon's link with a house through procreation. Antigone and the cave act, in a sense, as the agents of the powers of the house, earth, and death when they rob Creon of his last human ties. "You will give one of those from your own loins" (*splanchna*), Teiresias warns, "a corpse in exchange for corpses" (1066–67). Through Haemon Creon too feels deep physical and biological ties to the *splanchna*.[104] This word, as we have noted, generally denotes the womb and not the loins. It thus confuses Creon's rigid differentiation of male and female and thereby puts him in touch even more fundamentally with life and death.

Creon himself is deeply concerned with family solidarity, as his opening lines to Haemon make clear (639ff.). Haemon sensitively exploits this sympathy with his father: he begins his plea, "Father, I am yours" (635). But this concern on Creon's part only increases the pathos of his downfall through his alienation from every member of his house, living and dead (1302–1303). Exhibiting something of what Bergson called "intellect's congenital lack of comprehension for life," he disregards until too late what his blood kin might teach him about the meaning of familial ties. Hence his house, instead of being a locus of civilized values and the place that transmits new life from generation to generation, becomes, like the house of Antigone and Oedipus, a place of death and savagery, a cavern-like "harbor of Hades."

Fleeing his father's house for the cave, Haemon exposes that house to the terrible savagery which in the fourth stasimon occurs in a far-off Thracian setting at the very limits of civilization. Here too the act of savagery (see *agria damar*, "savage wife," 973) was directed against the eyes (*ommata*, 974; cf. *agria ossa*, "savage eyes," 1231). These "savage eyes" turned against the father by the son ironically echo the bitter father-son conflict earlier, where Haemon shouted out his bitter threat, "Never will you see my face as you look upon me with your eyes" (764). "Eyes" mark a progression from angry looks to deeds of bloody vengeance. Now "the evils in the house," *ta en domois kaka* (1279–80), are the last blow to the king's tottering strength. Deeper father-son hostilities lurk in the background (cf. the Freudian equation, eyes = penis), but we cannot discuss those here.

When Creon uses the language of procreation, it is only to reinforce his authoritarian principles. Thus in his encounter with Haemon, he praises "obedient offspring," literally "obedient births" (*gonai*, 642). "Begetting (*phiteusai*) useless offspring," he generalizes in his favorite mode of speech, only "sires" (*physai*) trouble for oneself and laughter for one's enemies (645–647). Haemon's reply about the gods' "planting" (*phyousi*) wits in men (683) takes a very different view of the process of birth as a metaphor for man's relation to nature.[105] This verb, *phyein*, involving growth, birth, procreation, not only points back to more mysterious aspects of birth (cf. 144, 866) but also includes Antigone's utterly opposite attitude toward birth, kinship, and "inborn nature" or *physis* (see 523, 562).

Creon's demand for obedience assimilates the order of the house to the order of the city and levels out the difference between them: lack of authority, *anarchia*, "destroys cities and overturns houses" (672–674). Scornfully dismissing ties of kinship with a slur on Antigone's reverence for "Zeus who looks after kindred blood" (658–659), he asserts his principle that the man who is good in the realm of the house will also be just in the city (661–662). Creon's word for "order" here, as elsewhere in this speech, is *kosmos* (660, 677, 730), the word used to describe Antigone's burial of the corpse (396, 901). The one subordinates kin ties to the "order" of the polis; the other defies the polis to "order" the rites owed to a dead kinsman.

Creon consistently incorporates kinship terms into his political framework. In his opening speech he calls the terms of his decrees about the corpse "kindred" (*adelpha*) or "brother" to his glorification of the *nomoi* of the polis (191–193). He phrases the question of his son's loyalty in terms of a "final vote" (632), a political "alliance" (740), or a "case at law" (742). On the other hand, Creon's rational civic authority, couched in the language of birth, begetting, and nurture (660) in this scene, contrasts sharply with the sinister and irrational sense of family in the second stasimon which immediately precedes (see *genean*, *genos*, 596). We should take note of the transition between that stasimon and the exchange of apothegms on political wisdom: the chorus introduces Haemon as "the last birth (*gennēma*) of [Creon's] children, grieving at the fate of his bride, pained to excess at the loss of marriage bed" (626–630). These words, immediately following the second stasimon, strike an ominous note that is confirmed at the end when Eurydice alludes to the earlier death of another son; now Creon alternates between "mother" and "child" in his response to the final ruinous blow to his house (1300).

In an early speech, Creon incorporated an image of growth into his political wisdom but in a negative sense: corruption in the state "flourished (*eblaste*) as an evil currency" (*nomisma*, 295–296). Later Haemon generalized, "What greater joy for children than the good fame of a father in the bloom of life (*thallōn*)" (703–704). But this expression of filial love ends in a horrible rupture between father and son: Creon later changes from one who "flourishes (*thallōn*) in the noble seed of children" to "a breathing corpse," scarcely "alive" (1164–67).

The root, *thall-*, recurs in the "newly plucked branches" (*neospasin thallois*) which Creon, too late, uses to burn the remains of Polyneices (1201–1202). This gift of just recently "flourishing" wood to the pyre continues the pattern of Creon's reluctance to confront the forces of life and death that lie beyond human control. It prefigures also the debt, hitherto stubbornly refused, which he owes and will so painfully discharge to the dead. As the belated and futile attempt to appease the outraged gods of the underworld by purification (1199–1200) leads into Creon's "Hades' harbor, hard to purify" (1284), so the newly plucked boughs of this reluctant rite are recalled in the "newly cutting blows" (*neotomoisi plēgmasi*, 1283) of the just dead queen, "all-mother of the corpse" who punishes Creon for the death of both his sons (1304–1305). Creon, so emphatic on the subordination of younger to older generation (639–647, 726ff., 728, 735), will lament the premature death of a son, "young with a young doom" (*neos neō(i) syn morō(i)*, 1266).

The word which denotes the ties of kinship throughout the play, *syn-haimōn* or *hom-haimōn*, means literally "sharing the same blood." Yet "blood," *haima*, also draws us back into the violent passions contained in houses less ordered than those which Creon envisages (658–662): Polyneices' thirst for the blood of his fellow citizens (121, 201); the "bloody dust" of the curse on the house of Oedipus (601–602); the horribly "bloody hands" in the savage house of Phineus (975–976). Creon's taunts of Antigone for her devotion to the family take the form of insulting the god who watches over those of kindred blood (*synhaimon*, 488, 659).

These scorned ties of blood have their revenge in the death of Creon's most vividly developed tie of blood, stressed by a grim pun on the name Haemon: "Haemon has perished, bloodied with his own hand" (*Haimon . . . autocheir d'haimassetai*, 1175). The inversions implicit in this play on *Haimon haima*, blood,[106] go even further in the depiction of Haemon's death as a parody of the act of generation: he "embraces" (1237) his bride in the dark places of the earth and "sprays out with his breath a swift stream of bloody drops upon her white cheek" (1238–39).

In the peripety the irrational forces contained within the house of Oedipus turn against Creon, not only the "blood" and *splanchna*, but also the "wailing" for the dead (*kōkytos*), which moves from Antigone to him (204; cf. 1227, 1316). The curse of a doomed family conveyed by the word *autocheir*, "with one's own hand," moves from Antigone's house to Creon's (1175, 1315).[107] The underground "shelter" (*stegē*, 1100) from which Creon would release Antigone, recurs in the "shelter" which Eurydice's lament will soon fill with the "grief belonging to (Creon's) house (*oikeion penthos* 1248–49; cf. *oikeion kakon*, 1187). The pollution which Creon hoped to keep outside the walls (172) enters not only the city (1015–18) but his house (1284, 1315). The brightness of public victory celebrated in the burst of light imagery in the parode (100ff.) changes to the dark look of Eurydice in her suicidal grief within the house (1301–1302) and Creon's wish not to look upon the light of another day (1328–32), the fulfillment of Teiresias' prophecy (1064–67).[108]

The play is truly a "fearful symmetry" in which Creon's undervaluation of blood ties and Antigone's overvaluation of them cancel each other out in a violent clash of Olympian and chthonic allegiances, narrowly exclusive male and female attitudes. The fates of Creon and Antigone, for all their differences, prove complementary. Antigone's willing sacrifice of life and marriage for those ties of blood which cannot be renewed by procreation produces a chain reaction which is irrational and yet logical. It destroys Creon through the procreative continuity of his own house: sons and mother are brought together in the disaster (cf. 1300).

Creon initially defines his house as a model of order and obedience, sharply opposed to Antigone's house. In Antigone he sees a viper lurking in his house (531ff.) and a source of accursed madness, *atē*, which he will not nurture (533;

cf. 660). But his house in fact contains its own *atē*. *Atē* characterized the curse on the house of Oedipus in the second stasimon (584, 614, 625) and also Antigone herself in her opening speech (4). Later Creon will have to claim *atē* as "not another's," but the result of his own "error" (1259–60; cf. 1096–97).[109]

Gradually Creon's house doubles with its chaotic opposite, the house of Oedipus from which he would carefully separate himself and the city. His encounter with Haemon reenacts the polluting strife between kindred blood in Antigone's house. Directly after the bitter exchange between Creon and Haemon the chorus sings an ode to Eros, whose power "stirs up this quarrel between those of the same blood" (*neikos syn-haimōn*, 793–794), an echo of the quarrel (*neikea*) between *Poly-neikēs* and his brother in the parode (110–111). The vocabulary of polluted killing of kin also moves from Oedipus' house to Creon's. His controlled iambic account of the death of Oedipus' accursed sons is echoed later in the cry of pain (in lyric meter) which his own suffering wrings from him:

> They in one day, in a double fate, perished smiting and being smitten with the pollution of their own hand. (170–172)

> O you who see those of the same clan (*emphylioi*) killing and being killed. (1263–64)

Finally Eurydice's Jocasta-like silent exit and death as she smites herself with her own hand reenact, within Creon's own house, the fate of the house of Oedipus (*paisasa . . . autocheir hautēn*, 1315; cf. *paisantes . . . autocheiri*, (171–172).

XII

It is part of the tragic situation of the play that neither house nor city proves a center of civilized values. Antigone's devotion to the house, like Creon's devotion to the city, spreads death and disaster rather than affirms life. Despite her splendid verse on her nature's bent toward love rather than hatred (523), she expresses that love in her relation to the dead rather than the living. "You have a warm heart for those who are cold" is Ismene's way of putting it (88).[110] She herself tries to rationalize it in her last speech (904–915), whose logic, or lack of logic, has so perplexed editors and commentators.[111]

Though we are badly informed on the legend prior to Sophocles, we cannot exclude the possibility that Sophocles himself invented the motif of Antigone's sacrifice of the future life of a new house to the curse of a dying house.[112] In a version of the myth contemporary with Sophocles, Antigone is still alive at the time of the Epigonoi's later attack on Thebes and is burned to death in a temple of Hera.[113] Euripides had his Antigone secretly marry and bear a son to Haemon.[114] If line 572, "O dearest Haemon, how your father dishonors you," is rightly attributed to Antigone (against the authority of the manuscripts), then her pull between life and death, marriage and Hades is stronger, but this tension, while it heightens her tragedy, does not mitigate her final choice of dead kin over living.

190

The house, on the one hand, is the catalyst for Antigone's love and heroism; at the same time, it is the vehicle for the mysterious curse and its dark burden of hatred and irrational evil. Allying itself with Creon at the moment when Antigone has confessed her burial of Polyneices, the chorus calls her "raw offspring of a raw father" (471, *gennēma ōmon ex ōmou patros*).[115] The word "offspring," *gennēma*, suggests the dark theme of birth earlier in *gonē* in the fourth stasimon (950, 981, 982) and in the root *phy-*, "grow," "beget." As the violence in the house of Oedipus spreads again from the slain brothers to Antigone and beyond, "birth" finds a sinister echo when the chorus, turning to Creon after their ode on the curses and madness (*atē*) in the house of Oedipus, introduce Haemon as "the last birth of your children" (*paidōn tōn sōn / neaton gennēma*, 626–627).

The "rawness" of Antigone as *gennēma*—birth, offspring—of a "raw father" in 471 forges a link between the imminent doom of the two houses. Creon's action has given her brother's corpse to "raw-eating dogs" (*ōmēstōn kynōn*, 697). From the chorus' point of view in 471, the "rawness" of the animal world outside the polis survives dangerously in the inward "rawness" lodged in the sheltered spaces of the house and in Antigone herself. But "raw-eating dogs" in 697—the only occurrence of this adjective in the extant Sophocles and the only other occurrence of "raw" in the play—are part of the defense of Antigone by the last offspring of Creon's house. This is the start of a division in Creon's house which is to prove as disastrous as that in Antigone's.

Teiresias, prophet of tragic doom, recalls the horror of the family curse when he describes the polluted altars "filled with the birds' and dogs' feasting (*bora*) on the fallen seed (*gonos*) of ill-fated Oedipus" (1017–18). The word *gonos* harks back to the sinister births of the preceding stasimon and of line 627, the destruction of the procreative capacity and biological continuity of the house. The emphasis on animals eating human flesh, "battening on the fatness of man's slain blood" (1022), throughout this graphic passage (1017–22) reveals in Creon's city a savagery at least as dangerous as the "rawness" (471–472) in Antigone's house.[116] "The law, whose political effect is mansuetude," Seth Benardete remarks, "shows itself as the instrument of bestialization."[117] If Antigone, in the chorus' view, pulls her house from its civilizing function toward the irrational violence of the family curse, Creon wilfully causes an even more fundamental violation in the anthropophagy gruesomely conveyed by Teiresias. In the passion and excesses of both figures, both house and city move toward a paradoxical union of opposites where each is civilized and savage at the same time.

The "rawness" which Antigone has from her father offers us the possibility of interpreting the family curse psychologically, a trait inherited from her ancestry, the violence and one-sidedness of emotional intensity handed down from generation to generation in the house of Oedipus. But it is also the survival of a more primitive past of the race, the taint of blood polluted by patricide and incest, into an age struggling to outgrow its archaic heritage and replace the irrational by reason, curse by law. In this sense the play continues the conflicts so powerfully raised in Aeschylus' *Oresteia*. In his last work, the *Oedipus at*

Colonus, Sophocles will continue the dialogue with Aeschylus, again focusing on the house of Oedipus but with a happier resolution.

Antigone's ambiguous relation to civilized values, as both their defender and their destroyer, is another manifestation of the profound tragic division within civilization itself, a division which the hero embodies and transforms into action. Viewed in historical perspective, the hero stands at the point where archaic and later strata in the society come together and conflict, where the older tribal values conflict with the cooperative, more rationally defined values of the polis.

Creon's exclusive allegiance to the polis is also allegiance to the ties created and maintained by the male society which by and large dominates the polis. Its public places, assembly, agora, and theater, are the places where men or exclusively male institutions have full autonomy, are fully independent of the female-dominated spaces of the *oikos*, of procreation, birth, nurture.[118] From the incongruous collocation of the life of the *oikos* and the life of the assembly or the theater, comedy elicits laughter, as Aristophanes does in *Thesmophoriazusae*, *Lysistrata*, and *Ecclesiazusae*. In tragedy this collocation marks the revenge of the *oikos* on those who would transcend it in the organized male activities of political life, the arts, or war.

Creon's aggressiveness toward women, then, is not merely another psychological detail of the authoritarian personality: his insistence on the supremacy of male over female exactly parallels that of city over house. Psychologically his attitude reflects the uneasiness and ambivalence which the Greek male in the fifth century seems to have harbored toward the mature woman.[119] Culturally it expresses the tension between the privileged autonomy of male intellect in a patriarchal society and the irrepressible and needed generative powers of subjected woman which throw the male back into dependence on the natural world that he would control.

The male characters, Creon and Haemon, embody different but interlocking ways of dealing with this tension. The young man, for all his avowal of loyalty to his father ("Father, I am yours," 635) abandons his own house, and its paternal authority, for the cavern-house, the perverted *oikos* of his bride-to-be. He thereby reverses the normal process of marriage, in which the bride leaves her house and goes to that of her husband. Departing from the cultural norm in the intensity of love for his betrothed, he overvalues his tie to the woman and with it reverses the usual movement between houses.[120] Creon, like Heracles in *Trachiniae*, undervaluing woman and the life-processes associated with her (569), had not reckoned on this destructive force of *eros* in his house.

The anomalous movement of the bridegroom to the house of his bride parallels an even more disastrous fusion: the nuptial chamber becomes the house of Death, and the bridal couch is the stone floor where no new life can be engendered (1204). The springs of that inversion lie deep in Antigone's own ambiguous relation to her house. Instead of conceiving of her house in a horizontal movement as one of those "unifying bonds of love," *desmoi philias synagōgoi*, which Protagoras cited as the necessary cohesive force in society,[121] she views her house in terms of a vertical movement, downward, in union with the *philoi* in Hades. *Philia* and *oikos* for her do not connect the individual with others, who live in a complex web of interlocking families, but bring isolation in a death-centered union with the single house. It is a further irony that Antigone's commitment to the unifying familial bond of *philia* is completed by this dissolutive *eros* of a *Liebestod* (cf. 781ff., 1234–43).

In this treatment of Haemon Creon shows himself caught between contradictory attitudes toward the house. On the one hand, he would subordinate the claims of the house to the absolute claims of the city, *oikos* to polis. On the other hand, he would assert the father's right to absolute obedience in the house.[122] The encounter with Haemon fully brings out this contradiction. Scornful of kindred blood where Antigone is concerned (658–659), Creon insists on Haemon's subservience to the father's will (*gnōmē patria*, 640; 644). His demand for obedient children (*gonas katēkoous*, 641–642) who have the same friend and foe as their father (*ex isou patri*, 644) reveals a conception of the house as narrowly patriarchal as that of the city. In his first speech he extolled the rights of the "fatherland" over those of kinship in terms which closely resemble his pronouncement to Haemon in 641–644: "Whoever holds a loved one (*philos*) of greater regard than his fatherland (*patra*), him I hold of no account" (182–183). Land and house both belong to the "father" (182, 640, 644).

Creon's word for his idea obedient children in 641 is *gonai*, literally "births." As we have seen, this root, *gon-/gen-*, evokes the mysterious power of female parturition and the sinister, uncontrollable force of family curse (see 598–599, 627, 981–982, 1018). Creon usurps for paternal authority a power beyond male control (641–642): "For this reason do men (*andres*) pray for births subordinate to them."

Behind the struggle of house against city, then, lurks also the struggle of mother right against father right. Antigone's view of the family extends far beyond the authority of the father per se. She values the ties of blood as such, not the house as the microcosm of patriarchal order in the city (897–899): "I nurture strongly in my hopes that when I come below, I shall come as one dear (*philē*) to my father, dear to you, my mother, and to you dear also, head of my brother." Even her expression for hoping is couched in terms of the woman's role within the house, "I nurture" (*trephō*). For this reason the role of Eurydice, defined as the quintessential mother (1282 and infra), is so important and so decisive in Creon's downfall.

In his need to perpetuate his line through the son who will succeed him as he succeeded Oedipus and his sons, "in accordance with proximity of kinship (*anchisteia*) to those who are dead" (174), Creon is dependent on the procreative power of the womb, the *splanchna* which represent Antigone's devotion to the ties of blood (511). As the struggle for the Theban succession has just shown, having offspring is a political as well as a familial matter; and Creon is threatened with the loss of "one from his own *splanchna*" (1066), his last offspring or "birth" (*gennēma*, 627–628).

The contradiction between Creon's subordination of house to city and his insistence on absolute patriarchy within the house finds a parallel expression in the plot structure, for Creon's ruin, paradoxically, is not that of a city, but of a house. That ruin, moreover, further undercuts his patriarchal definition of the house, for it takes place in terms of the close tie between child and mother. These are words wrung from Creon himself at the culmination of his disaster: "I see a corpse before me. Alas, alas, mother, unhappy; alas, child" (*pheu pheu mater athlia*; *pheu teknon*, 1300).

XIII

In the background of the house, now emerging into sudden importance, stands the dark figure of Eurydice, the archetypal grieving, saddened mother. When the Messenger announces her death, he calls her by the striking phrase, "the all-mother (*pammētōr*) of this corpse" (1282), a powerful juxtaposition of birth and death, the two forces that Creon has most scorned. This epithet, "all-mother," *pammētōr* or *pammēteira*, is rare in classical Greek literature. In Aeschylus it is the epithet of Earth, Gaia; later it is applied also to Night and to Rhea, Mother of the Gods.[123] Used of Eurydice, it seems to confer something of those elemental powers that Creon has violated, only to encounter them more fearfully in the hollows of Earth herself. Behind the figure of Eurydice, then, stand the mysterious female symbols of nature's ineluctable processes, recalcitrant to human control: Earth (Ge, Gaia) in the first stasimon; the Erinyes in the second; Niobe in the kommos; Phineus' "savage wife" in the fourth stasimon; the Eleusinian goddesses in the fifth.

Eurydice's brief allusion to an earlier death of a son, Megareus (1303–1305) suggests possible resentment and hostility between husband and wife. That tension has its deepest roots in a conflict between polis values and *oikos* values. In versions of the legend contemporary with Sophocles one of "the savage dragon's seed" (cf. 1124–25) has to sacrifice himself for the survival of the city. Only Creon and his children are eligible, and one of his two sons (called Menoeceus by Euripides) plunges to his death into the dragon's "precinct dark in its depths." Sophocles gives no details, but, as we have seen, he twice alludes to the death of Creon's other son (626–627, 1301–1305) and to an earlier tribulation for Creon and Thebes (993–995). Lines 1301–1305 hint obscurely at some disaster in the recent past. The Megareus of this passage is, presumably, to be identified with the Menoeceus of Euripides. Details are obscure and sinister, but Eurydice clearly blames Creon for the loss.[124] Eurydice's last word, "killer of sons" (*paidoktonos*, 1305) and her reference to "the glorious lot ["bed," *lechos*, manuscripts] of Megareus who died before" suggest the latent hostility and its origins in the sacrifice of sons to the polis. This bitterness of mothers who have lost offspring to male ambition and politics has a parallel in the Clytaemnestra of Aeschylus some fifteen years earlier (cf. *Agamemnon* 1415ff.).

The subdued earth of the first stasimon recurs more mysteriously in the Thebans' origin from the earth-born *drakōn*, where earth appears as the fertile womb of monsters and giants.[125] "Seed" or "sowing" (*spora*, 1125) evokes the theme of procreation around which there is so much ambivalence in the play. In the parode the chorus, firmly on the side of the city, celebrates the victory of Thebes over Argos as the triumph of the Theban snake (*drakōn*) over the Argive eagle (125–126).[126] The basic conflict between chthonic and Olympian is here crystallized into poetic image: the *drakōn* is earth-born; the eagle suggests Olympian Zeus (cf. 1039–40). The polarities blur, however, for the Theban polis also has chthonic associations, and Creon can insult Olympian Zeus. Megareus' story in particular evokes sinister elements in the myths of Thebes and its "Sown Men" (Spartoi, from the same root as *sperma* and *spora*). The *drakōn*, Theban autochthony, and Megareus' death point to powerful forces in the earth and the city of Thebes that Creon disregards.

Avenged by Eurydice, the fertile earth of Thebes eludes both Creon's male-centered political rationalism and the domination of nature in the Ode on Man. Not included in Teiresias' prophecy, the suicide of Eurydice confounds the patriarchal authority of the male rulers and the male authority-figures, king and prophet both. Their allegiance is to the Olympian gods; her connections are with the earth and the house. Her death defies the rational order of justice in the polis while fulfilling a justice of another sort. Hers is "a suffering that the city as such inflicts and no theodicy comprehends."[127]

In a sense Eurydice is an older Antigone.[128] Both women have lost, by violent death, two male kin, Polyneices and Eteocles in the one case, Megareus and Haemon in the other. Both losses are due to political reasons, and both are blamed upon the all-male polis world. Finally both women encompass the ruin of that male world through their association with an enclosed space, the cave on the one hand and the recesses (*mychoi*) of the house on the other (1279, 1293). Those inner spaces belong to the *oikos*, but they are also characteristically female, womb-like, the primal space where the male is utterly dependent on the female, the mysterious enclosed darkness of the womb before life and the darkness of the Underworld after life. Both Antigone and Eurydice have associations with the earth as the mysterious source of life and death: Antigone in being buried underground as Hades' bride (one thinks also of figures like Amphiaraus and Trophonius) and in her comparison to the petrified Niobe; Eurydice in the epithet "all-mother."

These forces of life and death underlie not only the motif of the cave (possibly Sophocles' invention), but also the transformation of Creon's house into a "Harbor of Hades." For Antigone the cave is associated primarily with the Underworld and with the blood kin, the *homosplanchnoi*, for whom she dies. For Eurydice the cave-like recesses of the house suggest rather the womb. But the two female figures and the two aspects of the cave—womb and Underworld—are complementary. In these inner recesses, whether of earth or of house, repressed female violence and passion can find their outlet, usually in disastrous form. Beside Deianeira we may think of Clytaemnestra and her carpet and net, Medea, Phaedra, and the dark tent of Euripides' *Hecuba*. Devoted to the house in "reverence for those of the same womb," Antigone opens Creon's ordered city, circumscribed by its seven gates and spiritually defended by its Olympian deities, to the darker powers under the earth and in the soul,[129] the darkness of life's beginning and ending in the unknown darkness of inner hollows, womb and earth.

The mythical background of the *Antigone* contains still another sinister mother-figure in all her terrifying power, namely the savage wife of Phineus in the fourth stasimon. She is another manifestation of the archetypal Evil Mother who inflicts blindness (symbolical castration?) on her two stepsons with the instruments of weaving (976), associated with the woman's space in the interior dark of the house. As in the case of Antigone and Eurydice, a woman's passion and potential violence is shown in relation to *two* male offspring (*dissoi Phineidai*, 971).

The cultural meaning of these female figures works together with their psychological significance. They embody the tragic failure of male-oriented rationalism in the face of the mysteries of death and the creation of life. This vengeance of the female through the children, as cunning Medea knew, wounds the male in his most vulnerable, most dependent place.

For all Creon's bluster the decisive acts of the play rest with women, with Antigone and Eurydice, and with the son who deserts the paternal house for the bond of *eros* in a dark cavern outside the limits of the polis. The king's house now fuses, literally and metaphorically, with the accursed house of the polluted rebel, Polyneices, and his sister, the criminal-pollution threatened with death by public stoning.

As Antigone emerges from the sheltered recesses of the house to stand alone against the entire polis (36),[130] she forces Creon to walk or "creep" the same ultimate "road" (807; cf. 1210, 1213, 1274). This is the path of *atē* creeping unexpectedly upon human life in the second stasimon (585, 613, 618). He is detached from the communal fastenings of the polis in descending into his cave, as Antigone is from those of the house in descending into hers, but his experience of this *principium individuationis* brings not a new heroic strength but a virtual annihilation to nothingness (1325).

"From Hades alone man will not escape" (361–362): death, finally, proves the measure of man, the touchstone of his humanity.[131] But civilization consists also in man's power to use reverently what an author writing in perhaps the generation after the *Antigone* called "the works of life," *ta erga tēs zoēs*.[132] To these both Creon and Antigone, for opposite reasons, stand in an ambiguous relation. By excluding from his *nomoi* the mysterious forces of birth and death and the irrational power which they can transmit, Creon suffers the loss of the rational structures which make him human; she, by sacrificing her capacity for life and love to the *nomoi* which belong to the dead, completes her identification with a paradigm of monumental but stony heroism. She thus realizes the destructive capacities of woman and the negative function of earth as the receiver of the dead rather than the source of new life. We may compare the grim nether world of the second stasimon and the Eleusinian Demeter's "folds common to all" in the fifth (cf. also 894).

XIV

"Hades alone will man not escape," sang the chorus in the last strophe of the Ode on Man (361–362). "You, Eros, no one of mortals or immortals can escape," concludes the first strophe of the third stasimon. The inescapability of love echoes the inescapability of death. But the force of the uncontrollable and the irrational has grown dangerously in the four hundred lines which separate these two statements. What was a small qualification in the Ode on Man, the inevitability of death, looms as a major element in the implicit definition of man which the play hammers out of the encounters in the orchestra.

The choral odes of this play also perform an important function in indicating the crescendo of the violence and irrationality parallel to the movement carried in the iambic trimeter of the dialogue.[133] Eros and Hades, Love and Death, are the two absolutes, at opposite ends of the spectrum, which man's civilizing arts cannot control. To them must be added Dionysus, the god of fusion with nature's energies, who plays a prominent role in the first and the last odes of the play.

After the darkness of the prologue and the literal and symbolical darkness of the night attack upon Thebes (16), the chorus enters, in the parode, singing of "the beam of the sun, loveliest light of all for seven-gated Thebes, eye of the golden day" (100–104). But beside this light we soon meet the blazing fire which signifies the destructive hatred of the attacker, Polyneices (124, 131, 135). Simultaneously the glittering panoply of heroic arms changes to bloody animality (contrast 106–109, 114–116 with 112, 120–121). These contrasts of light and darkness, civic joy and personal grief, epic warfare and bestiality, death-bent resolve and the renewal of life in the rhythms of night and day contain, in imagistic form, a microcosm of the tragic antinomy. Subsequent choruses are preoccupied with the extinction of light. A descent into the dark cave awaits both protagonists. The first ode ends with a call for "all-night choruses" in honor of Dionysus, patron god of Thebes (152–153). But Dionysus is a destructive as well as a joyful god. Earlier in that ode Dionysiac imagery described the divisive, not the unifying, forces in the city. Polyneices "raging, bacchant-like (*bakcheuōn*) with maddening rush, breathed upon us with the blasts of enemy winds" (135–137).

Of the first stasimon, the Ode on Man, nothing further need be said here.[134] The second stasimon begins with vivid images of the dark sea and the violence of nature to evoke the irrational violence of the curse on the House of Oedipus.[135] The uncontrollable sea here answers the confident nautical images of Creon's first speech about his "ship of state" and the control over the sea celebrated in the Ode on Man. The negation both of light and agriculture appears in the bold metaphor which describes the working of the curse, extending from Laius now to Antigone: "The light had been stretched over the last *root* in the House of Oedipus, but the bloody dust of the gods below *mows it down* along with madness of speech and the Fury of the soul" (599–603). The bloody dust recalls Antigone's sprinkling of dust over her brother's bleeding body. The mysterious springs of Antigone's deed and the mysterious curse on her house fuse together in symbols having to do with earth, darkness, agriculture and inverted fertility, the lower world.

Like the second stasimon, the third, on Eros, defines human life in terms not of what man controls, but what he cannot control. Not *eros* per se is tragic in the *Antigone* but the interplay, even the identification, of love and death. Creon's lines on Antigone's devotion to Hades (776–780) immediately precede the ode on Eros; the recurrent image of Antigone as the bride of Hades receives its fullest development immediately after.[136] Her nature's capacity for *philia* receives its fulfillment only in union with the dead *philoi* in Hades and in a passionate *eros* consummated in death (1236–43).[137]

Greek literature is full of warnings against Eros. Sappho describes Eros as an elemental force of nature, a whirlwind rushing down the mountains (frag. 47LP; cf. frag. 130LP). For Pindar the yearnings for "the unreachable loves" are among "the sharper madnesses" (*Nemean* 11.48). Plato holds out an ideal of a "musical *eros*," a love that reaches from the soul guided by reason to the eternal ideas of the Good and the Beautiful (*Rep.* 3.403A–C), and with playful seriousness he mythologizes Eros in the *Symposium*. Antigone's *eros* is more akin to that dangerous, unreachable type described by Pindar, "love for the impossible," the "unmasterable" (*amēchana*, 90).

Although the ode on Eros seems at first glance to relate only to Antigone and Haemon, it applies to Creon as well. He has treated with scorn the power of Eros, like all those elemental and therefore divine powers relating to birth and death (569, 633–644, 648–652, 746, 756). Eros "invincible in battle" (781; cf. 800) challenges Creon's aggressive outlook, until he learns that even he cannot "battle Necessity" (1105). Eros places man near the wild things. It falls on man and beast alike and is in the sea and in the "wild-pastured shelters" of beasts (785–786). Breaking down the barrier between beast and man, it attacks the rationalistic domination over nature celebrated in the first stasimon and implicit in Creon's world view. The sea in which Eros has his power (*hyperpontios*, 785) is not the subjugated sea of the Ode on Man.

The nocturnal vigil of Eros who "sits all night on the girl's tender cheek" (783–784) takes us once more into darkness. This all-night vigil contrasts with the public vigil of the citizens celebrating Thebes' victories in "all-night dances" in the parode (152; cf. 784). The power of the laws (*archai thesmōn*, 799–800) of Eros belongs to a far different world from those laws and power through which Creon exercises his rule in the city and in the family (cf. *archais te kai nomoisi*, 177; *anarchia*, 672). The chorus here sees itself drawn "outside of laws," *thesmōn exō* (802).

Early in the play Antigone, "in love with the impossible" (90) and "in love with death" (220), embodies this asocial, uncooperative *eros*. As the play moves further and further from the areas of human control, Creon too feels the chaotic power of *eros*, but it is an *eros* reaching for death, not life. At the point of reversal, *eros* and madness have their revenge and become the primary instrument of the disaster which overtakes him in the cave.[138] He then prays for death as something for which he feels love or desire: "All that I love (*erōmen*) I have included in my prayer," he says in his next-to-last speech (1336).

As Antigone is to descend into the literal darkness of the cave, the irrational violence associated with darkness becomes stronger. She says repeatedly that she will no longer look on the light of the sun (808ff., 878–880). In the fourth stasimon, one of the most complex odes in Sophocles, the madness brought by Eros yields to the madness sent by Dionysus.[139] The mastery of the sea by ships (954–946), the reference to the tower of Danae, the yoking of Lycurgus in his rocky cave, insulting speech and wild bacchantic fire (955–965) form a grotesque parody of the civilizing achievements in the Ode on Man as Creon himself, the proud ruler, begins to look more like the insolent Thracian king.[140] Lycurgus' northern setting, seen in even wilder aspect in the Bosphorus' dark rocks at the beginning of the second strophe (967ff.), is the utter negation of the sheltered civic space praised in the first stasimon and ostensibly defended by Creon in the parode.[141]

That northern setting is the abode of the savage wife who blinds Phineus' sons with the needles of her loom (966–976). Now the inner shelter of house as well as city fuses with the wildness which belongs outside. Simultaneously the peaceful womanly craft of that house, the age-old practice of weaving, becomes the means for a destruction of an even more basic function of the house, the protection and rearing of children.

The setting of this harsh external world correlates symbolically with the perverted inner realm of this deadly house: the "dark rocks" of this "twin sea" (another doubling in connection with the destruction of a house) are appropriate to the blinding inflicted there. As in the second stasimon, sea and darkness mark the irrational in human life. We may recall Antigone's "darkly meditated word" at the very beginning (20, with the sea imagery of *kalchainein*).

In the language of the fourth stasimon, "the accursed (*araton*) wound of blindness inflicted as vengeance (*alastores*) on eyes' round sockets" (972–974),[142] we are taken back to the curses on Antigone's house: the blindness of Oedipus (49ff.) and the "curse" on Antigone (*araios*, 867), with their symbolical extensions, as we have seen, in the sea and darkness of the second stasimon, so strikingly echoed here (cf. 966–967 and 589ff.). But the blinding also points ahead to the massive disruptions soon to overturn Creon's house (1231ff.). The savagery of the wife in the Thracian house and the natural setting there provide a mythic parallel to the violence which Antigone and Creon have both let loose into house and city. With a myth of this fearful extinction of sight ringing in our ears, the blind Teiresias enters (*typhloisi* in 989 takes up *typhlōthen* in 973) to announce the ominous extinction of the sacred fires at the altars (988ff.). Darkness now moves in upon Creon. He will not see many suns, Teiresias warns, before disaster overtakes his house (1064ff.).

As the human world is plunging into the darkness of subterranean chambers, the fifth and last stasimon celebrates Dionysus in terms of light flashing out of the darkness. The chorus dwells on the torchlight processions of bacchantic worshipers on Parnassus: "The glaring fire and smoke above Parnassus' twin-crested rock reveal you, Dionysus, there where Corycian Nymphs, devotees of Bacchus, dance" (1126ff.). They invoke the celestial aspect of Zeus, "deep-roaring" god of thunder and lightning, a spirit far different from Creon's scorn about his throne in the heavens (1117, 1139; cf. 1040–41). The ode ends with a brilliant image of Dionysus as "chorus-leader of fire-breathing stars" (1146–47). We recall the nocturnal fires of the Thebans behind their walls in the parode, celebrating their victory over the maenadic violence of fratricidal war (152–153). Now we move far beyond those walls. The worshipers in the fifth stasimon are women, not citizens, and they are out on the wild mountains. Their worship of the cosmic Dionysus has a calm and an expansiveness which elude the hate-ridden Thebans.

When we return from the Dionysus ode to the human action, this ode's movement from darkness to light reverses itself, a movement already anticipated in the first chorus' shift from "beam of the sun" (100) to "all-night dances" (153).[143] Just after this ode the Messenger announces Creon as a "living corpse" (1167) and tells of his descent into the cave. Creon says himself later that he has "entered Hades' harbor" (1284). Now he confronts the dark places of his own house where Eurydice's "dark lids," loosed in death, complete his ruin.

"Hades is the one who will stop this marriage," Creon announced coldly at the end of his interview with the captured Antigone. But far from "stopping her marriage," Hades consummates it (1235–41) and simultaneously destroys Creon's. As her "bridegroom," Hades brings a dark fulfillment to Antigone's *eros* for death (220; cf. 90). In death she is in a sense united with all her loved ones (897–902), whereas Creon is deprived of all of his.[144]

The emerging influence of Eros, Hades, and Dionysus in the last three choral odes complements, not contradicts, the human motivation, in accordance with the process of "double determination" or "overdetermination" frequent in Greek literature.[145] The increasing evidence of divine forces is another way of showing that human events have left the track of rational control and are in touch with the unknown. What we would call instinctive drives or buried psychological forces that finally break through a long-maintained resistance, the Greek poets view as an essential part of the cosmic order. These forces are, therefore, gods: that is, they are facts of power. "It is an idea that we meet over and over again in Greek tragedy," writes Kitto, "that when someone acts out of one of the fundamental necessities of life or in response to what we can call our deepest and most sacred instincts, he is working with the gods and the gods with him."[146]

XV

The deepest level of Antigone's tragic heroism and of her ambiguous relation to the positive values of life and civilization lies in her fearful acceptance of these elemental, divine powers, Eros and Hades, especially Hades. Antigone, the woman, is ready to close with the infinities which Creon's masculine rationality shuns. As the one who gives birth, the woman stands in the more immediate connection with life and death, and for Antigone kinship means the ties of birth. "It is noble," Antigone says, "to do this deed [i.e. bury Polyneices] and die" (72). She counts it a "profit" to die before her time (461–464). "You chose to live, I to die," she tells Ismene (555). And a few lines later she adds, "My soul has died long ago, so that my help is to the dead" (559–560). She feels an instinctive affinity for death and love because they, like her, reach into the timeless. The laws that she dies for "live always," as she says in her great defense of the unwritten laws (456–457); and it is in Hades that she will "lie always," as she says in the first scene (76).

Antigone's measure of existence is not the relative length of a man's life but the absolute, eternity. This is the *heroic* dimension of her devotion to Hades. She chooses the dead *philoi*, loved ones, over the living because they belong to eternity. She could have another husband or child, she explains in her last iambic speech but never another father or brother (905–915). The reasoning is emotionally, if not logically, consistent (for that reason so many scholars have sought to remove the speech as an interpolation), and this terrible emotional consistency is one of the basic qualities of Sophoclean heroism. It is not reasonable, refuses to be reasonable. Eternity, being and nonbeing, cannot be rationalized or comprehended within the categories of logical argumentation.

The power of Sophocles' tragic heroism lies in its passionate and fearless openness to the forces that challenge and threaten the orderly framework of human existence: time, death, hatred, love. For this reason the tragic hero is always in some sense beyond the pale of civilization, which can exist only by blocking out or delimiting those forces. It is part of the greatness of the fifth century that it allows the dialogue between the two sides to develop so fully. Tragedy is the outgrowth of this dialogue, this irresolvable dialectic, between the limited and the infinite, between man's civilizing, ordering energies and all that those energies cannot comprehend and master in the structures they so ambitiously create.

Nowhere is the contrast between the order and control of human civilization and the elemental forces beyond it more forceful than in the fifth stasimon, the ode to Dionysus.[147] It is curious that the poet usually taken as the exemplar of classic repose can write two of the most powerful odes in Greek literature on Eros and Dionysus. Here in the fifth stasimon the change from rationalism to ecstasy, from gnomic sententiousness to exuberant lyricism accompanies the breakthrough of supernatural forces into Creon's rigidly ordered polis.

This ode's maenadic lyric and bacchic dance opens a different perspective on the place of the polis in the natural world. The closing section of the ode lifts us beyond even human geography to the vast night sky and Dionysus' nocturnal choruses of stars (1146–54):

> O chorus leader of the fire-breathing stars,
> Watcher of the voices of the night,
> Child born of Zeus, appear, Lord,

With your attendant Thyads
Who, in the madness of their all-night dances,
Celebrate Iacchus the Dispenser.

This Dionysus is both a local and a universal god. He is the "joy of the Cadmean nymph," patron god of his "mother city of Thebes by the streams of the Ismenus" (1122–23),[148] but also the god "of many names" whose power ranges from Italy to Euboea (1116ff., 1126ff.). He is a god of the heavens in the last strophe but also identified with Iacchus, companion of the Eleusinian goddesses (1120–21), who had accomplished a descent into and ascent from the earth.[149]

Dionysus brings together the opposites which have been in tension throughout the play: Olympian and chthonic deities, city and nature, shelter and openness, light and darkness. His nature and attributes mysteriously unite polarities: the wildness of raging maenads and the distant tranquillity of the night sky. He is the god in whom the usual barriers erected between civilization and the wild break down.[150] His very being, as Euripides illustrates in the *Bacchae*, calls civilization itself into question.

The nocturnal setting of Dionysus' revels continues the darkness of Antigone's night burial of Polyneices and the darkness of imprisonment in the previous ode. But this darkness of Dionysus points to realms entirely beyond the civic context and the present tragedy. It is lit by the torches of the Corycian Nymphs (1126ff.) and the stars. After the themes of confinement in the previous ode and in the fate of Antigone, the expansive setting is exhilarating, but the final stage of the catastrophe brings a contrapuntal movement back into the dark spaces of cave and house (1204ff., 1279ff.). The threatening madness of war or passion is now joyful (1151).[151] The dissonant clash and screams of the attack on Thebes give way to the "voices of the night" which Dionysus leads in a choral procession (1146ff.). The god's music answers Lycurgus' insult to his "flute-loving Muses" in the previous ode (965): an expansive freedom and an inclusive harmony with nature stand at the opposite extreme from the underground rocky prison in which that violent monarch was "yoked" (958).

This ode recreates, but inverts, the elements of the first ode in the play. The bacchic wildness of Polyneices, "bearing fire" and "raging" (*pyrphoros, mainomenā(i) syn hormā(i)*, 135–136), and the "all-night choral celebrations" of victorious Thebes are now peaceful and cosmic rather than bellicose and defensive. The brightness in that limited civic context proves premature. For this Dionysus, leading choruses of Thyads and guiding the choruses of stars in the night, light and dark, reason and madness, coexist rather than clash destructively.

In balancing control over nature by sympathy with nature, reason by ecstasy, Dionysus also adds another dimension to the sexual antagonisms of the play. His divinity includes the maternal Demeter (1120) and bands of women followers, those "inspired women" (*entheous gynaikas*) whom a harsh king checked with force and insult (964–965), much as Creon behaved toward Antigone. Dionysus is to the limits of reason what Antigone's deeply feminine loyalties to the ties created by the womb are to the masculine loyalties toward the polis. He not only leads women outside of the house, their "proper" sphere, upon the open spaces of the mountains but also enables them, unarmed, to defeat men (*Bacchae* 758–764). Yet Antigone's intuitive sympathy with nature in comparing herself to Niobe (823–833) has none of the joy of Dionysiac fusion. She remains linked to the lower world, far from Dionysus' chorus of night stars.[152] Her struggle for the primordial oneness of the womb against the differentiation imposed by the laws of the city contrasts with the larger, cosmic oneness of Dionysus. Her efforts tend not to the open, starlit sky but to the endless darkness of the cave/womb of death.

The contrasts surrounding Dionysus extend to Thebes as well as to Antigone. The Thebans invoke Dionysus in the name of "the city and all its people" (*pandamos polis*, 1141) to come as purifier for the city's "violent disease" (1137–45). But what the city wants of the god and what the god actually gives are not necessarily the same. The chorus' prayer for help contrasts with the violent attributes of the god, especially the thunder which destroyed Semele (1139), a reminder perhaps of the power of Zeus which Creon has treated in so cavalier a fashion. The god is to come over "the groaning strait," *stonoenta porthmon* (1145): these, the last words of the strophe, are ominous: they evoke the sinister sea of the previous odes (cf. especially *stonos*, "groan," 593).

The ode begins and ends with the Eleusinian Dionysus, "in the folds of Eleusinian Demeter common to all" (1120–21), Dionysus as "Iacchus the Dispenser" (*ton tamian Iakchon*, 1154). Instead of the destructive, vengeful Dionysus who maddened and imprisoned Lycurgus in the previous ode, this hymn offers us a vegetation god connected with the richness of the vine (1133) and the renewal of life from death celebrated at the Eleusinian mysteries.[153] Antigone had invoked Hades "who receives all in sleep" (*pankoitas*, 810) and spoke of Persephone who "has received the greatest number" of her dead kin in her dark kingdom (893–894). But the death which Antigone envisages, unlike that of the Eleusinian Demeter and Iacchus-Dionysus, is eternal, not part of a cyclical rhythm of loss and rebirth. The maternal generosity of Eleusinian Demeter (see 1120–21) only sets off Antigone's desolation as a Kore who will not ascend from the dark Underworld to the bright sky. Her sterility as bride of Hades appears as all the more barren when seen in relation to the pairing of Demeter and Iacchus-Dionysus, dispenser of joy and wealth, child of the Eleusinian goddess and recipient of her bountiful maternity.

Antigone's death as bride of Hades contrasts not only with the cyclical renewal of nature associated with Demeter and Iacchus but also with the collective manner of worship: her loneliness against the choruses, whether of stars or maenads, fused in ecstatic togetherness. This contrast between divine and human action extends also to Creon and the citizens of Thebes: their hope to find in the god a divine patron for "purifying" the city of its "disease" (1142–44; cf. 1015) dissolves in the "harbor of Hades hard to purify" in the next scene (1284). The Olympian oneness of the sky in this last ode, then, moves back again to the chthonic oneness of death.

Dionysus' chorus of "fire-breathing stars" opens the ritual spaces of theater and the civic space of the polis to the infinities above, as Antigone opened the polis world of the play to the infinities which lie below. But Dionysus' astral regions have their dangerous aspect too, for "fire-breathing" implies the bestial destructiveness of a monster like the Chimaera. Dionysus may span Olympian and chthonic divinity, but his remote chorus of "fire-breathing stars" in the last antistrophe gives no clear assurance of mediation between the two realms, the eternal gods of Olympus and the eternally dead. This contrast in a sense reaffirms, in larger perspective, the oppositions of the second stasimon (603–610). The fusion of contraries which takes place around him cannot help the polarized oppositions of this tragic situation, until both sides are absorbed into the cavernous "nothingness" of Hades (1284, 1325).

The ode touches on still another tension within this city of sorrows. The chorus speaks of the primitive origins of Thebes from "the sowing of the wild dragon," *agriou epi sporā(i) drakontos* (1124–25). In the parode this "savagery" in Thebes' origins was part of the bestialized fratricidal struggle of a divided city: Thebes proved "the hostile dragon hard to subdue" (*antipalou dyscheirōma drakontos*, 126–127). In the last ode that savagery in Thebes' very origins coexists with the gentler landscape of the "mother city" and the "liquid streams" of its river, Ismenus (1123–24). Dionysus dwells (1123) in both places. Like Thebes' savage dragon, the god calls into question the clear limits of the polis. In both Dionysus and the dragon, as in Antigone too, what is at the center of the city's vital life reveals itself as somehow intractable to incorporation into the shelter of civilized space.

In its connection with the earth and with caves the dragon also continues the tension between upper and lower worlds, between the polis and those more savage, darker qualities of man with which it must somehow deal.[154] If we may reconstruct a hypothetical structure of spatial terms, Megareus/Menoeceus who sacrifices himself for the city (1303) stands at the very boundary between the city and the savage space outside, which is also the place where the savage dragon has his lair. His downward leap to the dragon's den attempts a mediation between city and earth which saves the city but leaves a destructive residue which Creon will encounter in the cave and in Eurydice's dark recesses, places where the sheltered structures of human civilization likewise are dependent on primordial forces of nature.[155] The dragon itself, from whose teeth, according to myth, the Thebans were sown (a mediation of the destructive and creative powers of the earth), can be viewed as a mythical attempt to bridge the gap between the city and the elemental world in which it stands. A human sacrifice is still needed to appease the subjected powers of earth.

In presenting Dionysus as the "chorus leader" of the stars, this last ode incorporates the performance itself and its place in civic ritual into the meaning of the tragic action. In the parode Polyneices appeared as a raging bacchant, breathing on the Thebans with the winds of hate. The removed Dionysus at the end leads the stars that "breathe fire," but this is not the totally destructive fire which Polyneices brings against his city. The citizens of the parode approach the temples of the gods in "all-night choruses" (152–153), but Dionysus' choruses of night stars are not to be confined in human spaces. The first ode of the play began with an invocation to the beam of the sun (100) before going on to the themes of madness, the night choruses, fire. The brightness in the limited civic context of that ode was premature. For this Dionysus, leading choruses of raging Maenads, yet guiding the steadier choruses of stars in the night, light and dark, reason and madness are not necessarily opposites. In extending the city's power over life and death, Creon had set a "day-watcher," *hēmeroskopos*, over the body on the wild hillside (253), a watcher whose sight is not keen enough. Here, near the end, the god whose rites involve the fusion of man with nature's energies is the "watcher" (*episkopos*) not of the mouldering corpse, but of the vast starlit skies of night (1146–48).

As the wild mountains and astral spaces of the ode expand the civic spaces of the polis, so the chorus of Nymphs and Thyads—the god's "immortal followers" (1134)—take us beyond the ritual celebrations of the citizen chorus of the parode (151–154) to a chorus composed not even of gods but of stars (1147). Here the ritual form of tragedy once more shows its capacity to embrace its own negation. The worship of Dionysus through choral dance in both the first and the last odes mirrors back the worship of Dionysus which is enacted in the performance itself, the dramatic festival held under the patronage of the god.

The worship of Dionysus here contains a contradiciton. The chorus whose ordered rhythms affirm a harmonious accord between the cosmos and the polis celebrate a Dionysus who transcends, if not actually shatters, the limits of the polis. This ode on Dionysus is the pendant not only to the civic, local celebration of Dionysus in the parode but also to the rational order extolled in the Ode on Man. On the one side stand the orderly civic spaces of wall and tower and the limits—spatial, religious, conceptual—that they impose; on the other side stand the vast, undefined spaces of mountain and sky. The ode helps indicate that the subject of this, as perhaps of all, tragedy is not just a specific event or a specific character, but the world itself, the permanent factors in the very makeup of the universe, the irreconcilable opposites between which all life is lived.[156]

Against the eternal clash of Eros and Hades, Life and Death, the civilizing power seems crushed, dwarfed. Yet the play shows not the collapse of human civilization but the opposing poles between which it is strung, the Olympian and Titanic sides of Dionysus, the celestial and chthonic Zeus. The progression which runs through the odes of the play shapes an increasing awareness of this tension.

Through its choral song the polis arrives at self-awareness of the tensions between which it exists. Embodying these tensions in art, it can confront them and work toward their mediation, even though mediation is not permitted to the tragic heroes within the spectacle itself. The play in its social and ritual contexts achieves for the society what it refuses to the actors within its fiction. Its context affirms what its content denies.

The Dionysus who leads the remote "fire-breathing stars" in the last ode is also the Dionysus celebrated by the performance itself. He is, as Bacchylides calls him, "the lord of the garlanded choruses" at the festivals held in his honor, leading the dithyrambic dance which celebrates his power (Bacch. 18.51). His role as the chorus leader of those stars and as the overseer of the night's voices mirrors the movements of the human chorus and the rhythms articulated by their voices in the orchestra. In the geometrically defined spaces of that orchestra the polis reaches imaginatively beyond itself to the undefined and unlimited spaces of the night sky and the wild mountainside. Its art and ritual form an orderly imitation of the ecstatic madness of the ambiguous god whom it is celebrating. The limits of aesthetic form and civic space become for a short time the containers of the limitless. The orchestra of the communal theater doubles for a moment with the orchestra of the universe where the stars perform their flaming dance.

If the human action shows us men and women pulled back into the darkness of an inherited curse, savagery, and hatred, the odes show us, at a few rare moments, glimpses of Olympian brilliance (610–611) and reveal that the world of nature holds both dark, turbulent waves and festive joy, both ecstasy and order. Yet they also reveal the savage fury of the attack on Thebes as a kind of released Dionysiac energy, a less peaceful aspect of the revels of the god celebrated in the final ode. Dionysus' intense union of serenity and ecstasy is not attainable by men or ultimately containable within the walls of the polis, except in the form of tragedy. Tragic art enables the polis to confront the contradictions which man's place in nature poses. It is that Dionysiac background, calm sky and nocturnal chorus of immortal stars, which forms the setting for the human actors' final agony.

7

Oedipus Tyrannus

 No figure in Greek drama more powerfully and tragically embodies the paradoxes of man's civilizing power than Oedipus. Ruler of a great and ancient city by virtue of his intelligence, vanquisher of a mysterious monster itself half-human and half-bestial, Oedipus sums up all that man can attain by mind alone. And yet this solver of riddles does not know the most fundamental thing about himself. He lacks the basic information about his origins that gives man his human identity and sets him apart from the undifferentiated realm of nature and the anonymous, unindividuated realm of the beasts.

Oedipus' very identity conceals a dreadful violation of civilized norms, the exposure of a first child by its parents on a savage mountainside. Though the exposure of a child was permissible in classical Greece, the exposure of a first-born son by the ruling pair of the city, not poor folk who had the excuse of poverty, is almost unprecedented.[1] Cast out from the shelter of the house, Oedipus is made a creature of the wild, a child of the mountain and a child of Chance. He is saved from death by shepherds, men who dwell beyond the pale of the city and occupy an ambiguous position between the wild and the civilized. Thrust from his *oikos*, he has no name, no rooted human identity, the most basic possession of even the humblest human being. The name which he does possess, "Swell-Foot," according to an etymology of which Oedipus himself is painfully aware, attests to the brutal act which separated him from the civilized world and gave him his anomalous place apart.

This outcast from home and city is destined to violate two of the most fundamental laws of civilization, patricide and incest. Contemporaries of Sophocles single out just these two taboos as the dividing line between human and animal behavior.[2]

And yet the Oedipus whose very name places him in the wild is also the quintessentially civilized man. His name can also be translated "Know-Foot" (from *oida*, "I know, and *pous*, "foot"); and in this etymology it recalls Oedipus' answer to the riddle of the Sphinx, which is the riddle of man's shifting, transient identity in time. The changing number of feet in the riddle (four, two, three) indicates the changeful quality of man's identity. Oedipus himself solves this riddle before our eyes, not in words, but in his enacted sufferings on the stage. Intelligent but irascible, humane but violent, compassionate but potentially ruthless (as in his threats to Creon and the old herdsman), Oedipus sums up all the essential paradoxes of man's nature. As Vernant suggests, he occupies simultaneously the highest and lowest places within his city, the role of king and the role of scapegoat or *pharmakos*, a figure whose associations are with what is "wild" or "savage," *agrios*.[3] His suffering enacts the city's ritual expulsion of its own latent savagery. Yet this ritual expulsion of the scapegoat becomes, in the dramatic fiction, also the expulsion, or attempted expulsion, of the irrational, uncontrollable forces that play so destructively about human life and about Oedipus' life most of all.

The ritual explanation of the play, however, is inadequate to the complexities and the paradoxes which Sophocles has wrought into its extraordinary structure. Even on the level of ritual action, Oedipus' expulsion as a *pharmakos* is ambiguous and problematical. As the play ends, he is not actually expelled. In the Homeric version of the legend, in fact, he continued to rule over Thebes.[4] In Sophocles' ending Oedipus remains suspended between expulsion and enclosure, between exile and the house which, on Creon's order, he reenters to hide his pollution from earth and sky. Thus in some sense Oedipus continues the ambiguities of his previous life. Yet at this point, when the hero, revealed as homeless, most desires exile and homelessness, he is made to feel most fully his responsibilities to and his protection by an *oikos*.

The impulsive violence of the punishment which Oedipus inflicts upon himself contrasts with the gentleness and restraint with which he is received by his family and fellow citizens and even by the new king of Thebes. When Oedipus stands before the city as the accursed outcast, he appears against the background of his warmest human ties in his concern for his children at the end. When the "savagery" of his place in the human world is clearest, in other words, he is most of all the civilized and civilizing hero, in the full, tragic ambiguity of that role.

The very first verse in the play presents the irony and the paradox of Oedipus' relation to civilization. The king addresses his assembled people who come to him in the ritual posture of supplication:

Children of Cadmus old the new progeny.

Ὦ τέκνα, Κάδμου τοῦ πάλαι νέα τροφή.

Trophē, "progeny, nursling brood," here used collectively (an unusual sense), also means "nurture."[5] It is the first and most fundamental benefit that a civilized house offers to its offspring, the benefit the outcast Oedipus has not received. This city, however, cannot now nurture its young, who perish in the womb (26–27) or on the earth (180).[6]

Oedipus' Theban subjects have a long-established communal past (cf. *palai*, "of old") which Oedipus, king but (as he thinks) outsider, shares only in an ambiguous and dangerous manner. The Thebans have a common ancestor, "Cadmus of old": Oedipus' ancestry, so far as he knows it, has its roots in Corinth. When he is called "a native-born Theban," *engenēs Thēbaios* (452–453), it is as an insult and prophecy of his doom. The collocation of youth and age in the city's stable continuity contrasts also with Oedipus' confusion of generations through his incestuous marriage. An orderly city integrates past, present, and future generations, but Oedipus runs together generations that should be distinct and successive.

Still within the prologue, Oedipus introduces himself as "I who am called Oedipus, glorious to all" (8). He does not say "I am Oedipus," as the Homeric Odysseus says "I am Odysseus, and my fame mounts to the heavens" (*Od.* 9.19). Oedipus' proud boast conceals the disastrous ambiguity of his name, "the (so-) called (glorious) Oedipus," *ho pasi kleinos Oidipous kaloumenos*. Everything about this hero, beginning with his name, reflects his ambiguous relation to the human community which should have provided his nurture.

The city pays for its nurture of Oedipus with the pollution, "nurtured in the land"—Creon's eagerly awaited news from Delphi (97)—which it must "drive out and not nurture unhealed" (98). Ironically, the city nurtures as a pollution the one citizen who has not received its nurture.

The opening scene stresses the civilized spaces within the city: the altars (16), market place or agora (20), the two temples of Athena, the oracular shrine of Apollo (20–21). Later the chorus will mention the temple of Artemis in the agora (161). But these civic spaces are threatened, as they were in the days of the Sphinx, by mysterious forces which, though "nurtured within" (97–98), also reflect a violation in the relationship between man and nature. The city is in danger of becoming deserted, *erēmos* (57). Oedipus' city, like Creon's in the *Antigone* (though from a different cause), is faced with extinction; the land becomes empty or barren (*kenē*, 54–55), since "a tower or ship is nothing if men do not dwell together within" (*synoikein esō*, 54–57). The shelter of the city is penetrated by a "storm of blood" (101): the violence of nature metaphorically breaches the walls. At the end of the play the king will remove this inner storm by bearing the full brunt of it himself in the "black rain and bloody hail" that fall from his injured eyes (1278–79).

Denied the proper nurture himself, Oedipus cannot comprehend Teiresias' apparent ingratitude toward the "city which nurtured him" (322–323). The truth which Teiresias does "nurture" will sever Oedipus' tie with his city (356). Though he taunts Teiresias with being "nurtured by one unbroken night" (374), Oedipus will find that his own nurture is his doom. It is surely more than accident that he reverses the natural order when, in recounting the oracles which drove him from Corinth, he calls Polybus "the man who nurtured and begot me" (827).

Oedipus gradually traces his nurture to a slave not purchased, but nurtured in the house (1123). But when he discovers himself as "the single best-nurtured man in Thebes" (1380; cf. 1142–43), he is simultaneously the polluted outcast, laden with all the evils that have a name (1284–85), "nursed" as a fair form with horrible sores festering beneath (1394–96). Even the slave was nursed in the house (*oikoi trapheis*, 1123); but Oedipus, expelled by that house, precisely because of that "best nurture" (1380), stands even below the slave. That superlative nurture paradoxically sets him outside "the town, towers, and sacred images of the gods" (1378–79) and sends him back to the mountain outside the city,

Cithaeron, the true place of his nurture, which "received" him as the house did not.

Estranged from the nurture of his house, Oedipus, though king, is also a stranger to the town or city he rules. With relentless irony Sophocles plays *xenos* and *astos*, "stranger" and "townsman," off against one another (see 219–222, 452, 455). Oedipus' fusion of nearness and distance ("stranger alike to the word and the deed," 219–220) will cause him to be cut off from stranger and towns-man both (816–819). In this same passage, when he fears that he may have killed Laius, he is still sheltered from the most fearful part of the truth by his assumption that Laius is a stranger. After telling how he killed the whole group at the crossroads, he concludes, "If Laius had any *kinship* (*syngenes*) with this *stranger* (*xenos*), who is more wretched than I?" (813–817).

Oedipus' "release" (*lysis*) of the "Cadmean town" has earned Oedipus his people's gratitude and recognition (35), and Oedipus repeats the boast later ("release for the townsmen," 392). But when he calls Thebes his paternal city, *patrōon asty*, he awaits exile in the wild mountains (1449ff.). He has blinded himself because he cannot bear to look on the town or towers of Thebes (1378). None of its townsmen (*astoi*) will now associate with his daughters (1489). The king who stands at the very center of the town (*asty*) creates distance all around him. We understand in retrospect how prophetic was the old Shepherd's wish to remove himself "as far as possible out of sight of the town" (*apoptos asteōs*) when Oedipus became king (762).[7]

By his extraordinary intelligence and will, Oedipus has transcended the brutal suffering and rejection of his infancy, passed from doomed babe to pow-erful ruler. Yet he is always, in a sense, held fast to the circumstances of those first terrible days of his life. He remains still the child of the "pathless mountain" where his parents "cast him out" (719, 1452ff.). Hence the rapidity and stub-bornness with which he concludes that Creon is trying to cast him out (*ekballein* 386, 399) without honor (*atimos*, 670). Sent away without honor, *atimos*, by Apollo from his oracle (789), he himself, not Creon, will cancel his great honors in Thebes (1202–1203). He can become free of that earliest and most deter-mining experience of his life only by reliving it, in a new but no less terrible form. His self-discovery as the source of Thebes' pollution is both the conse-quence and the reenactment of that initial banishment from the shelter of a civilized house.

The *skēptron* with which he kills Laius embodies the extreme polarities be-tween which Oedipus' tragic existence is strung. On the one hand it is the sign of regal authority; on the other it is the staff of the blind beggar with which, in Teiresias' prophecy, he will tap his way, poor instead of rich, a perpetual exile in a strange land (*xenēn epi gaian*, 455–456).

Having violated the taboos of incest and patricide, Oedipus, like Ajax, is deprived of the mediation between beast and god effected by the civilized forms of the polis. At the peripety, on the verge of the truth, Oedipus calls himself "a child of Chance, *Tychē*, the generous giver" (1080–81). Chance will not rob him of that honor (*timē*) which he so fears to lose (*ouk atimasthēsomai*, 1081; cf. 670,

787). The chorus interprets this hope to mean that he will prove the child of a god (1098ff.), as the mythical hero so often is.[8] But tragedy inverts the usual mythic pattern. To be a child of Chance can also signify to live below, not above, the human condition, to live as the beasts of the field, without order or limit.

Shortly before, Jocasta, trying to avoid the accumulating circumstantial evidence, appeals to "chance" and "randomness" in a tone of wistful simplification (977–983):

> What should a man fear, man for whom Chance rules, lacking clear fore-knowledge of anything. Best is to live randomly (*eikē kratiston zēn*, 979) as one can. Don't be afraid of marriage with your mother. For many men in dreams have slept with their mothers. He to whom these things are as nothing bears his life easiest.

From the notion of a divine providence revealed in the oracles, Jocasta leaps to the opposite extreme, the chaotic "random" life, governed by chance. In other fifth-century authors "to live randomly" in fact describes the disordered, "beast-like" life of precivilized man.[9]

The Chance which seems to govern Oedipus' life, then, contains the two extremes of divinity and bestiality. As a confident efficient king in the prologue, Oedipus joins *tychē* and Apollo (80–81): "Lord Apollo, by some saving chance may he (Creon) come bright as his eye is bright." But in the characteristically dense syntax of this play the lines may also mean, "May he walk bright in saving chance as bright in (saving) eye." At the end, when Apollo's oracle and chance seem to come to the same thing (cf. 1329), "walking," "brightness," and "saving" have been turned upside down. The "savior" king is the pollution who will curse his own savior (48, 1030, 1180, 1349–50). The chance by which Oedipus saved Thebes will destroy him (cf. 442–443), and he will prove Thebes' savior only by destroying himself.[10] Fulfilling Teiresias' prophecy, he will put out his "bright eyes" and walk in darkness (454–456, 1483; cf. 81).

Oedipus has his name from "chance" (1035–37):

> Oed.: Terrible the insult (*oneidos*) I received of my swaddling clothes.[11]
> Mess.: Yes, so that you were named who you are from that *chance* (*tychē*).
> Oed.: By the gods, was it my father or my mother? Tell me.

Here, for the first time in the play, Oedipus reveals the emotional charge which his infirmity holds for him. His ironic "terrible the insult" and his reference to the details of his infancy (swaddling clothes) express his deeply buried pain of having been cast out of his house into the wild.

On the verge of discovering the truth concealed in his name, Oedipus is preoccupied with naming. "For what reason, then, did Polybus name me his child?" (1021). His own name is a kind of antiname: It is a "reproach" or "insult" (*oneidos*). It is the "insult" of his name which, as he laments at the end, he will pass on to his daughters (*oneidos*, 1494, 1500). He left Corinth when he could not bear the insult of bastardy (784), but in trying to prove his legitimate name, he only fulfills the "insults" of the oracles (797). Later he proves true the insults which he exchanges with Teiresias (372–373, 412). "Insult me where you will find me great," was his proud challenge to Teiresias (441). But the very name of "Oedipus the great" (cf. 1083) proves to be an insult or reproach (1035–36). Oedipus' reversal is such as to excite insult or mockery from his former subjects; Creon, returning to the stage in 1422, is careful to forestall this possibility in his opening lines (1422–23).

"Named who you are from that chance": the irony deepens fifty lines later with Oedipus' confidence that he is a "child of Chance." He is a "child of Chance" in the grimmest possible way: he has his name from chance, not from the parents who exposed him before giving him a name. In the *Odyssey* the hero's humanity is inextricably bound up with his name. When he is treated like a beast in a cave, he loses that name and becomes *Outis*, No One.[12] In Herodotus the lack of individual names is an attribute of a savage people in the wilds of the Atlas mountains of North Africa (4.184). These same people, according to Pomponius Mela, who follows Herodotus closely here, also lack dreams that other humans see in their sleep (1.43). Not only is Oedipus denied this most basic mark of civilized identity, but his name is his curse: it points back to the initial expulsion itself. A "terrible-footed curse," *deinopous ara*, will drive Oedi-pous from the land, predicts Teiresias in one of the play's many grim puns on the name (418).

The horrible anomaly of Oedipus' place in the house confuses both the linguistic and the familial codes, both normal human relations and the names of kin ties (cf. 1214–15, 1256–57, 1405–1408). Similarly his ambiguous naming from chance confuses linguistic, familial, and spatial codes all together. Normally, the naming of a child took place at the rite of the *amphidromia*, when the child on the fifth day after birth was carried around the hearth and then placed on the hearth to receive his name.[13] Oedipus, however, receives his name not in the sheltered, domestic spaces of the house but out on the wild mountainside. The content of the name itself attests to the child's anomalous relation to house and parents.

"Named who you are"—the phrase echoes in Jocasta's penultimate words to Oedipus: "Ill-fated man! May you never know who you are" (1068). The meaning of the cry escapes Oedipus: he replies with a command to bring the shepherd (1069) and adds, "And let her rejoice in her rich family" (*plousiōi genei*, 1070). But that "rich family" includes Oedipus himself as her own child. The word translated "family," *genos*, can also have the concrete meaning "offspring," as well as the more abstract or collective meanings "kinship" or "race." By this point in the play all three meanings fuse, and all three have an ominous ring. Oedipus shuddered when he recalled the prophecy of the "unendurable race" or "family" that he was to bring forth (*genos atlēton*, 791–792). "Rich" also recalls the grim association of "wealth" and Hades in the prologue (*Plouton* and *ploutos*: cf. 29–30).[14] Earlier in this scene the word *genos*, "family," quickened Oedipus' search for "who he is": "Polybus is nothing to you in family" (*genei*), the Corinthian Messenger had said (1016). Polybus' remoteness in kinship is answered by Jocasta's excessive closeness. Her farewell line could also be translated, "Let her rejoice in her rich kinship." "Kinship," which seems to be moving to a safe distance, has a final ironic reverberation in his "kindred months" (*syngeneis mēnes*) at the end of the scene (1082–83).

Oedipus' destruction of the "difference" fundamental to the norms of civilization is especially marked in his multiple relation to "equality." Oedipus introduces a dangerous "equality" into language and kin ties, refuses to recognize the claims of "equality" in judicial procedure, and at one point approximates a position of dangerous "equality" with the gods.

Isēgoria, equality of speech, is one of the main achievements of Athenian democracy, and the principle of equality receives much attention from political thinkers in the fifth and fourth centuries.[15] In the *Politics* Aristotle points out that a citizen so preeminent as to appear a god among men must be expelled from the polis for the sake of equality (3.1284a11ff.). Ostracism is the Athenian mechanism to maintain this equality (3.1284a19ff.). In Oedipus' case, as Vernant suggests, the expulsion of the figure who exceeds at the upper limit (a god among men) fuses with expulsion of the figure who lies below the lower limit, the *pharmakos* or ritual scapegoat charged with all the pollutions of the city.[16] The Greek word *isos* spans both political status and logical identity; it connotes both "equality" and "sameness." In Oedipus' terrible equality, to be "equal to the gods" and "to be equal to nothing" coincide (cf. 31, 1187–88).[17] By proving equal to his earlier victory over the Sphinx (53), Oedipus answers that riddle in another form, and his equality with his earlier skill once more saves Thebes, though it destroys Oedipus.

This doubling of the saving with the destructive equality is particularly marked in the verbal play in the two near homophones, *exisōsei*, "will make you equal," and *exesōs(a)*, "I saved." In 425 Teiresias warns Oedipus that he does not perceive "the evils that will *make you equal* to your children."[18] In 443 Oedipus defends himself as the one who has saved the city, even at the cost of his own destruction (442–443):

Teir.: Just this chance (*tychē*) has destroyed you.
Oed.: But if I saved this city (*exesōsa*), I do not care.

The near coincidence of sound between the destructive "equality" of 425 and the saving solution to the riddle's "equality" in 443 places Oedipus simultaneously at the lowest limit of the human race as the city's pollution, "made equal to his children" in incest, and at the highest limit as the city's godlike savior (31). Moreover, Oedipus saved his city by resolving the Sphinx's specious differentiation of the three stages of human life (the riddle) back into the unity-in-difference of his answer, "man," the being whose evolution from the bestial life to near-divinity has made him and his microcosmic embodiment, Oedipus, both one and many.

Oedipus' encounters with Teiresias and Creon enact a destruction of juridical and political equality. Oedipus refuses his interlocutors the right of equal speech and equal hearing (408–409 and 544; cf. 627). One of Creon's points in his defense is the equality of honor, property, and power that he enjoys under Oedipus' rule (563, 579, 581; cf. 611). In this dispensation Oedipus has in fact shown himself a good ruler, dividing prerogatives equitably as Zeus, for example, does in the *Theogony*. But in reacting to the suspected breach of equality (cf. 635), he is not content merely with casting out Creon as Creon would have cast him out (386, 399 and 622) but would take the further step of putting him to death (623).

"Equal" is Creon's last word as he leaves Jocasta and Oedipus together (676–677): "I shall go, having found you unknowing, but myself in (the eyes of) these men equal." Creon means that he himself is still equal to his former honor (as the scholiast takes the passage) or that he is just in the eyes of the chorus (as Jebb takes it). In either case, Oedipus, "unknowing" but also "unknown" (*agnōs* here can have both meanings), stands in an ambiguous relation to the civic equality or fairness of the good ruler (cf. 61).

Teiresias began his first long speech with the juridical "equality" of the ruler (*tyranneis*, 408–409). Fifteen lines later that civilized equality in the city is contradicted by the chaotic "equality" that Oedipus has created in his house, "the evils which will make you equal to yourself and your children" (425). If Oedipus, as king and savior, was almost equal to the gods, "godlike," as a Homeric hero (31),[19] he is also near the beasts whose random procreation he has carried into a human family, begetting children "from the equals from which he himself was begotten," as he laments near the end (1498–99). "There is not one of you whose disease is equal to mine," Oedipus told the suppliants in the prologue (61). He speaks these words as the solicitous king comforting his people, but his "equality" in the "disease" as a native-born Theban puts him at the lowest, not the highest, point within the city.

"Equality" operates homologously in the several areas of civilized life, interrelated by the structure and language of the play. Oedipus inverts concepts of "equality" as applied to the family, the state, commerce, ethics, and ratiocinative activity in general. "He paid back no equal share," Oedipus says of his vengeance on the supposed stranger at the crossroads (810), using a metaphor drawn from commerce and justice. As a civilizing hero, Oedipus is the rational man who can calculate and distribute the "equalities" on which society depends, but he is also the man of passion who can repay an insult "with no equal share." He has saved a city and gained a throne by solving a riddle that has to do with equality, sameness, and number: "There is a creature on the earth with one name, two-footed, four-footed, three-footed."[20] In the course of the play Oedipus has to deal with another puzzling equality: "If he still says the same number, I am not the killer; for one would not be equal to many" (843–845). In this calculation, however, Oedipus fails. He unites the basic opposites of sameness and difference, unity and multiplicity, without the mediations that could protect him from the extremes of his nature or his situation.

Oedipus' search opens with a striking confusion of the one and the many. He asks Creon about Laius' escort on that fatal journey to Delphi (118–125):

Cr.:   They all died, except for *one*, who fled in fear and had nothing to
       say with certainty except *one* thing.

Oed.:   What? For *one* thing would often find out *many* if we should take a small beginning of hope.

Cr.:   He said that *robbers* (*lēistai*) killed him, coming on them not with the force of *one single man*, but with a *multitude* (*plēthos*) of hands.

Oed.:   How did *the robber* (*ho lēistēs*) come to such audacity unless he acted with money from here?

Oedipus' extraordinary error, "robber," after Creon's insistent contrast between "one" and "many," has often been noted, but its full force not brought out. The word "one" occurs four times in eight lines, the contrast between "one" and "many" twice within four lines, and still Oedipus says "the robber." With his great intelligence, he remains blind to a distinction between one and many, and so is blind to an even more crucial union of one and many in himself. Throughout the play, numerical patterns express this perplexing doubleness of identities. At crises Oedipus seems to count one-two-three: "one man . . . second things . . . nay, even third" (280–283); "one man . . . double flocks . . . three whole six-month periods" (1135–37). But all his counting, finally, equals zero (1188–89).[21]

"He said robbers" was Creon's report of the killing. It is with the same phrase, "He said robbers, as you related," that Oedipus pulls Jocasta up short in 842 (*lē(i)stas ephaske*, 122; *lē(i)stas ephaskes*, 842). But now the question of singular or plural is vital, and the matter has moved from the remoter third to the nearer second person. Now when Oedipus ponders the one and the many, it is a matter of vital consequences. Before that point is reached, however, he will wander in a futile search for robbers, misled by a confusion of unity and plurality, weakness and strength. He fastens on Creon as the "robber" (*lēistēs*, 535) of his kingdom but confidently believes that only a man with a multitude of friends and resources could essay its overthrow (540–542). Soon Oedipus will discover a different kind of multiplicity in himself, the "multitude (*plēthos*) of woes that makes (him) equal with (his) children" (424–425).

"Of all things that creep on the earth and move in the air and sea this alone changes its form (nature)," the ancient riddle went on. Oedipus' unique fate centers on that paradoxical and unstable middle term, the third foot. The act that cast him forth from house to "pathless mountain" (719) compels him to carry the "third foot" before his time. If he uses his scepter as a staff to aid his lameness, he goes on three feet at a period of life when most men go on two. Crippled for life by this maiming, Oedipus has, possibly, never gone on two feet at all. There is a grim justice—a Freudian might say a subconscious wish-fulfillment—that he should use the "third foot" against the man responsible for his bearing it at this stage of his life, a man who blocks his way as he "traverses his road" (*hodoiporōn*, 801) and tries to "pass by" (*parasteichōn*, 808; cf. *steichōn*, 798, "walking," "journeying").[22]

Oedipus is himself the anomalous third term,[23] the uneven number which bridges the gap between the four and the two and is also the differentiating term between bestial and human. Here, too, Oedipus, dissolving difference, stands "between." Beneath this arithmetical and locomotive peculiarity, however, lurks his life's far more sinister equation of one and many: king and scapegoat, son and husband, brother and father, knowing and not knowing, small and great. In the course of a single day (438) he will move through the three basic stages of human life, going back to his childhood and forward to helpless old age,[24] and in his fall he will simultaneously embrace the three biological conditions, god, man, and beast.

When opposites coalesce in this play they cancel each other out. Oedipus, who rests his hopes on the calculation of the difference between one and many, becomes as nothing in their sameness when the chorus makes another calculation (1186–88): "O generations of men, I number you as living equal to nothing" (to *enarithmō*, 1188, cf. *arithmos*, 844). The riddle plays upon sameness and difference in language; and its propounder fuses not only the different forms of locomotion but also the basic opposition of man and beast. Oedipus founds his innocence on a basic law of noncontradiction, the fundamental logic in man's apprehension of reality. Here, however, noncontradiction gives way to a fantastic, irrational "logic" of paradoxes in which opposites can in fact be equal and "one" can simultaneously be "many." "Equal to one" and "equal to many" come to yield the same terrible solution: "equal to nothing" (1186–88). But now Oedipus falls back on something more basic than his capacity for arithmetical calculation: he tries to break through the leveling of difference into sameness with a plea for his daughters. Entreating pity, he asks Creon, "Do not make them equal with me in my sufferings" (1507).

II

The riddle that both exalts and defeats Oedipus has to do with the anomalous position of man in the natural world. Not only has he evolved from the four-footed beasts to his unique two feet, but, thanks to his use of tools, he alone possesses that strange third foot. That third foot, however, can kill as well as support a lamed gait. Oedipus uses his staff (*skēptron*) both to kill his father, who is also the king, and to assert his own authority as king.[25] It both asserts and destroys order; as the beggar's staff at the end of the play (cf. 456), it brings together the other polarities which Oedipus spans: kingship and exile, power and helplessness, authority and dissolution of sacred bonds.

In Oedipus' hands "the third foot" contains the ambiguity of man's civilizing power and his destructive capacity: *homo faber* is also *homo necans*. Compensating artificially for his deficiencies in nature, man also does violence to nature in wresting from nature her hidden secrets, answering the riddle. Nietzsche saw the profound link between the "unnaturalness" of man's superiority over nature and the unnaturalness of Oedipus in his relation to nature's basic processes of birth and sexual union:

Oedipus, his father's murderer, his mother's lover, solver of the
Sphinx's riddle! What is the meaning of this triple fate? An ancient

popular belief, especially strong in Persia, holds that a wise *magus* must be incestuously begotten. If we examine Oedipus, the solver of riddles and liberator of his mother, in the light of this Parsee belief, we may conclude that wherever soothsaying and magical powers have broken the spell of present and future, the rigid law of individuation, the magic circle of nature, extreme unnaturalness—in this case incest—is the necessary antecedent; for how should man force nature to yield up her secrets but by successfully resisting her, that is to say, by unnatural acts? This is the recognition I find expressed in the terrible triad of Oedipean fates: the same man who solved the riddle of nature (the ambiguous Sphinx) must also, as murderer of his father and husband of his mother, break the consecrated tables of the natural order. It is as though the myth whispered to us that wisdom, and especially Dionysiac wisdom, is an unnatural crime, and that whoever, in pride of knowledge, hurls nature into the abyss of destruction, must himself experience nature's disintegration. "The edge of wisdom is turned against the wise man; wisdom is a crime committed on nature": such are the terrible words addressed to us by myth.[26]

Or, to quote Freud, "Man has become a god by means of artificial limbs, so to speak, quite magnificent when equipped with all his accessory organs; but they do not grow on him and they still give him trouble at times."[27]

Like Heracles in the *Trachiniae*, Oedipus has won a great victory over a bestial monster but confuses the boundaries between man and beast. Oedipus' marriage makes a chaos of the family structure (457–460, 1249ff., 1403–1408, 1497–99). His incest is a "yoking" which destroys rather than affirms, the distinctive qualities which separate human and bestial (826).[28] A yoking metaphor also describes the parents' unnatural behavior toward their child, for Jocasta uses it, a hundred lines earlier, of the piercing of the infant's ankles when they cast him out on the pathless mountain (718–719).

The metaphor of yoking correlates the inversions in the familial code with the superiority of man over beast in the biological code. In the prologue, we recall, the plague, which resulted from these pollutions in Oedipus' house, brings sterility to the earth, to animals, and to women (25–27).[29] The basic civilizing activities—agriculture, domestication of animals, the family—are therefore all implicated.

III

Incest in the royal house, the disruption of taboos relating to generation in the place most exemplary of the social order, causes a large-scale reversal of the relation between the human and natural order: plague and sterility.[30] In the imagery of the parode this disruption takes the form of the penetration of the city's boundaries by violent outside forces. This is the point in the play where we feel the pressure of the plague with greatest urgency. The ode moves from the sacred places that affirm order and civilization—Delphi, Delos, Thebes itself

(151–154)—to the civilizing goddess Athena and then to Artemis, here not the goddess of the wild, but of the city, she "who as the Fair-Famed (*Eukleia*) sits on her circled throne of the market-place" (agora, 161). Artemis and Apollo are invoked as gods who protect the boundaries of the city; when disaster (*atē*) struck, they "kept the flame away from the place, outside" (*ektopios*, 166).

When the chorus turns to its "numberless sufferings" and its "disease" in the next strophe, that fire is more threatening and the vast spaces outside are more ominous (174–177): "You would see (us) one after another like a swift-winged bird dash to outstrip the ravaging fire to the shore of the Western god." The fire here is the plague, and the flight of souls, like birds, to the West is a journey to the dark infinitude of death, the final negation of all human limit. The flight across the sea, then, is a concrete poetic image of the vastness of the outside that annihilates the orderly limits of city. "Whose city numberless is destroyed" is the next line of the ode (178–179), echoing the "numberless griefs" above (168). The threatening shore of the West is now within the city itself, for the "altar's edge" is literally the "altar's shore" (*aktan bōmion*, 183), a bold metaphorical confusion of inner and outer, polis and wild.

As the chorus dwells on the sounds of lamentation, the hostile world outside gains in force. The third strophe begins with Ares "blazing"; they hope that he may turn back to "Amphitrite's vast chamber" in the Atlantic Ocean (194–195) or "to the Thracian wave inhospitable of its harbors" (196–197). Here, as in the bird's journey to the Western shore earlier, fire and water combine with remote and unfriendly places at the limits of the civilized world to suggest the threats to the city whose borders (194) are violated.

The chorus then invokes Zeus, Apollo, and Artemis (200ff.), but all three appear with dangerous attributes: Zeus has "fire-bearing lightning bolts" (200), which recall the "fire" of the plague (166, 176) and the "fire-bearing god" who sends it in the prologue (27). Apollo has his shafts which, as in the first book of the *Iliad*, are also the shafts of the disease. Artemis, no longer a goddess seated in the agora, rushes over the remote Lycian mountains with fire-bearing brilliance (*pyrphoroi aiglai*, 206–207). Finally Dionysus, possibly appropriate as a god of purifications (cf. *Antig.* 1144), is invoked as the god of wine and ecstasy, the leader of the Maenads whose rites belong outside the city.[31] He is "ablaze," *phlegonta* (213), a word which recalls the sinister "blaze" (*phloga*, 166) of the plague. In the last line of the ode he is to "advance with torch upon the god dishonored among gods" (215). The reference is probably to the baleful Ares of 190ff.,[32] but Dionysus' own place among the Olympian gods is ambiguous, and in any case the closing image is one of strife rather than Olympian harmony. The torch of this "blazing" divinity still suggests the violence rather than the joyful release of the Maenads.

In a later ode harbor and field, the civilized ordering of earth and water, manifest the consequences of Oedipus' pollution. Not even the remote rivers of the Ister (Danube) or Phasis, the Messenger says, could cleanse the house (1227–28). The two rivers in the hyperbole stand for all the remote, barbarian lands beyond the limits of Hellenic civilization, and we are reminded of Ares'

Thracian seas in the parode. The gore from Oedipus' self-struck wounds is a "hail and rain" (1279) which, like the "storm of blood" inside the city (101), replace the rain which should nourish, not destroy.

Only by removing Oedipus, the anomaly in the natural as in the human world, can the city regain its fruitful relation with the larger world outside. At the end Creon would bring Oedipus within the house, so as not to show to the sun "such a polluted curse (*agos*) which neither earth nor sacred rain (cf. 1227) nor the light will receive" (1424–29).

The confusion of the boundaries between civilization and savagery is inward as well as external. It involves that "difficult nature" (674–675) of Oedipus as well as his ambiguous position between god and beast. Oedipus, who dwells with those he should not (414; cf. 367), also has terrible anger (*orgē*) "dwelling" with him that he does not see (337–338). This anger is "most savage," *agriōtatē*, Teiresias says (343–344), that is, it contains the inward dimension of the "savagery" of Oedipus' incest and patricide. At all the most crucial points of inquiry, where coolness and reason would be most appropriate, Oedipus gives way to passion or anger, *orgē*: with Teiresias, with Creon, with Jocasta (914), with the old Shepherd (cf. 1146, 1160). Anger rather than wisdom or knowledge becomes the driving force in the encounter between the two most august representatives of the civilized order, king and prophet.

Paradoxically, it is precisely Oedipus' intellectual achievements that dispose him to such passions. He is a self-made man facing men who have their position through inheritance or god-given inspiration; hence his defensiveness about his title and his merits (390ff., 440ff.), his sensitivity to any charge of weakness and inadequacy (536ff.). When Jocasta settles the squabble between Oedipus and Creon in almost motherly fashion (this is the first scene in the play which makes use of three actors onstage, 634ff.), she succeeds in calming Oedipus; but that very moment of calm is the point of recall for a more dangerous display of anger in the past, when, at the crossroads, he struck in anger (807; cf. 781).

Sophocles brings together the inward and outward savagery of Oedipus in a series of animal images. The first stasimon, shortly after Teiresias' charge of "most savage anger," reveals the unknown killer as "a bull of the rocks," prowling around the "savage woodland" (*agrian hylan*, 476–479). This is the first of a number of passages connecting the expelled or to-be-expelled Oedipus with deserted mountains (see also 719, 1391, 1451). The killer must flee "more swiftly than horses" (466–467), for Apollo "leaps upon him" (469), as Chance, in Oedipus' words, has "leapt" upon Laius (263). Oedipus by cleverness has defeated "the winged maiden" (507–510); but the oracles, like the Sphinx, have wings (482), and by their evidence Oedipus is already a lonely bull wandering on the mountains, a prophecy fulfilled when, at the peripety, he will "roar terrible things" (1265), a verb used elsewhere of a bull's roar (*Ajax* 322, *Trach.* 805).

"In the house or in the (wild) fields or in another land did Laius meet his death?" "In the house or in the field?" (*en oikois ē en agrois*, 112): the alternative between *oikos* and *agros* initiates Oedipus' search for the killer whose deed has let the force of the wild into the city. As Oedipus moves back in time to "hunt down" the temporal coordinates of his identity, the transformations of his self in time from outcast to king to outcast, he also recovers the spatial coordinates of that identity, city and mountain, house and wild.

These concerns are latent in the questioning which leads up to line 112 (108–111):

Oed.: Where in the land are they? Where will be found this track, hard to investigate, of the ancient cause?

Cr.: In this land (Apollo) said. What is searched for can be caught; what is neglected escapes.

Οι.: οἳ δ᾽ εἰσὶ ποῦ γῆς; ποῦ τόδ᾽ εὑρεθήσεται
ἴχνος παλαιᾶς δυστέκμαρτον αἰτίας;

Κρ.: ἐν τῇδ᾽ ἔφασκε γῇ· τὸ δὲ ζητούμενον
ἁλωτόν, ἐκφεύγει δὲ τἀμελούμενον.

In the splendidly dense second line, *ichnos palaias dystekmarton aitias*, the language of intellectual inquiry ("inference," "cause") overlies something more primitive, the "track," as of an animal, which leads to the secrets of Oedipus' identity in his own manner of walking. The juxtaposition, or interpenetration, of intellectual terms and animal references is more than a matter of style. It holds, in an as-yet-undifferentiated oneness, the contrasting extremes of Oedipus' tragic position, the proud "tracker" (cf. 221) and the hunted beast. Similarly in the next lines the neuter gender of the participle, *to zētoumenon*, "what is sought for," the "object of inquiry," blends with the neuter of the "caught" animal which "escapes."[33] The reversals of gender, from masculine to neuter, man to beast, parallel the reversal of number ("one" and "many") and of voice (the "hunter" and "tracker," the "hunted" and "tracked"): the "finder" is the one "found" (1397, 1421) or the "foundling," the object of discovery, *heurēma* (1106). Only after the tremendous suffering that attends the separation of the hero from his bestial double (cf. 476–478), can the language, taut with the pull between rational inquiry and imagery of beasts, break apart into differentiation once again.

Oedipus' two questions about place in 109 receive contrasting answers. The first, "where are the killers," is answered "in the land" (110). The second, "where did Laius meet his end," is answered, "away from the city," that is, outside (114–115). The two replies shape the structure that holds the paradox of Oedipus' identity. The servant who reported Laius' death was literally a "house-servant," *oikeus* (756), but the new king's accession to the throne makes that inner realm no longer habitable for him, and the man asks to live in the *agroi*, the fields and pastures, "to be as far as possible out of sight of the town" (761–762).

Oedipus' search comes to center upon figures who, like himself, occupy an ambiguous position between city and wild. At the climax of the search everything depends on "the one from the fields" (*agroi*, 1049, 1051). Only some twenty lines later Jocasta leaves the stage for the last time, driven by pain that is wild or savage, *agria lypē* (1073–74). The Shepherd, "nurtured in the house," as Oedipus was not (*oikoi trapheis*, 1123), will reveal the horrible truth of Oedipus' place between house and wild. When this exiled servant (761–762) comes back, literally, from the wild to the house for the interrogation, Oedipus makes that journey, metaphorically, in reverse, reenacting that anomalous passage of his infancy from palace to Cithaeron. The servant who initially saved him from the destructive intent of that journey fulfills that intent when he himself returns from mountain to city.

In the ode which follows, the chorus names Oedipus both the honored "ruler of great Thebes" and the pollution who "shares his house" (*synoikos*) with "savage infatuation" (1202–1206). Savagery is now shown to lie at the center of this house, as it lay at the center of the city and of Oedipus himself. "Sweet to the city" (*hadypolis*, 510) because of his cleverness or *sophia*, he is now, through his ignorance of himself, an outcast from his city with nothing "sweet" to look upon (1335; cf. 1339, 1390; also 151–152, 999). In the next scene, as he curses the man who took the fetters from his ankle, he views himself as a "wanderer," like the shepherd who found him (*nomas*, 1350; cf. 761). The *charis* of that act, the kindness which deserves gratitude (1352), like the *charis* invoked by the old Shepherd in asking for removal to the pastures (764), like the *charis* which Oedipus promises to the Corinthian Messenger (1004), becomes part of the destruction of civilized norms around Oedipus.

To the Greeks the child, not yet a fully civilized member of the city, has certain affinities with the "raw" world outside. Irrational, unable to speak, not yet in full command of his bodily functions, he is, as the Nurse says in the *Choephoroe*, "a beast."[34] Most peoples, the Greeks among them, have more or less elaborate rites of initiation to mark the passage from childhood to adulthood, from the savage realm to the civilized.[35] Oedipus' self-discovery in the play is a kind of initiation rite in reverse. Whereas the child's passage from infancy to adulthood is generally a passage from savage to civilized, nature to culture, Oedipus, in the retrospective knowledge that parallels the forward movement of the plot, moves from adulthood back to infancy, and simultaneously from his secure place in house and city to the savage mountain which is, in a sense, his parent (1092), "the place from which he was born" (1393). His anomalous condition confuses the normal routes of generational passage. That juxtaposition of "new" and "old" in the play's first line and near the climax of recognition (916) gains an increasingly ominous significance. When the Corinthian Messenger thinks that he is recalling Oedipus to his home ("so that I might do you a good service on your return home," 1005–1006), he is in fact recalling him not to a house or palace but to a barren mountainside.

Oedipus' recovery of his past centers on two places, both antithetical to the sheltered space of city or house, namely the mountain of his exposure and the narrow passage of his encounter with Laius. Jocasta mentions the two places, "triple road" and "untrod mountain," in close succession (716, 719). For the moment the mountain remains in the background, but the triple road is Oedipus' first clue.

The triple road is a no-man's land between cities (733–734), a mysterious place of dangerous transition, which even today retains its desolate, forbidding aspect. It is the appropriate setting for the deed of primal savagery enacted there. Though the first member of Laius' cortege whom Oedipus names is a herald (802), not a word is exchanged.[36]

The herald's silence, this absence of a civilized greeting or address, is the prelude to the awful savagery that follows. Laius' man tries to drive (*elaunein*) Oedipus from the road (804–805), a word appropriate to the driving of cattle (cf. 1139) which also recalls the terrible "yoking" of Oedipus' ankles in Jocasta's description shortly before (718). Laius strikes with his goad, *kentra*, another instrument for controlling beasts (809).[37] Oedipus replies with the staff or *skēptron*, the instrument which he carries because of the "yoking" of the feet which crippled him. The two instruments which mark man's distinctiveness from and superiority over beasts become the instruments of a deed which confuses those distinctions.

As the place where three converge on one, the crossroad is also the spatial analogue of Oedipus' anomalous place in nature, the appropriate place for him to act out with the *skēptron*, in its triple meaning of staff, scepter, and cane, the consequences of his—and man's—"unnatural" place. That narrow space cannot contain two such "natures" or "statures" (*physeis*, cf. 674–675, 740–743, 803).[38] Laius, old though he is, is as proud and irascible as his unrecognized son (805–813). The apparent opposites, chance and Apollo's design,[39] have converged to bring the two men together in that narrow passage, and it is here that man's subjection to chance draws him closest to the random life of the beasts. Two men of kingly rank act out a truly primal scene, father attacking son with the instrument used on beasts, son slaying father with the token of the hurt that the father caused to his limbs.

At the end of the play he addresses the triple roads, "which drank my blood, my father's, from my hands" (1400–1401). The place itself appears as a great savage beast, drinking the blood of its victims, like the bestial net and robe of the *Trachiniae* (1053–54). One is reminded too of the Sphinx who, in many versions of the legend, devours her victims. But the metaphorical savagery of that crossroads points to the inward savagery of the deed itself, the act which fuses the hero with his bestial double. Later, the goad with which Laius struck in that physical inversion of man and beast recurs in the inward "gadfly-sting of goads" (*kentrōn oistrēma*) of Oedipus' self-torment of memory and remorse (1317–18).[40] Yet there is a crucial difference: Oedipus feels his inward savagery here when, for all his misery, he is most human. At the crossroads his and Laius' outward acts, performed in ignorance, reduce both of them to bestial unreason and violence. Here Oedipus *knows*, and that knowledge transmutes brute pain into the human dimension of "memory," "grief," and "endurance" (*mnēmē, penthein, pherein*, 1318–20).

Oedipus' meeting with Laius at the crossroads literally and symbolically recapitulates his past. He is there, as a "single lone-girt man" (846–847) because he has left the house and city to which, after Apollo's oracle, he will never return.

It is as a result of Laius' act that he is there, alone, bearing his death-dealing staff/ scepter, seeking the house and the father which cast him out (cf. 718–719). The savagery of their encounter is both the consequence and the nightmarish adult projection of their earlier relationship.

Striking from above with a tool intended for beasts, the old king symbolically reenacts his old aggression against his son, as he sees him "passing by" on the road (*parasteichonta*, 808). The goad now aimed at the grown son's head, like the "yoke" on the infant son's feet, would prevent just this "passing by." But the new generation, insisting on its right to move ahead, pushes forward through the narrow passage with the same insistence that the baby pushes forward to be born. After meeting Laius, Oedipus will find his forward path blocked, again, by a creature whose name connotes "constriction" (*sphinx*, *sphingein*). The victory over Laius and the victory over the Sphinx are different encodings of essentially the same message about Oedipus' journey on his road or existence, the relentless drive to life and power against the resistance and aggression of everything in his environment, parents included.

"In the house or in the wild": the calm, controlled tone of that question about Laius' death (112) asked for the sake of the city gives way to desperate impatience as it turns from the city to himself (437, 1009). Oedipus' search for himself is a search both for his name and for his place. To know "who he is" (1036, 1068, 1184–85, 1273–74) is also to "know where he is" (367, 413). The "Know-Nothing Oedipus" (397) is also the "Know-Where Oedipus," since the name can be etymologized as "know where," *oidi-* (*oida*) *pou*.[41] Oedipus is continually asking where: Where are the killers (108); "Where are you the wise prophet?" (390); "Where is the land (of Laius' death)?" (732); and, finally, "Where am I?" (1309).[42] The question moves from the third to the second and finally to the first person (respectively 108, 367 and 413, 1309). When he asks this question in the first person, his first articulate word is "Unfortunate," *dystēnos* (1308), which was the final "name" that Jocasta had to give him (1071–72).[43] As he asks, "How does my voice flit around me, born aloft," this hero of intelligence and vision confronts the blindness of his total disorientation wherein even his own voice floats before him as if disembodied, no longer a part of himself. And in the next line he can only call out to that mysterious, nonhuman place "where (his) *daimon* leapt forth" (1311). At the end the old king has no place on earth or under the sky (1427–29), and the cautious new king will carefully feel out from the gods "where in need we stand" (1442–43).

Jocasta too asks "Where?" In her joy at the apparent good news from Corinth she exclaims, "O oracles, where are you? Listen to this man and then consider where the god's solemn oracles lead" (946–947, 952–953). But the oracles do not lie in Hades with the dead Polybus, as Oedipus in his transport of relief cries out (971–972); as the previous ode has suggested, they rule with the "high-footed laws" of the gods (863ff.), the opposite of that "foot" which gives Oedipus his ambiguous "place" on the scale between beast and god.

Like other divine foundlings—Romulus, Cyrus, Ion—Oedipus is the child of the god and the beast at the same time. The mountains where the infant Cyrus is exposed, to be brought up by Spako, "Bitch," are, as Herodotus twice insists, "the most bestial mountains," (*thēriōdestata*, Hdt. 1.110–111).[44] But Oedipus' tragedy is the foundling story in reverse. When he discovers where and who he is, it is to lose, not gain, a throne, to move not from the wild to the palace, but vice versa. Sophocles uses these folktale motifs not to assert the divinity of the hero but to explore the paradox of the "godlike" king's bestiality.

Oedipus is the outsider and stranger (*xenos*) who makes his way within, only to find that when he is truly an insider and citizen (*astos*) he must be cast out.[45] Whether he can retain his place inside comes to depend on whether the old Shepherd can "cast out" (*ekballein*) the tale he first told (848–849). The man who fought against being cast out (*ekballein*, 386, 399) discovers himself as the infant cast out on the pathless mountain (719) and begs the Thebans to cast him out (1290, 1412, 1436), since his place is outside (1410). Even the apparently trivial exchange with Creon and with the chorus about going outside and inside (676, 678–679) becomes part of a significant pattern. Creon's words near the end, "Bring him as quickly as possible within the house" (1429), echo both the chorus' words to Jocasta (678–679) and the blind Teiresias' words to his guide (444–445)—a guide whom Oedipus, no longer sure of his movements, will need.

IV

Oedipus begins and ends as a man without a house. His unknowing curse on himself requires that men drive him from their houses (241). Not knowing with whom he dwells or shares his house (414), he comes to share his house with "savage madness" (1205–1206) when he knows the final truth of his place within. His uncertainty of his identity has led him to leave his house at Corinth (998, 1010). It is at the very center of the house (1241, 1244; cf. 1262) that he confirms the discovery that makes him "a man who has his house outside the land," *ges apoikos*, as he says a few lines before the end (1518).

The first stasimon opened with the mountain as a place of god: the Delphian rock (*petra*, 464), seat of the oracle and therefore the place of mediation between human and divine. But the divinity of that oracle acts in the manner of a beast: six lines later Apollo "leaps out upon" the criminal (*epenthrōskei*, 469). The king is the criminal who prowls like "a bull of the rocks" (*petraios tauros*, 478) among the "savage woodland and the caves."[46] In the Ode on Man in the *Antigone* civilization "masters the beast of wild lair who treads the mountains . . . and yokes the tireless mountain bull" (*Antig.* 347–352). Here the king remains linked with the savagery of that mountainous setting (cf. 719). Found, the Messenger says, "in the valley-folds of Cithaeron" by one "tending his mountain flocks" (1026–28), Oedipus will discover himself as the child of the mountain, the mountain whom he will honor, the chorus sings, as "his fatherland and nurse and mother" (1091–92).

The premature joy of this great ode is one of the most brilliant pieces of irony in the entire play. This mountain does not open upon the serene rhythms of pastoral life in clear, silent air but in fact closes Oedipus more darkly into the secrets of the house which cast him forth. The chorus here gives the mountain three epithets of honor: "fatherland [or "paternal," *patriōtan*], nurse, and mother", but all three evoke the horror of Oedipus' identity. The divinities which the chorus names as possible parents of Oedipus in the next lines are all gods of the wild: Nymphs, Pan, Hermes, Dionysus "who dwells on the tops of mountains."[47] Apollo or Loxias also mentioned here is an ominous and ambiguous figure in the play. His "wild-pasturing uplands," which the chorus here says are dear to him, contrast, by a play on the word *nomoi*, "laws" and "pastures," with the *nomoi*, "laws," of the previous ode (865). These wild pastures (*agro-nomoi*) anticipate the pastures of Oedipus' infancy in the next scene, where Cithaeron and nurture will also have a more sinister ring (1127, 1134, 1143; also 1349–50).[48] When Oedipus later emerges from his house blinded and pronounces the name of his mountain, it is to affirm the truth of his removal from men and civilization and to wish for death (1391–93): "O Cithaeron, why did you receive me? Why did you not take me and kill me at once that I might never have shown to men the place from which I was born?" "The place from which I was born," *enthen ē gegōs*: the too intimate shelter of the incestuous womb and the desolate outer space of the mountain are both opposites and the same. In the collapse of difference between civilization and savagery, nurturance and rejection, fecundity and destruction, that most protected and inward of places holds for Oedipus the paradox that makes him both the king and the *pharmakos*.

After the peripety Oedipus asks not to have his house (literally, be a house-dweller, *oikētēs*) in his paternal city. His true home is on the mountains (1451–54): "Let me dwell on the mountains where Cithaeron here is named as mine, Cithaeron which my mother and father while alive established as my fixed and certain tomb that I might find death from those who tried to kill me." The bitter passage ironically echoes the joyful prediction of the third stasimon (cf. 1452–53 and 1091–92). The inversion of life and death parallels that of house and mountain. Oedipus calls Cithaeron "mine" because his parents established it while they lived as his place of death. The place which he should have inherited from his parents is not a house (cf. *oikētēs*, 1450; also 1374–75) but a mountain. The eagerly sought "parents who begot him" (436–437) become "those who tried to destroy him" (1454).

One expects Oedipus to reflect bitterly on receiving "death from those who gave me life" in 1454. But instead of the expected turn of rhetoric Sophocles wrote, "death from those who gave me—death." Parents are destroyers of children, children of parents. Oedipus killed "those whom he should not have" (1185). The broken lines at the actual moment of recognition run together "kill" and "give birth," *ktenein . . . tekontas* (1176). The similarity of sound stresses the paradox.[49] It is no accident that Oedipus uses the descriptive *tekousa*, "she who gave birth," instead of *mētēr*, mother, in his cry of compassion and sorrow for Jocasta (1175–76):

Οι.: τεκοῦσα τλήμων;
　　　　　Θε.: θεσφάτων γ᾽ ὄκνῳ κακῶν.

Οι.: ποίων;
　　　　Θε.: κτενεῖν νιν τοὺς τεκόντας ἦν λόγος.

Oed.: She (did it), the mother who gave birth, unhappy?
Mess.: Yes, in fear of terrible prophecies.
Oed.: What?
Mess.: There was an oracle that he would kill those who gave him birth.

We are reminded of the exchange between Orestes and Clytaemnestra just before the matricide in the *Choephoroe*. To Clytaemnestra's claim, "I nurtured you" (*ethrepsa*), Orestes counters, "Yes, but as the mother who bore me (*tekousa*), you cast me forth" (*Ch.* 913–914).

These strange reversals of giving birth and killing, of house and wild, of shelter and exposure partly account for the quiet, almost surreal horror of the exchange between Jocasta and Oedipus just before she realizes the truth (984–988):

Oed.: All this would be well spoken by you if the one who gave me birth (*tekousa*) happened not to be alive. But now, since she lives, there is every necessity, even if you speak well, to be afraid.
Joc.: And yet your father's death is a great boon (literally, "eye," *ophthalmos*).
Oed.: Yes, I agree, but there is still fear of her who lives.

So cool and logical is the development of the premises on which Oedipus' reasoning is based, so deeply are we involved in the logic of his search, that we scarcely attend to the hideous content of what is being expressed: a son's joy at the death of a father and uneasiness that a mother is still alive. Jocasta has just spoken her famous lines about sons sleeping with their mothers. Does not the exchange quoted above suggest a further release of unconscious fantasies? It is as if a miniature psychodrama of children's ambivalence toward parents were being acted out before our eyes.

The passage inverts the "normal" functions of the civilized house, preserving the life of children and caring for aging parents. In both respects the house of Oedipus, which, as the house of a king, should be exemplary, is the total reversal of civilized values. The parents' attempted murder of their infant son now finds its revenge, on the plane of unconscious feelings revealed in this dialogue, in the son's wish that his parents were dead. And that seems the most "natural" thing in the world, given the situation.

Intersecting what we may call this horizontal axis of antithesis between house and mountain is a vertical axis which runs between god and beast. Here too Cithaeron figures as one spatial pole. The other is Olympus. The two mountains define between them the two extremes spanned by Oedipus. The second stasimon sings of the "high-footed laws," *hypsipodes nomoi*, "begotten in the heavenly aether, laws of which Olympus alone is the father, nor did mortal nature beget them." Birth, the "father," and the epithet "high-footed" contrast with Oedipus, whose birth and "foot" contain secrets which drag him down below the human level and cast him out again to the "pathless mountain," Cithaeron, his "nurse and mother" (719, 1091ff.). Height and Olympian order are also connected with the excess and the dangerous "height" of *hybris*. *Hybris*, which "begets the tyrant" (another allusion to the charged theme of birth[50] and to Oedipus himself as *tyrannos*), if "filled to excess, mounts to the highest roof and dashes down against necessity with useless foot" (873–878). In the next scene this imagery of height fastens directly upon Oedipus who, Jocasta says, "lifts his spirit too high (*hypsou agan*) with grief of all sorts" (914–915).

In the Oedipus myth heights are dangerous. Literally for Jocasta and the Sphinx and metaphorically for Oedipus, death comes by a fall from high places.[51] Oedipus is an archer who has shot too high (1197), a "tower" (1200–1201; cf. 56–57) which protects the land but also by implication one who plunges from high rooftops (876–877; cf. *hyperopta*, 883).[52]

Oedipus is a man of superlatives, but the superlatives stand at opposite ends of the scale of human values without mediation between the extremes.[53] From first of men and the best of mortals (33, 46) he becomes the basest or most hateful of men (cf. 1344–46, 1433; also 334, 440, 1519). Even at Corinth he was the greatest of the citizens (776), but "Oedipus the great" (441) is simultaneously "great and small" (1083). The "great harbor" that received him (*megas limēn*, 1208) is the mark not of his skill as pilot (22ff., 46ff.) but of his curse (1209ff.). His ancient wealth and happiness (*olbos*) mask "all the evils that have a name" (1282–83).

The following diagram expresses the two axes which define Oedipus' identity:

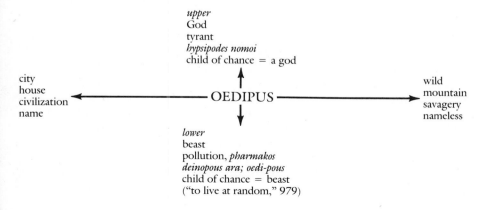

upper
God
tyrant
hypsipodes nomoi
child of chance = a god

city
house
civilization
name

OEDIPUS

wild
mountain
savagery
nameless

lower
beast
pollution, *pharmakos*
deinopous ara; oedi-pous
child of chance = beast
("to live at random," 979)

At the point when the opposite poles of the two axes are about to come together, "limitless Olympus" and Cithaeron are also juxtaposed (1086–92): "If I am a prophet and skilled in knowledge, O Cithaeron, not by limitless Olympus can you fail . . . to receive my honor as the fatherland and nurse and mother of Oedipus." In the previous ode Olympus was the upper realm of the "high-footed laws," safe from the flux of human generation and human time and change (865ff., 872). Olympus can be "limitless" because it is outside the conditioned, transient world of man. Seat of clearly defined anthropomorphic divinities, Olympus is associated with a rationally intelligible universe. Cithaeron, on the other hand, is connected with all the dark, irrational perversity of Oedipus' fate. This world order is not Olympian but daemonic. It reflects a "raw" or cruel *daimōn* (*ōmos daimōn*, 828), a word which belongs on the same scale of values as savage and bestial. The divinities here are not lucid Olympian forms but ambiguous powers who "leap" from hidden places (263, 469, 1300–1301, 1311–12).

As in the *Trachiniae* and *Philoctetes*, oracles mediate between the human and divine realms, between chaos and intelligibility. But in Oedipus' unmediated polarities, the oracles are destructive. Both the "speakable" and "unspeakable" spell doom (cf. 300–301, 1314). Teiresias would not speak beyond the limits (343), but Oedipus is no respecter of limits, whether of speech (1169–70) or emotions (673–674). Between Olympus and Cithaeron, Olympian order and dark chaos, Parnassus, with its "Delphian rock of Prophecy" (463–464) seems to stand as helpful mediation between god and man. But in Oedipus' case the Parnassian oracle will speak only "things unspeakable" (*arrēt' arrētōn*, 465); it is on that Delphian rock that the killer, Oedipus himself, will wander in the savage woodland, a bull of the rocks (475ff.). Oedipus' ambiguous relation to the mediation of the Delphic oracle continues to the end. While Creon calls for limits (1442–43) and would consult the gods (1438–39, 1518), Oedipus calls himself "the most hated by the gods" (1519). He thereby not only perpetuates the superlatives of his situation but also allows nothing between himself and the gods' hatred.

V

Time, like space, contains the contradictions which Oedipus' identity spans. "Time is where the real nature of things and people finally comes to light."[54] If ever a mortal experienced the tragedy of being in time, it is Oedipus. Like Ajax, he acts out the meaning of man's ephemeral nature, man as a creature of the day, never certain, as Pindar says, that he may "bring to fulfillment in peace a day, child of the sun, with unworn good" (*Olympian* 2.31–33).[55] This present day, Teiresias warns, will show him the pollution (351–352; cf. 374–375). "One day will give you birth and destroy you" (438). The verb "will give birth" evokes both the dark secret of Oedipus' birth and also the rhythms of time and change that govern all human life. At the end of the third stasimon "mortal nature," *thnata physis*, which can also imply mortal "birth," "coming to be," contrasts with the gods who are outside of time (869–872). "May I never see that day," says Oedipus of the oracles regarding his future (830–831). But this day leads not only to the future but also to the past. A man's life, unfolding in time, may suddenly end on a single day. "Not three days separated the child from birth," relates Jocasta of the exposure of her infant (717–718). Remembering his rescue of that child, the Shepherd wishes that he had perished on that day (1157). The single day has power to cancel out the slow movement of years. This is what Oedipus experiences and understands at the end (1282–85): "The previous wealth was justly wealth, but now, on this day, lamentation, infatuation, death, shame—all the names of suffering that there are, none of them is absent."

The operation of time in the play is not merely passive, aiding man to discover who he is, but mysteriously and dangerously active.[56] Time reveals and finds out. It dictates the rhythms of human knowing, as of human growth, but it also seems to reveal and find out as if it were a quasi-personified force. Creon's rather commonplace appeal to time to justify him ("Time alone shows the just man," 613–615) takes on a deeper meaning when the chorus tells the king who has prided himself on his powers of discovery, "All-seeing time found you out" (1213).

Oedipus makes time part of his calculations or "measurements," fitting the old Shepherd's years to the Corinthian's age (*xymmetros*, 1112–13).[57] But Creon's answer to Oedipus' question about the time since Laius' death splendidly conveys all the impenetrable remoteness of time (561):

μακροὶ παλαιοί τ' ἂν μετρηθεῖεν χρόνοι.

Years of time, long and ancient, would be measured out.

Being "co-measured with great time," as the Corinthian says of Polybus' passing, marks the limits of our mortality (*symmetroumenos chronō*(i), 963).

When Oedipus takes the measure of time, however, it is in an active, not a passive sense. He fled Corinth, in a step of decisive energy, "measuring the land of Corinth by the stars" (794–796):

τὴν Κορινθίαν,
ἄστροις τὸ λοιπὸν ἐκμετρούμενος χθόνα
ἔφευγον.

The weighty polysyllable, "measuring out," dominates the line, but the chilling word of exile, "I fled," held over to the next verse, contrasts with the cosmic sweep of "stars" and "earth." The diction suggests the wide purview of Oedipus' intelligence, and yet, as we know, he does not measure carefully enough. When he speaks as concerned and confident ruler in the prologue, he makes two "measurements" (*xymmetroumenos*, 73; *xymmetros*, 84). The first statement contains a double meaning typical of this play (73–74):

καί μ' ἦμαρ ἤδη ξυμμετρούμενον χρόνῳ
λυπεῖ τί πράσσει.

The surface meaning is, "The day, already co-measured with time, grieves me as to what he (Creon) is doing." But the lines can also mean, "[The] day grieves me, me who am co-measured with time." Oedipus is "co-measured by time" in the same ironical way in which he is "defined great and small" by the "kindred months" (1082–83). He goes on, in this latter passage, "Having such a birth (*ekphys*), I would not *come out* as someone different [and refuse] to learn my race" (*genos*) 1084–85. Earlier he used this same verb for the crucial calculation of "the time that has *come out*," or "passed by" since Laius' death (*chronos . . . exelēlythōs*, 735). The answer gave him his first thrill of fear as he suddenly glimpses mysterious forces playing about his life (738): "O Zeus, what have you planned to do with me?" At the moment of fateful recognition a related verb marks the clear emergence of the truth that time has revealed (1182): "Alas, alas, all things would *come out* clear."

"Chance was my mother; and the kindred months defined me small and great" (1082–83). "Defined," "set limits to," *di-(h)ōrizein*, belongs to the same vocabulary of intellectual terms as "measure," and here again Oedipus' calculations are disastrously wrong. Jocasta had used the verb in the play's first circumstantial narrative of the crimes of the past: "Such are the things that the oracles defined (*diōrisan*), and do you pay them no heed" (723–724). But the tale which she has just told (711–722) proves this advice about the "limits" of the oracle to be as mistaken as Oedipus' confidence about the "limits" of greatness and smallness.

It is not the space of months which "define" Oedipus' greatness and smallness but the single day of the *ephēmeros* (cf. 351, 1282–85). In the flux of time, great and small are interchangeable. Jocasta tells Oedipus and Creon not to expand their "nothing pain to something great" (*mega*, 638).[58] This pain (*algos*) which ought to be regarded as "nothing" will shatter Oedipus' expectations about "small and great" in 1082–83 and prove instead the nothingness of man (1187–88; cf. 1018). The chance which made Oedipus great (*megan*) will destroy him, as Teiresias repeats, on this day (438–442). The chance that preserved him from death has but "saved (him) for the greatest suffering" (*kak' es megista*, 1180).

Having answered a riddle about man's changeful passage from small to great, Oedipus' tragic experience enacts a darker riddle of change from great to small. Great and small are indeed the defining limits (1083) of Oedipus' life but in a sense opposite to the one he assumes. The "small Oedipus" of childhood will be uncovered behind the "great" Oedipus of Thebes, once "greatest" of the citizens of Corinth (776). The movement back to the "smallness" of his infancy is an overturning of his "greatness" in every sense. Only the god, as the second stasimon suggests, is "great," free of the movement between childhood and old age (*megas . . . theos oude gēraskei*, 872) which Oedipus grasped as an intellectual problem but has not understood as experience.[59]

In the ode which follows Oedipus' confidence about the limits of "great and small," the chorus sings of the happy revelation of Oedipus' divine paternity by "tomorrow's moon." But "tomorrow," *aurion*, rings an ominous change on the theme of man the *ephēmeros*. "Being a man never say what comes tomorrow . . . For not even of a long-winged fly is the change so swift," wrote Simonides (521P). The chorus exults in the conjecture that he will prove the child of "long-lived Nymphs" (*makraiōnes*, 1098), but Oedipus above all men will be revealed subject to the vicissitudes of human age or life (*aiōn*); and the chorus' hopes of divinity only set off his painful subjection to change and time. Even more than Ajax, Oedipus fluctuates between his "yesterday" and "tomorrow" without the mediation of a stable "today" that a secure identity confers.

Ironically, Oedipus' great success has been the joining of past and future in his answer to the Sphinx's riddle of the ages of man. But when new and old come together elsewhere in the play, it is to stress the precariousness of human identity. That juxtaposition of new and old (*nea palai*) in the first line of the play sounds ominously in the echo of the word "of old," *palai*, throughout.[60] Jocasta reproaches Oedipus with failing to "infer the new by means of the old" (916; cf. 666–667). In fact it is she who refuses to pull new and old together into a coherent pattern and chooses instead to "live at random" (979). She is quite wrong about Oedipus, for he does indeed "infer the new by means of the old." He will follow to the end that "track of difficult inference" to find the "old cause" (109). He has joined new and old in solving the riddle, and he joins new and old again in solving his personal riddle, when he presides over the inquiry which takes the old Shepherd back to his youth and leads his own maturity back to his infancy (1141–85).[61] Time on that Shepherds' mountain long ago, "from spring to winter, the time of six half-years," with the uneventful alternation of the seasons and change of pastures, is the large temporal backdrop to this tense scrutiny of Oedipus taking the measure of time, where every second counts. Time takes the form of steady regularity and continuity just when its discontinuity is to be so decisive for Oedipus.

Fitting the new to the old is the ever-renewed process of man's understanding of himself, and the succession of the new and old forms the natural succession of human generations. But Oedipus' collocation of new and old, from the play's first line on, expresses discontinuity and anomaly rather than orderly succession. His injury and the staff he bears confuse the natural progression in the stages of human life, and his incest confuses the orderly succession and separation of the generations within the family. Oedipus' sufferings make "the generations of men to live as nothing" (1186–88).

In one important respect, however, the chorus' pessimism is proven too severe at the end. As the daughters of Oedipus appear, Creon explains that he has summoned them (1476–77): "I am the one who offered you this, knowing your present delight (*tēn parousan terpsin*) which held you of old (*palai*)." Human time can create the bonds of love and can also lead men to understand and pity another's suffering. Both meanings seem implied by the placement of *palai*, "of old," at the end of the line so that it can go either with Creon's "knowing" or with the "joy" which Oedipus had in his children.

VI

The reversals implied in Oedipus' measuring of time form only a small part of the ironies that attend Oedipus' intellectual mastery as a civilizing hero. He is a knower who lacks the fundamental human knowledge of name, place, and birth; a plowman who plows a forbidden field; a hunter whose ingeniously "tracked" quarry is himself; a pilot lost in a dreadful harbor; a doctor unable to diagnose his own unspeakable disease;[62] a user of fire helpless before nature's elemental violence and the gods' power, symbolized by fire.[63] All the great achievements of human civilization are centered upon Oedipus, and all of them come to reflect the ambiguity of man's power to control his world and manage his life by intelligence.

The great achievement of that intelligence in the play is the solving of the riddle of the Sphinx. This, like Heracles' defeat of monsters, is a basic civilizing act, a defense of the city against threatening, half-bestial monsters from the "raw" world outside. For all the intellectual and Sophistic issues of the play, the Sphinx keeps her mythical status; she cannot be rationalized.[64] Her riddle points back to the mystery of human existence itself, the elusiveness of human identity in time, which intelligence cannot so easily solve.

The word for "solving" the riddle is *lyein*, literally to "loose" or "release" it.[65] In this play the sagacity of Oedipus as a "looser" of riddles is overturned by the "loosing" that took place on the wild mountainside. The Messenger who comes with the promise of "loosing" Oedipus from his old fears (1003) soon points back to that other "loosing" on Cithaeron (1034). That he "loosed" the riddle of the Sphinx is no guarantee that Oedipus can "loose" the god's oracle (see 407), which is in its own way a riddle (394, and see below, section VIII). The Messenger's verbal "loosing" of the riddle of Oedipus' identity (1003), his literal "loosing" of the fetters on Oedipus' feet (1034), the clever "loosing" of the Sphinx's riddle, the "loosing" of the city from the plague (101, 306, 392), the "loosing" of the god's mysterious oracle (407) reflect back and forth as in a series of mirrors. But they all focus on the primary riddle of Oedipus himself, the mystery of undeserved suffering and the inscrutability of human fate in an impenetrable world order. That is the riddle most in need of being "loosed." Jocasta prays to Apollo for a "cleansing release," a "loosing free of defilement" (*lysis euagēs*, 921), but the "loosing" that Apollo commanded (101) will show Oedipus as the "defilement" or *agos*.

In this world of collapsed polarities, saving and destroying are mysteriously the same. The old Shepherd's "loosing" on the mountains, like his present "loosing" of Oedipus' fears—and in a way like Oedipus' original "loosing" of the Sphinx's riddle—brings more harm than release. In the past as well as the present the Corinthian turns Oedipus' "safety" or "salvation" (*sōzein*) into a destruction worse than death (1179–80, 1456–57), and Oedipus comes to curse the man who "loosed" him from the "savage fetters" (1349–50). Oedipus himself, hailed as "savior" (48), like the other "saving" figures—Apollo (149–150), Teiresias

232

(304), the Corinthian, and the old herdsman—is the opposite of what he seems. The Corinthian's ambiguous "loosing" (1003, 1034) forces Oedipus to "loose" the riddle of the Sphinx a second time by confronting him with his earliest past. This time Oedipus knows that the answer is himself.

Even in the prologue Oedipus' "loosing" of the Sphinx's riddle is ambiguous. In appealing to him on the basis of that previous solution to Thebes' ills (35), the Priest explains that they do not "judge him as made equal to the gods, but as the first of men in the circumstances (fortunes, junctures) of life and in the encounters with divinities" (31–34):

θεοῖσι μέν νυν οὐκ ἰσούμενόν σ' ἐγὼ
οὐδ' οἵδε παῖδες ἑζόμεσθ' ἐφέστιοι,
ἀνδρῶν δὲ πρῶτον ἔν τε συμφοραῖς βίου
κρίνοντες ἔν τε δαιμόνων συναλλαγαῖς.

"First in the fortunes of life": these "fortunes" or *symphorai* can also mean "misfortunes" (see 99, 454, 833, 1347).[66] "For men of experience," the priest says a few lines later, "the fortunes of their counsels (*xymphoras . . . tōn bouleumatōn*) do most flourish" (44–45), after which he calls Oedipus "best of mortals," (46) as he called him "first of men" earlier (33). But the fortunes of Oedipus' counsels are to prove dark indeed; what "flourish" are the oracles (481), which will show the generations of men "flourishing" not as "equal to the gods" (31), but as "equal to nothing" (1187–88).

"First in encounters with divinities" (34) is even more ominous. The play shows no direct encounters with the gods: even the plague follows by a kind of law of cause and effect.[67] Oedipus deals with the supernatural, as with the natural world with intelligence and energy. But hidden encounters with divinities everywhere mock that success on which the Priest here congratulates him.

Encounters with divinities include the "hostile encounter" with the Sphinx, of which the Priest speaks immediately after. The word *synallagai* has that meaning in the *Trachiniae*, where the chorus uses it of the "encounter" between Deianeira and Nessus (845). Oedipus was victorious in that encounter, the Priest continues, "not taught by us nor having learned it, but with the help of a god" (37–39). But in Oedipus' version of his conquest the help of a god, literally, "the addition of a god," *prosthēkē theou*, is conspicuous by its absence.[68] He echoes the Priest's words—"the know-nothing" Oedipus, (397, 37)—only to leave the god's part out entirely. In fact he even contrasts his own human intelligence (*gnōmē*, 398) with the failure of divine solutions (394–398).

Synallagai, "encounters," can mean also "reconciliation" (cf. *Ajax* 732, 744). Yet any hope for reconciliation in Oedipus' relation with the divine disappears in the encounters that reveal his past (*synallagein*, 1110, 1130). His certainty of never having yet encountered (1110) the old Shepherd soon proves ill-founded; as it is undercut, so are all the intellectual terms of these lines ("weigh," "seem to see," "investigate," "measure," "knew," "understanding," 1110–16).

VII

"Not equal to the gods . . . first of men": the antithesis (reinforced by the Greek particles *men . . . de*) enframes Oedipus' identity as king in a context of limits and opposites that carry through the next lines: "fortunes of life . . . encounters with divinities" (33–34); "taught by us . . . aid of a god" (38); "report from gods . . . report from men" (42–43). These contrasts are not mediated by the rituals which, for most men, ease encounters with the gods. The suppliant citizens approach his altars, almost as if he were the god (16; cf. 31) but, as the *pharmakos*, at the opposite extreme, Oedipus has no right to any altars at all.

Oedipus' past is a tissue of violated or misconceived rituals. Laius disobeyed a divine warning about having children. The exposure of a child on a mountainside is a legalistic evasion of polluting oneself with kindred blood; we may compare Creon's immural of Antigone with just enough food "so that the city may avoid pollution" (*Antig.* 773–775).[69] In both cases, of course, the rationalistic expedient is a calamitous failure, and in Laius' case the result is an enormous pollution of house and city.

The play begins with an elaborate ritual of supplication. Oedipus' mention of suppliant seats, boughs, incense, garlands, paeans and lamentations in the opening lines reinforces the visual effect. At the end of the scene he bids the suppliants arise from their seated posture and take up their boughs of supplication. The whole scene is rounded off in something like a ring composition of ritual motifs (cf. "suppliant boughs" in 3 and 142–143). The scene is punctuated in the middle by the entrance of Creon, garlanded with laurel (83), another reminder of the ritual framework and the importance of the issues at stake in these encounters with divinity. The end of the play presents a very different kind of supplication, for now the king who received suppliants is himself a suppliant (*prostrepsomai*, 1446).

Purification is the major ritual of the play, and it contains an even more massive series of reversals. Here again the rite performed on behalf of the city at the beginning becomes personal at the end. "Drive out the miasma," Apollo's oracle commanded (97–98), saying nothing of Laius or his killer. Yet both Creon and Oedipus assume that Laius' killer is meant (100ff.), whereas the pollution has another and equally horrible source.[70] Their assumption is both correct and incorrect. While ostensibly pointing to the killer of Laius, the language of the oracle—"Drive out the pollution as *nurtured* in this land and do not nurture it beyond curing" (97–98)—points to the other source of pollution, the incest motif evoked by the verb "nurture." The public command hides an allusion to the most intimate and most hidden detail of Oedipus' life, the "nurture" which he never received from his parents.

The plague has "emptied the Cadmean house," the Priest says at the beginning (29). But by the end of the play that phrase has private reference to the afflictions of Oedipus' own house as well as to those of Thebes as a whole. The king himself is now subject to the curses which he uttered, early in the play, against Laius' slayer. These curses included expulsion from the communal rites, from "prayers to the gods, sacrifices, libations" (239–240). His daughters, he says at the end, will not enjoy the converse (*homiliai*) of their fellow citizens nor participate in the festivals (*heortai*). Instead of enjoying the public spectacles (*theōria*), they will sit shut in the house (1489–91). The *oikos* or house of the king, instead of being the symbolical center of the community, becomes a place of utter loneliness. Instead of being the focal point of health and prosperity, this house is the focal point of infection and disease, just as the union of King and Queen promotes a disharmonious and destructive rather than a fruitful relation between man and nature.

It is given in the tragic irony of Oedipus' situation that the rituals that the king must perform successfully can only destroy him. To be a savior of Thebes (*sōtēr*) (48) or to find the savior god (150) or the savior prophet (304) is to destroy himself. The only way he can save his city is to sever his own bond with it. Like Heracles in the *Trachiniae*, he must become one with his monstrous double and accept as "himself" the accursed infant exposed on the mountains, the murderer of the king "prowling in the wild woodland and the caves, a bull of the rocks" (477–478). By discovering and accepting himself as his fearful double, king and guilt-laden scapegoat at the same time, celebrant and sacrificial victim, he takes fully upon himself the responsibility for the violence created by the fusion and confusion of identities, of the doubles, in his life. With that act the violence is once more brought under control, and the gods are appeased.[71]

In the very center of the play, at the end of the ode on the "high-footed laws," the chorus meditates upon justice. "If the actions [of justice and reverence] are not honored," they sing, "why should I dance?" (895–896). The ritual act of the choral dance in the orchestra includes and symbolizes all the rituals performed in the play. It reminds us that the rituals in the orchestra represent ritual within ritual. The enclosed rituals within the fictional action of the drama are parallel and homologous with the larger, enframing ritual structure of the festival in which the play itself has its own ceremonial function. Through the reflected rituals of the tragedy the society is able to contemplate its own unity and the mediating functions of its own ritual/festive forms. Art and ritual, word and performed action, join in a momentary glimpse of the polis in its relations with the cosmic order. It is as if invisible bonds could now, in the magic of the performance, be faintly discerned.

Yet the fictional rites enacted or described in the orchestra are just the opposite of the larger ritual in which the spectators at the Dionysiac festival are participating. "Why should I dance?" the chorus leader asks. But of course in the orchestra dance *is* being performed. The fictional world within the boundaries of the orchestra is both the mirror and the negative of the actual polis world, the Dionysiac ritual, which includes it. There within the orchestra the ritual forms and the social and cosmic order which they celebrate are problematical; the harmony between man and the gods which the Dionysiac "dance" celebrates is disrupted. Hence the chorus moves back into the "fictional" rituals in the antistrophe, dwelling on the oracles. "I shall never go to the untouched navel of the earth," the chorus sings, unless these things prove true. "The old oracles of Laius are destroyed. Apollo is no longer conspicuous in honor. The divine perishes" (906–910). At once Jocasta enters, in a ritual of supplication (*hiketis*, "suppliant," 920), in word and deed echoing the suppliant ritual of the opening scene. The ritual is grotesquely out of place. It is an attempt to assert harmony where there is only dissonance. The echoes of the prologue measure how far we have come from the image of a well-ordered polis celebrating its rites. Jocasta asks Apollo for "a release that cleanses pollution . . . because all tremble with fear, seeing the pilot of our ship struck with confusion" (921–923). The imagery as well as the prayer of supplication take us back to the prologue with its storm-tossed city (23–24). But the pilot who could "right" the ship/city then (39, 46, 51; cf. 56) is now himself in trouble. The Corinthian Messenger's entrance, with his grim play on Oedipus Know-Where, is the answer to her prayer (924–926). Apollo does grant her prayer for "release that cleanses pollution" (cf. also 1003) but not in the way she means.[72]

That scene of fearful discovery is closed by the chorus' mistaken joy of the third stasimon. Cithaeron, they sing, "will be celebrated in their dances" (*choreuesthai*, 1093) as the nurse and mother of Oedipus. Once more the perversion of ritual points to the tragic disruption of man's encounters with the gods. This joyful dance answers the question of the previous ode, "Why should I dance?" (896). But the true answer is still hidden from all except Jocasta. The very misplacement of the ritual reflects the truth. This dance is not a rite performed in the safe communal spaces of the city; it is a figurative dance, on the wild mountainside, indeed, given the phrasing of 1091–93, a "dance" of the mountain itself. What is celebrated in the dance is not the polis, but its opposite, the mountain whose sinister presence haunts the action.

The appropriate ritual here is not the dance but the dirge, and that comes in the next ode. As the chorus looks in horror on the blinded Oedipus, they sing (1216–20): "O son of Laius, I wish I had never seen you, for I lament as if pouring forth the wailing dirge (*iēlemon*) from my mouth." Oedipus was the recipient of prayers and lamentation in the prologue (5). Now he is himself the subject of those prayers and lamentations.

VIII

In the pattern of mediation between man and god the oracles occupy a special place. Oracles and civic rites are closely interwoven at the end of the second stasimon: the chorus' question about its dance (896) is followed by concern for the honor of oracular shrines (898–910); then Jocasta appears as a suppliant asking for deliverance and purification (911–923).[73] The scene recapitulates the major ritual motifs of the play—supplication, purification, oracles—at the point when the king's relation to them is about to undergo a drastic reversal.

The play begins with Oedipus consulting the oracle on behalf of the whole city. As the action progresses, it takes us back to his lonely consultation of the oracle on his own behalf after the insult at Corinth. Not only is there a contrast between the solitary consultation of the now exiled Oedipus (794–796; cf. 787) and the cortege of Laius, but the solitariness of that journey to Delphi soon becomes a crucial point in his relation to his present city (see 846). The prophecies to both Laius and Oedipus also lead to the wild realm outside the city: Laius exposes a son on a wild mountainside (711ff.); Oedipus leaves the shelter of Corinth for the place where the two oracles join, the desolate crossroads (787ff.).

There are three oracles in the play: one to Thebes in the present, one to Oedipus in the past, and one to Laius in the still remoter past. They come together at the point when Jocasta, seeking to disprove the power of oracles (709–710, 723–725), inadvertently gives Oedipus the clue which proves their accuracy. Her crucial sentence about the triple roads begins, "Robbers killed him, as is the rumor . . . " (715–716). But that last clause, "as is the rumor," *hōsper g' hē phatis*, can also mean, "as (says) the oracle," for the word *phatis* means not only "rumor," but also "prophecy," "oracle," and in fact has that latter meaning in four of its five other occurrences in the play (151, 310, 323, 1440; cf. 495). Even in asserting the falsehood of the oracle, she affirms its strange truth. The "robbers" at the crossroad did indeed act in accordance with the "oracle/rumor." Public rumor is simultaneously one with the private oracle of Laius' house. Similarly the oracles that appear in the context of public cult (21, 151ff., 897ff.) show the leader of the polis as a lonely bull on the mountain, wandering apart in the "savage woodland" pursued by "every man" of the city (463–482).

This ode, the first stasimon, focuses a number of the central paradoxes raised by the oracles. We hear it with Teiresias' warning about his "intelligence in the mantic art" ringing in our ears (461–462). The brilliance of divine speech marked by the opening words of both strophe and antistrophe (463, 473–475) contrasts with the "unspeakable" things committed by the murderer (*arrēt' arrētōn telesanta*, 465). The animal imagery and the wild setting contrast both with the human world and with the revered sanctuary: "rock" (464, 478) refers both to the sacred place and its antithesis, the savage mountain. The loneliness of the bull/murderer is literally "widowhood" (*chēreuōn*, 479), whereas it is just the opposite, the too close marriage of Oedipus, the *gamos agamos*, "marriage no-marriage" (1214), that makes the king his bestial opposite, the hunted animal in the savage woodland, wandering with "wretched foot" (479). The metaphor of the ode makes him both the king responsible for the oracles and the guilty criminal exposed by oracles, both a suppliant at Apollo's shrine (through his proxy, Creon) and a wanderer in the wild forest outside that shrine, both inside the city and on the mountain.

Parnassus itself faces both ways. It is both a snowy mountain (473), a suggestion of desolation and remoteness, and the "mid-navel of the earth," a center of human concourse and a meeting place between man and God. Hence on the spatial axis of the events it occupies the place between Olympus and Cithaeron, the remote mountain of the eternal gods and the mountain which symbolizes the reduction of human life to bestial chaos. It reflects this antithesis in the geographical, ritual, and biological codes and, in cutting across them, helps link them together.

Within these antitheses and inversions of upper and lower limits, Apollo's oracles and the Sphinx's riddles both contrast and converge. The Sphinx exalts, Apollo abases him. Yet the victory over the Sphinx is achieved in a lonely encounter analogous to the first visit to Delphi. This victory makes Oedipus king but also wins him the marriage that puts him outside the human order. In his quarrel with Teiresias, Oedipus contrasts his solution to the riddle with the prophetic art (*technē*: 390–398; cf. 380). But the oracles of Teiresias are "riddling," *ainikta* (439; cf. *ainigma*, 393),[74] just as the Sphinx is oracular (1200). The Sphinx propounded a riddle which required "prophecy" (*manteia*, 394; cf. 462). Both need "loosing" (cf. 392; also 306, 407). According to a tradition preserved in a scholion to Euripides' *Phoenissae* (1760), "She was not a beast (*thērion*), but a propounder of oracles (*chrēsmologos*) who told the Thebans prophecies that were hard to understand, and she destroyed many of them who misinterpreted the oracles."[75] Riddle and oracle come increasingly to look like mirror images of one another. Both, when properly "solved" ("loosed"), spell Oedipus' doom.

Oracle and Sphinx stand at the fringes of the human world, the point where divine and human and divine and bestial intersect. Whereas the oracles point upward to a divine, albeit mysterious order, the Sphinx points downward to what is dark, monstrous, subhuman. The oracles mediate between God and man; the Sphinx between man and beast. Half-bestial in form, she is described as "savage" and "raw-eating." She devours her victims and rends her human prey with talons or savage jaws.[76] She violates the linguistic code in her riddle, biological order in her shape, kin ties in her incestuous parentage (Hesiod, *Theogony* 326ff.), the relation between city and wild in her affliction of the city from her vantage point on the "Sphinx Mountain" (*Phikeion Oros*) outside or, in other versions, her position on a pillar in the heart of the city.[77] Like Oedipus, her mixed form (lion, bird, woman) makes her mode of travel, like Oedipus', ambiguous. When the riddle is solved, she plunges from a high place to her death.[78] When Oedipus' riddle is solved, he plunges from the highest to the lowest place in the city (876–879). In her connections with mountains,[79] she belongs to the savage mountain world of Oedipus' exposure on Cithaeron. Yet her challenge to man is the confusion of human forms with their bestial opposites.

The Sphinx's inversions of oracular mediation are especially marked in the realm of language. To the chorus she is a *chrēsmōdos*, singer of oracles (1200); presumably her utterances, like the oracle's, are in dactylic hexameter. But she is a singer who is "harsh" (36), "of tricky song" (130), a "rhapsode-dog" (391), "hook-taloned maiden singer of riddling oracles" (1199–1200).[80] Euripides calls her songs "most unmusic" (*Phoen.* 807) and elsewhere dwells on her "musical" aspect. In a fragment of his lost *Oedipus* he describes the riddle as a horrible shrieking whistle.[81] Her song is just the reverse of a civilized art: it enables her to prey upon and destroy a human community. And yet this perverse combination of savagery and civilization parallels that in Oedipus himself. He is the man of intelligence and authority governed by a savage temper (344) and savage infatuation. The "harmony" he finds in the age of the Shepherd and his own past (*xynaidei*, 1113, literally, "sings in harmony with") leads to the dissonances of his bestial "roar" (1265) and fulfills Teiresias' prophecy that Cithaeron will echo in "harmony" with (*symphōnos*, 421) those shouts that mark his forfeiture of his place in the city, his loss of the right to the forms of address from its citizens.

Choral lyric could celebrate the "concordant peace," *symphōnos hēsychia*, of a coherent universe, as Pindar does in the *First Pythian* (1–40; 71). But the tragic universe has no place for those harmonies. Tragedy, unlike Pindar's "lordly lyre," does not celebrate the unity of city and gods in a secure communal space. The very juxtaposition of choral song and the iambics of the suffering protagonist in tragedy sets that communal order over against something else. The myths of tragedy, unlike the myths of choral lyric, are not exemplary of the city's safe relation to its heroes and gods. The chaos or disorder viewed by Pindar or Bacchylides is itself neutralized by the implicit security of the choral setting. But the tragic performance, like the tragic hero, confronts its own negation: "Why should I dance?" this chorus asks (896). The music of this chorus has its "bestial double," as it were, in the "harmonies" of Oedipus (421, 1113) and the chorus' misplaced celebration of Cithaeron in music and dance (1093). In the parode the song of communal solidarity is a song of grief (*stonoessa . . . homaulos*, 187). It is joined with a paean to Apollo that "flashes forth" (*paian . . . lampei*, 186) in a combination of sound and sight that prefigures the ambiguous rituals and prayers to this god throughout the play (473–476, 909, 919–920). The revelations of Apolline ritual song at Thebes, like Apolline speech at Delphi (187, 475), and also like the riddling revelations of the Sphinx outside Thebes' civic space, confuse rather than clarify the relation between appearances and reality.

The Sphinx's negative mediations in the linguistic order are homologous with those in the spatial order. Both involve Oedipus in inversions of upper and lower. Acclaimed for his victory over the "winged maiden" (508), the birdlike Sphinx, he is defeated by her Olympian opposite and analogue, the oracles which "hover" about the outcast (481–482) and their interpreter, a reader of bird signs (484; cf. 310, 395, 398). The "bird of good omen," *ornis aisios* (52), which Oedipus brought with him when he defeated the Sphinx, is also a "bird of ill-omen" (the phrase has both meanings). Earlier in the prologue the Theban children are like weak fledglings (16–17), and in the parode the Thebans themselves appear as birds fleeing a vast fire (175–178).

These bird images, all underlining the helplessness of men before the supernatural, counterbalance Oedipus' victory over the bird-maiden, the Sphinx. Jubilant at the apparent failure of the oracles, he dismisses "the birds above" (964–966); but he is mistaken about the father whom he believes "below" the earth (968). His own ambiguous position between high and low, already underlined by the second stasimon, is made even more dangerous by his being "lifted too high" (914). The chorus, in the first stasimon, "flits about with uncertain hope" (486–488), but that spatial disorientation becomes more than just fore-boding when Oedipus, after the peripety, does not know where he is and wonders at his voice "flitting about" as if disembodied (1308–10).

The oracles, Teiresias, the birds, and the Sphinx locate the ambiguous plane of human truth between animality (the Sphinx) and divine prophecy (Apollo and his "flitting" oracles and birds of omen). The Sphinx is a singer of oracles (1200), who yet points down to the beasts. Teiresias is a servant of Apollo but, like Oedipus, is caught up in an all-too-human anger.[82] He comes in obedience to Oedipus' summons but will not tell. He conceals as much as he reveals. He is both willing and reluctant, both majestic and irritable, both clear and myste-rious, both distant and petty. The manner of his revelation cancels out its cred-ibility. In him language is not simply the vehicle of truth; it contains truth in its complex, imperfect, riddling human form (439). In him, as in all human truth in this play, reality is veiled in illusion. To tear off the veil is to bring destruction as well as "salvation"; but it is the task of the tragic hero to do exactly this, to stand at the point of "fearful hearing" and press on (1169; cf. 1312).

The two men, Oedipus and Teiresias, reinforce one another in their blind-ness-in-vision. They unwillingly collaborate with the god in demonstrating the imperfection and ambiguity of human truth and human speech. The shifting status of the birds between Sphinx and prophet, beast world and Delphi, is then a function of the play's larger ambiguities of knowledge and ignorance, the intelligibility or chaos of the universe. Some of these relationships can be ex-pressed in the following diagram:

Lower (Beast)	*Oedipus*	*Upper (God)*
Pharmakos, pollution	← Defeated by riddles →	Solver of riddles, "godlike man"
Winged maiden = Sphinx		Birds of oracles
Sphinx (beast)	← Riddles / Oracles →	Apollo (god)
Anger, illusion	← Oedipus and Teiresias →	Clarity, truth
Non-signification	← Language / Language → as vehicle as instrument of confusion of truth	Intelligible discourse
Unintelligibility, chaos	← Oedipus proven / Teiresias proven → *sophos* in *sophos* in matter of birds interpreting (507ff.) bird signs	Orderly universe

The action of the play depicts the coincident opposites of the middle column. In this tragic space, as Vernant observes, the hero is himself a tension of opposites.

The paradox of Oedipus' sight-in-blindness throws all the familiar opposi-tions into confusion. Oedipus' blindness implies insight, vision into the darkness of ultimate questions: Why stay alive in the midst of such suffering? What is the value of life when it can contain such agony? It is in terms of eyes and sight that

Oedipus implicitly answers the question of why he did not commit suicide (1369–77, 1384–90).

Oedipus' tragic knowledge here may be contrasted with the Promethean technological knowledge. Aeschylus' Prometheus gives men "blind hopes," *typhlas elpidas*, to make life endurable, taking away foreknowledge of their deaths (*PV* 248–250). This negative gift strangely contrasts with Prometheus' other gifts of knowledge and vision (*PV* 442–444, 496–499). The Promethean mastery of the world requires a certain blindness to the ultimate questions of individual death. Hence it consists in a taking away of knowledge, a turning away from the inevitable end of every life.

The tragic knowledge of Teiresias, however, is the knowledge of death's certainty, which raises the metaphysical question about life's meaning. The price of this inward knowledge is blindness to the physical world. Prometheus and Teiresias embody opposite definitions of the tragic in human life. Becoming like Teiresias, Oedipus abandons control over others for knowledge of himself. To establish dominion over his world, he must first live in harmony with himself. The Promethean vision of the inner workings of the physical universe requires a determined blindness to the knowledge of death. To conquer nature, man must ignore death in himself and turn away from the dark and mysterious paths that lead to a full knowledge of the self.

IX

No play is more about language than the *Oedipus Tyrannus*. An expert at decoding difficult messages, the hero cannot decode the meaning of his own name. Human communication, parallel to the communication by ritual and oracle between man and God, is continually breaking down, either ceasing prematurely because of fears or knowledge that cannot be spoken, or running to excess because of passion and anger. Apollo's oracles from above and the Sphinx's riddle from below provide models for human discourse but both also short-circuit the significative function of language. The oracles are either too terrifyingly specific to be understood, or else conceal beneath apparent generality their precise import for Oedipus' life ("Drive out the pollution nurtured in the land," 97). The riddle, with its plural meanings for each signifier, undermines the denotative and differentiating function of language. It misuses, or perhaps overuses, language by exploiting its ambiguity rather than its precision. It thereby projects a world whose meaning corresponds to the shifting, uncertain, "enigmatic" quality of language rather than to the potential clarity, definiteness, intelligibility of language.

Language and reality reveal one another but also serve as symbols or analogues of one another. The play correlates personal identity, language, and the world order as multiple reflections of the hero's failure to find the mediating terms of civilized life. The oracle veers between images of the world order as chaotic and as deterministic; the riddle/prophecies veer between the undifferentiated and the overspecific; and Oedipus, guided by both oracle and riddle, moves back to the origins of his identity where he finds beginning and end condensed into a terrible oneness. As both son and husband, brother and father, he finds his childhood and his maturity collapsed together—just as they are in the riddle which he solved in the past and will solve again, with a profounder and more personal answer, in the action of the play.

"Human life," to quote Geoffrey Hartman, "like a poetic figure, is an indeterminate middle between overspecified poles always threatening to collapse it."[83] Oedipus' life parallels the struggle of language in the play. He attempts to draw forth differentiating order from his world of fused polarities. He creates the space or distance necessary for significance in a world where that space threatens to disappear under the threat of total nothingness, the zero of meaninglessness or the ungraspable plenum of gods who seem to direct and control everything. "The space Sophocles wrested from the gods," Hartman goes on, "was the very space of human life. That space is illusory, or doomed to collapse as the play focuses on the moment of truth which proves the oracle."[84]

Language, therefore, becomes the microcosm for all of man's means of understanding reality. It reflects the failure of the tools of his intelligence to grasp and order world and self both, to create and maintain difference in the face of chaotic sameness, and to assert warm familiarity in the face of coldly alien otherness. Oedipus, solver of verbal riddles, is led to defeat by the multiple riddles of his own being until he can find with his own life a deeper answer to the Sphinx's riddle, and that not with words alone.

Until that point is reached, words spoken with deliberate truth say "too much" to be understood (767–768, 841).[85] Language is "in vain," *matēn*, as characters evade or deny plain words (cf. 365 and 1057), but the dismissed *logos* returns with killing force. Word and deed, *logos* and *ergon*, form paradoxical relationships (219–220, 452, 517). The confused terminology of kinship carries its grim irony throughout the play (264–265, 928, 1214, 1249–50, 1256, 1403ff.). It becomes a matter of the first importance whether something is "speakable" or "unspeakable" (300–301, 465, 993, 1289). Oedipus himself, the authoritative speaker of a public proclamation (93, 236), comes to utter things unspeakable (1289, 1313–16) and falls under a ban of speaking or being spoken to (1437, 238). His first utterances after the peripety are the inarticulate cries *aiai aiai, pheu pheu* (1307–1308). His own voice seems disembodied (1310). Speech is now his only means of recognizing friends or loved ones (1326, 1472–73), so that his speech too, like his relation to the rituals and the oracles, moves from the public to the personal sphere.

The basic categories of speech become confused. The riddling Sphinx is a prophet (1200), and the oracles are riddles (439; cf. 390ff.). The decree of the king (*kērygma*, 350, 450) becomes the curse on the one who has spoken it (744–745). The Corinthian's speech of congratulation (*euepeia*, 932) reveals the "reproach" of Oedipus' name and leads to Jocasta's last word of address, the "only word" of her final address, fixing Oedipus forever in his new condition, "unfortunate" (1071–72).

Logos is here not the glorious achievement celebrated in the *Antigone's* Ode on Man (353) but something "terrible," *deinon*, in an even darker sense than in the *Antigone*. At the point where speaking and hearing stand at their peak of terror (*deinon*, 1169–70), the *logos* seems to take over and become almost independent of Oedipus. Sophocles uses a dramatic device analogous to the questioning of Lichas by the Messenger in the *Trachiniae* (*Trach*. 402–433).[86] The chief actor stands on the sidelines, a momentarily silent witness, for the most crucial *logos* of his life, while the solving of his riddle goes on, for a few crucial minutes, without the direct participation of the great riddle-solver himself.

Presenting himself as moderate in speech, Oedipus flies to the most violent extremes of language. "Neither bold nor fearful at the present speech" was his image of himself as he prepared to receive Apollo's words at Creon's return from Delphi (89–90). But when he prepares to hear another prophet, one who "knows things that may be taught and things unspeakable" (300–301), he changes from respectful address to acrid vilification within a few moments. Less than twenty lines from the end of his deferential welcome to Teiresias he is hurling insults at his head: "O basest of base men" (334).

The deepest irony of Oedipus' relation to language lies, of course, in his name. As an infant, Oedipus received not a name, a *logos*, but the scars left by his "yoking" on the mountain. His name is a reproach (*oneidos*, 1035–36). Oedipus "called the glorious" (8) will give his name to Cithaeron (1451–52), henceforth linked with him. Nothing could be less justified than this nameless ruler's pride in what he is "called" (8). To learn the truth of his name is, as he says at the end, to pronounce "the names of all the evils that there are" (1284–85). This fearful superabundance of "names" coincides with his own zero-point of naming, where name is insult, abomination.

By learning and accepting the truth of his name, Oedipus, like the hero of the *Odyssey*, reestablishes the structures of differentiation over the randomness of the animal world. But the recreation of civilization in tragedy is far more precarious than it is in epic. The end of Oedipus' quest is to fracture the "seeming" unity of his life and his language into its bipolar reality. He is not just king but also scapegoat, not just husband but also son, not just *tyrannos*, but also *basileus*.[87] It is his tragic destiny to replace apparent oneness with binary or ternary terms. The riddle's cancellation of verbal differentiation parallels the cancellation of other forms of differentiation—self and other, stability and change, reason and madness—that make up the moral and intellectual clarity of our world. It is the problem of the one being equal to many, as Oedipus says (845–847). For Sophocles, as for Plato, the relation of the One to the Many is the focal point for man's understanding of himself and the universe.

Violating the limits of speech, Oedipus also violates those of silence. At the crossroads he fails to utter the humanizing word that might have saved Laius and himself. "These things will come even if I conceal them in silence," Teiresias warns. "Then should you speak to me of what will come," is Oedipus' reply (342). There are some things which are "unspeakable," but Oedipus is no respecter of these constraints. Only Creon, the man of good sense, the untragic figure, knows how "to keep silence where I have no knowledge" (569). He makes this remark in his futile self-defence and repeats it, in a very different context, at the end of the play (1519). He would "give an account," *logon didonai*, in the reasonable atmosphere of forensic debate (583–584), but his attempt, like Teiresias' more spirited effort, fails before the savage wrath of Oedipus.

Confounded or puzzled by silence, Oedipus forcibly elicits speech. He repeats the pattern four times: first with the chorus in his decree about keeping silent (233–243); next with Teiresias (340ff.), whom he compels to repeat his fearful words not once, but three times (359–365), "making trial of words" (360);[88] then with Jocasta (1056ff., especially 1074–75); and finally with the old herdsman, where he actually uses physical torture (1153).[89] Yet the mysterious silence of the gods cannot be forced before its time, and it is this which defies all of Oedipus' most strenuous efforts. "How, how could the furrows of your father have borne you in silence (*siga*), miserable man, for so long?" (1210–12).

X

With the disintegration or confusion of the communicative function of language, the basic relation to physical reality is threatened. Speaking, hearing, and seeing are no longer taken for granted. It is as if the world of Oedipus contracts from his dominion over Thebes to the mountainside where the exposed infant is doomed to cry without being heard, without learning human speech.

Early in the play speaking and hearing (*klyein, akouein*) belong to the ruler's communication with his subjects: he speaks and they hear or obey (216–217, 235; cf. also 84, 91, 294–295). In the encounter with Teiresias the double function of hearing and speaking as cognition and communication begins to break apart. Accustomed to having others "hear" him, he will not "hear" Teiresias (429). "Blind in ears and mind and eyes," he calls the prophet (371), but Teiresias at once turns the line back upon Oedipus himself (372–373). The three terms correspond almost exactly to Oedipus' reply to the first mention of Laius (105): "I *know* by *hearing*, but I never *saw* him." In the first stasimon striking synaesthetic imagery combines sight and sound to describe the words of the Delphic oracle: the oracle (*phama*) appears and "flashes forth" (*elampse*, 473–475).[90] The chorus would "see an upright word" (505; cf. also 187). But neither sight nor hearing helps Oedipus. His refusal to "hear" plays an important role in the scene with Creon (543–544). In the next scene, with Jocasta, it becomes crucial for him to ascertain just what has been heard (729, 850), until he arrives at the point of "dreadful hearing" from which there is no return (1169–70).

Having dwelt in a world of illusionary seeing and hearing, of mistaken perception as well as false or incomplete communication, Oedipus now finds that he has no desire for the organs of cognition (1224): "What deeds will you *hear*, what deeds will you *see*?" cries the Messenger at the beginning of his description of Jocasta's death and Oedipus' self-blinding. His daimon, Oedipus cries, "leapt to a fearful place [*deinon*; cf. 1170], not to be heard, not to be seen" (1312). "Why then," he asks a little later, "should I want sight since when I saw there was nothing joyful to behold" (1334–35). If he could, he would have closed up the channels of hearing as well as sight "that I might be blind and hear nothing, for to house one's thought (*phrontida . . . oikein*) outside of evils is sweet" (1384–90).

The man who lost in infancy, and now in adulthood, the house (*oikos*) where the senses are trained to perception and communication, would now "house" (*oikein*) his mind outside of its sufferings by giving up all perception of reality. This act not only fulfills Teiresias' prophecy (371, 1389) but also has a more fundamental meaning, referring to man's existential and cognitive reality: cast out of the house, having no "place" among men, Oedipus does not "know where" (cf. 1309–11). His rhetoric acts out, inwardly and physically, both the parents' rejection of the child and the city's ritual expulsion of the *pharmakos* or pollution. His desire to shut out physical reality recapitulates his original expulsion from the human world and also corresponds to his newly discovered status as the pollution who cannot be shown to earth or sky (1425–28).

Yet Oedipus does not sever his bond with life. Touch and hearing remain, and are intimately linked with his human feelings of grief, pity, and joy. He can hear the chorus' voice in his darkness (1325–26).[91] When he hears his dear ones weeping, he realizes that Creon has pitied him "knowing," as Creon adds, his "joy" (*terpsin*) in his children (1471–77). Initially he seems to repeat the gesture of the old servant who touched the hand of Jocasta in a suppliant's request to be sent away from the house, "out of sight of the town" (760–762; cf. 1437–38, 1449–50). But a little later in this scene the polluted outcast asks to touch the hands of his dear ones and to weep over his woes with them (1466–67). The house is his curse, but it is the only space which can receive him now as seen and heard (1429–31); and it is still the place where he, the land's pollution, can exchange touch.[92]

Oedipus does not abandon his house as his house abandoned him. Though he is "made equal to his children" by the incest consequent on that earlier expulsion from the house (425), he asks that his children not be "made equal" to his sufferings (1507). Destroyed by the ambiguities of speech, he can now experience another quality of civilized speech in the friendly voice of the chorus who do not forsake him (1325–26) and the voices of his children whom Creon allows him to hear (1472). Time and knowledge, which were destructive while Oedipus was ignorant of his place in the house, can create understanding and compassion when Creon grants him the meeting with his daughters because he "knew of old" Oedipus' delight in them. Darkness and groping touch with hand (1466) or staff replace the apparent sight and scepter of the king. But at the same time a tender exchange of speech within a house which is now truly, if grimly, his own partially fills the gap between regal command and cry on the wild mountainside. In the dramatic reversal from strength to weakness, from sceptered king to blind beggar with his staff, Oedipus gives his final answer to the riddle of the Sphinx. Oedipus the King becomes Oedipus the man.

Oedipus becomes a second Teiresias. Yet he has the inner sight of his blindness not as a gift of the gods but as the hard acquisition of his human experience and suffering. In his seeing blindness he discerns not the future, like the old prophet, but the meaning of his past and the reality of his own condition of strength-in-weakness in the present.[93]

At the end of the play Oedipus' imperfect, proud knowing ripens into the "knowledge that he has been set apart for a unique destiny." He discerns and responsibly accepts the fact that his life has a shape, a pattern which it must fulfill, formed by the interlocking of internal and external determinants, character and chance both. After crying out that he would dwell on the mountains which his parents chose as his tomb (1451–53), he pulls back abruptly and makes his deepest statement of "knowing" in the play (1455–58): "But yet I know (*oida*) this much, that no disease or anything else can destroy me, for I would not have been saved from death except for some terrible suffering. Wherever my fated portion (*moira*) goes, let it go." It is at this point, after facing the possibility that his life may be a cruel joke played upon him by malignant gods, that Oedipus turns to Creon and asks about his children. In that gesture he finally leaves the bare mountainside which his own parents gave him instead of a house and turns back for the touch and the speech of those left in his own shattered house.

The pollution is still there. It is not overborne, as it is by the inward innocence of Heracles in Euripides' *Heracles Mad* or by Oedipus' own certainty of his place in the gods' will in the *Coloneus*.[94] Against the enormity of the pollution this last gesture of human contact and human love is, by its very naturalness, momentous.

Only when Oedipus joins the two ends of his life, infancy and adulthood, and becomes the incestuous patricide along with father and king, does his life begin to make sense as part of a tragic, yet intelligible pattern. At that point a design becomes visible which embraces his exposure on the mountain, his victory over the Sphinx, his consequent rule over Thebes, and his desire to be cast out upon the mountain. All the parts taken individually at any point and grasped in the totality of their interconnection exemplify his essential greatness-in-nothingness, strength-in-weakness.

Only man spans such conflicting opposites; only man, therefore, has a tragic destiny that includes also the capacity to bring the coexistence of opposites to consciousness. Oedipus answers and lives out, knowingly, in his own life, the riddle of the Sphinx, which is the riddle of man's existence in time and of his being both the one and the many simultaneously. The months which Oedipus says defined him great and small are truly proven his "kindred" (1082–83) because time and the changes that time brings not only mark man's tragic bondage to death but also the precariousness and the painfulness of self-knowledge.

Moving from king to pollution, from seeing to blind, from rich house to the savage mountain of the monstrous birth and rejected outcast, Oedipus becomes, even more deeply than Teiresias, a constellation of contradictions and opposites. He realizes his identity not as a stable unity but as a juncture of polarities. Replacing the blind seer as the paradigm of man's tragic knowledge, he joins these oppositions in conscious and agonized union rather than unconscious coincidence. Oedipus seeks the murderer of Laius, whom he fears as his own, and finds himself.[95] His sufferings in the play constitute a far more significant "answer" to the Sphinx's riddle than the one which he so confidently gave outside Thebes in his youth. By living out his answer, he becomes a more authentic civilizing hero, the bearer of the tragic meaning of civilization for men. Prometheus, the archetypal culture hero, gave men "blind hopes" along with the arts of civilization so that they could not foresee their death. Oedipus tears away the veil and by his self-chosen blindness gives men sight.

"That we are set into a 'blind destiny,' dwell within it," Rilke once wrote, "is, after all in a way the condition of our sight . . . Only through the 'blindness' of our fate are we really deeply related to the wonderful muffledness of the world, that is, with what is whole, vast, and surpassing us."[96] For Sophocles, however, that "muffledness" is not "wonderful," but terrible-and-wonderful, *deinon*. To exemplify the mystery of existence is not a blessing but a misfortune, a curse. Yet only through that blindness can the hero know the vast life of the universe in all its strange, remote workings.

Oedipus' fate in the orchestra mirrors back to the members of the audience their own experience, in the theater, of nothingness before time and change. As they watch the performance, they too pass from blind seeing to seeing blindness, from the comfortable certitudes of daily life to the shaken awareness of how fragile these certitudes are, how thin the film between reality and illusion. They, in firm control of their lives, are, like Oedipus, "struck" or "shaken," *ekpeplēgmenos* (922), a word used by Sophocles' contemporaries to describe both intense aesthetic and emotional reactions.[97] Each member of the audience, joined but also isolated in the silent crowd, celebrating a festival but also involved in the sufferings of the masked actor, temporarily loses his identity, his secure definition by house, position, friends, and becomes, like Oedipus, nameless and placeless, weighing the light accidents of birth, fortune, status above the void of nonbeing.[98]

Like all tragic art this play above all reveals the fragility of those structures—ritual, social, moral—that enclose it and are the sources of its life. In every sense, as Knox observes, personal, historical, communal, "the audience which watched Oedipus in the theater of Dionysus was watching itself."[99]

Yet what ultimately emerges from the *Oedipus Tyrannus* is not a sense of total chaos and despair but a quality of heroism in the power of self-knowledge. "No other mortal except myself can bear my sufferings," Oedipus says near the end. The verb *pherein*, "bear," "endure," is a leitmotif of the play. Like everything which touches Oedipus intimately, it spans the two poles of weakness and strength.[100] As the trusted ruler in the prologue Oedipus "bears grief for these my subjects here more than for my own life" (93–94). But this grief (*penthos*) at the end is located *in* his own life. He "grieves a double grief and bears (*pherein*) double woes" (1320). The same verb, *pherein*, describes both his heroic "endurance" (1293, 1320, 1415) and, in the play's typical transformations of actives into passives, his helplessness as he is "born aloft," "swept away" without place (*pheromai*, 1309–10). Both Teiresias and Jocasta, in different ways, urge him to "bear life easily" (320–321, 982–983). But by destiny and by temperament Oedipus does not exist in the middle ground where such bearing is possible. He has, as Creon tells him, a "nature most painful to bear" (674–675) and "bears ill" the half-knowledge of his encounter with Laius (770).

In a life where so much seems to have been chance or randomness (see Jocasta's *eikēi*, 979), Oedipus not only discerns pattern but creates pattern. His capacity to bear is connected with his determination to discover the shape which his life has within the mysterious order, or disorder, of the gods, to discern the coherence between the inner nature and the outward event, between the beginning and the end, the suffered and the inflicted injury. Whereas earlier Oedipus angrily rejected the pains (*pēmonai*, 363) which Teiresias had foretold for him, at the end he chooses them as his own (*authairetoi pēmonai*, 1230–31) and strikes with his own hand (1331ff.).[101] These "self-chosen pains" answer the "savage pain" of Jocasta (1073–74), who cannot face the suffering contained in her destiny, and contrast also with his own violent emotional oscillations when he "excites his spirit too much with pains of all sorts" (*lypai pantoiai*, 914–915).

For Oedipus, more than for any other Greek hero, ontogeny recapitulates phylogeny; the tragic hero is both anomalous individual and universal mythic paradigm. The Sphinx's riddle defines man and Oedipus sequentially in the normality of his passage through the stages of life; Oedipus, in answering the riddle, finds himself the simultaneous combination of all three stages, a monstrous abnormality. He does not solve the ultimate riddle, the meaning of the gods who remain as remote as the stars with which he, in the first step of the exile that will henceforth be his life's pattern, measures his distance from Corinth (779). But he follows this pattern to the end and completes it, as symbol and paradigm, by a self-inflicted suffering. To search for and accept his hidden origins and his darker self is to essay anew the riddle of the Sphinx, that is, enter the tragic path of self-knowledge.

Beyond the questions of time, change, and the multiplicity and fluidity of identity, Oedipus' tragedy also asks whether human life is trapped in a pattern of its own or others' making or is all random, as Jocasta says. He asks, in other words, whether the sources of such suffering lie in an overstructured or an unstructured universe, absolute necessity or absolute chance. That question can have no ultimate answer. But to confront the alternatives with such total and open risk is truly to encounter the demonic Sphinx and therewith to leave the safe, defined spaces of house and city and cross the dangerous boundaries between man, beast, and God.

8

Electra

Until recently critics have regarded the *Electra* as an affirmative, even an optimistic play. The matricide, they argue, is not emphasized; the Furies who avenge Clytaemnestra are not much in evidence; Sophocles is, therefore, giving a morally neutral, objective, "Homeric" rendering of a famous myth, the just and happy liberation of the House of Atreus from its sinful past. The first serious opposition to this view came from a series of essays by J. T. Sheppard published between 1918 and 1927 and promptly forgotten.[1] In the last two decades, however, an increasing number of scholars have expressed reservations about the play's combination of "matricide and good spirits," and Sheppard's position is no longer so isolated as it once seemed.[2]

I will confess at the start that it is to this darker view of the play that I adhere. The *Electra*, I believe, is concerned with the destruction of a personality once capable of love; a vengeance that has gone sour in an unheroic, embittered world; deceit and misunderstanding between those who do and should love one another; and the ambiguities of truth and illusion amid the difficulties of communication and the deceptiveness of language.

The matricide-punishing Furies, it is true, do not have the weight that they do in Aeschylus and even in Euripides. Yet they are sufficiently present in the text to give us serious qualms about a "scot-free vengeance, noble heroine, and affirmative drama."[3] After the *Oresteia* no tragedian had to lay much emphasis on the details, and even small touches are enough to convey both moral and psychological abhorrence. As George Gellie has recently reminded us, "The most famous Furies in tragedy were more interested in pursuing the killers of Clytaemnestra."[4]

Electra has a triple focus: the restoration of justice in a corrupt world, the emotional suffering and division within the chief protagonist, and the confusion or beclouding of the means by which men relate to one another, to the natural world, and to the gods, especially through language and ritual.[5] Electra faces a tragic choice between the compromises of Chrysothemis and her own fidelity to her father and to justice. But to accept her full commitment to the latter also involves a spiritual self-annihilation, the conversion of her capacity for love into its opposite.[6]

Electra's commitment to death over life is a condition not only of her soul but of her whole universe. It is to be understood, therefore, not merely in psychological terms (still the dominant mode of interpreting the play), but in the perspectives of myth and deity and the large question of a valid image of civilization. It is characteristic of what H. D. F. Kitto has called Sophocles' "religious drama" that the protagonist's inward struggle and veering between self-destruction and self-realization are inseparable from the larger question of man's relation to the natural and divine order.

As we have seen in the other plays, disharmony in the human world is reflected in the play's spatial axes: the relation between the inner space of house and city and the outer world of natural forces on the horizontal axis; the relation between upper and lower worlds, Olympus and Hades, on the vertical axis. In these, as in other respects, the *Electra* is closest to the *Antigone*.

Enclosed within the city and within the house, Electra awaits her brother, Orestes, who comes from a foreign city to bring deliverance. The first scene highlights this intersection of inner and outer space. Orestes and the Paedagogus enter Argos from the outside. The language of their exchange is expansive. Speaking of Troy and the shrines of Argos, they locate Agamemnon's house within the broad spatial and temporal perspectives of the city (1–14). They seem to stand on a height, commanding the city and its outer limits.[7] Their temporal horizons embrace the recent past of Agamemnon's campaign at Troy (1), Orestes' early youth, as he is brought up to be "the avenger of his father's death" (14), and the remoter antiquity of Argos and its legends (4–5) and the house of the Atreids (9–10). Above all, they speak of "act" and "acting," *ergon, erdein* (22, 60, 76, 83).

Electra, by contrast, makes her first appearance with a cry from inside. We are introduced to her as a helpless voice of lamentation trapped in the interior of the palace (77–79). To Orestes' impulse to stay and listen, the Paedagogus opposes the necessity of acting and the hope of victory and power (84–85). Where she laments to the chthonic deities (110ff.), Orestes and his companions speak of Apollo and the execution of his orders (35–37, 51ff., 82–83). This scene presents the basic antithesis of the play, an antithesis between the free, outer worlds where action is possible, and the enclosed world of the palace where the only form of action is sterile dirge (121ff.).[8]

In one respect, however, the tension between inner and outer realms differs from that of the other plays. There the hero either is initially outside the city, an exile or outcast (Ajax, Heracles, Philoctetes, the aged Oedipus), or else stands in a problematical relation to city and house as he or she moves from its center literally or figuratively to its fringes (Antigone, King Oedipus). Electra remains at the heart of house and city, defined by her relation to the *oikos* where she is imprisoned, both literally and metaphorically. As the chorus chants its final words about the freedom of the "seed of Atreus," Electra may be envisioned as standing before the house, alone, as at the beginning, and then following Orestes and Aegisthus into its darkness (1493ff.).[9]

In the other plays city and house embody the shelter and stability of civilization from which the hero, in his tragic isolation, is excluded. In the *Electra*, to be rooted in house and city is to be trapped in a suffocating atmosphere of evil and death.[10] Without Orestes' intervention Electra runs the risk of being enclosed "in an underground chamber, outside this land," where she will never "look upon the light of the sun" (380–382). Expulsion outside the city will only intensify the darkness and living death which she endures inside the house. Even the saving hero who comes from the outside is pulled into its inner darkness (1493–98). The initial polarity between inner and outer seems to give way to a circularity that makes the ultimate "liberation" ambiguous (see 1487–1500, 1508–10).

Though it is the setting for the action, the city itself has only a shadowy existence. But as in *Oedipus Tyrannus*, *Antigone*, and *Trachiniae*, disorder in the house is the microcosm of the disharmony in the political life of the community. The adulterous lover in Queen Clytaemnestra's bed also sits on the legitimate King's throne (266–274). On that bed she has ominous visions of a phallic generative power and its threatening fertility (410–423). Agamemnon, coming for "a second meeting" or "second union" (*homilia* has a sexual connotation), "grasps and fixes fast at the hearth the scepter which once he wielded, but now Aegisthus holds; from this a burgeoning vine bloomed upward, and with this all the Mycenaeans' land became dark with shadow" (419–423).[11]

In these inversions of fertility in nature the moral order too is conflicted and problematical. The murder of a father is avenged by the brutal killing of a mother. The "law" with which Electra answers Clytaemnestra's attempt at self-defense would only perpetuate the cycle of violence (579–583):

> Should he [Agamemnon] have died at your hand? By what law (*nomos*)? Watch out lest in setting up this law for mortals you set up pain and remorse for yourself. For if we kill one man in retaliation for another, you would be the first to die if you meet justice (*dikē*).

The last lines of dialogue in the play restate this "law" and "justice" with a similarly generalizing tone ("mortals," "all men"), but now Electra's warning has become reality, and the harsh *lex talionis* is unsheathed. Orestes, marching Aegisthus off at sword point, moralizes (1505–1507): "This should be the justice (*dikē*) for all, at once, to kill whoever wishes to act outside the laws (*nomoi*), for thus wrongdoing would not abound." Such a generalization provides no more satisfying a summation of the action than the equally youthful and impetuous Hyllus' angry incrimination of Zeus at the end of the *Trachiniae*. Earlier, in his eagerness to push on to action, Orestes, impatient with words, dismisses the question of his mother's morality (1288–89): "Let go excessive talk, and do not teach me that my mother is evil."

Electra's relation to justice is not without its ambiguities. She has no answer to Clytaemnestra's charge that Agamemnon killed his daughter (573–576). In her pent-up hatred for her mother she, like Orestes in 1289, dismisses the question of justice altogether (558–560): "You admit you killed my father. What statement could be more shameful than this, whether it [the killing] was done *justly or not*?"[12] And at the end of Electra's long speech the chorus describes her (if we read the text correctly) as "breathing passion" and expresses doubts about her concern with justice (610–611).[13]

The issue of justice is sharper still in her exchange with Chrysothemis later in the play (1041–43):

El.:   Do I not seem to you to speak with justice?
Chr.:   Yet there are places where justice brings harm.
El.:   Under such laws I do not wish to live.

Electra is right, of course, but the lines point up the tragic aspect of her concern for justice. In this city of violence and evil, commitment to justice and commitment to "life" (*zēn*) are mutually exclusive. Life values are in conflict with moral values, and Electra has to opt for the latter. What emerges is the inadequacy of a society whose system of justice rests on blood-vengeance, for here the avengers run the risk of coming to the same level as the criminals. In late fifth-century Athens such critical reevaluations of justice and punishment were in the air: we may recall the discussion in Plato's *Protagoras* and the fragment of "Truth" (*Alētheia*) ascribed to Antiphon the Sophist.[14]

II

In this conflict between life and justice Electra resembles Antigone. Yet the house to which Antigone can devote her life, though under a curse, is a place of love (*Antig.* 523), and through love she hopes to restore the shattered wholeness of her house. The violent rifts within Electra's house, however, are made irrevocable by her action. Indeed the excessive closeness of blood relations in Antigone's house is almost the exact opposite of the excessive distance in Electra's.

Electra's situation is the microcosm of the world around her. The basic rhythms of life are overturned. Nurture and destruction, fertility and death, bloom and decay, birth and killing are inverted. The basic situation was given in the myth and richly developed in the imagery of Aeschylus' *Oresteia* (see, for example *Ag.* 1382–98). The daughters, forcibly kept unmarried, can regain the "blooming" of their house only by joining with their brother in matricide (951–953, 961–966). For both the Paedagogus and Electra the nurture of Orestes to the ripeness of youth (*hēbē*, 14) or his "bloom of life" (*biō(i) thallonta*, 951–952) signifies primarily his readiness for murder (*phonos*, 14, 953). The inversions become especially powerful in Clytaemnestra's dream and prayers, where the darker truth of dream and vision forces its way through the rational control of consciousness and logical discourse (see 417–423, 635ff., 1404–1405, 1416–23).[15]

These inversions operate both as metaphor and as action. Orestes in the prologue expresses his qualms about being "dead in word" (59), alluding to legends like those of Salmoxis and Aristeas, whose mysterious disappearance and return embody an archetypal myth of death and rebirth, the cyclical renewal of nature after the sterility of winter.[16]

The narrower cycles of day and night parallel the inversions of the seasonal cycle. The play begins with the "bright light of the sun" at dawn (17–18), but the "failing of the stars' black night" in the next line puts the return of light in a curiously negative way. For Electra night and day lose their distinctness in the sameness of perpetual grief (86–94). The *Electra* ends with a slow, deliberate return to the darkness of the house and the evils which it is yet to "see" (1396, 1494, 1497).[17] The human act, stripped of its ritual absolution and legal resolution, presses with the full weight of its emotional violence and personal responsibility upon the human actors, who at the crucial moment are isolated both from one another (1398ff.) and from the gods (1424–25). Instead of a ritual procession to the sacred earth in a covenant between human and divine, as at the end of the *Oresteia*, Sophocles ends with a private "procession," of two men, alone into a curse-ridden house for a deed of cruel and bitter (1503–1504), if necessary, violence.

The house, with its nurture of the future generation and its power to commemorate and ritually memorialize the past generation, should hold the balance between living and dead, giving each its due. But in this play that balance is destroyed. The living members of the new generation are denied their proper nurture, and the dead cannot be laid to rest. Carried away in her denunciation of her mother. Electra almost imagines Iphigeneia, "the dead one," as alive and speaking (548) but only to bear witness against her mother.[18]

As in *Hamlet*, the dead king comes to life, as it were, to punish his murderers. The chorus adduces the parallel of the slain Amphiaraus who now, "in his full consciousness (*pampsychos*) rules in the Underworld" (841).[19] The return of the dead is then completed in the chorus' chilling vision as Clytaemnestra dies at the hands of her son (1417–21): "The curses accomplish. Those who lie beneath the earth live. Those long dead drain away from their killers the blood that flows in retribution."

Electra is the pivot for the inversion of upper and lower worlds (1090ff.), for the inversion of life and death. At one moment she even appears as a Fury of the lower world, "drinking down neat" the life's blood of her victim (785–786; cf. 1417–21). Like Antigone, she is devoted to the powers of the lower world but in a very different sense. Her relation with her living kin has its basis in shared hatred, not shared love (*Antig.* 523). Antigone enters the underworld darkness of the cave to honor a dead brother; Electra clings to the false ashes of a living brother and watches joyfully as he enters the house in what seems to be a ghostly procession into Hades itself (1384–97, 1417–21, 1491ff.).

In its failed mediation between man and the cosmic order, this city suffers also from a disintegration of both heroic spirit and heroic language. The collective memory of great deeds is weak. A worthy expression of the noble past which might call men to a higher vision of themselves is lacking. The play begins with a resonant evocation of Agamemnon and the Trojan war, the touchstone of heroism for Mycenae: "O son of Agamemnon, once general at Troy" (1–2). But Orestes, though eager for the honor that is his due (*timē*, *kleos*, 60, 64, 71), will obtain it by the unheroic means of "deceit" (*dolos*), "thievish trickery" (*kleptein*), and "secrecy" (*kryptein*) (37, 55–56). Such stratagems in Sophocles generally run counter to the noble nature (*physis*) of the true heroes: Neoptolemus in the

Philoctetes is the clearest example.[20] As the case of Neoptolemus and the related, though very different, case of Deianeira show, such schemes have a dangerous tendency to run away with their executors. Not only is there a discrepancy between Orestes' means and ends, but his means bring him dangerously close to those he would punish, for Agamemnon's murderers, like himself in 59–61, are repeatedly described as using trickery, lies, concealment.

Like Neoptolemus, Orestes is the bereft young son of a glorious father whom he has never seen. But there the resemblance stops. Neoptolemus resists the use of base means for ostensibly noble ends; Orestes proposes them to himself. Neoptolemus has a heroic model, in fact a plethora of models, to recall him to his inborn nature and great deeds. Orestes has only an old palace servant and an embittered maiden sister. The balance between heroic deed and potentially treacherous word that Neoptolemus manages to recover, thanks to his older mentor, at the end of his play, remains skewed and ambiguous for Orestes.

Whatever is heroic in the play rests with Electra. Yet her heroic stature involves yet another inversion of normal values, the exchange of male and female roles. She is isolated in a city where the legitimate king is replaced by a "valorless king" (*analkis*, 301) who "makes his wars with women" (302), not with the warriors of Troy (1). The first fully heroic utterance of the play occurs in an interchange between two women (393–403). Electra refuses to take the "sensible" (cf. *phronein*) position of compromise. In her second meeting with her sister she, a woman, will practice the valor of a man (997–998). To Chrysothemis' protestations of feminine weakness and cowardice she opposes the heroic values of honor and courage (literally, "manliness," *andreia*, 983). Taking an oath by the virgin, undomesticated Artemis, she scorns the traditional passivity of women (1238–42), but Orestes reminds her that in this house the martial spirit of Ares "lies with women too" (1243). As in Aeschylus, Clytaemnestra and Aegisthus seem to reverse sexual roles.[21] Yet there are hints of an ominous reversal for Orestes and Electra, too. Orestes, like the pusillanimous usurper, also "makes battle with women" (see 302).

The discordant mood of these inversions shapes a tragic necessity (*anagkē*) that hangs over the action and creates a pervasive sense of waste, made visually explicit in the wearing down of the heroine's nobility and beauty, her once "glorious form" (1177).[22] House, city, ritual, and language—four of the most basic areas of the civilized order—are called into question.

III

Here, even more than in the *Oresteia*, all the violations of the natural and moral order are concentrated in the house. Electra views her personal tragedy in terms of the destruction of her house. She will not have children to continue the line of Agamemnon (964ff.). In her grief at the sight of Orestes' urn she fuses her own loss with that of her whole family (*genos*, 1119–22): "Give me the urn," she begs, "that I may bewail myself and all my race together with this dust here."

At the climactic moment of the matricide, the chorus joins "family" and "city" in their ambiguous cry of triumph (1413–14). "Family," *genea*, takes up Electra's justification of the matricide in terms of avenging "the sire who begot (*gennēsas*) them" (1410–21):

> Clyt.: (*offstage*): My child, my child (*teknon*), pity the mother who gave you birth (*tekousan*).
>
> El.: But he received no pity from you, nor the father who begot (*gennēsas*) him.
>
> Cho.: O city, O race (*genea*), unhappy, now your fate of every day is wasting away, wasting away.
>
> Clyt.: (*offstage*): Alas I am struck.
>
> El.: Strike, if you have strength, a second blow.
>
> Cho.: The curses fulfil. Those who lie below the earth live, for the long dead drain their killers' blood, flowing in retribution.

The act that seals the destruction of the house, son killing mother to avenge the murdered father, is consummated through repeated words for birth, siring, family: *teknon . . . tekousa, gennēsas . . . genea*. Both the mother-*genetrix* and the father-*generator* are destroyed. The inversion is signalled in the strange oxymoron of 1413–14: the liberation of the house appears as the "wasting away" of its doom. The next lines, 1415–16, echo the death scene of the *Agamemnon* (*Ag.* 1343–45), and at once the chorus evokes the curses of the house in an Aeschylean vein (1417–21; cf. *Ag.* 1509–12; *Cho.* 65–69, 400–404, 886). In Aeschylus the lines on striking the blow are in the passive voice and are uttered by Agamemnon dying at the hands of Clytaemnestra. Here they are put in the mouth of Electra so that her emotional participation in the matricide may have full scope.

In its evil and suffering, house dwarfs city. The chorus cries out, "O City" (1413), but all the force of the passage rests with the house. The chorus' hopeful evocation of the "glorious land of the Mycenaeans" early in the play (161–162) or Aegisthus' authoritarian reference to "all the Mycenaeans and Argives" near the end (1459) gives us little concrete impression of the larger political entity. The public landmarks given in the prologue—the temples, the agora—are overshadowed by the ominous "much-destroying house of the Pelopids" as Orestes' goal (10–16).

Orestes' part in the action describes a movement from the outside, public world to the darkness of the house. For him the house has an almost living reality. He addresses it near the end of the prologue after invoking his native earth and the gods of the land (69–72): "O house of my father, for I came as your cleanser (*kathartēs*) in justice, sped by the gods. Do not send me away from this land without honor (*atimos*), but rather as the ruler of my wealth and founder of my house." Yet his "purification" of the house involves one of the most celebrated pollutions in Greek tragedy.

Whereas Orestes, like Clytaemnestra (648), emphatically asserts his title to the material status and possessions of the house, Electra scorns its wealth (452, 457, 960) and speaks only of her emotional ties to it, her complex inward bonds of hate and love. She is totally defined by her relation to the house. Her first utterance in the play is a cry from inside, heard by the Paedagogus, who attributes it to "some servant" (78–79). His supposition, possibly a cover to keep Orestes undistracted from the task at hand, has an ironic truth. Electra is in fact treated as a servant, as she herself soon laments (189–190), held in a kind of slavery (*douleia*, 814, 1192). Prohibited passage outside the doors (310ff., 328ff., 516ff.), she is badly dressed, ill-fed, forced to serve at tables which are "empty" for her, the king's daughter (190–192).[23] To these physical sufferings, however, is added the emotional suffering of having to associate with and share house with (*synoikos*) her father's killers (262–265, 817–818).

Within the house Electra witnesses the violations of its sacredness: the new king's possessions of her father's clothes, throne, bed (266–273), the impious rites that celebrate the murder of a husband (271–281), the cruel treatment and mockery of a daughter who weeps while the murderess-wife laughs (277, 283). The most holy places of the house, hearth and bed, are desecrated by these sacrilegious "libations at the heart" (*parhestioi loibai*, 269–270). The mother at the hearth blocks both her son's and the daughter's passage to adulthood. Usurping the masculine authority of the house, Clytaemnestra transmits that authority not to the son of her womb but to her lover, an older male who prevents the legitimate heir from acceding to his father's property. This usurper, at the masculine center of the violated interior of the house, also stands in an anomalous, indeed an outrageous, position: instead of taking a wife to his own hearth, the usual practice in the patrilocal society of the fifth century, he has moved to hers and borrowed her authority along with her *oikos*. Only in terrifying nocturnal vision does the legitimate king take up his scepter "at the hearth" of his unfaithful wife, his murderess (419–420).[24] Not only can the daughter not share the house with the mother (818), but the mother finds it equally horrible to share the house with her daughter, who seems more a destructive daimon or a Fury than a living person (784–786).[25]

The choral odes create a larger mythical frame for these perverted family relations within the house: the tales of Procne and Itys, a mother killing a son to avenge a husband's rape of a sister (107, 148–149); the story of Eriphyle, similar in its essentials to that of Clytaemnestra and Orestes (837–847); and the earlier history of the Pelopids themselves (504–515). Virtually every ode in the play deals with the destruction of a house. In the parode Electra brings together the stories of Procne and of Niobe (145–153). Though the latter is an unlikely parallel for a childless girl, she too has a tomb-like existence of perpetual weeping (151–152). Like Procne, Electra might be called "one who loses children" (*tek-noleteira*, 107), though the adjective can suggest also the unnatural behavior of the maternal figure in this doomed house.

What belongs outside the house is mistakenly applied to the most intimate bonds within. Thus the son is "an exile from his mother's nurture" (776), a disturbing collocation of political and domestic language which in turn implies the confusion of the civic and familial codes. The mother herself is a "tyrant" or "ruler" rather than a mother (*despotis*, 597–598). What Electra "learns" or has "by nature" from her mother is shamelessness and the capacity for violence and evil (307–309, 343–344, 605–609, 619–621).[26]

In the Procne myth of the parode a human house collapses into the savagery of nature. In the second stasimon (where the nightingale of 1077 recalls Procne) wild creatures paradoxically honor the sanctions which fifth-century anthropology regarded as distinctive of human civilization.[27] Niobe is a natural emblem for Electra's fixity of grief; yet in this myth the barriers between the human and natural worlds break down, and in Electra's eyes the rock-like eternity and dumbness of nature lift Niobe even to the level of godhead (150–152): "Alas, all-enduring, pitiful Niobe, you I hold a god, weeping, alas, in your tomb of stone."

The inversion of wild and civilized space also marks Electra's opening lamentation. She cries out to the light and the sky and then speaks of her "hateful bed within her grief-filled house" (92–93), sole witness of her dirge-like cries for "the unfortunate father whom bloody Ares did not receive as guest (*exenisen*) in a barbarian land, but my mother and her bed-sharing mate, Aegisthus, split his head with bloody axe as woodcutters an oak" (94–99). The striking verb *xenizein*, "receive as guest, offer hospitality to a stranger," inverts the relation between safe house and hostile soil. Ares, the most savage and least civilized of the gods, detested even by the other Olympians (*Iliad* 5.890–891), would have offered the king kindlier hospitality than his own house. We may recall the second stasimon of *Trachiniae*, where Ares, named at the point of dangerous transition between city and wild (*Trach.* 647–654), offers grimly ironic "release" to the "citiless" hero. In Electra's simile the foreign battlefield and the life-giving interior of the house, the barbarian shore and the homeland of safe return, exchange places.

The Homeric simile for Agamemnon's murder, "like woodcutters splitting an oak" (98–99), creates another deadly convergence of opposites. The civilizing work in the forest doubles with the savage act inside that destroys a king in his own house. Later Electra laments for her supposedly dead brother as one "snatched away like a storm wind" (1150–51). She views the death of a beloved member of the house as an invasion of safe human space by nature's violence. The Homeric associations of this, as of the woodcutting simile, compound the inversion of wild and civilized space with an inversion of heroic values.[28]

Electra exemplifies interiority carried to its extreme.[29] The chorus admonishes her early in the play that her grief is excessive (*perissos*), beyond what the others inside suffer, though their loss is the same (154–158).[30] Penned within the house (326–328), treated as a domestic slave (814, 1192), free to venture outside only when Aegisthus is also outside in the country (310–315; cf. 516–518, 627), she is threatened with a negative form of both interiority and exteriority: imprisonment "in an underground chamber outside this land" (381–382). To the well-meaning and alarmed Chrysothemis who reports Aegisthus' plan she bitterly wishes for its rapid fulfillment "that I might flee as far away as possible from all of you" (391).

In the first half of the play the recurrence of the verb "send," *pempein* and compounds, underscores these movements between inner and outer. The rulers will "send" Electra where she will never see the sun (380). Clytamnestra has "sent" Chrysothemis to bring libations (406, 427) because Agamemnon has "sent" a fearful nocturnal vision (460). But Clytaemnestra's attempt to bridge the distance between house and tomb, the two major sacred, and polluted, spaces of the play, turns into Electra's first victory: for the first time she foils the attempt of those within the house to reach the outside and persuades her sister to leave Clytaemnestra's offerings "where none of them may ever approach the resting place [literally, "bed," *eunē*] of our father" (434–438).

In the middle section the answer to Clytaemnestra's secret prayer is a stranger (*xenos*), "sent," he says (*epempomēn*, 680) to tell the "truth" of Orestes' death. At this point Electra, though about to be restored to "life," feels herself as "dead"; "strangers" are the closest friends; those from "outside" simultaneously save and destroy the inner space of the house and its one faithful guardian (676–680):

> Paed.: I declare both now and then that Orestes is dead.
> El.: I am destroyed, O misery. I am no longer anything.
> Clyt. (*to El.*): Do you do as you like. But, you, stranger, tell me the truth. In what way did he meet his doom?
> Paed.: For just that was I sent. I shall tell you the whole tale.

Soon after, Clytaemnestra invites within the stranger bearing the news of her son's death, while she harshly tells her daughter to stay outside and cry out "her own and her dear ones' woes" (802–803). We are reminded of Aegisthus' threats of the sunless chamber where Electra, "outside this land, will sing her song of woes" (382). But Clytaemnestra's security inside her house has never been more precarious than at this moment. Her inversions of inner and outer, "loved ones" and "strangers," will soon issue into the culminating inversions of the house, "deserted of loved ones, of destroyers full" (1404–1405).

This scene ends with Electra's nadir of despair and greatest point of crisis. As Clytaemnestra and the "stranger" enter the house, Electra, outside, "bereft of loved ones," is ready to die at the hands of "any of those within" (817–822). Yet in accepting this position at the gate, cut off from the inner space of the house, she also asserts a new heroic strength. Now she refuses "to go within to share the house with" the murderers (*ou . . . synoikos eiseimi*, 817–818). That strength takes the form of a determination to act which overcomes her sister's timidity as she orders Chrysothemis to go inside to her mother while she will carry out the vengeance alone (1052; cf. 1033).[31]

These multiple inversions meet and interact in the token that gives access to the house, a burial urn borne by a putative stranger confirming the son's final removal from the house. When Orestes requests that someone announce his presence to those within (1103), the chorus points to Electra as "the nearest one" (*anchistos*, 1105), a word which can also mean "nearest of kin."[32] Physical distance, however, stands in inverse relation to the emotional distance which brother and sister must traverse to reestablish their original proximity as *philoi*, "loved ones," within the house. Holding the urn of her "dead" brother while her living brother stands beside her, Electra laments the futility of having sent forth her brother to save him from death within the house. She repeats the verb "sent forth," *ekpempein*, three times in five lines (1128, 1130, 1132): what she sent forth to save she receives back dead (1128). He died "outside of the house, an exile in another land, apart from (his) sister" (1136–37), his corpse not washed by the dear hands of his sister (1138–39). Now her proud separation of herself from the destructive inner spaces of the house collapses as she apostrophizes the "dead" man and asks him to "receive" her into the small chamber (*stegos*) of the urn (1165; cf. 1142). This culminating point of her grief recapitulates the tyrant's threat of imprisonment in an underground chamber (379–382). But now that enforced quasi-death of enclosure is an emanation of Electra's own suffering spirit as she sees her last hopes for love and justice obliterated by death.

In these inversions of inner and outer space a simple statement like "the mother is in the house" (*mētēr d'en oikois*, 1309) is electrifying: it signals the destruction of the protected realm inside. Conversely, the threatened emergence of those within (*endothen*) to the outside (*exodos*) puts Orestes and Electra on guard (1323–24). Electra then bids the "strangers" to "go in, especially as you bear what no one would drive away from the house, nor yet receive with joy" (1323–25). The relation of inner and outer at this point becomes a tactical problem in the execution of the matricide (1367–74).[33] Orestes' obeisance to the ancestral seat of all the gods who inhabit this court before the gates (*propyla*, 1374–75) and obeisance to the "father's abode" (*patrōa hedē*, 1374) precede the killing of the mother in the inward space characteristically hers.

When Orestes is inside the house, Electra strains to hear. The scene is an exact inversion of the prologue; now brother and sister have changed positions (cf. 77ff.). The darkness and mystery of that inner space are all the greater for its invisibility. "Someone cries within," Electra says, in answer to Clytaemnestra's address to a house "bereft of loved ones, full of destroyers" (1404–1406). These are the first words heard from within. They can be taken as the stage directions for a shriek that leaps out now like an electric spark across the void between inner and outer space. Brother and sister are joined on either side by the sounds that signify the murder of their common parent.

In this violated interior space Ares, whose proper sphere is the exterior realm of the battlefield (cf. 95–96), "breathes blood of harsh strife" (1385) as the murderers' "bloody hand drips with the sacrifice to Ares" (1422–23; cf. 1243). When Orestes reenters from inside and announces, "The things in the house (*ta en domoisi*) are well if well Apollo oracled" (1425), we cannot but think of all the horrors of these "things in the house."[34]

The last act of the vengeance continues these relentless inversions of inner and outer space. When Aegisthus returns and questions Electra, she replies (1448–49): "I know very well. For otherwise I should be *outside* (*exōthen*) of the fortunes (*symphora*, also "misfortunes") of those dearest to me (*philtatōn*)." Asked where they are, Electra replies with grim and studied irony, "Within, for they have made their way to a hostess dear to them" (1451). Then the doors open and the horrors of what lies within are brought forth as the still veiled body of Clytaemnestra is wheeled out on the ekkyklema, "a very grim sight," as Electra says (1455).[35] The vengeance is only complete when Aegisthus is forced to go inside (1491), another echo of the ominous command which has resounded through the play (cf. especially 1373). The literal entrance of killer and victim within the darkness of the house (1493–94), though poetic justice for Agamemnon's slaughter, also recalls the passage of the gods of the lower world within the Hades-like darkness of the house (1384–97, 1417–21).

The former passage is especially relevant to the final movement into the interior darkness (1395–98): "Hermes, son of Maia, conceals the guile in darkness and leads them to the very goal and no longer waits." "Goal," *terma*, a term from athletics, recalls the expansive and brilliant race at Delphi. But that freedom of movement, itself part of the trick to enable Orestes to enter the house, contracts to this grim passage in a dark and narrow space. Along with the "evils of the Pelopids" (1498), it also evokes Pelops' ancient horserace (504ff.), when "outrage, bringing pain in plenty, never departed from this house" (513–515).

As Clytaemnestra replaces the language of kin ties with the language of politics (see below), the "strangers' " approach to the house ominously conjoins its political and familial aspects.[36] Like the Corinthian Messenger in the *Tyrannus* (*OT* 925), the Paedagogus enters asking "the foreign women" (*xenai gynaikes*) if "this is the house of the ruler Aegisthus" (*tyrannou dōmat' Aigisthou*, 660–661). Clytaemnestra, whom he "conjectures" to be his "wife," *damar*, a word that must sound bitter on his lips, has, he says, the appearance of a ruler (*tyrannos*, 663–664). He is bringing "sweet words from a man who is dear" (*philos*) to her and her spouse (666–667), but of course the sender is a *philos* in a very different sense, and the *logoi*, so ambiguous in this play of false and distorted messages, are far from sweet (cf. *pikron*, "bitter," 1504). When Orestes himself enters, in disguise, he addresses the chorus as "women," dropping the Paedagogus' "foreign." More significant still is his omission of the title "ruler" when he asks "where Aegisthus has his dwelling" (1101). The very presence of Aegisthus in that house, of course, is an abomination, and Orestes' search for his house has indeed been, as he says in 1101, his object "of old" (*palai*).[37]

For all her inversions of the maternal role, however, Clytaemnestra is not entirely without motherly sentiments. She wavers in her hatred as Electra never does. She feels guilt and hesitation, and even the relief she feels at the news of Orestes' death is mingled with the pain of a mother's loss (766–771):

Clyt.: O Zeus, shall I call this happy, then, or terrible (*deina*), but gain (*kerdē*)? Painful indeed if by my own sufferings I save my life.

Paed.: Why are you so downcast at this present tale?

Clyt.: Terrible it is to be a mother, for not even when your child hurts you is there hatred toward him.

By revealing this tender and maternal side of Clytaemnestra, Sophocles lets us take the measure of what the matricide involves both for the house as an institution and for the emotions of the human beings within it. Earlier Clytaemnestra accused Agamemnon of being able to "endure" sacrificing his daughter (*etlē*, 531).[38] The end of the play will again stir the deep emotional resonances in the closest of all blood ties when the mother implores her son to spare her life. As the repeated *deinon*, "terrible," insistently stresses the conflicting emotions of Clytaemnestra on hearing the news of her son's death, a three-fold repetition of the root, *tek-*, "give birth," in a cry of shattering simplicity, emphasizes the horror of the deed (1410–11): "My child, my child (*teknon, teknon*), pity her who gave you birth (*tekousan*)."[39] Clytaemnestra's "Painful it is to be a mother" (*tiktein*, literally "give birth," 770) proves prophetic in an unexpected way. Her "gain" of controlling the house as a locus of power, possessions, and sexual satisfaction— the things she prays for a hundred lines earlier (649–655)—clashes with *to deinon* of the maternal bond, a fearful or awesome force whose hold no amount of rationalization or calculation can shake.[40]

The destruction of the love relationships that the house should foster appears also in the realm of sexuality. The death struggle between husband and wife appears as a kind of perverted sexual battle (see 493–494), as it had already in Aeschylus (*Agamemnon* 1388–92). The mother purchases her sexual license at the price of her sexually mature daughters' reluctant virginity (962–966, 1183; cf. 164–166). Consorting with Aegisthus, as Electra bitterly points out, Clytaemnestra bears new children and rejects the old (587–590; cf. 97, 272). She herself, on the other hand, whose very name means "wedless,"[41] "consorts always with many sufferings" (599–600; cf. 562, 652). Her hatred of Clytaemnestra has its roots not only in the latter's unmotherly and unwifely behavior but also in a deep sexual rivalry and resentment. For her the "ultimate outrage" (*hybris*) is "the murderer in the father's bed . . . the mother sleeping with the murderer" (271–274). The image has a graphic reality for her; it is something which she virtually "sees" (271). The struggle extends even to the body of the dead father. She would keep her mother's offering from "the bed of her father" (436) and would dedicate there not only a lock of her hair but also her belt (*zōma*, 452), the symbolical offering of virginity.

Instead of reinforcing the distinctions between the generations, this house confuses them. The daughter is involved in a conflict with her mother that centers in part on the father's "bed." What she learns from her mother are "things not seemly to her" (*proseikota*, 618). Hostility, force, and compulsion replace love as the mode of parental instruction (*dysmeneia, anagkē, bia*, 619–621). Electra is still Clytaemnestra's daughter, and her tragedy is in part just this paradoxical resemblance to the mother she hates (see 608–609). "It is as though Electra recognizes in herself an evil inheritance from her mother," Gordon Kirkwood remarks, "and it tortures her."[42]

Electra's very passion for revenge brings her perilously near the crime which she is avenging (608–609, 619–621).[43] Both women are carried away to the point of madness in their emotions (135, 294–299, 1153). Electra is "too much conquered by joy" at Orestes' "return" to life (1278), as Clytaemnestra was "mad with joy" at his "death" (1153). It is perhaps more than poetic justice that Electra's prayer at the end recalls Clytaemnestra's in 643ff., or more than fortuitous resemblance that the exhausted Electra of the last scene seems very much like the exhausted Clytaemnestra of Aeschylus' *Agamemnon* (*El.* 1483ff.; *Ag.* 1654ff.). Even more strikingly, Electra's vicarious participation in the murder of Clytaemnestra echoes the Aeschylean Clytaemnestra's murder of Agamemnon (1415–16 and *Ag.* 1344–45).[44]

This tendency of the avenger to draw close to the criminal is not nearly so marked in the *Electra* as in the *Oedipus Tyrannus*. Yet here, as there, this theme is the dark side of the recognition or anagnorisis. For all the steadfastness of Electra, identity is elusive and problematical. The "doubling" of mother and daughter, though valid enough in psychological perspective, is not to be understood solely in psychological terms. It also reflects the collapse of polarities that involve language and the human capacity to understand reality.

IV

"Time," says the chorus, "is an easy god" (179). This is the facile advice that they give to an Electra who can never forget the past. Time in this, as in every Sophoclean play, is not "easy."[45] The past, like the dead who seem to come alive (1417ff.), cannot be laid to rest; it returns as terrifying nocturnal vision and as indelible hatred. Such is the old hate (*palaion misos*) that has melted deep into Electra's face and soul (1309ff.). Clytaemnestra cannot escape her past as the mother of Orestes; so, in the twisted parental relationships of this house, she still cannot find enough hatred (*misos*) toward the child who has apparently wronged her to cancel out the pain of losing the child to whom she gave birth (770–771; cf. 775ff.). She feels time "standing over her" (*ho prostatōn chronos*, 781–782) with the threat of punishment for her guilty past. Ironically, *prostatōn* means not only "standing over," "imminent," but also "protecting."

At moments time seems to have stopped and the characters seem trapped in an almost compulsive repetition of actions. Even after the news of Orestes' death, for example, Clytaemnestra includes him with Electra as if he were still alive (794–795):

El.:   Go on insulting, for now you are, by chance, the one fortunate with success.

Clyt.:   Won't you and Orestes stop this then?

Clytaemnestra's dual form (*pauseton*, "won't you two stop this?") reenacts her drawn out struggle with the avenging pair as if no new events had intervened, as if she cannot quite free herself from the fear with which she has lived for so long. The atmosphere of timelessness reflects that inner world of guilt and anxiety in which she is caught, a world insensible to the inflections of time and change. Thus her words reenact a domestic squabble between a mother and her children, while at another level they reflect an isolation in guilt that blurs or cuts off her contact with reality.

This circularity, this thickness, of time for Electra express her heroic determination to keep the past alive (86ff., 164–172, 784ff.). Yet this static quality of time informs the spirit of other characters and events as well. Agamemnon's grave is "ancient" (*archaios taphos*, 893), as Chrysothemis calls it when she describes the "newly flowing" (*neorrhytoi*) streams of milk mysteriously offered there (893–895); yet the crime is as fresh as if it occurred yesterday, and at the end fresh streams, now of blood, not milk, "flow again" (*palirrhyton*) as those "slain in the past" (*hoi palai thanontes*) "live" and avenge their murder (1417–21). Orestes, "dead in word" (59), returns to life, as it were, with an action which seems but the continuation of something long ago performed. Returning to the stage after the news of his "death" and bearing the urn which supposedly contains the ashes of Orestes, he asks the chorus (1101):

Αἴγισθον ἔνθ' ᾤκηκεν ἱστορῶ πάλαι.

Of old have I been seeking where Aegisthus has his dwelling.

It is as if Orestes is asking a question which he has asked many times in the past. The single, specific action in the present seems to exist as an act repeated with an almost obsessive force. Similarly the debate between Clytaemnestra and Electra in the first third of the play, though arising from a single moment of the dramatic situation, reenacts a dialogue which has gone on, spoken or unspoken, between them for years. The scene catches them as if frozen into the timeless posture of their relationship to one another, bound together in that interdependence of hatred and guilt, fear and vengeful bitterness which has filled their every meeting and stamped their every day together in that house.

Eager as she is to escape the past and find release (*lysis*, literally "loosing," 447, 635ff.), Clytaemnestra is as much bound to the past as Electra. Her association with Aegisthus is a daily reminder of it (see 652–653). According to Electra, in fact, she celebrates the day on which she killed Agamemnon (278–281) and sees, mistakenly, in the present moment "this day" that will bring "release from fear" (783). The phrase "this day" or "this one day" recurs to mark a decisive change of state from life to death (so for Electra in 674 and 1149 and for Chrysothemis in 918–919, both mistakenly), or from hate to love (1363). Yet the act which seems to mark the long-awaited change in "the day-by-day fate" of the house is ambiguous both in word and deed (1413–14). In each case the unique "day" of dramatic change is also, at some level, the "day" of endless cyclical succession. The Paedagogus relentlessly cuts short the recognition between brother and sister and pushes them into the matricide in these terms (1362–66):

El.:   For know that in the space of a single day I have come to hate and love you most of all men.

Paed.: Enough! As for the tales of what's in between, many the days and equal nights in their circles of succession that will reveal them to you in all clarity.

Cyclical time is here superimposed on Electra's experience of soul-wrenching change in the short space of one day. At the very moment when she seems to be escaping that world of dead, stale time enclosed in the house, she is pulled back into the mood of unchanging, repetitive, hopeless acts with which she began (86ff.).

Even in the joy of discovering her brother alive, Electra still affirms her suffering which is "not to be released, not to be forgotten" (1246–48, 1287). She thus reiterates the themes and words of her despair before there was any intervention from outside ("not forgetting": 146, 168; "no release": 447; cf. 635). The "just now" of her present freedom to speak (1256) is qualified by her need for all of present time to tell of her sufferings (1254–55). Orestes uses almost exactly the same phrase a little later but in the opposite sense. Stressing the urgency of the present moment of action, the *kairos* (1292; cf. 1368), he asks her to "show what will suit the time now present" (*paronti nun chronō(i)*, 1293). Electra, by contrast, dwells on her constancy in the unchanging old hatred (*misos palaion*, 1311) which serves, as she says, "the present fortune" (*parōn daimōn*, 1306).

This ambiguous oscillation between the fixity and changefulness of time pervades the ending of the play. On the one hand the action moves to an "end," an "accomplishment," *telos*, the last word of the play, as the chorus describes the "seed of Atreus . . . perfected in accomplishment (*teleōthen*) by the present effort." On the other hand there remains a feeling of entrapment in the hatred and evil of the Pelopid house in Aegisthus' last, prophetic speech (1498). The positive side of this fixity appears shortly before when Electra, in response to Aegisthus' gloating over her apparent submission, speaks ambiguously of "accomplishment" (*telos*, 1464–65): "And so my part is being fulfilled, for in time I got sense (*nous*) so as to agree with the stronger (better)." Verbal legerdemain enables Electra to conceal the heroic fixity of her spirit (*nous*) in an apparent acceptance of change (*nous* as "good sense," "reasonableness"). Thus to Aegisthus her reply means something like, "All is over with me: in time I have learned to be sensible and submit to the rulers." Her real meaning is, "My actions have reached their *telos*, fulfillment; and my enduring spirit (*nous*) has, in time, found its true alliance (*sympherein*) with the better and nobler side."

For all this teleological sense of time, however, her last speech contains a difficult and ambiguous statement about time, time as circular and heavy with futility. As Aegisthus pleads for leave to speak even for a little, Electra cuts him short (1482–86):

μὴ πέρα λέγειν ἔα,

πρὸς θεῶν, ἀδελφέ, μηδὲ μηκύνειν λόγους.
τί γὰρ βροτῶν ἂν σὺν κακοῖς μεμειγμένων
θνῄσκειν ὁ μέλλων τοῦ χρόνου κέρδος φέροι;

In the gods' name do not let him speak, my brother, nor lengthen out his words. For since mortals are mingled with suffering, what profit of time (*kerdos tou chronou*) would he gain who is about to die?[46]

The dense syntax and the generality of the diction make these lines difficult and ambiguous. Neither deletion (on most slender textual evidence) nor emendation is satisfactory. Here, as in 1464–65, the two meanings depend on the different values of time. On the one hand, Electra is referring specifically to Aegisthus and the immediate situation and recommending the swift execution of justice. This is the sense emphasized by Jebb in his translation, "When mortals are in the meshes of fate, how can such respite avail one who is to die?" On the other hand, "mortals mingled with sufferings" (or "with evils") include also Orestes and Electra. Kells, stressing this point, translates, "For when mortals are enmeshed in troubles, what benefit can he who is sure to die win from (allowance of) time?"[47]

To the very end Orestes' linear conception of time, the seizing of the *kairos* of action to accomplish a specific purpose, remains in a dialectical relationship with the circularity of Electra's view. Similarly, his ambitious reckoning of "profit" in the prologue (*kerdos*, 61) here meets her darker vision of the ultimate futility of all human striving for "profit."[48] Behind the moment of triumph lies her tragic vision, expressed with her usual spiritual courage, of man doomed to suffering under remote or indifferent gods. The thought and diction recall the tragic insight of another heroic figure at his last great moment of unflinching clarity, Achilles in the last book of the *Iliad* describing the jars of Zeus from which no mortal receives good unmixed with suffering.[49]

"Time is an easy god," said the chorus in the prologue (179). For the women of the house, sheltered by their very collectivity, uttering the voice of normality, urging acquiescence in life's injustices, time can bring oblivion, heal pain, help us return to the regularity of daily tasks and rewards. But not for Electra, nor for any Sophoclean hero. Her nature is suspended over what Hofmannsthal called "the deep-grounded contradictions over which existence is built . . . : whoever wants to live must escape beyond himself, must change: he must forget. And all human dignity is bound up with sticking firm ("beharren"), with not forgetting, with fidelity."[50] Thus Electra's part in the tragedy cannot be circumscribed by the single moment of success; she cannot narrow her sense of time to the "moment" (*kairos*) of present action or the "profit" of future success, any more than she could narrow her sense of time before Orestes' arrival to the daily round of household activities and block out the terrible past. Time for her embraces not only memory but also eternity, "all time," with its vastness and threat of ultimate nothingness.

In the *Electra* as in the *Ajax* the hero's vision of eternity remains beyond the grasp of other men. Civilization serves to mediate between the limitless time of eternity or death and the measurable span of the individual human life with its finite sorrows and satisfactions, that "profit of time" which Electra denies. Civilization breaks down all time, *ho pas chronos*, into meaningful, graspable units. Tragedy threatens those structures and forces man to confront again the threat of meaninglessness raised by the endless cycles of nature or the undifferentiated time of eternity:

Why day is day, night night, and time is time
Were nothing but to write day, night, and time. (*Hamlet*, II.ii 88–89)

Nontragic figures, like Orestes here or the Odysseus of the *Ajax*, live in a different dimension of time, sheltered from the disturbing visions of "all time," and so accomplish their deeds and achieve the gain (*kerdos*) that they seek.

Electra's lines 1485–86 closely parallel two other passages in Sophocles, one spoken by Ajax, the other by Antigone. Both are akin to Electra in choosing death over compromise, the permanence of their vision of the world over the limited, compromised happiness of "normal" life. Ajax reflects on the relation between time, life, and joy as follows (*Ajax* 473–480):

> To want long life is base for a man who has no variation in suffering. For what joy has day to add to day, advancing him to death and then drawing him back again? I would not buy at any reckoning a mortal warmed by empty hopes. The man of noble birth must live well or die well. You have heard my whole speech.

Ajax is here stating the absolute demands of his heroic ethic. He is already entertaining the death to which his heroic code condemns him. His yearning for the timeless "imperishable glory" of the Homeric warrior (Homer's *kleos aphthiton*) and his sense of failure and guilt at his present weakness combine in this bleak vision of time as an empty procession of joyless days, where the prospect of life unfolding the normal cycle is but delusion.

Like Electra in her rejection of Chrysothemis' compromising common-sense logic and life values (stigmatized by Ajax as the "warmth of empty hopes"), Antigone also looks beyond the immediate "profit" of time to the timeless realm of death (*Antigone* 460–464): "I knew that I would die—why not—even if you had not set forth your decrees. But if I die before my time, I call that profit (*kerdos*). For whoever lives, as I do, in many evils, how does he not gain profit by his death?" Unlike Electra, however, Antigone does not merely state the futility of life but implicitly contrasts its limited span with the "unwritten laws of the gods" that "live always" (*Antig.* 454–457). For Ajax too there is an implicit contrast of the transience of mortal life and the timeless world of fame to which the man of noble birth aspires. Electra has no such positive counterfoil to her view of time and death.

Electra makes this utterance at the very end of her play, in her last lines on stage. For Ajax and Antigone a full course of heroic action still lies ahead. For Electra it is coming to an end. Her lines lack a ring of heroic affirmation, a swing upward to decisive energy and self-realization. Instead, they mark a trailing off into futility and uncertainty.

Electra's last speech reiterates, on a small scale, the contrasts of the prologue and of the Paedagogus' long speech on Orestes' death. In both these passages the two male figures share the companionship of concerted action focused on the *kairos* of deeds, while Electra stands by in her lonely agony or prolonged silence.[51] At the end the suffering is both subtler and more deeply tragic, for it rests not on error and emotion but on Electra's certain knowledge. It is just this knowledge that negates the "profit of time" which Orestes now enjoys (see 61). Paradoxically, Orestes' purposive time, the *kairos* of deeds not words (1335ff., 1372–73), is on Electra's side, working to fulfill her strongest desires. But for a moment Electra glimpses a darker truth about time and act hidden from every one else. After this she speaks no more.

On this reading of the last scene, Electra's isolation becomes spiritual and inward rather than enforced and physical. She is more finally and hopelessly isolated by the loneliness of her tragic realization than she was by literal imprisonment within the house. There is the hint of a new barrier between her and the brother with whom she desired union as her savior. The Paedagogus' circles of equal nights and days, Orestes' entrance into the dark house, Aegisthus' conjunction of the present with the future evils of the Pelopids efface the distinctions between progress and regress. The abyss of cyclical time threatens to engulf the protagonists' effort to restrict the sameness of repetitive guilt.

V

In the *Electra*, as in the other plays, tensions between culture and nature are important, but they are not projected on a phantasmagoric mythic world of half-monstrous creatures, as in the *Trachiniae*, nor on a vast, desolate landscape at the margins of the civilized world, as in the *Ajax* or *Philoctetes*. The *Electra* is closer to *Antigone* and *Oedipus Tyrannus* in focusing on the royal house of a great city and the personalities and relationships which, in that interior space, create a microcosm of the conflict between savagery and civilization within man.

The myths of Niobe and Procne with Electra invokes (107–108, 147–152) transfer the sheltered realm of maternal love and child-rearing to the wild realm of forest or mountain. In the same ode she compares the murder of her father in the house to the splitting of an oak by woodcutters (97–98). Later she compares the loss of Orestes to the effects of a violent storm (1150–51). The loss of control over the sea recurs throughout the play in a number of metaphors describing various facets of Electra's isolation: the cowardliness of her sister who "sails with lowered canvas" (335), Pelops' murder of the charioteer Myrtilus (504–515), the death of her brother in "the wave of horses" or the "shipwreck of horses" (733, 1444), her own "tossing in a storm" when she seems totally alone (1074), Clytaemnestra destroying the house by "bilging out" its wealth (1291).

The Delphian chariot race which occupies such a conspicuous place at the center of the play as the pivot of Orestes' plot to regain his house is a glorious celebration of man's control over brute force. But in terms of the symbolic truth which this fictitious race contains, that control is insufficient for the beasts' unruly violence. The nautical imagery of this disaster (see, for example, 733) fuses together two important areas of man's control over nature, also singled out in the Ode on Man in the *Antigone*: sea and horses. The infamous race of Pelops brought together sea and horses, for the treacherous charioteer is "drowned in the sea" (*pontistheis*, 508), and the chorus views this act as responsible for the "much-suffering outrage which never leaves this house" (514–515). The two races are related as cause and as paradigm.[52] In both cases guile and deceit serve personal aggrandizement and the power of the house. Orestes in fact seems virtually a second Myrtilus, an innocent victim of Pelopid misfortune. The chorus describes his death, like Myrtilus', with the same word, "cut off at the root," *prorrhizos* (512, 765). Yet his manipulation of a horse race for his own advantage also suggests the perpetuation of Pelopid treachery, the deceit or *dolos* to which he commits himself, albeit with misgivings, in the prologue (36ff., 59ff.).

Metallurgy plays a small but not insignificant role in the inversions of civilized arts. Bronze and gold have a special prominence. Both point to the disruption rather than the establishment of civilization. An "all-bronze" or "bronze-smiting" axe fells Agamemnon (195, 484–485). Retaliation comes through the "bronze-flanked urn" and the "bronze-footed Fury" (54, 491). Gold, mark of wealth and the settled order which makes possible its accumulation, is even more sinister. The grandiose phrase, *Mykēnas tas polychrysous*, "Mycenae rich in gold," at the beginning (9) suggests power and stability but "the much-destroying house of the Pelopids" in the next line, beginning with the same compounding element (*polyphthoron*, 10), points to the darker side of Pelopid wealth, the greed, passion, and hatred which that gold inspired. Further back in time lurk the "all-gold chariot" of Myrtilus (510) and, in the parallel story of Eriphyle, the golden necklace which becomes the "gold-linked net" to entrap her husband, Amphiaraus (*chrysodeta herkea*, 838).[53]

Mycenae's ancient wealth (72, 648) suggests corruption and violence rather than stability. Aeschylus, drawing on the archaic anxiety about the danger of great wealth, had already exploited this aspect of the Pelopid theme.[54] Sophocles is echoing him when he takes over the unusual adjective *archaioploutos*, "wealthy of old," and applies it to Orestes' house at the crucial moment of his reentrance, guided by the Furies and Hermes (1393).[55] The legitimate heirs are not only disinherited ("cast out," 589–590) but half-starved and squalidly dressed (191, 361–364, 1177–96). Attempting to persuade Chrysothemis, Electra will adduce "the possession of their father's wealth" as an argument, linked as it is to the daughter's eventual marriage (960–966); but of course to "save their father's house," wealth and all (978, 960), they must violate the sanctity of the mother's place in the house.[56]

Although the imagery of the *Electra* is far less exuberant than that of the *Oresteia*, here too inversions of man and beast reflect the precariousness of the civilized order. The ancient Argos of Orestes' longing in the prologue has at its center the grove of a maiden turned into a beast ("gadfly-stung" Io, 5), a wolf-killing god, Apollo Lykeios (6–7), and a "glorious" temple of Hera, goddess of marriage in a city whose royal house is living up to its adulterous past.[57] These are the emblems of the corrupt world which Orestes is to enter. Even so, the Paedagogus' nagging temporal words—"now," "already," "before," "no longer"—truncate admiring contemplation of "glorious" temples or squares.[58]

We are invited to see the house and its doors as a threatening space from which an enemy may emerge at any moment (20).

Undaunted, Orestes compares his companion to an old but spirited horse which "does not lose his mettle (*thymos*) in frightening circumstances (*deina*), but pricks up his ears" (25–28). The simile of the battlefield and its terrors, though invoking the useful, domesticated animal, marks another grim contrast with the ostensibly peaceful order of city and house.

The image of the mettlesome horse looks ahead to the lie about the race at Delphi which Orestes mentions here for the first time. He instructs the Paedagogus to tell that he "was killed . . . at the Pythian Games, hurled from the wheel-driven chariot" (48–50). The scene of horses out of control forms the most vivid part of the Paedagogus' narrative when Orestes' ruse is put into operation (723ff.). This violent and dangerous aspect of the Delphic festival contrasts with its quieter, more intellectual side, the rendering of oracles (32ff.). In like manner and civilized quality of the "noble horse" showing his true spirit in dangerous circumstances contrasts with the violence of the horses out of control at Delphi. Both verbally and thematically that fictive loss of control over horses recalls the sinister, murderous tone of Pelops' horserace at Olympia, where deception is also involved (504–515; cf. 510, 50). The "outrage" (*aikeia*) of that race, the beginning of the crimes of the Atreid house, follows closely upon the "outrage" of Agamemnon's murder (511, 515 and 488), and its continuation of Electra's "outrageous" treatment (191). The false race at Delphi answers those crimes with a restoration of justice, but it also perpetuates the violence and deception which pursue the house from Pelops to Orestes. As in the fatal horserace of Pelops, success and failure are ambiguous. Victory in the present proves to be eventual disaster.

The uncontrolled horses of Orestes' lie are located in far-off Delphi, in the public realm of competitive athletics. The animal imagery surrounding the house and its curse, however, brings the bestial into the very heart of the *oikos*. Not only is Electra a bird that has lost its young (107, 243–244), but her mother views her as an animal that has been let free (516) and later as a creature that drinks the blood of its victims (783–784).[59] Human speech within the house, like the love or *philia* that should exist there, reverts to bestial wildness as Clytaemnestra "barks" in her fear and her threats (299). Further in the past, as Electra somewhat naively reconstructs it, Agamemnon treated his daughter as a "beast" (*thēr*, 572), sacrificed to the goddess of wild animals and the hunt (566–576).

The second stasimon gives a surprising turn to these inversions, for here birds are models of the reciprocal help and affection between parent and child so signally lacking in the human world.[60] But if wild creatures can appear more civilized than men, the inanimate blow of the axe can take on a monstrous animal identity: as the offspring begotten of cunning and lust, it "rushes forth" like a living creature. The chorus asks whether god or man was the agent, but the context suggests the unnamed alternative, something between man and beast (196–200).

Even the divine power in this play can veer to its opposite pole and assume a bestial aspect. Besides Artemis' demand for the sacrifice of the King's daughter as a substitute for the beast (571–572), the avenging Furies enter the house like dogs which track down men (1387). This inversion of the hunt echoes the capture of Amphiaraus "in the nets" (839–840) and prefigures the capture of Aegisthus "in the nets" (1476). At his reappearance onstage Orestes, seeking Aegisthus, is also "tracking" him (*mateuein*, 1107). Here, as at the matricide, the avengers are hunters but hunters of men, soon to be hunted in their turn if the Aeschylean echoes of 1387–97 are relevant.[61] The description of Ares "breathing blood" applies a bestial image to a god (1385). All these details help us envisage the matricide as violating not only the sanctions of family but also the biological hierarchy separating god, man, and beast.

The nets which trap Agamemnon in Aeschylus are woven by the Furies or by Justice (*Agamemnon* 1580, 1611). But these are Aegisthus' metaphors, and we sympathize with the slaughtered hero's plunge from godlike king to slaughtered animal. In the *Electra*, however, the nets which entrap Aegisthus are distinctly man-made, as he cries, "Into what men's nets have I fallen" (1476–77). The Aegisthus who claimed divine sanction for his crime in Aeschylus' play (his "nets of Justice," *Ag.* 1611) is here caught by a human instrument. The shift is characteristic of the ambiguity of the divine justice in Sophocles' world. Euripides, typically, widens the discrepancy between the two poles. Clytaemnestra parades the trappings of a civilized order, "shining in her dress and chariot" at the moment when she "marches straight into the nets," a beast about to be caught (Euripides, *Electra*, 965–966).

The man-beast inversions of the play include most of the basic relationships within the house: mother killing son (Procne and Itys); wife killing husband (Amphiaraus caught in the nets); son killing mother (the Furies as beasts in 1386); and father killing daughter (Iphigeneia as sacrificial beast in 566–576).

The closing scene extends these reversals from the house to the city. Sophocles here exploits the homology between civic and domestic order which the *Oresteia* had so richly developed. Ordering the gates flung open, Aegisthus uses the metaphor of the bit, confident that his political, as his domestic, authority is now secure (*stomion*, 1462). His lines echo the speech of Aeschylus' Aegisthus, who describes his newly gained power with a metaphor of controlling horses (*Ag.* 1624, 1632, 1639–40).[62] The parallel is not particularly flattering to this Aegisthus, and in any case the bit has been ineffective: we recall the "bitless colts" of the Delphian race (724–725). Aegisthus, would-be controller of beasts, is soon caught like a beast in the "nets of men" (1476). His entrapment "in the nets" is an ironic answer to his own attempted inversion of human and bestial status.

Although justified in killing Aegisthus, the new rulers, representatives of *dikē*, also overstep the limits between the human and bestial, for Electra's last speech calls for a violation of one of the most fundamental sanctions separating man and beast, the rites of burial (1487–88): "Kill him, and when you've killed him throw him to the buriers that he deserves." We feel no pity at all for Aegisthus, but this deliberate outrage of his corpse casts doubt upon the restoration of a fully civilized order in the city.[63]

VI

Sacrifice stands next to burial in the play's violations of the ritual order of a civilized city. Sophocles draws upon the rich and complex inversions of sacrifice in the Aeschylean version of the myth.[64] Sophocles' account is remarkable for the fact that the story of Agamemnon's sacrifice of his daughter is told by the king's staunchest supporter, Electra. She assumes that the necessity to expiate Artemis' anger by the sacrifice of a daughter instead of an animal exonerates the king entirely. Given the context of the impassioned hatred of this speech, it is unlikely that we should accept this simplification at face value. The naive acceptance of a man-beast violation here raises similar doubts about the violation of burial rites at the end and about the absolute justice of her acts.

To create the more condensed, trimmer effect of his single character-centered play, Sophocles vastly reduces the complex Aeschylean theology of cause and effect, freedom and responsibility, inherent in the sacrifice of Iphigeneia. Even so, the motif of the human sacrifice stands out as arbitrary, oppressive, cruel. Wilamowitz' instinct was right: there is something disturbing and puzzling about the whole episode.[65] Even if our present view of Sophocles' tolerance of dissonance and unresolved suffering allows us to see it as something other than an infelicitous intrusion into his serene grandeur, its violations of the ritual, familial, linguistic, and social order are still shocking. There is not even a clear indication of the goddess' command, only a clause of purpose, expressing her alleged intention which Agamemnon carried out (570–576):

> From this (boast) the goddess in her wrath held back the Achaeans so that my father might sacrifice his own daughter in compensation for the beast. For there was no other release (*lysis*) for the army, either homeward or to Ilion. Therefore with constraint and much protesting he sacrificed her, not for Menelaus' sake.

The last phrase, "not for Menelaus' sake," seems almost trivial. The verb of sacrifice in 572, the compound *ek-thyein*, implies "some cruelty or violence."[66] Euripides uses it in the *Cyclops* (371) to describe the "pitiless" monster's cannibalistic devouring of men who are also suppliants, a scene replete with grisly details of butchering and eating human flesh (*Cyc.* 369–373). Immediately after, Electra invokes the bloody *lex talionis* against her mother, "You would be the first to die if you should get justice" (582–583).

On the other side, Clytaemnestra has repeated Agamemnon's perverted sacrifice in the ritual slaughter of cattle that celebrates her husband's murder (280–281), adding insult to the maltreatment of a daughter (282–286). After the debate with Electra, she calls for "full-fruited offerings," *thymata pankarpa* (634–635), but tokens of fruitfulness have an ironic ring in a place where legitimate sexual union and fertility are turned to death. Her daughter's insistent presence also interrupts the ritual silence (*euphēmia*, 630, 641–642); and the sinful nature of Clytaemnestra's desires prevents the open utterance of her prayers (637–654).[67] If Agamemnon's violated ritual involved too brash an address to divinity (569–570), Clytaemnestra is too covert in addressing the gods.

The climax of this central concern of the play, ritual and moral order, is the matricide, which appears as a monstrous rite of sacrifice. Ares presides over it, and it is violent and bloody (1422–23): "The bloody hand drips with the sacrifice to Ares."[68] Ares belongs on the battlefield not in the house. One is reminded of the ominous implications of Orestes' battlefield image in his first speech (25–28) and his warning later that "Ares lies in women too" (1243–44). The remote and ambiguously oracular Apollo (What's in the house is well if well Apollo oracled," 1424–25) pales beside the very present and violent Ares. Ares' bloodthirstiness, in close association with chthonic powers, in fact frames the matricide (1384–88, 1417–23). The play's last word may then continue the sacrificial imagery if, as Kells suggests, *teleōthen*, "perfected," recalls *teleios*, "used of beasts ripe for sacrifice."[69] If so, the avengers of one perverted sacrifice become, in their turn, the sacrificial victims of another.

Torn apart by the *sparagmos* of his false death (748) and mourned in the ritual cry of the *ololygmos* (750),[70] Orestes may be viewed against the pattern of a victim sacrificed for the restoration of order and fruitfulness in this blighted city. Like the "sages" who feigned death to achieve greater glory—Pythagoras, Salmoxis, Aristeas—, Orestes will descend into the darkness of the Underworld only to be reborn into a brighter light, "shining like a star" (66). As in Euripides' *Helen*, whose male protagonist, Menelaus, he closely resembles in his own ruse, Orestes undergoes a ritual death that purges the burdens of the past and issues into a rebirth of energy and vitality (see *gonai*, "births," 1232).[71] But, as we have noted, the purification of this house is highly ambiguous (69–70), and the bright light of the star is closed in the house, dark with its past crimes and guilt, at the end. The cathartic force of Orestes' submission to death in the trick is grimly offset by his role as a sacrificer, not a victim, at the end (1422–23).

Hating and killing stand in counterpoint to purification and renewal. Thus the more positive mythic pattern of death and rebirth emerges only as a faint imprint upon the narrative beneath which death and destruction are outlined all the more sharply.

Ritualized beginning and completion frame the entire action. In the prologue the Paedagogus speeds Orestes on his way to "doing" (*erdein*) with a verb connoting a solemn ritual of beginning (*archēgetein*, 83) as they proceed from Apollo's oracles to the offerings for Agamemnon. Immediately afterwards Electra describes her dirges of grief ironically as "all night festivals," (*pannychides*, 92).[72] This is the first of a series of disrupted, perverted, or falsified rituals. Clytaemnestra prevents her from performing the proper rites for her dead father, while she herself treats the day of the murder as a festal celebration (275–285). The dirge or *thrēnos* that ought to be an expression of communal or familial grief, like the mourning over Hector in *Iliad* 24, is here the furtive lamentation of an isolated woman (94, 100–101, 285–286, 1122). Only by the dangerous deed of killing the usurper, Electra tries to persuade Chrysothemis, can the legitimate heirs hope for a place of honor at the public festivals (982–983).

Prayers and the ritual silence which should attend them are equally ominous. Clytaemnestra's concealed prayer to Apollo near the center of the play has a dark pendant, Electra's prayer, to the same god, just before the matricide (637–659, 1376–83). Electra has won the highest prize "for her piety toward Zeus" (1095–97), but this piety still has to take the form of bloodshed, matricide, and the exposure of a human body.[73] Hence the answer to her prayer to Apollo is Ares breathing blood and the Erinyes entering the house in darkness and stealth (1384–97). Just before Electra's prayer, Orestes' obeisance to the ancestral "seat of his father" (*patrōa hedē*, 1374), like Electra's appeal, earlier, to the "father's wealth" and the salvation of "the father's house" (960, 978), ignores by omission the mother's share in that house and its gods.

The rites for the dead king and father reveal the violated social and cosmic order of Electra's world. For Aeschylus, as Gilbert Murray once wrote, the maltreatment of Agamemnon's body was "almost the central horror of the whole story. Wherever it is mentioned it comes as something intolerable, maddening; it breaks Orestes down."[74] In Aeschylus the knowledge that the murderers deprived his father of these ablutions whips up Orestes' passion for vengeance. In a scene of ritualized responsion Orestes and Electra pray to the chthonic powers (*Choephoroe* 489–492):

Or.: O Earth, send up my father to oversee the battle.
El.: O Persephone, grant lovely victory.
Or.: Remember the ablutions from which you were kept away, my father.
El.: Remember the net.

For Sophocles the religious significance of these rites, though by no means negligible, takes second place to their emotional and psychological impact and to a subtle interplay of character and imagery. Only in the figurative language of excited prayer, under the stress of the impending matricide, will the restless, desecrated dead come back to life (1417–20).

Funeral rites become an element in the scenic action, the emotions they arouse displayed powerfully on the stage in Electra's reactions to the ruse of the death and burial of Orestes. The very plot of the *Electra* advances the emotive force of these rites to a new freshness and immediacy of feeling. The grief for a long-dead father in the *Choephoroe* now receives reenforcement and reduplication in the grief for a newly dead brother, a grief that time has not yet been able to temper (cf. *Cho.* 433ff. and *El.* 864ff.).

Orestes' initial service to the dead takes place in the context of his all too easy readiness to cross the barriers between life and death. "What pain (*lypē*) is there if I die in word but in deed win salvation and glorious fame?" he asks in the prologue. His plan does indeed bring pain (*lypē*) to Electra (822, 1170). She, however, refuses even great advantage if it means pain (*lypē*) to him (1304–1305).[75] This combination of pain and advantage in the matters of death and burial defines the moral and emotional dilemma of Clytaemnestra too. "Shall I call this fortunate or terrible, yet advantageous (*kerdē*)? It is painful (*lypēron*) if I save my life through my own woes," she says at the news of Orestes' death (766–768). In the process of bringing new life to the house through false burial rites, Orestes inflicts an emotional death on Electra (1152, 1163–70), with all the pain (*lypē*) such a death brings. She longs for death because she "sees that the dead have no pain" (1170).

Apollo had commanded Orestes to honor his father's tomb with "libations and rich offerings of cut hair" (52), a pointed contrast to Electra's poor offerings of hair and belt, the latter "adorned by no rich luxury" (452; cf. 360). In like manner Orestes, allegedly killed in a foreign land, receives from strangers the rites that Agamemnon was denied at home (757–760, 445). Agamemnon would have fared better had he died at Troy: at least he would have received honorable burial (95–96) and not the outrage of *maschalismos*, the fearful mutilation of the corpse which prevents his ghost from walking (445). Yet he does return "to the light," in dream, and thereby indirectly aids the revenge for his death (417–423).

At the end of the prologue Orestes and the Paedagogus leave to pour libations (*loutra*) to the dead king (84), as Apollo had ordered (*loibai*, 52). His word in 84, however, *loutra*, means literally "washing" or "ritual ablution," and its usage in the sense of "libations" is exceptional.[76] This strange usage suggests still another desecration of the rites of burial, for Electra describes later how Clytaemnestra, after mutilating the body, "wiped off the bloodstains on the head for ablution" (*epi loutroisi*, 445). The attempted purification implied in these macabre ablutions can only deepen the stain of blood and render it more horrible. The detail confirms Electra's statement, some ten lines before, that Clytaemnestra has no right to bring funeral offerings or purificatory libations (*loutra*) to the dead king's grave.

Electra's relation to ritual action, like that of all the other characters, remains ambiguous and paradoxical. In the prologue, to be sure, her lyrical *thrēnos* to the dead father (86–120), passionate, hopeless, and futile, contrasts with the practical, goal-oriented gestures of reverence by the Paedagogus and Orestes (60–61, 84–85). Yet her first significant action in the play is to thwart a ritual. In dissuading Chrysothemis from carrying their mother's offerings to their father's grave she wins an important initial victory but also confirms the violated ritual and familial order. The rites that should unite the members of a house in commemoration of common ties of blood and a common grief express hatred and fear. Sister joins with sister against mother. The mother's libations would be "hostile" (*dysmeneis choai*, 440). Dishonored and mutilated "like an enemy" (*dysmenēs*, 444), the father who should be "the most beloved of mortals" (*philtatos brotōn*, 462) is instead "the most hostile of mortals" (*dysmenestatos brotōn*, 407). The love or *philia* that should exist in the security of the interior realm of the house is replaced by the "enmity" proper to the battlefield.

When the rites of burial are first introduced in this scene, Sophocles stresses the special intimacy of kin ties (324–327):

Chorus: I see now your sister *by blood* (*homaimon*), in birth (*physin*) of the same father, and also of the [same] mother, Chrysothemis, bearing in her hands offerings from the house for a tomb, the customary offerings for those below.

The language of 325–326 is particularly striking:

τὴν σὴν ὅμαιμον, ἐκ πατρὸς ταὐτοῦ φύσιν,
Χρυσόθεμιν, ἔκ τε μητρός · · ·

The proper name "Chrysothemis" is placed between "father" and "mother" in an expressive hyperbaton, and the adjective "same" is omitted from the second member, "mother," so that the lines mean, literally, "(I see) . . . your blood-sister from the same father by birth, Chrysothemis, and of (her/your) mother." Both the language of kin ties and the circumstances of the ritual separate the sister from the mother.

The attempt of Clytaemnestra to reach outside the house to the tomb of the slain husband and appease the angry spirits of the dead (417ff.) would reestablish some measure of harmony between the house and the gods, the closed interior world and the cosmic order outside. Intercepting the emissary sent forth from the house (*pempei*, 406, 427) on the road which she travels (404–405), Electra blocks both the spatial communication between inner and outer and the ritual communication between the living and dead of this house.

In this scene Electra begs Chrysothemis to "conceal (*krypson*) [the offerings] in winds and deep-dug dust" (436–437). The zeugma of the verb, strained between winds and earth, expresses on a syntactical level these offerings' failure to effect mediation between upper and lower worlds, interior and exterior, house and open air.[77] Electra sarcastically remarks of Clytaemnestra's offerings, "But when she dies, let these (libations) remain stored up for her below" (437–438).[78] What will arise "from the earth" (*gēthen*, 453) where these "hostile" offerings (440) are poured will be the "propitious helper" to whom Electra makes a far simpler offering (451–454). In her next line she prays that Orestes return "alive" and leap "with force of upper hand" (*ex hyperteras cheros*, 455) upon his enemies. Then they would "deck out" (*stephein*, "crown," 458) Agamemnon with richer offerings than now (455–458).

In the choral ode that follows, Justice herself, Dikē, will "bear in her hands" something more dangerous for Clytaemnestra than the offerings which the weak Chrysothemis carries, namely "just force" (*Dika dikaia pheromena cheroin kratē*, 476; cf. 431). The hope persists even after Orestes' "death" as the chorus, in a later ode, pray that Electra "may live as much above (*kathyper*) your enemies in force of hand and wealth as you now dwell beneath their hand" (*hypocheir*, 1090–92; cf. 1265). But before that point is reached Electra must participate in a ritual that seems to strip her of all hope and strength as she receives the urn from her disguised brother and bears him in her hands now as "one who is

nothing" (1129). The urn scene seems initially to reverse her successful interference with Clytaemnestra's offerings to Agamemnon. Now what Electra has
"sent forth brilliant from the house" (1130) returns in darkness (cf. 405–406,
419ff.). She herself, reduced to nothing like the ashes of the urn, will dwell
forever "below" (1165–66; cf. 438).

Clytaemnestra's rituals, like her prayers, seek "release" (*lysis*) from the murderous, polluted past. Electra's aim is unerring when, after describing Clytaemnestra's grisly ablutions (*loutra*) on the hair of the mutilated corpse, she asks her
sister, "Do you think that these can bring her release (*lytēria*) from the killing?"
(446–447). The similarity in sound between *loutra* and *lytēria*, "ablutions" and
"release," in consecutive lines only points up the gap between them. This perverted "cleansing" of the mutilation preempts any possibility of the "release" that
it was supposed to effect and also cancels out the expiatory libations of 434,
where *loutra* is used in its proper, nonmetaphorical sense. There can be no washing away—ritual, moral, or psychological—of these pollutions. The dead will
remain outraged and hostile, *dysmeneis* (407, 440, 444). In the next scene Clytaemnestra's "prayers for release" (*lytērioi euchai*, 635–636) will not dispel the
darkness, literal and figurative, that envelops her and her world. Ironically Electra's prayer for "release" (*lytērion*, 1490) at the end seems to have little more
hope of fulfillment.

Orestes' "death" in the center of the play makes the perversion of the burial
ritual an immediate, dramatic experience. When Clytaemnestra invites her
daughter "to cry forth *outside* (*ektothen*) both her own and her loved ones' woes"
(803–804), she neglects the fact that Electra's *philoi* are also her own. Electra
replies with a taunt about her mother's "laughing" instead of "weeping" over
her dead son (804–807), an inversion which harks back to her "laughter" over
her murdered husband as she celebrates the day of his death (277).[79] The care
that Orestes' body received from "strangers" at Delphi elicits a deep cry of pain
from Electra (865–870; cf. 749–760, 1141). But what is part of a carefully
thought-out plan on the part of Orestes and the Paedagogus is immediate emotional experience for Electra. She wants to touch with her hands (866), and we
are reminded of the emphasis on hands and on touching and holding the offerings
at Chrysothemis' first entrance (326, 431, 458; cf. 455, 476).

When Chrysothemis enters for the second time, it is to announce the performance of a funerary ritual, the pendant to the interrupted ritual of her first
appearance (893–896): "For when I came to my father's ancient tomb, I saw at
the top of the mound milk fresh-flowing and my father's grave adorned in a circle
with flowers of every sort." The happy exuberance of flowers takes us by surprise.
But Electra's conviction of death does not allow the joyful note to last long.
What "blooms" in this world are indeed the flowers of evil (cf. 43, 422; 260,
952). Chrysothemis is certain that the offering must be from Orestes and not
Electra because the latter is "not permitted to leave this house even to visit the
(shrines of the) gods without smarting for it" (911–912). Electra's life in the
palace, far from providing the protection that a woman should receive from her
philoi, constitutes a violation of one of the basic relations among *philoi* and an

important function of that relation for women in the house, namely the ritual lamentation over their dead.

Chrysothemis' account makes it seem as if Orestes has propitiously fulfilled his wish to "crown" the tomb, as he said he would in the prologue (*stephein*, 53; cf. *peristephēs* of the "crowned" tomb in 895). Conversely, his act seals the failure of Clytaemnestra's attempt to "crown" (*epistephein*, 441) it with a morally repugnant offering. As Electra had hoped, the grave is "crowned" with richer hands than hers (*stephein*, 457–458). But, as is typical of this play, exaltation soon changes back to sorrow. Later these "new-flowing streams of milk" (*neor-rhytoi pēgai*, 894–895) are answered by the "streams of blood that flow back in retribution" (*palirrhyton haima*, 1420), the final offering that Orestes makes to the tomb of his father.

Unperformed funeral rites (the aborted offerings of Clytaemnestra) joined the two sisters, whereas Orestes' successfully completed ritual divides them. Rituals once more fragment rather than reaffirm *philia*, until Electra's mistaken ritualized lamentation over the empty urn brings together those who would naturally be united in the ritual community of the house.

Orestes enters holding the urn in his hands, as Chrysothemis entered holding the grave offerings of Clytaemnestra. In both cases an intended rite for the dead is interrupted. The disproved truth of Chrysothemis' reported offerings, however, is made good by the revelation of the false rites involving the urn.[80]

Although Orestes and Electra do not meet until the urn scene, they have been unknowingly joined all along by furtive actions involving funerary rites. Orestes makes covert offerings at his father's grave and must "conceal" the urn (55); Electra seeks to "conceal" her mother's offerings in wind or dust (436). Both make secret offerings of hair at their father's tomb, with hope of "wealth" in future times (52–53, 72; 457–458).

The interrupted rite of the urn scene, unlike the interrupted rituals earlier, momentarily breaks through the hatred and murderous vengeance which engulfs *philia*. Initially, however, the urn brings Electra to her most painful reversal of life and death (1165–70):

> Receive me into your urn, nothing into nothing, that for the rest [of time] I may dwell with those below. For when you were here above, I had equal shares with you. Now too in death I long not to leave your tomb. For the dead, I see, have no pain.

With its false ashes and its manipulation of the relation between living and dead, the urn caps the theme of inverted funeral rites. But the urn is also the appropriate token of recognition for this separated pair; it is the symbol of Electra's life-in-death and also of the falsehood, deceit, and distilled hatred in which she and Orestes are forced to live. The urn expresses the tragic nature of this recovery of love and "life" in a world dominated by hatred and death.

Yet in giving up the urn Electra relinquishes something of her tremendous bond to the dead. "O births, births of bodies dearest to me," she exclaims as she accepts the truth of Orestes' presence (1232–33). Orestes hitherto has regarded the urn only as a necessary tool, a means of utilizing the conventional attitudes toward death for his "advantage" and "glory" (59–61). Now he recognizes in the wasting of Electra's "glorious form" (1177) the fearful emotional and physical toll which his stratagems have taken.[81] "So then I knew nothing of my own evils," says Orestes in a sudden flash of insight into what Electra's past has been (1185). As in the *Philoctetes*, an eager youthful hero finds his initial plans qualified by an experience of suffering. But in the *Philoctetes* the young hero really alters fundamental aims and attitudes; here the corresponding figure only delays his aims and slightly changes his ends.

VII

The urn performs several functions. It represents the conflict of appearance and reality, life and death, strength and weakness. It is the operative element in the most moving deception and the most pathetic interchange of truth and falsehood in the play. What is "inside" the urn is really "outside." The "little vessel" which contains the dust and ashes of Orestes—"a small weight in a small container" (1142; cf. 757–758, 1113)—is actually the receptacle of something infinite. Its very materiality (we are several times reminded of its size and weight) stresses the incommensurability between its quantitative dimensions and the human feelings which it arouses.

Through the urn Orestes and Electra recognize one another not merely in external form but in essential natures.[82] The urn is the token of love found and shared in the midst of evil and death. It holds the remaining substance of whatever love Electra has felt and can still feel. It brings together, at their greatest intensity, the two primary forces in Electra's world, love and death. More inwardly still, the urn brings together the opposite extremes of Electra's emotional nature. In her wish to die and enter the narrow confines of the urn (1165ff.), she plunges into her greatest depths of human suffering, only to surface again to equally great joy, darkened in its turn by the background of murder and sorrow.[83] Measure of her utter weakness and "nothingness" (1166), the urn is also the means of her "rebirth" (1232-33) to full strength when the true relationship of inner and outer, life and death, is revealed. The sequence of near collapse when she receives the putative remains of Orestes and exultation when she receives the real, living Orestes in her arms corresponds to a rhythm of disintegration and inner renewal established earlier: when she hears the news of Orestes' death at Delphi she sinks down without desire for life (804ff.), but then afterwards she gathers her energies to a new firmness of resolve when she takes the task of killing Aegisthus into her own hands (947-1020).

If the urn brings together brother and sister, however, its original function is to separate forever children and mother. Its affirmation of *philia* comes only as an unexpected, unplanned, and even unwanted interlude. The lock of human hair, freshly cut from her living brother's head, fails to convince Electra, whereas the cold bronze at once wins her credence. This inversion has its visual enactment on the stage as Electra clings to the metal container of her brother's ashes, as she thinks, while the living brother stands before her.

The power of the urn to deceive is not merely a convenient device of the plot but, as one interpreter suggests, "an artistic principle which has the force to shape new situations that have the same reality as non-deceptive situations."[84] Between the Paedagogus' long speech and Orestes' reappearance with the urn, there is no one left onstage able to distinguish between truth and falsehood. Neither Electra nor Clytaemnestra is the deceiver in the messenger scene, but both, unknowingly, further the power of the lie.[85]

Chrysothemis recognizes Orestes' presence by the token of the hair which she calls an *aglaïsma* (908), something that "brightens," "a thing of joy." For Electra, however, this word has associations with the darkness of her hatred: she had prayed that the killers "may have no profit of their bright joy" (*aglaia*, 211; cf. 1310). For her, too, grave offerings have a very different meaning (cf. 405ff.), and those which Chrysothemis has seen are for her proof rather of "Orestes dead" (932–933). The joy of Orestes' physical presence which the offering suggests to Chrysothemis is for her not an appropriate means of recognition. Her reunion begins with the darker bond established by the urn. To her the urn is the "clear token" (*emphanes tekmērion*, 1108; cf. 1115) that replaces her sister's "token" (*tekmērion*, 904) of the hair. Her final "clear" (*saphes*) token will then be the "signet ring of the father" (1223), appropriately the symbol of the authority which she and Orestes will reclaim and vindicate.[86] The recognition for Chrysothemis is primarily personal and emotional, the flutter of joy in her soul when she sees the familiar form (900–906), whereas Orestes and Electra meet under the sign of the house and its patriarchal power.

The doubling of the token of recognition, the urn and the seal ring, fulfills the pattern which the entire play has developed. The ring, symbol of male power and possession, answers to and supersedes the woman's fruitless lamentation over an empty object, sterile monument of a destroyed loved one. The realm of the father and king, action and property, contrasts with the vibrant tenderness and vulnerability to the pain (*lypē*) which Orestes' stratagem unthinkingly caused.

The urn's inversions of the normal love between blood kin continue with a darker pathos at the matricide itself, for Clytaemnestra is adorning the urn for burial at the very moment of Orestes' attack (1400–1401). The mother who flagrantly violated the rites of mourning (804–807) is now herself a victim of the son whose burial she ostensibly prepares.[87] Instead of completing the burial of the dry ashes of her son, she spills her own blood in a long-awaited human sacrifice to the gods below (1422–23).

Finally, at the very end of the play, Aegisthus hypocritically offers to participate in the ritual dirge over the dead, "so that kinship (*to syngenes*) may receive its due of lamentation (*thrēnoi*) from me too" (1469). But he soon falls victim to the corpse he supposedly laments and suffers an outrage of funerary rites (1487–89). Given the ominous associations of such violations throughout the play, it is hard to believe that this deed, Electra's final piece of work in the play, will in fact effect the "release of ancient evils" for which she prays (1489–90, cf. 635–636).

VIII

The prologue presents the vengeance as the manifestation of Apollo's will. Orestes tells how he went to Delphi to inquire "in what manner I might exact just punishment for my father from those who killed him" (33–34). He reports Apollo's answer, that he should use guile and deception to catch Aegisthus unawares and unarmed and thereby accomplish the "justified slaughter" (*endikous sphagas*, 36–37). In shifting between singular and plural ("killers" in 34; the possibly "poetic" plural, *sphagai*, "slaughters," in 37; but "him," Aegisthus, in 36), Orestes leaves the issue of the matricide unclear. Other factual matters are also left vague: we are not sure which are Apollo's words and which are Orestes' interpretation.[88] The problem of whether Orestes has in fact begged the question by asking "how" to exact vengeance from the "killers" (plural, presumably including his mother) rather than *if* he should exact such a revenge has been much discussed, and scholars are not likely to agree on the answer. So much, however, is clear: the precise details of the oracle are left vague, and nowhere in the play does Apollo give explicit and unambiguous sanction for the matricide.[89]

In the second half of the prologue Orestes reports oracles enjoining rites to the dead: he is "to adorn his father's tomb with libations and offerings of cut hair, as he [Apollo] commanded" (51–53). Then at the end of the scene the Paedagogus reminds Orestes as he vacillates at Electra's cry, "Let us attempt no act before trying to accomplish the things of Apollo (*ta Loxiou*) and make our beginning from them, pouring out libations to your father. For these things, I say, bring us victory and power in what we do" (82–85). Apollo's command for such an obvious act is, as Wilamowitz noted, peculiar.[90] The precision about this rite contrasts with the vagueness about the matricide. Even here, however, the Paedagogus' closing words put success, "victory and power," above piety.

In the Pelopid house oracles are notoriously dangerous, as Aegisthus points out at the end (1500). He should know, for his father, Thyestes, followed Apollo's advice that he seduce his brother's wife, thus avenging cannibalism by incest, with dire results. Sophocles dramatized this myth in his *Thyestes* (frag. 247P = 226N)[91]; that play, along with plays like the *Oedipus Tyrannus*, *Trachiniae*, and *Philoctetes*, warns us not to expect oracles to provide a simple clarification or justification of complex moral issues. Within the *Electra* itself there is the example of Orestes' father, who relied on Artemis' authority to sacrifice Iphigeneia. The prophet in this play is Justice, *Dika promantis*, and she brings violence (475–476). Rather than resolving conflicts of guilt and responsibility, oracles in Sophocles seem to throw them into sharper relief, and Orestes' appeal to the oracles immediately after the matricide does nothing to dispel this ambiguity (1424–25).

The gods of the *Electra* are as remote and mysterious as those of any other Sophoclean play. Of the Olympians themselves we hear little. It is as if contact between earth and Olympus is broken off, and instead the divinities of the lower world are free to invade house and city, led by the destructive Ares (1243, 1385, 1422–23) and Hermes, guide of dead souls (1391–97).

Apollo is the most important god in the play. In addition to his function as a god of oracles, he is also the god whose image stands before the house (637), a god of purification (in Clytaemnestra's prayer of 645ff.) and, in Electra's last prayer, Apollo Lykeios, the destroyer of one's enemies (1379ff.).[92] This god of light and purity sponsors intrigue and chicane (37) and sanctions the polluting act of matricide.

Like the Apollo of the *Tyrannus*, this Apollo is, among other things, a symbol of the inscrutability of reality, of that "necessity" which requires a certain task of a certain person at a given time. His presence behind the action points to the mystery of that conjunction of events that gives a human life its peculiar destiny and stamps it with its tragic shape. He is in part the objectification of that supernatural compulsion which dogs the life of most tragic figures, like Hamlet's

> The time is out of joint. O cursed spite,
> That ever I was born to set it right!

That inward struggle against one's destiny does not rise to full consciousness in the *Electra*, but the "necessity" is there as an objective force whose power is both rooted in Electra's own emotional vehemence and is also projected, in part, upon Apollo and his oracles.

A thunderbolt-brandishing Zeus should visit punishment upon the guilty, as the chorus repeatedly prays (823–825, 1063–65); but Zeus is little more than a name in this play.[93] The chorus congratulates Electra for her piety to Zeus (1097), but we may recall her own sense of the necessity which keeps her from such piety of action (307–309).

Artemis, dangerous and spiteful according to Electra's account of the becalmed fleet at Aulis, appears only as a goddess of wrath, *mēnis* (570), a jealous protectress of the wild who is yet not averse to the sacrifice of human young. Sophocles does not stress the disproportion between her anger and Agamemnon's offense, but it is there nevertheless, and we may recall the remote and spiteful Chryse of the *Philoctetes* or, on a larger scale, the ambiguous paternalism of Zeus in the *Trachiniae* or the agency of Apollo in the *Oedipus Tyrannus*.

The use to which Orestes and the Paedagogus put the god's Delphic celebration parallels the use to which they put his Delphic oracle. The glorious assembly and its brilliant games, the public exploit and its loud proclamation (683–684) contrast with the "concealment," "trickery," and silence that attend the actual deed which is now under way.

The Delphic festival has its reality only in the baroque eloquence of the Paedagogus' oratory, exemplification of the power of language to spin gripping fictions with no substance behind them. The Homeric, Pindaric, and Bacchylidean echoes in this speech create the play's sharpest division between *logos* and *ergon*, language and action. Heroic language, bearer of the city's noblest values, is undercut by the situation it serves. On the plane of poetic diction, the high registers of epic and epinician poetry play against the low registers of lie and deception.[94]

Holding "the greatest body in its small bronze" immediately after the account of the race (757–758), the urn is the material emblem of this paradox. Made of solid bronze but empty of the true Orestes, the stage prop for an elaborate fiction capable of eliciting Electra's most intense emotions, the urn symbolizes the ambiguity of language, its power to distort and manipulate, as well as to represent, reality.

In the lie itself, as in the tragic striving for justice and order throughout the play, heroic greatness is hemmed in by meanness, as within the house Electra's love is held to hatred and death amid the evils of her world (307–309). In more than one sense the vessel is out of proportion to its contents. Yet only by the success of the lie, which will insure the reception of the empty urn, can justice, however clouded, reenter the house.

The Paedagogus first describes the games as "Hellas famous showpiece of a contest" (Kells), *to kleinon Hellados / proschēm' agōnos*, (681–682); but the phrase means also "the glorious pretext (or pretense) of a contest." *Proschēma* is something "held up before," which conceals rather than reveals. Clytaemnestra used the word in that sense to counter Electra's accusations in 525. Whereas Orestes uses the outward show or "pretense" of this "glorious" event to win back, by unheroic means, his heroic status, Electra has maintained her heroic spirit intact beneath the wasting away of her "glorious form" (*kleinon eidos*, 1177). The *proschēma* at this middle point of the play obscures the truth of heroic and moral values (cf. Clytaemnestra's request for "truth," *alēthes*, in 679).[95] The lifting of the veil (*kalymma*) at the completion of the vengeance brings together appearance and reality (1468). Now the "contest" will be openly avowed to be one of life and death: "For this is not a contest, *agōn*, of words, but of your life," Orestes tells Aegisthus in 1491–92. Yet clarity and vision of the truth remain still ambiguous (1493–1500).

The lie about the Delphic festival at the exact center of the play is a paradigm for the corrupted ritual and civic order. It reflects this society's incapacity for valid public rituals. In contrast to the public lamentation for Orestes, the *ololygē* of the crowd of strangers in 750, stand the mother's ambivalent reaction in her house (760ff., 791–807), Electra's recognition of the loneliness of her grief both here (813ff.) and in the urn scene, and finally the hidden, private cry of pain "within" (1404ff.). In like manner the new rulers' mocking celebrations and choruses in honor of Agamemnon's death (266–281), like the "unchorused reproaches" to be brought to the dead below (*achoreuta oneidē*, 1068–69), are a travesty of healthy public ritual and public discourse.

The ambiguity of ritual and language at the midpoint of the *Electra* reflects the ambiguity of the aesthetic and moral order shaped by tragedy itself. The Paedagogus' speech self-consciously creates a public, agonistic ritual, just as Orestes' entrance with the urn self-consciously creates a fiction within a fiction. As at the Dionysiac festival itself, an order-asserting rite encloses a fiction, and the capacity of speech to shape images of truth and order stands in tension with the capacity of speech to shape falsehood and images of chaos and violence. Like the Delphic *agōn*, and later the urn, tragedy seeks to affirm the truth by concealing truth, to overcome disorder through a temporary immersion in disorder.

For us, the spectators, as for Electra, the participant, the task is to distinguish true from false, good from evil. Only through the anguish, vicarious or represented, of this test are clarity about justice and greatness of soul finally attained. Here, as in all of Sophoclean tragedy, the dissolution of difference is paradoxically the means by which differentiation is reestablished; the confusion of moral and psychological truth helps us in eventually unveiling a deeper truth. As elaborate *logos* gives way to a direct and forceful *ergon*, the concealment of vigorous new life in the narrow confines of the urn is counterbalanced by the triumphant "uncovering" of a real corpse, whose death has been encompassed by justice (1442–80). Through the Paedagogus' magniloquent lie the tragic *logos* asserts its civilizing power by calling into question the basic institutions of civilization. A celebratory ritual, its underlying divine and civic order, and its heroic values appear only as the framework for a falsehood that inverts life and death. And yet the false *logos* and the unholy deed for which it prepares are necessary to restore justice. The urn is the concrete manifestation of this truth-speaking deception. It packs into the smallest compass (757–758) a representation of life as total suffering and deprivation in order to release a truer image of the strength, endurance, and commitment that can right wrongs and maintain fidelity not only to necessary hate but also to truth and love.

IX

The point of intersection between true and false speech and between word and act, the urn points up the function of the *logos* virtually as a participant in the vicissitudes of the action. Language is not merely a means of communication but a dangerous weapon. It is Electra's most powerful weapon against her enemies. They attempt to constrain her speech (see 310–313, 382, 554ff.). Possession of the *logos* about Clytaemnestra's dream gives her her first advantage in her struggle for vengeance (417). Her silence and her sister's are crucial for the completion of the deed.[96] Clytaemnestra experiences Electra's *logoi* as "painful" (557) or an act of outrage (*hybris*, 613; cf. 522–523, 794), but they are her only means of answering her mother's "deeds"; and in this play "The deeds find out the words for themselves" (624–625).

The middle portion of the play is in fact a tense battle of *logoi* whose hostility reveals the violent inversion of the mother-daughter relationship (516–629). The Paedagogus' contrived *logos* about Orestes' death answers Clytaemnestra's muffled prayer (680ff.); his opening promise, "I shall tell all" (*to pan*, 680), counterbalances Clytaemnestra's necessary "silence" (657) as she counts on the gods "to see all" (*panth' horan*, 659; cf. 639). Even though Electra is devastated by the effect (unintended so far as she is concerned) of this *logos*, she still inspires Clytaemnestra with fear for her speech: "Great would be your value, stranger, if you had stopped her from her full-tongued shouting," Clytaemnestra tells the Paedagogus, repeating the phrase from her prayer shortly before (*polyglōssos boē*, 641 = 798).

Just as "base speech" or "insult" separates mother and daughter (*kakōs legein, kakostomein*, 523ff., 596–597), so "right speaking" separates the two sisters (*eu legein*, 1028, 1039ff.). Electra cannot accept her sister's "words" (1050, 1057), any more than her sister can accept her "ways" (*tropoi*, 1051). They reenact here the disharmony of "words" and "ways" at their first meeting (397, 401). No lasting communication proves possible. Even Electra's attempt at persuasion rests on the suppression of speech, withholding the name of "Clytaemnestra" beside "Aegisthus" (955–957). It may be, as Gellie suggests, that "Electra always tells the truth,"[97] but she does not necessarily tell the whole truth, and in this play it is lies that bring success. Her concealment, despite the promise of 957, "No longer must I conceal anything from you," recalls Orestes' evasiveness about killing his mother in the prologue (33–37; cf. 14).[97] The most essential words cannot be spoken, as Clytaemnestra too shows in her "concealed speech" (638) which she yet expects the god to understand.

Orestes' return to "life" seems to restore the viability of *logos* as communication between loved ones. Yet even this restoration of open speech is short-lived. There is "dirge" on the one side (1122ff.) and "ill-omened speech" (*dysphēmia*, 1182) on the other. Although the action moves beyond the hypocritical attempt at *euphēmia* by Clytaemnestra (630) and the too easy *euphēmia* of Chrysothemis (905), Orestes' promise of holy speech (1212) is still far from realization. Even when she has won "a free tongue" (1256), Electra is still constrained to silence (1236, 1238, 1262, 1322, 1335ff., 1288, 1353). In the closing scenes, however, it is she who will advise "silence" in the tense expectation of the cry from the house (1398ff.). When the cry breaks forth, the chorus shudders at the hearing of "things that should not be heard" (1406–1408). Speech remains oppressed by fear to the very end as Electra pleads for an end of speaking (1483ff.) and Orestes impatiently terminates discussion (1501–1502) with Aegisthus.

Throughout the play Electra veers between immoderate speech and immoderate silence. In her images of grieving in her initial choral lament she envisages her grief either as the eternally repetitive "Itys, Itys" of the transformed Procne or the eternally inarticulate weeping of Niobe, water dripping on rock (147, 151–152). She is equally ready to sink down in frozen, deathlike silence at the palace gate (817–822) or to raise wild cries of joy in total defiance of the risks to the person she would most protect (1232ff.). Her attempts to engage in rational debate (with Clytaemnestra) or logical persuasion (with Chrysothemis) end, like Oedipus' encounters with Teiresias and the shepherds, in violent outbursts that throw rationality and even the characteristic human power of speech to the winds (294, 299).[98] In the first situation initial agreement on rules of reasonable discourse gives way to threats and insults (552–557, 601–609). "Word" and "deed" are confounded (613–633), Electra "breathes fury" like a wild beast (609–610),[99] and finally rejects speech altogether for hostile silence (633). In the second scene initial harmony turns into a divorce between speech and intelligence (1038–39; cf. 1048) and finally a rejection of speech (1050–51, 1056–57). Both scenes erode the middle ground for speech as a form of civilized communication.

In the scene with the urn, however, the failure of *logos* has a more positive meaning. For once Orestes, cool manipulator of *logoi* (cf. 59–60), loses control of his tongue and is "helpless in words" (1174–75).[100] He now falls into Electra's vocabulary of helplessness (cf. 1161), lack of strength (cf. 1175 and 604, 1415), and lamentation (1184). But he soon recovers his control, and checks the exuberance of speech with his firm pressure for deeds, *erga* rather than *logoi* (see 1251–52, 1292–93, 1353, 1372–73). Instead of the release in words that Electra's starved emotions crave (1364–67), she is hurried toward deeds. But words have destroyed her too, as she complains to the Paedagogus, even when the deeds were sweetest (1359–60). Present on the stage is also a third male figure, the mute Pylades, figure of pure action who speaks no word (see 1372–73).

With the success of Orestes' goal-oriented *logos*, Electra becomes fully immersed in the violence of *ergon*. This is the tragic price of the "freedom" (1509) which her *ergon* achieves. When she was entirely in the realm of *logos*, she retained a nobility, grandeur, and even a certain tenderness: hence her association with the maternal paradigms of Procne and Niobe. When word fuses with deed the grim actuality of the latter predominates over the integrity and nobility of spirit kept alive in the former. Thus with her cry, "Strike if you can a second blow," at the climax of the deed (1415–16), Electra moves from the perpetually lamenting *mater dolorosa*, Procne or Niobe, to a different mythic paradigm, the destructive, vengeful female, the Clytaemnestra of the *Agamemnon*, whose act she here symbolically repeats (cf. *Ag.* 1343–44). Totally eclipsed by act, *logos* loses the autonomy whereby man might transcend the closed circle of blood vengeance. The act absorbs everything. There is no room for fresh visions beyond the present dark foreground (see 1493–94, 1497–98) and its necessity (*anagkē*, 256, 309, 1497).

Orestes closes the play with an insistence on the all-absorbing present moment (*euthys*, "at once," 1505) and the act of killing which fills it (*kteinein*, 1507). Only Aegisthus looks beyond to "the future" (1498). Orestes twice mentions prophecy in this scene, in both cases derisively (1481, 1499). Prophecy is a mode of speech which does indeed transcend the present moment, but it is the most ambiguous of all *logoi*. For all his confident manipulation of *logos*, Orestes both in the prologue and at the matricide itself is dependent on this most difficult and uncertain form of speech (31ff., 1424–25).

Aegisthus, an unlikely prophet, foretells "the present and future woes of the Pelopids" (1498) which qualify both Electra's hopes for a "release from the woes of old" (1489–90) and Orestes' single-minded concentration on the immediate moment of the *ergon* (1501ff.). Guilty agent who is justly punished, Aegisthus doubles for a moment with prophetic victim, the Cassandra of the *Agamemnon* who marches inside to be killed speaking truths that no one else can grasp or acknowledge.

The character of Electra is the field in which the opposing movements between *logos* and *ergon* and the ambiguities within *logos* have their fullest scope.[101] For her the gap between truth and falsehood, love and hatred, intimacy and distance yawns with the widest, most desperate abyss. As Electra, bearing the tragic burden of the swing of the *logos* between appearance and reality, nearly becomes one with her evil opposite, Clytaemnestra, so the *logos* itself threatens to become one with its destructive opposite, the *ergon* of treachery and murder.

The triumph of deceptive *logos* brings a final confusion to those distinctions which it is the task of civilization to maintain: loved one and enemy, man and beast, living and dead, nobility and evil. The last anagnorisis ("recognition") in the play is Aegisthus' grasp of the riddling "word" that identifies opposites (1476–79):

> Aeg.: In what man's nets have I fallen, O miserable?
> Or.: Don't you see that in your speech you have long since been equating the living with the dead?
> Aeg.: Alas, I have understood the saying (*to epos*).

What is "unveiled" here, as in the *Trachiniae*, is man's capacity for violence, destruction, possibly self-delusion (cf. *ek kalymmatōn, Trach.* 1078; *pan kalymma, El.* 1468). With the removal of that "veil from the eyes" of both living and dead (the "eyes" of 1468 could refer to either), the last act of the tragedy can be performed, a just killing carried out, or at least initiated, before the uncovered body of the murdered mother.[102]

This recognition, like the others in the play, does not dispel the ambiguity that clings to speech. *Logos* retains its power of deception to the very end. It is as much a distorting mirror as a clear glass. The recurrence of words like "visible," "clear," "proof" (*emphanes, saphes, tekmērion*), along with the persistent emphasis on "concealment" (*kryptein*), stresses the difficulty of breaking through appearance to truth.[103] Thus the urn, so essential for reestablishing justice, also confuses death and life. The *mēchanai* or "devices" which make Orestes dead and alive by turns (1228–29) have taken Electra through an infinitely more painful experience of the same cycle of truth and falsehood, life and death.[104] As she says near the end of the recognition scene, *logos* has nearly destroyed her when "fact," *ergon*, held her greatest joy (1359–60).

As I noted earlier, the *Electra's* concern with appearance and reality in relation to speech and language is closely paralleled in Euripides' *Helen*, probably written within a few years of Sophocles' play (cf. *Hel.* 1049–52 and *El.* 59ff.).[105] But in the *Helen* the power of *logos* to deceive is balanced by its power to restore. Whereas the convolutions of true and false *logoi* subject Electra to a living death (see 804–823), Helen uses the artfulness and grace of her speech, as of her person, to create a ritual of death and rebirth which in turn enacts a *mythos* of happy return across mysterious seas, ascent from a Hades-like exile, and a sacred marriage.[106] Nothing could be further from the movement into the dark, death-filled house which concludes the *Electra*. "The glorious form" of Electra (1177), unlike Helen's, has been preserved by no divine magic. And the *logos* of the *Electra*, unilluminated by the grace and beauty (*charis*) of a Helen, cannot transcend the cycle of hatred, revenge, and sterility in which the house and its members are entrapped. In Euripides' play Helen's trickery, neutralized by the life-giving function it serves and separated from the lustful cloud-Helen that went to Troy, can symbolize the magic of art's restorative power; deceitful beauty becomes a true vision of beauty, nobility, and fidelity in human affairs. In Sophocles' play, however, tragic art celebrates its paradoxical power to condense the suffering of life into its most concentrated essence and simultaneously to represent the spiritual force that can triumph through and above a world that appears as total suffering.

The urn is perhaps the play's richest symbol of this paradox. It fuses the opposites of great and small, heroism and deceit, substance and shadow, reality and symbol. A symbolical token of fictitious death, it is the means of bringing Orestes back to "life." Confronted with the tangible object, not Chrysothemis' report in words just before, Electra is able to break through the constructions of *logoi* that have separated her from her brother. Temporarily, at least, she converts this instrument of deceit and falsehood (54ff.) into the means for recreating truth and love.

The urn is the appropriate emblem for the ambiguous function of language in the play, itself a work of art whose fiction contains truth and reveals truth. An elaborately shaped work of plastic art (cf. *typōma chalkopleuron*, 54), the urn has false contents, but through its falsehood restores truth. Even so, only when Electra puts down the artifact and embraces the living body can the truth be revealed, as if the fiction itself must be dissolved and transcended once it has done its work.

This crossing of fiction and reality in the symbolism of the urn, like the false suicide leap of *King Lear*, is a fundamentally *theatrical* or visual exploration of the nature of dramatic fiction.[107] We, the audience, see Electra wracked with pain over the inanimate object while the real brother is standing there alive before her. In order for the scene to have its full dramatic force, she must invest the urn with the intensity of emotion due to the "real" Orestes until she is persuaded to relinquish the false symbol for the living person. Only by totally succumbing to the illusion and the emotions which it raises is she able to call illusion into truth. At the same time we, the spectators, are undergoing an analogous process, surrendering to the emotional power and even the pain of a fiction in order to benefit from its ultimate truth in the reality which it restores. This paradox is the paradox of all literary fictions but here finds a uniquely visual and theatrical equivalent: urn and living person, tangibly before us at the same moment, concretely embody the tension between the "fiction" of the surface and the "truth" of what may lie beneath. "Meaning" then exists in the tension between the falsehood and the veracity of the represented image.

The urn's functions as a mediator between appearance and reality and between language and action justify its status as a symbol for art itself. Understood more broadly, the urn refers to the two-sided nature of man's symbolic representation of reality in general. Having no inherent value, valued only for what it contains and signifies in accordance with the *logos* of which it is an adjunct, the urn points to the ambiguity of the signifier in the signified/signifier relationship. Language and other symbols are arbitrary, manipulable tokens; they can be enlisted equally on the side of truth or propaganda, justice or oppression. Initially Orestes uses the urn as an amoral means to power and success. At the end he must put down the urn to allow his sister to hold in her arms not the false ashes in the metal container, but the warm, living form of her real brother. Fortunately the emotional resonances of the urn for Electra transcend the cold rationality of its use by Orestes. Its function as a cultural symbol, in other words, emotionally charged with religious and familial ties, outweighs its function as a symbol of the power of the *logos*, a counter in the manipulation and control of reality by language.

The urn's function does not end with the recognition scene. Put aside momentarily for a "rebirth" of love between brother and sister (1232–33), it is then taken into the house to work a final deception, now between mother and son. Initially the urn evoked strong feelings in Clytaemnestra too ("A fearful thing it is to give birth," 770–771), but these never break through the deceitful *logos* enveloping the urn to reach the true Orestes who bears it. To the last the urn remains for her an instrument of guile, the token of violated *philia*.

Although the urn has already served its purpose of admitting Orestes to the house, its effect upon the other members of the house lingers. Clytaemnestra remains involved with it and, in fact, is represented as focusing her attention on it at the moment of the matricide: she is decking it out for burial when Orestes makes his attack (1400–1401). The symbol here reveals its full ambivalence, which corresponds in turn to Clytaemnestra's own ambivalence of attitude toward the "dead" Orestes. The two main antagonists, Electra and Clytaemnestra, each receive the truth of family relationships that they are able to perceive in the urn.

Chrysothemis, on the other hand, unable to commit herself to the struggle between justice and evil, never meets the urn at all. She encounters Orestes only through the offerings laid on the father's tomb, far from the house. Even here the *logos* which she brings back from that vision is never embodied in a concrete, visual symbol, like the urn. Though factually true, her *logos* is overthrown by the false but emotionally more intense *logos* of Electra which, for all its objective falseness, has a deep symbolic truth, namely that life and hope have died out in Argos. Only the shattering encounter with the symbol of death itself, the urn, and the inversions consequent on this, can finally reverse this paradoxical relation between a lie that has its truth and a death that signifies life.

For the last act of deception in the play, namely the tricking and killing of Aegisthus, the urn is abandoned. Aegisthus, presumably, had not been told that the messengers came with the *ashes*, not the body, of Orestes. Hence he is ready to accept as Orestes the figure veiled under the covering. Clytaemnestra's body, of course, makes for a more dramatic scene. But stage effects flow from but do not preclude deeper meaning.

Invested with the strong emotions of *philia*, associated with the ties of blood, an object that can be taken up, touched, handled by loved ones, the urn would be an inappropriate instrument for vengeance upon the outsider, Aegisthus. Aegisthus, therefore, is not to meet his end through the token of the joy and pain which blood kin within the house experience at the loss and recovery embodied in the urn. His death comes through the veiled form of the woman who is both the prize and the instrument of the wealth and power which he enjoys in Mycenae. It is a sign of the play's movement from the realm of *logos* into pure *ergon*, from deception to direct action, that the false ashes within the vessel are replaced by a real corpse outside.

In one sense, then, the play moves closer to truth and tangible reality as it progresses through its three main instruments of deception: first the Paedagogus' elaborate deception speech at the center of the play, then the urn with the fictitious ashes, and finally the actual body of Clytaemnestra.[108] The physical actuality of death moves closer as we progress from tale to visible symbol and from container to real corpse.

The movement from appearance to reality, from artifact to person, however, is still ambiguous. The possibility of manipulation and symbolic distancing of reality and emotion advances a stage further each time. It is a final, more horrible token of the disrupted values of this corrupted world that son and daughter can use their mother's corpse as the ruse for the final act of violence and "justice." On the one hand, using Clytaemnestra's body as bait for Aegisthus is poetic justice for her maltreatment of her husband's body in consort with her new spouse (267–281, 442–447). On the other hand, this act can appear as one more outrage against civilized behavior, the holiness of blood ties and the rites of burial (1487–90).

X

The dramatic power of the *Electra* derives in large part from the richness of the main character, a woman of extraordinarily intense emotions, whose capacity for love has been turned toward death and hatred. In this corrupt world the compromising Chrysothemis could survive and likewise the ambitious Orestes, but not Electra.

The inversions of life and death and of *logos* and *ergon* in the play, however, generalize the tragedy from the personal suffering of Electra to the tragedy of a whole city, a whole civilization. The failure of *logos* is not only the failure of personal communication but also the failure of man's civilizing powers: it reveals the problematical side of man's ability to distance himself from reality and manipulate it through the mental structures of *logos*.

These inversions are symbolized by the urn. It is an artifact through which man seeks to control his apprehension of reality; a semi-religious object that can be invested with the most intense emotions; the substitute for the love and joy in life that seem unattainable; the highly wrought vessel that is both the instrument and the symbol of a complex stratagem of words and acts. For all its solidity, it may contain nothing at all; but as pure symbol it can reveal truth or delude, estrange in terrible loneliness or work toward recognition, affirm love or help kill a mother.

The shifting values of *logos* reflect not only on the peculiar status of art and tragic discourse, but also on Athens in the last decades of the fifth century.[109] The great city, like the great-souled heroine, is caught by "necessities" (cf. 256, 309, 620) which constrain and distort its nature and its aims. We are reminded of Thucydides' view of the war as a "teacher by violence," a "harsh teacher," *biaios didaskalos*, which turns the creative capacities of the city to destructiveness. In the play the "glorious temple of Hera" (8), the "glorious earth of the Mycenaeans" (160–161), and the "glorious showpiece of contests at Delphi" (681–682) are but the settings for the impious piety (308, 1097) that Electra must practice. As these "glorious" (*kleinos*) settings contrast with the ignoble actions which they enframe, so the heroic language of the Pythian games contrasts with their function as deception; grim private aim contrasts with public, festive function. That scene is the microcosm of the more general discrepancy between "the glorious army of Hellas" (694–695) led by its great general (1–2, 695) and the unheroic action of the disinherited prince. Yet these public glories are not the only things to be lost or marred. Their reduction is summed up and symbolized visually in Electra herself, her "glorious form" (*kleinon eidos*, 1177) wasted by years of waiting, her beauty blighted by joyless concentration on an action which can bring no positive good in itself but only a release from past evils (1489–90) that is not without qualifications and ambiguities.

The failure of the forms of mediation between man and the natural and supernatural worlds leaves the human action of the *Electra* bare and isolated. The foreground of the action absorbs us almost entirely. The triumphant choral song and ritual procession that end the *Oresteia* are here reduced to ambiguous discourse and reluctant, private movement toward a house whose contact with the divine order is clouded and uncertain. Sophocles seems to have deliberately stripped away the rich mythic perspectives which Aeschylus had so elaborately woven into his version of the story. The lyrics are sparse and for the most part restricted to discussions of the immediate situation. The few myths that do occur are briefly told.[110] The divine perspective is the most reduced of any Sophoclean play. The narrow spatial limits—so different from the *Oresteia* with its grand beacon speech or even from other Sophoclean plays like the *Trachiniae*, *Tyrannus*, or *Ajax*—correspond to the shallowness of the mythic and divine planes. The human figures are left to themselves, but in this highly concentrated and barren world they seem to have little scope for regeneration.

In the action of the play violations of the civilized order are encoded in the terms of space, of ritual, family, animal and plant life, and of language. All give the parallel message of a distorted personal, political, and natural world. What is exceptional about the *Electra* is the convergence of these distortions upon the personality of a single character and their austere limitation to a narrow field of space and action. In the characterization of Electra, as Virginia Woolf has said, Sophocles has "cut each stroke to the bone":

> His Electra stands before us like a figure so tightly bound that she can only move an inch this way, an inch that. But each movement must tell to the utmost, or, bound as she is, denied the relief of all hints, repetitions, suggestions, she will be nothing but a dummy, tightly bound. Her words in crisis are, as a matter of fact, bare; mere cries of despair, joy, hate.[111]

In his last two surviving plays, the *Philoctetes* and *Oedipus at Colonus*, written probably within a decade of the *Electra*, this narrow, reduced world once more opens up. The gods, so remote in the *Electra*, move again to the foreground. Human action once more takes its place in a larger supernatural frame, fulfilling broader, if no less mysterious, divine purposes.

This deepening of the religious dimension of human action does not, paradoxically, imply a lessening of man's civilizing power. For Sophocles that power is never autonomous. As the Ode on Man in the *Antigone* implies, man is truly civilized not only as he develops and recognizes his own extraordinary powers of heart and mind, but also as he acknowledges the vast rhythms of the world around him and the mystery of the divine forces which play incessantly about his life.

9

Philoctetes: The Myth and the Gods

 On Philoctetes' "sea-girt Lemnos" there are, it would seem, no altars. Not only has Sophocles indulged the poetic licence of making a populous island uninhabited, but in creating a hero whose struggle for survival reflects early man's establishment of civilization, he omits the institution of worship of the gods, a fundamental point in fifth-century speculation on the origin of culture.[1] In this respect, as in others too, the hero is *agrios*, "savage," rude, uncivilized, an epithet with which he himself and others describe his character (226, 1321).[2] His "savagery" is "over-determined," moreover, by the "savage disease" (*agria nosos*, 173, 265), which is both cause and effect of his exile on his deserted island. For ten years, says the chorus, he has lacked bread, "the seed of the sacred earth" (707) and wine. The latter, described as "the joy of the cup and its libations" (*oinochyton pōma*, 714–715), appears particularly in terms of its religious usages. Lacking bread, he is deprived of the most distinctive item of a civilized diet and of a basic token of the generosity of the earth, itself divine or "sacred."[3] Lacking wine, he has not the means of performing the simplest offering to the gods.

In its inversions of civilization and savagery, as well as in the common presence of Heracles, the *Philoctetes* has affinities with the *Trachiniae*. Both plays unfold against a background of elemental savagery: the beast world of archaic monsters on the one hand; the deserted island and the rude life of its one inhabitant and his savage disease on the other. Only in these two plays, with the partial exception of *Ajax*, the civilized space of the polis is kept in the background, and a wild landscape of mountains, rivers, desolate sea holds the foreground. In both plays brutalizing pain brings the hero harshly in touch with the realities of his own animal nature. Sickness makes Heracles of the *Trachiniae* all body. He loses articulate speech not to divine inspiration, like Cassandra in the *Agamemnon*, but to sheer physical suffering. This pain is itself animate, a "devouring beast" in the imagery of both plays (*Trach.* 1084, *Phil.* 7). In his life, as in his art, Sophocles seems to have been concerned with the relationship of illness and its cure to both bestiality and divinity. He received the god of healing into his house in the form of a snake and for this act was himself worshiped as a divinity of sorts under the title of the hero, Dexion, Receiver, after his death.[4]

The Heracles of the *Philoctetes* stands in somewhat the same relation to the Heracles of the earlier play as the Oedipus of the *Coloneus* stands to the Oedipus of the *Tyrannus*. In both cases the earlier hero has now fully separated himself from his "bestial double" and successfully spanned the distance between beast and god. Through Heracles and his bow that distance is a crucial issue in the *Philoctetes*. In both plays the hero moves from a beastlike existence to the fulfillment of a destiny emanating directly from the gods' will; his task is to understand and accept his life in the light of the divine purposes. In both works these purposes manifest themselves as violence done to the hero's own will or autonomy; but in the *Trachiniae*, as we have seen, the gods' purposes are much more obscure and the violence done to the hero much greater. The Heracles of the *Trachiniae* is a paradigm of all human suffering: he longs for ease and eternal life but ends in pain and death. His only "release," the apotheosis, is itself clouded by uncertainty. In the *Philoctetes* suffering is also strong, but the transcendence of pain in a higher destiny, the achievement of "immortal excellence" (*Phil.* 1420), is a much clearer hope. In both cases, however, the release from suffering lies in the validation of a part of the self that exists on a plane outside the ordinary limits of life. That validation is associated with Heracles' transcendence of his mortal and physical being, ambiguous in the *Trachiniae*, assured and paradigmatic in the *Philoctetes*.

Heracles' civilizing role, so precarious in the *Trachiniae*, is reinvested in his erstwhile companion and now symbolic alter ego, Philoctetes. The earlier Heracles is now the clarified archetype of the civilizing hero. The violent killer of monsters is now fully socialized and unambiguously divinized. He can therefore bring the civilizing power which he has himself attained only by the ordeal of his death (cf. *Trach.* 1259–63). His return marks Philoctetes' inner achievement of these qualities after the trials, both physical and spiritual, of the years of hardship on Lemnos. The nine long years are symbolically condensed into the single day of endurance, vicissitude, and choice represented in the play. But those years of combat with the wild, like Heracles' years of wandering and battling monsters in the *Trachiniae*, brutalize as well as temper the soul. It is the task of Heracles in the later play to show that those years of endurance are not wasted on Philoctetes, that even bare survival, for a human being, must have a spiritual, civilizing component.

The attributes which enable man to subdue the natural world vacillate between opposite poles. Fire, the basic instrument of civilization, in both plays also symbolizes destructive, beastlike passion in man. The Hydra's venom in the *Trachiniae* was the tool of further subjugation of the monstrous on the earth but also symbol of the monstrosity within Heracles' soul. The bow, once the weapon for taming the earth, is now, initially, Philoctetes' means of perpetuating his savage life on Lemnos, until Heracles, the wounded and bestialized hero of the earlier play, shows him how to make it the means of healing, not retaining, the wound of the beast.

In mood and style the two plays are vastly different. To most readers the *Trachiniae* seems the most archaic in its myth and execution, the *Philoctetes* the most modern. The beast world of the *Trachiniae* stands out like some troglodytic survivor amid what we fondly imagine as the lucid rationalism of the Classic Enlightenment. The *Philoctetes*, at first glance, seems almost entirely free of those ghostly mastodons of a primitive past. Here no dimly remembered ancestral curses force themselves upon us, as they do in the Theban plays. Instead human relationships and human decisions seem to fill the entire stage. Modern-looking too is the tension between the alienated individual, repulsive but indispensable, and the society that needs and (ab)uses him, the tension between "the wound and the bow," in Edmund Wilson's celebrated formulation.[5]

And yet this modernity is deceptive. Like all of Sophocles' work, the *Philoctetes* is more than a study of character or human relationships, important as these are. True, the growing friendship between Philoctetes and Neoptolemus, the latter's search for his heroic identity and a valid father-figure, the former's paradoxical relationship to his own heroic past and to society are major themes. But, as in the other plays, the purely human elements constantly interact with the divine. The human condition and its social setting are never autonomous. The question "What is man?" in Sophocles is never fully separable from the question "What is God?" Hence character in Sophocles consists as much in the realization of a larger destiny as in the possession of a unique, idiosyncratic personality.[6] To be a hero in Sophocles is to have a destiny, to bear and painfully realize fate, given by the gods—that is, given by something beyond his immediate comprehension—that sets him apart from the mass of men and makes him simultaneously both exemplary and fearful.

The combination of its social and personal issues and ancient mythic patterns makes the *Philoctetes* a work of many-layered meanings. The bow is both a symbol of technological power and a magical talisman of a great, dead king. Lemnos is a microcosm of the wild where primitive man battles a hostile environment, but it is also one of those fabled islands of the mythic journey of the soul: it is a place where an old self dies and is reborn and a new world order is symbolically regenerated.[7] The wound is the psychological illness of an "ensavaged" soul but also the debility which signifies the waning vitality of a wounded world order where the legitimate king, or in this case the legitimate bearer of the heroic and moral values of kingship, is injured, enfeebled, and exiled.

The three elements that have most embarrassed contemporary readers and critics, the oracles, the wound, and the *deus ex machina* at the end, are the most Sophoclean features of the play and therefore the hardest to understand in modern terms. The two levels of the action, human and divine, are inseparable aspects of the total cosmological consciousness with which this tragedy surrounds the mythical events it represents. Not only does it end with the appearance of a deity onstage, but its last iambic trimeters are an exhortation to the "piety" which does not pass away (1440–44).[8] It is with prayers and invocations to divine powers both near and remote that the main figures leave the stage (1445ff., 1454ff., 1464ff., 1469ff.).

Like the heroes of the other plays, Philoctetes bypasses the mediated, civilized point between the two extremes of beast and god. He possesses a weapon endowed with godlike power but uses it only to maintain a bestial existence, a lonely hunter's life of bare survival in a cave. Whereas civilized man learns to inhibit his destructive and aggressive drives and turn them to socially useful purposes, Philoctetes, separated from his society, leads the life of a lone predator, a hunter/killer whose lack of social forms keeps him closer to the beasts he hunts than to the men whom he regards as his enemies. Yet he is destined to win the deathless glory of capturing Troy.

The renewal of the bonds of friendship through the bow, which Philoctetes possesses only because of his past friendship with Heracles, accompanies the renewal of ritual action, the exchange of the gestures and words appropriate to "holy things" (*hosia*, Philoctetes' word in 662) when he hands the bow over to Neoptolemus who would "do obeisance to it as to a god" (657). Not only does the exchange of the bow seal heroic friendship, as it did between Philoctetes and Heracles in the past, but it is also a symbolic renewal of ritual, the absence of which constitutes one aspect of the hero's savagery on Lemnos.

This double perspective, religious and secular, of Philoctetes' savage exile also characterizes his relation to his environment. He is a prototype of early man, battling inhospitable nature to procure the essentials of life. But his landscape is truly an *entgötterte Natur*, a place as remote from divine providence as is the hero himself. Neutral, impersonal, unhallowed, and silent, it resembles the de-mythicized world of the Atomists or the challenging physical environment of Sophistic anthropology, awaiting human domination and exploitation.[9]

II

We first see the absent hero through his humble possessions, token of his will and his struggle to survive. There are the rudiments of food and shelter, "the nurture that makes a dwelling" (*oikopoios trophē*, 32), kindling wood (36), and a cup carved from a single piece of wood (*autoxylon ekpōma*, 35), where the adjective stresses the rudimentary quality of the implement. Both the subject matter and the vocabulary (for example *technēmata*, "device" or "handicraft," used of his cup) suggest Sophistic culture-history. In his own account of human civilization in the *Antigone* Sophocles extols man's "skillful device of craft and art".[10] Finding evidence of Philoctetes' diseased foot, which Neoptolemus notes with disgust (38–39), Odysseus, characteristically attuned to the resourcefulness of human intelligence, conjectures that he has some curative plant or anodyne (44) which he may even now be gathering.[11] Philoctetes later confirms the existence of such primitive remedies (649–650; cf. 698), and we are reminded of the place of medicine in Sophistic anthropology, a topic also mentioned in Sophocles' Ode on Man (*Antig.* 353–354).[12]

Like early man, Philoctetes dwells in a cave.[13] Neoptolemus finds kindling (36), and Philoctetes later tells him in detail how he (re-)invented fire, essential to his survival (297), by striking stone against stone (295–299). He uses almost the same phrase, "stone upon stone," for his attempted suicide when he sees himself betrayed and trapped (cf. 1002 and 296). He could hold out against nonhuman nature, but betrayal by men renews his old wound at its cruelest and drives him to that ultimate act of despair from which he held back for nine years.

Philoctetes can rightly be proud of the strength of heart (*eukardia*) that enabled him to wrest a life from this rocky island. Survival under such conditions is itself an heroic achievement. All the more striking, therefore, is the contrast between the wretched *technēmata* of his survival and the "evil artfulness" (*technē kakē*, 88; cf. 80) which Odysseus, "man of many devices" (*polymēchanos*, 1135), practices not against rude nature but against his fellow men. Neoptolemus does not escape the charge of exploiting the baser potential of human inventiveness when Philoctetes excoriates him for his "most hateful artifice (*technēma*) of clever roguery" (926–927).

The older members of Sophocles' audience might have recalled the opening of Euripides' *Philoctetes* of some twenty years before. There the hero, entering unkempt and "clothed in the skins of wild beasts," won the pity and sympathy of Odysseus (Dio Chrysostom 59.5). The Sophoclean Odysseus' cold, intellectual description of Philoctetes' "arts," as he assesses the risk to himself of a sudden return (41–47), lays the foundation for one of the central paradoxes of this play.

Like Ajax in the early play, Philoctetes is in a sense the last of the heroes. He possesses an uncompromising fidelity to his ideals, a firm sense of justice, a warm and ingenuous humanity, and a tenacity of life that recalls the heroic virtue of endurance, *tlēmosynē* or *karteria*. He has also known and befriended a race of heroes that has passed from the earth.

Like all the great heroes in Sophocles, however, his identity consists of opposites. If he is the most "civilized" man of his time, he is also the most bestial. To him, the desolate Lemnian landscape reflects a world order characterized by harshness, indifference to suffering, cruelty. Struggle and conquest rather than the gifts of the gods sustain his life.

Philoctetes' reinvention of technology is both a reenactment of primitive man's victory over nature and a regression to a world deprived of the potential graciousness and benevolence of the gods. This mode of life has achieved basic physical survival but neither the arts nor the community of civilized life. It is analogous to the precivilized stage of human life in Protagoras' myth, when men lived scattered, *sporadēn*.[14] He lives alone (*monos*) and deserted (*erēmos*). The latter word, as John Jones says, "tolls like a bell through this play."[15] Without friends and without city (*aphilos erēmos apolis*, 1018), he lacks both the private associations of *philia* and the public associations of the polis. As enfeebled as "a child without his dear nurse," in the chorus' description (702), he is deprived of the nurturing aid of an *oikos* in a setting which has no domestic, mothering females, only the dangerous Chryse in the remote past. Born "of one of the first houses" (*prōtogonoi oikoi*, 180–181), he dwells "apart from others with the dappled and hairy beasts" (183–184). The spatial frame of his life comprises the hostile sea on the one side and the wild, rocky terrain where he hunts on the other, both spaces beyond the pale of civilization.

Philoctetes: The Myth and the Gods

The responsibility for Philoctetes' loneliness lies with the Greek army at Troy. His life on Lemnos is the sign of men's deafness to one another, their inaccessibility to one another's needs.[16] The hero's desperate plea to Neoptolemus, "Do not leave me deserted thus apart from the track of men (*anthrōpōn stibou*), but take me to your house (*oikos*) thus saving me (486–488)," echoes Odysseus' opening description of Lemnos, "with no track of mortals (*astiptos*), no habitation" (2). The attributes which Odysseus gave the island now recur in the mouth of its only human inhabitant. His very eagerness to leave his lonely condition makes him vulnerable to deception and manipulation. Thus the enforced "savagery" of his external life is both a symbol of and a foil to the inward "savagery" of his disease. The same paradox is present in the bow: the weapon which sustains him in his brutalized life is a gift of the gods and a token of his own capacity for friendship. What makes the arrows so fatally effective is the poison of the bestial Hydra, monster of the swampy earth. But their unerring aim presumably derives from the bow's divine origin and association with Olympian Apollo.

Philoctetes' island life, then, like his soul, contains these two extremes. But it depends on the men who approach him whether they will evoke the capacity for bestiality or divinity, the spirit of death or the movement toward the "eternal *aretē*." When he addresses the rocky and marine setting, the beasts, and the cave of his primitive life (952, 936–937), he reenacts his return to the solitary, beast-like life. Now he has no companions with whom he could speak (938), and his companionship or associations (*synousiai*) are only with the beasts of the mountains (936), as previously it was with his disease (*tēs nosou synousia*, 520), which is also "a beast" (cf. 173, 265, 313, 698). Only with the renewal of trust in human friendship at the end can he reopen his converse with the divine, both in himself and in the world.

Every aspect of Philoctetes' status as a civilized man is ambiguous. He walks upright and hunts beasts, but he is also prey to the beastlike disease, because of which he limps. If *L*'s reading, *agrobatas*, is correct at 214, there is something savage about his walking too (cf. the "mountain-walking beast," *oreibatēs*, 955). As a hunter, he has a mode of life that belongs to the more primitive food-gatherers, not the *aneres alphēstai*, the truly civilized men who are tillers of the soil, according to the chorus' description at 707–711.[17] The word used of his "food" here, *phorbē*, connoting prey or carrion, recurs throughout the play in contexts that stress either the effort necessary for bare survival or the captured prey of the hunt.[18] So precarious is this reduced life that with the loss of the bow hunter may become the hunted and himself provide the *phorbē* to those on which he fed (*epherbomēn*, 957). His lonely life is like that of a shepherd, himself a marginally civilized figure, but his bucolic music is not that of the oaten flute: it is the "fearful shouting" of his pain (213–218; cf. 188–190).[19] The margin of survival on Lemnos has no surplus of energies left for song (see 209–218).

Philoctetes has invented shelter, but it is the savage shelter of a cave, like that of the Cyclopes who "dwell in caverns, not the shelter of houses" (Euripides, *Cyclops*, 118) and also lack wine, agriculture, organized civic life, and the means and knowledge of navigation (Homer, *Odyssey* 9.125–129, 275–278; Eur., *Cyclops* 113–124).[20] In Homer Odysseus must prove his human identity by escaping from a cave, whose savage inhabitant would devour him raw, as a lion devours its prey (*Odyssey* 9.292–293). In the anthropology of the Sophists early man "dwelt in mountainous caves and sunless gullies (Moschion, frag. 6.4–6, Nauck), "like beasts" (*Homeric Hymn* 20) until Athena and Hephaestus taught them the "shining works" of civilization.

Philoctetes' cave constitutes a "house" (*oikos*) of sorts, but it is a paradoxical "house that is no house" (*aoikos eisoikēsis*, 534) and does not provide "the nurture that makes a human house" (*oikopoios . . . trophē*, 36).[21] Made habitable by fire (*oikoumenē . . . pyros meta*), it furnishes everything except respite from the disease (298–299). Its rocky nature associates the lone inhabitant's dwelling with the desolation of the island itself (16, 159–160, 272, 952, 1002, 1262). It is an *aulion*, "a word suitable to rough or temporary quarters as to a bivouac";[22] even that is "most full of pain" (1087). The snake of the "raw-minded" divinity who embodies the cruelty of the place (*ōmophrōn*, 194) is the "housekeeper" (*oikourōn ophis*, 1328) of the shrine whose trespass has reduced the hero to this state. *Oikourein* elsewhere suggests the domestic life of a human *oikos*,[23] but here it denotes a venomous serpent whose "house" is open to the elements ("an uncovered shrine," 1327) and lacks the warmth of a human dwelling. Over against this paradoxically savage "housekeeping" stands the rekindling of human sympathies through Neoptolemus, whom Philoctetes comes to trust as "the unbelievable housekeeping of my hopes" (*oikourēma*, 867–868).

Although the movement back to a human *oikos* will not be easy, Philoctetes retains that sense of a "house" which marks a civilized man. His distant *oikos* on Malis represents "salvation" from savagery which he longs for but cannot attain (311, 487, 496). Reaching out of his loneliness and abandonment (470–471), he invokes those basic ties of civilized humanity from which he is cut off. He calls Neoptolemus *teknon*, "child," and entreats him "by your father, by your mother, by whatever in your house (*oikos*) is dear to you" (*prosphilēs*, 468–469). For all the rudeness of his house that is no house, this castaway can movingly convey the affection or *philia* that a house should contain (468, 492). His own example, finally, will recall the younger man to the heritage of his noble house, the *gennaiotēs* or "innate nobility" passed on from father to son in a house (475, 799, 1402; cf. 51, 995–996). In fulfilling his promise to send Philoctetes back to his house (*pempein pros oikous*, 1368, 1399), the fatherless youth both revives truly civilized values and recovers the heroic spirit of his own house.

Civilization as basic survival and civilization as personal and social morality come together in the symbolism of the bow. Philoctetes has the use of it as a material possession, a piece of technology essential to his survival. But so far he lacks the inward responsibility to the larger order, both human and divine, represented by the bow. The gift of Apollo to Heracles, the bow helps make the earth safe for civilized life and enables man to participate in the Olympian struggle against chaos and violence.[24] Heracles, according to Pindar, used it against the Giants (*Isthmian* 6.33–35), but Philoctetes uses it to hunt the small game that sustains his miserable and solitary existence. In the prologue of Euripides' *Philoctetes*, the hero pointed out to Odysseus how the bow provided his "nurture and clothing" (Dio Chrysostom 59.11). Drawing possibly upon the Euripidean or Aeschylean version, Accius has the hero lament how he uses "these arrows against a feathered, not an armored body, all glory thrown away"—lines which Cicero poignantly applies to himself on his retirement from public life.[25] This contrast between the heroic glory (*gloria, kleos*) of the bow's past and its unheroic uses on Lemnos seems to be a major element in the tragic conception of the myth.

The bare physical nurture (*trophē*) which the bow provides (32, 953, 1126, 1160) stands very far from the kind of nurture which it was meant to give its bearer. This latter "nurture," in the secondary sense of "education" or "upbringing," is a leitmotif of the play, from the very first sentence, where Odysseus addresses Neoptolemus as "nurtured (*trapheis*) by the best of fathers" (3). But it is the literal, not metaphorical, nurture with which Philoctetes must be primarily concerned. His possession of the bow only parallels the overall pattern of his life on Lemnos: the primitive hunter and food-gatherer's arts of bare survival, lacking the deeper civilizing art that Plato's Protagoras calls *politikē technē*, the skill that makes civic and communal existence possible and shapes "the ordered structure of cities and the unifying bonds of friendship" (*Protagoras* 322c).

In the course of the action the bow undergoes a twofold development. The hero's meeting with Neoptolemus renews that capacity for human warmth and affection which originally won him the bow from Heracles (see 654–670). Heracles' message at the end enables him to regain the divinity in the bow and in himself. Heracles restores Philoctetes' spiritual right to possess the bow and bring back together in him the parts of the bow, hitherto disjoined, necessary for civilization: technical proficiency (*technē*), and heroic companionship and personal responsibility (*philia*).

Neoptolemus' reciprocal recognition of the bow's "glory" (*kleina toxa*, 654) and divinity (his "revering it, as a god," 657), sets into motion his own rite de passage to heroic adulthood, after the pattern of his illustrious father, Achilles.[26] Leaving behind his "false" father, Odysseus, he also leaves behind the Odyssean conception of the bow, an instrument of success obtained through guile, lying, and treachery. This narrower, instrumental view of the bow—shared, albeit in different ways, by both Odysseus and Philoctetes—gives way to its broader meaning as a gift of the gods, immortal and bearer of a god-given destiny.

The bow has its rightful place on the field of battle at Troy not on barren Lemnos. Yet Troy is not worthy of the bow until its bearer creates a human and heroic basis for its return, and this he does in reestablishing with his young companion the kind of *philia* which Heracles had once established with him.[27] Odysseus' attempt to gain the bow by "hunting down" its rightful owner both reflects his unworthiness to bear it and undercuts the supposedly civilized order constituted by the army at Troy. As in the earlier plays—and particularly *Antig-*

one, *Oedipus Tyrannus*, and *Trachiniae*—the civilized place is open to the savagery of the wild, and the two polarities cross over into one another before a valid definition of civilization can emerge.

III

Seen in such terms, the *Philoctetes* closely parallels the *Antigone* and the *Oedipus Tyrannus* in its critique of man's pride in the autonomous power gained through rationalism and technology. The pacification of the natural world still leaves man brutalized, ensavaged (227), unless he also finds his way to a larger order that gives his life a meaning beyond physical survival, *sōtēria*. Participation in this larger order constitutes one aspect of the undying piety or reverence, *eusebeia*, which Heracles enjoins on Philoctetes and Neoptolemus in his closing lines (1440–1444).[28] Without this reverence Philoctetes must remain "diseased." A dwelling warmed by fire is the best that Philoctetes can achieve on his island and that "provides everything except not being diseased" (298–290).

Worship and piety are a touchstone for the quality of civilized life. But if, in Heracles' injunction, reverence accompanies the enlargement of the hero's perspective from survival to things eternal and divine, it also points up the hypocrisy in the society which cast him out. Besides alleging that he was only following orders (6), Odysseus uses worship as his excuse: the army could not perform libations or sacrifices with that terrible screaming, the "savage cries of ill-omen" (*agriai dysphēmiai*, 10). When he learns that he has been tricked into going back to Troy against his will, Philoctetes throws that argument back in Odysseus' face (1031–34): "O man most hated by the gods, how am I not lame and foul-smelling for you now? How, if I sail, can you burn your offerings? How make your libations any more? For that was your excuse for casting me forth." Leaving Philoctetes on Lemnos now without the bow not only reenacts the original abandonment but even exacerbates the cruelty. Then as now, on Lemnos as on Troy, with or without the bow, Philoctetes stands as a reproach to the supposedly civilized society which can expose an invalid on a deserted island and promote an Odysseus.

The theme of hunting focuses the ironies of civilized values in the play. As his one means of procuring food, hunting is an indication of the hero's fortitude as well as his misery. But on the scale of civilized values hunting occupies an ambiguous place.[29] The chorus, as we have noted, contrasts his meager hunter's diet, "food for his belly" (710), with the "crops sown in holy earth . . . by gainful men," tillers of the soil (706–707). Regarding hunting as a lower stage of culture than farming, they exhibit the familiar Greek attitude: agriculture is the civilized activity par excellence, the model for all stable, orderly social life.[30] Like Euripides' half-savage Cyclops (Homer's has wine), he does not "sow Demeter's grain" or enjoy "Bacchus' drink, the flowing juice of the vine" (*Cyc.* 121–124).

The chorus pities his ten years of enforced abstinence from wine, a deprivation all the more striking as Lemnos from Homer on was famous for its wine.[31] Its divinities, the mysterious Cabiri, were protectors of wine and wine-making, and Thoas, its mythical king, is the son of Dionysus. Its barrenness in the play, however, is further set off by contrast to "Peparethus rich in grapes," where the pseudo-merchant is heading "home" (548) in a speech carefully concocted to deceive Philoctetes. Thus even this simple activity is drawn into the ambiguity which surrounds all civilized institutions in the play.

Philoctetes is, of course, far worse off than the Cyclops. He is compared to a shepherd but lacks both herd and music (213–219). The "track" which he "plows" to secure his food is only the mark of his diseased foot, a "furrow" from which nothing can grow (cf. 162–163). What "blooms" for him on this barren island is the "disease" itself (258–259) which cuts him off from civilized life and civilized food. Like the blooming "flower of madness" in *Trachiniae* and the "burgeoning" of evils in *Electra*, this inverted agricultural imagery touches the nerve of the hero's tragic suffering.[32]

Removed from the fruitfulness and regularity of agriculture, Philoctetes leads the lonely life of the hunter, apart from others but close to the "dappled or shaggy beasts" on which he preys (182–187), crying out like them and to them (186–187, 936–939), neither hearing nor speaking human words.[33] Odysseus' guile reduces Philoctetes to a stage even below this: deprived of the bow, he will become a prey to those he preyed on, a hunter tracked down and eaten by the beasts he used to hunt (956–958). Literally to be "hunted" by the beasts, he and his bow are metaphorically "hunted" by Odysseus. In the prologue Odysseus speaks repeatedly of "catching" (*labein*) Philoctetes or his bow.[34] He envisages his meeting with the castaway in the same terms (*heloito, labein*, 47). This general vocabulary of catching, however, passes, by way of talk of trickery (*kleptein*, 55, 57, 77), into a full-fledged metaphor of the hunt. Whereas Odysseus takes refuge behind a screen of words for theft, device, craft, and gain,[35] Neoptolemus blurts out the truth: "The bow must be hunted then (*thēratea*, 116) if this is so." Later the false merchant, with Neoptolemus standing by, calls Odysseus' capture of the prophet Helenus "a fine hunt" (*thēran kalēn*, 609). The metaphor characterizes the underlying brutality of the man and his methods. Men are objects to be pursued for specific goals. The hunting image connects this instrumental view of human beings with the general inversion of civilized values that it implies. It overturns that basic subordination of beast to man which constitutes one of the definitions of civilization.

Neoptolemus' changing attitude toward Philoctetes also changes his relation to the theme of hunting. At the point when Neoptolemus sees beyond Odysseus' selfish interpretation of the oracles he also rejects the reduction of Philoctetes to subhuman status that the hunt implies. In his new perception of Philoctetes' rights, announced in oracular and heroic hexameters, he begins to doubt the validity of this "hunt" (839–840): "I see that we have this hunt (*thēran*) for the bow all in vain if we sail without him." With the success of Odysseus' plot, however, Philoctetes, the captured prey, bitterly applies the hunting image to himself twice in rapid succession (1004–1009):

> My hands, what you suffer lacking your own bow, hunted down (*synthērōmenai*) by this man here. You, incapable of a healthy or free thought, how you crept stealthily upon me, hunted me (*ethēraso̅*), taking this boy here as your screen (*problēma*), unknown to me, unworthy of you but worthy of me.

Philoctetes has been cornered, stalked, caught, and tied up so that he has not even the power to kill himself, again like a trapped animal. True to his instrumental attitude to human beings, Odysseus, as Philoctetes sees him, has even made use of Neoptolemus as the "screen" or "blind" behind which he could lie in wait for his prey, whereas Philoctetes views the lad in terms of his worth (*kataxios*, 1009).

Moving from metaphor to reality, hunting becomes grimmer as Philoctetes first recognizes the betrayal and pictures the degradation of the hunter now hunted (957–958): "Dead, I shall provide a feast (*daita*) to those on whom I fed, and those I hunted before will now hunt me." Soon afterwards he addresses the beasts as hunters ("winged hunters," *ptanai thērai*, 1146), and elaborates the details (1155–57): "Come creeping now, to sate your jaws at last taking your fill of my quivering flesh, death in return for death." "Quivering flesh," *sarkos aiolas* (1157), might refer, as Jebb thinks, to his diseased skin, spotted and unsound. But the primary connotation of the adjective is the rapid, shimmering effect of glancing light, and it suggests rather the rapid movement of beasts of prey, darting about the white body as they tear it apart. In any case, the gruesome detail reflects the horror of seeing himself as a piece of carrion. It may also hint at Philoctetes' own proclivity to identify with the forces of the wild and with the self-destructive qualities in himself which that identification, that "inner" savagery, implies. Neoptolemus' pity for the man reverses the image of the hunted beast. Odysseus the stalker (1007) now finds himself "stalked by fear" as his whole hunt proves futile and Neoptolemus gives back the bow.[36]

Even earlier, however, Neoptolemus' burgeoning compassion for this savage hunter begins to reverse the meaning of hunting and to establish different possibilities of human association. As Philoctetes suffers a sudden attack of his disease, he lets forth a series of terrible shrieks (745–746, 754), after which he entrusts the bow to his new-found friend (762ff.). At the second outcry Neoptolemus asks, "Is this the terrible whistling on (*deinon to episigma*) of the disease," to which Philoctetes replies, repeating the word "terrible," *deinon*, "Terrible and not speakable. But pity me" (755–756). "Whistling on," *episigma*, is a metaphor of hunting.[37] It is used of calling hounds to the prey. But on the heels of this hunting metaphor comes the direct, simple appeal of one human being to another, "But pity me," three straightforward words, in Greek as in English. Neoptolemus, the first character to use an explicit hunting image (110), is confronted by an appeal in the face of which he cannot retain the role of hunter pressed upon him by Odysseus. His agitation appears in the sharp question of tragic decision, *ti drasō*, "What shall I do" (757). Then he cries out in compassionate response to the other's suffering: "Alas, alas, poor, miserable man, shown truly miserable through your many sufferings" (759–760):

ἰὼ ἰὼ δύστηνε σύ,
δύστηνε δῆτα διὰ πόνων πάντων φανείς.

Not only does the exclamation *iō iō* break into the middle of the line, but the repeated "miserable," *dystēne*, and the alliteration of *d* and *p* intensify the emotional effect. In this response of the young "hunter" Odysseus' schemes meet a double reversal: the hunter feels compassion for his prey, and he actually returns the once hunted object (116), the coveted bow, to its rightful possessor. What was before hunted treacherously is now bestowed, in compassionate spirit, freely and in trust.

The image of 755 has another significance for the hunting theme. This hunter of wild animals is already "hunted" by his own disease. His disease, like Heracles' in the *Trachiniae*, is called "devouring" (*nosos diaboros*, 7; *adēphagos nosos*, 313) or "biting" (*dakethymos*, "biter of the soul," 706), and he himself is "devoured" by it as by a ravening beast (745; cf. 313 and *boskein*, 1167).[38] His foot is *enthēros*, "the dwelling of a beast" (698).[39] Metaphorically, then, he is the prey of a nonhuman force and thus doubly removed from the human hunting practiced by Odysseus. As a hunted creature he is doubly deserving of compassion: he is hunted by men as a victim of Odysseus' plot, and he is hunted by his disease as part of a mysterious divine destiny. This second significance of the hunt opens the way to a new relation between him and Neoptolemus, as the hunter, finding his prey already hunted in another sense, gives up the relation of hunter-animal agreed on in the prologue (116) for a fellowship of men who can entreat and bestow the uniquely human gift of pity (756).[40]

IV

Sophocles' great ode on civilization in the *Antigone* begins with man's conquest of the sea. To Philoctetes, cut off from humankind on "sea-girt Lemnos" (1–2), sailing is the means of rejoining civilization. But this art, like that of commerce closely associated with it, raises the question of who is civilized, who savage. It recurs repeatedly in connection with the hero's cruel betrayal by his erstwhile comrades-in-arms. He recreates for Neoptolemus the terrible moment ten years ago when he awoke on Lemnos and "saw the ships with which I sailed (*naustolein*) gone, all of them, and no man in this place to aid me or share the toil of the disease with which I suffered" (279–282). Neoptolemus, serving Odysseus' plot, has to fend off his victim's eagerness to set sail. He comes up with a lame excuse about contrary winds (635–640), but Philoctetes pessimistically moralizes (641–644):

> Phil.: Sailing is always good when you flee evil.
> Neopt.: No, but [the breeze] is adverse for them as well.
> Phil.: Robbers and pirates never have an adverse wind when there's a chance to steal and plunder by force.

At the moment of betrayal, Philoctetes throws it in Odysseus' face that his sailing to Troy was marked by deception and compulsion (*klopē, anagkē*), whereas Philoctetes himself sailed willingly—only to be abandoned in misery and dishonor (1025–28). At the end, however, Neoptolemus, ready to sail back to Greece with Philoctetes, makes good the previous deception in his promise with an echo of the very words of that deceptive sailing earlier (645 and 1402). But this voyage, though an important restitution to the hero and necessary for the reestablishment of trust on the human level, is countermanded by Heracles. Philoctetes' final sailing (*euploia*, 1465) from Lemnos is directed not by personal aims alone but by "the great Destiny" (*megalē Moira*) and the counsel of friends and the all-ruling divinity" (1466–68). The chorus' concluding "Let us go" recalls the earlier use of that word to urge departure under false pretenses (cf. 645 and 1402 with 1469). Their prayer to the Nymphs of the sea as "saviors in their return" (1470–71) then moves the theme of sailing from the human to the divine, from amoral technology to the acknowledgment of powers other than human rationality.[41]

Sketching Lemnos' topography early in the play, Philoctetes stressed the lack of harbors, the rarity of passing sailors, the lack of "profitable traffic" (300–303). These deficiencies mark the savagery of the place. In Thucydides' "Archaeology" the absence of trade is a mark of the ruder days of Greece (1.2.2).

The sea image of the "storm" of Philoctetes' disease which came from Chryse of the sea (*pontia Chryse*) is in keeping with the uncivilized aspect of the island. On the other hand an elaborate sequence of metaphors reveals commercial and maritime activities as a negative aspect of civilization.[42] Odysseus is unscrupulous in pursuing gain or profit (*kerdos*, 111). The merchant (*empolos*), instrument of his guile, awakens Philoctetes' suspicions by "holding a dark traffic of words" with Neoptolemus (578–579). A little earlier Philoctetes had insulted his old enemy as "the son of Sisyphus, bought in traffic (*empolētos*) by Laertes" (417). "I am sold" (*pepramai*, 978) is his indignant cry when he sees how he has been tricked. His captured bow even appears as a kind of ship, "rowed" (*eressesthai*) by the overinventive man of many devices (*polymēchanos*, 1135). That negative implication of craft or device (*mēchanē*) also characterizes Neoptolemus' Odyssean lie about his sailing to Troy, on an "elaborately fitted ship" (*poikilostolos naus*, 343). The first part of the adjective, *poikilos*, frequently connotes craftiness and trickery. It has exactly this sense in Odysseus' mouth when he describes his stratagem of the merchant to Neoptolemus in the prologue (130).

Always a matter of some suspicion in the land-based values of the Greek aristocracy, these metaphors of sailing and trade contribute to that blurring of the division between the civilized and the savage in this play. The intelligence that directs ships to the inaccessible coast of Lemnos is manipulative and self-seeking; the castaway, helpless before the sea-tossings of his disease (271), has a more humane and civilized spirit than the master of sea traffic, profit, and calculation.

V

Philoctetes' reinvention of fire, as we have seen, reenacts early man's triumph over nature by artifice (295–297). Yet here, as throughout the play, the themes of Sophistic culture history reflect a paradoxical coexistence of strength and weakness. In the prologue Philoctetes' "treasury" contains kindling among the "artifacts of the man of wretched works" (*phlaurourgou . . . technēmat' andros*, 35–36), in Neoptolemus' phrase. The untranslatable adjective *phlaurourgos*, "sorry craftsman" (Jebb), "worker in lowly arts," and Odysseus' ironical term "treasury" or "storehouse," *thēsaurisma* (37), suggest both the achievement and the limitation of this neotechnology. Fire, as Philoctetes says himself, brings survival, *sōtēria*, but no cure for the disease (297–299) which is both the cause and the condition of his ensavaged state.

In addition to fire as an instrument of human technology, there is the elemental fire of Lemnos with its volcanic associations. This is the so-called Lemnian fire of 799–801. Here the hero, in the grip of his disease (cf. 299), asks Neoptolemus to "burn" him "with that Lemnian fire that one calls upon in prayer."[43] This Lemnian fire belongs not to the heavens and the Olympian gods but to the earth and indeed to its mysterious depths, for it is associated with the volcanic fires of Mt. Mosychlos on the island. We may recall the association of volcanic fire with savagery and monstrosity in Euripides' *Cyclops* (297–280) and Pindar's *First Pythian Ode*. Antimachus of Colophon uses this Lemnian fire as an image of the violence of passion (frag. 46 Wyss = 44 Kinkel).[44] Death by fire, however, recalls Heracles' pyre on Mt. Oeta through which that hero passed upward to Olympus. Philoctetes, in fact, explicitly draws the parallel between his request that Neoptolemus burn him and his kindling of Heracles' funeral fire (801–803): "Burn me, noble lad; I too once deemed it worthy to do this to the son of Zeus, in return for these arms which you are now keeping." In this context Oetean pyre and Heraclean bow are pathetic and ironical. Some seventy lines earlier the chorus, abetting Neoptolemus' ruse, had sung of his return to his homeland "where the bronze-shielded hero draws near to all the gods, all-shining with divine fire (*theion pyr*) above the hills of Oeta" (727–729). But the death by fire for which Philoctetes entreats Neoptolemus here is a travesty of his old friend's death on the pyre. Instead of an upward mediation to Olympian gods and heroic fame, the Lemnian fire invoked here points downward to the earth, to a bare, animal existence, and to an inglorious death in sickness and misery on a deserted island. By recalling the divinity of the bow and the nobility of Philoctetes in winning it (668–670), the present passage both holds out the hope of reenacting that earlier heroic model and simultaneously measures the distance from it.

Entrusting the bow to a friend (804) is an important step toward that heroic and divine Oetean fire. When that trust is betrayed, Philoctetes expresses his bitterness in another image of fire (927–929): "You fire and utter monster, most hateful devising (*technēma*) of fearful villainy. What have you done to me! How have you deceived me!" The close collocation of fire and craft (*pyr, technēma*) repeats the pattern of the prologue (cf. 36–37).[45] But now that collocation signifies the breakdown of civilization. A few lines later Philoctetes makes his famous address to the harbors and headlands of his deserted island, "For I have no one else to whom to speak" (938). Fire and technology are here manifestations not of the intelligence, resourcefulness, and trust that can shape civilized human communities but of the craftiness, deceit, and cold, immoral calculation that attend their disintegration.

A little later in the same scene Philoctetes replies to Odysseus' threat to take him back to Troy by force with another imprecation involving fire (986–988): "Lemnian earth and the all-conquering, Hephaestus-fashioned flash, is this to be endured, if he will take me from your realm by force?" This cry parallels his insult of Neoptolemus in terms of fire in 927. Philoctetes seems to turn increasingly away from the fire of civilization. If he has reenacted early man's mastery of fire, he also remains in touch with that still unmastered fire of brute nature. Like the god of fire whom he resembles in his lameness, he is set apart by a closeness to fire's elemental, destructive force.

If this elemental, tellurian fire of Lemnos marks Philoctetes' alienation from men, the sacred fire of sacrifice indicates Philoctetes' alienation from the gods. The fire of his invention cannot cure his disease (299). Interrupted burnt offerings are Odysseus' excuse for casting Philoctetes off on Lemnos (8–11). Philoctetes' fire of bare survival on Lemnos is a measure of his distance from the divine fire on Oeta, but the excuse of interrupted fire-offerings at Troy (8–11, 1031–34) is another measure of the Greek host's ambiguous relation to civilized values and to the gods.[46]

This contrast between these two aspects of fire, the divine and the elemental, is analogous to that of the *Trachiniae* between the corruptive fire at Cenaeum and the purifying fire of Oeta. Before the onset of Philoctetes' disease the chorus associates this purifying fire with the hero's return to his homeland and its local divinities, the Nymphs of Malis (727–729). Possibly the "all-shining flash" of Heracles here is recalled in the "all-conquering flash" of the "Hephaestus-fashioned fire" in 986. But that Lemnian fire of Hephaestus is associated with violence, treachery, and the continued "savagery" of the disease. Thus when Philoctetes invokes the Lemnian fire in his request to Neoptolemus (799–803), it is to ask for death not to attain immortal life. The elemental fire of destructive hatred and passion figures in his final defiance of Odysseus, (1197–99): "Never, never will I go, not even if the fire-bearing hurler of lightnings comes here to set me ablaze with the flashes of his thunderbolt." As before, divine fire is only a destructive element (801–803, 927–929, and 986–987), even though he is now able to affirm his uncompromising integrity in terms of Olympian divinity. Earlier the heroic and divinizing fire had been only part of a plot to deceive (727–729). Its full celestial meaning remains hidden from Philoctetes until Heracles descends from Olympus and reawakens in Philoctetes' soul the meaning of the fire that he once kindled on Oeta.

It is part of the paradox of Philoctetes' tragedy that the elemental fire which sets him apart from the civilized world in the impoverished life on Lemnos is also the sign of his heroism: the vehemence of his passions, the uncompromising force of his ideals, the indomitable energy of his spirit. In touch once with the divine fire (728) that sent Heracles upward to Olympus, he now lives in a cave, both literally and metaphorically close to the elemental Lemnian fire of his deserted island. Human civilization is located at a point equidistant between Heracles' Olympian fire and the Lemnian fire of the wild landscape. At this mediate point belong the domestic fires of hearth and the sanctified fires of altars. But, as we have seen, it is just hearth and altars which the cave-dwelling hero so pathetically lacks.

VI

This tension between civilization and savagery has a rich background in the myths and cults connected with Lemnos. As a hellenotamias (state treasurer) in 443/2 and as a general in the Samian Revolt of 441–439,[47] Sophocles had ample opportunity to become familiar with the local cults and myths of the eastern Aegean. Lemnos had been an Athenian possession since Miltiades' conquest of the island a century before, and its cult of Hephaestus may have been influential in Athens.[48]

The destruction of civilized life is a major theme in the best known myth of the island, the Lemnian women's murder of their husbands. Aeschylus makes this deed one of the great paradigms of criminal violence in the central ode of the *Choephoroe* (629ff.). Sophocles wrote a *Lemnian Women*, in which "Chryse" seems to be the name of a city on the island (regarded, in that play, as inhabited).[49] This mythical atrocity has a kind of historical analogue in later times, when the "Pelasgians," the pre-Greek inhabitants of the place, kill their Athenian concubines and children (Herodotus 6.138). Both stories probably reflect the vicissitudes in the Greeks' struggle to possess the island, overcoming the hostility of its indigenous (female) powers. Possibly the conquest of Troy and the conquest of Lemnos served as parallels, both historic and mythic, for Greek expansion to the northeast. In both cases the result of violence is barrenness and the destruction of civilization. The Lemnian women's crime results in the extinction of all fires on the island. In an annual festival known as the Pyrophoreia, or "Carrying of Fire," the altars, fireless for nine days, were rekindled by sacred fire brought anew from Delos.[50] The Pelasgians' deed, like that of Oedipus in the *Tyrannus*, brings a plague upon the land: earth, animals, and women cannot bring forth (Herodotus 6.139). Yet it is by sacrificing to the Lemnian Nymphs, that Medea is able to end a famine that afflicts Corinth.[51] The Lemnian Nymphs at the end of the *Philoctetes*, we may recall, mark the hero's return from desolation and certain death to life and honor.

As this last detail suggests, Lemnos functions both as a real place and as a mythical point where opposites converge. The mysterious Lemnian fire, twice mentioned in the play, connects the island with the elemental power felt in volcanic places like Aetna or the Lipari islands.[52] Yet the island was also famed for its fertile vineyards. In the *Iliad* Jason's son exports its wine in a regular and profitable manner. It is a crossroads between Greeks and barbarians as well as between myth and history. In Demodocus' tale in the *Odyssey* Hephaestus deceives Aphrodite and Ares with the lie about a journey to its "well-built city," "the dearest of all lands to him" (*Odyssey* 8.283–284); but, as the duped Ares remarks a few lines later, its inhabitants are "the savage-speaking (*agriophōnoi*) Sintians" (8.294).

As a place where savage and civilized meet, where human *technē* emerges from the raw wilderness of nature, Lemnos is appropriately the birthplace of Cabirus, son of Hephaestus, whom one ancient source calls the first man.[53] Here Hephaestus, the fire god, lands when Zeus hurls him from Olympus. Here Prometheus brought to men the fire which he stole from the gods.[54] Although close to the major centers of Greek and Anatolian civilization, Lemnos is the place where Hera finds the god Sleep, whose usual abode is at the ends of the earth, in the "house of black Night."[55] It has the epithet "goodly," *ēgatheē*, but also a more ambiguous epithet, *amichthaloessa*, which may mean "inhospitable" or "misty," "smoky" (*omichlē*, "mist"). It is the site of important, unifying events like the Greek oath against the Trojans (*Il.* 8.230). Already in the *Iliad* it is the island where Philoctetes "suffers strong pain" (2.722), though there it is still called "goodly," not barren. It is also the place where Achilles sells the sons of Hecuba whom he has captured, including Lycaon (*Il.* 21.40–41). Possibly these varied and often contradictory mythical associations helped Sophocles turn into a desert an island whose non-inhabitants he had himself assessed to pay a yearly tribute of 900 drachmas some 35 years before writing *Philoctetes*.[56]

The inhuman savagery which surrounds Philoctetes on his island is closely bound up with the mysterious goddess, Chryse, "the golden," called *ōmophrōn*, "raw-minded," "savage" early in the play (194). Interestingly, it is not Philoctetes, but Neoptolemus who gives her this epithet, as he tries to comprehend Philoctetes' sufferings. They are "divine" (*theia*, 192) the work of the gods (*theōn meletē*, 196), in his judgment, an affliction awaiting the fated time when Troy should fall beneath his arrows (196–200). The theological explanation for suffering is not very cogent, nor is it clear where and how the cruelty of Chryse fits into such "work of the gods."[57] His later attempt, though propounded in a more confident tone, is not a great improvement: Philoctetes suffers "as a result of divinely sent fortune" (*theia tychē*, 1326) when he approached the snake that guards Chryse's shrine (1327–28).[58] Despite the gods' direct intervention at the end, Chryse remains a symbol of recalcitrant, impenetrable harshness, the embodiment, perhaps of the hostile, untamed spirit which protects these northern islands and their treasure (the "gold" of her name) from the invaders who would seize them.[59] Other fifth-century representations of the biting of Philoctetes suggest that possibly Chryse herself is a milder figure, an innocent bystander of sorts.[60]

Beside the Lemnian Nymphs mentioned at the end of the *Philoctetes*, there are traces of kindlier goddesses, a great goddess, Lemnos, who gives her name to the island, and Cabirian Nymphs connected with fertility.[61] But of these there is little trace in the play, and the nurturant abundance of Ge or Gaia, Mother Earth, is ambiguous or remote (391ff., 700). Instead of the generous mother, the sole female figure of the play is the distant, mysterious Chryse. Violating her holy places, guarded by a dangerous snake (the threatening power of the phallic mother?), is a serious trespass, punished by a debility in the foot (symbolic castration).

Although vaguely associated with the civilizing goddess, Athena,[63] Chryse has much closer affinities with the Tauronian or Brauronian Artemis, the goddess who guards the sea approaches to the land and protects it stubbornly from invaders.[64] Philoctetes calls the goddess *pontia*, "of the sea" (269–270). She may even be a form of the Thracian Bendis, the goddess whom the indigenous inhabitants would invoke against the Greek invaders.[65]

The three major mythic expeditions to the northeast begin with a heroic warrior appeasing this goddess by founding an altar to her. Jason, Heracles, and Agamemnon all have to undertake this task.[66] She seems to be a power, then, that adventurers in these alien and perilous shores have to confront. Through Chryse the land's implacable recalcitrance to conquest reasserts itself and avenges itself on its conqueror.

The bite of Chryse's snake not only causes but prefigures abandonment on this desolate, alien shore: the hero encounters the full savagery of nature and of men. Not only is Chryse "raw-minded" (194), but she has this epithet in a context that stresses Philoctetes' isolation, as he "suffers without men to care for him" (*kēdemōnes*, 195, which implies kinship as well as caring). In her association with the sea (269–270), she is almost a personification of the Lemnian setting which cuts Philoctetes off from human society. The very next line takes up the sea theme (*salos*, 271) but now as a metaphor for the disease which keeps the hero isolated on his inhospitable island, by the shore in the sheltered rock (272).

The fact that Philoctetes is attending or cleansing Chryse's altar, as some versions have it, does not mitigate the indifferent, irrational cruelty of her attack. In one version, however, she wounds him as he is attempting to found an altar to Heracles:[67] the goddess presumably repulses the conquering Hellenic hero invading her soil.

Chryse is the name not only of a goddess but also of a small deserted island near Lemnos. Sophocles mentions it in his lost *Lemnian Women* (frag. 353N = 384P). Some ancient sources even locate the biting or the abandonment here rather than on Lemnos itself.[68] An altar to Philoctetes was to be seen there as late as the first century A.D.[69] Sophocles has transferred to Lemnos the barrenness of Chryse island, but he has left the goddess Chryse her role as an active emanation of the unassimilable wildness of the area. In this connection we can better understand the reintegrative role of Heracles at the end: he is not only the successful male warrior overcoming another threatening female power,[70] but also the characteristically Greek civilizing hero whose efficient Olympian helpfulness answers the hostile sea and malevolent earth of Chryse and her snake.

Over against this mysterious goddess of wild places stand the civilizing figures connected with Lemnos itself. Chief among these is Hephaestus, associated with the island's Lemnian fire.[71] When Zeus hurled him from Olympus, he was received on Lemnos by the Sintians, whom, as we have noted, Homer regarded as half-barbarous, "speakers of a savage tongue" (*agriophōnoi Od.* 8.294). According to Hellanicus (*FGrHist* 4F7la), they invented fire and the forging of weapons, activities also attributed to Hephaestus. Accius, in his *Philoctetes*, possibly following Aeschylus, makes Lemnos the place where Prometheus brought fire to mortals.[72] Like Elba, also renowned for its metals, Lemnos was called Aithalea, "Blazing Isle," and its chief city was named Hephaistias.[73]

Users of fire, like the Sintians, frequently have a sinister aspect, perhaps because they are felt to stand too close to its elemental force.[74] Other mythical craftsmen of the area, like the Rhodian Telchines (from *thelgein*, "enchant," "charm") and the Idaean Dactyls, have the baleful powers associated with magicians.[75] Another set of mythic Lemnians, the Cabiri, are connected with the beginnings of technology.[76] Their name seems to derive from a Semitic word meaning "Great Gods." They had a major sanctuary on Lemnos near Hephaesteia, as well as in nearby Samothrace. Said to be the children of Hephaestus, they are also called Karkinoi, "crab-like," an epithet which suggests that they share his lameness, the distinguishing trait of smiths.[77] Divinities of wine, they are involved with agricultural as well as metallurgical technology, and they have "Mysteries" involving Dionysus' dismemberment. Like the Sintians they are connected with the very origins of man as a civilized being, user of fire and tiller of the soil. When human civilization is negated by the crime of the Lemnian women, they abandon the island.

All this may seem to take us far from the *Philoctetes*. Yet Philoctetes has some remarkable affinities with the Lemnian fire god of the island whom the Greeks identified with Hephaestus.[78] His lameness, like Hephaestus', belongs to the magical smith or worker of metals, set apart from his fellow men by his special power over fire and molten metals. Like Hephaestus, Philoctetes is exiled from his society through an embroilment involving a female divinity and brought back only with difficulty.[79] In both cases the return is necessary because the god or hero possesses an indispensable technical skill connected with the kindling of a magical fire. We may recall too his special pride in reinventing fire on his island (295–299).

Between Hephaestus and Philoctetes the mythical tradition established a number of explicit connections. In one legend Philoctetes is cured by the Lemnian earth on which Hephaestus landed when he fell from Olympus.[80] A variant of this story attributes his cure to one Pylios, a son of Hephaestus,[81] or to the priests of Hephaestus on Lemnos, who are especially successful in treating the bite of the water snake or hydros.[82]

Philoctetes may have begun as a divinity of the Troad connected with fire and smiths.[83] But Sophocles, perhaps building on the lost work of his predecessors, Aeschylus and Euripides, transforms and humanizes this remote mythical material. This culture hero stands outside of society not because of the taboos attaching to the quasi-magical art of using fire, but because of human cruelty and the long-term effects on his character of that treatment by his fellow men. He is not a demonic power like the Telchines or Cabiri nor a god like Hephaestus, but a man with human responses and sensibilities. Whatever magical power over fire the Lemnian god may have possessed is for Philoctetes a hard-won achievement. The primal power of Lemnos and its divinities lies far from him; the Lemnian fire did not help him in his battle to survive. If the lame smith represents the technological skill through which civilization advances, Philoctetes has that skill only in its most basic and reduced form and only after a hard struggle. Far from conferring any supernatural powers, fire, like his magical bow, is but another aspect of his miserable, fragile life and in fact places him at the very opposite pole of existence from those Lemnian fire gods to whom he may have owed his origins.

A central detail in Philoctetes' story links him closely with another important Lemnian myth, namely the foul smell of his diseased foot. This bad smell, *dysosmia* or *dysōdia*, also plays a major role in the myth of the Lemnian Women. Refusing to worship Aphrodite, they gain this unsocial affliction as a punishment from the goddess.[84] The result is a profound disruption of civilized life: the men refuse to sleep with their wives, and the women kill the male members of their households. The legend was kept alive in cult. "Even up to now," the fifth-century Lemnian historian Myrsilus wrote, "there was one day a year on which the women kept away their husbands and sons because of the bad odor."[85] In another sector of the Lemnian myth the Cabiri leave "because of the women's reckless deed" (*tolmēma*).[86] Thus both within the house and outside it civilization disintegrates.

Philostratus describes the rite of purification by which the Lemnians symbolically recreated civilized life each year: "In consequence of the crime perpetrated by the Lemnian women against their men . . . , Lemnos is cleansed, and once a year fire on the island is extinguished for nine days, and a sacred ship carries fire from Delos." After the proper ritual purification, this pure fire (*katharon pyr*) brought from over the sea is distributed to households and craftsmen, and "they say that they begin a new life from that point."[87] With the extinction of fire that results from the Lemnian women's crime, rudimentary civilized activities like cooking, offerings to the gods, the gathering of the family around the hearth all disappear. The importation of pure fire establishes them anew.[88] In this rite, as in the Lemnian myths which we have been discussing, the island appears as a place where the boundary between civilization and savagery nearly disappears, where wild nature thrusts itself more violently upon man.

Here, then, the basic elements of civilization stand out in sharper outline, more precious and also more exposed.

In this perspective the relation of Lemnos to Philoctetes' reduced mode of life becomes clearer and more significant. Like the Lemnians, he suffers a total breakdown of civilization in his abandonment on the island and has to recreate laboriously its basic element, fire (295–299). A number of legends establish specific connections between Philoctetes and the (historically earlier) crime of the Lemnian women. During the siege of Troy he was said to have attacked various islands off the Anatolian coast in the company of Euenos, Jason's son by the Lemnian queen, Hypsipyle.[89] In another account, the altar of Chryse, where he is bitten, is founded by Jason. The younger Philostratus tells the tale:

> Sailing to Troy and touching at the islands, the Achaeans searched for the altar of Chryse which Jason had founded when he sailed to Colchis. Philoctetes, from his memory of one of his adventures with Heracles, showed it to them, when a water snake approached him and shot its venom into one of his feet.[90]

The bad smell which leads to a disruption of sacrifices on Lemnos, for both Philoctetes and the Lemnian women, is the antithesis of the sweet savor which, in proper rituals, mounts up to the Olympian gods. We recall the thick smoke of the perverted sacrifice in the *Trachiniae* (766) and the smoky, sputtering altars in the *Antigone*, with its violated rituals of burial (*Antig.* 1006–1008). Philoctetes' alleged disruption of the fires of sacrificial rite (cf. 8–9) makes his savagery too a failure of civilized mediation between beast and god.

When he cited the interruption of rituals as the reason for leaving Philoctetes on the island, Odysseus displaced the disgust at the disease from smell to hearing the "savage cries of ill-omen" (*agriai dysphēmiai*) of his "shouting" and "groaning" (9–11). But in returning to this motif later, Philoctetes specifically cites the foul smell (*dysōdes*, 1032). In the earlier, treacherous discussions of taking Philoctetes on board, both parties allude more delicately to the smell (473–475, 483, 519–521). Neoptolemus' word, *synousia*, "association," "fellowship," in the last passage (520) can also refer more generally to the basic converse among men in society which such an affliction destroys. When Neoptolemus has withstood the test of the disease's virulent outbreak, Philoctetes joins smell and sound: it is a mark of the young man's "noble nature," he says, that he stood by "though filled with the shouting and the bad smell" (*boēs te kai dysosmiēs gemōn*, 876; cf. 520). When Neoptolemus offers his own and his followers' aid in helping the stricken man to get up, Philoctetes refuses the latter, "lest they be weighed down with the bad smell (*kakē osmē*) sooner than necessary, for the toil (*ponos*) of sharing a dwelling place with me (*synnaiein*) on the ship will be quite enough for them" (890–892). Here he concentrates on smell alone; and his word *synnaiein*, "live with," stresses the basic disruption of communal life that smell causes. Ironically, however, it is not the smell that detains Neoptolemus here. His ease or difficulty (cf. *eucheres*, 875) in having Philoctetes with him on the ship lies in a moral or spiritual dilemma, not a physical cause (902–903).[91] Sophocles plays the inward, emotional significance of the detail off against its physical, ritual meaning in 9–11.

Remote from the gods and the rites that could reach them, Philoctetes on Lemnos, like the worshipers in the Lemnian fire festival, suffers an eclipse of civilization. The Lemnian fire of his desolate landscape is, as we have seen, closely associated both with his brutalizing pain (800–801) and with the violence of his own hatred and anger (927, 986–987). It stands far from the pure fire of the Lemnian cult that marks the renewal of light and life at an annual celebration, far too from the divine fire which brought Heracles, "all-shining," to Olympus (727–729). The descent of Heracles from Olympus to Lemnos at the end touches the deserted island and the abandoned hero with the revitalizing fire of new life and puts the hero again in contact with the purer ritual fire which he himself once kindled on Oeta.

A number of related myths connect the theme of fire on Lemnos with an opposition between chthonic and Olympian and between death and rebirth (see Appendix). The snake which bites Philoctetes is named after water, *hydros*. Not only do Hephaestus and his priests have the power of curing this bite, but this "watery" snake's wound is, according to Philostratus, the only kind of snakebite which the fire god's Lemnian earth can cure.[92] This opposition between fire and water, familiar from Hephaestus' battle with the river Scamander in *Iliad* 21, is also an opposition between earth and sky:[93] the snake makes his appearance from the earth; Hephaestus arrives on Lemnos from the sky and after a period of exile on the island makes his way back to Olympus.

In a version of the Philoctetes legend told by Servius (on *Aeneid* 3.402), but possibly quite old, Philoctetes is wounded not by a snake, but by the *falling* of one of Heracles' arrows, poisoned by the Hydra's venom, on his foot. The reason is his disclosure of Heracles' burial place in the earth by stamping it with his foot, thereby denying Heracles' upward movement, through Hephaestus' fire, from earth to Olympus. He is punished by a serpentine creature (the Hydra) whose associations are with water and with the darkness of the earth. The later result is Philoctetes' loss of that civilizing fire which establishes an upward mediation between gods and men.

Philoctetes' sufferings on Lemnos parallel not only Hephaestus' (exile and return), but also Heracles': recall to life, through fire, after the deathlike exile of his life on Lemnos. His return to "life" in fact takes the specific form of being called forth from the dark cave, the place of certain death as well as removal from a civilized existence. Philoctetes' kindling of a holy fire on Oeta facilitated Heracles' upward movement to Olympus. His lighting of that fire in the past bears witness to those cooperative virtues of friendship, compassion, and reverence which Heracles' presence renews in him. A rite on Oeta in fact joined Philoctetes and Heracles together to commemorate this deed: burnt offerings to both figures were placed annually on an altar at the top of the mountain.[94]

Rebirth and renewal play an important part in the myths of Lemnos, obviously in the case of the Lemnian women and the renewal of the fire, which, as Burkert has shown, corresponds to a familiar type of ritual that celebrates the return of joy and vitality after a period of desolation and mourning.[95] The mysteries of the Cabiri too have affinities with agrarian rites of renewed fertility. Georges Dumézil has recognized in Cabirus himself the familiar figure of the fertility god who ritually dies and is brought back to life each year with the sprouting of the crops.[96] The healing properties of the Lemnian earth, especially with its Hephaestean associations, probably belong in the same context.[97] A myth told by Hesiod relates how the blinded Orion goes to Lemnos and there meets Hephaestus who has him led to the Sun who restores his sight.[98] Hephaestus himself suffers a nine-year exile on Lemnos, during which he acquires his magical powers, before his return to Olympus.[99] We may recall the annual cycle of the nine-day extinction of fire on Lemnos, as well, of course, as Philoctetes' own nine years of desolation.

What is straightforward, regular, and assured in myth and cult is ambiguous and problematical in the tragic recasting of the myth. Although an underlying pattern of death and rebirth is important in the play, it appears only in paradoxical form: Neoptolemus' initial restoration of the hero to "life" is a trick, and the true act of calling him forth from the cave to return the bow does not produce the desired result. To be sure, there is nothing like the drastic inversions of life and death that we have seen in the *Electra*, but even with the "happy ending" the expected pattern takes surprising turns. In the tragedy the antitheses of the mythic background give way to ambiguity. Fire, for example, is not simply a saving, civilizing power but has a violence that corresponds to the violence of Philoctetes' savagery (cf. 800–801, 927–928, 986–987) and thus to the paradox of his role as a civilizing, Hephaestean hero.

Thus no simple opposition of civilization and savagery will suffice to interpret this play. The ostensibly civilized world has its savagery, and vice versa. The limping figure, echo of a remote fire god, leads a life of wretched survival, subdued by fire's opposite, the watery elements of sea and water snake, while his own civilizing fire has its antisocial, savage side.

We cannot, of course, say for certain how many of these mythical elements entered actively into Sophocles' conception of the play. Much of the humanization of the myth had been done long before, by Homer, the Epic Cycle, Pindar, and of course his immediate predecessors in dramatizing the story, Aeschylus and Euripides. Still, Sophocles' familiarity with the myths and history of Lemnos may well have had something to do with his setting of the play, abandoned island and all. Lemnos' crippled and exiled smith god, its mysterious healing earth, its remote demigods of fertility and technology like the Cabiri and Sintians, its implacable local goddess and her dangerous snake with its chthonic and watery associations, the fearful crime of the Lemnian women, and the cult of lost and then renewed and purified fire offered rich and suggestive material. Here Sophocles would have found a focal point for his themes of loneliness and society, anger and friendship, the rise and cancellation of civilized values, and the ambiguities of the civilizing power itself.

VII

Philoctetes, we have suggested, is *agrios*, savage, not only in his relation to human society but also in his relation to the gods.[100] In his last attempt to persuade Philoctetes, Neoptolemus says that the disease comes from the gods, "from god-sent chance" (*ek theias tychēs*, 1326). He explained, a few lines before, that while men must endure "the fortunes given from the gods" (*tas ek theōn tychas dotheisas*, 1316–17), Philoctetes' ensavaged state (*ēgriōsai*, 1321) consists in clinging to his own misfortunes and in stubbornly rejecting well-meant advice, good will (*eunoia*), and friendship (1316–23). In his climactic plea Neoptolemus again brings together men and gods: "Trusting the gods and my words, sail away from this land with this man here, your friend" (*philos*, 1374–75). To sail from the barren, deserted island is to accept his place simultaneously in the divine order and in men's society. To do that is to become human again, to leave an existence of bare, animal-like survival and to accept goals and obligations that, as Heracles propounds, reach toward the timeless.

Heracles' speech, which does finally reintegrate Philoctetes into both the social and the divine order, exactly complements Neoptolemus', but at a higher level. Neoptolemus offers a present human friendship and speaks in general, remote terms of the gods (1316–17, 1326–28). Heracles himself embodies the presence of the divine and the immortal in human life. The friendship that Heracles recalls and renews, however important it is as a paradigm of heroic association (cf. 662–670), is now but a remote memory. And yet that memory, so important for human culture, is a vital and active force. It must be kept alive, and hence the importance of Heracles' specific instructions that Philoctetes bring the spoils of Troy to his pyre, "as a *memorial* (*mnēmeia*) to the bow" (1432).

As a spokesman of the divine will in which Philoctetes will again have a role, Heracles has his opposite in Odysseus. Like some of Sophocles' other less sympathetic, authoritarian characters, for example, Menelaus in *Ajax* and Creon in *Antigone*, Odysseus is quick to identify his own aims with the gods' and to make the gods an extension of his own will. His treatment of the oracles shows the same tendency to subordinate reverence to expediency.[101]

Philoctetes, to be sure, has his bitterness, natural enough, toward the gods. But he has also an instinctive sense of reverence (662, 738) and respect for the rights of a suppliant (773, 930, 967). The very intensity of his repeated demand for divine justice implies a depth of religious concern, embittered though it is, far above Odyssean manipulation of divine enunciations.[102] The passionate blasphemer is often the believer's hidden side; the man of cynical and superficial observance may be the more truly irreligious spirit. Even in his bitterest, most lonely moment Philoctetes has an insight, albeit obscure, into divine purposes working behind the present events (1035–39):

> Having done injustice to me, you will perish, at least if the gods care for justice. But I know full well that they do care, since you would not have set forth on this expedition for a wretched man like me unless some god-sent spur (*kentron theion*) for me drove you.

In the light of such a passage Heracles' closing words about reverence and the imperishable piety (1440–44) do not fall on an entirely unreceptive spirit. Here, as elsewhere in the play, Heracles is the voice of Philoctetes' nobler, truly human, civilized self.

Philoctetes' wound, Neoptolemus tells us, comes from "divinely sent chance" (1321; cf. 1315–16). But this cruel affliction from a remote, arbitrary goddess also has, or assumes, significance as an emanation of human character and human emotions.[103] The suppurating ulcer which makes him an abomination to men is the festering of his own hatred. In this respect the play deserves a place beside Mann's *Magic Mountain* as one of the great studies of the corrosive effects of illness on the human soul.

The disease is not merely a symbol. It has an objective existence as a divinely inflicted punishment. Here, as in the *Oedipus Tyrannus*, we are left with a complementation of internal and external causation, human and divine factors. Like Oedipus, Philoctetes may have begun life with a nature that is its own source of pain or suffering (cf. *OT* 674–675). As in the case of Oedipus, the circumstances of Philoctetes' life, his fate or destiny, have pushed that nature into its present path. Yet for Sophocles the converse also holds: such a nature draws to itself its appropriate destiny; it shapes its own gods. The question of what factors conspire to make us what we are is never fully answerable in Sophocles. Something always eludes our grasp, and that is the daimon or the "divinely sent chance" or "the divine spur" which lies behind the controllable and rationally explicable movements of men's lives.

Outwardly the wound is an affliction that results from a goddess' mysterious wrath. Inwardly it is the correlative of Philoctetes' bitter soul, the poisonous hatred rankling in him all these years. In this inward significance the wound itself is *agrios*, savage (176, 265), the reflection of that trait in Philoctetes' character. Likewise the pain, *algos*, which the hero feels refers both to inward, emotional state and to physical suffering.[104] *Algos* alternates between the two meanings throughout the play, and in at least one passage includes both dimensions of Philoctetes' sufferings (339–340).

When Neoptolemus unsuccessfully attempts to persuade him to leave his island, the two meanings occur within twenty lines of one another. Unable to reconcile himself with the Atreids at Troy, Philoctetes says (1358–59): "It is not so much the pain (*algos*) of things gone by that bites me (*daknei*), but I seem to foresee what I must still suffer from those men." He then asks Neoptolemus to take him home to Greece, not Troy; but Neoptolemus urges him to go instead to Troy, "to those who will stop you and your suppurating walk from pain (*algos*) and save you from the disease" (*nosos*, 1379–80). Both the inward and the outward pain, like the emotional and physical disease, must be healed together. The literal bite of the divinely sent snake (cf. 265–267, 705) parallels the "bite" of "things gone by" in 1358 (cf. also 378). That metaphorical biting recalls also the animal metaphor of the disease as savage or bestial. To heal Philoctetes, Neoptolemus must feel again his initial pain at Odysseus' deceit (86; cf. 66) and refuse to serve as the screen for those "unhealthy" plots (*mēden hygies phronōn*, 1006).

Pain and disease are not only the projections of Philoctetes' inner savagery: they are also literal emanations of the gods' will. Hence the full cure must be both literal and metaphorical. It must combine reconciliation with both men and gods. The prerequisite, on the human level, for his sailing to Troy is, as Neoptolemus says in this scene, "trust in the gods *and* in my words" (1374).

The very mysteriousness of the wound is basic to the meaning of the play. Lessing long ago grasped this point better than some modern scholars:[105]

> How wonderfully the poet has known how to strengthen and deepen the idea of bodily pain! He chose a wound (for the circumstances of the story may be considered by us as dependent upon his choice, inasmuch as, on account of these advantageous circumstances, he chose the whole story), he chose, I say, a wound and not an internal malady, because he was able to make a more vivid representation of the latter than of the former, however painful it may be . . . This wound, moreover, was a divine punishment; a poison worse than any to be found in nature incessantly raged within him, and it was only the vehement access of pain which had its appointed limit and then the wretched man fell into a stupefying sleep, in which he was obliged to refresh his exhausted nature in order that he might again enter upon the same path of suffering . . . A natural poison working for nine years without causing death is infinitely more improbable than all the fabulous wonders with which the Greek has ornamented his story.

Philoctetes cannot return to the human world with his burden of hatred and bitterness symbolized by the mysterious wound. He must come to terms with his past, with the society which rejected him, and with the gods from whom the wound originates. Even being healed at Troy does not wipe out the ten years of frightful suffering.

Sophocles never fully clarifies the exact reason for Philoctetes' wound. In Euripides' version, some twenty years before, sacrifice at Chryse's shrine was necessary to the success of the war; only Philoctetes, who had been there earlier with Heracles, knew its location.[106] Ironically, Philoctetes' solidarity with the aims of the expedition is rewarded with total isolation. Though Sophocles does not describe the circumstances in which Philoctetes was bitten (details which Odysseus would not want to clarify in any case), he does have the hero bitterly contrast his willing service on the expedition with Odysseus' reluctance (1025–28). His early zeal to further the army's success is now matched by an equal intensity of refusal to help. Forced to serve as a kind of ritual scapegoat for the army—a parallel with an earlier human victim, Iphigeneia, comes to mind—, he now considers it his bitter enemy.

In the strange shapes of the gods' justice, however, the army's earlier need for the hero is now reenacted in the oracles about the bow. Once again, Philoctetes possesses something indispensable for the success of the war against Troy.

But now the pain and disease that separate him from gods and men have a new meaning in the divine scheme. Earlier Neoptolemus had dimly realized that to Philoctetes belonged the crown of glory at Troy (841). That human and heroically defined reward gives way before a more basic task at Troy, the cure of his "disease" in both its literal and its metaphorical sense. This reward is for Philoctetes alone, not for the army. It belongs to the area of divine causation and supernatural events (cf. 1437–38) and has nothing to do with the original aims of the expedition.

The wound and the divine chance which causes it embody the unknown, arbitrary-seeming circumstances that stamp a human life with its peculiar destiny. That interaction of circumstance and character makes us what we are. In this sense the wound partially resembles the curse of Oedipus. Both express Sophocles' conviction that "life is dangerous and its issues momentous."[107] Those who do not themselves suffer can label this arbitrariness "divine chance," as Neoptolemus does, or "compulsive chance" as Tecmessa does in the *Ajax* (*Ajax* 485, 803, *anankaia tychē*). Neoptolemus, and even to some extent Tecmessa, can accept the arbitrariness, for their concern is with life and continuity in the world as it is. What defines the tragic hero, however, is his hopeless nonacceptance of the world. For him, as for Oedipus, Jocasta's "life at random" is not acceptable. Chance or necessity is not a valid explanation, unless, as in Philoctetes' case, divinity suddenly intervenes to reveal some other dimension of the gods' will, some meaning of life in this world which has remained hidden up to now. At that point, when the conflict is resolved and the world yields to the hero, he ceases to be tragic.

This is what happens to Philoctetes at the end of the play. He is an Ajax to whom the gods yield at the eleventh hour. He is not forced to the ultimate conflict with an intransigent reality that would condemn him to a life of suffering, diseased and isolated to the end of his days. But the gods can yield only because Philoctetes, unlike Ajax, has a Heracles in his past and a Heracles alive somewhere within him now. The spark of that heroic companionship is still there to draw Neoptolemus, who can find it and rekindle it into the saving warmth of life.

VIII

Like the wound, the bow has both a psychological and a theological significance. As the focal point of personal transactions between men, it is the reward of Philoctetes' benefaction to Heracles (670) and the token of growing trust in Neoptolemus: he will let him handle it with a generosity that he extends to his other possessions too (658–659). At the onset of his disease Philoctetes hands the bow to Neoptolemus not merely out of helplessness but as a reminder of the reciprocity of trust between them (762–766): "Take this bow . . . *as just now you asked me for it.* Keep it and guard it until the present pain of this disease abates." As the wound links human and divine in a negative way, manifesting the rage of a violated divinity, the bow is the source of special favor from the gods and ultimately serves to reconcile an embittered hero with angered divinity.

Thus the wound and the bow have interlocking and complementary mediating functions. The wound, which removes Philoctetes from gods and men, is answered by the bow which joins him both with the gods through Heracles and with men through its heroic future at Troy. The wound effects a downward mediation. It reduces Philoctetes to beastlike status on Lemnos and is itself beastlike: it bites and devours him as if it were a beast of prey attacking its victim. If recent interpreters are right about *enthēros* in 698, that diseased foot appears as inhabited by the "beast" of the disease.[108] The bow, on the other hand, is not only the gift of Heracles on his upward movement from the pyre to Olympus but also, as the civilizing gift of Apollo to Heracles, the weapon for exterminating bestial and monstrous violence from the world of men. Initially only the means of subduing the beasts of Lemnos for food and bare survival, the bow eventually enables him to leave the deserted island and to achieve the immortal excellence promised him at Troy by its previous owner (1420). The bow, then, mediates between man and god as the wound mediates between man and beast. As the wound brings Philoctetes into contact with the elemental fire of Lemnos (799–800), the bow puts him in touch with the divine fire of Heracles' pyre (727–728).

Each major figure in the play defines himself through his relation to the bow.[109] To Odysseus it is an instrument of war, a necessary acquisition, the key to success. To Neoptolemus it carries an aura of the remote, glorious heroism of his nobler aspirations. It opens to the wider horizons worthy of his lineage and brings him his first glimpse of the world where men like Achilles and Heracles have wrought their great deeds, where he too is destined to find his path (see 654–675). Although initially he seeks the bow as part of Odyssean "profit" (*kerdos*, 111), he finds in it the stirrings of his Achillean *aretē*. Instead of being the goal of calculation and deceit it arouses passionate desire (*erōs*, 660).

Moved by the younger man's ardor, Philoctetes feels again the divine and heroic effulgence of the bow's past. In sharp contrast to the food-getting functions to which he has, perforce, reduced the bow on Lemnos (932–933, 1126, 1282), he now speaks of excellence (*aretē*) and benefaction (667–670). Sophocles takes up Heraclitus' play on *biós* "bow" and *bíos* "life," "livelihood" (931–933, 1282);[110] but his point is not the philosopher's dark presentation of the mysterious laws of the cosmos but the reduction of a heroic weapon to unworthy tasks.

In one respect Philoctetes' use of the bow resembles Odysseus'. Both men, in different ways, evade and pervert its divine and heroic meaning. The one uses the civilizing gift of a god to perpetuate a life of savagery and isolation on a deserted island; the other does violence to a helpless cripple and takes advantage of a noble nature.

Ironically, Philoctetes evokes the bow's heroic past ("the holy arms of Heracles, born of Zeus," 942–943) at the moment when he turns away from human companionship and back to his associations with the beasts of the mountains (946ff.). This passage marks the low ebb of personal friendship and heroic values in the play. Betrayed, as he thinks, by the man to whom he entrusted the bow in a bond of friendship and benefaction analogous to that which existed between him and Heracles (670), he sees the total victory of villainy, craftiness, and deceit (*panourgia, technēma, apatē*, 927–929), the exact opposites of the heroic values for which the bow once stood. What a falling off there is from this heroic spirit is measured by the contrast between the bow as mark of heroic identity in 260–262 and the bow as object of present desperate need in 932:

> Child, son born of Achilles, your father, I am he of whom you have heard tell, perhaps, the master of the arms of Heracles.

> Give back, I beseech you, give it back, I entreat you, child.[111]

Later, deprived of the bow and utterly alone, Philoctetes addresses the bow as he had just addressed his rocky dwelling (1081ff., 1087ff.) and endows the lifeless object with the love and compassion that he finds lacking among men (1128–31): "Beloved bow, forced from loving hands, . . . perhaps, if you have any consciousness (*phrenes*), you look pityingly upon me." Yet some of that harshness rests with Philoctetes, for at this furthest remove from men he rejects the human friendly feeling (*philotēs*) of the chorus (1121–22) for the *philia* of the inanimate weapon. To move back to the heroic significance of the bow requires the risks of lonely daring and brave decisions. This task now rests with Neoptolemus, and when it is accomplished the bow can again become a bond of trust, compassion, and friendship between men.

In the past the bow served the most panhellenic of Greek heroes, one who championed Greek against barbarian, for Heracles also fought at Troy. Yet Odysseus fears that Philoctetes will use it against him, a fellow Greek (75–76, 104–107). His fears are realized late in the play when Philoctetes prepares to let fly one of those "invincible shafts" (105) against his old foe (1299–1304). Neoptolemus, having grasped something of the heroic obligations which the bow confers, intervenes: "For neither you nor me is this a noble act" (*kalon*, 1304). It is as inappropriate to use the bow to serve private revenge as to maintain bare survival. Neoptolemus' new relation to the bow proves him the son of Achilles, an Achilles purged of his divisive and solitary spirit. We see, in retrospect, that Philoctetes was right in instinct to entrust the bow to his care.

Philoctetes' offer to use the bow to defend Neoptolemus against Greek reprisals (1405–1408) pulls back to the vindictive, isolating side of the heroic character. Although the bow, so used, would now help another man and not merely procure bare existence for a solitary castaway, this proffered use would still keep alive the old quarrel and disrupt rather than create civilized order. It would cancel out whatever the war has so far achieved and foment dissension among the Greek states once united at Troy. It would but extend the use to which Philoctetes has put it on Lemnos, contravening the ordering spirit in which his mentor wielded it and passed it on to him. His offer to Neoptolemus just before Heracles' appearance would enclose even his new-found friendship in the narrow confines of his hatreds. Caught in an insoluble dilemma of conflicting loyalties and values, Neoptolemus accepts Philoctetes' offer of the bow, the only honorable choice. Heracles' appearance shows it to be a tragic choice and from his perspective the wrong choice. The god can speak for the bow's deepest meaning and cut the knot that prevents the realization of that meaning in the complex, conflicted world of men.

When Philoctetes and Neoptolemus participated in the quasi-ritual which affirmed their fellowship of the bow (654–675), its heroic aura embraced only the two of them. Though they stand at a moment of high emotion, the discovery of nascent friendship and trust, they are still isolated individuals on a deserted island. That incipient reconciliation with Philoctetes' heroic past will be enlarged to a public restoration of heroic values and society, and this Heracles does. Heracles completes the process begun by Neoptolemus. A hundred lines after the ritual of the bow Philoctetes would "do obeisance" (*proskyson*) to divine envy (776–778): "Do obeisance to the envy (of the gods) so that the bow may not be a source of many sufferings to you and may not be to you as it was to me and its possessor before me." Philoctetes here views the bow as a source of suffering and divine malevolence. The bitterness of his disease isolates him from the positive meaning of the bow. But, as we have seen, Neoptolemus had shown him that other side of the bow, the heroic glory to which it calls and the "obeisance" as to a god which it invites (657, *proskysai*).

While both Philoctetes and Neoptolemus call the bow divine or holy (191, 657, 743), neither, as yet, knows the reason for its divinity, Neoptolemus because at this point he is still an instrument of Odyssean guile, Philoctetes because the gesture through which he won the bow belongs to a distant past which he must recover. Heracles' presence at the end makes the bow once more a link between God and man and recalls Philoctetes to what it means to have practiced the kindness or benefaction (*euergetein*, 670) that originally won him the weapon.

Part of the bow belongs to divinity, the inward divinity of the hero's *aretē* and the external, mysterious aspect of the divine will that makes the bow and its owner indispensable for victory at Troy.[112] Another part belongs to human ties: heroic companionship and social responsibility. If Heracles recalls Philoctetes principally to the divine potential of the bow, Neoptolemus recalls him to its human meaning.

At the beginning of the play the bow embodied a false relation between men, a relation based on deceit, manipulation, and self-aggrandizement. Now it becomes the token of a new friendship and a new trust, requiring decision, courage, and self-sacrifice. Where Neoptolemus initially acquiesced in capturing the bow "as a thief" (*klopeus*, 78), Philoctetes gives it openly, as a friend. "Taking the bow, as you asked me just now, until this present pain of the disease abates, keep it and guard it," Philoctetes entreats the young man (762–766). The same phrase, "taking the bow," in the same metrical position, recurs some hundred and fifty lines later to mark the test which that new friendship now undergoes on both sides: "Taking the bow you have deprived me of life. Give it back, I beseech you; give it back, I supplicate you, my child" (931–932). The language of "taking" harks back to Odysseus' language in the prologue, "taking" (*labein*) the man and "taking" his weapon, reminding us again of the instrumental, dehumanizing attitude which Neoptolemus has had to overcome.[113]

The appearance of Heracles takes place, in a sense, for Neoptolemus as well as for Philoctetes. He revalidates heroic action and heroic companionship in a debased world. Heracles addresses both the older and the younger man (1409–1433, 1433–37). At the end he includes them both in dual or plural "you" (1436–37, 1440–41, 1449). Neoptolemus as well as Philoctetes gives his formal assent (1448).

Sophocles does not indicate that Philoctetes' earlier benefaction (670) extended beyond loyalty to a single man. Heracles, however, sets that personal loyalty into its largest frame. Like all divinity in Sophocles, he throws a human life open to its widest, if also most threatening, horizons. Earlier Philoctetes had entrusted the bow to Neoptolemus with warnings of the divine envy (*phthonos*) and the many sufferings (*ponoi*) that it had brought to him and to Heracles (776–778). At the end, Heracles explains those sufferings as part of the heroic quest for immortal excellence and a life of glory (*athanatos aretē, eukleēs bios*, 1418–22). In restoring Philoctetes to the larger human and divine world that the bow potentially embraces, Heracles adduces his own sufferings as a possible paradigm for those of Philoctetes. He thereby provides a kind of catharsis of their pain. Turning Philoctetes' regard outward once more to grief and pain other than his own, citing events beyond those which have led to the narrow confines of his desert island, he essentially effects an emotional healing of the wound that both precedes and parallels the physical healing which he promises at Troy (1437–38).

IX

Sea-girt Lemnos is both a real and mythical place. In this latter aspect it resembles the mysterious islands of the *Odyssey* or the remote Egyptian shore of Euripides' *Helen* or Prospero's island in *The Tempest*, places where hidden contradictory aspects of the self are called forth or a zero point of identity from which a new self is reborn. For both Philoctetes and Neoptolemus it is the place where a lost nobility can be recovered. The aura of heroism that surrounds Philoctetes and his weapon has become obscured by the savagery of the island. Thus when he introduces himself to Neoptolemus he laments the loss of his glory (*kleos*, 251).[114] The momentary flash of his heroic past fades before the bitterness of his abandonment (*erēmos*, 265, 269) and the savagery of his disease (265, 267). Although he can view himself as an *esthlos anēr*, noble and worthy of Neoptolemus' friendship and aid (904), that heroic self has retreated behind its "bestial double," the ensavaged cave dweller on Lemnos. The island and the disease, *nēsos* and *nosos*, have done their work. Like Heracles in the *Trachiniae* and Oedipus in the *Coloneus*, his task is to find his place in the larger order of the gods. To do that he will have to shed the savagery of his bestial other self and reclaim the true *kleos* for which the possession of the bow has marked him out (see *kleos hypertaton*, "highest glory," 1347; also 1422).

The *Philoctetes*, like the other plays, establishes symbolic identification or affiliation between the setting and the hero.[115] Except for the elemental "Hephaestus-fashioned fire" (987), the island seems, initially, untouched by the presences of gods as they are felt in long-inhabited places. Trapped on this unhallowed coast, Philoctetes looks back in hopeless longing to the sacred stream (*hieran libada*, 1213–14) of the Spercheios in his homeland. Outward savagery of place both mirrors and exacerbates inward savagery of affliction. Suffering from the "beast" in his foot, from the savage disease that bites his spirit, he turns to the beasts of the island when he feels himself betrayed by men (936ff., 1080ff., 1146ff.). The rocky cave where he lives and the rocky setting in general are an aspect of his own harsh "soulscape," the granitic quality of his heroism and his savagery both.[116] In his indignation and hatred at seeing himself trapped by Odysseus he threatens to dash out his brains against the rock by leaping from the rocky ledge of the cave (*petrā(i) petras anōthen*, 1002). It is from his rocky cavern (*petrēreis stegas*, 1262) that Neoptolemus will call him forth, from death to life, from rancor to trust.

The sea which physically cuts Philoctetes off from other men is not only an essential feature of the island's remoteness but also an extension of that in him which cuts him off from gods and men.[117] "Alone, he listens to the wave-beaten surge" which echoes back to him only the resounding groan of his own pain (*stonos antitypos*, 694). When he envisages a less forbidding aspect of the sea, it is only as the setting for his archenemy's mocking laughter (1123–26): "Alas, he sits somewhere by the sea's hoary strand, laughs at me, brandishing in his hand my poor means of sustenance." The reminiscence here of the seascapes of Homer, and especially of Achilles' solitary beach in *Iliad* 1.349–350, suggests the ironic negation of the heroic world.

This sea, as we have seen, functions as a means not of civilized communication, but of Odyssean guile and "profit." A professional seafarer or merchant has, in fact, a major role in the execution of that guile. The two extremes in man's use of the sea, commerce and piracy, come together in Odysseus, the first just as negative as the second.

At the end, when Philoctetes takes leave of his island, he addresses the rocky headland's "male smiting" of the sea where his cries often echoed as his head was lashed by wind and wave (1453–60). But now, with his reintegration into the human and divine order at Heracles' appearance, he sees a landscape imbued with divinity once more. He addresses the Nymphs who preside over stream and meadow (1454), the nature gods who oversee the fresh water on which his life depended. The sea which isolates (304ff., 1123ff.) is a means of communication once again. He prays for fair sailing (*euploia*, 1465), now with more hopeful prospects than in the earlier request to Neoptolemus (641). Beside the Nymphs of fresh water (1454) stand also the Nymphs of the salt sea. The chorus' prayer to these sea Nymphs, *Nymphai haliai*, now "saviors of the return journey" (*nostou sōtēras*), in fact ends the play (1469–71). The dehumanizing Lemnian landscape proves to harbor divinities who can help toward the saving return.

The Nymphs of fresh water at the end (*Nymphai enydroi*, 1454) are a reminder that Lemnos is not without deities nor without physical amenities. Odysseus in his initial reconnoiter of the cave had an eye to its habitability, including the presence of a spring of water (16–22; *poton krēnaion*, 21). Describing the hardship of survival there, Philoctetes gives a rather different picture of what it meant to find drinkable water (292–295; cf. 712–718). Yet at the end he includes the springs, personalized in direct address, in his farewell, and he even has a specific holy name for the spring, named after Apollo Lykios (1461–62). In most of the play, however, Lemnos is devoid of divine beneficence. The parode ends with the Nymph Echo, but it is only the shrieks of his "bitter cries" that she returns to him (188–190).

As in the *Oedipus Tyrannus*, the shepherd has an ambiguous place between civilized community and the wild, but Philoctetes is even more savage (*agrios*) than the "wild-pasturing" herdsman (*agro-botas*, 214). He is a hunter, not the keeper of domesticated herds. When he turns back to the beasts in his despair at men, it is beasts of the mountains not the fields or valleys which he addresses (*thēres oreioi*, 937; *ouresibōtas*, 1148). When he contemplates dragging himself back to his cave now denuded of his bow, he laments his inability to kill winged bird or beast which walks the mountain (*thēr oreibatēs*, 955) but foresees his own death as the prey and food of such creatures (957–958). The shepherd may go hungry if his flocks fail, but Philoctetes will be killed, torn, and eaten if he loses his control over the animals on whom his life depends (955ff.). The "economy" of Philoctetes' island, therefore, is not a matter of subsistence only but the truly savage condition of raw nature: eat or be eaten.

Like the sea, the earth of Lemnos is bare of both divine benignity and human cultivation. The chorus sings an ode to Earth, "Goddess of Mountains, all-nourisher, mother of Zeus himself, keeper of great Pactolus, rich in gold" (392–394).[118] Aside from serving as a cover for Neoptolemus' lie, this ode extols not the tilled earth of the plains but the Earth of the mountains (*orestera*, 391), the mountains where Philoctetes has his ambiguous companionship with his hunted prey (937, 955, 1148). How different is the feeling about Earth in the great ode of *Antigone*: an adjunct of human civilization, she is still, even when subdued by man and his plows in his annual tillage, "highest of gods, Earth, deathless, unwearied" (*theōn . . . tan hypertatan, Gan aphthiton, akamaton, Antig.* 338–342). Pactolus and its gold here may also suggest a luxury too far from Philoctetes' condition to be helpful; again the image is of a sterile, metal-bearing rather than a fertile, grain-bearing earth. Not only is the softness of Lydian wealth ironically inappropriate for Philoctetes, but gold might also suggest the area of profit and gain associated with the negative aspects of civilization as embodied in Odyssean machination. The rather jarring intrusion of Odysseus' patronymic, "son of Laertes," into the attributes of Earth in the last line (402) is a reminder of Odyssean guile and of the practice of that guile in the very lie which this ode attempts to support. Earth's attributes here as "mistress of bull-killing lions" (400–401), though relevant to the syncretistic fusion of Gaia, Rhea, and Cybele on which Sophocles draws, plunge us back from the civilizing arts of agriculture to the savage violence from which Philoctetes, vainly, here seeks escape. The ode then reinforces the impression that the image of civilization embodied in Odysseus is, at this point, still deceptive and inadequate.

The next ode, sung between the ritual introduction of Neoptolemus to the bow and the onset of the disease, presents a more positive image of earth. The nurturing earth (*phorbas gaia*, 700) furnishes Philoctetes with the gentle leaves or herbs that he applies to his beast-ridden foot (698–699). Yet some fifty lines before, Philoctetes himself was more spare in describing the provenience of that healing herb (649–650): "There is a certain leaf with which I lull to sleep this wound, making it tame and gentle." Here he gives no credit to a beneficent earth. The plant simply exists as the needy hero finds it (*phyllon ti moi parestin*, 649).

Even the "nurturing earth" of 700 is qualified in the next strophe's description of Philoctetes' actual way of life (707–718):

> Taking no food sown of the holy earth such as we men tillers of the soil enjoy except if ever he wins some food for his belly from his swift-shot arrows, with his winged missiles. O poor soul who for ten years had no joy of the wine-poured drink, but dragged himself along to whatever standing pool of water he had spied and found out.

Agriculture is mentioned only as a foil to the life of the savage hunter which Philoctetes leads. His nurture (*phorbē*, 707) comes not as a gift of "holy earth," but as harsh prey, nurture for his belly (*gastri phorban*, 711), killed by his winged arrows (711) under circumstances which may suddenly make him food for the beasts he hunts (*epherbomēn*, 956; cf. also 43, 1108).[119]

When Philoctetes himself addresses the earth, it is to emphasize his desolation. After the choral ode cited above, he cries out to the earth as he feels the attack of pain coming upon him, and it is the earth as tomb, not the source of life and nurture (819–820): "O earth (*gaia*), receive me in the state of death that I am. For this woe does not let me be straightened up." Later, when he is robbed of the bow, his cries of desperation all associate the earth not with life but with death. He will go, he says, "seeing my father": "Where in the earth?" asks the chorus, "In Hades," Philoctetes replies (—*poi gas*,—*es Haidou*, 1211). Never will he go to Troy, he declares, "as long as I have this cragged pedestal of earth" (*gēs tod' aipeinon bathron*, 1000); and it is against this rocky ground that he would dash out his brains in his next lines (1001–1002).

After his second address to the wild inhabitants of Lemnos in 1146ff., Philoctetes goes on (1160–62): "Whence will I have a source of life (*biota*)? Who is nourished so on the winds, having dominion (*kratynōn*) over none of what is sent by earth, giver of life (*biodōros aia*)." His verb here, *kratynōn*, "conquering," still indicates an aggressive attitude to the earth, a relation of necessity, struggle, conquest. Even the bounty of this life-giving earth refers to animal food, the prey he hunts by the bow not the grain or fruit that earth itself produces as a gift (-*dōros*, 1162).

His earth of Lemnos (*Lēmnia chthōn*, 986) implies not the gentle and nourishing holy earth of the chorus in the first stasimon (707ff.) but an elemental force, here coupled with the "all-conquering flash" of "Hephaestus-fashioned" fires, the mysterious earth-fires of Lemnos. This fire reflects the savage violence of his own spirit and points to a deeper source of energy in the midst of this uncompromising harshness. When he phrases his refusal of Odysseus in terms of defying even Zeus, "the fire-bearing hurler of lightnings" (1197–99), his hyperboles recall the hybristic oaths of Creon in the *Antigone* (486–487, 1039–41). But they also bespeak the grandeur of a hero worthy to rekindle the divine fire which brought Heracles to Olympus ("Oeta's hills where the bronze-shielded hero drew near the gods, he all ablaze with godlike fire," (726–729). In both its savagery and its violent beauty, its cliffs, sea, and strange fires, the landscape of Lemnos is the landscape of Philoctetes' heroic self, rugged, precipitous, and desolate, but also in its fierce outlines strong, unmovable, majestic.

Fire and Water and Other Oppositions in the Myth of Philoctetes

The positive associations of fire for Lemnos and Philoctetes are counterbalanced by the negative associations of water. Not only does the sea cut Philoctetes off from men (*Phil.* 1–2), but the snake whose bite causes the disease is, as we noted, a water snake, *hydros*. Its wound is cured by the Lemnian earth, with its Hephaestean and therefore fiery associations. This snake is also notorious for its bad smell (cf. Nicander, *Theriaka* 421–425, 429–430, with the scholia on 421, 422, 429), and thus it takes its place with the Lemnian women and Philoctetes' suppurating wound among the antisocial, savage elements of the Lemnian myths.

The opposition between fire and water is particularly marked in the *hydros*. It has a natural affinity with the cold and the wet, but it also becomes particularly dangerous when afflicted by heat, the element hostile to it. Nicander reports that it is at its worst "when Siris parches the water . . . Then it goes on land . . . warming its baleful body in the sun" (*Theriaka* 367ff.; cf. *Schlange*, *RE* II. A.1 [1921] 556). Quintus of Smyrna, describing the wound of Philoctetes, says that the *hydros* which bit him is particularly destructive "when the force of the sun parches it as it goes upon dry land" (9.384–387). Aggravating its poison, heat and dryness reappear in the effects of its venom, namely a "thirsty madness" which "parches" its victims (Nicander, *Theriaka*, 428, 436).

If heat and fire aggravate this snake and thus render it more dangerous, water, this snake's proper element, also intensifies the disease which it causes. A scholiast on *Iliad* 2.723 reports that the wound festered when sea water touched it (*legousi de katechein autou tēn sēpsin prosrainomenēs thalassēs hydōr*).

A second area of associations links together Philoctetes as hero, Heracles, Hephaestus, and fire on the one side over against snake, water, and savage monstrosity on the other. The *hydros* which reduces Philoctetes to his deathlike existence on Lemnos is etymologically, at least, akin to *Hydra*, the multiheaded snake whose venom both gives Heracles his arrows and, through Deianeira's robe, reduces him to weakness and ultimately death. This association between Philoctetes' *hydros* and Heracles' Hydra occurred to Eustathius (on *Il.* 2.723, Leipzig 1827, vol. 1, p. 267.44). There is a more specific link between the two venomous creatures in the version, mentioned by Servius on *Aen.* 3.402 (see *supra*), in which Philoctetes' foot is poisoned by one of Heracles' arrows, tipped with the Hydra's venom, which falls upon it in punishment for his revealing that hero's burial in the earth, not immortality on Olympus. The story of the Hydra too involves an opposition of fire and water: it inhabits a watery marsh and can be vanquished finally only by the application of fire (*pyraktein* is Nicander's verb, *Theriaka* 688). Just as a companion at the end of his life helps Heracles with the fire which assures his movement from human to divine, so another companion earlier helps him with the fire in the deed that accomplishes one of his most important victories over the beasts: Iolaus cauterizes the Hydra's decapitated necks so that they do not grow back.

The civilizing fire of Lemnian Hephaestus, the fire which enables Philoctetes to survive the bite of the *hydros* on Lemnos, and the fire on Oeta which, in another way, enables Heracles to defeat the fatal poison of the Hydra all belong together as part of a constellation of motifs which oppose the watery *hydros*, its sinister patron, Chryse, and Philoctetes' moribund existence on an island cut off by water from human civilization. Integrating these motifs with those of the other Lemnian myths discussed above results in the following diagram:

Savagery	*Civilization*
Chryse	Hephaestus, Heracles
Earth; water	Olympus; fire
Philoctetes made lame and "savage" by watery snake (*hydros*); brutalizing force of "raw-minded" Chryse and "destructive-minded" snake (*Il.* 2.723)	Philoctetes cured by (a) Lemnian earth where fire god, Hephaestus, landed on Lemnos; (b) priests of Hephaestus, who cure only this kind of snakebite; (c) intervention of Heracles from Olympus because Philoctetes lit his pyre; (d) friendship, good will (*eunoia*)
Bad smell (*dysosmia*) and destruction of civilization by savagery	Sweet savor of proper sacrificial rites
(a) In Lemnian crime, destroying fire in hearth, altar, etc.	Renewal of civilization with pure fire from Delos
(b) In Pelasgian crime, leading to plague and barrenness (Hdt. 6.87)	
(c) In Philoctetes' wound, leading to desolate, deathlike existence on Lemnos, without rituals (*Phil.* 8-11) (downward mediation toward bestial life)	Lighting of pyre on Oeta and reestablishment of reverence (*Phil.* 1440–44) (upward mediation, toward gods)
(d) Bitten while tending or founding altar	Healed by Heracles because lit fire at Oeta
(e) Wounded by Heracles' arrow, tipped with Hydra's venom,	Final victory over poison of bestial Hydra and apotheosis on Olympus
which falls *down* on his foot	*Upward* movement from beast to god at pyre on Mt. Oeta
because he shows Heracles' grave on *earth*	Apotheosis on Olympus aided by Philoctetes
implying denial of his immortality by Philoctetes	Advice about immortal *arete* and immortal piety from Olympian Heracles to Lemnian Philoctetes (1420, 1443–44)

10

Philoctetes: Society, Language, Friendship

 In order to become once more a participant in society, Philoctetes must leave behind both the spiritual and physical contours of the savage Lemnian landscape. The task however, is not one-sided. Society must also be reshaped to receive the hero whom it once so cruelly rejected. The social order conceived by Odysseus is based on success in achieving specific goals irrespective of individual protest or suffering. This cannot be the spiritual home of the pain-wracked outcast, nor could Philoctetes accept a place in such a world.

Odysseus' concept of society rests on the subordination of inferior to superior, of individual to group. He extends his authoritarian ranking of leader and subordinate (cf. 15, 53) even to the gods, for he regards himself, self-righteously, as the "subordinate helper" (*hypēretēs*) of Zeus (990). His attitude, resembling those of the Atreids in the *Ajax* and Creon in the *Antigone*, introduces conflicts similar to those of these earlier plays.[1] In his opening lines Odysseus affirms that in abandoning the sick Philoctetes on his island he was only following orders. The spirit of this supposed justification contrasts with the heroic terms of his address to Neoptolemus (1–7):

> This is the shore of sea-girt Lemnos, untrodden by mortal men and uninhabited, where, O son of Achilles, Neoptolemus, you who had your nurture from the best of the Hellenes, I once cast forth Poeas' son, of Malis, appointed to do this deed (*tachtheis*) by those in command (*anassontōn*), his foot dripping with the devouring disease.

Philoctetes later takes a very different view of following orders and excuses Neoptolemus on the grounds that "he knew nothing but to do what he was ordered" (*to prostachthen*, 1010). Neoptolemus himself does not accept such an easy solution. When he disobeys military authority, he invokes Zeus in a spirit far different from the smugness of Odysseus in 990, abjuring Odyssean deceit (*dolos*, cf. 1288) by an oath to "pure reverence for highest Zeus" (1289; cf. 990).

Before this late stage in the action, there is no real alternative to Odysseus' view. In their first ode, the chorus accepts this hierarchical conception of authority. Echoing a Hesiodic sentiment, they pronounce regal authority as validated by "the rule (*anassetai*, cf. 6, 26) of the divine scepter of Zeus" (138–140; cf. Hesiod, *Theogony* 80–96). This authority they call "primordial rule" (*kratos ōgygion*), and they hold it to be the basis of their subordination and obedience (*hypourgein*) to their leader Neoptolemus (141–143). Later, they defend Odysseus in terms of his own authoritarian premises: he is but one of many, acting only under orders (*tachtheis*, 1144; cf. 6, 1010).[2] The supremacy of the counsel (*gnōmē*, 139) of the one who possesses Zeus's regal scepter is severely shaken at the end of the play when "Zeus's purposes" (1415) are revealed as not entirely congruent with Odysseus'. The counsel (*gnōmē*) that brings the requisite return of the hero to Troy is not that of the ruler wielding the symbol of authority (139) but the counsel of friends (*gnōmē philōn*, 1467).

Neoptolemus' instinctive distaste for Odysseus' instrumental view of human relations (86ff.) opens the central conflict. Gradually this widens to a conflict between the objective needs of the society and the spiritual and emotional life of its individual members. Even in his acquiescence to Odyssean authority Neoptolemus does not see eye-to-eye with his leader. He regards himself not as a subordinate (15 and 53) but as a co-worker (*synergatēs*, 93). In the same breath he rejects Odysseus' willingness to purchase victory at the cost of baseness (*nikan kakōs*, 94), even though he acknowledges his own obligation not to be a traitor to his cause (92–93). Lured by the promise of being the vanquisher of Troy, he momentarily yields to Odysseus' characteristic argument of profit (*kerdos*, 108–120), but the tension remains.

Although Neoptolemus repeats Odysseus' lies, he expands the Odyssean view of personal responsibility (385–388):

> I do not blame Odysseus so much as those in command (*tous en telei*), for the whole city and the whole army (*sympas stratos*) belong to the leaders. It is through the words of their teachers that men who behave in disorderly ways (*akosmountes*) become bad (*kakoi*).[3]

Neoptolemus here evades the issue of Odysseus' responsibility in terms that might in fact convict Odysseus. As he finds new "teachers," he also finds a different notion of social order. There is an intermediate stage when he is torn between obedience to the army and compassion for Philoctetes. He cannot, he says, return the bow, "for justice and advantage make me heed those in authority (*tōn en telei*, 925–926; cf. 385 above). His final decision contravenes that authority and defies the whole army which Odysseus repeatedly invokes (*sympas stratos*, 1243, 1250, 1257, 1294; cf. 387).

The independent and vitriolic spirit of Philoctetes and then later the defiance of Neoptolemus force Odysseus into a harder, more brutal expression of his authoritarian views. When Philoctetes refuses to go to Troy, Odysseus curtly replies, "But I say you must; this must be obeyed" (994). With pride and accuracy Philoctetes answers that this is the relation not between free men but between master and slave (995–996). Odysseus' bullying tone undercuts his counterargument that at Troy Philoctetes will enjoy equality with the best (*aristoi*, 997). When he leaves the stage at the end of the scene with the threat that he does not need Philoctetes at Troy, only his bow, he imposes a peremptory silence on his captive: "Answer me nothing in reply, for I am departing" (1065). The gesture repeats in microcosm his initial responsibility for Philoctetes' injury, robbing him of civilized discourse with his fellow men (see 180–190, 225, 686–695).

Odysseus takes the same high-handed tone toward Neoptolemus as the latter prepares to return the bow. First he invokes the authority of the whole army, then fear and threats of punishment (1250–51, 1258), and finally he draws his sword (1254–56). His last attempt to prevent the return of the bow is a futile reassertion of brute power: "But I forbid it," he shouts, invoking the gods and, once more, "the whole army" (1293–94). His last utterance in the play is, ironically, a threat to "ship Philoctetes off to Troy's plains by force, whether Achilles' son is willing or unwilling" (1297–98). The resort to force echoes the earlier part of the scene with Neoptolemus (1254ff.) and is equally futile. This man of guile, careful speech, and clever persuasion is reduced to angry blustering about force, which, in any case, is quite ineffectual: he retreats with prudent rapidity as Philoctetes prepares to fit an arrow to his bow.

How different are Neoptolemus' responses in the immediately ensuing lines. He invokes the gods as he begs Philoctetes not to shoot (1301) and then cites the principle of nobility which embraces both of them ("Neither for you nor for me is this noble," 1304). He can acknowledge the other's praise of his inherited, Achillean nature (1310), and then set forth with good will (*eunoia*, 1322) the advantages which Philoctetes will reap from going to Troy (1314–47). Neoptolemus' *eunoia* goes beyond the categories implied in Odysseus' outlook: superior-inferior, means-end, hunter-prey, deceiver-victim, and the use of intelligence and speech to manipulate men.[4]

In slowly forming their bond of friendship, Philoctetes and Neoptolemus create in miniature the ties of a more wholesome and humane society. The task of recreating a valid form of society when the old is corrupt is also one of the chief concerns of Plato two or three decades after the *Philoctetes*. What Werner Jaeger has said of friendship and society in Plato can also be applied to this play:

> When society is suffering from a great organic disorder or disease, its recovery can be initiated only by a small but basically healthy association of people who share the same ideas and who can form the heart of a new organism. That is exactly what Plato meant by friendship (*philia*).[5]

A heroic society based on good will, friendship, and respect rather than force and guile is the human precondition of Philoctetes' return and necessarily precedes the divine intervention of Heracles. A more humane and responsive social order, if only in miniature, necessarily precedes the indication of a more generous and intelligible divine order. First Philoctetes renews his trust in men; then he can once more come to trust the gods.[6]

Like Ajax, Philoctetes embodies an older heroism which the meaner, more pragmatic, more changeable world has difficulty in assimilating.[7] In both cases the hero rejects the society offered by the Greek army at Troy, his peers and fellow warriors. But in the *Ajax* the new society can only mourn and commemorate the hero's greatness after he is gone. Such a heroism must necessarily end in death: Ajax' society no longer has a place for his kind of intransigence. It needs compromise and adaptability rather than unbending fixity in heroic glory. In the *Philoctetes*, however, the hero is still necessary to his society. Communication between the older and newer vision of social organization is still viable. Neoptolemus performs this role, taking over the mediatory function of the Odysseus of the *Ajax*, the voice of compassion and compromise.

Yet ultimately even Neoptolemus' purely human good will is not enough. Final persuasion rests with the immortal heroism of which Heracles is the paradigm. Indeed, it is important that the symbol of that heroism is not the protagonist himself (as in the *Ajax*) but a figure outside the frame of the human action: the human hero of this play will be able to survive his heroism. Despite himself, he will prove useful to his society and to himself. The seeds of this view are perhaps present in the "enduring" (*pherein*) of Oedipus at the end of the *Tyrannus*. Its culmination is in the *Coloneus*. Oedipus there, trailing the intractable harshness of an old world of narrow, implacable domestic hatred and conflict, can create a new kind of bond, based on mutual respect and compassion, with his virtually adopted son, Theseus, in an adopted city. In like manner Philoctetes vents his destructive, hate-filled "old" heroism on the figure of his past, Odysseus, and leaves that archaic, intransigent heroism behind on Lemnos. In the more adaptable (and ultimately more pious or reverent) heroism, he can join in a new bond with his virtually adopted son, Neoptolemus. This creative power of the hero—possibly felt by Sophocles as akin to the creative power of art itself—has its roots and strength in a dark and violent part of the soul and a dark and violent past. But it will undergo transformation to help the hero shape a new world. Oedipus will leave blessings to Athens; Philoctetes will bring back to Troy the heroism which lies "dead" there now (cf. 331ff., 412ff., 446ff.). By killing Paris, the cause of the war (1426), he will definitely put an end to the ten-year struggle through which Greece has been stripped of nobility and left only with what is mean and base (412–452).

If "Odyssean" society rests on absolute obedience, subordination of individual to group, manipulation, and force, the new miniature society of Philoctetes and Neoptolemus rests on friendship (*philia*), trust (*pistis*), compassion (*oiktos, eleos*), and good will (*eunoia*). The persuasion (*peithō*) which results from this combination is very different from Odyssean guileful persuasion which seeks self-interest rather than the good of the person being persuaded. Odyssean society constitutes an ironic inversion of civilized values—ironic because Odysseus, "twisted instrument of the divine plan," is, after all, attempting to restore Philoctetes from the savagery of Lemnos to human society.[8] Odysseus' means cancel out his ends. Undoing his earlier relegation of Philoctetes from Troy to Lemnos, he veers between coercion and persuasion or seems to use them indiscriminately (593–594). Initially unmoved at the evidence of Philoctetes' suffering (37–47),[9] he lacks the good will to perceive, as Neoptolemus does, that the oracle means benefit to Philoctetes and not just success for the expedition.

To take the simplest of the civilized qualities to be reconstituted, friendship, *philia*, has become an instrument of Odyssean trickery. Friendless, *aphilos*, on his desert island (1018), Philoctetes welcomes with open arms the friendship he has so long lacked (509–510, 530ff., 671). Reflecting on the world he knew at Troy, he laments the disappearance of all his old *philoi*, all that was dearest to him (421ff., 434). The new *philia* with Neoptolemus is not only based, initially, on a lie but also rests on the opposite of friendship, a common hatred, alleged on Neoptolemus' part, of the Atreids and Odysseus (509, 585–586, 665–666). This mutual enmity, a "clear token" of having suffered at their hands, forms the initial bond between the two strangers (403–404). Near the end Philoctetes' offer to help Neoptolemus with his bow against the Greek army (1406ff.) is the final expression of this isolating, ultimately negative aspect of their *philia*. Olympian Heracles, however, evokes a past friendship of a more expansive and heroic nature. He can then recall Philoctetes to a comradeship rooted not in mutual hatred but in cooperation in a major enterprise of large, historical import and, we must assume, for the common good of all Greece.[10]

Before that point is reached, Philoctetes will go through a zero point of total friendlessness, turning away from the corrupted *philotēs* of men to wild nature, the animals, and to the bow itself (*toxon philon*, 1128–29; cf. 1004). Odysseus not only uses a false friendship to entrap Philoctetes but has no scruples against abjuring his friendship with Neoptolemus: "We shall make war not against the Trojans but against you," he threatens as he prepares to draw his sword on his erstwhile ally (1253–54). But Neoptolemus, here ready to fight Odysseus, will save the life of this friend turned enemy some fifty lines later as he prevents Philoctetes from shooting the bow (1300ff.).

With the return of the bow, Philoctetes calls Neoptolemus not just friend but dearest child (*philtaton teknon*, 1301). The endearment appropriate to blood relationship expresses the newly realized spiritual kinship. Even this *philia*, however, is weaker than the bond of hatred for the Greeks at Troy (1374–85). Only the divine *charis*, kindness or grace, of Heracles can effect that change (1413).[11] But Philoctetes' closing words show that the younger man's movement from pretended to genuine friendship has not been without its effect: in acquiescing to join the army at Troy, he now places the counsel of friends, *gnōmē philōn*, prominently beside the powers of great Destiny and the all-conquering deity.

Trust, *pistis*, undergoes a similar process of destruction and regeneration. Odysseus exploits the trustful converse, *homilia pistē*, that Neoptolemus will be able to establish with Philoctetes (70–71). In due course that trust grows between the two men and is sealed by a pledge of hand (*cheiros pistin*, 813). At this point Neoptolemus' relation of trust with Philoctetes is about to undergo a critical change. When Philoctetes sees the younger man still there after the attack of his disease, he calls it "an unbelievable housekeeping of my hopes," *elpidōn apiston oikourēma* (867–868), an untranslatable phrase which joins two basic elements of civilized association, personal trust (*pistis*) and the bonds of a house or *oikos*. Feeling himself betrayed, Philoctetes bitterly throws Neoptolemus' breach of trust in his face: "Yes, you were a trusty friend (*pistos*) but in secret full of bane" (1272). The return of the bow recreates trust. "Trust," fuller communication in words, and good will then all come together when Philoctetes, in his turn, reaches a moment of tragic decision (1350–51): "Alas, what shall I do? How can I not trust (*a-pistein*) in the words of this man who gave me counsel with good will (*eunous*)?"

II

As this last passage makes clear, the problem of civilization in this play is intimately bound up with the status of language.[12] Communication erodes with the breakdown of trust and honesty, and like them has to be built up afresh on a new basis. As the plot moves from manipulation to true sympathy, from harsh authority to noble generosity, it also moves from the echoing cliffs of a savage island to the welcoming voice of a friend who can persuade.

The exchange between Odysseus and Neoptolemus in the prologue at once raises the problem of language: Neoptolemus' reluctance to be called (*kaleisthai*) traitor (93–95) clashes with Odysseus' willingness to be called anything if it means success (64–65, 84–85, 119–120). For Odysseus language is a carefully crafted tool to attain definite ends. In this aspect it reflects some late fifth-century Sophistic theories of language as an amoral medium for winning one's case, a *technē* or skill to be exercised without regard for law or justice.[13] It is in fact a means of subverting justice for personal advantage, as Strepsiades in Aristophanes' *Clouds* hopes to use the "Stronger Argument" to elude his creditors.

Philoctetes' view of persuasion is very different. When he asks Neoptolemus to be persuaded to take him back to Greece, he invokes the religious sanctity of supplication (484–485). His request, "Put me where I would least give pain (*algynei*) to fellow passengers" (482) embodies a view of human association higher than Odysseus', to whom it gives no pain (*algynei*) to go to the furthest extremes of base speech (64–66). For all his external savagery, the outcast has both a capacity for deeper communication and ultimately a truer power to persuade than the artful persuader, Odysseus.

On the other hand, the savagery of Philoctetes' disease consists partly in its destruction of intelligible speech. It manifests itself in a beastlike whistling (755) and the cries or groans of inarticulate pain (752, *iygē*, *stonos*), represented in the text by a string of repeated syllables, *a, a, a, a*, or *pheu pheu*, or *papai*.[14] Like Aeschylus' Io and Cassandra, like the Heracles of the *Trachiniae*, the stricken hero's intensity of suffering places him at the border between human speech and animal cry.[15] At the low ebb of his return to the savage life of Lemnos he addresses the beasts and landscape of the wild, and only rocks and mountains echo his voice (936ff., 952ff., 1080ff., 1146ff.; cf. 1458). The musical metaphors or similes that describe this lonely silence early in the play set off by contrast the inhuman reduction of his speech (cf. 188ff., 213–215, 405). Hence the mere sound of a human voice thrills him with delight (225, 234–235).

Philoctetes' ambiguous relation to language and communication reflects the hero's ambiguous relation to civilization in general. His disease deprives him of one of man's great civilized achievements, celebrated in the Ode on Man in the

Antigone along with agriculture, sailing, and medicine. Language, of course, enjoys a privileged position in the other culture histories of the period.[16] Philoctetes' reaction to the report of Helenus' oracle shows this ambiguity. He warns against being persuaded by Odysseus' soft words (*malthakoi logoi*, 629), a precaution more justified than he knows, given the deception involved in Odysseus' use of the oracle (628–633):

> Is this not terrible, my child, that Laertes' son should ever expect, by means of soft words, to lead me out of his ship and show me off among the Greeks. No! Sooner would I harken (*klyoimi*) to the viper that made me thus to lack a foot. But for him all things are sayable (*panta lekta*); all things can be dared (*tolmēta*).

Philoctetes' resistance to *logos*, here associated with the viper, the wound, and the poisonous hatred bred by the disease in both its literal and metaphorical sense, is part of the savagery which keeps him apart from gods and men.[17] And yet that very refusal to be persuaded is, paradoxically, just as essential to a genuinely humane communication as Odysseus' glib rhetoric. Odysseus' world view is based on the plasticity of men and words. Everyone is amenable to persuasion; everything "can be said, can be dared."[18] For Philoctetes, however, resistance to persuasion is vital to integrity of spirit. His stubborn refusal of persuasion is an aspect of his savagery, a sub-human quality. It is also an aspect of his heroic nobility, and as such it is in touch with the super-human qualities of Olympian divinity and immortal glory. Neoptolemus approached him armed with Odyssean persuasiveness, and Philoctetes must teach him when to reject the changeability of this persuasion. But he must himself learn from the youth which *logoi*, and whose, can be heeded. This crisis of language creates an impasse which only Heracles' pronouncements, involving speaking and hearing on a new plane, can break.

The failure of *logos* lies on both sides. The oracle spoke of persuading Philoctetes by word (612), but Odysseus is ready to apply force (594, 1297).[19] On the other hand even after the clarification of the oracle and the return of the bow (the deed which negates the trickery of Odyssean word), Philoctetes refused to listen to words spoken with good will (1321–22, cf. 1268–69, 1350–51, 1373–74, 1393–96), and this refusal constitutes an aspect of his ensavaged state (*ēgriōsai*, 1321).

This reduction of speech by savagery contains still another paradox. Those terrible bestial shrieks in fact are the first steps toward a genuine human communication. When he hears these cries, Neoptolemus must confront the reality of what he is doing to a fellow human being, never more human than when he lies at his feet writhing in agony.

The paradox is already present in the play's very first scene. Odysseus views Philoctetes' rags, still wet with the discharge of his infected foot, as evidence from which to infer his proximity to the cave (40–44, and note the legalistic *saphōs*, "clearly," 40); Neoptolemus' response is the inarticulate cry, *iou, iou* (38), the first of several such cries that he will utter as he moves closer to the disease and the feelings, conflicts, and decisions which it forces upon him (see 759, 895). Already here in the prologue the monosyllabic utterances are pregnant with a greater humanity than Odysseus' logically inflected, incisive sentences. These incoherent cries of pain are what finally persuade Neoptolemus, whereas the developed—indeed, overdeveloped—arts of speech practiced by the wily Odysseus not only fail but in fact betray civilized values.[20] As Neoptolemus repeats such syllables at his own points of spiritual crisis later in the play, he reaches an agony almost equivalent to that which extorts these cries from the sick outcast.

The contrast between Odysseus' smooth syntax on the one hand and these terrible cries on the other is related to a major Sophistic debate, whether language exists by human convention (*nomos*) or by nature (*physis*).[21] Odysseus' speech embodies a view of language as part of the slowly evolved imposition of rational form upon brute matter, conscious articulation upon a rude, unbroken stream of sound. Philoctetes' broken cries imply a kind of natural language, reduced to the level of bestial howl but at least free of manipulative rationalism. In its very rawness and wildness it can touch a chord of instinctive communication lost in a world of ruthless cleverness and pitiless artifice. That the young Neoptolemus, disciple of a master-rhetorician, should find out the true worth of words and communication from a half-savage outcast on a desert island is the dramatic emblem of these inversions of language.

When language, corrupted, becomes the tool of a social leadership that has lost touch with its best ideals, the young, especially the gifted and sensitive young, are left the most confused, disoriented, alienated. Neoptolemus' hesitation about Odyssean wiles in the prologue (86ff.) reveals a malaise which the actual execution of Odysseus' methods will only deepen. Rational language cannot point the way out, for it is the very source of the corruption. To cut beneath his Odyssean training and reach a mode of action more authentic to his character, Neoptolemus needs to experience a totally different level of discourse. This comes about through the negation of language in Philoctetes' sudden silence (730–731, 741) and then the paroxysms of agony, the "whistling on of the disease" which brings a direct appeal to his humanity more moving than any word (755–757):

Neopt.:   Terrible the whistling on of the disease.
Phil.:   Terrible and *not to be spoken*. But pity me.
Neopt.:   What then shall I do?

Philoctetes' cries elicit from the young bystander a question not about words but about deeds: *ti drasō*, "What shall I do?" (757). It is a question of crisis that echoes again and again through the latter half of the play. He continues with an emotional exclamation of his own: "Alas, alas, you unhappy man, unhappy" (*iō iō dystēne su, / dystēne*) in a heavily alliterated sequence of *d*'s and *p*'s (759–760). At this point the distanced relation of word and logic that marked Odysseus' reaction to the signs of the disease in the prologue (40ff.) gives way to the emotion-filled physical response of touching: "Do you then want me to hold you and touch you?" (761). The tentative form of this question (deliberative subjunctives, *dēta*, "then," and the delicate and untranslatable *ti*, literally "touch you in some respect," *thigō ti sou*) indicates, with all that wondrously natural subtlety of Sophoclean dramatic art, the slow growth of a new range of feelings in Neoptolemus. Fresh possibilities of relating to others, and therefore to himself, begin to stir in him.

This scene culminates in the first great deed or *ergon* of the play, Philoctetes' surrender of the bow, which will be answered by the "manifest deed" of its return. Taking an oath that he is abjuring the guile (*dolos*, 1288) that goes with the Odyssean mode of language, Neoptolemus proclaims, "The deed will here be manifest (*tourgon parestai phaneron*). Stretch forth your right hand and command your weapon" (1291–92).

Between these two points occurs the play's most violent crisis of *logos*, delineated in part through Neoptolemus' echo of Philoctetes' cry of inarticulate pain, *papai*, and his echo of his own question about action, "What shall I do?" (895; cf. 797). At this point Philoctetes, troubled, asks, "Where have you gone off in speech?" The other answers, "I know not where to turn my pathless word" (*aporon epos*, 896–897). This *logos*, in contrast to Odyssean certainty of direction, has reached an *aporia*, with no place to go, quite literally, unless it cancel itself out by a drastic reversal. Philoctetes' anxious question, "Has then the ugly harshness of the disease *persuaded* you not to bring me as a sailor on your ship?" (900–901), only underlines the paradox that just this harshness of the disease, with its wild cries of pure pain, has persuaded Neoptolemus. Where Odysseus' wily rhetoric fails, the nonverbal persuasion of the disease succeeds.

Philoctetes' silence at the onset of the disease is now echoed in Neoptolemus' own silence of shame (934) and then in the long silence of a hundred lines (974–1074). Beginning to practice a different form of discourse, Neoptolemus loses his capacity to speak when his old master of *logoi*, Odysseus, appears. Speaking and doing are tightly intertwined in this scene. The chorus frames the issue of action in terms of the kind of *logoi* that one should heed (963–964): "What will we do (*ti drōmen*)? With you, my lord, now rests our sailing and going over to this man's words (*tois toude proschōrein logois*)." Neoptolemus and Philoctetes then exchange a brief discourse of pity (*oiktos deinos . . . eleēson*, 965–968), culminating in the former's *oimoi ti drasō*, "Ah me, what shall I do?" (969). The silences of this scene, combined with the savage cries of pain which preceded it, form a zero point of *logos* from which a more genuinely communicative *logos* will be reconstituted.

"The concealed words of a wily mind" is Philoctetes' description of Odysseus' plot (*krypta epē doleras . . . phrenos*, 1112). As they break through deception to valid communication, both Philoctetes and Neoptolemus reciprocally neutralize this Odyssean concealment. "I shall no longer be able to conceal the evil from you" (*kakon krypsai*), Philoctetes cries as he feels the attack of the disease approaching (742–743). This dropping of concealment about a *kakon* has a pendant soon after when Neoptolemus confesses (908–909): "O Zeus, what shall I do? A second time I shall be taken as base (*kakos*), concealing (*kryptōn*) what I must not and speaking the most shameful of words." Now changing

336

places with Philoctetes as the one "caught" or "taken" (*lēphthō*) instead of "taking" (*labein*, 101, 103, 107), he meets him halfway on the new ground of forthright speech. "I shall conceal nothing from you," *ouden se krypsō*, he decides six lines later (915), echoing Philoctetes' first open avowal in 742–743. In both cases the *kakon*, when confronted and confided honestly, unites rather than isolates.

This regaining of true communication by abjuring a deceptive plot has a close parallel in the urn scene of the *Electra*. Here the deceptive *logos* of Orestes, visually embodied in the empty urn, confronts the visual truth of another order, the wasted form of Electra before him on the stage. At that point, Orestes encounters a tangible and manifest suffering that, like Philoctetes', hits below the level of *logos*. He then loses control of his *logoi* in almost the same way as Neoptolemus (*El.* 1174–75): "Alas, what shall I say. At a loss for words where (in words) can I go? For I can no longer master my tongue." We may compare the exchange at *Philoctetes* 895–897:

Neopt.: Alas, what would I then do from here?
Phil.: What is it, my child? Where have you gone off in word?
Neopt.: I do not know where to turn my pathless speech.

It is perhaps characteristic of the respective plays that the confusion of word is reciprocal in *Philoctetes*, one-sided in *Electra*. The two men are joined together in this confusion, even as it will, momentarily, draw them apart. In *Electra*, however, confused *logoi* rest primarily with Orestes, who has used guileful *logoi*, and a tension between the desire to speak and the possibility of speech marks the ensuing dialogue. In both plays blockages in communication can be cleared away only by something more basic than language itself.

The *Philoctetes*, however, is more optimistic in healing the breach between *logos* and *ergon*. Neoptolemus not only performs the manifest deed (1291) of returning the bow but also speaks the noble word (*gennaion epos*, 1402) at the end, fulfilling his earlier false promise of restoring Philoctetes to Malis (645) and answering the deceptive *logoi* of Odysseus (55, 1112, "hidden words from guileful mind"). Overcoming false speech, Neoptolemus and Philoctetes together reestablish a bond of nobility and heroism resting upon the generous deeds of *eu-ergetein*.

Heracles' appearance confirms and completes the new level of discourse toward which the human characters have been groping. His is the discourse of immortal things, "the immortal excellence" and the "piety that dies not with mortal men" (1420, 1443–44), and his the final, authoritative speaking in the play. His words possess an absolute effectiveness. Where Neoptolemus' persuasion and good will have failed, his command instant obedience. Heracles designates his speech by the term *mythoi*, not *logoi*, the only place where this term occurs in the play.[22] The shift in terminology indicates this new power of language. Divinely sponsored *mythos* resolves the impasse in the social and moral order caused by faithless and deceitful *logos*. *Mythos* is here truer than *logos*. Yet this *mythos* emerges only after the two human protagonists, struggling to make human *logos* once more a vehicle for trust, honesty, and compassion, have spoken the words that confirm one other in their complementary strengths: willingness to abandon deceitful words for a deeper commitment to moral values on the one hand, the old firmness of heroic integrity on the other.

Neoptolemus receives from Philoctetes the lesson of inflexibility in clear moral values that he needs to overcome his earlier pliancy, albeit reluctant, to Odyssean guile. Yet Philoctetes' continued intrasigence remains a problem for the resolution of human *logos*. Heracles' appearance is both a victory and a defeat for Philoctetes. Possibly Sophocles intended us to perceive the different responses of different generations. Neoptolemus' uncertainty about the proper model can be resolved in human terms and through human *logos*. His noble nature, turned in the right direction, will throw off bad training and reveal its full heroic potential. Philoctetes' deeply imbedded bitterness cannot be so easily overcome. Indeed, the end of the play suggests that it is impermeable to the processes of social interaction and can be healed only by the figure who symbolizes a buried layer of his own capacity for relation, full trust, and communication, that is, only by something which lies deeply buried within himself.

It is important to note that Heracles does not merely announce his words from a great emotional distance. Even if he speaks from the raised platform, or *theologeion*, above the actors, he shows concern that Philoctetes "hear" or "understand" his words. "Do not go," he says, "until you hear our words, son of Poeas; deem that you both heed in your hearing (*akoē(i) klyein*) the voice of Heracles and see his sight" (1409–12). He then gives a personal motive for his descent: "I come for your sake" (1413). He concludes this prologue with another injunction about hearing: "Hear my words" (1417, *mythōn epakouson*). Hearing, like speaking, stands on a new level of interaction.

Throughout the play "hearing" has been authoritarian obedience or the passivity of Neoptolemus' hearing with pain a scheme unworthy of his nature (86) or else unacceptable compromise ("sooner would I hear the viper," said Philoctetes, 631–632). When Philoctetes, after long years of silence, heard the human voice he had so longed for (225, *phōnēs akousai boulomai*), it was part of a trick. But now that premature joy of the cry "O dearest voice" in the early scene (*Ō philtaton phōnēma*, 234) is legitimate; Philoctetes echoes that cry in his exclamation at the end of Heracles' speech, *ō phthegma potheinon*, "O longed for speech" (1445).

Twice disconcerted by unexpectedly hearing Odysseus' hateful voice (977, 1295–96), Philoctetes now hears the voice of his soul's longing (*pothos*). The dubious value of speech for trustworthy communication is made good by the visual certainty of pure presence: Heracles' appearance as in an epiphany (1411–12; cf. 1445–47) brings the unmediated vision of instinctively known and felt truth.

Philoctetes does not merely see and hear but for the first time is persuaded and obeys (*ouk apithēsō*, 1447). It is appropriate, therefore, that Heracles should use a new term not only for speaking (*mythoi*) but also for hearing. When he first commands the hearing of his *mythoi*, he uses the verb *aïein*, (1410), not the familiar *akouein* or *klyein*. This verb, like its noun, occurs only in this part of the play and nowhere else. Heracles speaks the words that Philoctetes has been waiting to hear, in this special sense of heedful perception and acceptance. Only he, with his aura of heroic companionship and generosity from Philoctetes' own past, when he still believed in men and society, can command and elicit from Philoctetes the kind of hearing that will make him return to Troy.

Heracles' appearance, however, has a meaning that extends beyond the personal situation of Philoctetes. It also implies the ability of the *logos* of tragedy to reach a plane of truth, clear of the ambiguities and sophistries of Odyssean rhetoric and trickery. As the influence of Odysseus wanes, *logos* gives way increasingly to *ergon* (deed), until finally the figure who most embodies direct heroic action and straightforward relations with men and the world appears on the stage, uttering *mythoi*, not *logoi*. The appearance of Heracles is in itself an epiphany of the divine power of heroic myth, still alive and potent in a corrupt world. Speaking the language of the old heroism ("immortal excellence," "toil," "life of glory," 1419–22), Heracles is both the paradigm and the symbol of all that is threatened with extinction in a world where Odysseus rules and Philoctetes lives in savagery on a desert island. His validation of the meaning of the bow also validates the truth that myth has to convey (*mythos*, 1410, 1417, 1447) and restores the coherence of a spiritual universe where symbolic thought and mythic paradigms have power.

Heracles' appearance is analogous in some ways to the heroization of Oedipus in the *Coloneus* two or three years later. It is a statement about the saving power of tragedy: its ability to make contact and keep vital a lost nobility, grandeur of aspiration, and integrity and to bring lost or absent divinity back to the human world. It is, then, in part, a reassertion, for tragedy itself, of that civilizing power which has been redefined and recreated through the bond between Philoctetes and Neoptolemus. Heracles' appearance regenerates the possibility of absolute values in the tragic *logos* and *mythos*. It does this through its validation of pure symbol (the epiphany itself) in a realm of ambiguous, shifting, and relative *logos*.

The efficacy of persuasion by word in a corrupt society also invites comparison with the *Ajax*. In *Ajax* verbal debate threatens to dissolve into force until the appearance of Odysseus, a very different Odysseus, effects a compromise. This earlier Odysseus embodies some of the best qualities of a democratic polis: compassion, reasonableness, adaptability, skill at negotiating differences. The victory of Odyssean persuasiveness and humane intelligence gives the dead Ajax some measure of dignity and honor. It effects at least a partial reconciliation between the splendid but harsh intransigence of the old heroism and the flexibility demanded by the new society of the fifth-century polis.

In spirit (as in date of composition) *Ajax* stands closer to the end of Aeschylus' *Eumenides*. It shares its confidence in democratic institutions, logical debate, the beneficial effects of persuasion. Half a century later, *Philoctetes* reflects a mood of mistrust in the declining democracy. The failure of the *logos* between men here is the expression of a deeper rift between the personal and the social *logos*, between barren social forms and the need for individual bonds of trust, friendship, communion. Over against this breakdown of communication within the larger society stand the integrity and compassion of personal friendship on the one hand and a more generous divine order on the other. From that personal friendship, though established in hard defiance of the authority-figures, the rest of the society will, ultimately, benefit, since Philoctetes' return assures the capture of Troy and the success of the expedition.

Two major points, however, remain unresolved. First, Philoctetes' repugnance about helping his old enemies and his demand for justice are overridden. Second, even the sincerity and good will of Neoptolemus cannot get beyond short term goals (Philoctetes' return to Greece) and past hatred. It takes the fiat of Olympian *mythos* to command assent by opening again a path to absolute values and things eternal.

III

Language itself, therefore, even persuasion with good will (*eunoia*, 1322), is insufficient. Action, resolution of conflict by decision, and the risk and effort involved in change are also vital. The mounting agony of the question, "What shall I do?" (*ti drasō*), speaks emphatically to that point (757, 895, 908, 962, 969, 1063, 1351). The two scenes of crucial change, first Neoptolemus' as he debates within himself whether to hand over the bow to Odysseus, and then Philoctetes' as he wonders how to respond to the good will proven in the return of the bow, both frame the decision in terms of the question, "What shall I do?" (908, 962, 969, 974, 1351). As Neoptolemus repeats this question, he sees more clearly the inadequacy of the moral terminology which he had accepted as part of his Odyssean training. Though he reveals the truth ("I will hide nothing from you," *kryptein*, 915), he still finds it not possible to return the bow, "for justice and advantage make me heed those in command" (925–926). The closely repeated "What shall I do?" however (962, 969, 974), shows that his generalization uniting justice and advantage does not resolve the question of action. As that question sharpens, Neoptolemus finds that he must choose. He has to sacrifice advantage to justice. They will not coalesce as easily as this protégé of Odysseus once thought. At the crucial moment Neoptolemus will stand fast by his resolve and prefer justice to Odyssean cleverness (1246): "With justice on my side, I do not tremble at your threats of fear." His path of acting (*dran*, 1227, 1231, 1241, 1252) is no longer obscured by words. Obedience to the army no longer keeps him from doing what he knows to be right (see 1243, 1257).

The active component of the good will that Neoptolemus can eventually offer Philoctetes consists in part in help, *ōphelein*, a quality in which Odysseus' society is bankrupt. His followers had set the crippled sufferer ashore with but "a little help of food" (*ōphelēma smikron*, 274–275), whereas Neoptolemus' presence at the attack of the disease, "present and sharing in help" (*synōphelounta*, 871), is both the sign of the noble nature (*physis*) on which Philoctetes congratulates him (874–875) and the basis for the later decision to act in a new way. Help here accompanies Neoptolemus' capacity for "enduring pityingly" the stench and cries of the disease (*tlēnai eleinōs*, 879), something which Philoctetes' sworn brothers-in-arms could not endure (*etlēsan*, 872–873).[23] This direct action reveals the cleavage between word and deed which Neoptolemus, unlike Odysseus, cannot bridge. Philoctetes, disturbed by this gap between saying and doing, focuses it on the question of help. He thus brings the young man to his first full realization of the momentous choice he can no longer evade (903–913):

Neopt.: There is difficulty every way if one leaves his own nature (*physis*) and does what is not fitting (*dran*).

Phil.: But you at least are neither *doing* nor saying anything inconsistent with the father who sired you if you help a noble man (*epōphelōn*).

Neopt.: I am shown disgraced (*aischros*); this has long been my pain.

Phil.: Not at least in what you are *doing*. But in what you are *speaking* I have fears.

Neopt.: O Zeus, what shall I *do*? For a second time I shall be caught in baseness (*kakos*), hiding what I should not hide and speaking the most shameful words.

Phil.: This man, unless I am base in judgement, is likely to betray me and leave me and set sail.

Neopt.: Not by leaving you; but lest I escort you with greater grief, that has been my pain for a long time.

Moving from Odyssean *logos* to the *ergon* of real help, from concealment (*kryptein*, 915; cf. 909) to honesty, Neoptolemus finds that leaving Philoctetes (912) and leaving his own nature (903) come to the same thing. Under Odysseus' tutelage in the prologue, his question was about words (cf. 54–55), and his doing (*to dran*, 118) consisted in using words: "What else are you ordering me (to do) except to speak lies (*pseudē legein*, 100)?" Now seized by pity, which he experiences almost as a fearful (*deinos*) being that "has fallen upon (him) not for the first time, but long since" (965–966), Neoptolemus' questions are all about action, and his onstage silence of over a hundred lines is one of the most dramatic in Sophocles (974–1080).[24] The repeated word, *palai*, "long since," in this scene (806, 913, 966) gives a temporal dimension to this conflict in Neoptolemus' soul.[25] It suggests the slow growth of his pity and his attempts to resist it, until it overwhelms him, finally, with the hard question of active spiritual revaluation, "What shall I do?" (895, 908, 963, 969).[26]

In his final attempt to persuade Philoctetes, Neoptolemus subordinates words to the active benefits of his friendship and help (1373–75): "Your arguments are reasonable, and yet I wish you to obey the gods and my words and *sail* from this land with me, *your friend*." When Philoctetes still balks at the hateful destination, Troy (1376–77), Neoptolemus cites the specific benefit to him, the end of pain in his infected foot and salvation from the disease (1378–79). But Philoctetes still resists being helped himself (*ōpheloumenos*, 1383) if it means benefit (*ophelos*) to the Atreids (1384),[27] a statement which recalls his warning, some twelve lines before, against helping base men (*kakous epōphelōn*, 1371). Neoptolemus' last effort is the affirmation of friendship (1385): "I speak as a friend (*philos*) to you, and such too is my word." The active qualities of help and friendship are then completed in the actual offer to take him back to Greece, in defiance of the army (1402ff.). So long friendless (*aphilos*, 1018), Philoctetes will need Heracles' expression of archetypal friendship to recall him from hatred and disease to the help and salvation that he deserves.

Conflict, decision, and action are so hard precisely because they contain the possibility of error; this, too, Neoptolemus, bearing the responsibility for his own acts, must face. The verb *hamartanein* means both "miss" or "fail" in a neutral sense and "err" in a moral sense.[28] The two meanings are perhaps already implicit in the doing or acting (*dran*) to which Neoptolemus somewhat reluctantly agrees when he tells Odysseus, in the prologue, "I prefer to *fail* in noble acting (*kalōs drōn*) rather than succeed in base (*kakōs*)." At his first major crisis, revealing the truth of his plot to Philoctetes, he must confront, from the older man, the painful (*algeinon*) impact of the error he has made (1011–12). Later he not only acknowledges that error before his old mentor (1224–26) but undoes it by trying "to make up the shameful error in which I erred' (1248–49). Now Neoptolemus is willing to accept failure in Odyssean terms (94–95) to win a more important success in moral terms. At his first encounter with Neoptolemus, when he was only a strange, but welcome voice, Philoctetes had said, "Answer, for it is not likely that either I should mistake (fail) you in this, nor you me" (230–231). And in truth the older man neither errs nor fails in respect to the younger, for even in his terrible anger he does not mistake the other's underlying nobility of nature (1004–12). That recognition of inner essence is reciprocal, for that expression, "either you . . . or me," recurs in Neoptolemus' mouth when he tries to hold Philoctetes back from shooting Odysseus and then when he tries to persuade him to return to Troy: "For neither *you nor me* is this noble" (1304); "the things which I see as best in their fulfillment *for you and me*" (1381). The instinctive recognition of inborn nobility and particularly the emphasis on friendship, help, and good will suggest the mood of Athenian optimism in the early years of the Peloponnesian War. In his Funeral Speech Pericles had stressed the active, enterprising initiative of the Athenians in winning allies.[29] Democritus' contrast between good will (*eunoia*) and fear (B268) resembles the contrast embodied in the treatment of Philoctetes by Neoptolemus and Odysseus respectively. Fragment 255 urges the strong to be kindly to the weak. "If they have the courage and boldness (*tolmē*) to do this, the result is pity (*oiktirein*) and not being isolated (*erēmoi*) and being companions, and mutual help and the concord of citizens and such other good things as one could scarcely list."[30] Similarly Plato has Protagoras, in his myth, place the warmer, more personal unifying bonds of friendship (*philia*) beside the more legalistic order of cities (*poleōn kosmoi*) as the benefits of Justice and Reverence (*Protagoras* 322d). This spirit in the *Philoctetes* is part of that mood of nostalgia that pervades the early part of the play (cf. 410ff.).

Neoptolemus' final gesture of friendship to Philoctetes reflects another characteristic Athenian quality, flexibility. Changing one's mind is a major theme in this play. Indeed, the *Philoctetes* is unique among the extant plays in representing a tragic hero changing his mind.[31] The spirit in which such changes occur, however, is crucial. Neoptolemus' task is to find his way back to the constant elements of his nature in the midst of the adaptability asked of him by Odysseus. Despite his temporary acquiescence in Odyssean shiftiness, something deep within him remains unchanged.[32] The moment is unripe for either genuine change or the pity that can take the form of action. The change (*metatithemenos*) and pity which the chorus seems to advocate in the lyrics of 507–518 only support the ruse. Also serving that ruse, Neoptolemus, in replying immediately after, makes clear the importance of real, inward change (519–523): "Watch out now that you are easy (*eucherēs*), but when you have your fill of the disease in close association (*synousia*) you show yourselves the same as your words say."

When Philoctetes fears Neoptolemus' hesitation because of "the ugly harshness of the disease" (*dyschereia*, 901–902), Neoptolemus replies, "There is harshness (*dyschereia*) every way whenever one deserts his nature (*physis*) and does what is unfitting." Neoptolemus thinks of constancy, not change, but it is constancy not to Odysseus' ruse but to his own nature. The word translated "harshness" here, *dyschereia*, is the opposite of the "pliancy" (*eucherēs*) about which Neoptolemus warned the chorus when he was still acting as Odysseus' agent in 519ff. He must move from a false "pliancy" back to a part of himself which he cannot change or can change only at the price of his moral integrity.

Sophocles forces his characters to the point where the paradoxes of change and constancy become the center of the spiritual *agōn*, the conflict of basic values for each. At the climax of the discovery scene Philoctetes checks his curse on his deceiver with the words, "May you perish—but no, not until I learn if you will change your mind (*gnōmēn metoiseis*); and, if not, may you die miserably" (961–962). Pitying long since (*palai*, 966), Neoptolemus reveals that time has been working toward a changefulness very different from that envisaged by Odysseus.

Still full of pity (cf. 1074), Neoptolemus cannot make the decisive change himself but can only wait, hoping that the other may change his mind ("take a better mind, *phronēsis*, toward us," 1078–79). The hope is futile: soon after, Philoctetes meets the chorus' question about a change of mind (*gnōmē*, 1191–92) with a "firmly fixed" (*empedon*) reply, "Never, never" (1197ff.). Neoptolemus' courage in changing his own mind is an important step toward establishing a change that implies not weakness but strength in the certainty of his deepest, most essential nature. "Is it not then possible to change one's mind again?" Neoptolemus asks the older man after he has returned the bow. He finds the older man still suspicious of persuasion by his words (1268ff.). Yet the model of flexibility based on good will and benefiting others (*eunoia, euergetein*) realized by Neoptolemus works in the present as Philoctetes' experience of these qualities works, through Heracles, from the past.

This capacity for change is a concomitant of the compassion and integrity that make Neoptolemus, like the Odysseus of the *Ajax*, the bearer of truly humane, civilized values.[33] It is as a paradigm of civilizing heroism that Heracles descends from Olympus to make those values effective in Philoctetes once more. Odysseus, the man of change (cf. 1049), Homer's "man of many turnings" (*polytropos*), proves the least flexible character in the play.

IV

As change and firmness shift meanings, so do other basic value terms: "Baseness" and "nobility," *kakos, aischros*.[34] Neoptolemus' final decision in the play is to hold firm to his change from Odyssean obedience. Deserting the army at Troy is, as Philoctetes says, noble, *gennaion* (1402). The "corruption" of Neoptolemus in one sense is his "redemption" in another; this effects the redemption of Philoctetes too.[35] Through a process of lonely choice, isolation, and sacrifice, Neoptolemus comes to repeat in his own experience what both Philoctetes and Achilles have lived. This process constitutes a kind of initiation into heroic society.[36] Like the older men, he finds youth's bright expectations dimmed by complexity and bitterness.[37] But by relinquishing his initial ambitions, he acquires a more authentic heroism than he could have won in his yearned-for success at Troy under Odysseus (114ff.).[38]

Amid the deaths of so many of the great heroes, Philoctetes would die too, were it not for the still uncorrupted nature of Neoptolemus. By himself Neoptolemus cannot persuade Philoctetes, any more than he could initially resist Odysseus. Heracles serves as the necessary mediator between lonely asperity and instinctive nobility. Spanning the two poles of the time-bound and the eternal, Philoctetes' past benefaction and the immortal excellence (1420), Heracles enables the complementary strength and weakness, intransigence and tractability, of the two protagonists to work together rather than cancel out one another.

Beneath the superficial brilliance of success offered by Odysseus, Neoptolemus comes to discern a sordidness unworthy of his own character. Beneath the misery, fetor, foulness of Philoctetes he comes to perceive the last glow of Achillean heroism in this world of ghosts (946–947, 436ff., 446ff.). The older world of Philoctetes' heroic firmness has something to teach the new world of youthful fluidity and adaptability. But youthful trust, compassion, and flexibility have a lesson for embittered old age. "Learn (*didaskou*) not to be harsh in your ills," Neoptolemus advises the older man (1387).[39] This reversal of pupil and teacher roles is then reenacted on the stage in the appearance of Heracles. Now it is as if Philoctetes himself returns to his youth, to the point where Neoptolemus now stands, a young man listening to the words of an older, mature man who is his model.

Heracles, as we observed earlier, comes not merely as the messenger of the divine will but as a friend giving helpful advice to a younger friend ("I come for your sake," 1413).[40] At his first encounter with Neoptolemus, Philoctetes was overjoyed at the sound of a "longed-for voice . . . after so long a time" (234–235). This desired "voice" belongs not to Neoptolemus but to Heracles, who can

344

restore him to his humanity in a fuller way than he could have guessed at that first hearing.[41] The premature recognition of that earlier "longed-for voice" is made good, and Philoctetes now finds the wise counselor (*symboulos*, 1321) whom he could not accept in the younger man, one who will tell him the counsels of Zeus (1415; cf. 1442–43).

In its flexible viewpoint, the *Philoctetes* represents a striking change from the *Ajax* of perhaps some forty or even fifty years earlier. There the hero's rigidity defined a doomed, if compelling, code of values obsolescent in the newer world of democratic institutions.[42] Here the old world, open to communication with the new, proves ultimately educable, albeit only through a miracle from the gods.

In still another way Neoptolemus and Philoctetes undergo parallel experiences in their relation to heroic father-figures of their past. Each is robbed of heroic arms that rightly belong to him, Neoptolemus in pretense (assuming that his story about being robbed of Achilles' arms is a lie), Philoctetes in fact.[43] Neoptolemus' lie (359–381), however, contains a hidden truth: in becoming Odysseus' protégé, he has, in a sense, lost his right to his father's god-given arms and the heroic world which they exemplify.[44]

The lie about Achilles' arms recurs, rather surprisingly, near the end of the play. Wavering for a moment under the effect of Neoptolemus' reasoned and well-meaning plea that he return to Troy, Philoctetes replies that neither of them should go. The army's leaders, he argues, "insulted you, stripping you of your father's prize of honor (*geras*) and in the judgment of Achilles' arms decreed unfortunate Ajax as inferior to Odysseus" (1364–67). Why should this now irrelevant detail recur? Possibly Sophocles wishes to remind us of Neoptolemus' shame in having stooped to lie when he was under Odysseus' influence. If so, the repetition calls attention to the scars which falsehood has left on heroism, even after falsehood is abandoned. Neoptolemus' fidelity to his originally deceitful promise to Philoctetes does not entirely expunge the error bred by the initial deception. The chagrin for Neoptolemus is all the greater, for just before this passage Philoctetes warns against the ill effects of being educated by base men (1360–61).

In taking Philoctetes' side, Neoptolemus now ranges himself with Ajax and Achilles against Odysseus and Agamemnon. His lie about the arms paradoxically prefigures the nobility which he will in fact attain at the end. In his fabricated speech he related how he stood up, to face the whole assembly (367–377). That gesture recalls Achilles' defiance of the army in *Iliad* 1.[45] At the end, Neoptolemus acts out that gesture on the stage, defying Odysseus and returning the bow in the name of honor, nobility, and truth. Like Achilles, he is ready to draw his sword against superior authority if necessary (1255–56; cf. *Iliad* 1. 188ff.). In thus defying his base teacher to defend the new teacher whom he has found, Neoptolemus, presumably in possession of his father's arms all along, has at last shown himself worthy to inherit them.[46]

Heracles' arms pose a similar trial to Philoctetes. He introduced himself as "the lord of Heracles' weapon" of whom Neoptolemus has perhaps heard (261–262).[47] For both him and Neoptolemus heroic weaponry symbolizes an as yet hidden or not fully realized aspect of identity to which both must gain access. For Philoctetes this happens literally, for Neoptolemus metaphorically. Each set of weapons should be a token of nobility, but each becomes involved in unheroic falsehood. Neoptolemus has to relive his initial falsehood about the armor in 1365–67. Now, however, he makes the lie good as truth: he changes his feigned rejection of Odysseus into a firmly fixed decision. He has separated himself from the spirit as well as the person of Odysseus. He now stands ready for a still more courageous conversion of lie into truth, fulfilling his false promise to take Philoctetes home.

At the midpoint of the action Philoctetes called the bow "a thing of much suffering," *polypona* (777). At the end, through the example of his own suffering (*ponoi*), Heracles reveals the bow as the means to immortal *aretē* and a life of glory (*eukleēs bios*, 1418–22). Heracles' *ponoi*, in their association with the bow, are a paradigm not only of suffering but also of release from suffering.[48] The hopeless, brutalizing *ponoi* of Philoctetes' disease (508) or the cowardly *ponos* of the chorus' acceptance of Odysseus' scheme (863–864) give way to the heroic *ponoi* of the bow's past and future.

"The sailors will not begrudge you their pain" (*ponos*, 887, also "trouble," or "effort"), Neoptolemus reassures Philoctetes as he offers to have him carried on board. Still under Odysseus' influence, Neoptolemus is approaching his moment of crisis and decision, in which *ponos* takes on a new importance. He has just witnessed, pityingly, the agonizing *ponos* of the disease, from whose spasms Philoctetes has only now recovered (867ff.). Astonished and relieved to see the young man still there after his collapse into unconsciousness, Philoctetes has reservations about the sailors (890–891): "Let them be, lest they suffer the affliction of the fetid smell sooner than necessary." He has a more realistic estimate of the pain (*ponos*) connected with the wound (891–892): "Their pain (*ponos*) on the ship, in dwelling with me, will be enough." Sophocles plays on the range of meanings of *ponos*: the physical effort of carrying the injured man to the ship, the suffering endurance of a voyage made unpleasant by a screaming and foul-smelling invalid, the agony of the wound, the toil and effort of a great hero.

The *ponos* that Neoptolemus dismisses so easily here (887) will have a very different significance for him later. "Did you too then share in that pain (*ponos*)?" Neoptolemus' disingenuously asked Philoctetes about the Trojan expedition early in the play as he began to spread his net of Odyssean guile about his victim (248). He will have a much deeper knowledge of the suffering and the sharing as he leaves the stage, destined to join with Philoctetes in the enterprise that will bind them together in heroic fellowship (1436). The result is, factually, the same as that plotted by Odysseus in the prologue (113–115), but the emphasis is not on Odysseus' success, but Philoctetes' reward. He returns to Troy under the aegis not of Odyssean guile but of the Heraclean *ponoi* that lead toward *aretē*, glory, eternity (1418–24).

Heracles functions not only as the symbol of Philoctetes' greatness of soul, that part of him still in touch with heroic *aretē* and timeless things, but also as the spokesman for a larger order in which that heroism is needed and is destined to play a major role. He is Philoctetes' link with the divinity in himself[49] and with the objectively existing divine order and its demands.[50]

The spatial field of the play comprises not just the tension between Lemnos and Troy, but a triangular tension between Lemnos, Troy, and Malis-Oeta.[51] By line 1409 Philoctetes has secured his journey from Lemnos to Malis, but he is to return to Malis via the heroic exploits of Troy. He is to recover not the Malis of Poeas but the Malis which has Heracles' mountain, Oeta, in its territory. He must bring the prize of glory (*aristeia*), Heracles tells him, "to his father Poeas, to the plain of his fatherland, Oeta" (1428–30) and he is to dedicate the spoils awarded him by the army "at my pyre, in memory of my bow" (*toxōn emōn mnēmeia*, 1432). In following the destined route of the Heraclean bow, Oeta–Lemnos–Troy–Oeta, Philoctetes brings the rewards of achieved *aretē* back to its symbolical center in the play, back to the source of heroic generosity in Philoctetes himself (*euergetein*, 669–670).

In the first half of the play Oeta is only Philoctetes' homeland (453, 479, 490, 664). Its significance changes after he initiates Neoptolemus into the heroic meaning of the gift of the bow. When the chorus mentions Oeta now, it is to celebrate the place of Heracles' movement from man to god, "all ablaze with divine fire" (727–729). From this point on, Oeta signifies that there is something more in Philoctetes' past than the mortal, isolated, local aspect of the homeland to which he wants to return. His dedication of the Trojan spoils on Oeta closes the circle and completes for him, as the Oetean pyre did for Heracles, the movement from the beastlike life of his savage isolation to immortal excellence, from the elemental fire of Lemnos to the divine fire of Heracles' apotheosis. Heracles' careful instructions about the spoils and the prize of valor show how utterly mistaken Odysseus was in his threat to leave Philoctetes on Lemnos and his fantasy that the army might award Philoctetes' prize (*geras*) to him (1060–62). It simultaneously validates, once and for all, Neoptolemus' burgeoning insight into the meaning of the oracle: the crown belongs to Philoctetes (839–841).

In these instructions and prophecies, Heracles in a sense makes Philoctetes the gift of the bow a second time, just as he sends him to Oeta a second time. This second "gift" of the bow consists not in handing it over physically but in recalling him to its true meaning as a symbol of heroic action. As the fire of Oeta once separated the bestial from the divine Heracles, so the recollection of that purifying fire through the gift of the bow separates the ensavaged from the heroic Philoctetes, the noble from the bestial self.

Here again Philoctetes and Neoptolemus complement one another. Both are vouchsafed an insight into the workings of the divine will, Neoptolemus through his perception of the true meaning of the oracle in 839–841, Philoctetes through the speech of Heracles. In both cases this god-sent voice corresponds to a more truthful, more authentic inward voice, the voice of each man's essential nobility and inborn heroism. This voice speaks a truth greater than the truth contained in Philoctetes' hatred and embittered refusal.

Sophocles does not completely close the gap between the divine plan and the justice for which Philoctetes screams, between noble heroes and the base men who have victimized them.[52] Although he and Neoptolemus have reconstituted the heroic bond which once existed between Philoctetes and Heracles, that bond does not necessarily extend to the leaders of the Trojan host. There is reconciliation neither with the Atreids nor with Odysseus, and there is no final answer to the moral outrage that Philoctetes feels in bringing help or benefit to his loathed enemies (1383ff.). Nor is there any suggestion, within the framework of this play, that the Atreids and Odysseus are punished for what they have done to Philoctetes.

It would be utterly mistaken, however, to read the appearance of Heracles as constituting a mockery of Philoctetes or the futility of his will against an overriding divine force.[53] By stressing his gift of the bow, his relation to his old companion as friend and model, and his return to Oeta, Sophocles has gone out of his way to present Heracles' prophecies as the fulfillment of the latent nobility of the hero, in its civilizing not its savage face. The tone of heroic greatness overshadows our knowledge that full justice has not been done. But one meaning of Sophocles' difficult ending is that the desires of the envenomed, ensavaged Philoctetes cannot and should not be fulfilled. He will go to Troy, but not at the order of the Greek generals nor even as a result of human persuasion. He will obey only the divine voice that comes to him, personally, "for his sake" (1413), from Olympus. The demand for heroic recognition can ask little more. Sent to Troy in the spirit of Heracles' immortal excellence, he will not be infected by Odyssean or Atreid baseness.[54] He may accomplish the ends of Odysseus and Agamemnon, but that is only because all of them must fulfill the gods' will. The spirit of that accomplishment and its rewards remain Philoctetes'; that too is the significance of dedicating the spoils of that accomplishment at Heracles' Oetean shrine.

Both Heracles and Philoctetes triumph over a brutalizing disease which would reduce the hero from his human to his savage self. Heracles, whose end, thanks in part to Philoctetes' presence at the pyre, embodies the upward movement from beast to god, reappears to validate the true meaning of the bow and thereby to cancel out the destructive confusion of man and beast in the wound. With the heroic and divine use of the bow restored, the wound can be cured, the savagery of the disease defeated. To this restored order in the hierarchies of the animal and social order corresponds a restoration of order in language and ritual. The first takes place through the proper understanding of the oracles, the second through the fulfillment of the divine will and the prayers that end the play.[55]

V

In having Philoctetes refuse to go to Troy and in insisting on Neoptolemus' fidelity to his oath to return him to Malis, Sophocles is testing not only Philoctetes but also Neoptolemus. In the last scene Neoptolemus is made to choose one last time between the familiar heroism of winning the prizes of war at Troy and a more difficult, far less obvious heroism that brings no material rewards, no external, public recognition, but rather the reverse. This is the last teaching which Philoctetes has to give the younger man before himself receiving from Heracles his own re-initiation into heroic *aretē*.

The language of the last scene reflects the changed view of heroic behavior. In his lie to Philoctetes early in the play Neoptolemus had used the Homeric formula, "brilliant Odysseus" (*dios Odysseus*, 344).[56] At the end, when Heracles affirms the new bond between the two men, based now on truth, pity, and endurance rather than falsehood, expediency, and moral compromise, Homeric language returns: "Do you guard him and he you," Heracles says, "like two lions joined together" (*leonte synnomō*, 1436–37).[57] Neoptolemus has now earned the right to be included in this heroic simile by the greatest of heroes. When Philoctetes had promised the bow to his young companion for the sake of *aretē*, his last words were, "My disease longs to take you as a helper who stands by" (*symparastatēs*, 674–675). But at the end, their association, with the falsehood now expunged, rests on strength, not weakness, on health, not disease. Instead of needing one who stands by with him, Philoctetes is himself one of a joined pair of powerful creatures, their unity expressed in the dual form, who "take a share" (*syn-*) in the protection of the other. This change, expressed through the figurative language of an epic simile, is already prefigured in the dialogue just before Heracles' appearance, for now it is Philoctetes who proffers help (*prosōphelēsis*, 1406) to Neoptolemus.

In the prologue Odysseus described Neoptolemus and the bow as interdependent ("Neither you without the bow, nor the bow without you," 115), but the emphasis was entirely on the aim of sacking Troy and the isolated, individual gain (*kerdos*) of Neoptolemus (112–115):

> Neopt.: What gain is it for me, then, that this man [Philoctetes] should go to Troy?
> Odyss.: This bow alone will take Troy.
> Neopt.: But am not I, as you kept saying, the one to sack the city?
> Odyss.: Neither you without that bow, nor that bow without you.

Odysseus here subtly modulates from Philoctetes to the bow. The coordinate construction, "Neither you without the bow, nor the bow without you," brackets Neoptolemus and Philoctetes together under the physical objective of the bow. As Neoptolemus himself begins to act, however, the syntactic pattern of coordinate pronouns refers to the two men, not the man and the bow. This shift expresses the movement from deceit to honesty, from manipulation to trust, from materialism to heroic idealism.

Philoctetes' initiation of Neoptolemus into the heroic meaning of the bow foreshadows this change. "It will not be given except to you and me," Neoptolemus promises as he receives the bow from Philoctetes' hand (*soi te kamoi*, 774–775). Philoctetes gives it with a warning to propitiate the envy of the gods, "so that it may not be a source of suffering to you, nor such as it was to me and to its possessor before me" (776–778). Neoptolemus seconds the prayer with the dual form of the personal pronoun, "we two," (779), which now joins the two men as one under the sign of the bow, with its great owner of the past in the background (778). This joining however, is premature, for Neoptolemus' receipt of the bow and promise of propitious voyage in the next lines (779–781) have behind them not the nobility of Heracles, but the guile of Odysseus.

The attack of the disease interrupts the execution of Odysseus' plan. When Neoptolemus once more prepares to set sail, he repeats the pattern of coordinate personal pronouns but with a different significance. He offers his sailors' assistance in carrying the wounded man aboard, "since to you and me it seems best to do thus" (*soi t' edox' emoi te dran*, 888). But this doing is far less easy than it once seemed. Neoptolemus' painful, "What should I do?" occurs soon after (895). This is the crisis in his relation to the man and the bow. When the collocation "I and you" next recurs, it is under the aspect of nobility (*kalon*) and mutual help. Philoctetes, repossessed of his bow, prepares to let fly an arrow at Odysseus; but Neoptolemus stops him with the line, "But neither for me nor for you is this noble" (1304). Their premature conjunction through the bow implied in the earlier scene is fulfilled (774–80), but now Neoptolemus recalls the other to the heroic values implicit in ownership of the bow.

Neoptolemus stresses Philoctetes' capture of the city and the bond of heroic action which links the two men: he defines Philoctetes' task as "sacking Troy's citadel with this bow and with me" (1335). That line (1335) harks back to Odysseus' formulation of the prologue (115) but exactly inverts its meaning. A little later in the scene Neoptolemus reaffirms his conviction that he is persuading his friend to do what he sees as "best both for you and for me" (1381).

The rapid exchange that follows 1381 is the climax of the conflict between the persuasion of friendship and the intransigence of bitterness. Here the intertwining of the two personal pronouns is even more tense and more critical (1388–89, 1393–96):

Phil.:   You, I know, are destroying me with your words (*oleis me, gignōskō se*).

Neopt.:   Not *I*, but I say that *you* refuse to learn . . . What then should we do, if we cannot persuade you in words to do anything that I am saying? Easiest *for me* to cease my words and *for you* to live, as you live now, without being saved.

Neoptolemus' painful but decisive "Let *us* go" (1402) finally validates the union of "I" and "you." Philoctetes' offer to aid with the bow expresses the active, risk-taking help (1406) of his friendship. Upon that pledge of heroic (though ultimately narrow) friendship follows the entrance of Heracles, paradigm of heroic bonding, who joins the two mortals together in epic comradeship (1437–38): "Like twin lions, he guarding you and you him." These lines ennoble their tie of reciprocity and lift it into the heroic radiance of the Homeric simile, albeit with an ambiguity about lions to be discussed below. The coordinate pronouns "neither you without him nor he without you, he guarding you and you him," are now brought together in a more emphatic expression by a third person who stands above both and joins both in a visible gesture of union as friendly and caring as it is authoritative and definitive.[58]

What the syntax of the personal pronouns expresses on the verbal level scenic imagery expresses on the visual. The two men are bound together under the sign of the bow; the three actors on the stage, two mortals and a god, form a triangular configuration whose apex is the mythic embodiment of heroic values throughout the play. Present only in words and symbol in the earlier bonding by the bow (667–670, 727–729), Heracles is now visible in the achieved clarity of scenic action. The luminous emblem of heroic friendship and commitment to man's hidden divinity totally outshines the devious complexity and concealment of Odyssean plotting.

In the prologue, as Neoptolemus took up Odysseus' suggestion, one man would hunt the other (116). Now each will guard the other. The word which expresses their bond in 1436, *synnomos*, means "feeding together" and so suggests the continuation of the savage life on Lemnos, so often described in terms of eating or being eaten. The word also contains the root of *nomos*, "custom-law," "social usage"; elsewhere in tragedy *synnomos* expresses intimate human relationship in civilized institutions, like that of husband and wife (*OC* 340).[59] At one level, then, the simile of the joined lions brings the purely animal associations (*synousiai*, 936) of Philoctetes' life on Lemnos to a new stage, beyond savagery to the divinity of his past and the renewed humanity of his present and future.

At the same time, lions, though evocative of epic heroism and martial courage, are also paradigms in Homer and elsewhere of violence, wild rage, and destructiveness. In the *Odyssey* Homer chooses a simile of a mountain-reared lion to describe the monstrous Cyclops as he eats Odysseus' companions raw, bones, entrails, and all (*Od.* 9.292–293). In the *Iliad* lions dwell in desolate forests or mountains, prey on flocks of sheep and cattle, and fight or kill the shepherds. Thus the lion simile may suggest an element of unresolved bitterness in Philoctetes' return to the Greek host. How can one return from ten years of the most painful exile without some trace of rancor? True, his future association with the Atreids and Odysseus at Troy is outside the frame of the play; yet there is here perhaps some hint of its emotional complexity, as there is also of Neoptolemus' irreverence at the sack of Troy (1440–41). Neoptolemus has jeopardized his future relation with the Greek army in his brazen defiance of one of its leaders and his expectation of armed conflict when he returns home (1404–1408). Restored to the army at Troy by divine command, he and his companion will remain at least partly marginal figures, something of their bond still in touch with the savagery of wild creatures suggested by the lion simile.

Heracles' speech does not really tell us anything new. Neoptolemus has already set forth the essentials in the preceding scene (1329–47). Critics have found this illogical. But Neoptolemus cannot speak with the same authority as

Heracles.[60] What he avers on the authority of Helenus, "best of prophets" (1337–38), Heracles affirms as the counsels of Zeus (1415). Neoptolemus promises that Philoctetes will be judged the best (1345); Heracles says that he will be judged first in *aretē* (1425).[61] Neoptolemus had promised him the highest fame (*kleos hypertaton*, 1347); Heracles says that he will win a life full of fame (*euklea bion*, 1422). But Heracles announces this fame as something owed (*opheiletai*, 1421) to Philoctetes. More important, Heracles can cite his own suffering (*ponoi*) as the paradigm for the achievement of immortal *aretē* (1418–22). This vision of an ultimate meaning of suffering in the perspective of eternity and heroic values carries Philoctetes beyond the static hopelessness of his view of suffering when he tells Neoptolemus, "Let me suffer what I must suffer" (1397). Only Heracles speaks of *ponos* in this larger framework. Only Heracles speaks of *aretē*; Neoptolemus never utters the word.

Neoptolemus gives Philoctetes good advice: "Mortals should endure the fortunes given by the gods" and not "cling to their injuries of their own accord" (1316–20). Yet where the human companion and advisor chides him for his savagery (1321, *ēgriōsai*), the divine friend affirms things eternal (1440–44):

> When you sack the land, bear this in mind, to be pious in what pertains to the gods, since father Zeus holds all else in second place. For piety (*eusebeia*) does not die along with mortal men. Whether they live or die, it is not destroyed.

Heracles opens Philoctetes' sufferings and future achievements into the timeless. These are his last iambic trimeters and the last iambic lines in the play, but like the first trimeters of his speech (1418–22), they contain a vision of his life *sub specie aeternitatis*. His appearance marks the paradox that in this life of savagery, isolation, and misery there lies a hidden strength, like that within the enfeebled Oedipus of the *Coloneus* soon after, which reaches toward the brilliance of the gods[62] and after suffering is illuminated by something like Pindar's "Zeus-given radiance" (*Pythian* 8.96–97).

Heracles is the mediator not only between Philoctetes' past and his future at Troy, but also between man and god, between deceptive human *logos* and divine *mythos*, between illusion and truth.[63] His presence marks the healing of the disease and the relinquishment of savagery in a double sense, both psychological and theological. It restores Philoctetes to himself as a man who can move beyond his bitterness and his envenomed hatred to join with his fellow men once more in heroic companionship and heroic enterprise. Simultaneously, it restores Philoctetes to his place in the larger divine order. To wield the bow sound of limb and heart at Troy is part of his role in a historical pattern. His life, even when purged of its bitterness and isolation on Lemnos, does not exist in isolation, but has its place within the social frame of the Greek expedition and the theological frame of the gods' will.[64] As we have seen elsewhere, it is the task of the Sophoclean hero to recognize that his life has a shape, a place in some larger order which he must fulfill. In the perception and free acceptance of his role in that pattern lies one of the essential qualities of Sophoclean heroism.[65]

VI

As Philoctetes returns from brutalized isolation to human society, from his bitterness toward the gods (254) to piety, he also gains a new feeling for what may be divine in the barren landscape in which he has lived.[66] Obeying Heracles' command for a swift departure from Lemnos (1449–51), Philoctetes takes a last farewell of his island (1453–71):

Phil.: Farewell, chamber that shared the vigils with me and you meadow Nymphs of the waters, and the male beating of the sea's headland, where often my head in the (cave's) inner recesses was drenched by the south wind's buffeting. Often the Hermaean mountain sent back to me, as I was caught in the storm (of my pain), the echoed groan of my voice, beaten back to me. But now, you springs and Lycian water, we are leaving you now, leaving you, never having reached this expectation before. Farewell, you sea-girt plain of Lemnos. May you now send me forth without complaint and with fair voyage, there where the great Destiny is bringing me and the counsel of friends and the all-conquering divinity who has brought these things to fulfillment.

Chorus: Let us then go all together, having prayed to the Nymphs of the sea to come as the saviors of our return.

Philoctetes does not forget the harshness of the sea surrounding Lemnos, the storms, the wind, the rocky setting of the cave where he sought refuge from the elements, the danger of exposure, the wild sounds. And yet he can also see his island as imbued with divinity. For the first time he addresses the Nymphs of the place (1455) and gives local names to a mountain and a spring of water (Hermaean Mountain, Lycian water).

Homer's Odysseus, we may recall, recognized his native land through its springs, the water nymphs, and their worship (*Od.* 13.355–360, 17.204–211). Earlier the chorus had mentioned Nymphs in Philoctetes' native land, Malis (724). Then he was given a false promise of return. Now, when his departure from Lemnos, though for a different destination, is assured, he recognizes the existence of Nymphs on Lemnos, too. He thereby acknowledges Lemnos as something other than a place of bare, savage survival: it is also the place where he was to find the way to his own great destiny (1466). Like Ajax in his final address to the setting around him (*Ajax* 856–866), he can discern a saving as well as a harsh, elemental quality in this world; but, unlike Ajax, the saving power predominates, for the gods themselves intervene to restore the hero to a world in which he now has a necessary place.

How different is Philoctetes' prayer from that of Odysseus at the beginning of the play. Odysseus invoked as his saviors Hermes, the god of trickery (*Hermēs dolios*), and Athena as goddess of victory and civic life (Athena Nikē and Polias, 133–134). Whereas Odysseus remains within the limits of his goals and his confident manipulation of deceit, Philoctetes moves to the vastness of the gods' presence in nature and in man.

Philoctetes bids farewell to both the inner and outer spaces of his savage life. He addresses both the cave (1453) and the deities of the landscape outside. Earlier, at his false and premature departure, he directed his reverent gesture only to the savage aspect of the setting, implied in the paradox of the dwelling that is no dwelling (*aoikos eisoikēsis*, 534).[67] Here, that gesture takes in the divinities of nature, too, although of course he does not forget the harshness of wind and water (1454–60). But that hard life, exposed to cold and wet, and the sound of battering waves endured within the recesses of the cave (*endomychon*, 1457) are tempered, in some small degree, by the sacral dimension of water and its Nymphs outside (1454, 1470).

Civilized habitation involves not just mere survival but establishing relations with the sacred powers of the place through holy names, ritual, and prayer. So far, this sacralization of place has been foreign to Lemnos. "All-nurturing mother Earth" was a remote Asian goddess (391ff.), and the holy earth that gives man the gift of grain was reduced to the barren earth of the hunter (707–708). Nymphs and sacred water belonged to distant, unreachable Malis (725, 1215). In his final address to Lemnos, Philoctetes begins to perform for his earth the civilizing, sacralizing functions that he could not perform while entrapped in its savagery and his own. The farewell expresses, perhaps, a residual bond with the savagery of the island, as if a part of himself were still attached to it.[68] But in addressing Lemnos' Nymphs and springs and not just its wild beasts or its rocks as earlier (cf. 936ff., 1146ff.), he is leaving behind that savage aspect of his island which cut him off from men and gods.[69] He is also bringing to Troy and the spiritually depleted Greek army that intransigence, determination, integrity, and fortitude with which the rocky landscape also has an affinity.

In the perspective of the "great Destiny . . . and the all-conquering divinity who brought these things to pass" (1466–68), barren Lemnos reveals other features. Now the lonely tread or beat (*ktypos*, 201) of one torn with pain (202) has, beside the "male beat" (*ktypos*, 1455) of the sea, female Nymphs (1454) and the "longed-for voice" (1455) which overcomes the bleakness of these wild echoes (1460; cf. 186ff., 694–695, 938). The juxtaposition of male and female (1454f.) is perhaps of significance in a play of exclusively masculine characters. In another legend the Lemnian Nymphs are associated with fertility and salvation from famine: Medea prays to them and to Demeter to end famine in Corinth.[70] Here, as deities of meadows and springs, they preside over the sacredness of fresh water once so hard to obtain.[71] Water, like the sacred earth and the beloved land of Oeta (391ff., 664–665), now becomes part of the hero's own final view of Lemnos, fixed for the future in this more welcoming aspect.

Echoing Odysseus' "sea-girt Lemnos" of the opening line (cf. 1464 and 1), Philoctetes now reverses the meaning of the island for himself and also for Odysseus: he has found in it access to powers in himself and in the world that lies far beyond Odysseus' ken. The crossing of the sea to Troy, envisaged only as the hard-won achievement of human guile, is fulfilled as the plan of remote, mysterious divinities. The closing prayer to the Nymphs of the sea makes good the false or unfulfilled prayers for favorable voyage throughout the play (464, 528f., 627, 782, 1077). Man's contrivances to master nature here issue into a prayer to the now divinized powers of nature. This reversal is perhaps the culminating paradox of the play, that the divine order, and not human *technē*, ultimately permits man to master the savagery of nature and win *sōtēria* (1471).[72] Before he can do that, man must master the savagery in himself.

The closing prayer also widens the meaning of the safety or salvation, *sōtēria*, sought in the play. It consists either in Odysseus' confidently and unscrupulously plotted success (cf. 134–135 and 1109, salvation through falsehood) or Philoctetes' bare survival (for example, "fire which saves me always," *sōzei*, 297).[73] Overcome by the agony of his disease, he prays, in vain, for the gods to come, saving and mild (738–739). But now at the end the gods really are saviors (1471). The promised safety, pursued in prayers that are either false or premature (528–529), has been hindered by Odysseus' deceit or Philoctetes' own obduracy (919–920, 1391, 1396). But now it opens as a gift from Olympus as Philoctetes has access once more to his own blocked humanity and the larger order of the gods.

That double restoration of the hero both to society and to the divine order is reaffirmed in his last words, for he joins the supernatural forces impelling him to rejoin the army with the human. The simple copula *te*, "and," links "the advice of friends" with "great Destiny" (*megalē Moira*) and "the all-conquering divinity who has brought these things to pass" (1466–68).[74] Philoctetes' hateful portion or destiny (*Moira*, 681–682) and his bitterness about the gods or *daimones* (254, 447, 1116, 1187–88) are now subsumed into a larger vision which has some share in the counsels of Zeus (1415) and in those more mysterious powers of these closing lines.[75] In asking that this fair voyage be made without blame, *amemptōs*, 1465, Philoctetes adds the further qualification of moral probity. Along with his closing prayers to the Nymphs, these words suggest that he is well on his way toward heeding Heracles' warnings about piety toward the gods (1441) and his instructions about the piety that does not die with mortal men (1443–44).

VII

The resolution implied in Heracles' descent from Olympus and Philoctetes' farewell to Lemnos is not total. The great Destiny and the all-conquering divinity who brought these things to pass retain that inscrutability characteristic of Sophocles' God.[76] That same god-given fortune which caused his sufferings, in Neoptolemus' view (1315–16, 1326), will also relieve them and compensate for them, but not punish the human agents, Odysseus and the Atreids. Heracles intervenes out of concern and friendship. And yet he is there also as a sign that there is something intransigent about the demands of the gods, something not entirely congruent with human justice. Philoctetes' refusal, though an aspect of his stubborn savagery, is also a reflection of his nobility and his moral integrity, his constancy to his ideals of justice. He feels an instinctive repugnance at participating in an endeavor that will cause the wicked to prosper, even though he thereby prolongs his own suffering.[77]

By resorting to the *deus ex machina* Sophocles shows his recognition of this moral dilemma. But the device does not necessarily mean that the "true" meaning of the myth is Philoctetes' refusal.[78] Euripides might indeed have ended the play at 1408. But the terms in which Sophocles casts Heracles' appearance, as we have seen, are quite different. It both fulfills an inward potential which has been there since his first meeting with Neoptolemus and also signifies that his life has a place in a larger scheme. The entrance of the divine into the human world in Sophocles is always disturbing. The Sophoclean gods do not exist to make us comfortable. Their presence means that a life is touched by something beyond itself that is never fully circumscribed by human terms.

Neoptolemus had told Philoctetes that men "must of necessity bear the fortunes given by the gods" and that his own disease comes from just such divine necessity (1315–16, 1326). Heracles says that the hero must be pious toward the gods (1441ff.). Comparison of the two injunctions might suggest irony or cynicism about the gods. But we must take Heracles' privileged knowledge of Zeus's counsels (1415) at face value. The contrast between his immortal piety and Neoptolemus' divine chance is analogous to the contrast between Heracles' final vision and Hyllus' limited perception at the end of the *Trachiniae*. Neoptolemus' reconciliation of his companion's suffering and the divine will remains conventional and superficial. After Heracles' speech he can only join in the briefest assent (1448).

Philoctetes has a dim premonition of that divine justice when he affirms that the gods must be concerned with justice since their "divine spur" (*kentron theion*, 1039) forced the Atreids to seek him out on Lemnos (1035–39).[79] But the gods' justice spans a wider purview than Philoctetes'. He had conceived of this divine spur in terms of private bitterness and vengeance. Heracles' vision moves back to take in the first sack of Troy (1439–40) and the crime of Paris (1426–27): "With my bow you will deprive of life Paris, who was responsible (*aitios*) for these evils."[80] The gods' concern is not just with the immediate sufferings but with a larger pattern of guilt and retribution that extends back to the beginnings of the Trojan war. Paris signifies little for Philoctetes, but his crime is the source of those evils which have afflicted not only Philoctetes but all of Greece. To the mortal characters the issue of causality or guilt (*aitios*) has been dark with deception (385, 590) or threats (1404). For the god it is lucid and unambiguous; it demands simple, direct action of just the sort Heracles undertook in life. Placing Philoctetes' past suffering and future glory in the perspective of eternal things, Heracles introduces a larger reality over against the illusion to which human perception is so often limited.[81] In this larger perspective Philoctetes' return to Malis, though just, would be an error.

The very existence of this division between the broader and the limited vision, truth and delusion, the larger and the private justice, the whole and the part, implies a tragic view of life. Through Heracles' eyes we see that there is rightness both in Philoctetes' refusal and in his acquiescence. But the complex moral vision that can reconcile this contradiction and lead the hero to a resolution between them belongs not to men but to the gods. Literally and figuratively Philoctetes passes from death to life, but that life has its final meaning only in Heracles' purview of immortal things.

The world symbolized by Troy is marked by death and decay. The great heroes are all dead; only the mean survive and flourish. The point is repeated several times in the early dialogues between Philoctetes and Neoptolemus (412, 417–420, 428–429, 436–437).[82] It is logical that Thersites should still be alive, "since nothing base ever perishes" (446), as Philoctetes says.[83] Neoptolemus assents, alleging that he has left Troy as a place where the worse man has greater strength than the good, and what is noble wastes away, and the coward rules (456–457). What "bloom" (*thallein*) in this morally rotten world are Philoctetes' disease on Lemnos (259) and the corrupt leaders at Troy (420).

Philoctetes' life of bare survival on Lemnos is in fact a living death. He is, as he says, "a mere corpse, the shadow of smoke, a wraith and nothing more" (946–947). So he describes himself, addressing not men but the rocks and beasts of his island, as he reflects bitterly on the irony of leading him, a man of strength (*andra . . . ischyron*, 945), forcibly to Troy. But of course here, as elsewhere in Sophocles, the terms of strength and weakness are not necessarily physical. The Greeks cast him out, he continues later, "friendless, abandoned, citiless, a corpse among the living" (1018). His living death here corresponds to the savagery of his reduced life. "Why do you want to take me back," he asks a dozen lines later, "for I am nothing and died for you long ago?" (1030). Determined on death, literally as well as figuratively (1001–1002, 1204ff.), he will seek his father in Hades and will never see his native city again (1216–17). The loss of his polis and his death go together. Refusal to leave Lemnos is tantamount not only to the risk of death by starvation but also to the continuation of the living death of his savagery.

As in the *Electra*, the inversion of life and death which centers on the hero involves not merely personal survival but the health or corruption of the cosmic order. And, as also in the *Electra*, the return of the enfeebled hero from life to death might be read as a statement of hope about the spiritually and physically impoverished Athens in these last years of the Peloponnesian war.[84]

In his misplaced joy at Neoptolemus' false promises, Philoctetes tells him, "You alone have vouchsafed me to look upon the light of the sun" (663–664; cf. 867–868). But Neoptolemus' courage and innate nobility will later transmute this hyperbole into literal fact when he leads the deceived man forth from the darkness of the cave (1261–62).

When Philoctetes feels the onset of his disease he invokes death and the Lemnian fire (796–801). Fainting, he lies "stretched out in night" (*nychios*, 857), "like one in Hades" (861; cf. 883–885). "Light" is the first word he utters as he awakens (867). He regards the present event as reversing his earlier betrayal by the Atreids (872–873; cf. 276ff.), only to find it later a bitter reenactment, in fact a return to an even surer and crueler death (1017–18, 1084ff.). And yet the forces of life are secretly at work, for this very deathlike sleep stirs in Neoptolemus the compassion that will enable him to overcome the dark talk of Odyssean plotting (578; cf. 581), just as the flash of the Oetean pyre (727–729), symbol of rebirth from death into immortal life, shines as a beacon of radiant heroism that will ultimately flash the light of things eternal into this world of death and corruption.

This "rebirth" of Philoctetes is dependent on a prior "rebirth" in Neoptolemus. The youth who came to Troy "out of desire for the dead" (*tou thanontos himerō(i)*, 350), the desire to look on the body of the great father whom he has never seen (350–351), has to find his way to the living truth of Achilles in himself. The host at Troy, on seeing him, swore they saw the dead Achilles alive again (357–358). Serving Odysseus by the lies of this very speech, he does the reverse of bringing Achilles back to life. In abandoning his own nature, as he gradually comes to realize (902–903), he suffers a death of the self comparable to Philoctetes' dying to his own heroic past in the ensavaged self he has become on Lemnos, "a wraith and nothing more."

In the reversal of life and death that takes place in the play, Philoctetes' deathlike coma (cf. 797) starts the process of recalling to life Neoptolemus' dead Achillean *physis*. The praise which Philoctetes bestows on him after the return of the bow does indeed suggest that he has brought Achilles back to life (1310–13): "You have shown the noble nature from which you sprang, my child. Your father was no Sisyphus, but Achilles, who, when he lived, had the noblest repute among the living and now among the dead." Praising the heroic fame that spans the division between the living and the dead, Philoctetes sounds a little like Heracles at the end, with his pronouncements about "immortal *aretē*" and "a life of glory" (1418–22). What Neoptolemus does with respect to Achilles, Philoctetes will soon do with respect to Heracles. Each man will revivify the dead hero of his past and thereby effect a "rebirth" for both himself and his new friend. Yet neither figure can do that alone. Neoptolemus needs Philoctetes, Philoctetes needs Heracles' actual presence. Neoptolemus' mention of the highest glory that Philoctetes will win at Troy (1336) wrings from the other a plunge back into "death" (1348–53): "O hated life, why, o why do you then keep me here above and not let me go down again to Hades?" The realization of Neoptolemus' good will then elicits the cry, "Alas, what shall I do? Shall I yield then? But how, ill-starred as I am, shall I do this and go into the light? To whom shall I speak?"[85]

Philoctetes' death-in-life finds its visible emblem in the scenery itself, the cave always in view as the reminder of his savagery.[86] Like the cave of the *Antigone* and the threatened immersion in a cavernous space in *Electra*, the cave of the *Philoctetes* is a place of both physical and emotional death.[87] It is by the cave's vaulted rock that Philoctetes was initially abandoned in the deathlike sleep of his disease (271–273); it is against the rock of this cave that he would dash his head in a desperate access of bitterness when he sees himself betrayed a second time by erstwhile friends and allies (1000–1002).

Philoctetes' figurative death to the heroic world (1018, 1030) and the literal death which he faces on his harsh island are brought together through the motif of the cave. Treacherously stripped of his bow, he returns to his cave, doomed to what he foresees as certain death by starvation (952–954): "O double-gated rocky shape, I shall return to you stripped, without nurture (*trophē*), but alone in this abode I shall wither away." An echo of this passage later marks an even clearer association between the figurative death of his savagery and the literal death in the cave which is the locus of that savagery. Left alone with the chorus, he begins his lyrical lament by addressing the cave of hollow rock (1081; cf. 952) which he endows with the feeling which he has found lacking among men (1082–85): "Alas, I was destined never to leave you, but you will share the knowledge of my death."[88] Neoptolemus' return replaces that address to a rock with a real human voice and real human compassion (1261–64):

> Neopt.: O Poeas' son, Philoctetes, do you come forth, leaving this rocky shelter.
>
> Phil.: What sound of a cry arises here by my cave? Why do you call me forth?

The final cancellation of Philoctetes' death-in-life would be even more vivid if Heracles, as some have conjectured, made his appearance from the cave itself.[89] In that case the place and the symbol of Philoctetes' social and physical death would be negated by the god who points him toward "life" in the largest possible sense, the deathless glory and the immortal piety. However that may be, the return of the heroic spirit from death to life and to eternal things extends the significance of "rebirth" beyond Philoctetes himself to the world of men as a whole, where, as the early scenes make clear, true nobility has died and only baseness flourishes.

Philoctetes' two-mouthed cave recalls that of another hero who is making his way back from a deathlike state to life and his heroic identity, namely the hero of Homer's *Odyssey*.[90] The misty cave of the nymphs on Ithaca marks his mysterious transition back to human life and human society after wandering and loneliness. This cave also has two entrances (*Od.* 13.103–112). A part of the natural world, it contains, in petrified form, the tokens of the civilized, productive life of the palace to which Odysseus will make his way: cups, amphoras, looms, fine garments (*Od.* 13.105–107). Unlike Philoctetes' cave, however, this cave of a hero now returned after trials to his native land, stands between the civilized and the wild, between gods and men. Its vessels, like its magical looms, are of stone and thus belong still to nature. But it is here that Odysseus renews his contact with the divinities of his homeland, divinities, like Philoctetes' Heracles, who define a rich life of human associations from which the hero has long been separated. He will meet those nymphs again at the point of his final journey to the palace. In a grove where cool water flows from a rock there is an altar of the Nymphs, where all wayfarers make offerings (*Od.* 17.208–211). Is it mere coincidence, then, that in his last address to his cave Philoctetes joins cave and water nymphs (1453–54): "Farewell O chamber (*melathron*) which shared my watchful vigils; farewell, Nymphs of waters and meadows." Just as he can sense on barren Lemnos the presence of previously unnamed divinities, so here, at this point of return from savagery to civilization, he gives that rude cavern of his bare survival the name of a civilized dwelling, *melathron*, "chamber," "house." Retrospectively, the word revalidates his existence on Lemnos as a proto-civilized rather than an utterly uncivilized life. That cave has seen terrible sufferings and has certainly been the setting for a reduced and miserable existence. Yet for all its deprivation that existence has been recognizably human. Philoctetes' efforts to survive have, in the end, added up to more than the savagery of bare survival.

In the prologue Odysseus first described the cavern as "a two-mouthed rock" (*distomos petra*, 16). He and Neoptolemus soon discover the traces of rudimentary artisanship and technology, the wretched "treasure" (*thēsaurisma*, 37) of the inhabitant's possessions (32–39). In that glimpse of the cave the savage aspect predominates, but, as we have seen, it shelters a nobility more civilized, in certain essential ways, than the military organization at Troy. Philoctetes' last words to the cave show it to us in this paradoxically civilized light. Having kept himself alive there by endurance and ingenuity, having furthermore not lost his hope of hearing another human voice or his capacity for human association, and finally having received from Heracles the knowledge of the value of the suffering which he has endured in the paradigm of that hero's own *ponoi*, he has the right to call his rude cavern by the name of a civilized dwelling.

Ready to persevere in his wraithlike existence (946–947) and suffer what he must suffer, (1397), the hero, at an earlier stage, passes through death and nothingness to the deep sources of his humanity, which, paradoxically, are also the point where he touches divinity. The experience is analogous to that of Antigone, Heracles in the *Trachiniae*, Electra, and Oedipus in both his plays. In the agony of this passage the *Philoctetes*, despite its happy ending, has a fully tragic spirit. The immortal *aretē* and the undying piety are reached only through a bitter eclipse of God and a long immersion in the subhuman life of the beastlike, ensavaged self.

There is, as at least one scholar has suggested,[91] an affinity between Antigone's famous speech on the unwritten laws which live always (*Antig.* 455–457) and Heracles' lines on the piety which does not die with mortal men. In both cases man is brought into contact with a dimension of existence that lies beyond his humanity, yet makes him truly human. Without that contact he would remain like the beasts, possessed of physical survival but lacking the *sōtēria* without which life is brutish and meaningless (cf. 1397–98). Thanks to Neoptolemus' courage and good will and the gods' final dispensation in Heracles' appearance, the man potentially friendless, abandoned, citiless (1018) can be returned to life, society, and the gods. Behind the bestial form of Chryse's snake, mysterious agent of obscure divine vengefulness and jealously guarded prerogatives, emerge the familiar form of the now divinized Heracles, the helpful sons of Asclepius who will effect the physical cure at Troy, and the remoter divine powers, the Great Destiny and the all-conquering divinity, in whose will the whole action ultimately resides.

Philoctetes: Society, Language, Friendship

To look beyond the desert island of hatred and bitterness to these larger powers is itself to be pious with respect to the gods (1441). This is the piety that Heracles teaches Philoctetes at the end. It includes also the recognition of the daimon of one's destiny in its largest terms. That is the hard knowledge to which the gods call the tragic hero in Sophocles when they force their abrupt entrance into his life. Those who do not attain the dubious privilege of this knowledge are left in the semidarkness of the human perspective alone or die before they can convert their suffering into knowledge. Into this latter category fall Creon in the *Antigone*, Hyllus and Deianeira in the *Trachiniae*, Jocasta in the *Oedipus Tyrannus*, and perhaps Orestes in the *Electra*.

What is remarkable about the *Philoctetes* is the combination of this larger knowledge with the final yielding of the gods, the last-minute reconciliation between human sympathies and obscure divine purposes. How the aged poet arrived at this vision we shall never know. Little of it can be traced in the *Electra*, written probably only a few years before the *Philoctetes*. Yet we should not read the end of *Philoctetes* too optimistically. We should recall the ambiguous lion simile of 1436. Left to himself, the hero would suffer the pain of his physical and emotional wound to the end of his life. That is the darker side of the bright aspect of immortal *aretē* and deathless piety which Heracles opens before the intransigent Philoctetes.

The *Philoctetes* cannot be read simply as a play about individual isolation or social or psychological maladjustment. It is, rather, a profound reflection on the nature of man as a civilized being, on the bonds, needs, and obligations that hold men together. Its double but unified subject is what Plato calls "the unifying bonds of friendship" (*desmoi philias synagōgoi*, *Protagoras* 322c) *and* simultaneously the relationship of those bonds to the elusive and mysterious divine order, which in Sophocles is the final touchstone of man's strength and weakness.

The psychological, social, and theological meanings of the wound and of the bow are inseparably fused. They are each parallel to the other, and they all work together to explore what becomes of men who live in an unhallowed world, a world of brute nature, bare survival, where human beings are treated as means. It is a world which, mutatis mutandis, we easily recognize as our own. But unlike the *entgötterte Natur* in which modern man lives, Sophocles' world contains immortal heroes who remind man of what is divine in himself. Philoctetes' world is inhabited by nature deities and by *daimones* who embody, after all, the sacredness of the soil on which he walks (1464) and the sea over which he passes (1470) with his now trusted companions as he accomplishes his God-given great Destiny.

11

Oedipus at Colonus: The End of a Vision

 In the three late plays, *Electra*, *Philoctetes*, and *Oedipus at Colonus*, personal relationships play a crucial role in articulating a new image of civilization.[1] The *Philoctetes* and the *Coloneus* treat an outcast's reintegration into society. As Philoctetes needs to separate himself emotionally from the hatred of his past and accept a present friendship that reaches back to the health of his pre-Odyssean and pre-Trojan self, so Oedipus must separate himself from the city of his embittered past, with its feuds and curses, and accept friendship and trust in a new city. Forcibly dragged back toward the old city of violence and pollution, Thebes, he chooses the enlightened piety of Athens. The contrast between the two cities and the two images of society that they embody is essential to an understanding of this play.

The *Oedipus at Colonus* begins, in a sense, where the *Philoctetes* leaves off. Instead of struggling against the all-ruling divinity of his destiny (*Phil.* 1467–68), Oedipus foreknows and accepts that destiny from the beginning.[2] Like Philoctetes, he has the savagery of his anger, but he also possesses initially the *philia* that forms the inward and personal basis for his return to society. This outcast is not alone. He has with him the companion of his wanderings, Antigone. She is the child of the accursed marriage which drove him from Thebes but also the sign of his continuing bond with humanity. If his past has maimed him, it has also given him a support for those wounds. This support is not Philoctetes' magical weapon of a remote and now divinized hero but a frail human being whom he loves. She is the extension of that part of himself which can reach out to others. Thus she attends his crucial passage back into society and gives that saving counsel about listening and yielding (170–173) which the intransigent Philoctetes can receive from no mortal companion. The question for Oedipus is not, as it is for Philoctetes, whether he can be restored to civilization at all, but rather what kind of society can admit him.

Oedipus is an awesome, forbidding figure. His very appearance awakens the fear of pollution and touches off hard thoughts about the hidden workings of the gods. Only the city that is able to receive him and offer him shelter can also receive the mysterious blessings which he brings.

Set on its deserted island, the *Philoctetes* starts from a zero point of civilized values from which the two protagonists will have to rebuild a basis for human association. The *Coloneus* begins with the prospect of a towered city, approached through solemn, venerated places of great antiquity. The private microcosm of a heroic society realized between Philoctetes and Neoptolemus here expands to a full-fledged depiction of civil life under a noble leader, a society worthy of Oedipus' greatness. Unlike Heracles at the end of the *Trachiniae*, Oedipus' call from the gods at the end gives him a place at least partially within the framework of the polis.

Oedipus' return to society is also immersed in a setting of house and family. The bond of father and son provides a model for the association of Philoctetes and Neoptolemus; yet, despite the allusions to Philoctetes' home in Malis, family life is remote. The *Oedipus at Colonus*, however, deals directly with the interactions and tensions of a close-knit *oikos*: the loyalties of daughters, the neglect by sons, the anger of a father. The division of the son-archetype into two figures, Polyneices and Theseus, the accursed and the pious son, in turn reveals two aspects of the father, the angry patriarchal father who calls down the wrath of the gods of his house, and the generous, grateful father whose blessings bring continuity and security.

If the theme of accepting an outcast into the city links the *Coloneus* with the *Philoctetes,* the theme of the family curse links it with the *Electra*. The two works are in some ways mirror images of one another. In the *Coloneus* a polluted wanderer from outside the city frees himself from his curse when he enters a city and bestows on it his mysterious strength and blessing. In the *Electra* a figure coming from outside brings hope of release but also evokes the dark, continuing curses of the past (*El.* 1493ff.) and certainly does not confirm the city in its civilizing power with the clarity with which Oedipus' alliance with Theseus does. Whereas the *Electra* presents a disrupted mediation between man and god and between city and nature, the hero of the *Coloneus* is himself a powerful mediator between the city and the gods and between Olympian and chthonic divinity. In the *Electra* the Furies remain ominously in the background; in the *Coloneus* the powers of the Underworld, though no less mysterious, confer blessings as well as curses. The *Electra* is dominated by evil kingship, the *Coloneus* by an idealizing image of the good king. Electra is an exile in her own city, facing a precarious future (*El.* 1498); Oedipus, an exile, finds a place of honor in a city whose future he helps secure. In the *Electra* only the isolated heroine is left to set right the corrupted moral order. In the *Coloneus*, as in the *Philoctetes*, the gods' role in the reestablishment of civilization is direct and visible.

Like the Oedipus of the earlier play, the aged hero of the *Coloneus* still occupies a position at the boundary between order and chaos, civilization and the wild. But unlike his younger counterpart, he enters the city not to call the civilized order into question but rather to deepen and strengthen it. The demonic forces with which Oedipus has his mysterious affinity already have an established place in the city he is about to enter, and this city is able to recognize and accept his special relationship to the supernatural.

Unlike Ajax, the hero is welcomed back into society before his death. Unlike in the *Antigone* and the *Tyrannus*, a false or illusory image of civilization does not have to be shattered by a catastrophic destruction and the sudden, violent revelation of a new truth.[3] Unlike Heracles (in the *Trachiniae*) and Philoctetes,

Oedipus commands his oracular knowledge before the dramatic action gets underway. For him the point of return to the shelter of a city is also a transcendence of it. His place of reentrance is not a desolate island, a lonely cave, or the remote summit of a mountain but a sacred grove which serves as the border between city and wild. Like Oedipus himself, it is both part of the civic order and outside of it; and, like Oedipus, it combines both threatening and benign divinity, both dread and reverence.

Oedipus' reacceptance into the polis, however, is not a given. The opening scenes, in fact, pose one of the central problems of tragedy itself: how can the ordered structures of society confront and incorporate their negation? Oedipus contains in himself something irreconcilable with the city. He is more exposed than other men to the mystery and enmity of the gods, to the irrational in the universe, to the extremes of brightness and darkness with which the divine presence touches human life. Like the heroes who precede him, he stands at the intersection of fundamental polarities: man and god, upper and lower worlds, human weakness and impersonal power, the destructive and the creative force of blood ties, the stain of blood-guilt and inner purity, curse and blessing. His cult status as a hero in the technical sense is itself the religious expression of this fusion of polarities, for he possesses elemental, demonic power, sheer *numen*, in both its destructive and its life-giving manifestation.[4]

The first half of the play dramatizes the movement of the citiless Oedipus into the city, as he changes from being *apolis* or *apoptolis*, "without city," "outside the city" (208, 1357), to *empolis* ("in the city," 637). The polluted scapegoat or *pharmakos* of the earlier play must again be accepted as a "suppliant of the gods" (558). The hero who was once called "savior" when he was the hidden pollution of the land (*OT* 46–48) now, as the polluted outcast whose very name awakens horror (210–236), will bring profit, help, and salvation to the city, even though his former "help" to a city involved his own destruction (cf. 541).[5]

The play begins with Oedipus' inquiry about the inhabitants of the city which he and Antigone are approaching (1ff.). The first clear image is a city seen from outside. Looking at a distance (*prosō*, 15) Antigone describes the "towers which crown a city" (14–15). This initial statement of the setting marks Oedipus' place at the boundary point between wandering outside and enclosure within. The spatial configuration of the action is emblematic of Oedipus' situation. He stands at the edge of a sacred grove, heavy with numinous power, itself between city and wild. "Nowhere else in Greek tragedy," John Gould has recently remarked, "does the primitively mysterious power of boundaries and thresholds, the 'extraterritoriality' of the sacred, make itself felt with the force precision that Sophocles achieves in the *parodos* of the *Oedipus at Colonus* (especially 117–198)."[6] The grove is part of Athens, yet apart from it: "Athens I know," says Antigone, "but not this place" (24). As Oedipus once entered forbidden places as the pollution of a city, so here, as future savior of a city, he walks where the native inhabitants dare not tread. The chorus' repeated cry, "You pass beyond the limits" (155–156), refers to more than just spatial movement or ritual "transgression."[7] It sums up the hero's tragic road of life.

Oedipus' curse, we will learn later, would keep him at the limits or boundaries of Thebes (*horoi*, 400),[8] a place at, but not quite within the frontiers between the civilized and the demonic. Still further back in his past lie his voluntary advances to dangerous powers, to save, not infect a city, namely his approach to the Sphinx on the mountain outside the city of Thebes. Both aspects of his past, the cleansing and the polluting, are reenacted in his entrance to the grove of the Dread Goddesses.

Traversing the fringes of civilized space, Oedipus is repeatedly called "wanderer," *alētēs*, *planētēs*.[9] The problem of stationing this wanderer in a fixed place, or seat in the opening lines (9, 11, 21) holds the nucleus of the whole play: overcoming movement by rest, homelessness by fixity, the conditions of the stranger or the citiless man by the right to dwell among men (for example, 637). The play's very first lines juxtapose the wandering Oedipus with a polis of settled, secure life (2–3). His life has followed the tragic long road of life (cf. 20, 87ff.); now, finally, coming to its calm end in a haven appointed by the gods, the place at the end of the goal (*chōran termian*, 89),[10] the stranger (*xenos*) finds a place of rest for strangers (*xenostasin*, 90). Here he discovers his "road" not as placelessness but as direction, as a path given by the gods. His words bespeak the strength, certainty, and confidence that Sophocles' heroes have only at the end of their lives (96–98): "For now I came to know that it was a faithful omen from you (gods) that led me forth on this road into this grove."

To reach her father, Ismene has had to make a long journey also, and the geographical imagery (the Sicilian horse, Thessalian hat, the exposure to the sun, 312ff.) stresses wandering and distance. Oedipus compares his children to the remote Egyptians, where the women venture outside and men stay at home (337ff.). His bitter comparison inverts not only male and female roles but also interior and exterior space. He has had to wander with his daughter in the wild forest (*agria hylē*, 348–349), a possible echo of the earlier play, where Laius' murderer is said to wander like a mountain bull in the wild woodland (*hyp' agrian hylan*, OT 476–477). He is an exile and a beggar outside (*exō*, 444), while his sons remain inside. The daughters, like men, provide that nurture (*trophē*), which the sons should have provided for their father.[11] Instead, the daughters endure harsh toil (*ponos*, 345; cf. 1368) outside, where they do not have their proper portion of marriage, given from one house to another but run the risk of rape in the no-man's land where they are a prey to the passing wayfarer (751–752). It is, appropriately, the imperious Creon, who carries off one of these girls by violence and who raises this last point. But Ismene has already established the connection between the reversals of inner and outer space, house and wild, kindred and strangers, when she describes her efforts in finding where Oedipus "houses his nurture" (*katoikein trophēn*, 362).

We are reminded again and again of Oedipus' exposure to the wild. As Ismene, seeking him, is exposed to the sun (314), he is himself, as his son says later, exposed to the winds, his hair flying uncombed (1261). To Creon he is a quarry to be hunted (1026).[12] To the chorus, reflecting philosophically on the place of human life between being and nonbeing, he is like a rocky headland beaten on all sides by wintry winds (1240–50). The simile recalls the wave-lashed headland of Philoctetes' savage retreat (*Phil.* 1455ff.) and the rocks beaten by the dark sea, symbol of the irrational doom of an inherited curse, in the second stasimon of the *Antigone* (586–593). In both cases, the associations are with figures who stand in savagery, outside the norms of human association.

Like Philoctetes, Oedipus cannot make his way back to society on the old terms. He cannot rejoin the city he left. To Thebes he is still a curse. The stain of blood bars him from burial in that soil (406ff.). Hence he must be kept at the boundaries (400), for the continuing pollution of incest and patricide endangers house and city.[13] The elaborate descriptions of painful movement in the first scene focus on the difficulty of this crucial passage from wild to city. The chorus' concern and horror center on the place where Oedipus is or dwells (117–119, 137). They must learn whether he belongs inside the place (*enchōros*, 125) or outside (*ektopos*, 233; cf. *aphormos*, 234).

Oedipus' reentrance to human society threatens to reenact his initial expulsion. He might be driven forth again, blind and helpless. But he is not to repeat the pattern. The time has come for him to win back his rightful title to the shelter of civilization. The grove, he says, in a phrase of untranslatable richness of meaning, is "the token of my destiny," *symphoras synthēm' emēs* (46), which can also mean, "watchword of my disaster." The grove of the Eumenides/Furies faces both ways, as does Oedipus' *symphora*, his destiny/disaster. But the double *syn*-compounds, pronounced by the Teiresias-like old man, denote a coming together and a harmony where earlier there was separation and dissonance.

Once Oedipus knows that he is at the end of his journey in the sacred grove, he is determined to keep the place that has welcomed him. "Let them receive the suppliant propitiously," he says of the Eumenides, "for I would not again go forth from this your seat" (44–45). The mysterious, forest-like place of the Dread Goddesses is a seat where a ritual of supplication can be enacted. Supplication is itself a ritual of crucial passage between territories, states of being, conditions of life: we recall Odysseus' suppliant gestures as he enters the palace of the Phaeacian king in the *Odyssey*.[14] As John Gould points out, the rite of supplication is closely connected with the community's acceptance of the stranger from the potentially dangerous realm outside. One of its functions is "to bring an aberrant human being within the norms of the social order and to mitigate or resolve the crises which result when the community or its representative agent is confronted with what is 'outside'."[15] Hence the paradoxical status of Oedipus as a totally helpless, feeble, blind old man on the one hand and a potent danger to the community on the other. Crossing "the threshold of what is not permitted" (157),[16] he threatens the society with a confusion of the sacred and the profane. His very presence calls into question the boundaries between inviolable space and the place where ordinary mortals may tread (167–168): "If you have any speech in converse with us, depart from ground not to be trodden upon (*abata*), where it is lawful custom for all (*pasi nomos*): but before that, keep off."

From the very beginning Oedipus' relation to the sacred contains that polarity of wonder and terror, purity and pollution, which reaches its strongest expression in the seeing blindness of the end. The hero's hard rejection of his son's supplication later is the foil to his own successful supplication of the Athenians in this first scene.[17] Oedipus will now play the role of the supplicated divinity or king. Refusing to grant the suppliant "seat," he sends his unfortunate son back into the exile and the pollutions of the curse from which he himself emerged in his early suppliant scene. Polyneices now has no fixed place in a city, and he enters the realm of the wild, the curse, the pollution that are to be his doom.

Making Oedipus stand or sit is the first scenic action.[18] "If you see any resting place (*thakēsis*), make me stand or sit me down" (*stēson, exhidryson*) is his first command in the play (9–11). "Sit me down now" (*kathize me*), he asks a few lines later (21). Then he asks, "Can you tell me where we have come to stand" (*kathestamen*, 23). Making him change his place of standing is the chorus' chief concern (*metastathi*, 163; *metanastas*, 175). The actual moving of the blind old man proceeds for almost thirty lines of excruciating detail (173–201). The Thebans, as noted, would make him stand (*stēsousi*) near but not in his homeland (399–400). He feels keenly that he is uprooted, *anastatos*, literally "made to stand out of his home" (429–430). It is the same word that described the exiled Heracles and his family in the *Trachiniae*. Polyneices promises to make his father "stand" in his house (*stēsō*, 1342), but for his own purposes not Oedipus' good. Theseus' welcome had a different spirit. He expresses pity (556) and asks, "With what supplication of me and the city do you come to stand by us (*epestēs*), you and the unfortunate one who stands by you" (*parastatis*, 558–559). "Terrible indeed," he goes on, "would be the matter from which I would stand apart" (*exaphistaimēn*, 561).

Oedipus' cautious, halting movements from within the grove to outside (*exō*, 226; cf. 193) gradually expand to a wider spatial field as he comes to view his whole life of wandering outside (444). This movement between interior and exterior is both literal and metaphorical. Oedipus' new understanding and security about inner and outer, purity and pollution, fortify him against Creon's specious plea that he conceal his shame at home (*oikoi*), in Thebes, his old nurse (*trophos*, 755–760). In his earlier Egyptian analogy he laid bare Thebes' hypocritical reversal of inner and outer in the matter of nurture (337–341). At the end of the *Tyrannus* Creon, not yet made rigid and proud by an authority of which he was not capable, could make a similar demand about concealing shame and pollution within the house (*OT* 1424–31). But the later Creon's order is vitiated by his own transgression of the boundaries between inner and outer territory. Athens, not Thebes, will uphold Oedipus in his right to move freely in the open light and air of civic space. Creon, not Oedipus, will now be expelled outside, (*exō*, 824; cf. 341), driven from the land as unholy (*exelan ton asebē*, 823).

There are three attempts to move Oedipus. All involve nurture in a city as opposed to exile: first the chorus of the elders of Colonus at the grove: then Creon's attempt by force; and finally Polyneices' supplication. His admission of his deficient nurture for his father at the start predetermines his own failure to regain a settled place in Thebes later (1263–66). His behavior when he held the throne and scepter of royal power in Thebes (1354) violated the father's right to polis and *oikos* both. "You drove out your own father and made him citiless (*apolis*)" Oedipus accuses (1356–57). He hammers in the charge a few lines later: "You made me to be nurtured (*entrophon*) in this suffering . . . ; you drove me out" (1362–63). His daughters, who gave him the nurture that the sons should have provided (1365, 1367; cf. 338ff.), will have Polyneices' seat (*thakēma*) and throne (1380). Made fatherless, (*apatōr*, 1383; cf. 1356), Polyneices has lost his place figuratively in house and city, as he has already lost his literal place there, a fitting return for his expulsion of Oedipus from both nurture and city (1355–63). The son will be stained with kindred blood as the father was before (*haimati miantheis*, 1373–74). The only way he can return to his city is to overthrow the city, but Oedipus aborts that endeavor in advance by the very terms in which he formulates it (1371–74): "There is no way that you shall overthrow that city, but first you will fall stained with blood (*haimati*), and your brother (*synhaimos*) equally."[19] The ties of "blood" in the house now lead to pollution, exile, savagery, not settledness and civil or domestic order. The play on "pollution by blood" and the "blood tie" of brotherhood in *haimati . . . synhaimos* brings together the outwardly directed violence of war and the inwardly turned violence of fratricide. Polyneices' attempt to regain the interior space of the city will destroy all that such space signifies. Civil war and fratricidal bloodshed are homologous destructions of polis and *oikos* respectively. Citiless and fatherless, Polyneices will revert to the position from which the old, polluted Oedipus is now emerging.

The road is the single most dominant spatial metaphor of the play.[20] "You have wandered forth on a long road for an old man," Antigone tells her father in the prologue (20). We must understand this verse in its fullest, most pregnant meaning. It is the whole long road of this tormented hero's life that now nears its final destination. The "bronze-footed threshold" near the grove with its crossing of three roads (1590–93) closes the long journey that began on that other triple road long ago (*OT* 733).[21] Here Oedipus can feel that he has at last found rest (*paula*, 88) and his goal (89), "rounding the turn on the hard road of his life" (91). Confirming Oedipus in a destination which offers shelter, Theseus gives commands about the "double-mouthed roads" where strangers enter the land (900–901). Later his restoration of the kidnapped daughters who put an end to his previous unhappy, deserted wandering (1113–14) definitively closes off the exile of Oedipus' past and prevents the recapitulation of earlier lonely wandering. His journey can no longer coincide with the roads of his Theban life, either Creon's or Polyneices' "road of unhappiness" (1399–1400; cf. 1397).

Oedipus' long road of life leads him from suffering to purification (see 20, 91, 1551). Over against his journey stands Polyneices' literal and figurative path of doom (1397–1401, 1432–34 and 1439–40).[22] To Theseus, however, Oedipus can promise a new fortune of the road (*tychēn hodou*, 1506). At the great finale this imagery receives stirring visual enactment: the blind, helpless figure, so painfully guided to a place of ease and rest (173–201), is now himself the leader (1520–21, 1542, 1588–89) on a road between earth and underworld, life and death (1590), between the accursed past of the triple roads (1592) and an unknown future where the curse is removed.

Beside stationing and the road, the third spatial metaphor of major importance is the boundary, *horos*. The entire play can be viewed as a situation of passage: entrance into and passage out of the civilized locus, Athens, via points of mysterious transit: the grove at the beginning and the crossroads by the broken threshold at the end (1590–92). The sanctity of the holy place (*chōros hieros*) from which blessings will eventually emanate for all of Athens is not confined to the grove of the Eumenides alone (54–63):

> This whole place is sacred. Revered Poseidon holds it. In it is also the fire-bearing god, the Titan Prometheus. The ground you tread upon is called the bronze-footed threshold of this land, the bulwark of Athens. The fields nearby claim to have as their leader the horseman Colonus, and giving themselves his name they bear it all in common. Such are these things, stranger, honored not in words, but rather in the shared association.

The brazen-footed threshold in 57 obviously prepares for the supernatural event at the brazen steps at the end (1591), where Oedipus pauses for his final purification. These brazen steps evoke not only supernatural powers like brazen-shouting Ares (1046) or the brazen-footed Erinys of the *Electra* (490), but also the ancient mythical boundaries between elements of the cosmos: day and night, earth and Tartarus, sea and sky. In Hesiod a brazen threshold, "rooted in the earth" like Sophocles' brazen steps (1591), marks the limits between these cosmic territories (*Theogony* 748–750, 811–813).[23] Behind the verdant landscape stand the timeless elements of sea, fire, earth, bronze.

The Thorician Rock, the hollow pear tree, and the tomb of stone nearby (1595–96) are obscure details, but they too may have to do with a point of crossing between life and death. Just before, the Messenger refers to Theseus' journey to Hades to bring up Peirithous through a hollow in the earth (1593–94). This is a myth of descent and renewal like that of Persephone, which in fact the scholiast on 1593 adduces as a parallel. At Colonus itself a hero's shrine marked the site of Theseus' descent and return (Pausanias 1.30.4).[24] The tomb in 1596 is related to death, whereas the Thorician Rock and the pear tree have associations respectively with the procreative power of male seed and the restoration of lost virility.[25] Mythical emblems of death and life, sterility and fertility, descent and return thus mark the place of Oedipus' last passage. His strange end, which brings him neither to Hades nor to Olympus, characteristically blurs the division between these opposite and mutually exclusive categories. Though safely enclosed within the civilized space of the polis, he is also beyond its familiar human limits.

Oedipus is both there and not there. We hear repeatedly of a tomb (*taphos, tymbos, thēkē*); yet Antigone says that he was snatched away in an invisible fate

(1681–82), and Ismene cries that he is "without tomb" (*ataphos*, 1732).[26] The resting place of the body which brings blessings upon the land is, in any case, concealed from all living men but one. The hero's own passage to the world beyond the grave, like that of Romulus-Quirinus, is not death but a mysterious summons from the gods that hides him from all mortal vision.[27]

Unlike Heracles in the *Trachiniae*, however, Oedipus remains involved in earth and its mysteries. His is not the path of transcendence on the remote mountain top. As Sophocles' fullest embodiment of tragic knowledge, he repeats Creon's plunge into the dark cave in the *Antigone* and the earlier Oedipus' entrance to Jocasta's womb-like chamber of death in the *Tyrannus*, but with a different meaning. With his blind man's knowledge of those dark places, Oedipus can now transform the chthonic goddesses of those places into his allies. He can reenter their earth without losing contact with the Olympian order of the polis. Despite the fact that this play will end with Oedipus' heroization, it has none of the mythic remoteness of the *Trachiniae*. This hero, far from being aloof from human ties, is an all-too-human sufferer whose tragedy unfolds in the civilized spaces of house and city.

The male protagonists of the two earlier Theban plays, Creon in the *Antigone* and Oedipus in the *Tyrannus*, champions of the male-oriented polis, meet destruction in the inward enclosures of earth, house, and womb, the darkness and mystery of the female creative power, which is also connected with the unknown and with the irrational. Likewise Heracles' doom in the *Trachiniae* is tied to the inner recesses of the *oikos* where Deianeira has harbored the Centaur's poison in the dark. Oedipus in the *Coloneus*, however, spans both Olympian and chthonic knowledge. Led by the female figure who defends reverence for the chthonic in the *Antigone*, he is also under the special protection of the ambiguous female divinities of the dark grove and the Underworld. Unlike the younger Oedipus, he is not the active riddle-solver, proud of his intellectual triumph over nature's mysteries. His knowledge in the *Coloneus* has reached its furthest distance from the Promethean knowledge as conquest of the otherness of the world. It has become a fully tragic knowledge, self-knowledge, and it comprises a potential harmony with the mystery of nature, reconciliation of the cosmic opposition between Olympian and chthonic.

Oedipus' antagonist in this last play is rightly Creon and not his older self of the *Tyrannus*. His present tragic knowledge is a natural development of the self-knowledge which ends that play. He contrasts not only with the Creon of the *Antigone*, overwhelmed by the female-dominated forces of house and cave, but also with the cautious Creon of *Tyrannus* who must consult the oracle of Olympian Apollo before further action. The Creon of the *Coloneus* is a more rigid form of the Creon of the *Antigone* (without the lesson of his fall); but that confident masculine rationalism is also nascent in the Creon of the last scene of the *Tyrannus*. Theban Creon lacks just that spirit of reverence which might have helped his evolution into a just ruler like the Athenian Theseus. Thebes' doom is written in the ossification of a potentially good monarch. The reasonable Creon at the end of the first *Oedipus* becomes a self-righteous and violent tyrant. His discomfiture in the *Coloneus* gives us the pleasure of seeing the unjust king defeated by the just.

II

Oedipus' movement back within the shelter of a civilized community involves political as well as supernatural boundaries. The Thebans, concerned primarily with control of Oedipus' body (*kratein*, 400) will not let him dwell within the actual boundaries of the land (*gēs horoi*, 400). Yet, as Theseus points out with the same verb as that which described Oedipus' exclusion from Thebes' boundaries in 400, Creon has violated the boundaries of Athens (924). The excited choral ode which marks the interval between Theseus' orders to set that violation right and the recapture of Oedipus' daughters lists the sacred boundaries of Attica, including the place of the solemn rites of Eleusis (1050ff.), which, like the Eumenides' grove, is a place of holy contact with the mysteries of earth and the realm beyond death. Oedipus, whose last moments on earth are spent near a hill sacred to Demeter Euchloos, Demeter as protectress of what springs green from the earth,[28] has a deeper knowledge of those mysteries of which the chorus speak only in passing.

This ode comes at the point when a city is acting decisively to protect the suppliant whom it has received. It thus reaffirms Athens' role as a place of piety and shelter, its frontiers protected by the gods' holy places. In allowing the polluted suppliant his place in the Eumenides' grove, Athens itself extends the sacred protection of its boundaries to him, and at the end he will repay Athens by constituting himself another such sacred place, again at the boundaries of the land. Yet this place, politically the most important place in the play, is hidden from all men except King Theseus. The physical boundaries of Attica, central to the dispute between Creon and Oedipus and between Creon and Theseus, now give way to the spiritual boundaries, the point between human and supernatural realms.

The grove by which Oedipus enters Attica stands at the fringes of the city but is not entirely of the wild. Like him, it has both gentle and harsh aspects.[29] It belongs to both upper and lower worlds, life and death. Like him, too, in his future role, it is a bulwark of Athens. As Oedipus brings both curses and blessings, so the goddesses of the grove are both Erinyes and Eumenides, both fearful and sweet (39, 106), both dread-visaged and "gracious" (84, 144; cf. 126ff.).[30]

Though we are ill-informed about the history of the local cults of Attica, it is not impossible that Sophocles has endowed this grove with an importance beyond actual cultic significance.[31] He makes it the emblem not only of the ambiguity of Oedipus but also of the mysterious place of tragedy on the confines of structure and chaos, the familiar and the unknown, civic order and the infinities of death and the gods. Sunless and silent, the grove suggests the nothingness of death. Yet it is also alive with the vital movements of nature. Both physically and metaphorically it stands between the polis and the hidden sources of energy that give Athens its special strength and its favored relation to the gods.

On the horizontal axis the grove is the point of intersection between the wild outside and the interior space of the polis. On the vertical axis it is the place where Olympian and chthonic powers converge to welcome Oedipus back into the society of men and gods and to bring his mysterious blessings to the city whose land (*chōra*) occupies the surface world between the gods of the heavens and the gods of the Underworld. This aged Oedipus, like that of the younger Oedipus of the *Tyrannus*, stands at the point of intersection of the two axes. This is also the point where the activities of "horizontal man," dominating the surface of the earth by the rational powers celebrated in the *Antigone's* first stasimon, intersect the powers less amenable to human control, both above and below.

In the temporal dimension of Oedipus' life, as in the religious dimension in general, the grove is the point where an ancient curse is transmuted into benediction, weakness into power, horror into welcome. It is the place of transition between Thebes' tragic past and Athens' happy future,[32] between a city of strife and a city of piety, between the pollution of the *pharmakos* and the blessings of the hero, between guilt and atonement.

Though initially defined by the distant towers of Athens (14–15), the grove, with its bird-song and vegetation, also belongs to the *agros*, the uncultivated space outside the polis. Whether or not it and its surroundings are inhabited is a major question in the opening scene (27–28, 39, 64ff.). As we see it through Antigone's eyes, it contains the olive and the vine, but nearby stands the "unpolished rock" (19) bearing no marks of a tool (*askeparnon*, 101; cf. *autopetron*, 192–193, if the text is right). The goddesses who dwell there receive no wine (101); but Oedipus, invoking them, sets their "ancient darkness" beside the more luminous aspect of Pallas Athena and her city (106–110): "Come, sweet children of Darkness old, come, Athens, called of greatest Pallas, of all cities the most esteemed, pity this wretched shadow of Oedipus the man." Whereas the deserted, savage island of the *Philoctetes* was entirely under the sway of an implacable, vaguely defined divinity, the dangerous female powers of this grove can be placed in close proximity to the Olympian daughter of Zeus. Thus the dread power of the mother, particularly baleful for Oedipus, can be neutralized by the city's patron goddess whose alliance, in Aeschylus' *Eumenides*, is with the male and the Olympian rather than the chthonic world.[33]

This passage and the scenery of 14–16 defines Athens, "most esteemed of cities," as a place of harmonious accord between man and nature, upper and lower worlds. But to Oedipus it is something more. As soon as he hears that the grove belongs to the Furies, he recognizes his kinship with the place.

After the Athenian stranger's identification Oedipus makes his second mysterious pronouncement: he must see the king, and he promises "great profit for small succor" (72). Asked what profit can be expected from a blind man, Oedipus answers with the solemnity of the mysterious inner vision that he now knows to be his (74): "All that we shall speak has eyes and sees." The contrast between the obvious helplessness of the blind old man on the stage and the authority of his words is itself a first visual enactment of the play's central paradox.

This place holds the secret of Oedipus' return to the civilized world, and he knows it. He enters and leaves through this no-man's land of the daughters of darkness, the bronze-footed threshold (57, 1590–91). Even in the prologue, although he recognizes the goddesses by the darkness of their underworld abode (39, 106), he knows that it will be "earthquake, or thunder, or a flash of Zeus" that will call him (95). He recognizes the place by the cosmic opposites that it contains, and these will come together even more actively at the end.

The presence of "the terrible" in Oedipus, *to deinon* (141), threatens to exclude him once more from the dwellings of men. But the potential exclusion never happens. Antigone's role here is crucial. Submitting to her guidance, he painfully makes his way out of the grove to a place where civilized discourse is possible. The chorus says (184–187): "Stranger in a strange land, unhappy man, have the courage (*tolma*) to hate what the city has nurtured as outside of friendship (*aphilon*), and revere what it holds a friend (*philon*)." The words "city," "nurture," "friend" strike a hopeful note. Oedipus replies with talk of piety (*eusebia*) and exchanging speech and hearing (188–191). Fearing to be called "lawless" (*anomos*, 142), he has entered the realm of law (*nomos*), where speech is possible (167–168).

Mediating between Oedipus' past and his future, his isolation and his humanity, Antigone will reestablish human contact through appeals to reverence, pity, supplication, and kindness (*charis*) which the chorus had nearly abrogated (cf. 232 and 249). She can look at them as her blind father cannot (244). Her plea, in the more emotional lyric meters (237–253), establishes the human basis on which Oedipus can conduct his defense to the now pitying chorus (255) in the calmer iambic arguments of guilt and innocence (258ff.). The crucial transition between wild and city passed, we move from dread pollution to the legal and rational discourse that can contain it and absorb it, the language of civilized men. The famous ode on the grove at Colonus, the first stasimon, 668–719, comes just at the moment when Theseus has accepted Oedipus with the solemn pronouncement, *chōra(i) d' empolin katoikiō*, "I shall make you dwell as a citizen within the land" (637). For all its lushness the grove is sunless and windless like a place of death (676–677). The nightingale whose song fills it (671–673; cf. 17–18) is generally a bird of sadness and doom in Sophocles.[34] The civilizing and Olympian associations of the vine, Dionysus, golden Aphrodite, Zeus, and Athena are balanced by the chthonic associations of Dionysus, the Great Goddesses, and the narcissus (683), the flower associated with Persephone's disappearance into the Underworld and with death and sterility.[35] The narcissus brings together celestial and chthonic, light and dark, fertility and the mystery of the earth (681–685): "Beneath the dew of the skies blooms each day always the narcissus with its lovely clusters, ancient crown of the Great Goddesses, and the gold-flashing crocus." The springs of the Cephisus in the next lines (685–691) take us back to the familiar places of Attica and the bounty of the tilled earth which gives the farmers "swift birth" of crops (*ōky-tokos*, 689). Yet these springs are, like Oedipus, "wanderers" (*nomades*, 687); and swift birth also suggests mortality.

The second strophe moves more strongly to civilized order and control. The first strophe began with the song of the nightingale and ended with Dionysus and his "nurses"; the first antistrophe ends with choruses of Muses and Aphrodite of the Golden Reins. We thus move toward the Olympian brilliance of music and love. Aphrodite's epithet leads into the second strophic system, where the arts of civilization are more in evidence: mastery of the sea and the horse and the olive trees sacred to Zeus and Athena. Conquest of the sea and the use of the bridle recall the *Antigone*'s Ode on Man (*Antig.* 334–341) and, within this scene, Theseus' metaphorical reference to the sea in his promise to defend Oedipus (661–663).[36]

Yet the relation between man and nature in the ode is more complex. Dionysus, the bacchic god revelling with his divine nurses (678–680), is both the god of wine and vegetation and the god of wild ecstasies on the mountains, where the boundaries between man and nature are dissolved.[37] The olive springs up by itself and is uncultivated by human hand (*acheirōton*, 698).[38] The conquest of sea and horse is attributed not to human intelligence, as in the Ode on Man in the *Antigone* but to divine gift, in fact the "gift of the great divinity" (*daimōn*, 709), a phrase which recalls the Great Goddesses, Demeter and Persephone, of 683. The oar which ends the ode is not a device of human technology but an element in a mythical world and its inhabitants: it is called "attendant of the hundred-footed Nereids" (717–719). Sea and earth both, then, appear as the haunt of divinities. The ode reflects not man's conquest of nature nor even his accord with nature, but the point where human civilization touches the mysterious forces of divinity, where the "surface" world which man controls by agriculture and navigation is bisected by the vertical line connecting man with the imponderables above and below.

Having now incorporated Oedipus, the city reaches out to embrace that element of "the terrible" which he carries with him (141, 1651). The city too becomes involved in that passage between things human and things divine which centers upon Oedipus. For Sophocles, writing during Athens' near-exhaustion at the end of a long war, it may have seemed as if Athens was engaged in a perilous crossing between an old and a new existence, between material and spiritual greatness. Athens, like the aged Oedipus—and perhaps also the aged Sophocles—throws off the outer covering of its battered form to be reborn in the inner strength of its spiritual power.[39] Its civilizing achievement is no longer in its might and dominion but in its spiritual radiance, its privileged openness to divinity.[40]

Oedipus' grove, like Athens, is a place where new life arises in the midst of death.[41] Close to death, like Oedipus, it holds a secret vitality that leads to rebirth. The singing nightingale in the sunless, windless grove, the beauty of the narcissus, the light of the crocus amid the dim foliage suggest a crossing of life and death not only for Oedipus and not only for Athens, but also for Sophocles' art:

something in touch with the sources of vital energy that lie beyond human control, a promise of transfiguring brilliance in the midst of darkness.

The parallels between the double aspect of the grove and its goddesses and the double aspect of Oedipus grow stronger in the course of the play. Their grove, like Oedipus, is "untouchable" (*athiktos*, 39; cf. *thigein*, 1132–35). They are "dread-visaged" (*deinōpes*, 84); he is dreadful to see, dreadful to hear (*deinos*, 141), and he awakens dread (*deos*, 223) in those who see him. His name, like theirs, inspires awe or fear (41, 265, 301, 306); he too has a dread nature or origin (*aina physis*, 212). They are daughters of Earth and Darkness (40; cf. 106); Oedipus at the end will be "clothed in the eternal darkness under the earth" (1701). They are the all-seeing Eumenides, *panth' horōsas* (42); Oedipus, though blind, utters words which have sight (cf. *panth' horōnta*, 73–74). Oedipus' certainty that divine guidance has led him to the grove marks his sympathy with its goddesses in the collocation, "I undrinking to you wineless ones" (*nēphōn aoinois*, 100).[42] As he hears about them, he begins to understand that he, like them, is a bulwark of Athens (72ff.; cf. 58). Later, with even greater confidence, he can identify with their positive attributes: he, the pollution, can declare himself holy, *hieros*, like them (287–288; cf. 15, 54) and a source of protection to Athens. His mysterious place of burial will have some of the same qualities as the Furies' grove, and a tradition even located his tomb within their sanctuary (Pausanias 1.28.7).[43] In the prologue and the Colonus ode the Eumenides are associated with the beneficent aspect of Earth and the Great Goddesses (106, 683); at the end Oedipus' final resting place lies near the shrine of Demeter of the Green Shoots (Demeter *euchloos*, 1600).

As Oedipus becomes increasingly sure of his power and his destiny in the middle portion of the play, he calls upon these goddesses as his own protectresses against his enemies (864ff., 1010ff., 1389ff.). As he can identify with the Eumenides' beneficent power as a bulwark of Athens, so he can appear, at moments, in their ominous aspect, as a vengeful Fury, drinking his enemies' hot blood (621–622; cf. *El.* 1420–21).[44] His body, as he tells Creon, will be buried in Athenian soil as a source of blessings to that people, but his spirit will be "there" (*ekei*, 787) in Thebes as an avenging spirit or *alastōr* (788). The gentle benignity of sainthood is not part of being a hero.[45] Protecting the Athenian earth, to his Theban sons he will give "just so much a share of earth as is enough to die in" (789–790), an echo of the archaic Aeschylean theme of the family curse (*Seven against Thebes*, 785–790).

His defiance of Creon and his terrible curses upon his sons show the dread aspect of his emerging numinous power in its kinship to the goddesses of the grove. But in these curses he is also beginning to pull away from his polluted past, separate it out as a distinct, clarified part of his life, and discharge it, expel it as a kind of *pharmakos* or scapegoat, upon the city of violence and guilt.[46] His power to bless and his power to curse, like that of the Eumenides, remain inseparable. When he joins with Athens' king in his resistance to Creon, he is already helping the Athenians by the spiritual force of his just anger; he invokes the goddesses of the grove in Athens' behalf, so that Creon "may learn what sort of men guard this city" (1010–13). Oedipus' kinship with the goddesses has moved from a place at the boundaries of the land to a place within it. He thereby brings the dreaded familial, chthonic curse of the Furies into the service of the polis in its civilizing function, a shelter of suppliants, the old, and the weak.

It is now clearer why Oedipus should hail the Eumenides' grove as "the token of my (mis)fortunes" (46). Acceptance into this grove is not only the appropriate sign of his own position at the border between civilization and savagery and of his passage from the wild into the city: it also stamps as holy and meaningful in a larger order of things that dread (*to deinon*) in the suffering that has dogged his life.

In the Eumenides' grove misfortune or disaster becomes the "fate" (another possible translation of *symphora*) that completes his destiny and makes him not the outcast, but the civilizing hero that Sophocles felt him to be. Oedipus reenters civilization by this grove because the polarities which meet in the Eumenides are also those which meet in him. In the grove these contradictions can come together in a richly symbolical but also highly traditional nature poetry, to be then transcended in the larger destiny above tragedy which Oedipus fulfills.

III

The chorus of Muses who frequent the sacred grove in the Colonus ode (691–692) alludes to the great public festivals through which the city expresses its consciousness of its civilizing functions, its cohesiveness, and the harmonious bonds between itself and the gods on which its physical and spiritual existence depends. These expressions, like Antigone's reference to Athens as "a place most eulogized in praise" immediately after the ode (720), have their first level of reference to the celebration of Athens within the play; but their significance extends also to all the choruses of tragedy, dithyramb, or communal song that have celebrated and continue to celebrate Athens as a place where the Muses and their arts can find a home.[47] When Antigone here, directly after the chorus, calls out (720–721), "O place most eulogized in praises, now it is yours to reveal (*phainein*) those shining words (*ta lampra tauta . . . epē*)," the implication is that the rhetoric of the ode will be realized in deeds as dramatic enactment. In the "revealing" or "showing forth" (*phainein*) of the ode's "shining words," the play both celebrates the ritual which affirms the civilizing role of the city and simultaneously includes the creation of joyous song within its framework of ritual, political, and aesthetic order. The play itself calls attention to its function, as a communal art form, to celebrate the city's consciousness of its civilizing power and also to reflect on the mystery of its origins.

The next stasimon of the play marks out the sacred places that bound the Attic land and insure its political and religious integrity (1044ff.). The third stasimon returns to darker images of death, isolation, exposure to the violence of nature. Here, as in the *Antigone* and the *Oedipus Tyrannus*, the odes veer deliberately between the upper and lower limits of human power, the city's confident enclosure in its ordered spaces and its openness to the unknown which lies beyond. In the Colonus ode death and the Underworld, through the allusions to the chthonic Dionysus and Persephone, form part of the mysterious rhythms of loss and renewal. In the third stasimon, a "song of the fundamental and total sadness of human life,"[48] death appears as the blackness of utter negation, the desolate emptiness of non-being. The defined, local geography of the previous two odes (668ff., 1044ff.) gives way to the remoteness of the four corners of the earth, defined in terms of elements of nature: the sun's setting and rising, its beam (*aktis*) in the middle of the sky, and the dark Rhipean mountains of the north (*ennychiai Rhipai*) (1245–48). The familiar yields to the remote, the earthly to celestial phenomena, and within the ode day to night.

As opposed to the Muses' choruses and shining words that praise Athens in and just after the Colonus ode (691–692, 720–721), there is no music, only the "unhymned, unlyred, unchorused portion of Hades" (1221–22). The Muses' choruses of the first stasimon incorporate but transcend death: joy, harmony with a benign nature, order, and community predominate. Here, in the third stasimon, "not to be born wins at every accounting" (1225). The play, as an affirmation of meaning and structure, ultimately refutes this pronouncement and thereby parallels the ultimate meaning of Oedipus' life in the action which it dramatizes, transcendence of suffering in a mysterious light that comes from the darkness which his seeing blindness has plumbed. Yet the presence of Oedipus' worn body on the stage and the lyrical evocation of his sufferings in the third stasimon's powerful simile of the exposed and beaten shore at the end (1239–48) keep the path of the city's civilizing power open to the unknown spanned by tragedy and its quintessential, accursed hero.

As in the *Oresteia*, the civilizing power of Athens in the *Coloneus* lies in its reverence for the gods. Here, as in Euripides' *Heraclidae* and *Suppliants*, Athens is particularly distinguished for reverence and piety.[49] The prominence of the grove of the Eumenides indicates the city's ability to incorporate the darker side of the divine powers.

Theseus, Athens' civilizing hero par excellence, is solicitous in his worship of the Olympian gods. His sacrifice to Poseidon Hippios is a recurrent motif in the play. He too has made his descent to the chthonic realms, as we are reminded in the description of Oedipus' place of purification, "where lie the ever-faithful pledges of Theseus and Peirithous" (1593–94). The word for these "pledges," *synthēmata*, is the same word that Oedipus uses for the "watchword of (his) destiny" at Colonus (46). Contact with the mysterious realms beneath the earth links the two heroes, the one rooted at the center of his polis, the other driven from every polis, yet both possessing a mysterious closeness to the divine. Oedipus was once an effective ruler like Theseus, although his piety was not so lucid nor his kingship so stable in the face of unexpected events. King Theseus at Athens is the happy mirror image of King Oedipus at Thebes.

Theseus recognizes Oedipus as accursed (552ff., 571ff.), but "the bloody destruction of his eyes" (552) stirs pity rather than horror (556). He can then accept him through the rites of supplication and the laws of hospitality or *xenia* (558, 565ff.). Like Odysseus in the prologue of the *Ajax*, Theseus stresses the frailty of the human condition which joins them as fellow sufferers (561–568; cf. *Ajax* 121–126). His nobility (569) consists in affirming this common human bond between himself and his suppliant. By accepting Oedipus as an equal, he implicitly sanctions the inward purity that Oedipus has been asserting (287–288), the prerequisite for the externalized ritual purity necessary for his return to civilized society. Later, when Theseus has restored to him the daughters through whom he reaches out to others, that bond of suffering nearly overcomes the separation enforced by the pollution: he would embrace Theseus in gratitude, "For only those mortals experienced in such things (*empeiroi*) can share in suffering them" (*syntalaiporein*, 1135–36).

Yet to the secure ruler of a well-ordered city, acquainted though he is with suffering, Oedipus brings a knowledge of time—*chronos*, an important word in the play—which Theseus lacks (see 607ff.).[50] It is the tragic hero, not the established king, who has been most dangerously exposed to time and its vicissitudes. Whereas Oedipus' life has confronted an ultimate nothingness (cf. 393), Theseus speaks of nothingness only in his confident achievements as king and as defender of his suppliant: "You considered me as equal to nothing," he proudly taunts the discomfited Creon (918).

IV

Athens, city of law and reverence, contrasts with Thebes, city of violence and bloody faction. Just before Theban Polyneices arrives in Theseus' Athens, the chorus lists "envy, discord, strife, battles, and slaughter" (*phthonos, stasis, eris, machai, phonoi*, 1234–35). Evil strife, *eris kakē*, for rule and power (*archē, kratos*) characterizes Thebes (372, 400, 405, 408, 448ff., and so forth). Thebes' hold on Oedipus is based on *kratos*, force, not compassion.

Where Athens is reverent, Creon is shameless, irreverent (*anaidēs*, 863, 960). Where Theseus has been compassionate toward Oedipus' pollution, Creon and Thebes have been coolly legalistic (cf. 368).[51] Creon interrupts sacrifices (887ff.) and violates the rights of a suppliant (922–923). In both situations Theseus and his city are scrupulous and honorable. Creon tries to manipulate Athenian piety to his own advantage; Theseus, preferring the spirit to the letter, is willing to leave his sacrificing to aid the suppliant. It is in fact Theseus who accepts Polyneices' suppliant posture as binding on Oedipus (1178; cf. 1164). Antigone utters her personal plea for her brother on the basis of blood ties (1181ff.), but Theseus sums up the father's religious and legal obligation. It is Theseus who gives Polyneices the just procedure of speaking and listening (*lexai t' akousai*, 1288), which is the right that Oedipus won from the chorus when he left the shelter of the grove at the beginning of the play (190).

Like the ambitious Odysseus in the *Philoctetes* and the unscrupulous Atreids in the *Ajax*, Creon views piety as a matter of human convenience. And, like Odysseus in *Philoctetes*, he is proven colossally wrong. The *Coloneus* goes beyond *Philoctetes*, however, in removing the barrier between the divine plan and the hero's desire. From the first the two are striving to realize the mysterious harmony between them. The antagonist, Creon, is left even further outside the divine plan than Odysseus in *Philoctetes*, for the latter at least gets what he wants, if not in the way he wanted it.

Creon has come in the name of a polis (733–741), but he has violated the most basic rights of a polis, its boundaries between outer and inner space, tame and wild. That space Theseus defends as sanctioned by law and justice, *nomoi* and *dikē* (907–916). Violating law by force (*bia*, 916, 922), Creon will be kept by force (*bia*) as a foreign resident in the land he has invaded (933–935).

Creon's territorial violations apply to Oedipus even more than to Athens. He claims the right to "nurture" Oedipus (*trephein*, 943) but will not allow him the proper nurture of a house (*domoi*) in his own land. Instead he will keep Oedipus as a *paraulos*, one who has his dwelling beside or outside that of other men (784–785). Nor will he allow him to be covered by his native earth in proper burial (406–407), a denial of a basic property of civilized communities that recalls the Creon of the *Antigone*. Theseus, on the other hand, firmly offers citiless Oedipus (*apoptolis*, 208) both house and city, *oikos* and polis, in the line, *chōra(i) d'empolin katoikō*, "In this land I shall establish your dwelling (*oikos*) as one within the city" (637).[52] Creon, then, who would maintain Oedipus' relation of marginality to the land, will get Oedipus only as an avenging spirit (*alastōr*) for the land (788; cf. 410), whereas Athens will receive his blessings.

In the imagery of the play too Creon appears as a perverter of civilized values. He is a hunter, but one who hunts men. His pursuit of Oedipus is so described twice (950, 1026), and it is answered by the Athenians' invocation to "hunter Apollo" (1091) as they plan the hunt-like ambush that will foil Creon's plans (*euagros . . . lochos*, 1089–90, "the ambush of good hunting"). The "flashing bridle" (1067) echoes the Colonus ode (714) as Athena, here Mistress of Horses, Hippia, and Poseidon of the sea come to their aid (1070–73). Bridle, horse, and sea recall the double gifts of Poseidon in the Colonus ode (711–719), gifts which adorn Athens as the quintessentially civilized city.

Creon's connections with sea and seamanship are also negative. In an implicit allusion to maritime war Oedipus warns him, "Do not stand at anchor and watch in the place where I shall dwell" (811–812). We may recall the images of the violent sea which describe the lonely life of the outcast in the ode on death (1239–51), the opposite of the tamed, useful sea which Poseidon has made available to Athens (716–719).[53] As a user of device, *mēchanē*, a word which characterizes the arts of civilization (*Antig.* 365–366), Creon also perverts human intelligence to a shifting craftiness (*mēchanēma poikilon*, 761–762; cf. 1035).

As in *Ajax* and *Philoctetes* and negatively in *Electra*, civilization is confirmed through the establishment of human ties of warmth and love, what Protagoras, in Plato's myth, calls "the unifying bonds of friendship" (*Protag.* 322c). In the

Coloneus the key term is not the *philia* of the *Antigone* or the *eunoia* of the *Philoctetes* but rather *charis*, a rich and evocative word which can be translated "kindness," "grace," "favor."[54] It applies both to the gods' grace toward men and to reciprocal trust, generosity, and benefit between men. It denotes the love between Oedipus and his daughters (see 1106); and it is in the name of this familial bond that Antigone entreats her father to receive Polyneices (1182–83).

The movement from the rancor of family strife in the past, however, toward *charis* in the present is far from smooth. Antigone's plea for *charis* toward her brother has to overcome the bitterness of Oedipus, for whom the news of his son's arrival is "an utterance most hateful for a father" (*echthiston . . . phthegma . . . patri*, 1177). Antigone functions as that side of Oedipus which is potentially open and loving, whereas his male children pull him back toward all the violence and homicidal hatred which the house of Laius contains, a hatred particularly directed by fathers against sons. Even here, on the verge of a *charis* that will overcome the curse of Laius, Oedipus is still drawn to reenact and perpetuate it.

Charis, however, denotes the possibility of a new relation not only within the house but within the city. Oedipus' right to enter Attic territory and receive the rights of a suppliant from its citizens depends upon establishing a bond of *charis* rather than using deception (*apatē*, 229–233). Antigone's plea for his respect (*aidōs*) and *charis* as a suppliant (247–249) wins from the chorus an expression of pity (255) which in turn encourages Oedipus to make his first full defense of his innocence, a major step in separating himself from the curses and pollutions of his past (258ff.). But the *charis* that Oedipus entreats can be granted only by the ruler of the city (294–295). When Theseus arrives, the bonds of respect (*aidōs*) and *charis* are easily and spontaneously established, and Oedipus now feels no shame (the negative side of *aidōs*) in setting forth his situation in the briefest terms (569–570). Theseus in turn regards Oedipus' request for burial, a request refused by Thebes, as an easily granted *charis* (here "favor," 586). That *charis*, as Theseus' formal proclamation makes clear, includes granting him a place in Athens: "Revering (*sebistheis*) these (claims), I shall never cast away his *charis* ["spurn his grace," Jebb], but I will settle him in the land as a citizen" (*empolin katoikiō*, 636–637).

The contrast with Creon in the next scene is striking. Creon repeatedly violates just such *charis* as Oedipus receives from Theseus. "When it was my pleasure (*terpsis*) to be exiled from the land," Oedipus says, "you were unwilling to give that *charis* to me, willing though I was" (766–767). Instead, Creon granted that favor when it brought no joy, "when *charis* bore no *charis*" (779). His *charis* negates itself in its diametrical opposite, *bia*, force or violence.[55] Overvaluing kin ties now, for ulterior motives, as he undervalued them in the past, Creon would replace the harmony and gentleness fostered by *charis* with its disruptive antithesis. He accuses Oedipus of giving favor (*charis*) to his anger, in violence to his friends (*bia philōn*, 854–855), but in a sharp exchange some twenty lines earlier we have seen Creon's own anger and violence toward "his own" ("I am taking those who are mine," *tous emous agō*, 832). Creon's perverted *charis* holds Oedipus within when he wishes to go out (766–767). It would forcibly place Oedipus at the edges of a city after Theseus' *charis* has assured him a secure place at its center (*empolis*, 637) and indeed in the very home of the ruler (*domoi*, 643).

It is characteristic of Oedipus' detachment from full inclusion in house or city that he prefers the marginal space of the grove to the ruler's palace (643–646). Receiving his *charis* from Theseus, he remains in a sense where Creon would have put him, at the outer limits rather than the secure center of a city, but in a very different spirit, thanks to Theseus' offer of 636–637. Here Oedipus will reverse his earlier relationship to Thebes. Choosing grove over palace, he declares prophetically, "Here I shall have power (*kratos*) over those who have cast me out" (646). Thus he anticipates his rejection of Creon's ambiguous *charis* of 766–767 and intimates the failure of that physical violence against kin that Creon tries to exert (832).

The last movement of the play sees the final confirmation of the promised *charis* between Theseus and Oedipus. With a view to more limited aims, the frightened chorus prays to Zeus that its *charis* for helping Oedipus may not be profitless (*akerdē charin*, 1484). Oedipus, however, with larger vision, promises the fulfilled *charis*, *telesphoron charin* (1489), "a requital . . . fraught with fulfillment (of my promise)," as Jebb translates. The phrase suggests that concern with the mystery of last things, things involved with *telos*, which distinguishes Oedipus throughout the play. As *telesphoros* is general active, however, the phrase also means "fulfillment-bringing grace," "the favor that grants accomplishment." Thus it prefigures the mysterious power of Oedipus as one who grants *telos*. When the chorus, in the next lines, describe this *charis* as a just favor, "a just recompense for benefits" (1497, Jebb's translation),[56] they draw *charis* back into the more familiar territory of social bonds, the reciprocity of men held together by mutual need and respect.

In his last lines in the play Theseus fulfills his half of this civilizing bond of *charis*, promising aid to Oedipus' daughters and *charis* to the departed hero himself (1773–76). When applied to Oedipus, however, as the *telesphoros charis* of 1489 implies, *charis* reaches beyond the clearly defined ties of reciprocity between man and man to a wider and more mysterious realm where the human impinges upon the divine. Oedipus' share of the bond of *charis* near the end is clothed in figurative language. Theseus consoles Oedipus' daughters (1751–53): "Cease your lamentation, my children. For where the favor of those below (*chthonia charis*) is stored up (as a benefit) in common (both to Oedipus and to Athens), one must not grieve. It would provoke the gods' anger."[57] This "favor of the lower world," *chthonia charis*, is the culmination of that mysterious favor which Oedipus confers. As a common favor both to himself and his adoptive city its reciprocity is perfect: the hero's grace in his newly acquired chthonic status is a source of strength to the city which sheltered him at the last; but it is also a grace for himself. The power to confer blessings on those who have shown him *charis*, the basic kindness owed between men, compensates for the terrible curse he has suffered and his years of loneliness outside the pale of common humanity and civilized life.

The mystery of this chthonic *charis*, still locked into the tensions of opposites that surround Oedipus, contrasts with the simpler warmth of *charis* for which Antigone, out of love for her father, begged the chorus (237–253) and the generous *charis* which Theseus, out of nobility and compassion, bestowed (569ff., 636–637). The contrast at the end between the *charis* of Theseus for the living (1773–76) and Oedipus' favor of those below (1752–53) perpetuates the ambiguity of Oedipus' gifts, between curse and blessing. The *charis* that he receives as a suppliant from a city of strangers he withholds from the son of his own flesh. His moving joy in the *charis* which restores his daughters (1106) only just precedes the reluctance of yielding to Antigone's plea for *charis* toward Polyneices (1183).[58] The request of *charis* for a suppliant here repeats the pattern of the first half of the play, but now Oedipus is in the position of bestowing rather than requesting *charis*.

This reversal not only exemplifies Oedipus' shift from weakness to strength, suppliant to savior,[59] but also clarifies his problematical relation to human ties. Even when he is restored to a place in a humane and pious city, Oedipus remains in touch with a numinous power from which flow both love and hatred, both blessing and curse, both life-fostering saving (*sōtēria*) and destructive vengeance.

Closely related to *charis* in the play is *terpsis*, joy. Oedipus connects the two words in his onslaught on Creon in 766–767: when Oedipus' joy was in leaving Thebes, Creon's favor of keeping him there against his will was a perverted *charis*. Creon's kindness brings no real joy or pleasure (*terpsis*, 775; *hēdonē*, 780), just as his soft speaking conceals hard things (*sklēra malthakōs legōn*, 774). Whereas Creon can only offer this joyless friendship to an unwilling recipient (cf. 775), the true *charis* of a civilized city restores Oedipus to the deep joy (*terpsis*, 1122, 1140) of a father in his children. And yet this joy, like the grace which accompanies Oedipus, is also entwined with the dark hatreds of the house. Oedipus knows that in time joy becomes bitter between men (615). He calls his yielding to Antigone to hear Polyneices a heavy pleasure, *bareia hēdonē*, (1204). Antigone hopes, in vain, that Polyneices' appeal to his father may bring some joy (*terpsis*, 1281–83). But the result of the meeting, Oedipus' curses on his son, leaves the onlookers with no sharing of joy (*syn-hēdomai*) in what they hear (1397–98).

The third stasimon, which comes between the heavy joy of his reluctant acquiescence in Antigone's request (1204) and the entrance of Polyneices deals with the negation of joy in death. Hades, "without marriage, without lyre, without dance" (1221–22), is equally the negation of all that gives joy (*ta terponta*, 1217–18) and of all the bonds fostered by civilized life. These lines have a close parallel with the ode in *Ajax* where the Salaminian sailors lament their loss of joy at the death of their leader (*Ajax* 1199–1205, 1210–22). There, as here, this loss of a joy rooted in ties of loyalty and affection is conveyed in images of the wild. In both cases the suffering hero's precarious relation to this joy of civilized society is symbolized by exposure to the violence of nature, especially the sea (*Ajax* 1217–22; *OC* 1240–48).

V

With Polyneices' appearance the threats to human relationships first acted out in Creon's abduction of Oedipus' children gain in turbulence and complexity. Both Creon and Polyneices would draw Oedipus back into his Theban past, with its violence, inherited curse, and shedding of kindred blood. The hero's efforts to separate himself from this past, which earlier in the play centered on ritual and on political issues with the elders of Colonus and with Theseus respectively, now become more deeply emotional as he meets his own son. Coming from his own flesh and blood, the backward pull of Polyneices' plea is more powerful than Creon's force. It comes not only from his ancestral city but also from his ancestral house. Now, however, Oedipus has the strength to resist both polis and *oikos*. In this most painful of confrontations with his past, he is stronger, clearer, and more definite than before. Yet that denial necessarily involves a loss of human warmth and sympathy as well. Previously, as Oedipus became stronger in denying the twin pollution of incest and patricide, he moved from intense lyric to logical argument (207ff., 265ff.). Later, in defying Creon, he subsumes residual guilt into well-placed anger. Finally, in confronting Polyneices, the last temptation of his past, his anger does not even need a champion like Theseus but is itself effective as curse.

Oedipus' encounter with Polyneices closely parallels that with Creon. In both scenes a stranger comes from abroad and interrupts Theseus' rites of sacrifice (887ff., 1157ff.). But in the space between the two scenes Oedipus' situation has changed. Accepted into a civilized community, no longer an exile, he is surer of his authority and reveals flashes of his newly acquired heroic power. In the early scene Creon, as Oedipus observed, "spoke harsh things softly" (774); now, as Polyneices laments, it is Oedipus who utters the harsh things (*sklēra*, 1406).

If the interview with Polyneices parallels that with Creon, it also stands in contrast to it.[60] Oedipus, the helpless suppliant, is now the one to hear prayers of supplication (1309; cf. 1237). By the end of the scene Oedipus' curses, in Antigone's comment, have gained the power of divine prophecy ("such things as he prophesied," *thespizein*, 1428). Like an epic hero or an angered divinity, he has his heavy wrath (*mēnis bareia*, 1328; cf. 964–965, 1274), which, though harsh, has its justice. Creon, a suppliant who issued commands rather than uttered prayers, vitiated the suppliant ritual.[61] Polyneices' supplication, though more respectful of the forms, is almost a parody of Oedipus' own supplication at the beginning of the play.[62] Polyneices claims to be an exile driven from his land, seeking a place of rest (1292, 1296, 1330). He identifies himself with Oedipus as beggar, wanderer, stranger, a man with the same daimon of misfortune as his father (1335–37). But it is he who had driven out his father (compare 1363 with 1296 and 1330). He is no isolated wanderer but a general with allies at his back (1310), the fearless army of Argos (1325) in which he takes pride. His lengthy warrior–catalogue of the mighty Seven (1311–22) seriously undercuts his suppliant prayers (1309) and his claim to be the wronged victim.[63] These lines not only remind us of his involvement with martial glory, but, recalling

Aeschylus' *Septem*, evoke again the image of Thebes as a city of violence and tragic doom, a city of curses which are now enfolding the quarreling sons.

Ismene had described these martial preparations early in the play, including Polyneices' hope "to reach the heavens" if victorious (377–381). We are thus already prepared to recognize the hypocrisy of these pleas of beggary and helplessness. Polyneices' conventional invocation of the god as "helper" (1285–86) contrasts with Oedipus' deepening knowledge of the divine will. His appeal to oracles, immediately after his resentful cry for "vengeance against the brother who has driven me out and stripped me of my fatherland" (1329–31), contrasts with Oedipus' mysterious knowledge of oracles and his own growing oracular power (cf. 1428, *supra*). Correspondingly, the self-pity of his farewell to his sisters, implicitly inviting them to take the risks which they will have to run in burying him (1405–10), contrasts with Oedipus' concern for their welfare (1634ff.). In like manner, his last embittered and despairing farewell, "You will never again see me alive" (1437–38) stands on a plane far below Oedipus' acceptance when he recognizes the signs from the gods and takes his final farewell from his daughters in a deeply moving appreciation of their loss and his love (1610–19; cf. 1437 with 1612).

The Polyneices scene reaches back not only to the beginning of the play, reversing the roles of suppliant and supplicated, but also to the very beginnings of Oedipus' tragic career. It echoes the opening of the *Oedipus Tyrannus*, where the Theban elders approach Oedipus with suppliant rites and gestures as one almost equal to the gods (*OT* 31).[64] Now, no longer a proud king in his prime but a blind and battered wreck of a man, Oedipus is far closer to being equal to the gods and has a greater right to receive supplication. The scene with Polyneices, while not softening Oedipus' uncompromising hardness and hatred, is also an implicit answer to his embittered question of 393, "When I am no longer, then am I a man?"

With Polyneices Oedipus reenacts also the Teiresias scene of the *Tyrannus*, but now with Oedipus in the role of the blind prophet and Polyneices taking the part of Oedipus' younger self.[65] Oedipus is now not the accursed but the curser; and he has begun, while living, to acquire the awesome power to shelter or reject suppliants which in the *Ajax*, perhaps half a century earlier, accrues to the hero only when he is a corpse.

The length of the Polyneices scene has puzzled critics.[66] It is, however, absolutely necessary to Oedipus' growth and his return to a place of power in a civilized community. It is the penultimate stage of his confidence in his new-found authority and his paradoxical strength-in-weakness. "I know," says Oedipus (*eg' oida*, 452), putting together the new and the old oracle like Heracles in *Trachiniae*, in deepened understanding of his destiny. "You do not know (Creon's) threats," he had warned Theseus (656) and is proven right. "I have come here, holy and pious and bringing benefit to these townspeople," he proclaimed in an early intuition of his new powers (287–288). "I arrive here to make you a present of my wretched body, in appearance not worth consideration, but the profit from it is greater than a lovely physique," he tells Theseus (576–578). With this deepened perception of the relation between weakness and strength, transient exterior and lasting value, he is an Oedipus no longer confused by the paradoxes of appearance and reality.

His speech on time a few lines later confirms that perception of the paradoxical contrast between the frail body's blessings and the waning strength, in time, of a powerful body or a mighty land (609–610). At the end the gifts which Oedipus will confer are, as he prophesies, "untouched by the pain of age" (*gērōs alypa*, 1519). His dim sense that his body (*sōma*) is somehow a concern to the gods and has a place in the divine plan (354–355, 384, 389ff.) ripens into the defiant certainty which he throws in Creon's face that he has a better understanding (*ameinon phronō*) of Thebes' fortunes insofar as he more clearly hears Phoebus and Zeus (791–93).

The oracles of Apollo spoken of old (453–454) are no longer riddling, as in the *Tyrannus*, no longer destructive but helpful. In the earlier play these oracles revealed his hidden weakness when he was outwardly strong. Now they do just the reverse: they point to his hidden strength when he is outwardly weak.[67] Now he himself possesses oracular power in its darker side, the power to utter curses which will be fulfilled. His commanding presence at the divine call at the end, finally, fulfills in verbal and scenic action that early premonition of the gods' care (385ff.).

The Polyneices scene also provides a visual review in small compass of Oedipus' life. It forms a concentrated tableau of the principal figures in his tragedy and in its resolution, each one illuminated in a characteristic posture. Theseus urges the sanctity of the suppliant and the obligation of listening (1175–80), just as Theseus himself listened to Oedipus earlier (574–575; cf. 551). Antigone stresses the ties of blood. "You begot him," she says simply (1189). For her these ties should supersede the abstract principles of justice and vengeance (1189–91). She recreates in miniature the configuration of her tragedy of kin ties which Sophocles had developed thirty-five years earlier. Oedipus now passes through and beyond that tragedy, leaving his children still to face the curse of their blood.

VI

The entire play enacts Oedipus' rite of purification, both literal and figurative. It is a highly complex version of what Arnold Van Gennep called "liminal" rites, rites of entrance, reintegration, and separation.[68] Oedipus performs the lustral rites which purify the holy grove of his intrusion. Simultaneously he purifies himself of his pollution, both in words and in ritual deeds.[69] The ritual act of purification for entering the grove is also a symbolical purification of that entrance to a forbidden place which is part of his curse. Thus the ritual ablution is itself closely linked to the moral purification. Following close upon this rejection of Polyneices, it is the external, visible sign of his separation from the city of strife that belongs to his past and confirms his place in the well-ordered city of Theseus.

Joining the hands of his daughters and Theseus in a bond of trust (1631–35; cf. 1639), Oedipus moves beyond both the violent touch of Creon earlier which violates all piety (856, 863) and his own reluctance to touch Theseus with his polluted hands (1132ff.).[70] His initial declaration that he was holy and pious, *hieros*, *eusebēs* (287–288), is vindicated not only by the holy libations touched with pure hands (469–470; cf. 1598ff.), but, more important, by an inward purity validated by the gods themselves.

Polyneices entreats his father's aid for exactly the wrong reasons. "Shall I weep over my own woes first or his, my old father's?" he begins (1254–56). The note of self-pity dominates his speech. "I shall bring you to your house and establish you there," he promises (1342–43); but in the very next clause he goes on, "And establish myself there too, throwing out that other by force" (1343).[71] Like Creon, he stresses force and power, *bia* and *kratos*. Oedipus' new *kratos* impresses him now. The oracle, he says, declared that "the side to which you joined yourself would have the *kratos*" (1332). This is just the aspect of Thebes which Oedipus has most resented and resisted, the desire to "dominate" him (*kratein*) and use him as a kind of magical talisman, an instrument of success, in the way that Odysseus would use Philoctetes. "They say that their sources of power (*kratē*) lie with you," Ismene had told Oedipus early in the play (392). Creon and his men came, she had said, "to get power (*kratein*) over you and place you on the border of their land (399–400). "They want to join you to themselves near their country so that you may not even have power over yourself" (*sautou krateis*, 404–405); Polyneices disastrously echoes her hateful verb, "join yourself to us," in trying to "win over" Oedipus (1332). Replying to Ismene earlier, Oedipus had sworn that "they never will have power (*kratein*) over me" (408), and he reaffirms that determination even as he accedes to Antigone's request, asking from Theseus assurance that "no one have power (*kratein*) over my life" (1207).

In the play's reversal of inner and outer strength, the sons who chose thrones and scepters over their father (448; cf. 1354) get only the curse as their patrimony (cf. 425), whereas the daughters, who were Oedipus' true "staff/scepter" (*skēptra*, 848, 1109) will gain the "power" (*kratein*) of the throne (1380–81).[72] The words "throne" and "scepter" throughout recall the curses upon strife-riven Thebes (cf. 367–376, 392). But Oedipus' power or *kratos* is now spiritual rather than physical. Creon would deprive him of the intimate, personal *skēptra*, his daughters (848). Their safe return by Theseus seals Oedipus' security in Athens and assures his blessings on the pious rather than the violent city. Certain of rest in Athenian soil, Oedipus will exercise his mysterious, divinely granted *kratos* over his enemies. When he explains his request for burial to Theseus, he says, "This is the place . . . in which I shall have power (*kratēsō*) over those who cast me out" (644, 646).

Polyneices' language calls up also the bitterness of Oedipus' own violent past just when he is seeking to free himself from it. Winning a throne by the shedding of kindred blood evokes Oedipus' own grim accession to the throne of Thebes. The gall of domestic hatred rises again and again as Polyneices speaks of exile, expulsion, all-ruling throne, vengeance (1296, 1293, 1329, 1330). The thought that his younger brother (1295) has stripped him of his privileges (1330) and sits, a tyrant in the house (1338), rankles most bitterly and forces from him the cry, "O me miserable" (1338). As he spoke twice of being driven out (1296, 1330 in the same metrical position), so he returns twice to the pain of being laughed at or mocked by his brother (1339, 1423). Like Ajax, he smarts most from this laughter of one whom he regards as an enemy. Returning to the point that he is the elder brother, he becomes more and more fixated on the quarrels of childhood, the intense, narrow rivalries of a house whose enclosed rancors and excessively intense kin ties are its curse. Incestuously begotten, he consumes his life in a kind of narcissistic involution of sibling rivalry.

Bending all his energies toward expelling his brother from the place which he desires for himself, he fires his resentment again and again with the symbols of power, throne and scepter (1293, 1354, 1380–81). The violent acts of losing and gaining power, even if they mean the destruction of his city and his house, hold him in a morbid fascination that he cannot break. His small detail of how Eteocles got the city on his side, using persuasion rather than force (1296–98), speaks worlds about his desperate thirst for vengeance and power. How totally different are Theseus and the Athenians, ready to speak and hear reasonable arguments. We pity Polyneices the man and his hopeless situation; but Sophocles is relentless in demonstrating that his doom is irradicably ingrained in his character.

Polyneices perpetuates all the worst values of Thebes, all of its corruption of human relations. Ismene, the first messenger from that accursed city, told of its internecine struggle for power (361ff.). Her grim talk of evil strife, tyrant's power, expulsion, exile (367–381) is echoed and confirmed in person by Polyneices. In his presence, Oedipus relives aspects of his own curse but turns it against his son, a new *pharmakos*. He throws Polyneices' own language of power and hatred back against him: "Never to conquer (*kratēsai*) your native, kindred land by the spear, . . . but with hand of kindred race will you slay and be slain by the one by whom you were driven out" (1385–88). "By whom you were driven out": with a keen sense of his son's vulnerability, he touches the part that hurts most.

Oedipus is harsh, but he is also just. Polyneices entreated him in the name of "Reverence that shares the throne of Zeus for every deed" (1267–68). Oedipus answers with "Ancient Justice who sits beside Zeus's ancient laws" (1381–82).[73] Polyneices' appeal to this solemn Olympian "throne" of Reverence has already been undercut by his concern for the more earthly throne of Thebes and its all-ruling power (1293). It is no coincidence, then, that Oedipus, just before invoking Justice, pronounces Antigone and Ismene's right to that seat and throne of secular power which Polyneices so desperately covets. Oedipus' certainty of Ancient Justice (*palaiphatos Dikē*, 1381–82) confirms his certainty of knowledge about Apollo's ancient prophecies earlier (*manteia palaiphata*, 453–454). In both cases the hidden and terrible ways of the gods become his.

Polyneices and Creon together form the negation of the two central institutions of civilization, house and city. Theseus' introduction of Polyneices as one who "has no share in a city (*empolis*), but shares kindred blood" (*syngenēs*, 1156–57) echoes his own offer of city and house in admitting the homeless hero to the shelter of Athens (*empolin katoikizein*, 637). Oedipus accuses Polyneices of having driven him from both city and house and made him citiless, *apolis* (1356–57). In his culminating curse he calls his son fatherless (*apatōr*, 1383) and combines city and house in the doom which he prophesies: Polyneices is to lose the land of his race (*gē emphylios*, 1385) and die by kindred hand (*cheri syngenei*, 1387). The last phrase severs that tie of kinship by which Theseus introduced him as a suppliant. He then calls upon the "grim paternal darkness of Tartarus" to "unhouse" Polyneices (1390). His verb, *apoikizein*, "drive from the house," is the opposite of Theseus' *katoikizein* in 637, "house in the city."

Like Oedipus at an earlier stage, Polyneices will be cut off from the human world, abhorred (*apoptystos*, 1383, literally "spit back") and forced to dwell in the fearful darkness of the family curses beyond the pale of civilized humanity. Tartarus' hateful darkness, here called "of the father," *patrōon* (1390), again associates Polyneices' fate with the ancestral curses of the house.[74] What Polyneices will inherit as the privileges of rank from his father, (*gera*, 1396) should include both the prerogatives of the house and the royal power, but they are replaced by death outside the city at the hand of a brother (1387–96).

Polyneices' first speech had shown his ambiguous relation to the *oikos* which should have sheltered his father (1256–63):

> [My father], whom I have found in a strange land, driven out here with such clothing: its filth, hateful (*dysphilēs*), has long made its abiding home with him, old with an old man, befouling his body; and on his head, deprived of eyes, his hair uncombed flutters in the wind. Sisters to these (*adelpha*) it seems, he carries nurturing sustenance (*threptēria*) for his miserable belly (*nēdys*).

All the words point up his failure as a son in an *oikos* to whose ruin he has contributed.[75] The filth is *dysphilēs*, the negation of the *philia* of love. It dwells with the wandering beggar as if it shared house with him (*syn-oikizein*, 1259), the house denied him by his sons. His food is *threptēria*, a word which also refers to the "nurture" given by children to aged parents or by parents to children. The adjective, *adelpha*, "sister," instead of a more general word for 'likeness," reinforces the familial connotation. Even the word for "belly" is not the common *gastēr*, but *nēdys* (1263), which properly means "womb." Both "nurture" and "begetting" play a significant role in Oedipus' curse: he uses these words five times in eight lines (1362–69).

After Oedipus' terrible curse Antigone entreats Polyneices (whom she calls "child")[76] not to attack his brother, but Polyneices can only think of his claims of primogeniture (1420–23):

Antig.: Why need you be so full of anger, O child. What profit is there in razing your fatherland?

Polyn.: Exile is shameful, shameful for me, the elder, to be laughed at (*gelasthai*) by my brother.

The key words, fatherland and brother, enmesh political with personal motivations. The rivalries within the house are both beneath and parallel to the clash of armies from different states.

This pattern of language concentrates in Polyneices both the lure of this-worldly power, "thrones and scepters," and the awful pollutions of the family curse. By successfully resisting both, Oedipus completes his rite of separation. In his ritual ablutions soon after, Oedipus takes off just those filthy robes which his son cited at the beginning of his speech as the token of his father's misery and exile (*dyspineis stolas*, 1597; *dysphilēs pinos*, 1258–59). Literally divested of this garb of accursed exile and accursed Thebes, Oedipus is ready for the ritual cleansing that immediately precedes his heroization.

The exchange between Polyneices and Antigone after Oedipus' curse is a miniature Sophoclean tragedy. It is a scene we have encountered before: the doomed hero is unshakable in his violent resolve and his self-destructive passions, and a loving woman tries to call him back to life.[77] "Polyneices, I beseech you," she cries, "be persuaded by me" (1414). But she cannot persuade any more than Tecmessa could persuade Ajax or Jocasta Oedipus. "Do not persuade me of what you must not" is Polyneices' almost final word (1442). "Miserable, unfortunate, if I am deprived of you" is all Antigone can reply (1442–43). Yet Polyneices does not break. He answers with the tragic hero's acceptance of his daimon, the god's will: "That rests with the *daimōn* of fortune, that things should be thus or otherwise" (1443–44). His last words have the noble calm of the doomed man who has turned his face to death but looks back in compassionate sorrow to those whom his death will hurt (1444–46): "But I pray the gods that you two [his two sisters] may not meet suffering. For you are undeserving to have ill fortune in everything."

From all this Oedipus stands apart. Through this figure, involved and yet distant, Sophocles seems to be reflecting on the essential nature of his tragic art from a perspective which includes but is above tragedy. As the chorus of Athenian citizens reflects the situation of every tragic audience beholding man's encounter with the divine, "the chance encounters of life and the junctures with the *daimones*" (*OT* 33–34), so the position of Oedipus, removed in high and impassioned power amid the suffering and the doomed companions of his life, reflects the situation of the poet himself, shaping tragic destinies with knowledge and justice.

For all his tragic pathos, then, Polyneices can only partially engage our sympathies. Not he, but Oedipus is the center of attention and concern. For Oedipus the meeting is part of the accelerating rhythm toward the mysterious power of heroes. Entering the realm of the *daimones*, with their terrible anger and that remoteness of divinity whose retaliatory punishment, as Oedipus' own life attests, stands in no exact measure to guilt or even confuses the guilty with the innocent, Oedipus passes beyond the limits of normal moral judgments.[78] His curse has the fearful elemental justice of the gods.

Polyneices' arrival marks the second interruption of Theseus' sacrifice. The third comes immediately after, as the thunder and lightning tell Oedipus that the time is at hand to summon his friend (1457ff.). This third interruption, climaxing the other two, is the final stage of Oedipus' recognition of that token of his fortunes with which he began (46). Now, however, the summoning of Theseus is made in Oedipus' strength of certain knowledge. Not an outsider who arrives fortuitously, but Oedipus himself initiates the request.

The Polyneices scene is the watershed between Oedipus' human weakness and his heroization. The ode just preceding sings of the barrenness of death: "Not to be born exceeds all accounting" (1224–25). Here Oedipus, as we have seen, appears in the image of the exposed shore battered by the wild sea (1240ff.).[79] Polyneices takes us momentarily back into this realm of desolation and chaos, only to free us from it in a final blast of purificatory violence. Oedipus passes from the darkness of Rhipean night in the ode (1248) to the flash of Zeus-sent lightning as Polyneices departs. The supernatural luminescence that marks the epiphany of a god now succeeds the darkness of death and the darkness of the curse on the house of Laius. Inner vision replaces the moral blindness of the young Oedipus and the young Polyneices. In *Antigone* 586ff. that curse had appeared in imagery very similar to that of the ode on death, the dark violence of sea and storm. This ode of the *Coloneus* occurs as the hero approaches the transition from darkness to light, passing through curse to blessing. He comes to ever closer grips with ultimate things, being and non-being (*phynai* and *mē phynai*: cf. 1224–25). In this widened perspective, this *largior aether*, he leaves behind the bitterness of family quarrels, the jockeying for royal power, the strife over privilege, and the rancor of exile. Oedipus, himself meting out the awful retaliation which is given by the gods, comes closer than any mortal in Sophocles to seeing eye-to-eye with the Ancient Justice of Zeus (*palaiphatos Dikē*, 1381–82).

Earlier Oedipus has passed through a succession of liminal rites, first in entering the Eumenides' grove, then in gaining a sanctioned position in Athens itself. He has two stages of moral purification from incest and patricide, first to the chorus and then to Creon; these carry their benefit through the middle section of the play. The actual rite of purificatory libations, however, was interrupted by Creon's abduction of Ismene, who was to fetch the water from the holy springs (469ff., 495ff., 818ff.). Creon's interference with this rite is more than a physical obstruction: it would block the purificatory act, literally as well as symbolically, by pulling Oedipus back into the orbit of Theban violence and Theban pollution.

Polyneices, we recall, began his speech to Oedipus with pity and horror at his foul clothing. Oedipus turns Polyneices' pity for his dirt-encrusted raiment back upon him as the accusing mark of his son's pollution (1357–61). These foul garments have associations with Oedipus' *miasma* as the visible mark of the curses on his house. They are a reminder of his power to continue those curses through his deadly imprecations upon his sons. Now, as the ritual is finally performed,

Oedipus looses his filthy robes (1597). With the lustral rites (*loutra*, 1602) and new clothing (1603), he is ready to assume his new identity, a hero freed of the terrible impurity which has stamped his life.

Suspended for more than the thousand lines spanning the central action of the play (465ff., 1597ff.; cf. 478 with 1599), the purificatory rite essential for Oedipus' entrance to the holy grove finally intertwines acceptance into the sacred place of the goddesses with acceptance into the civic space of Athens. Here at the end another mysterious transition, now in the form of a passage across a numinous threshold to another world (1590ff.), answers and supersedes the earlier transition from savagery to civilization via the grove of the chthonic deities at the outskirts of Athens. Oedipus' solemn exit from known civic space at the end leaves him, paradoxically, with a firm place in its religious life and under its physical protection.

Passage, journey, road are important themes in the existence of the tragic hero. But this hero, moving beyond tragedy, possesses the most deeply rooted fixity that a mortal may attain. Oedipus' earlier speech on time (609ff.) recalls that of Ajax some half a century earlier, but Oedipus' end is completely different. His life has been defined by wandering, by unstable movement outside of house and city; but his movements of entrance and exit in the play finally come to rest in a space which, for all its ambiguities, is defined in the great ode on Colonus as peaceful, reverent, beautiful, musical, fertile, in harmony with the gods and with physical nature.

The grove is a forbidden place. Entrance to tabooed places, especially those associated with the earth and female, maternal powers, is as potentially dangerous for Oedipus in the present as it had been in his past. Now, however, he enters not to contract a *miasma*, as he did when he entered that secret place of his sowing in the earlier play, but to put away the *miasma*.[80] Initially "untouchable," *athiktos*, like the goddesses (39), blind Oedipus gains the power to find his resting place "without the touch of a guide" (*athiktos*, 1521). The meaning of "untouchable" undergoes a complete reversal from the beginning to the end of the play (39 and 1521). Hesitant to pollute others by his touch (*thigein*, 1133), he can now ask for the touch of hands in ancient pledge (1632). Likewise the helpless appeal of the blind man in the first scene as he asked for his daughter's guiding hand ("Touch me now—I touch you even so," 173) gives way to a confident laying on of hands conferred as a blessing and source of strength to those who sustained him. Like the newly blinded Oedipus at the end of the *Tyrannus* he touches his daughters with those once dreaded "blind hands" (1639), as he exhorts them to the endurance and nobility (*to gennaion*, 1640) which have been the distinguishing traits of his life (cf. *to gennaion*, 8).

In his uncleanness Oedipus had to pour holy libations (*hierai choai*, 469) to the Eumenides with holy hands (*hosiai cheires*, 470). At the end he himself gives the order for those libations (1598). The quality of holiness passes to him. His tomb is a holy place (*hieros*, 1545, 1763). His startling, improbable declaration, "I am here, holy and pious" (*hieros, eusebēs*, 287), is not only proven true but sanctified by solemn rites. Holy in part because of his suppliant status earlier, he is proven holy at the end because of the sacred force in the body which the holy tomb will shelter.[81] The holy weakness of the suppliant is replaced by the holy strength of the savior (see 460, 463, 487). He totally rebuffs Creon's accusations that he is unholy or impure (*an-hosios*, 946, 980, *an-hagnos*, 945). He can end this encounter with his accursed past, as he ends the next one too, by invoking as helpers and allies the goddesses who should pursue him as stained with kindred blood (1010–13; cf. 1391). Even the dreaded name, "Oedipus," loses its horror. Protecting him by his own name (667), Theseus can call him "son of Laius," as if that appellation has lost its terrifying force (1507; cf. 220, 553). A hundred lines earlier Oedipus could still use his name to curse (1395); but the god at the end calls him by the name which has been the token of his suffering and his pollution, "You, that Oedipus" (1627).[82]

VII

Here as elsewhere in Sophocles the quality of civilized life is measured by the capacity for human communication. *Logos*, language in all its aspects, is a major concern. Oedipus' first trial in the play is the establishment of speech, the right to speak and hear, with the citizen of Athens (190). Concealed in the grove, he will keep silence (113) until he learns what words the inhabitants of Colonus will speak (115–116). The grove of the Eumenides by which he makes his fresh contact with a civilized community is a place where speech reaches its furthest limits, where experience pushes into that which cannot be spoken. The first man Oedipus meets there tells him of the names of the place and informs him that what is there is "honored not in words (*logoi*), but rather through the sharing of association" (*synousia*, 63–64). The chorus enters singing of the goddesses "of whom we tremble to speak" (*tremomen legein*, 128), whom "we pass by sightless, speechless, wordless, moving the mouth in thought of propitious utterance" (130–132). The grove itself is "unutterable" (*aphthenktos*, 157). To speak, the chorus tells Oedipus, he must move beyond the *abata*, the places not to be trod upon, where "speech is lawful for all" (166–169). In this place of forbidden speech he reenacts his life's place on the fringes of society. Outside its frame of communication, he must leave the grove, the place of silence, and return to a common ground of speech with other men.

His opening exchange with the chorus gives his speech the mystery and awe of his whole being. It is by speech that he sees, as he tells the chorus. This use of speech for a function alien to it expresses, on the level of *logos*, Oedipus' affliction. "Fearful to see, fearful to hear" is the chorus' reply (141). The dialogue centers on hearing or heeding (the verb is repeated several times: 169, 172, 181, 190, 194), until the fateful speaking, the solemn *phatizomenon* of 139, leads to promises of the exchange of speech (190) and culminates in the chorus' tense cry, "Speak," *audason*, "O unhappy man, who among mortals are you?" (204–205).

The short lyrical lines of this scene create a suspenseful drawing near and retreat from speech (208–212) that has close parallels with the climax of the *Oedipus Tyrannus*. Once more, speech stands, literally, in the realm of the ultimate things: "Speak," Antigone encourages him, "since you come to the last things" (*ep' eschata baineis*, 217). Oedipus here reenacts those "last things of speech," the "point of terrible speech" when the old Shepherd spoke the final clue in the *Tyrannus* (*OT* 1169). Here too Oedipus finds the courage to pass beyond that point: "I shall speak, for I have no means of concealment" (*OC* 218). Now the status of speech in extremis comes at the beginning rather than at the end; it is the opening stage of the process of reintegrating the hero into civilized life not the final push beyond the pale.

When Oedipus, a few lines before, begs, "No, no, no, do not ask me who I am, nor search out beyond with further seeking," (210–211), he verbally echoes Jocasta's request, in the *Tyrannus*, that he search no further when the horrible results of further speech are all too plain to her (*mē mateuseis*, *OT* 1060–61; cf. *pera mateuōn*, "searching further," *OC* 211). This searching further was just what Oedipus refused to do for so long in his earlier play. But now he is the one to make those demands. Taking over the role of the frightened interrogators of the previous drama, he can finally possess the knowledge to answer the question, "Who am I?" (*tis eimi*, 210–211). Passing the point of terrible speaking does not shut him off from the civilized world, as earlier, but reopens channels of communication, painful as this is. Though the words wring from him the repeated cry *oimoi* (199, 213, 216), he can face openly the dread tale of incest and patricide. Speech can neutralize the ancient terror.

The next scene shows Oedipus liberating speech from the mute terror of the curse. Still trembling with fear of the gods, the chorus is reluctant to "utter anything beyond what we have now spoken to you" (256–257). But Oedipus, who had previously addressed only the goddesses of the grove at such length (84–110), now makes his second great speech, clearing his name of the taint of willful evil and moral guilt (258–291). The chorus acknowledges the impressiveness of this speech (293–294).

The arrival of Ismene opens another level of human discourse for the old outcast. To her, father and sister are the dearest words of address (*hēdista prosphōnēmata*, 325), and they exchange the terms of intimacy and endearment ("Father," "child," 326ff.). Language, like kinship, however, remains ambiguous for Oedipus as he calls his daughters "seed of kindred blood" (*sperma homaimon*, 330). The phrase reminds us that their incestuous birth gives a darker side to both paternal address and paternal love. In this same speech he calls his sons too by the terms of the curse of incest, "youths of the selfsame blood," (*authhomaimoi neaniai*, 335): language and kinship are destructively interwoven in this accursed family. Denouncing his sons soon after, Oedipus anticipates the darker side of his power of speech: he now perpetuates that very curse from which he exonerated himself in his defense of his inner purity. Love for daughters and hatred for sons mingle in this two-sidedness of Oedipus' speech, affection and curse. Those two sides continue through the scene with Ismene (see 421ff.).

Having admitted Oedipus to the fellowship of a common discourse, the

393

chorus pities him (461) and offers instructions about the purificatory ritual which will solemnize his reentrance to the community of men (466ff.). The emotional response of pity precedes its formal validation in the rite of purification. The expression of human feeling and the ritual act are parallel aspects of the same message, Oedipus' passage from the wild to the civilized realm. The horror of men and the anger of the gods lift at the same time and include him again in full human discourse.

Oedipus, however, struggles still with the terrible words of his past. He has to face once more the agony of uttering these awful names (see 528), satisfying the chorus' request for the "right hearing" (517). Once more he must hear and pronounce accursed words, the bed of sinful name (*dysōnyma lektra*, 528), which it is death to hear (529), children begotten of his own mother's womb (533), daughters who are also sisters (535), and disease upon disease, the killing of his father (542–545). In these painful, choppy lyrics, Oedipus reenacts, in miniature, the confusion of language and kinship developed in the earlier play. His present situation, however, has an answer to that destruction of differentiation in the linguistic and familial codes. He can steel himself to pronounce these awful words and simultaneously declare his innocence. His own growth and the proximity of Theseus' Athens give him a confidence in a rational human justice which undercuts the inexorable irrationality of the curse. "I shall speak," he says firmly in the last lines of this lyric dialogue. Then in two clear, firm lines he recapitulates the moral innocence he asserted in his long defense earlier: having acted without knowledge and in innocence, he is pure in the eyes of law, *nomō(i) katharos* (546–548).

With this affirmation, access to the city through speech is open. The change to the dialogue meter of iambic trimeters after the broken lyrics as Theseus enters marks a new ease of speaking. Oedipus feels such trust in Theseus' nobility, matching his own (cf. 8 and 569), that he feels no need to speak at length (or, with Pearson's emendation, feels no shame, *aideisthai*, in speaking briefly, 569–570). The trust between the two men obviates the need for a formal oath: Theseus' word (*logos*) is enough (650–651).

In the ode on Colonus which follows this scene, speech is raised to its highest function, a hymn of praise and celebration. "O land most hymned in praises (*epainois eulogoumenon*)," Antigone says as the choral song fades, "now is the time to show forth (*phainein*) your brilliant words" (*lampra epē*, 720–721). The contrast between words and real acts which the stranger cited in the prologue as part of the worship of the grove (62–63) is now put to the test. Over against the hymn of praise and Antigone's eulogizing (720–721) stands Creon's entrance speech, with its harsh and hypocritical tone (see 758–759, 774). Oedipus is then once more pushed to embittered speech: accusations of tricky speech (761–762), refusal of persuasion (802–803), and another eloquent defense of his innocence (960–1002). If Theseus' nobility permitted Oedipus to abridge speech, Creon's baseness has just the opposite effect: it compels speech (979) and pulls us back into the violent speech of which Oedipus is also capable.

Like Tecmessa in *Ajax* and Neoptolemus at the end of *Philoctetes*, Antigone is the voice of Oedipus' capacity for reconciliation over against the bitterness that draws the hero apart from men in doomed isolation. Unlike those earlier plays, however, the protagonist is in agreement with this part of himself from the beginning. Where Ajax and Philoctetes remained adamant, Oedipus yields. In the scene with Polyneices near the end, as in the scene with the elders of Colonus at the beginning (see 217), it is Antigone who swings the balance in favor of speech: "What harm is there," she pleads, "in hearing words?" (1187). Yet for Polyneices Oedipus' speech will prove more terrible even than the ominous silence (cf. Polyneices' uneasy "Why are you silent" at 1271).

Antigone views the *logos* not as legalistic debate or accusation, but as a healing incantation which can "charm" men out of a flawed nature (1192–94): "Some men have a bad origin and a sharp temper, but when they are reproached by the charmed speech (*epō(i)dai*) of friends, they are charmed out of their nature (*exepa(i)dontai physin*)." With this age-old, naive concept of language as a curative magical spell,[83] she would persuade Oedipus to address Polyneices in the spirit of fatherhood, using words to guide, chastise, improve. Asking Oedipus to listen to his son (1175–76), Theseus only elicits his refusal to yield (*eikathein*), the reaction typical of the intransigent tragic hero. Oedipus reiterates the hatefulness of his son's voice (*echthiston phthegma*, 1177). Only Antigone actually effects the exchange of speech. Ironically, Oedipus, who himself begged for an exchange of speaking and hearing at the beginning of the play, nearly refuses that same boon to another homeless suppliant. His rejection of Polyneices' appeal as "a voice most hateful" in 1177 inverts those "voices most sweet" with which Ismene addressed him and Antigone in 325. The contrast once more expresses the ambiguity of language in the sphere of the tragic hero. Like the hero himself, it veers between gentleness and harshness, blessing and curse, openness and rigidity, with that coexistence of opposites which is so essential, and so difficult, a part of Oedipus' character in this play.

Restraint in speech is also a mark of civilization. The silence demanded by the Eumenides' "soundless vale" (57; cf. 128ff., 489) indicates the reverence accorded to these goddesses who are both within and without the civilized order. Beside their holy silence stands also the silence demanded by the Eleusinian deities. As a later ode sings, a "golden key" seals the tongue of their priests, the Eumolpids (1051–53).

The sanctity surrounding speech reminds us of another sacred *logos*, the oracles which come from the gods. Here Oedipus finally comes into his own as one who speaks true and important *logoi*. Hesitant to speak at all in the first scene, he becomes increasingly authoritative as the prophet of the gods' will (450ff., 787–794).[84] At the end his curses have the force of oracles (1372ff., 1425, 1428). His oracular directives command King Theseus' obedience: "You persuade me," Theseus says, "for I see you uttering oracles (*thespizonta*) and no false prophecies" (1516–17). Oedipus himself used this verb, *thespizein*, in a query about oracles (388). Later other characters use it of his numinous utterances, both his curse (1428) and his understanding of his destiny (1516).

Having rejoined civilization through the effort of painful speech at the beginning, Oedipus transcends human speech at the end as he passes not outside but beyond the bounds of the polis. No longer the accursed *miasma* who cannot be addressed in speech (cf. *OT* 238), he is the bearer of the sacred *logos* of the gods which human speech cannot fathom.

The gods' calling of Oedipus raises speech to a new level of power and mystery. An awesome, thunderous voice, "Zeus-hurled and unspeakable" (*aphaton*, 1464), frightens the townspeople and summons Theseus once more (1500–1501). Oedipus who "saw by voice" and was "terrible to see, terrible to hear" (139, 142) now interprets the great crashing sounds which leave the others gasping, "Look! Behold!" (1463–64, 1477–79). The intersensal imagery (the combination of sound and sight) which initially reflected Oedipus' deprivation of normal perception recurs here at the end to signify a perception of a sphere hidden from ordinary mortals.[85]

Like the Eumenides, Oedipus now commands the power of sacred silence; and that silence, like theirs, has the power to protect and save (1530ff.). There is a close parallel with the grove at the beginning, but Oedipus is now the center of these mysterious sounds. The Eumenides' numinous power, like their power to curse, is increasingly associated with him. Where the others are confused, he is calm. To him the thunder and lightning speak with thrilling clarity (1511–12): "The gods themselves are heralds and bring word to me, with no falsehood in the signs that stand before us." Theseus, a few lines later, gives Oedipus' oracular utterances this same divine attribute of freedom from falsehood (*ou pseudophēma*, 1517; cf. *pseudontes ouden*, 1512, *ou pseudomantis*, 1097). What he has to tell Theseus is instinct with holy power: it can be spoken to very few (1522ff.).

Language itself is not easily adequate to the events of Oedipus' end: no brief tale (*mythos*) can tell what happened (1581–82). Silence and speech reinforce one another as the entrance of the divine into the human world forces language and emotion to a new plane (1623–28):

> There was a silence. And of a sudden the voice of someone shouted out for him, so that everyone's hair stood bolt upright of a sudden in fear, for the god calls him, a much repeated manifold call: "Oedipus, Oedipus, why do we hesitate to go? Of old has been the delay on your side."

It is the high point of the play, and one of the highest points of the Greek theater. The accursed name, "Oedipus," earlier so reluctantly pronounced (207ff., esp. 221–222; cf. *dysōnyma*, 528), is now the token of the outcast's divinity. With the call from God, *ek theou kaloumenos* (1629), human speech reached its outer limits. The stylized *mythos* of the Messenger's speech is scarcely adequate to contain it (1581–82). Like Socrates' enigmatic closing words of the *Phaedo*, with their calm, mysterious glimpse into the unknown, it takes its verbal form beyond the limits of its familiar function.

The transcendence of the human *logos* in the *Coloneus* is just the opposite of its annihilation in the earlier plays.[86] There the mediating function of language breaks down as men sink below the level of their humanity or experience the divine afflatus as destructive. In the *Coloneus* the *logos* also pales before elemental forces, but the direction is upward rather than downward, toward divinity rather than bestiality. The mediating function of speech in an orderly polis is dissolved in transcendence. Closest in time and in mood are Heracles' *mythoi* at the end of *Philoctetes*. The civic leader, characterized throughout by openness and plainness of speech, must keep silence about this final event. The well-being of his city, outstanding for its accessibility to reasonable *logos*, depends on his not speaking, even to those with whom Oedipus has shared the most intimate and humanizing of words, "the one word" of love (*philein*, 1615–19).

The transcendence of *logos* in the last scene is all the more forceful because what precedes it is a virtual destruction of civilized discourse. In the scene between Oedipus and Polyneices, language comes close to breaking down. The father nearly refuses to speak to his son (cf. 1173–74, 1177). When they do address one another, it is in set speeches, punctuated by awkward silence (see 1271).[87] The line-for-line or phrase-for-phrase exchanges of stichomythia or *antilabē* take place only between Antigone and Polyneices.[88] Oedipus stands silent for the ninety-odd lines of Polyneices' speech. After six lines of restrained third-person utterance in a lofty periodic style (1348–54), his first word of direct address is crushing: "You basest of men" (*ō kakiste*, 1354). Hearing these words, Oedipus said, will never bring cheer to his life (1353). These are words which Polyneices will not be able to tell to any of his followers (1402–1403). Instead, he will have to return in silence (*anaudos*, 1404; cf. 1429–30). "Who will dare to follow you," Antigone realistically asks, "when he hears what this man has prophesied?" (1427–28). Polyneices exits soon after with a futile prayer and a final refusal of persuasion (1441–42) as he remains unmoved by Antigone's entreaties.

As the culminating failure of *logos* in Sophocles, this scene is not only the foil to the finale's brilliant transfiguration of tentative human speech into the divine call, but also the natural completion of the contrast between the language of Athens and the language of Thebes. Ismene, crossing the borderland between Thebes and Athens, brings with her the fearful speech of her native city (see 333, 357, 377), full of strife and hatred and terrible deeds (367ff., 383–384). Creon's small attempt at persuasion in the center of the play (736, 740, 802–803) soon yields to the deeds of force and outrage (*bia, hybris*).[89] The silence which Creon brusquely commands (864) is, literally, in another world from the god-given silence enjoined by the grove or by the gods at the end (1623). His is a shameless voice (863) and an unholy mouth (981), which is prepared to say anything, the speakable or unspeakable word (*rhēton t' arrhēton t' epos*, 1001). In his mouth speech quickly degenerates to insult (*oneidos*, 967, 984, 990) or ranting threats (*apeilēmata*, 817, 1038; cf. 659–660). He and Oedipus engage in a sharp stichomythy on right speaking (806ff.). Words for foul-mouthing recur repeatedly (794–795, 963, 981, 986). For Creon the just or noble word (762, 1000) is trickery or hypocrisy. He is ready to flatter the noble name of Theseus (1003). Like Odysseus in *Philoctetes*, from every just argument (*logos dikaios*) he would make a crafty device (*mēchanēma poikilon*, 762).

Athens, by contrast, hallows the reverent silence of the Eumenides' grove

(128ff.), treats speech and listening as a matter of law and justice (168, 190), and defies the bluster of Creon. Where Creon compels Oedipus to speak a long defense and break his moderate speech for bitter curses (864ff., 1010ff.), Theseus' nobility makes lengthy explanation unnecessary (569–570). The Athenian ruler's speech is characterized by intelligence (*nous*, 659ff., 936; *gnomē*, 594), freedom from boastful exaggeration (*kompein*, 1149) or falsehood (1127, 1145).

The right relation between word and deed that is part of Athens' reverent attitude in the prologue (honoring the grove not in words, but by shared association, 62–63) is also inverted in strife-torn Thebes. There, as Ismene tells Oedipus, words become terrible deeds (382–383). Carrying that perversion of *logos* and *ergon* to Athens, Creon offers Oedipus things noble in word, but in deed base (782) and resorts to force and deeds when defeated by words (815, 817). Oedipus suffers in deeds, but defends himself in words (872); Creon does just the reverse: suffering by words, he retaliates with deeds (*antidran*, 953). A terse *antilabē* sums up their duel of words and deeds (861):

> Cho.: Terrible is what you *say*.
> Creon: As what I will now *do*.

In disengaging himself from Thebes and entering Athens, Oedipus establishes a new relation of word and deed: "My deeds lie in suffering rather than doing" is one of the cornerstones of that new conviction of inward purity that enables him to leave his polluted Theban past (266–267; cf. 538ff.). His encounter with Creon tests that defense (872, 953, above), and though momentarily defeated in deeds, Oedipus is yet the winner in words. Theseus' energetic command of both deed and word restores the healthy relation between them that exists at Athens. "Enough of words" is his curt, effective answer to fruitless verbal ranting (1016). "Not by our words more than our deeds do we strive to attain a life of brilliant glory," he claims when his deed, the rescue of Antigone, is an accomplished fact (1143–44).

Cutting through the corrupt *logos* of Creon's Thebes is the "one word" of love (*philein*) in Oedipus' farewell to his daughters, which, he says, "looses all the sufferings" of the past (1615–19).[90] This simplest and briefest of terms contrasts with the distorted communication and tangled human relationships in both Oedipus' Theban past and Creon's Theban present. It also forms a leitmotiv which runs throughout the play. He grants at the end to his daughters that "one word" which his sons withheld from him in Thebes (443–444): "But for the sake of a small word I wandered, outside always, an exile, a beggar." That refusal rebounds on them when Theseus announces the elder son's arrival, "a tale . . . small to tell (*logos . . . smikros eipein*), but worthy of wonder" (1152). He goes on (1161–63):

> Thes.: I know one thing only (*hen*). He asks, they tell me, a brief word of you(*brachyn mython*), not full of weight (*onkos*).
> Oed.: What sort of word? For this seat of supplication is not a matter of small account ("small word," *smikrou logou*).

The reversal acts out that mutation of human fortunes and sentiments which Oedipus, from his own experience, understands so well (607–615). In a happier context, however, Oedipus can count on Theseus' nobility to obviate the need of all but a small word (*smikros logos*, 569). He gives Theseus a lesson in the changefulness of human affairs wherein allies can become enemies as a result of a small word (*smikros logos*, 620). When Theseus has weathered this change and proven his loyalty to the suppliant whom he has received, the small word recurs as a sign of Oedipus' fatherly concern for his daughters (1115–16): "Tell me what happened as briefly as you can, since for girls of your age a small word suffices." In a new ease of speaking, Oedipus can ask his host, "Do not wonder if with such eagerness I lengthen out my speech (*mēkynō logon*, 1120–21) to my children, whom I see here beyond my hope." With sympathetic understanding Theseus finds no difficulty in this length of words (*mēkos tōn logōn*) in the other's joy (1139–40).

VIII

The *philia* or love of Oedipus' "one word" as he takes leave of the human world is another dimension of the civilized life sheltered by Theseus' city. Here in Athens and at the end of Oedipus' life the hero cursed as an enemy to those close to him, both those above ground and those below (*OT* 415–416), recovers the love that reconciles him both with his living *philoi* and with the powers below the earth.

Oedipus returns to human society by a route just the opposite of Philoctetes'. Exiled by his wound from gods and men, Philoctetes needs to experience the friendship and good will of his young companion before he can fulfill the gods' design and heal himself at Troy. Oedipus will not only share the Athenians' feeling about what "the polis has come to hold as dear (*philon*)" and what it regards as "friendless" (*aphilon*, 184–187), but will guide and aid Athens in those mortal vicissitudes wherein friends turn to foes (605–628).

In moving from Thebes to Athens Oedipus' chief task is disentangling love and hate. The daughters who emerge finally into the simplicity of *philein* are also the twin curses or disasters (*atai*, 532) of his incestuous marriage. Longing for her life with her father despite the pain it involved, Antigone heaps up the paradoxes of their *philia* (1697–1703):

> Even for woes is there somehow desire. For what was in no way loved (*philon*) is loved, when I held him, O my father, my dear one (*philos*), in my arms, O clothed in the eternal darkness beneath the earth. For never will you be unloved (*aphilētos*) by me or by her here, far away though you are.

Against this tangible human warmth of *philia* stand Oedipus' mysterious union of opposites and ambiguous relation to civilization: light and darkness, sky and earth, (1456ff., 1471, 1556ff.), upper air and Hades, curses in the name of Tartarus and call from the aether (1389–90, 1464–71), Zeus of the lower world

(*Zeus chthonios*) and "Demeter of the green shoots" (1600–1605), benefit to the city and reaching something beyond mortal ken.[91]

As the miraculous thunder and lightning and the awesome call from the gods die away (1621–30), there comes almost at once a different sound, the familiar wail of lamentation (1668–69): "They are not far, for their voices, not unmarked by wails of grief, show (his daughters) rushing hither." Oedipus himself did not lament at his end (*ou stenaktos*, 1663, in an active sense), but these voices of grief recall the bitter voice of his daughters' cries as "they fell at their father's feet and wept and would not let up their beatings of breast or long-drawn-out cries of woe" (1607–10). He takes his farewell, however, with the firm knowledge of his destiny and the simplicity of his "one word" of love (1612–19).The embrace of his daughters here (1611), important in a play where touching has been so problematical, is a visual and tactile assurance of his love, but, hero that he is, he does not let his feelings obscure his clarity of vision and definiteness of purpose. Comparison with the *Ajax*, written over half a century earlier, is instructive. There is the same firm lucidity of choice and unshakable will, but this hero's attitude to those whom he is leaving behind and to the divine powers surrounding his life shapes a gentler, far more conciliatory mood.

This clash of the turbulent emotion of the survivors and the calm of the hero who is passing out of the human realm is Sophocles' fullest expression of the different planes of human and divine knowledge. It develops, but goes far beyond, Heracles' moment of understanding at the end of *Trachiniae* (1143–78). The Messenger attempts to render the full wonder of Oedipus' passing: there was no thunder or storm from the sea, "but either some messenger from the gods (took him), or else it was very earth's foundation, the place of the lower gods, standing apart in good will for him without pain" (1661–62).[92]

This mysterious good will and painless, parturient division of the lower world leaves little trace in the limited understanding of the hero's immediate survivors. He met his end, Antigone laments, not in war nor on the sea, "but the viewless fields snatched him off, borne away in some unseen doom. But for us two a destructive night has come on our eyes" (1679–85). Antigone has recourse here to the familiar language of myth, wherein the deceased is snatched away (*marptein* is her verb) by some creature of the air. True, she speaks of the unseen fields as doing the snatching, but her language is still that of archaic myth, like the Harpies, snatchers of the dead in Homer and early Greek art,[93] and not the wondrous, (1665) painless riving of the earth "in the kindness of the chthonic dark" for Oedipus in the Messenger's account. She sees only destructive night, not the mysterious alternation of light and dark, Olympian and chthonic forces, which the Messenger described.

Antigone and Ismene are present at the end, however, not just to round out the legend.[94] It is rather that Sophocles refuses to leave us on the plane of divine knowledge only, in a pious stupor at a holy miracle, all passion spent. We may recall here that disturbing speech of Hyllus (or the chorus) that closes the *Trachiniae*. Even the gods' summons has its peremptory note of harshness.[95] Over against the now familiar human survivors mourning visibly in the orchestra stands this unknown, nameless and remote "voice of someone," a *theos*.[96] The love (*philia*) of the survivors exposes them to a pain from which the immortal gods are exempt. The public benefit which Oedipus' death confers, like his death itself, has this quality of exemption from pain (*alypos, alypētos*, 1519, 1662, 1765); but the call from the gods is soon drowned out in the wailing of the all too human, grief-stricken *oikos*.

The heroization of Oedipus does not have the last word in the play. It does not silence the children's cries for a dead father. Though free of the burden of providing their father's nurture (*trophē*) and sharing his wanderings, Antigone bewails the life of wandering that she sees before them (1685–87) and asks how they will get their nurture (*trophē*, 1688).

IX

Despite Oedipus' instructions (1528–29), Antigone's first desire is to see the tomb (1725ff.). She accedes to Oedipus' order forbidding it (1761ff.); but the very phrase she uses to describe the tomb, *tan chthonian hestian* (1727), indicates her distance from the heroized father. The phrase means not merely "resting place in the ground," as Jebb paraphrases, but "chthonic altar," the place of a divinity, not a man. For Theseus the tomb is a locus of mysterious power, a holy memorial (*thēkē hiera*, 1763), a source of benefit to Athens (1764–65). For Antigone it is a place where she can vent her sorrow and her violent emotions of loss. Theseus does not mourn. For him Oedipus' death is the fulfillment of a divinely established destiny and part of the history of Athens. The contrast between the two cities is again strong. The Theban girls see only the personal and familial side, the suffering and loss (1668–69); Theseus sees a mysterious *charis* (1752) and for his country "good fortune . . . and a land forever without pain" (*aien alypon*, 1764–65).

Theseus' explanation of Oedipus' final wish has a calming effect on Antigone (1768). Yet the passion and violence of the Theban past still pull Oedipus' kin toward suffering. Images of wandering, the sea, the wild (1684ff., 1746) surround the distraught Antigone, in contrast to Theseus' authoritative vision of holy events and divine injunctions. "Cease your lamentation," he tells them, as he speaks of the strange grace of the chthonic powers (1751–53).

The two sisters surrender to the "destructive night" of their grief (1684) and "are ablaze" in their impassioned sorrow (1695). This destructive night covers Antigone's eyes as she thinks of the obscure fate of her father (1681–84). Oedipus himself, however, at the end has an inner sight in his blind eyes. His daughters are covered by darkness; he, who began in night, ends in a Zeus-given brightness. At the miraculous celestial thunder that heralds his end, the chorus cries out to Time, his deadly enemy in the earlier play: now Time sees all things (1454–55), and what is seen is the "light that is no light" of the hero's new, supernatural vision (*phōs aphenges*, 1549; cf. 1481).

After much travel on the road of life (20, 91, 96) Oedipus has come to a numinous "threshold broken sheer" at three roads' crossing where he makes his mysterious passage to peace and to power (1590ff.). Antigone, having escaped the roads which would have brought her prematurely to Thebes (cf. 990ff., 1506), has, like Polyneices, a hard road ahead of her (cf. 1397–98, 1432). Oedipus has his escort, *pompos*, from the gods (1661, 1664; cf. 1548). Antigone asks for escort (*pempson*, 1770) back to "primeval Thebes," *Thēbas tas ōgygious* (1769–70). For the survivors of tragic events—one thinks of Agave in the *Bacchae*, of Theseus in the *Hippolytus*, of Hyllus in the *Trachiniae*—life is often "a burden in many ways worse than the release of death."[97]

Both the Athenian king and the elders of Colonus urge the sisters to put an end to lamentation. They try to soothe their immediacy of raw grief with the grace of the chthonian powers below (1752) or the final validating order (*kyros*) of the divine plan: "Cease your lamentation, children. For where the grace of those below (*charis chthonia*) lies stored as a common good, we must not grieve: it would be subject to divine anger (*nemesis*)" (Theseus, 1751–53). "Cease, then, nor awaken grief in greater degree. For in every way these things have final validity" (Chorus at the end, 1777–79). In both cases, however, the spectacle, audial and visual, of the girls totally gripped by their suffering confronts transcendence with immanence, checks distant consolation with present lamentation (*thrēnos*, 1751, 1778). Oedipus has his tomb, Athens its blessing. Antigone and Ismene stand totally alone, between a city that is not theirs and a house disintegrating in bloody ruin.

Deprived of her father's last moments of life, barred from the actual experience of his death which would give it emotional reality, Antigone is left with only the emptiness, the non-presence, of the dead, perhaps the most painful residuum of losing a loved one. She does not even have the body to mourn over. In keeping with the character which Sophocles had given her in her own play thirty-five years earlier, she tries to fill that emptiness with the concrete, tangible presence of the tomb.[98] It is a consolation that is denied.

In withholding his place of burial from his children (1528–29), Oedipus passes beyond the ties of family and blood. He leaves behind him those intense bonds of love and hate which have caused him, and those close to him, so much suffering. He becomes part of a larger order, beyond the family, an order which perhaps anticipates a different kind of civic life even as it shows the fifth-century polis in a final, transfiguring glory. The concealment of his place of burial from those who would give it the rituals and the tears that only blood kin can is the last purgation of the curses of his past. His efforts at purification early in the play were inward and moral, still directed toward the familial pollutions of father-murder and the incestuous bed (525–548). Now that purification is choral and communal. The fate of Oedipus passes from a house to a city. Henceforth he belongs to a polis, not to an *oikos*; to Athens, not to Thebes.

Oedipus here resolves old tensions between polis and *oikos*, but in a spirit exactly antithetical to that of the *Antigone*. There the Olympian and male-oriented polis represented by Creon failed to transcend its biological roots in the house and so was pulled back into the violence and destructiveness of those immanent bonds of blood and the womb. The *Coloneus* breaks those bonds. Freed of the necessity of human rites of burial, not placed in a conspicuous tomb which can become an object of family veneration, like the grave of Agamemnon in the *Electra*, Oedipus has moved outside those ties of blood and family which have been his curse. At the price of giving up his *oikos*, he becomes the hero of a polis alone, his grave known only to the male ruler of a city to which he has no ties of blood.

Antigone's request for "escort to primordial Thebes," *Thēbas ōgygious*, in her last speech, however (1769–70), draws us back to the city of strife which Oedipus has left, back to the hatreds and conflicts generated by the family curse. The contrast between Athens and Thebes is sharpest here at the end, when the hero himself has transcended it. Antigone will return to that Theban world. Her motivation is characteristically generous and protective of life: she and her sister hope to "prevent the slaughter (*phonos*) coming upon those of our own kindred blood" (1771–72). "Slaughter," *phonos*, is a brutal word. It echoes the chorus' grim, general pessimism about the place of envy, civil disturbances, strife, battles, and slaughter in human life (1234–35). It also echoes Oedipus' specific curse, about to be fulfilled, of "being killed and killing" (*thanein ktanein te*, 1388). Antigone's very word contains a premonition of her failure. Even her cry, some forty lines before the end, "Take me there [to Oedipus' grave] and then kill me" (1733) contains her heritage of Theban violence which, as we know from the earlier play, will not end the curse but continue its work to the end.

In keeping with her conciliatory role between father and son here, Antigone must try to prevent this catastrophe (cf. 1193–94). In keeping with her tragic role she must fail. Her inability to persuade Polyneices in the earlier scene already intimates the outcome (cf. 1414ff.). Polyneices there foreshadowed her own share in the curse of Oedipus (1407–10): "If these curses of my father have effect and there is a return to our house, do not, by the gods, leave me in dishonor, but place me in the grave with due burial rites." We know at what cost Antigone will honor this plea, and we know too the irony and futility of his departing prayer (1444–46): "For you two girls I pray to the gods that you meet no evil. For you do not deserve to have misfortune in all things."

Theseus can offer the daughters aid in the name of his city's bond of reciprocal favor or grace to Oedipus (*pros charin*, 1777), a last reflection of Oedipus' mysterious grace of the chthonic powers (*charis chthonia*, 1752). But the play does not end as a ringing paean to the mercy of the gods. Oedipus' *charis* can bless Athens but can do nothing for his own accursed city and its past, that primordial Thebes where Antigone, bound to return, will fulfill the last act of the tragic history of this house.[99]

Oedipus has met the threefold test of his separation from this curse: inward and moral in defending himself to the guardians of the grove; physical and political in resisting Creon; emotional and familial in arming himself against

Polyneices. His separation at the end is definitive, and it is marked by his very absence from the stage. All of those pulls back into the past are to some extent embodied in Antigone. Her voluntary return recalls Creon's violence to take her back to Thebes in the middle portion of the play. That scene also adumbrates the enmity between her and Creon which will be operative in the next phase of the story. And her vain hope to prevent the slaughter (1771) also reminds us that the curse which Oedipus has miraculously transcended retains its ineluctable grip on his house, thanks in part to his own agency, his own malediction upon his sons.

Yet the hopeless destinies of those still bound to Thebes' accursed past are distanced from us. In the foreground stands Oedipus the Hero, not Oedipus the King. He becomes for Sophocles the figure in whom is finally resolved the long conflict between human passion and divine will, between searching intelligence and the unlimited and unknown, between the laws of civilization and the mysterious justice of the gods. In every sense we reach the end of a vision, and we feel that we have arrived at the limits of human understanding.

"It is the last things of life you ask for; the things between, you either are forgetting or hold of no account": these words of Theseus to Oedipus early in the play (583–584) apply to more than just the request for burial. His last things of life, *ta loisthia tou biou*, mark the ultimate fusion of greatness and nothingness and the ultimate fulfillment of the Sophoclean pattern by which suffering becomes strength. The blindness becomes the inner sight which can guide Athens' seeing king to a place of mysterious union with the powers of light and darkness beyond the grave. This final vision is true to the ambiguity and complexity of the hero's relation to the city, and to tragedy's relation to society.

Sophocles' vision of the gods' unfathomable justice brings Oedipus back, by a long road, to that civilizing and saving power to which his subjects appealed when we meet him first in the prologue of the *Tyrannus*. His last moments and the mysterious passage which they comprise effect the ultimate mediation between Olympian and chthonic powers that civilization needs and creates.[100] The hero who in the *Tyrannus* was caught in a helpless, unmediated swing between the upper and lower limits of his nature, between god and beastlike pollution, between Apolline riddles and Sphinx-given oracles, is now the figure in whom transpires a mysterious unity between humanity and divinity.

Oedipus, we are repeatedly told, is summoned both by the Olympian gods and the powers of the nether world; Theseus, at the climactic revelation, "reveres at the same time and in the same utterance both earth and the Olympus of the gods" (1654–55). In this coincidence of upper and lower worlds the dark forces of life come together with the cultural and intellectual achievements of Athenian humanism, prelogical belief with Olympian religion, the primitive magic of the hero cult, demanding the physical presence of the potent bones, with the new feeling for the power of the individual and his spiritual endurance of suffering.[101]

No play is more insistent on its rootedness of place than the *Coloneus*. This is emphasized also by the cult of the hero, who can confer his benefits only by virtue of his body's presence. In its patriotic concern with the invulnerability of the Athenian land (*chōra*, 1765), and its use of the cults and topography of Colonus and its grove, the play is among the most parochial of Greek tragedies. Its appeal to the localism of its original audience is strong.[102] And yet no other Sophoclean play leaves us with a greater and more deliberate vagueness about place. The mystery surrounding Oedipus' final resting place obliterates the narrow localism of the prologue and raises the action, ultimately, to a universality as independent of place as of time. Oedipus has not merely moved from being the mythical hero of one polis to being the protective divinity of another: his final moments are a larger triumph of suffering and will. The grove and the tomb are not only features of local Athenian cult, but places of transition between worlds where a towering and tested spirit strides to the very limits of human experience and passes beyond.

It is characteristic of Sophocles' last two plays that the will of the gods is more immediately manifest and intervenes more visibly in human affairs. Theseus' announcement establishes the hero's place in the quintessentially civilized city. The hero of no certain place in a city earlier as he traced his path from Corinth to Delphi to Thebes and to Mount Cithaeron, he is now definitively housed as *empolis*, "within a city" (636–637). But the magnitude, mystery, and full legitimization of that place in the polis are confirmed, finally, not by human decree but by nothing less than the awesome thunder of the gods. This too is part of the "age-old Justice who sits beside the Ancient Laws of Zeus" (1381–82).

As in Aeschylus' *Eumenides*, Athens becomes the place where archaic bloodguilt is purged by reason and piety. But this polluted outcast, unlike Aeschylus' Orestes, has no further wandering awaiting him, and he confers blessings as great as those which he receives. Here civilization can expand in insight and generosity to accept the outcast hero; and the hero who remains beyond the pale of civilization can return to it without relinquishing his greatness or his demonic violence. In the final justice of Sophocles' vision Oedipus emerges as the civilizing hero that he was all along: savior of the city, destroyer of the fearful monsters that terrify its people, father who claims his children's deepest love and most bitter mourning at his death.

As in Aeschylus' *Eumenides* Athens embodies a civilized order which can mediate chthonic and Olympian powers.[103] Sophocles' Athens, like Aeschylus', can accept Oedipus' defense of his moral cleanliness, but still retain the awe and reverence that make a lasting civic order possible. Yet Sophocles, writing half a century after Aeschylus and at a very different point in Athens' fortunes, stresses not so much the city's capacity to receive the outcast as the mysterious power which years of suffering have conferred on the polluted hero himself. The triumph at the end is *his* rather than the city's. The blessings now come not from the Eumenides, as in Aeschylus, but from the hero himself, the ancient sinner, exile from all cities, now made a divinity of this just and pious city. As the blessings are his rather than the Eumenides', so the curses, in the previous scene, are the just overflow of his bitterness and the sign of his power and his suffering rather than the instrument of divine vengeance.[104]

X

In moving from feeble exile to heroized savior, Oedipus reverses the pattern of his earlier play, with its movement from king to beggar, godlike authority to pollution and misery. By returning to this figure whose life contains the most extreme of tragic reversals, Sophocles seems to be consciously reflecting upon and transcending the tragic pattern which he did so much to develop. His earlier Oedipus was "a tragic king who was to bear the weight of the whole world's suffering . . . , an almost symbolic figure, . . . suffering humanity personified."[105] At the end of the *Coloneus* Oedipus sums up and visually enacts the tragic road of life, now traveled to an incomprehensible end, through and beyond tragedy to a virtual apotheosis. It is an apotheosis not only of the tragic hero but of tragedy itself.[106] With the passing of Oedipus the tragic age of Greece, with its taut, ever-shifting balance between irrational archaic curse and rational humanism, is both fulfilled and comes to an end.

The hush of the onlookers within the play is an element in the dramatic fiction, but it also mirrors back to the spectators who watched the play their own situation and their own emotions within the theater. For Oedipus' blessings to Athens are the gift of tragedy itself. Tragedy emerges as the civilizing power which bridges the gap between the unsayable and the common traditions of the panhellenic past, between the experience that transcends or lies below the level of human speech and the communal, ritualized forms of public festival, public language.[107] The play asserts the victory of continuity and the shaped energy of music and chorus over the "lyreless and danceless" realm of death (1222). It celebrates the happier music that resounded within the dreaded grove which Oedipus enters. Yet, as in the last ode of the *Antigone*, this closing reflection of the communal experience unfolds against the infinities from which those communal rites shelter and protect. Tragedy contains both the protection and the exposure; in the opposing directions of its context and content it also shapes a powerful tension between them.

Like Oedipus, tragedy confers its blessings by plumbing the depths of the unknown: the most fearfully alien becomes beneficently familiar. As Athens can welcome the ancient Theban pariah, so the spectators, whether Athenian or contemporary, in the course of the play come to something like familiarity, friendship, understanding with figures as foreign as the accursed scions of the Theban royal house, raging demigods, the proud victors of the Trojan war. Like Oedipus, tragedy passes through the darkness of ominous places at the borders of civilization and converts into lucid, intelligible, even paradoxically pleasurable forms the fearful powers of the unknown, the irrational, the awesomely terrible. Through tragedy the archaic curses and the formless horror in which they dwell are named, visualized, and shared in the formed, geometric space of the civic theater. The terror is purified—purged, as Aristotle said—by the verbal, spatial, and musical articulation and by the expression of community in the confrontation with the dreaded unknown. Private nightmare becomes the shared humanity of suffering. The curse of Oedipus, the most horrible of maledictions, can be ban-ished in the enactment of a civic rite in which the spectators are, in every sense, involved.

The hero's life retains its sadness and the impenetrability of the unknown in which tragedy deals; but he, like tragedy itself in this last manifestation of its full power, is transfigured.[108] Oedipus and Theseus, the essentially tragic hero and the spirit of Athenian civilization, are joined together in a final mystery which is the mystery of the cathartic, restorative, and transfiguring power of art itself. The onlookers' awe within the play, then, not only reflects the reactions of the spectators sitting on the benches in the Dionysiac theater, but also fixes the power of tragic art in one of its most intense, essential, and awesome functions, the reliving and undoing, through aesthetic participation, of archaic evil.

The hero who in the *Tyrannus* enacted the power of tragedy to confront the dissolution of all difference and the confusion of all the codes of the civilized order—the riddling nature of language, the loss of personal identity in the paradoxes of illusion and reality and the paradoxes of the theatrical masks which unmask truth—becomes in this last play a symbol of the dark blessings of tragedy to the city and perhaps to mankind as a whole.

This new civilizing function of the hero not only reflects the spiritual power of Athens at a time when it is outwardly ruined and enfeebled,[109] but also locates that power in the art of tragedy itself. The tragic hero and the tragic art and probably also the aged tragic poet are all bound up together.

Writing the *Coloneus* in the last years of his long life, Sophocles, like Oedipus, is also at the threshold of a great crossing. For himself, as for his hero, power and existence reside in the spirit and in art:

> An aged man is but a paltry thing,
> A tattered coat upon a stick, unless
> Soul clap its hand and sing, and louder sing,
> For every tatter in its mortal dress . . .[110]

Sophocles' tone, however, unlike Yeats's, is religious and communal rather than private or defiant.

Standing at the crossing of civilization and savagery, life and death, superior and subterranean powers, humanity and divinity, tragedy, like Oedipus, is rooted in local attachments but moves beyond them to the hidden places where the boundaries between man and God give way, where the biologically and socially conditioned passes into the timeless. The paradoxical status, the liminality, of Oedipus, both within the polis and beyond it, reflects the paradoxical position of Greek tragedy, which is both rooted in its local institutions and structures and yet detached from them in its fundamental questioning of all structure. He is the ultimate example—and the ultimate resolution—of that tension between context and content in tragedy's representation of myth discussed in the third chapter.

Within the work of Sophocles the heroization of Oedipus marks a significant step beyond the problematical divinization of Heracles in the *Trachiniae*. Ambiguous and uncertain in the earlier play, Heracles' apotheosis was based on physical conquest of the beast world. The heroization of Oedipus, totally unambiguous, rests not on the extermination of monsters by brute force but on his spiritual power, inner vision, and mysterious contact with the unknown. In presenting this heroization of the archetypal tragic sufferer, Sophocles also suggests the divinization of his tragic art. The tragic poet becomes a kind of culture hero who confronts the darker mysteries of life and by his art, like Oedipus by his god-given power, transmutes the pollutions of an accursed past into blessings for his fellow citizens. Both hero and poet reach into the horrors of existence and bring forth a mysteriously acquired boon that can be dispensed to all who partake of the community whether of the land or of the dramatic performance, the citizens of the fifth century or the spectators of the twentieth.

At the hidden place, near the haunt of dread goddesses and an entrance to the Underworld, a blessing emanates from an old outcast's once polluted body and goes forth upon the whole land of Attica. This place is itself the locus and the emblem of the cathartic, regenerative quality of tragic art.

In effecting the collaboration of chthonic and Olympian powers to give Oedipus his final honor, tragedy reunites fear and intelligence, man's helplessness before the mysteries of the universe and his confidence in his unique power of spiritual vision. The last moments of this old sufferer in the magical circle of Dionysus recapitulate and condense the experience of a hundred years in that privileged space where the mythical and the unreal are the most intense of realities. The heroization of Oedipus is nothing less than an aged poet's insight into the divinity of his art seen in its timeless healing and civilizing power, even as it is viewed against the historically conditioned background which gave it birth.

Abbreviations

Notes

Selected Bibliography

Index

Abbreviations

Periodicals and Reference Works

AC: L'Antiquité Classique
AJA: American Journal of Archaeology
AJP: American Journal of Philology
Anz Alt: Anzeiger für Altertumswissenschaft
APA: American Philological Association
A.u.A.: Antike und Abendland
Austin: Austin, Colin, ed., *Nova Fragmenta Euripidea in Papyris Reperta* (Berlin 1968)
    = *Kleine Texte für Vorlesungen und Übungen*, vol. 187
BICS: Bulletin of the Institute of Classical Studies, University of London
CJ: Classical Journal
C&M: Classica et Mediaevalia
CP: Classical Philology
CQ: Classical Quarterly
CR: Classical Review
CW: Classical Weekly, Classical World
DK: Diels, Hermann and Walter Kranz, eds., *Die Fragmente der Vorsokratiker*, ed. 6
    (Berlin 1952), 3 vols.
Edmonds: Edmonds, J.M., ed., *The Fragments of Attic Comedy* (Leiden 1957–1961)
FGrHist.: Jacoby, Felix, ed., *Die Fragmente der griechischen Historiker* (Leiden 1954ff.)
G&R: Greece and Rome
GRBS: Greek, Roman and Byzantine Studies
HSCP: Harvard Studies in Classical Philology
HThR: Harvard Theological Review
JHS: Journal of Hellenic Studies
K: Kock, Theodor, ed., *Comicorum Atticorum Fragmenta* (Leipzig 1880–1888)
Kaibel: Kaibel, Georg, ed., *Epigrammata Graeca ex lapidibus conlecta* (Berlin 1878)
LEC: Les Etudes Classiques
Lesky, *TDH:* Lesky, Albin, *Die tragische Dichtung der Hellenen*, ed. 3 (Göttingen 1972)
LSJ: Liddell-Scott-Jones-McKenzie, eds., *A Greek-English Lexicon*, ed. 9 (Oxford 1940),
    with supplement (1968)
MD(A)I: *Mitteilungen des Deutschen Archäologischen Instituts, Athenische Abteilung*
MH: Museum Helveticum
MLN: Modern Language Notes
M-W: Merkelbach, R. and M. L. West, eds., *Fragmenta Hesiodea* (Oxford 1967)
N, Nauck: Nauck, Augustus, ed., *Tragicorum Graecorum Fragmenta*, ed. 2 (Leipzig 1889);
    supplement, B. Snell (Hildesheim 1964)

Abbreviations

NGG: Nachrichten der Gesellschaft der Wissenschaften zu Göttingen, Philosophisch-historische Klasse

NJbb: Neue Jahrbücher für das klassische Altertum

OCT: Oxford Classical Texts

P, Pearson: A. C. Pearson, ed., *The Fragments of Sophocles* (Cambridge 1917), 3 vols.

Page, *PMG:* Page, Denys, ed., *Poetae Melici Graeci* (Oxford 1962)

PCPS: Proceedings of the Cambridge Philological Society

PMG: see Page, supra

PP: La Parola del Passato

P.Oxy.: Oxyrhynchus Papyri, ed. Grenfell and Hunt et al. (London 1898ff.)

QUCC: Quaderni Urbinati di Cultura Classica

RE: Pauly-Wissowa-Kroll, eds., *Realencylopädie der classischen Altertumswissenschaft* (Stuttgart 1894ff.)

REA: Revue des Etudes Anciennes

REG: Revue des Etudes Grecques

RhM: Rheinisches Museum

RFIC: Rivista di Filologia e di Istruzione Classica

Ribbeck: Ribbeck, Otto, ed., *Tragicorum Romanorum Fragmenta,* ed. 3 (Leipzig 1897) (= *Scaenicae Romanorum Poesis Fragmenta,* vol. I)

Roscher, *Lexicon:* Roscher, W.H., ed., *Ausführliches Lexicon der griechischen und römischen Mythologie* (Leipzig 1884–1937)

SB Wien: Akademie der Wissenschaften, Vienna, Philosophisch-historische Klasse, *Sitzungsberichte*

SMSR: Studi e Materiali di Storia delle Religioni

SO: Symbolae Osloenses

Studia Vollgraff: Studia Varia C.G. Vollgraff a Discipulis Oblata (Amsterdam 1948)

TAPA: Transactions of the American Philological Association

TrGF: Tragicorum Graecorum Fragmenta, vol. I, ed. Bruno Snell (Göttingen 1971); vol. IV, *Sophocles,* ed. Stefan Radt (Göttingen 1977)

UCPCP: University of California Publications in Classical Philology

WS: Wiener Studien

YCS: Yale Classical Studies

ZPE: Zeitschrift für Papyrologie und Epigraphik

Short Titles of Works Frequently Cited

Adams: S. M. Adams, *Sophocles the Playwright, Phoenix,* supplement 3 (Toronto 1957)

Bowra: C. M. Bowra, *Sophoclean Tragedy* (Oxford 1944)

Gellie: G. H. Gellie, *Sophocles, A Reading* (Melbourne 1972)

Girard: René Girard, *La violence et le sacré* (Paris 1972)

Jones: John Jones, *On Aristotle and Greek Tragedy* (London 1962)

Kirkwood: G. M. Kirkwood, *A Study of Sophoclean Drama,* Cornell Studies in Classical Philology 31 (Ithaca, N.Y., 1958)

Kitto, *Form:* H. D. F. Kitto, *Form and Meaning in Drama* (London 1956)

Knox, "Ajax": B. M. W. Knox, "The *Ajax* of Sophocles," *HSCP* 65 (1961) 1–37

Knox, *HT:* B. M. W. Knox, *The Heroic Temper,* Sather Classical Lectures 35 (Berkeley and Los Angeles 1964)

Knox, *Oedipus:* B. M. W. Knox, *Oedipus at Thebes* (New Haven 1957)

Lattimore, *Poetry:* Richmond Lattimore, *The Poetry of Greek Tragedy* (Baltimore 1958)

Abbreviations

Lesky, *TDH:* Albin Lesky, *Die tragische Dichtung der Hellenen*[3] (Göttingen 1972)

Letters: F. J. H. Letters, *The Life and Work of Sophocles* (London 1953)

Musurillo: Herbert Musurillo, *The Light and the Darkness* (Leiden 1967)

Reinhardt: Karl Reinhardt, *Sophokles*[3] (Frankfurt a.M. 1947)

Rosenmeyer, *Masks:* Thomas G. Rosenmeyer, *The Masks of Tragedy* (Austin 1963)

Vernant, *MP:* Jean-Pierre Vernant, *Mythe et pensée chez les Grecs*[2] (Paris 1969), here cited in the two volume reissue by Maspero (Paris 1974)

Vernant, *MT:* Jean-Pierre Vernant and Pierre Vidal-Naquet, *Mythe et tragédie* (Paris 1972)

Vickers: Brian Vickers, *Towards Greek Tragedy* (London 1973)

Vidal-Naquet, *MT:* see Vernant, *MT,* supra

Whitman: Cedric H. Whitman, *Sophocles. A Study of Heroic Humanism* (Cambridge, Mass., 1951)

References to the commentaries of Jebb and Kamerbeek and to a few other specialized works are given in full at the first occurrence in the individual chapters and then cited by author's name only.

Notes

1 Tragedy and the Civilizing Power

1. For the temple and its site, see Vincent Scully, *The Earth, the Temple, and the Gods: Greek Sacred Architecture* (New York, N.Y., 1962; revised 1969) 123–125 with figures 235–237: "It is the god as savior of humanity making his presence felt in the heart of the wild" (p. 123). For the rite of Zeus Lykaios, see Plato, *Rep.* 8.565d.

2. See Sigmund Freud, *Civilization and Its Discontents* (1930), trans. Joan Riviere (Garden City, N.Y., 1958) chap. 3.

3. The most likely possibilities: *nomos* and *ta nomima*, which imply the established institutions, the customs and norms of the society; *politeia*, which refers to the form of government, especially constitutional government; and *paideia*, which refers to culture as manifested and transmitted through poetry and art.

4. Giambattista Vico, *The New Science*, trans. from the third ed. (1744) by T. G. Bergin and M. H. Fisch (Garden City, N.Y., 1961) 53 (book I, sec. III).

5. See W. K. C. Guthrie, *In the Beginning* (Ithaca, N.Y., 1957) and *A History of Greek Philosophy* II (Cambridge 1965) 471–474 and III (1969) 60ff.; E. A. Havelock, *The Liberal Temper in Greek Politics* (New Haven 1957); Thomas Cole, *Democritus and Greek Anthropology,* APA Monograph 25 (Cleveland 1967); Fabio Turato, *La crisi della città e l'ideologia del selvaggio nell'Atene del V secolo* a.C. (Rome 1979). Further discussion below, chapter 2, section VII.

6. For Sophocles' interest in culture history, see Wilhelm Nestle, "Sophokles und die Sophistik," *CP* 5 (1910) 134–137. For the *Triptolemus* see frags. 539–560N = 596–616P and *TrGF*.

7. See Felix Heinimann, *Nomos und Physis* (Basel 1945); Guthrie, *History of Greek Philosophy* II, 340, 353–354, 495–496 and vol. III, chap. 4. Further discussion and bibliography in A. Battegazzore and M. Untersteiner, *Sofisti, testimonianze e frammenti,* fasc. 4 (Florence 1962) 72ff.

8. For this more individualizing spirit in Sophocles, note the usage of *psychē* in *Ajax* 154, *Antig.* 177, *Trach.* 1260, *Phil.* 1013; frag. 97N. See in general Guthrie, *History of Greek Philosophy* (above, note 5) III, 467–468; E. A. Havelock, *Preface to Plato* (Cambridge, Mass., 1963) 197–198, 211n3, and his "The Socratic Self as It Is Parodied in Aristophanes' *Clouds,*" *YCS* 22 (1972) 5–9, 15–16.

9. Freud (above, note 2) 61–62.

10. René Girard, *La violence et le sacré* (Paris 1972), trans. P. Gregory, *Violence and the Sacred* (Baltimore 1977). See the interesting review by Carl Rubino, *MLN* 87 (1972) 986–998 and the issue of *Diacritics*, vol. 8, no. 1 (spring 1978), devoted to Girard, especially Hayden White's review of *Violence and the Sacred,* pp. 2–9. Though I find Girard's focus on the problem of "degrees" and differentiation helpful, I do not agree

with all of his speculation about the mechanism of purification and scapegoating in Greek tragedy.

11. See e.g. Alvin Gouldner, *Enter Plato* (New York and London 1965) chap. 2.

12. Walter Burkert, "Jason, Hypsipyle, and New Fire at Lemnos: A Study of Myth and Ritual," *CQ* n.s. 20 (1970) 15–16.

13. See e.g. Jones 93; Vickers 110ff., 158n11, and 230ff. For qualifications see P. E. Easterling, "Character in Sophocles," *G&R*, ser. 2, 24 (1977) 121–129, and "The Presentation of Character in Aeschylus," *G&R* 20 (1973) 3–19.

14. For the dangers of interpreting characters in Greek tragedy in terms of personal realism and idiosyncrasy, see Wolfgang Schadewaldt, "Aias und Antigone," *Neue Wege der Antike* 8 (1941) 110; Kurt von Fritz, "Zur Interpretation des Aias," *RhM* 83 (1934) 116, 126; Peter Walcot, *Greek Drama in Its Theatrical and Social Context* (Cardiff 1976) 86–93 (Euripides' technique, like Sophocles', is "impressionistic rather than representational"; p. 87); John Gould, "Dramatic Character and Human Intelligibility in Greek Tragedy," *PCPS* 204, n.s. 24 (1978) 43–67 (character in Greek drama is part of "a 'world' of metaphor which transcribes and reshapes our experiences in a new mould"; p. 61). For an attempt to balance the two approaches, see Easterling's essays (above, note 13).

15. See in general Vernant, "Tensions et ambiguïtés dans la tragédie grecque," *MT* 39–40; A. von Blumenthal, "Sophokles (aus Athen)" *RE* A III A 1 (1927) 1092–93.

16. For the comparison see J. C. Kamerbeek, "Sophocle et Héraclite," *Studia Vollgraff* 98, also Vernant, *MT* 29–30.

17. See John H. Finley, Jr., "Euripides and Thucydides," *HSCP* 49 (1938) 35ff. and "The Origins of Thucydides' Style," *HSCP* 50 (1939) 51ff.

18. For this formal aspect of plot construction in Greek tragedy, see Anne P. Burnett, *Catastrophe Survived: Euripides' Plays of Mixed Reversal* (Oxford 1971).

19. In structuralist terminology, we could perhaps attribute this difference to the predominance of the syntagmatic plane of the narrative in epic and of the paradigmatic in tragedy: see Jonathan Culler, *Structuralist Poetics* (London 1975) 13.

20. Jean Cocteau, *La machine infernale*, act 3.

21. See Murray Krieger, "Mediation, Language, and Vision in the Reading of Literature," in C. S. Singleton, ed., *Interpretation: Theory and Practice* (Baltimore 1969) 234.

22. A. C. Schlesinger, "Tragedy and the Moral Frontier," *TAPA* 84 (1953) 164–175; see also Gellie 208.

23. *Apoptolis: OT* 1000, *Trach.* 647, *OC* 208; *apolis: Antig.* 370, *Phil.* 1018, *OC* 1357.

24. See George Gellie, "The Second Stasimon of the *Oedipus Tyrannus*," *AJP* 85 (1964) 123; Pierre Vidal-Naquet, *Sophocle: Les tragédies* (Paris 1973) 29.

25. See Th. 2.40.1 and also 2.39.4, 2.43.4–6.

26. Albin Lesky, "Sophokles und das Humane" (1951), in Hans Diller, Wolfgang Schadewaldt, and Albin Lesky, *Gottheit und Mensch in der Tragödie des Sophokles* (Darmstadt 1963) 85.

2 A Structural Approach to Greek Myth and Tragedy

1. See Vernant, *MT* 126 and 121.

2. See G. E. R. Lloyd, *Polarity and Analogy* (Cambridge 1966); Norman Austin, *Archery at the Dark of the Moon* (Berkeley and Los Angeles 1975) chap. 2, esp. 90–91; Vidal-Naquet, "Les jeunes: Le cru, l'enfant grec et le cuit," in J. Le Goff and P. Nora, eds., *Faire de l'histoire* (Paris 1974) 3.149–150, citing also Arist. *Metaphy.*

A.5.986a22–26; Paula Philippson, *Genealogie als mythische Form, Symbolae Osloenses,* suppl. 7 (1936), especially 14, 34ff.

3. E.g. Vernant, "Ambiguïté et renversement: Sur la structure énigmatique d' 'Oedipe-Roi,' " *MT* 101–131; J. T. Sheppard, *The Oedipus Tyrannus of Sophocles* (Cambridge 1920) 101; Knox, *HT* 42–44; R. P. Winnington-Ingram, *Euripides and Dionysus* (Cambridge 1948) chap. 12.

4. See G. S. Kirk, *Myth: Its Meaning and Function,* Sather Classical Lectures 40 (Berkeley and Los Angeles 1970) 42–83, 132–171, and *The Nature of Greek Myths* (Harmondsworth 1974) 81–91; Vickers chap. 4; Pietro Pucci, "Lévi-Strauss and Classical Culture," *Arethusa* 4 (1971) 103–117. For a useful bibliography, see John Peradotto, *Classical Mythology: An Annotated Bibliographical Survey* (Urbana, Ill., 1973) 40–47. For some applications see Vernant, *Mythe et pensée chez les Grecs*² (Paris 1974) and *Mythe et société en Grèce ancienne* (Paris 1974), esp. 226–250; Vernant and Vidal-Naquet, *MT* passim; Marcel Detienne, *Les jardins d'Adonis* (Paris 1972); Vidal-Naquet, "The Black Hunter and the Origin of the Athenian Ephebeia," *PCPS* n.s. 14 (1968) 49–64 and "Le mythe platonicien du *Politique,* les ambiguïtés de l'âge d'or et de l'histoire," in J. Kristeva, J.-C. Milner, and N. Ruwet, eds. *Langue, discours, société, pour Emile Benveniste* (Paris 1975) 374–390, English trans. in *JHS* 98 (1978) 132–141; Claude Calame, "L'analyse sémiotique en mythologie," *Revue de Théologie et de Philosophie* 2 (1976) 81–97; Walter Burkert, "Analyse structurale et perspective historique dans l'interprétation des mythes grecs," *Cahiers Internationaux de Symbolisme* 35–36 (1978) 163–173; B. Gentili and G. Paione, eds. *Il Mito Greco* (Rome 1977); Charles Segal, "The Raw and the Cooked in Greek Literature: Structure, Values, Metaphor," *CJ* 69 (1973/74) 289–308; idem, "Pentheus and Hippolytus on the Couch and on the Grid: Psychoanalytic and Structuralist Readings of Greek Tragedy," *CW* 72 (1978/79) 129–148. Excellent concise introductions to Lévi-Strauss's thought in English are Edmund Leach, *Lévi-Strauss* (London 1970) and *Culture and Communication* (Cambridge 1976), and Michael Lane, *Introduction to Structuralism* (New York 1970) 11–39. For the problems of literary application, see Jonathan Culler, *Structuralist Poetics* (London 1975); Robert Scholes, *Structuralism in Literature* (New Haven and London 1974); Frederic Jameson, *The Prison House of Language* (Princeton 1972); R. Macksey and E. Donato, eds. *The Structuralist Controversy: The Languages of Criticism and the Sciences of Man* (Baltimore 1972); Terence Hawkes, *Structuralism and Semiotics* (Berkeley and Los Angeles 1977); Philip Pettit, *The Concept of Sructuralism* (Berkeley and Los Angeles 1977).

5. Jane Ellen Harrison, *Reminiscences of a Student's Life* (London 1925) 83; see also Robert Ackerman, "Jane Ellen Harrison: The Early Work," *GRBS* 13 (1972) 209–230, esp. 228. For a useful brief survey of the development of the study of myth in the nineteenth century and the conflict between the "scandal" of primitive "savagery" and a "science" of mythology, see Marcel Detienne, "La mythologie scandaleuse," *Traverses* 12 (Sept. 1978) 3–18.

6. Roland Barthes, "The Structuralist Activity," in R. and F. DeGeorge, eds., *The Structuralists from Marx to Lévi-Strauss* (Garden City, N.Y., 1972) 153.

7. Claude Lévi-Strauss, *The Raw and the Cooked: Introduction to a Science of Mythology,* I, trans. J. and D. Weightman (New York 1970) 16.

8. See Albert Cook's *Myth and Language* (Bloomington, Ind., 1980), and also "Lévi-Strauss and Myth: A Review of *Mythologiques,*" *MLN* 91 (1976) 1099–1116.

9. Michael Nagler, *Spontaneity and Tradition: A Study in the Oral Art of Homer* (Berkeley and Los Angeles 1974) chaps. 1 and 2, esp. 16ff., 45ff.; Austin (above, note 2) chap. 1.

10. Walter Ong, S. J., foreword to Pedro Laín Entralgo, *The Therapy of the Word in Classical Antiquity* (New Haven 1970) xii: "First, in a culture without writing, speech serves not only to express what is lodged in the mind, but in its various stylized configurations—its themes, formulas, proverbs, epithets, and the like—also to store and retrieve verbalized knowledge. Without the storage systems which writing later provides, knowledge has to be constantly regurgitated and uttered ("out-ered") or it simply disappears. Speech has to be given special patterns of a mnemonic sort, for man knows only what he can recall, and the only resource for verbal recall in an oral culture is memory."

11. See Roman Jakobson, "Linguistics and Poetics" (1960), in DeGeorge, *Structuralists* (above, note 6) 85–122, esp. 111ff.; see also Culler (above, note 4) chap. 3.

12. Lévi-Strauss, "The Structural Study of Myth," in *Structural Anthropology*, trans. C. Jacobson and B. G. Schoepf (Garden City, N.Y., 1967) 226–227.

13. On the principle of redundancy in myth, see Richard S. Caldwell, "Psychoanalysis, Structuralism, and Greek Mythology," in H. R. Garvin, ed., *Phenomenology, Structuralism, Semiology, Bucknell Review,* April 1976 (Lewisburg, Pa., 1976) 209–230.

14. See Segal, "Pentheus and Hippolytus" (above, note 4) 136; idem, "Curse and Oath in Euripides' *Hippolytus*," *Ramus* 1 (1972) 165–180.

15. See e.g. Martin Nilsson, *Geschichte der griechischen Religion* I² (Munich 1955) 120–121.

16. I have drawn on my essay "Raw and Cooked" (above, note 4), especially in sections VII–VIII and X–XI. See also Paolo Scarpi, *Letture sulla religione classica: L'inno omerico a Demeter* (Florence 1976) esp. 47ff.; Vickers (above, note 4) 196–197; F. Turato, *La crisi della città e l'ideologia del selvaggio* (Rome 1979) 65–88.

17. Lévi-Strauss (above, note 12) 226.

18. See Vickers 250–251.

19. On this liminal function of mediating figures, see Leach, *Culture and Communication* (above, note 4) 71–75.

20. See Sheila McNally, "The Maenad in Early Greek Art," *Arethusa* 11 (1978) 101–135. See also in general Henri Jeanmaire, *Dionysos* (Paris 1951) 280–281.

21. See e.g. Men. frag. 620K (= 534 Edmonds), and Carl Schneider, *Geschichte des Hellenismus* (Munich 1967) I, 151–152.

22. For more details see C. Segal, "The Homeric Hymn to Aphrodite: A Structuralist Approach," *CW* 67 (1973/74) 205–212.

23. In Hesiod, *Theog.* 224, Deceit and Love, *Apatē* and *Philotēs*, are closely associated among the brood of destructive Night. See Vernant, *MP* I, 52–53.

24. See Scarpi (above, note 16) esp. 47–137.

25. For other aspects of the myth, see Joseph Fontenrose, *Python* (Berkeley and Los Angeles 1959) 13–22, 252, 365–374; Ileana Chirassi Colombo, "Heros Achilleus-Theos Apollon," in Gentili and Paione (above, note 4), esp. 244–247, 258–263.

26. See Froma I. Zeitlin, "The Dynamics of Misogyny: Myth and Mythmaking in the *Oresteia*," *Arethusa* 11 (1978) 157ff. with further bibliography there; C. Segal, "The Menace of Dionysus: Sex Roles and Reversals in Euripides' *Bacchae*," ibid. 185ff.

27. J. Tynjanov and Roman Jakobson, "Problems in the Study of Literature and Language" (1928), in L. Matejka and K. Pomorska, eds., *Readings in Russian Poetics* (Cambridge, Mass., 1971) 79–80.

28. See David Sansone, "The Sacrifice-Motif in Euripides' *IT*," *TAPA* 105 (1975) 293ff. For the issue in general, with further bibliography, see *Grecs et barbares*, Fondation Hardt, Entretiens sur l'antiquité classique 8, (Vandoeuvres-Geneva 1962).

29. See G. Dumézil, *Le problème des Centaures* (Paris 1929) 182ff.; Kirk, *Myth*

(above, note 4) 152–171; Victor Turner, *Dramas, Fields, and Metaphors: Symbolic Action in Human Society* (Ithaca, N.Y., 1974) 253; Page duBois, "Horse/Men, Amazons, and Endogamy," *Arethusa* 12 (1979) 35–49.

30. Further discussion and references in Segal, "Raw and Cooked" (above, note 4) 291–292. See also the interesting study of Herodotean ethnography from this point of view by Michèle Rosellini and Suzanne Saïd, "Usages des femmes et autres *nomoi* chez les 'sauvages' d'Hérodote: Essai de lecture structurale," *Annali della Scuola Normale Superiore di Pisa,* Classe di Lett. e Filos. 8.3 (1978) 949–1005.

31. Jacoby, *FGrHist* 715F27b.

32. See Rosellini and Saïd (above, note 30) 998ff.; duBois (above, note 29) 44: "The Amazon myth was used in part to sustain ideas of sexual difference by representing a deformed alternative to the ideal of the polis. In the classical period it also served to supply a definition of man as the sole significant figure of human culture, as the subject of marriage and civilization."

33. See in general Marcel Detienne, *Dionysos mis à mort* (Paris 1977) pt. 2. As an aristocratic pursuit, however, hunting can define the gentlemanly life of leisure, especially in the fourth century: see Werner Jaeger, *Paideia*, trans. Gilbert Highet (New York 1943) III, 177–178 apropos of Xenophon's *Cynegeticus*.

34. For Atalante see Detienne, *Dionysos mis à mort* 81ff., 101–117; Giampierra Arrigoni, "Atalanta e il cinghiale bianco," *Scripta Philologa* 1 (Milan 1977) 9–47.

35. See Vidal-Naquet (above, note 2) 159–160. Cf. Plato, *Laws* 7.808d; Plutarch, *De Audiendo* 2.38d.

36. See Laurence Kahn, *Hermès passe* (Paris 1978), esp. 41–73.

37. See Winnington-Ingram (above, note 3) chap. 7, esp. 92 and n3.

38. See in general C. Segal, "Le structuralisme et Homère: sauvagerie, bestialité et le problème d'Achille dans les derniers livres de l'Iliade," *Didactica Classica Gandensia* 17–18 (1977–78) 191–203; James Redfield, *Nature and Culture in the Iliad* (Chicago 1975) 93, 103, 183, 200ff. with reference to the hero's marginality.

39. See Kirk, *Myth* (above, note 4) 166–171; Vidal-Naquet, "Valeurs religieuses et mythiques de la terre et du sacrifice dans l'*Odyssée,*" *Annales, Economies, Sociétés, Civilisation* 25 (1970) 1285–86.

40. For the story of Heracles and Pholus, see Apollodorus 2.5.4 and Kirk, *Myth* (above, note 4) 161.

41. Further examples and discussion in Segal, "Raw and Cooked" 297 and 300–301.

42. See Vidal-Naquet, *MT* 155; R. F. Goheen, "Aspects of Dramatic Symbolism: Three Studies in the *Oresteia,*" *AJP* 76 (1955) 136.

43. Further discussion and references in Segal, "Raw and Cooked" 297–300; Redfield (above, note 38) 197ff. These associations of tameness and agriculture with civilization remain vital into Hellenistic times: see Albert Henrichs, "The Sophists and Hellenistic Religion: Prodicus as the Spiritual Father of the Isis Aretalogies," *Proceedings of the VIIth Congress of the International Federation of the Societies of Classical Studies* (Budapest, forthcoming). I am grateful to Professor Henrichs for allowing me to see this paper in advance of publication.

44. *P.Oxy.* 3151, frag. 13b3, with Haslam's note *ad loc.* See also Soph., frag 731.5N = *TrGF* 799.5; Eur., *HF* 889, *Tro.* 436, *Ba.* 139, frag. 472.12N. See below, section X.

45. E.g. Eur., *Suppl.* 201–204; Critias 88B25DK; Democr. 68B5.1DK; Pl., *Protag.* 320c–322e; Isoc., *Nic.* 6, *Antid.* 254, *Bus.* 25. See in general above, chapter 1, note 5; also Redfield (above, note 38) 191.

46. See Josef Mattes, *Der Wahnsinn im griechischen Mythos und in der Dichtung bis*

zum Drama des fünften Jahrhunderts (Heidelberg 1970) 54–57; further discussion in Segal, "Raw and Cooked" 301ff.

47. Further details of imagery and structure in Jacob Stern, "Bestial Imagery in Bacchylides' *Ode* 11," *GRBS* 6 (1965) 275–282; C. Segal, "Bacchylides Reconsidered: Epithets and the Dynamics of Lyric Narrative," *QUCC* 22 (1976) 122–128.

48. See Aesch., *Ag.* 1407–21; Dem. 25.33. See K. J. Dover, "Some Neglected Aspects of Agamemnon's Dilemma," *JHS* 93 (1973) 59.

49. See Mattes, *Wahnsinn* 71–72, 87, 93, 99 for further examples.

50. E.g. Virg., *Ecl.* 6.48–51; see A. Henrichs, "Die Proitiden im hesiodischen Katalog," *ZPE* 15 (1974) 300–301. Note also the contrast between their wandering movements in the wild and the ordered dance at the established ritual in Bacchyl. 11.112, between agriculture and herding (70, 95), and between harsh and gentle speech (50–52, 90). The wandering of the Proetides in Hesiod's *Catalogue*, frag. 37.15M-W is probably metaphorical; that in Bacchyl. 11.93, literal (Mattes 107 and also 63–69, 97 on wandering). One thinks also of Lear on the heath or Titus Andronicus; see Northrop Frye, *Anatomy of Criticism* (Princeton 1957) 223.

51. Hunting: Eur., *HF* 898 and *Ba.* 977; storms: Aesch., *PV* 883–884; Soph., *Ajax* 206–207; Eur., *HF* 1091, *Or.* 297; honor: Aesch., *Suppl.* 562–563, *PV* 599. See Mattes, *Wahnsinn* 61–62, 95, 111–113.

52. Cf. the similar myth of Clymenus and Harpalyce in Parthenius, *Erot. Pathem.* 13; see N. B. Crowther *CQ*, n.s. 20 (1970) 325f.

53. For the myth of Lycaon, see Giulia Piccaluga, *Lykaon, un tema mitico* (Rome 1968), who views him as an historical reflection of a preagrarian (and therefore precivilized) phase of human culture (pp. 84ff.). Walter Burkert, *Homo Necans* (Berlin 1972) 98–108, stresses the themes of savagery and cannibalism and notes the massive and complex reversals of normal civilized customs; see also Detienne, *Dionysos mis à mort* 135–136.

54. See Marie Delcourt, "Tydée et Mélanippe," *Studi e Materiali di Storia delle Religioni* 37 (1966) 139–188, esp. 164ff.

55. See W. Burkert, *Homo Necans* 45ff, 71ff; *Griechische Religion der archaischen und klassischen Epoche,* Die Religionen der Menschheit 15 (Stuttgart 1977) 104–105, with the references there cited; "Greek Tragedy and Sacrificial Ritual," *GRBS* 7 (1966) 87–121. For a structuralist interpretation, see Detienne, *Jardins d'Adonis* (above, note 4) 71–113; *Dionysos mis à mort* 139ff., 164–207.

56. Hes., *Theog.* 535ff; *Erga* 42ff.; see Vernant, *MP* I,32ff., 51–52, and below, note 59.

57. Jean Rudhardt, "Les mythes grecs relatifs à l'instauration du sacrifice: Les rôles corrélatifs de Promethée et de son fils Deucalion," *MH* 27 (1970) 14.

58. See Burkert, "Greek Tragedy" (above, note 55); Anne Lebeck, *The Oresteia: A Study in Language and Structure* (Washington, D.C., 1971) 60–73; Vickers 356–359; Froma I. Zeitlin, "The Motif of Corrupted Sacrifice in Aeschylus' *Oresteia*," *TAPA* 96 (1965) 463–508 and "Postscript," *TAPA* 97 (1966) 645–653.

59. See Vernant, *Mythe et société* (above, note 4) 177–194; "Sacrifice et l'alimentation humaine à propos du *Prométhée* d'Hésiode," *Annali della Scuola Normale Superiore di Pisa,* Classe di Lett. e Filos. 7 (1977) 904–940.

60. See Carl A. Rubino, "Le clin d'oeil échangé avec un chat: Some Literary Presentations of the Problem of Self and Other," *MLN* 88 (1973) 1238–61, esp. 1243, 1258ff.

3 Kingship, Ritual, Language

1. Shakespeare, *Hamlet* I.iv.69ff.; *King Lear* IV.vi.57 and 25 respectively. See Gellie 88: "As a king he [Oedipus] must extend himself beyond the safe limits, he must use his wits and his imagination to jump the gap between the known and the knowable."

2. Seneca, *Oedipus* 1054, 1058, 1059–61. For an elaboration of points in this paragraph, see C. Segal, "Tragic Heroism and Sacral Kingship in Five Oedipus Plays and *Hamlet*," *Helios* 5 (1977) 1–10.

3. Corneille, *Oedipe* V.ix.:

Là ses yeux arrachez par ses barbares mains
Font distiller un sang qui rend l'ame aux Thébains.
Ce sang si précieux touche à peine la terre
Que le couroux du Ciel ne leur fait plus la guerre,
Et trois mourans, guéris au milieu du palais,
De sa part tout d'un coup nous annoncent la paix.
Cléante vous a dit que par toute la ville . . .

4. Voltaire, *Oedipe* V.vi:

Peuples, un calme heureux écarte les tempêtes;
Un soleil plus serein se lève sur vos têtes;
Les feux contagieux ne sont plus allumés;
Vos tombeaux qui s'ouvraient sont déjà refermés;
La mort fuit, et le dieu du ciel et de la terre
Annonce ses bontés par la voix du tonnerre.
      (Ici on entend gronder la foudre, et l'on voit briller les éclairs.)

5. Horapollo, *Hieroglyphica* 2.56, cited by W. Headlam, *CR* 16 (1902) 436. On the isolated position of the tragic king, see also Bowra 189.

6. See Masao Yamaguchi, "Kingship as a System of Myth: An Essay in Synthesis," *Diogenes* 77 (1972) 43–70, esp. 62; Northrop Frye, *Anatomy of Criticism* (Princeton 1957) 207: "The tragic hero is typically on top of the wheel of fortune, halfway between human society on the ground and the something greater in the sky."

7. On this point see, in general, Jacques Lacarrière, *Sophocle dramaturge* (Paris 1960) 103–130, esp. p. 123: "L'Oedipe d'*Oedipe à Colone* sera entouré des mêmes signes que l'Oedipe d'*Oedipe-Roi*, mais ces signes attesteront désormais l'alliance des dieux—et non plus leur malédiction."

8. See Henri Hubert and Marcel Mauss, *Sacrifice: Its Nature and Function* (1898), trans. W. D. Halls (London 1964) 58–59 and 97.

9. Gregory Nagy, "Phaethon, Sappho's Phaon, and the White Rock of Leukas," *HSCP* 77 (1973) 151; Mircea Eliade, *Patterns in Comparative Religion* (Cleveland and New York 1963) 419–423, 428–429.

10. E.g. Hom. *Od.* 10.80ff.; Hes. *Theog.* 743ff., Parmenides 28 Bl.9ff.DK; Pi., *Ol.* 2.61ff. See in general Leonard Woodbury "Equinox at Acragas," *TAPA* 97 (1966) 605–616.

11. See Gilbert Murray, "Hamlet and Orestes," in *The Classical Tradition in Poetry* (Cambridge, Mass., 1930) 233, for a psychological view.

12. Aesch., *Ag.* 651, 958–960; also 773–778 and 800ff. for the plunge from high to low.

13. Yamaguchi (above, note 6) 51. For the pattern of sacral kingship and sacred incest in relation to Oedipus, see Lowell Edmunds, "The Oedipus Myth and African Sacred Kingship," *Comparative Civilizations Review* 3 (fall 1979) 1–12.

14. Girard 154; Girard goes on (p. 155), "[Le roi] est une machine à convertir la violence stérile et contagieuse en valeurs culturelles positives. On peut comparer la monarchie à ces usines, généralement situeés sur les marges des grandes villes et qui sont destinées à transformer les ordures ménagères en engrais agricoles."

15. Ibid. chaps. 2 and 3; Vernant, "Ambiguïté et renversement: Sur la structure énigmatique d' 'Oedipe-Roi,' " in *MT* 115ff. Walter Burkert, "Greek Tragedy and Sacrificial Ritual," *GRBS* 7 (1966) 87–121; Jean-Pierre Guépin, *The Tragic Paradox: Myth and Ritual in Greek Tragedy* (Amsterdam 1968), esp. 16ff., 24ff. See also above, chapter 2, notes 40, 67.

16. See Yamaguchi (above, note 6) 67; Girard chap. 6, esp. 222ff.; on the coincidence of savior and *pharmakos*, see also Murray (above, note 11) 64–66.

17. Victor Turner, *The Ritual Process* (1969; reprint Harmondsworth 1974) 42ff.

18. Heraclit. 22 B102DK and see also B40, 41, 72, 78, 93, 114; for application to Sophocles, see J. C. Kamerbeek, "Sophocle et Héraclite," *Studia Vollgraff* 84–98; Hans Diller, "Göttliches and menschliches Wissen bei Sophokles" (1950), in Hans Diller, W. Schadewaldt, and A. Lesky, *Gottheit und Mensch in der Tragödie des Sophokles* (Darmstadt 1963) 26–27.

19. See Reinhardt 204; Vernant, *MT* 110.

20. See Peter Szondi, *Versuch über das Tragische*[2] (Frankfurt a.M. 1964) 23; E.-R. Schwinge, *Poetica* 3 (1970) 621, 629, quoting Theodor Adorno: "Die Stärke eines Iches bewährt sich darin, dass es fähig ist, objektive Widersprüche in sein Denken aufzunehmen und nicht gewaltsam wegzuschaffen."

21. Victor Turner, *Dramas, Fields, and Metaphors* (Ithaca, N.Y., 1974) 253; see also his "Metaphors of Anti-Structure in Religious Culture," in Allan W. Eister, ed., *Changing Perspectives in the Scientific Study of Religion* (New York 1974) 63–84.

22. See, in general, Turner, *Dramas* (above, note 21) 255ff.

23. See Yamaguchi (above, note 6) 59.

24. Thomas Gould, "The Innocence of Oedipus: The Philosophers on *Oedipus the King*," pt. 3, *Arion* 5 (1966) 522–523.

25. See A. C. Schlesinger, *The Boundaries of Dionysus,* Martin Classical Lectures 17 (Cambridge, Mass., 1963) chap. 5, esp. 57–64.

26. Girard 181ff.; R. P. Winnington-Ingram, *Euripides and Dionysus* (Cambridge 1948) 176–177; Walter F. Otto, *Dionysus, Myth and Cult* (1933), trans. R. B. Palmer (Bloomington, Ind., 1965) 110ff., 120ff.; Jeanne Roux, *Euripide, Les Bacchantes,* 1 (Paris 1970) 63: "Dieu cosmopolite, il organise sa religion en dehors des cadres habituels de la vie civique, famille, tribu, phratrie"; p. 64: "Il ne tient pas compte de la rigoureuse hiérarchie sociale, fondée sur la logique et le sens commun, qui assigne à chacun son rôle dans la communauté civique."

27. See Winnington-Ingram (above, note 26) chap. 7; C. Segal, "Euripides' *Bacchae:* Conflict and Mediation," *Ramus* 6 (1977) 103–120.

28. Winnington-Ingram 176–177.

29. See Paul Vicaire, "Place et figure de Dionysos dans la tragédie de Sophocle," *REG* 81 (1968) 351–373; Louis Gernet, *REG* 66 (1953) 392–393.

30. Such is certainly the implication of Euripides' *Bacchae* and the view represented by the *logos* of Plato, *Laws* 2.672a-b.

31. See Winnington-Ingram 152ff.; E. R. Dodds, *The Greeks and the Irrational,* Sather Classical Lectures 25 (Berkeley and Los Angeles 1951) 270–282; Alvin Gouldner, *Enter Plato* (London 1965) 110ff., 116ff.; Laszlo Versényi, *Man's Measure* (Albany, N.Y.,

1974) 112–114: "[Dionysus] represents life exploding beyond all boundaries, life undifferentiated and formless, life disjointed, disoriented, disorganized" (p. 113). Also C. Segal, "Sex Roles and Reversals in Euripides' *Bacchae*," *Arethusa* 11 (1978) 186–188; James Hillman, *The Myth of Analysis* (1972; reprinted, New York 1978) 258ff.

32. See Henri Jeanmaire, *Dionysos* (Paris 1951) 294–295.

33. See Versényi (above, note 31) 114–115.

34. See Girard 233; Victor Turner, *The Forest of Symbols* (Ithaca, N.Y., and London 1970) 105.

35. This formulation owes something to the Prague and Russian formalist schools: see Roman Jakobson, "Linguistics and Poetics," in R. and F. DeGeorge, *The Structuralists from Marx to Lévi-Strauss* (Garden City, N.Y., 1972) 92ff.; Robert Scholes, *Structuralism in Literature* (New Haven and London 1974) 26ff.

36. On the ambiguity of the ritual, see C. Segal, "Pentheus and Hippolytus on the Couch and on the Grid: Psychoanalytic and Structuralist Readings of Greek Tragedy," *CW* 72 (1978/79) 138–139. On Medea, see Pietro Pucci, *The Violence of Pity in Euripides' Medea* (Ithaca, N.Y., 1980) chap. 4, esp. 131–136.

37. Aristotle, *Poetics* 1453b34–54a4; see Gould (above, note 24) 514–523.

38. The list of subjects in Aristotle's *Poetics*, chap. 14, is illuminating.

39. Roland Barthes, *Sur Racine* (Paris 1963) 67.

40. For the hierarchies of beast-man-god in comedy, see Cedric H. Whitman, *Aristophanes and the Comic Hero*, Martin Classical Lectures 19 (Cambridge, Mass., 1964) 44–46, 48–52.

41. Ibid. passim, esp. chap. 2.

42. Soph., *Ajax* 394; cf. *Antig.* 74 and 924, *OT* 1214; *El.* 768. Cf. Kamerbeek (above, note 18) 95.

43. E.g. Aesch., *Ag.* 1026, *Ch.* 461; Soph., *El.* 1424f.; see Vernant, *MT* 15–16; Kirkwood 137–143 and 240–241; Vickers 27; Joachim Dalfen, "Gesetz ist nicht Gesetz und fromm ist nicht fromm. Die Sprache der Personen in der sophokleischen Antigone," *WS* n.s. 11 (1977) 5–26.

44. See C. Segal, "Shame and Purity in Euripides' *Hippolytus*," *Hermes* 98 (1970) 278–299.

45. Soph., *Ajax* 317–322; Shakespeare, *King Lear*, V.iii.369–370.

46. Aesch., *PV* 566ff., 588–589; Pierre Pachet, *Poétique* 12 (1972) 543, speaks of Io's aphasia here as "une retombée dans l'animalité."

47. For the importance of *perissos* in Sophoclean tragic heroism, see Knox, *HT* 24–25.

48. See Winnington-Ingram (above, note 26) 69, 137.

49. Gerhart Hauptmann, *Iphigenie auf Aulis*, III.i, in *Sämtliche Werke*, ed. Hans-Egon Hass (Frankfurt a.M. 1965) III,899.

50. Shakespeare, *Hamlet* I.ii.150; see also IV.iv.35ff.

51. See Knox, *Oedipus* 53–57.

52. See Rosenmeyer, *Masks* 126: "With Aeschylus language is not an instrument, but an entity, a vibrant self-sufficient thing, working in close harmony with the brilliant objects filling the stage of the *Oresteia*. The word textures pronounced by the chorus, like the sentence patterns of the actors' speeches, stir the audience as violently as the sight of a crimson tapestry or the vision of evil Furies on the roof."

53. See John J. Peradotto, "Cledonomancy in the *Oresteia*," *AJP* 90 (1969) 17, 20–21.

54. B. M. W. Knox, "Aeschylus and the Third Actor," *AJP* 93 (1972) 111, and see also 116–117 on the dramatic significance of Cassandra's silence; Oliver Taplin, *The Stagecraft of Aeschylus* (Oxford 1977) 318–319.

55. Emil Staiger, *Grundbegriffe der Poetik* (1946), 8th ed. (Zürich and Freiburg i.Br. 1968) 190; also p. 183; Szondi (above, note 20) 54–55.

4 Trachiniae

1. For a fuller study of the general problems of interpretation and bibliography, see my essay, "Sophocles' *Trachiniae*: Myth, Poetry, and Heroic Values," *YCS* 25 (1977) 99–158. For some of the issues raised in this chapter, see also my "Mariage et sacrifice dans les *Trachiniennes* de Sophocle," *AC* 44 (1975) 30–53. I shall refer to these henceforth as "Segal, *YCS*" and "Segal, *AC*" respectively.

2. Plutarch, *De Prof. in Virtute* 7.79B; C. M. Bowra, "Sophocles on His Own Development," *AJP* 61 (1940) 385–401 = *Problems in Greek Poetry* (Oxford 1953) 108–125; Lesky, *TDH* 170.

3. For the dating see Segal, *YCS* 103–104, with the literature there cited; Lesky, *TDH* 192–193, 207–208, who places the play shortly after the *Alcestis* of 438. Fullest discussion in E. R. Schwinge, *Die Stellung der Trachinierinnen im Werk des Sophokles,* Hypomnemata 1 (Göttingen 1962), who dates the play before 450, and Kirkwood 289–294, who dates it between *Ajax* and *Antigone.* Thomas F. Hoey, "The Date of the *Trachiniae,*" *Phoenix* 33 (1979) 210–232, provides a thorough survey of recent literature and also argues for the early date.

4. Aristotle, *Politics* 1.1253a3ff.; Knox, *HT* 42–44. See above, chapter 2, section I.

5. See especially Pindar, *Olympians* 3 and 10; *Nemean* 1.

6. Philip Slater, *The Glory of Hera* (Boston 1968) 387–388.

7. Jean-Pierre Vernant's preface to M. Detienne, *Les Jardins d'Adonis* (Paris 1972) xi; cf. xxvi.

8. "Beast": 556, 568, 662, 707, 935; "beast Centaur": 680, 1162, cf. also 1059, 1096. In Bacchylides 64.27 Snell (Pindar, frag. 341.25 Bowra) Nessus is "the savage beast," *phēr agrios.* In *Iliad* 1.268 the centaurs are "mountain-dwelling beasts": Chiron, teacher of Jason, however, is the "divine beast," *phēr theios,* in Pindar, *Pyth.* 4.119. For centaurs in general see above, chapter 2, section V, and in regard to the *Trachiniae* now Page duBois, "Horse/Men, Amazons, and Endogamy," *Arethusa* 12 (1979) 35–49, who interestingly focuses on the question of endogamy and exogamy, the races with whom exchange of women is permissible and those where it is not.

9. See M. P. Nilsson, *Gesch. d. griechischen Religion* I³ (Munich 1967) 120–121; Vernant, "Hestia-Hermès," *MP* I, 140–141; cf. Plutarch, *Coniugalia Praecepta* 42, p. 144B.

10. To see how the thing should be done, we may compare Apollo's zealous inquiry about the nymph Cyrene's ancestry when he falls in love with her on Mt. Pelion: Pindar, *Pyth.* 9.33–34. Vulnerable though the girl is in this remote spot, the god's love is holy (39), touched by modesty (*aidōs,* 41), and its "keys" are "secret" (39).

11. See Vernant, *MP* I, 156–158.

12. See in general Vernant, *MP* I, 124–170, esp. 129ff.; and the remarks on the *aretē* of the fifth-century wife in T. E. V. Pearce, *Eranos* 72 (1974) 21ff. See Eur., *El.* 73–76; Lysias 1.7; Xenoph. *Oec.* 7.3; Plato, *Meno* 71e. Some have derived *damar,* "wife," from *dōma,* "house": cf. E. Benveniste, *Le vocabulaire des institutions indo-européennes* (Paris 1969) I, 296, 305.

13. See Vernant, *MP* I, 156–158.

14. On *aparchē* see Jean Rudhardt, *Notions fondamentales de la pensée religieuse et actes constitutifs du culte dans la Grèce classique* (Geneva 1958) 219–221.

15. For the vegetarian nature of these offerings, see the schol. on 237–238 and also Johannes Haussleiter, *Der Vegetarianismus in der Antike, Religionsgeschichtliche Versuche und Vorarbeiten* 24 (Berlin 1935) 14–15 ("aus Blüten and Früchten bestehendes Räuchenwerk").

16. See Rudhardt (above, note 14) 228–229. In Hindu rites "the construction of the altar consists in describing a magic circle on the ground": Henri Hubert and Marcel Mauss, *Sacrifice: Its Nature and Function* (1898), trans. W. D. Halls (London 1964) 28. On establishing boundaries for religious rituals in general, see Edmund Leach, *Culture and Communication* (Cambridge 1976) 85–93.

17. See J. C. Kamerbeek, *The Plays of Sophocles*, Part II, *The Trachiniae* (Leiden 1959) *ad loc.*

18. For a good appreciation of the verbal difficulties and ambiguities of this speech of deception, see Ursula Parlavantaza-Friederich, *Täuschungsszenen in den Tragödien des Sophokles* (Berlin 1969) 26–29.

19. See Girard 66: "On admet sans peine que ses terribles travaux aient pu accumuler sur Héraklès une quantité prodigieuse d'impureté." See in general Hubert-Mauss (above, note 16) 56–59, esp. pp. 58–59: "It is already a remarkable fact that, in a general way, sacrifice could serve two such contradictory aims as that of inducing a state of sanctity and that of dispelling a state of sin . . . Thus we shall see rites of sacralization and expiatory rites combined in one and the same sacrifice."

20. Ibid. 98.

21. In other versions of the myth Heracles asks Deianeira for a ritual robe to be used especially for the sacrifice ("the robe and cloak which he was accustomed to use for sacrifices," Diodorus 4.38.1), or for a "bright garment" (Apollodorus, *Bibl.* 2.7.7).

22. Hestia's place is at the very heart of the domestic place, "in the middle of the *oikos*" (Hom. *h. Ven.* 5.30), marking the fixity of the house in the earth, its continuity and permanence as well as its interiority: see Vernant, *MP* I, 125–126; Benveniste (above, note 12) 305–306.

23. For this doubling of the god of light and order and his "chaotic adversary" in myths that relate to sacrifice, see Hubert-Mauss (above, note 16) 86–89.

24. For other such reversals of the fire at the altar or hearth, see Pierre Pachet, "Le bâtard monstrueux," *Poétique* 12 (1972) 542.

25. For hearth and altar as marking "la route des échanges avec les dieux d'en-bas et les dieux d'en-haut," see Vernant (above, note 9) I,168. For such "communication systems" implicit in rituals of this nature, see also the work of Bellah summarized by Vickers 127–128 and 159 n17.

26. "Skin," *chrōs*, occurs only in these two places in the play and only twice elsewhere in the extant plays and fragments of Sophocles.

27. For this inverted significance of music, cf. also Eur., *Phoen.* 786–790, 1028, 1489–91; *HF* 871, 878–879, 891–892. See in general Pachet (above, note 24) 542; A. J. Podlecki, "Some Themes in Euripides' *Phoenissae*," *TAPA* 93 (1962) 369–372.

28. See also *Ajax* 706 and Kamerbeek (above, note 17). Unless otherwise indicated, further references to the commentaries of Kamerbeek and Jebb are to the lines under discussion.

29. Dio Chrys. 60.4 seems aware of this dimension of the encounter when he

interprets Nessus' "violence" to Deianeira as his seductive arguments to win her over (*logoi epitēdeioi*). For the text and interpretation of 660–662 generally, see Kamerbeek (above, note 17) Segal, *YCS* 112 and 40.

30. a. πέρσας πόλιν (750 and 244)

b. νίκης ἄγων τροπαῖα (751)
καὶ ζῶντ' ἐπίστω καὶ κρατοῦντα κἀκ μάχης
ἄγοντ' ἀπαρχὰς θεοῖσι τοῖς ἐγχωρίοις· (182–183)

c. ἀκτή τις ἀμφίκλυστος Εὐβοίας ἄκρον
Κήναιόν ἐστιν, ἔνθα πατρῴῳ Διὶ
βωμοὺς ὁρίζει τεμενίαν τε φυλλάδα (752–754)
ἀκτή τις ἔστ' Εὐβοιίς, ἔνθ' ὁρίζεται
βωμοὺς τέλη τ' ἔγκαρπα Κηναίῳ Διί· (237–239)

d. ταυροκτονεῖ μὲν δώδεκ' ἐντελεῖς ἔχων
λείας ἀπαρχὴν βοῦς· (760–761)
τέλη τ' ἔγκαρπα (238)
ἀπαρχάς (183)
ἡμέρᾳ ταυροσφάγῳ (609)

31. See Girard (above, note 19) 66–67.

32. See Detienne (above, note 7) 73ff.; also above, chapter 2, section XI.

33. See Segal, *AC* passim, esp. 40–41.

34. Note too the absence of the flute at the perverted ritual of Aesch., *Ag.* 152: see Anne Lebeck, *The Oresteia* (Washington, D.C., 1971) 34.

35. Cf. the *ololygmos* in Aeschylus, *Ag.* 594–597, 1235–37 and see Eduard Fraenkel, *Aeschylus, Agamemnon* (Oxford 1950) ad locc. (I, 296–297, II, 572–573); also Lebeck (above, note 34) 61; S. G. Kapsomenos, *Sophokles' Trachinierinnen und ihr Vorbild* (Athens 1963) 57–68.

36. On the ritual inversion in the *euphēmia*, see R. C. Jebb, *Sophocles, Part V, The Trachiniae* (Cambridge 1892) and Kamerbeek (above, note 17).

37. Cf. also the "altar most thronged with strangers" in Pindar, *Ol.* 1.93.

38. The rocky setting is even more prominent in Ovid, *Met.* 9.204ff., where a touch of pathos is added in Lichas' attempt to hide in a cave: *ecce Lichan trepidum latitantem rupe cavata / aspicit, Met.* 9.211–212.

39. Cf. Paul Stengel, *Die griechischen Kultusaltertümer*, Müller Handbuch d. Altertumswiss. 5.3³ (Munich 1920) 108–109.

40. See Burkert, *Homo Necans* 63–64; Marie Delcourt, "Tydée et Melanippe," *SMSR* 37 (1966) 169–173.

41. For the literal and metaphorical significance of the "disease," see Penelope Biggs, "The Disease Theme in Sophocles' *Ajax, Philoctetes, and Trachiniae*," *CP* 61 (1966) 223, 228ff.; P. E. Easterling, "Sophocles, *Trachiniae*," *BICS* 15 (1968) 62–63; Segal, *YCS* 113ff.

42. See Kamerbeek on lines 1050–52; H.D.F. Kitto, *Poesis*, Sather Class. Lectures 36 (Berkeley and Los Angeles 1966) 176.

43. Seneca admired and imitated this irony: *Hercules Oetaeus* 794–797.

44. For the sexual implications, see Segal, *YCS* 110–111; D. Wender, "The Will of the Beast: Sexual Imagery in the *Trachiniae*," *Ramus* 3 (1974) 1–17.

45. With Kamerbeek (above, note 17) and against Pearson's *OCT* I keep the mss. reading, *entethermantai*, at 368; cf. *entakeiē*, 463.

46. Cf. Deianeira's grove of maidenhood, sheltered from the "sun-god's heat" (*thalpos*, 148) and cf. Aesch., *PV* 590–591, 649–650. See also Sophocles, frag. 474P (*Oenomaus*), where the lovers are "warmed" (*thalpetai*) and "roasted" by *eros*.

47. See Kamerbeek. Deianeira's "warm tears" in 919ff. are an echo of an Homeric formula, but here too warmth is connected with an inverted or dangerous aspect of sexuality, in this case the farewell of a bridal bed which will see a consummation not of love, but death. I cannot agree with the attempt to emend 1046 by B. Jaya Suriy, *CR* n.s. 24 (1974) 3.

48. See Gregory Nagy, "Six Studies of Sacral Vocabulary Relating to the Fireplace," *HSCP* 78 (1974) 71–106, esp. 76 and 99ff.; Paul Friedrich, *The Meaning of Aphrodite* (Chicago 1978) 37.

49. For time in the play, see Segal, *YCS* 107–108.

50. Ibid. 143–145.

51. See above, chapter 2, notes 40 and 70.

52. Cf. 304, 306, 359, 401, 420, 549.

53. E.g. 28, 108, 325, 893–895; C. Segal, "The Hydra's Nurseling: Image and Action in the *Trachiniae*," *AC* 44 (1975) 612–617; Easterling (above, note 41) 59: "In a normally happy marriage one would expect the nourishing to be concentrated on the children, not on fears." See also Wender (above, note 44) 5. For the equation of marriage and agriculture, see above, note 9.

54. See Kamerbeek (above, note 17) on lines 841–846.

55. See Wender (above, note 44) 13.

56. Cf. *pothos*, "longing," in 103, 107, 629–632; *tēkein*, "melt," in 463, 662, 836. For the erotic sense of "melting" see Soph., frag. 941.7P, with Pearson's note. Cf. also Pindar, frag. 123.10–13 Snell. Cf. also the adjective *takeros* in Ibycus 287.2, Anacreon 459, Alcman 3.61 (all Page, *PMG*).

57. This speech wins from Lichas praise of Deianeira for "having mortal thoughts," (473), i.e. being reasonable, whereas her thoughts are mortal in a very different way.

58. On the monstrosity of Achelous' shape, see Segal, *YCS* 105 and 26; Paolo Vivante, *The Homeric Imagination* (Bloomington, Ind., 1970) 113, cites *Il.* 21.237 and observes how much more primitive, in a way, Sophocles' description is. Archilochus too was more restrained (frag. 270 Lasserre-Bonnard).

59. The change may also suggest that the rape has gone less far: cf. the "wanton hands" in 565. On Sophocles' transformations of this part of the legend, see Charles Dugas, "La mort du Centaure Nessos," *REA* 45 (1943) 24–25; Bruno Snell, "Drei Berliner Papyri mit Stücken alter Chorlyrik," *Hermes* 75 (1940) 177–183; Franz Stoessl, *Der Tod des Herakles* (Zürich 1945) 52–56.

60. See G. Dumézil, *Horace et les Curiaces* (Paris 1942) 57–58, who calls attention to parallels with Cuchulain and remarks," C'est toute la Femininité qui tente sa chance contre toute la Virilité représentée par un exemplaire de choix."

61. For Heracles and Omphale in satyr plays, see Ion of Chios frags. 18–33 N, esp. 29 and Achaeus frags. 32–35. The theme appears prominently on the volute-crater of the Pronomos-painter in Naples at the end of the fifth century: see Erika Simon, "Die Omphale des Demetrios," *Archäolog. Anzeiger* (1971) 199–206; B. Snell, *TrGF* I,189, with the review of Snell by T.B.L. Webster, *Gnomon* 44 (1972) 739. Heracles dressed in Omphale's Lydian robes while she carries his rude club becomes a favorite motif in Graeco-Roman art. See in general C. Caprino, s.v. "Onfale," *Enciclopedia dell' Arte Antica* V (1963) 695–698.

62. See Easterling (above, note 41) 61–62.

427

63. Other versions of Heracles' mode of life in Trachis were available: see Dio Chrys. 78.44. Other sons seem to be present in the Nurse's address to Deianeira in the prologue, and cf. frag. adesp. 126N (Dio Chrys. 78.44).

64. See Hom., *Od.* 6.7; Th. 1.12; R. P. Winnington-Ingram, "Tragica" *BICS* 16 (1969) 45; Segal, *YCS* 104.

65. See Slater, *Glory of Hera* 376–377.

66. As in the *Odyssey* also, much of the action of the play concerns a prayed-for arrival of a father: cf. 285–287, 655, 757. For other connections with the *Odyssey* see G. Schiassi, *Sofocle, Le Trachinie* (Florence 1953) xxiv-xxv; Stoessl (above, note 59) 35.

67. There may be another inversion of "nurture" if we keep the mss. reading, *trephei* in 117. Jebb, who with most editors prefers *strephei*, "turns about," cites a possible parallel in Eur., *Hippol.* 367, "O toils that nurture mortals."

68. See T. F. Hoey, "Sun Symbolism in the Parodos of the *Trachiniae,*" *Arethusa* 5 (1972) 143.

69. He seems here "a mythical giant rather than Deianeira's human husband," suggests Kamerbeek (above, note 17) on line 50. See also H. Lloyd-Jones, "Sophoclea," *CQ* 48 (1954) 91–93.

70. For this landscape of childhood innocence, see also *Ajax* 552–559, frag. 583P, and the *Ichneutae* generally. Cf. also Musurillo 33–34.

71. Cf. Eur., *Hippol.* 73–87; Segal, *YCS* 148–149 and also *HSCP* 70 (1965) 121–124.

72. *Od.* 6.41–46, 7.112–31.

73. In the terms of Vernant's important essay (above, note 9), which is highly applicable to the *Trachiniae*, the male and female aspects of the house, instead of being complementary, cancel one another out. The mobility of the male leads to dangerous infidelity and instability; the interiority of the female becomes entrapment. The kind of integration necessary for the successful blending of *oikoi* is deformed. Cf. Vernant, *MP* I, 147–148: "Hestia nous semble avoir en effet pour fonction spécifique de marquer l'incommunicabilité des divers foyers: enracinés en un point défini du sol, ils ne sauraient jamais se mélanger mais restent 'purs' jusque dans l'union des sexes et l'alliance des familles. Dans le mariage ordinaire, la pureté du foyer se trouve assurée par l'intégration de l'épouse à la maison de son mari (. . . dans le mariage et dans la procréation, elle cesse de représenter son foyer; on pourrait dire qu'elle est 'neutralisée': elle ne joue plus de rôle, elle est purement passive; l'homme seul est actif)." In the *Trachiniae* the interaction of the husband and wife reverses this situation and brings out only its destructive potential. By violating the sacred interiority of the hearth with Iole, Heracles, excessively active, stirs Deianeira from her "proper" passive role and undoes her "neutralization." The resultant release of demonic sexuality anomalously sexualizes the virginal space of Hestia and at the same time creates a destructive form of "incommunicability" which now excludes and kills the father.

74. For this dangerous aspect of inner space, see also 542, 579, 610–613, 686, 689.

75. For the meaning of 952–953, see Kamerbeek.

76. Note also the association of Heracles' "last things" with the public realm and the forces of nature in 1149 and 1256. Cf. also his embittered reference to his defeat of the dragon at the earth's farthest places, *eschatoi topoi* (1100).

77. See Detienne, *Jardins d'Adonis* 165ff. and above chapter 2, section V.

78. Macchiavelli, *The Prince,* chap. 18: "The parable of this semi-animal, semi-human teacher is meant to indicate that a prince must know how to use both natures."

79. Cf. *King Lear* IV.vi.124ff.: "Down from the waist they are Centaurs,/Though women all above;/But to the girdle do the gods inherit,/Beneath is all the fiends."

80. Susan Woodford, "More Light on Old Walls: The Theseus of the Centauromachy in the Theseion," *JHS* 94 (1974) 162.

81. *Kentaurou* here can also go with *nephela* (see Kamerbeek, above, note 17) so that 831–832 could also mean, "If necessity anoints him with the deadly cloud of the Centaur." A number of critics have called attention to the fact that the "cloud" here recalls the origin of the centaurs from Nephele, the cloud-image fashioned by Hera to thwart Ixion's attack in Pindar, *Pyth.* 2. 36–37: see Letters 78. Thus it reinforces the association of Nessus with unruly, destructive lust.

82. For these inversions of technology, see Segal *AC* 46.

83. See Eur., *Hippol.* 509ff.; Segal, "Shame and Purity in Euripides' Hippolytus," *Hermes* 98 (1970) 278–299.

84. See Kamerbeek on line 701: "The fate of the wool must be considered an omen, a prefiguration of Heracles' own fate."

85. Kamerbeek remarks on *prosharmozein* (494): "The verb . . . makes us think of the peplos or of the philtron (cf. 687) or of both; at the same time the verb, with *dōra*, can be understood as meaning: 'to make a suitable return gift.' "

86. Ibid. on lines 1066–69.

87. For fire in the play, see Segal, *YCS* 141–143. Note also the sacred fire of Artemis "with a torch in each hand" (*amphipyros*, 215): this fire celebrates in a prematurely happy rite a reunion which the destructive fires of lust, poison, and perverted sacrifice will destroy.

88. For the hearth fire's ambiguous fluctuation between inner and outer space, see 206, 262, 607, 954. Vernant, *MP* I, 129–130, points out the contrast between the pure fire of the hearth and the generative, less pure fires associated with male desire and sexuality.

89. See Segal, *YCS* 109, 137; Kamerbeek on lines 839–840. For the metaphorical usage, cf. Herodotus 7.13.2; Soph., *OC* 434. Cf. also Plutarch, *Amatorius* 24.769F: "But Eros seems to cause a kind of seething (*zesin*) as of liquids running into one another."

90. For the theme of ferrying in Nessus' activities, see Snell (above, note 59) 178 n1; Bacchyl., frag. 64.9 Snell (Pindar, frag. 341.7 Bowra); Segal, *AC* 46.

91. For a brief discussion of the sea imagery, see Musurillo (above, note 70) 65–66.

92. For *eu prattein* cf. 230–231, 297, 1171; also *eutychēs praxis* in 293–294 and *eutychein*, 192.

93. See in general S. Eitrem, "La magie comme motif littéraire chez les Grecs et les Romains," *SO* 21 (1941) 39–41. For a larger range of this ambiguity, see Jacques Derrida, "La pharmacie de Platon," *Tel Quel* 32 (1968) 3–48.

94. Whitman 116 remarks, "One suspects Heracles' new illness of being only a continuation of the old one."

95. For the veering of the disease between physical and emotional disorder, see Biggs (above, note 41) 230–231. If the mss. reading, *synkratheis*, is retained at 662, there may be a further inversion of a medicinal drug: instead of the drug being "mixed," the victim is "mixed" with the ointment. Elsewhere in Sophocles this verb is used metaphorically with words of emotion like "grief" or "pity": *Antig.* 1311; *Ajax* 895 and cf. frag. 944P with Pearson's note and also Pindar, *Pyth.* 5.2. One should note too the powerfully suggestive use of "anoint" (*chriein*) and compounds throughout the play: 661, 687, 689, 832.

96. Cf. Hom. *h. Cer.* 237; Apollon. Rhod., *Arg.* 4.870–871. See N. J. Richardson, *The Homeric Hymn to Demeter* (Oxford 1974) on lines 237ff.

97. This word occurs here for the first time and nowhere else in tragedy: see Kamerbeek (above, note 17); also Segal, *YCS* 111.

98. On this bestialization of the disease, see P. Rödström, *De Imaginibus Sophocleis a Rerum Natura Sumptis,* Diss. Uppsala (Stockholm 1883) 27.

99. *Paradise Lost* 2.542–547:
As when Alcides, from Oechalia crowned
With conquest, felt the envenomed robe, and tore
Through pain up by the roots Thessalian pines,
And Lichas from the top of Oeta threw
Into the Euboeic sea.

100. See C. Segal, "Synaesthesia in Sophocles," *Illinois Class. Studies* 2 (1977) 88–96.

101. On the motif of writing, see Segal, *AC* 48–49.

102. See J. Lacarrière, *Sophocle dramaturge* (Paris 1960) 51–52, "Séparés l'un de l'autre dans la vie comme dans la mort, Déjanire et Héraclès se parlent littéralement 'd'une ère à l'autre.' Quand Déjanire dit 'amour,' Héraclès comprend: 'sexe.' Quand elle dit 'femme,' il comprehend 'femelle' " (p. 51). See also T. F. Hoey, "*The Trachiniae* and the Unity of Hero," *Arethusa* 3 (1970) 11.

103. The erotic implications of "persuasion," *peithō,* need hardly be stressed: see J. de Romilly, "Gorgias et le pouvoir de la poésie," *JHS* 93 (1973) 161 and nn 35–36; Segal, YCS 111–112.

104. The mss. reading, *phasmati,* is surely right and stresses the phantasmagoric nature of the poison: cf. 509 and the "deadly cloud" of 831. See H. Lloyd-Jones, "Notes on Sophocles' *Trachiniae,*" *YCS* 22 (1972) 266; A. A. Long, "Poisonous Growths in *Trachiniae,*" *GRBS* 8 (1967) 276–277; Segal, *YCS* 118.

105. In 662 I follow Pearson in adopting Paley's *parphasei:* see *YCS* 112–113 and 40. *Parphasis* is another erotically colored word: cf. *Iliad* 14.216–217 and also 208.

106. On the theme of secrecy, see Kirkwood (above, note 2) 232–233. One should add *lathraios* and *lathrāi* in 384, 533, and Deianeira's remark about doing things in the dark, 596–597. See Segal, *YCS* 144.

107. E.g. Th. 2.64.8, 3.38.2ff.

108. Th. 3.82.5ff.; 3.83.2–3.

109. Note also the remarks about the "trusting" of tales and oracles in the prologue, 67 and 77.

110. For this verb of fastening and related ideas, see Segal, *YCS* 138. There is another aspect of distorted communication in the play on *stellein,* "send,": and *stolos,* which means both "robe" and "entourage" or "accompaniment" for the journey. Deianeira says that "it is not just for Lichas to go back empty having come with so great an entourage" (495–496; cf. 226); the result is the "adorning" (*stellein*) of Heracles in the robe (611–612), which conveys the "sending of words" (*logōn epistolas,* 493) that Deianeira would have Lichas bring. That adorning, in turn, harks back to that first sending from her father (*patrōon stolon,* 562), when she, as the new bride, first encountered Nessus and acquired the poison.

111. See Kamerbeek on line 620.

112. On the oracles see especially Kirkwood 78–79; H. Weinstock, *Sophokles* (Wuppertal 1948) 27ff.; Lacarrière (above, note 102) 15–16.

113. See Kamerbeek; Jebb, Appendix 203ff.; Lesky, *TDH* 209 n66.

114. Kirkwood, "The Dramatic Unity of Sophocles' *Trachiniae,*" *TAPA* 72 (1941)

209 points out that there is another contrast between Deianeira and Heracles in her silence in death and his silence about her, another contrast between selfishness and unselfishness.

115. Cf. Pindar's *phēr theios,* "divine beast," *Pyth.* 4.119.

116. For Heracles' comprehension of the oracles at the end, see Segal, *TCS* 133–134; also Kirkwood, *Study* 50: "Only for Heracles can the baffling and misleading oracles and the truthful lie of Nessus give meaning and pattern. For Deianeira to become involved in this unmanageable sweep of events means destruction."

117. The need for someone other than Heracles to light the pyre is strongly emphasized in the mythic tradiiton: see Diodorus 4.38.4 and Apollodorus, *Bibl.* 2.7.7.

118. E.g. Pindar, *Pyth.* 4.270; see LSJ s.v. *paian.*

119. For the problem of the apotheosis and bibliography, see Segal, *TCS* 138ff.; B.M.W. Knox's review of G. Ronnet, *Sophocle, poète tragique,* in *AJP* 92 (1971) 694–695; Walter Burkert, "Die Leistung eines Kreophylos," *MH* 29 (1972) 74–84, esp. 83–84 on the epic tradition.

120. The legend was also enshrined in local cult: see Arrian in Stobaeus 1.246.18 Wachs.: "It is told that sacrifice is made each year on the summit of Mt. Oeta to Heracles and Philoctetes in memory of the ancient event, and the ashes remain in place on the altar." For the archaeological evidence, see M. P. Nilsson, "Der Flammentod des Herakles auf dem Oite," *Archiv f. Religionswissenschaft* 21 (1922) 310–316.

121. See Evelyn B. Harrison, "Athena and Athens in the East Pediment of the Parthenon," *AJA* 71 (1967) 43–45, 57.

122. See Segal, *TCS* 140.

123. Hubert and Mauss (above, note 16) 85.

124. Ibid. 97.

125. See Girard 223; Segal, *TCS* 146–148.

126. See J. K. MacKinnon, "Heracles' Intention in His Second Request of Hyllus: *Trach.* 1216–51," *CQ* n.s. 21 (1971) 33–41. I cannot, however, accept MacKinnon's view that Hyllus is to take Iole merely as a concubine. Not only is the usage of *damar* in the play against this view but so is the mythical tradition: see Apollodorus 2.7.7 and the note *ad loc.* of J. G. Frazer, *Apollodorus, The Library,* Loeb Classical Library (London 1921) I, 269.

127. MacKinnon (above, note 126) 41; also Kamerbeek on lines 1225–26; Kitto (above, note 42) 170–172; Weinstock (above, note 112) 24 (Heracles' act "bleibt ganz im Bilde des naiven Ichmenschen"); most recently Christine E. Sorum, "Monsters and the Family: The Exodos of Sophocles' *Trachiniae,*" *GRBS* 19 (1978) 69ff.

128. See Bowra 192–193; Segal, *TCS* 151–152 and 110; Easterling (above, note 41) 67–68 has a sensitively balanced view.

129. In this respect Heracles does not differ from the usual "outsized" Sophoclean hero: cf. Knox, *HT* chap. 1, esp. 24ff.

130. On 1246, with a somewhat more positive view, see Easterling (above, note 41) 67.

131. For a more detailed study of this passage, see Segal, *TCS* 136–138. also my "Eroismo tragico nelle 'Trachinie' di Sofocle," *Dioniso* 45 (1971–1974) 107ff.

132. Note, too, the use of the metaphor of the bit for civic control and authority: Soph., *Antig.* 109 and *El.* 1462.

133. *Psychē* as the center of moral consciousness occurs in the early fifth century, even though it is usually associated with Socrates: cf. Pi., *Pyth.* 3.61; Soph., *Ajax* 154, *Antig.* 177. Further references in Segal, *TCS* 136 n89.

134. Ibid. 141ff. and *AC* 47ff.

135. For this circle of man's fate, see Kamerbeek on lines 129–131; cf. *El.* 1365–66.

136. For the association of the circle and circular movement with the feminine realm of the hearth, see Vernant, *MP* I, 148ff.

137. For Deianeira and cyclicity, see Hoey (above, note 68) 142.

138. For this point see Segal, *YCS* 156.

139. This paragraph recapitulates the argument of Segal, *YCS* 158.

140. Compare the similar sense of supernatural powers behind the action in *Ajax* 1028–37 and *Electra* 1420ff., 1477–78. See Jean Carrière, "Sur l'essence et l'évolution du tragique chez les Grecs," *REG* 79 (1966) 13–16.

141. See Jebb and Kamerbeek. Also Jebb's Appendix 207.

142. Heracles' command to Hyllus in 1224, *prosthou damarta,* "Take her to wife," also recalls the callous willfulness of his attempt to introduce her into the old *oikos* as a kind of second "wife," *damar,* 428–429.

143. The attribution of the closing lines is, as often, confused in the mss. Though some scholars assign them to the coryphaeus addressing the chorus of Trachinian women (so Kamerbeek, Mazon and Dain in the Budé edition, Lesky *TDH* 217, Easterling [above, note 41] 68), I feel little doubt that they belong to Hyllus. Only he has sufficient stature to pronounce them; and only in the mouth of this young man, whose life has been so deeply touched by the tragedy of the house—a tragedy in which he is called upon to perform the final act—can they have their full dramatic significance.

5 Ajax

1. See Segal, *YCS* 25 (1977) 121–123.

2. See Rosenmeyer, *Masks* 181.

3. See J. Starobinski, *Trois fureurs* (Paris 1974) 19–26.

4. On the themes of time and change in the play, see the excellent studies of Rosenmeyer, *Masks* 155–198, and Knox, "Ajax," 1–37.

5. For the problem of the play's "diptych" structure, see W. B. Stanford, ed., *Sophocles, Ajax* (London 1963) xliiiff.; A. C. Pearson, "Sophocles, *Ajax* 961–973," *CQ* 16 (1922) 128ff.; Gellie 23ff.; James Tyler, "Sophocles' *Ajax* and Sophoclean Plot Construction," *AJP* 95 (1974) 24–42. Whereas some (e.g. Gellie and Pearson) allow the relevance of the last part but see it as embodying a fall off of dramatic power through (necessary) forensic debate, Reinhardt, seems closer to the truth in insisting on the importance of the last section not only for the fate of Ajax' body, but also for the presentation of "jene falsche Gegenwelt . . . , an der Aias hatte Rache nehmen wollen" (p. 42).

6. For good discussions of the motif of the single day, see Whitman, 67ff. and Rosenmeyer, *Masks* 166, who sees in the theme a reflection of the meaninglessness of time.

7. Cf. *Ajax* 399 and *Antig.* 789–790. See Michael Wigodsky, "The Salvation of Ajax," *Hermes* 90 (1962) 150–151; Jacqueline de Romilly, *Time in Greek Tragedy* (Ithaca, N.Y., 1968) 96. On the concept of man as *ephēmeros,* "creature of a day," in early Greek poetry, see Pindar, *Ol.* 2.31ff. and *Nem.* 6.6ff.; Hermann Fränkel, "Man's 'Ephemeros' Nature according to Pindar and Others," *TAPA* 77 (1946) 131–145.

8. See Whitman 70–71.

9. The question of the intentions of Ajax in this speech is one of the most widely discussed issues in the play. There are useful surveys of the arguments over the years in Ignacio Errandonea, "Les quatre monologues d'*Ajax* et leur signification dramatique,"

LEC 36 (1958) 23–27; H.-F. Johansen, *Lustrum* 7 (1962) 177–178; Knox, "Ajax" 11ff. and nn 70–75, pp. 32–34; John Moore, "The Dissembling-speech of Ajax," *YCS* 25 (1977) 47–66; Martin Sicherl, "Die Tragik des Aias," *Hermes* 98 (1970) 14ff. (now translated as "The Tragic Issue in Sophocles' *Ajax*," *YCS* 25 [1977] 67ff.); Stanford (above, note 5) Appendix D 281–288; Kurt Von Fritz, "Zur Interpretation des Aias," *RhM* 83 (1934) 113ff.; A.J.A. Waldock, *Sophocles the Dramatist* (Cambridge 1951) 67–79. Gellie (above, note 5) 12 concisely states the dilemma of the interpretation: "Ajax cannot change and Ajax cannot lie": if he cannot change, then he is lying; if he is not lying, he has changed. Scholars fall, by and large, into two camps. The one view goes back to F. G. Welcker, "Über den Aias des Sophokles," *RhM* 3 (1829) 43–92, 229–364, who argues that Ajax does not intend to deceive any one, that he is still unyielding, that he consciously chooses death, but that Tecmessa and the chorus, eager to hear what they want to hear, delude themselves into believing that Ajax means to yield. Variants of this view are championed by Kirkwood 161–162; Kitto, *Form* 190–191; I. M. Linforth, "Three Scenes in Sophocles' 'Ajax,'" *UCPCP* 15.1 (1954) 10–20; Eilhard Schlesinger, "Erhaltung im Untergang: Sophokles' Aias als 'pathetische' Tragödie," *Poetica* 3 (1970) 374–375. The other view maintains that Ajax, though still unyielding in his determination to commit suicide, takes pity on Tecmessa and deceives her and the chorus in order to die unhindered: see Adams 34; Whitman 74–76; Letters 138ff. Von Fritz and Knox have raised important objections to this view of an intentionally deceiving Ajax. Some scholars, while granting that deception is somewhat out of place, have fallen back on dramaturgic necessity: Sophocles, caught in an impasse between the necessity that Tecmessa and the chorus be deceived and the certainty that Ajax means to die, had, at the least, to let the others deceive themselves: so Waldock 78–79, and with variations Gellie 14–15; Lesky, *TDH* 184–185, 190 with further bibliography; Tycho von Wilamowitz-Moellendorff, *Die dramatische Technik des Sophokles*, Philol. Untersuch. 22 (Berlin 1917) 62–65. Of this approach, in terms of dramatic machinery, Knox's solution, that the speech is entirely a monologue and not meant to deceive anyone, is the most engaging, but, while satisfying our sense of Ajax' firmness of will, does not change the fact that the chorus behaves as if Ajax is changing his mind. Others of those accepting the speech as intended to deceive have stressed the contradiction as an essential part of Ajax' tragedy: especially influential here is Reinhardt 34ff., and see also Von Fritz 118ff.; Moore passim; Sicherl 17ff.; Lattimore, *Poetry* 71 ("That everything he says deceives through truth, that there is a double edge to everything puts the language into the oracular manner, the puzzle of daemonic dreams and portents"); Georges Dalmeyda, "Sophocle, Ajax," *REG* 46 (1933) 6 (Ajax is "obligé de feindre," but does so "avec une ironie amère").

10. This point is well stressed by Moore (above, note 9) 56.

11. See Von Fritz (above, note 9) 124; Whitman 75; Gustav Grossmann, "Das Lachen des Aias," *MH* 25 (1968) 84.

12. Lattimore, *Poetry* 71; see also Kitto, *Form* 190: "The very splendour of the imagery speaks of his unbroken pride."

13. In this joy the chorus is "pathetic in its hopes," remarks Moore (above, note 9) 65. Tecmessa's remark in 807–808, however, indicates, retrospectively, that she is not completely deceived about Ajax' "salvation."

14. Reinhardt 37.

15. See Knox, "Ajax" 14ff.; Stanford 285.

16. See Reinhardt 35; Edward Fraenkel, "Zwei Aias-Szenen hinter der Bühne," *MH* 24 (1967) 82: Tecmessa and the chorus "haben seinen [Ajax'] Inhalt in den Grenzen ihres

Sinnes, der nicht der Sinn des Aias ist, erfasst . . . Wir haben es also in dem Hauptteil der Rede mit einem schillernden, einem zweispältigen Gebilde zu tun: Einsamkeit des Redendes und zugleich Wirkung auf die andern, deren Anwesenheit er nicht beachtet."

17. See Von Fritz (above, note 9) 120.

18. See Moore (above, note 9) 57ff.

19. For the Iliadic parallels, see G. M. Kirkwood, "Homer and Sophocles' *Ajax*," in M. J. Anderson, ed., *Classical Drama and Its Influence, Studies Presented to H.D.F. Kitto* (New York, N.Y., 1965) 51–70; also Bowra 21–22; S. M. Adams, "The *Ajax* of Sophocles," *Phoenix* 9 (1955) 101–102; W. Edward Brown, "Sophocles' Ajax and Homer's Hector," *CJ* 61 (1965–66) 118–121, who also points out the similarities and contrast in the treatment of the bodies, the one whose burial, refused by the enemy, is achieved by the strenuous effort of his *philoi;* the other, refused burial by his own side and saved by a man he supposed his foe.

20. It is true, as Knox says, "Ajax" 27, that Ajax's "final words are addressed to things eternal, unchanging, timeless"; yet the adjectives also point back to his human associations and kin ties.

21. See J. C. Kamerbeek, *The Plays of Sophocles,* Part I, *Ajax* (Leiden 1963) *ad loc.,* on taking *homilei* in zeugma with both clauses.

22. The importance of the shield as part of Ajax' identity is well brought out by Fraenkel (above, note 16) 84–86; see also Kirkwood (above, note 19) 60, 63; Stanford 277–278; Rosenmeyer, *Masks* 180–181; most recently David Cohen, "The Imagery of Sophocles: A Study of Ajax's Suicide," *G & R* 25 (1978) 24–36, and Oliver Taplin, *Greek Tragedy in Action* (Berkeley and Los Angeles 1978) 85–87. Note also the verb *proteinō,* where the "risking" of his life (*psychē*) also suggests his characteristic Homeric gesture of "stretching forth" the great shield in the service of his comrades.

23. The translation is that of Stanford in his excellent note on 1408.

24. On the fixity of the sword and its implications, see the good remarks of Knox (above, note 4) 20. On the element of personal responsibility in Ajax' planting the sword, see Cedric H. Whitman, "Sophocles' *Ajax* 815–24," *HSCP* 78 (1974) 67–69.

25. Illustrated in Taplin (above, note 22) figure 11 (Metropolitan Museum, New York, Bareiss Collection L.69.11.35). For a more detailed discussion, see my "Visual Symbolism and Visual Effects in Sophocles," *CW* 74 (1980/81) 128–129.

26. The uses of *kyklos* and derivatives are as follows: 19 (Odysseus' cautious tracking of Ajax); 353 (the wave of Ajax' madness); 672 (the hostile cycles of nature); 723 (hostile encirclement of Teucer by the army); 749 (Calchas' emergence from the "circle" of leaders to announce the fatal prophecy).

27. So Odysseus' "wandering" in 23 and the chorus' mistaken image of Ajax as "wandering" in 886, as opposed to his direct "exit," *exodos* in 798 and 806.

28. See Pi., *Nem.* 6.9–11 and *Nem.* 11.37–43. The closest Ajax comes to anything similar is his reference to the "lovely-fruited summer" in 671, where however, the notion seems temporal rather than spatial.

29. See Adam Parry, "The Language of Achilles," *TAPA* 87 (1956) 1–7; and, in more detail and subtlety, Paul Friedrich and James Redfield, "Speech as a Personality Symbol: The Case of Achilles," *Language* 54 (1978) 263–288, esp. 266ff.

30. On Ajax' growth toward tragic knowledge, see Sicherl (above, note 9) 37: "Seine Grösse beruht darauf, dass er die Wahrheit, die ihn vernichtet, aber auch rettet und erhöht, in vollem Bewusstsein ergreift—nicht anders als Oidipus." Reinhardt (above, note 5) 36 observes the tragic irony of the dawning recognition of the hero's maladaptation to the world ("Erkenntnis eines ewigen Zerwirfnisses des Helden mit dem Lauf der Welt"). See

also Kitto (above, note 9) 188–189 and Michael Simpson, "Sophocles' Ajax: His Madness and Transformation," *Arethusa* 2 (1969) 88–103.

31. See Knox, "Ajax" 21 and also *HT* 24–25.

32. On the tragic aspect of Ajax's yielding, see Von Fritz (above, note 9) 124–125 and Moore (above, note 9) 59. On the correlation of political and natural order in the "prerogatives," see Knox, *HT* 24.

33. On the oracles see Wigodsky (above, note 7) passim, with the literature there cited; Schlesinger (above, note 9) 375ff. De Romilly (above, note 7) 16–21 stresses the function of the oracle in creating a sense of the pressing urgency of time.

34. Gellie 192.

35. See Musurillo 20–21; Helmut Kuhn, "The True Tragedy," pt II, *HSCP* 53 (1942) 80–83.

36. Ibid. 83: "Even the cosmic space opening up around him to receive his complaint is a symbol of his tragic solitude and freedom"; see also 61–62.

37. I accept Kamerbeek's interpretation of *aianēs* (above, note 21), as now Stanford does also, "Light and Darkness in Sophocles' Ajax," *GRBS* 19 (1978) 193 and n8. "Diuturnitate molestum et grave" is Hermann's paraphrase, quoted by F. Ellendt, *Lexicon Sophocleum*[2] (Berlin 1872) s.v.

38. For Ajax as *deinos,* see also 366 and in general Sicherl (above, note 9) 30.

39. Note the parallels between 650–653 and 667–670, which further associate Ajax with the forces of nature.

40. The image is perhaps that of the balances of a scale (see Kamerbeek), but an image of gaming pieces is also possible. J. C. Kamerbeek, "Sophocle et Héraclite," *Studia Vollgraff* 89–91, suggests parallels with the Heraclitean doctrine of universal flux. This hero, Rosenmeyer remarks (*Masks* 168) "does not count, he lives, and when life becomes a sordid business of ticking off days, he sacrifices life." His protest against time has nothing of the bleak, resigned acceptance of the kind of popular pessimistic philosophizing that one finds in this lapidary text (438 Kaibel): "All things the earth makes grown and covers up again in turn. Let one therefore not complain when he goes from the earth down into the earth. When you die, that is the end." The first line, πάντα χθὼν φύει καὶ ἔμπαλιν ἀμφικαλύπτει, resembles the second line of Ajax' great speech (χρόνος / φύει τ' ἄδηλα καὶ φανέντα κρύπτεται 646–647, but the shift from Ajax "great time" to "earth" is significant.

41. The first passage, 600–605, stands in an even closer relation to Ajax' speech on time through the verbal echo, *chronos . . . mēnōn anērithmos* (600–601) and *kanarithmētos chronos* (646).

42. Cf. also Deianeira's image of the sheltered meadow of girlhood (*Trach.* 144ff.), couched in similar language and equally precarious.

43. For the hunting metaphor, see Stanford 274; Knox, "Ajax" 21 and 105.

44. Note also the connection of his mad attack with darkness, night, blackness: 21, 47, 231, 376, 1056. The symbolism of light and dark has been much discussed: Stanford 275–276 and "Light and Darkness" (above, note 37) 189–197; Musurillo 10ff., 20; Schlesinger (above, note 9) 366.

45. For the interpretation of these two passages, see Kamerbeek and Stanford *ad loc.*; for the latter passage, also John Ferguson, "Ambiguity in *Ajax,*" *Dioniso* 44 (1970) 15–16.

46. Sicherl (above, note 9) 30 suggests, but does not develop, a possible connection between the alternation of light and dark in 393ff. and the rhythms of life and death in the great central speech on time (646ff.).

47. See Schlesinger (above, note 9) 367.

48. Note the repetition of *horan*, "see," in 118 and 125; see Schlesinger 364–365.

49. Cf. Phaedra's concern with seeing and being seen and the theme of looking another in the face in Eur., *Hippol.* 280, 416, 662, 720, 947 and cf. also 321; see my remarks in *Hermes* 98 (1970) 282 and n3, 288–292.

50. Cf. also 977: This "dearest eye" for his loved ones is a "grim sight," "hard to look at" (1004). For the possible play on *omma* here, see Ferguson (above, note 45) 21–22. Note too Athena's revealing the disease as "very visible," *periphanēs*, in 66 and "glorious Salamis . . . visible always," *periphantos aei*, in 597–599.

51. *Paraulos* might also mean "discordant" (*aulos*, "flute") as well as "near the shelter or dwelling" (*aulē*). The scholia give both; the latter is supported by *OC* 785 and *Phil.* 158. Possibly a play on both meanings is intended: cf. the grim "pipes" of 1411ff.

52. Cf. 985, where Teucer gives orders to fetch Eurysaces, who is alone by the tents, *monos para skēnaisi*.

53. E.g. Eur., *Hippol.* 141–150 with W. S. Barrett's commentary, *Euripides, Hippolytus* (Oxford 1964) on lines 141–144.

54. See Michel Foucault, *Madness and Civilization,* trans. Richard Howard (1965, reprint New York 1973) 193: "For Madness, even if it is provoked or sustained by what is most artificial in society, appears in its violent forms as the savage expression of the most primitive human desires." See also Rosenmeyer, *Masks* 179: "In a throwback to primitiveness he chooses to live in a world where man and animal are not distinct."

55. See above, chapter 2, section X, with the references there cited.

56. For the "storm of madness" see also Aesch., *PV* 883–884; Eur. *HF* 1091, *Or.* 279–280. See in general Josef Mattes, *Der Wahnsinn im griechischen Mythos* (Heidelberg 1970) 112–113.

57. Georges Dumézil, *The Destiny of the Warrior* (Chicago 1970) 141. See also Pierre Pachet, "Le bâtard monstrueux," *Poétique* 12 (1972) 533, who stresses the warrior's need for this "énergie tumultueuse et brûlant . . . qui permet au héros de triompher des adversaires les plus redoutables, avec le risque toutefois de devenir pour sa propre cité un danger incontrôlable." Following Dumézil, Pachet suggests that one of the functions of a myth like that of Heracles (and, we may add also, like that of Ajax) is to show by what rituals and sequences of confrontations (especially with women) "the superabundant energy of the hero can be put to the service of the community, reintegrated on each occasion into a social group whose limits, by definition, this energy exceeds" (p. 533).

58. Dumézil (preceding note) loc. cit.

59. For the madman's loss of honor, see Aesch., *Suppl.* 562–563 and *PV* 599; also Mattes (above, note 56) 95, 98–99 on Ajax.

60. See Lattimore, *Poetry* 73.

61. See Penelope Biggs, "The Disease Theme in Sophocles' *Ajax, Philoctetes* and *Trachiniae,*" *CP* 61 (1966) 224ff.

62. For this experience of Ajax's night of his madness, cf. Foucault (above, note 54) 111 on such madness as potentially also opening on a tragic experience of "the profoundest day of being . . . It is to this degree that tragic man, more than any other, is engaged in being, is the bearer of his truth since, like Phèdre, he flings in the face of the pitiless sun all of the secrets of the night, while the madman is entirely excluded from being."

63. Such a formulation, however, does not indicate that Ajax is mad throughout, as is suggested by Erik Vandvik, "Ajax the Insane," *SO,* suppl. 11 (1942) 169–175. Simpson's view of a development or clarification of the meaning of the madness in Ajax (above, note 30, passim) is far more likely. See also Biggs (above, note 61) 226.

64. On the various aspects and functions of Athena, see Whitman 66–71, esp. 70: "It is wholly in keeping with the plasticity of Greek polytheism that the figure of Athena can be used here to symbolize the inner being of the two men, painted large and timeless at the beginning of the play." See also Adams (above, note 19) 97–98; Gellie, 4–5; Grossmann (above, note 11) 76 on Athena in the first scene particularly; Schlesinger (above, note 9) 382–383; Simpson (above, note 30) 91; Tyler (above, note 5) 24–31; Ruth Camerer, "Zur Sophokles' Aias," *Gymnasium* 60 (1953) 310.

65. See Adams (preceding note) 100.

66. For the madness as disease, see Biggs (above, note 61) 224ff.; Gellie (above, note 5) 7–8; Vandvik (above, note 63) 172.

67. See Biggs (above, note 61) 226.

68. Ibid. 227.

69. See Knox, "Ajax" 21; Biggs (above, note 61) 224. Stanford xxviii–xxix cites Pacuvius' *Armorum Iudicium* on Ajax' *ferocem et torvam confidentiam.*

70. Jan Kott, *The Eating of the Gods* (New York, N.Y., 1972) 59.

71. The metaphors are briefly listed and discussed by Stanford (above, note 5) 274–275. See also Schlesinger (above, note 9) 363–364.

72. *thērasthai,* 2; *kynēgetein,* 5; *kynagia,* 37; *kyōn,* 8; *ichneuein,* 20; *ichnē,* 6 and 32; *basis,* 8 and 19.

73. "Klang- und Bilderfülle aus der ritterlicher Welt," remarks Reinhardt aptly, 27.

74. On the implications of man-beast reversal in this "driving," see also Aesch., *PV* 309, 580, 681–682, and in general Otfried Becker, *Das Bild des Weges,* Hermes Einzelschrift 4 (Wiesbaden 1937) 179, n69 and 195–196.

75. "Er entfernt sich wie ein krankes Weidetier von der Herde," says Mattes (above, note 56) 99.

76. For the double meaning of *syrinx* here, see R. C. Jebb, Sophocles, *The Plays and Fragments,* Part VII, *The Ajax* (Cambridge 1907) *ad loc.* Stanford *ad loc.* also has a useful discussion.

77. The text of 169 is not entirely certain. I have followed the majority of editors in inserting *d'* after *aigypion.* Compare the eagle simile of *Antig.* 110ff. and Aesch., *Ag.* 49ff. See in general P. Rödström, *De Imaginibus Sophocleis a Rerum Natura Sumptis* (Stockholm 1883) 32. *Aigypios* can frequently mean a vulture as well as an eagle. Though it probably has the latter meaning here—see Stanford (above, note 5) and Kamerbeek (above, note 21)—, one wonders if the choice of this rather ambiguous term (instead of *aietos,* for example, which in fact is connected etymologically with Ajax' name by Pindar, *Isth.* 6.50–54) may not connote the destructive and self-destructive aspects of Ajax' heroism.

78. For the yoke see Ferguson (above, note 45) 13 and 15; for the importance of verbs of "going" in the speech on time, see Becker (above, note 74) 205ff.

79. Earlier, however, a hunt separates Teucer from Ajax and prevents him from reaching him in time to protect him from his savage, lonely impulses: at the moment of the catastrophe Teucer is off on a hunt (*thēran*) for the enemy (564).

80. "Iron," *sidēros,* and compounds occur four times in *Ajax,* only twice in all the other extant plays, and only twice in the fragments.

81. See Camerer (above, note 64) 308–309.

82. The exact meaning of the expression in 650–651 has been questioned. The most probable interpretation is that Sophocles refers to the hardening of iron by dipping, not giving the metal greater suppleness. Thus the simile of 651 will be taken with *ekarteroun* in the previous line. See Jebb *ad loc.* and Appendix 229–230; Fraenkel (above, note 16) 79–80; Camerer (above, note 64) 316–317, who calls attention to the parallel with *Trach.*

1259–62, where, however, the metallurgical imagery is far less ambiguous, as Heracles seems to be moving toward, not away from, his civilized role. Kamerbeek (above, note 21) admits the possible ambiguity, which, I believe, is an important aspect of the phrasing.

83. Note the combination of *chalkeuein* and *dēmiourgos* in Plato, *Rep.* 3.395a. *Chalkeuein* is, in fact, the first example which Plato lists in the practice of the crafts in a city.

84. For the *topos* see A. Kleingünther, *Prōtos Heuretēs, Philologus,* suppl. 26.1 (1933). For the form of the passage, cf. Horace, *C.* 1.3.9ff. with the parallels of Nisbet and Hubbard (Oxford 1970) *ad loc.*

85. For Ajax' difficulties of communication, see Reinhardt 22f.; Gellie 14; Biggs (above, note 61) 225.

86. Pindar, *Nem.* 7.24ff.; *Nem.* 8.22ff.; *Isth.* 4.36ff.

87. See Reinhardt 30.

88. See Knox, "Ajax" 22; John H. Finley, Jr., "Politics and Early Attic Tragedy," *HSCP* 71 (1966) 11–12; Norman O. Brown, "Pindar, Sophocles, and the Thirty Years' Peace," *TAPA* 82 (1951) 18ff.

89. See 762–777 and also 386, 423. Bowra 32 suggests an echo of Aeschylus' Capaneus in *Septem* 424–425; I cannot, however, agree with Bowra's view that Teucer's account of Ajax' "excessive speech" is not to be credited. The first scene between Ajax and Athena, with its talk of boasting, has carefully prepared us to accept Teucer's story as truth. Teucer even echoes this theme of boasting from the prologue (cf. 766 and 96).

90. See 367, 382–384, 454; also 956–961, 969, 989, 1043.

91. See Grossmann (above, note 11) passim, esp. 79–83; Gellie 281 n6, remarks, "The laughter in line 303, reported by Tecmessa, provides a retrospective stage direction for the prologue."

92. See Reinhardt 31–32.

93. See Wigodsky (above, note 6) 153ff., esp. 157.

94. As Rosenmeyer, *Masks* 190 puts it, "The rhetoric of the soul gives way to the rhetoric of the forum."

95. Violent and quarrelsome speech is heavily underlined throughout: 1110, 1116, 1124, 1142, 1147.

96. On the contrast of force and persuasion, a frequent *topos* of the fifth century, see Democritus 68B181DK; it is a major theme in the *Philoctetes:* see below, chapter 10, section II.

97. Cf. 1335, 1342, 1343, 1344, 1363, and 1390. Contrast 1118–19, 1125–26, 1130, 1136. Cf. also the association of effective speech with the justice of the good king, whose authority comes from Zeus, in Hesiod, *Theogony* 79–97.

98. Kamerbeek remarks on line 522, "Nowhere is the reciprocity of *charis* better realized than here." See also Kirkwood 105ff. Note too that Ajax's cry for his son, *iō pai pai* (339), is his first articulate utterance after the repeated "Woe, Woe is me," of grief in 333, 336, a touch that Adams 30 considers "amongst the finest of Sophocles' dramatic effects."

99. See 830, 965, 1054, 1333, 1388, 1392.

100. The latter paraphrase of 577 is Stanford's. Note also the use of *koinos* in 267ff. and 284.

101. See Knox, "Ajax" 18.

102. Knox, "Ajax" 20 connects the "flowing" of 523 and 1267 to show the contrast with the fixed, irrevocably earth-planted sword of Ajax in 815, 819, 821, 907.

103. For the notion of reciprocity in *charis* here, see Kamerbeek.

104. With Kamerbeek and Stanford I follow the mss. in distinguishing between Ares and Enyalios in 179. For the ominous significance of Ares, see also *Trach.* 653.

105. Kamerbeek calls attention also to 712 and 970; Jebb cites Eur., *Phoen.* 947–948.

106. Besides 219 and 546 see also 815, 841, 898, 919. For the sacrificial sense, see *Trach.* 756. Where *sphazein* occurs elsewhere in Sophocles, it denotes either the killing of animals or half-animals (*Trach.* 573, 717; *El.* 568) or a violent killing that pollutes or destroys a house (*El.* 37; *Antig.* 1291; *Trach.* 1130). For further discussion and parallels, see J.-P. Guépin, *The Tragic Paradox* (Amsterdam 1968) 1–4; Lattimore, *Poetry* 75–76 and 26; Adams 36; Sicherl (above, note 9) 36.

107. See Jebb and Kamerbeek on line 220.

108. Cf. Soph., *El.* 435–436; Eur., *Suppl.* 1205–1207: See in general Sicherl (above, note 9) 23, 36 n3; Camerer (above, note 64) 310.

109. Cf. 407–409. For stoning as the punishment of the polluted outcast, cf. Aesch., *Sept.* 199; Soph., *Antig.* 36 and *OC* 435; Eur., *Or.* 50 and *Ion* 1222; in general Pearson (above, note 5) 130–134; Guépin (above, note 106) 104.

110. The solemnity of effect is further enhanced by the repetition of *tethnēiken* in something approximating ring-composition in 966 and 970.

111. See Knox, "Ajax" 11 and n65; Sicherl (above, note 9) 23.

112. Charles W. Eckert, "The Festival Structure of the Orestes-Hamlet Tradition," *Comparative Literature* 15 (1963) 321–337.

113. Ibid. 330, with the further references there cited.

114. Burkert, *Homo Necans* 64–66, 206–207.

115. Simpson (above, note 30) 92.

116. Ibid. 96 stresses Ajax' development from confusion, conflict, inarticulate madness to greater clarity and verbal skill, an "ascent to a higher vision of reality which becomes his justification for suicide." Jones 178ff. frames the change in terms of the shift from a shame culture to a guilt culture.

117. Eckert (above, note 112) 335–336.

118. Note, by contrast, the immovable fixity of the sword: 815, 819, 821, 907. See Knox, "Ajax" 20 and above, note 102.

119. Ajax, of course, was one of the ten eponymous heroes: cf. Hdt. 5.66 and Pausanias 1.5.2. There are numerous accounts of special dedications to him, including one after the battle of Salamis (Hdt. 8.121): cf. also Pausan. 1.35.3, schol. on Pindar *Nem.* 2.19. Though a few scholars have denied the relevance of the hero cult of Ajax to the play (e.g. Pearson, above, note 5, 129; Kitto, above, note 9, 182), the majority opinion, with which I concur, favors its importance: Rosenmeyer, *Masks* 186–189; Whitman 61, stressing the possible influence of the recent death of Cimon; Letters 139–140; Adams 24; Bowra 16; Jones 188–189; Dalmeyda (above, note 9) 14.

120. Knox, "Ajax" 20.

121. Musurillo 22.

122. N. O. Brown (above, note 88) 18ff. has convincingly shown that there is not one type of heroic *aretē* in the play, but two, involving a historical crisis between an older and a newer definition of values. This point is well developed by Knox, "Ajax" 24ff., stressing the anachronism of an Ajax in the age of democracy. See also Whitman 45ff. and Rosenmeyer, *Masks* 171–172.

123. Peter Burian, "Supplication and Hero Cult in Sophocles' *Ajax*," *GRBS* 13 (1972) 151–156.

124. See Kirkwood 94–96.

125. Such, in part, is the function of the funeral speech or *epitaphios logos,* pronounced over the dead: see Th. 2.43.2–3; Plutarch, *Pericles* 8. See Whitman 262 n71.

126. The text of 1417 is uncertain, and some editors have suspected the line: see Jebb *ad loc.* and Appendix, 239–240. He cites Seyffert's esteem for this verse as *unum ex pulcherrimis, ut nobis videtur, poetae ornamentis.* Possibly *thnētōn* in 1416 is corrupt. I take *Aiantos* in 1417 as a genitive of comparison with *lō(i)oni.*

127. For Ajax' grim *eros* for death, see Sicherl (above, note 9) 27.

128. In 1211ff. Sophocles may be alluding to a simile in the *Iliad* (17.746) where the two Ajaxes, holding back the enemy, are compared to a wooded headland holding back the waters of a flooding river. If so, the reminiscence would serve to reinforce the valued, cooperative aspect of Ajax as he appears in Homer.

129. See Knox, "Ajax" 17; Helen North, *Sophrosyne,* Cornell Studies in Classical Philology 35 (Ithaca, N.Y., 1966) 61.

130. See Kirkwood 107; Dalmeyda (above, note 9) 13.

131. On this aspect of Odysseus in *Philoctetes,* see my essay, "Philoctetes and the Imperishable Piety," *Hermes* 105 (1977) 138–142.

132. Cf. Aesch., *Eum.* 696ff. Lesky, *TDH* 187 remarks, "Was in den *Eumeniden* im Munde Athenes die grosse Weisheit von dem Werte heilsamer Furcht war, wird hier im aufdringlicher Wiederholung des Stichwortes *deos* (1074, 1079, 1084) zur leeren Phrase eines selbstgefälligen, kleinen Despoten."

133. Menelaus' lashing out at Teucer's *labron stoma*—possibly another oligarchical *topos:* cf. Pi., *Pyth.* 2.87—in 1147 is another indication of the breakdown of reasonable discourse. Note also the beast imagery of *daknein* ("bites") in 119 and *kentein* ("prick," as a goad) in 1245.

134. See Whitman 78.

135. The repetition of "straight" or "upright" (*orthos*) by Agamemnon in 1254 (cf. 161) is perhaps another ironic undercutting of the Atreid position. On the theme of great and small, see Biggs (above, note 61) 226.

136. Odysseus, says Knox, "Ajax" 25, exemplifies the "tolerance and restraint which is the mood of the new age, and of Athenian democracy at its best." See also N. O. Brown (above, note 88) 21; Whitman 65–66. On the fundamental contrast of world view between Ajax and Odysseus, see Rosenmeyer, *Masks* 194–198; Kirkwood 101–102; Gellie 26–28.

137. The fact that, as Whitman 71–72 points out, Odysseus for all his reasonableness, is still no yardstick with which to measure Ajax, is another indication of the Sophoclean hero's ambiguous relation to civilization. Reinhardt 25–26 compares the contrast between Odysseus and Ajax to that between Ismene and Antigone and between Creon and Oedipus in the *OT.*

138. The first phrase belongs to Knox, "Ajax" 25; the second to Kirkwood 108. See also Jones 187 (comparing Theseus in *OC* 565–568) and Kamerbeek on lines 124 and 1366.

139. If we read Pearson's emendation, *kinei,* in 1357 instead of the *nika(i)* in the mss. For the problems of the line, see Jebb.

140. On these shifts see Knox, "Ajax" 9–10, 19–20. We may also compare Calchas' change of position, both literal and metaphorical (*metastas,* 750), as he steps forth from the circle of the chiefs to offer help to Teucer in 749–752.

141. See Sicherl (above, note 9) 35: "Dadurch wird das Freund-Feind-Denken des heroischen Zeitalters in einer neuen, höheren Humanität aufgehoben. Damit schwindet aber auch die Möglichkeit einer Tragik wie der des Aias." See also notes 136–137 above.

6 Antigone: Death and Love, Hades and Dionysus

1. For a good comparison of Creon and Odysseus, see J. H. Kells, "Problems of Interpretation in the *Antigone*," *BICS* 10 (1963) 59–61.

2. For Creon and sophistic rationalism see Wilhelm Schmid, "Probleme aus der sophokleischen Antigone," *Philologus* 62 (1903) 1–34; R. F. Goheen, *The Imagery of Sophocles' Antigone* (Princeton 1951) 152 n28 with the further literature there cited (this book will be referred to henceforth as "Goheen").

3. I. M. Linforth, "Antigone and Creon," *UCPCP* 15, no. 5 (1961) 199. Though Linforth sees in the ode "a note of sincere admiration," he recognizes also the hints of danger which become explicit later: pp. 196–199.

4. See Eilhard Schlesinger, *"Deinotēs," Philologus* 91 (1936–37) 59–66; the term, he suggests, denotes man's "kulturschaffende Tätigkeit," which, while enabling man to subdue nature, also joins him with the elemental forces of nature which he would tame: "Sophokles übernimmt diese Auffassung, dass der Mensch das Ungeheuerste sei, aber dieses besteht für ihn nicht so sehr in den entfesselten Tiefen der menschlichen Natur [as, e.g., for Euripides] als in dieser zwei Möglichkeiten in sich schliessenden Anlage, die das ungeheuerste Naturphänomen darstellt, weil sie den Menschen sowohl auf den Gipfel der Kultur führen kann, je nach der Beschaffenheit des *ēthos* des Handlenden." See also Paul Friedländer, *"Polla ta deina," Hermes* 59 (1934) 54–63; Gilberte Ronnet, "Sur le premier stasimon d'*Antigone*," *REG* 80 (1967) 100–105; Giacomo Bona, *"Hypsipolis* e *Apolis* nel primo stasimon dell' Antigone," *RFIC* 99 (1971) 131–133; Goheen (above, note 2) 53 and n1, 141; C. Segal, "Sophocles' Praise of Man and the Conflicts of the *Antigone*," (1964) in Thomas Woodard, ed., *Sophocles. A Collection of Critical Essays* (Englewood Cliffs, N.J., 1966) 71–72 (cited henceforth as "Segal"). Note too Creon's reference to fearful profit (*ta deina kerdē*, 326) just before, if we keep the better attested reading against Brunck's *deila*, which most editors accept: see R. C. Jebb, *Sophocles, The Plays and Fragments,* Part III, *Antigone* (Cambridge 1891) and J. C. Kamerbeek, *The Plays of Sophocles,* Part III, *Antigone* (Leiden 1978) *ad loc.*

5. For these images see 113–114, 116, 140, 423–425, 998ff., 1039–40; and, in general, Goheen 26–35.

6. See Kamerbeek.

7. For Creon's reactions by insult, see Segal 74–75. Note also Lycurgus' *kertomiai glōssai,* insulting tongue, 962–963. For Creon see 280ff., 565ff., 740ff., 1033–63.

8. For madness see 135, 492, 790, 959–962, 1151; note too how the interview between father and son from the beginning teeters on the edge of the madness and anger (see 633, 765–766) in which it finally ends (1228ff.).

9. Note the usage of *symmetros* in *OT* 1113, discussed below, chapter 7.

10. For the theme of the "road," see R. di Virgilio, *RFIC* 94 (1966) 31–32 and n1. The ambiguity of the compounds of *poros,* "way," "path," as well as "resource," in 360–361 would be even greater if, as the late Cedric Whitman suggested in a public lecture at Brown University in October, 1978, those lines can be translated "Resourceless man comes to the nothing(ness) that is his future." Note too the association of *poros* with limit and direction over against the limitless chaos of unformed space in the cosmogony of Alcman, frag. 5.2, col. ii Page, on which see J.-P. Vernant and Marcel Detienne, *Les ruses de l'intelligence* (Paris 1974) 134ff.

11. For the ironies in Antigone's comparison of herself to Niobe, see Segal 73; Emil Staiger, *Grundbegriffe der Poetik*[8] (Zürich and Freiburg i. Br. 1968) 155: "Antigone in ihrem Schmerz vergleicht sich nicht mit andern Jungfrauen Thebens, sondern mit Niobe,

die auf den Höhen des Sipylos vor Schmerz zu Stein geworden ist"; also Seth Benardete, "A Reading of Sophocles' *Antigone,* II," *Interpretation* 4 (1975) 49–50. The parts of this careful and interesting reading of the play are I, *Interpretation* 4.3 (1975) 148–196; II, ibid. 5.1 (1975) 1–55; and III, ibid. 5.2 (1975) 148–184; I shall cite these henceforth as "Benardete 1,2,3" respectively.

12. Note Antigone's special concern with "always," eternity in 456, 892, a trait which she shares with other Sophoclean heroes: see Knox, "Ajax" 18–19.

13. See above, chapter 4, note 7.

14. The chorus' repetition of *kerdos,* profit, at the end, "You say what is profitable, if profit there is in woe" (1326) marks the total reversal of Creon's calculations for profit. On the importance of *kerdos* in the play generally, see Goheen 15ff.; Segal 66; Kamerbeek, Introduction 35.

15. See Reinhardt 94, 100–101, who stresses Creon's tragedy of "late learning."

16. See Vickers 539: "In allowing the body to become rotten, food for animals, Creon is reversing the process of civilization, man's triumph over the hostile forces of the environment, a triumph which has been celebrated in the great first stasimon." See also Segal 82–83; Gellie 33.

17. Yet her personal vision is objectively verified in the widening implications of the unburied corpse in Teiresias' description, 1016ff.

18. Note the recurrence of *bora* in 1017 and 1040. Cf. also Eur., *Suppl.* 46–47, *Phoen.* 1603, *IA* 423. On the connotations of the word, see my remarks in *Hermes* 97 (1969) 297–298; Vidal-Naquet, *M T* 148 and n73.

19. The phraseology of the "sweet treasury" is remarkable; Schneidewin-Nauck, Sophokles, *Antigone* (Berlin 1886) would delete it; cf. Anna Parodi, "Antigone nel prologo della tragedia di Sofocle," *Dioniso* 35 (1961) 95 and n28. For the potentially solemn and religious evocations of the word, cf. Pindar, *Pyth.* 6.8 and Hdt. 1.14.2. Benardete 1.153 takes a different view of the word, as indicating "the preciousness of Polyneices even though dead."

20. E.g. *Iliad* 11.453–454; 22.67, 207, 347; 24.212–213. See in general C. Segal, *The Theme of the Mutilation of the Corpse in the Iliad, Mnemosyne* suppl. 17 (Leiden 1971) 61.

21. See the discussion of *Trach.* 765ff., above, chapter 4, section II; also T. F. Hoey, "Inversion in the *Antigone,* A Note," *Arion* 9 (1970) 337–345; Michael N. Nagler, *Spontaneity and Tradition, A Study in the Oral Art of Homer* (Berkeley and Los Angeles 1974) 156–159.

22. See Jebb; Benardete 3.160–162.

23. Cf. Aristophanes, *Clouds* 1423–29 and *Birds* 757–759. See K. J. Dover, *Aristophanes, Clouds* (Oxford 1968) on the former passage (pp. 260–261).

24. In Sophocles' *Phaedra* (frag. 619.3N = 680.3P), diseases, god-sent, must be borne as we can (*theēlatous nosous*). In Hdt. 7.18.3 Xerxes' dream is *theēlatos,* and its divinity is a matter of considerable importance and discussion, 7.16.2ff.

25. I do not believe, with Kamerbeek on lines 429–431, that the double burial is a "fictitious problem": see my review in *Phoenix* 33 (1979) 271. For useful surveys see D. A. Hester, "Sophocles the Unphilosophical," *Mnemosyne,* ser. IV, 24 (1971) 25ff.; Marsh McCall, "Divine and Human Action in Sophocles: The Two Burials of the *Antigone,*" *YCS* 22 (1972) 103–117; Th. Zielinski, *Tragodoumenon, Libri Tres* (Cracow 1925) 16–18; R. P. Winnington-Ingram, *Sophocles: An Interpretation* (Cambridge 1980) 125–126 and n31. *Pace* Winnington-Ingram, I do not believe that Antigone's "curse on those who have done the deed" in 428 rules out the possibility of divine burial. Antigone's

admission to both burials in 434–435 also does not necessarily mean that she performed both, as Robert Coleman argues in an otherwise excellent study, "The Role of the Chorus in Sophocles' *Antigone*," *PCPS* 198 (1972) 10–12. Her confession to "both acts," ambiguous in any case, makes as good sense as part of her defiant spirit as a statement of what really happened. Note the similar ambiguity in her defiant confession of 443 and her possessive reaction to the deed at Ismene's eager confession in 536–539. Is it possible (assuming Antigone did not perform both burials) that her willful exclusion of the gods from the burial, paradoxically parallel to Creon's, is another aspect of her problematical impious piety?

26. See Reinhardt 80, 82.

27. McCall (above, note 25) 103–107; also S. M. Adams, "The Burial of Polyneices," *CR* 45 (1931) 110–111; H.D.F. Kitto, *Sophocles, Dramatist and Philosopher* (London 1958) 56–57 (the divine burial is an "unobstrusive miracle").

28. For the text of 376–377, see Kamerbeek and Jebb. For the contrast with the Ode on Man, see Benardete 1.196, who connects the "divine prodigy" of 376–377 with Antigone as the source of the *deinotēs* of the Ode.

29. Antigone, however, does use a "carefully welded pitcher of bronze" for her libations in 430.

30. There is ample evidence for nonburial as the punishment for traitors: Th. 1.138.6 Xen., *Hellenica* 1.7.22; Hyperides, *For Lycophron* 20: see A. C. Pearson, "Sophocles, *Ajax*, 961–973," *CQ* 16 (1922) 133–134; Hester (above, note 25) 19–21; L. A. MacKay, "Antigone, Coriolanus and Hegel," *TAPA* 93 (1962) 168 and n6; Coleman (above, note 25) 7.

31. See Arist., *Pol.* 1.1254b 5ff.; Isoc., *Nicocles* 6–9. See also Democr. 68B5DK; Pl., *Protag.* 322a; Jebb on line 354; and in general below, chapter 10, note 16.

32. For the associations of *kalchainō* with the sea, cf. Goheen 45.

33. E.g. *Republic* 3.410d–e, 412d–e, 8.565d–66a.

34. Creon's verb, *kōtillein* (756), which occurs only here in Sophocles, also suggests a womanish wheedling and coaxing: cf. Hesiod, *Opera* 374 and Theocritus, *Idylls* 15.89; cf. also Theognis 363.

35. For the theme of wailing over the dead, cf. also 423–427, 883, 1179, 1206.

36. See Jebb on line 487.

37. Cf. especially 1284ff. and the ominous new tale (*logos*) at 1289; also 1320. Note too Eurydice's great cry in vain (*boē*) in 1252 and Haemon's wretched cry in 1209. She opened her speech with fear at the "sound of woe for our house" (1187) and is given a report in which the sound of Haemon's voice plays a crucial role (1214, 1218). Cf. also the theme of wailing, *kōkyein*, which becomes increasingly insistent toward the end: 1079, 1206, 1227, 1302, 1316.

38. The "harbor of refuge" for the birds recalls, of course, the other area of rational control or lack of control in the play, the sea: cf. 334–337 and its connection specifically with Creon's confidence of power and its collapse in 290 and 1284.

39. For the "barbarization" of the birds and their language, see Benardete 3.160–161.

40. On the savage eyes of 1231–32, Goheen 34 notes the irony that "the son in subhuman rage glares now at the father who has been so prone to assign bestial characteristics to others but who would not, too late, make atonement."

41. The asyndeton and bare simplicity of 1214, *paidos me sainei phthongos*, add to the effect of sudden horror.

42. Creatures breathing fire in Greek myth are generally monstrous, dangerous, and

powerful, for example the Chimaera (Hom., *Il.* 6.181–182 and Hes., *Theog.* 319) or Typhos (Aesch., *Sept.* 493, 511): see in general Hoey (above, note 21) 344 and for the significance of fire in the play Benardete 3.162–163.

43. So Kamerbeek on line 1007. Possibly too the threat of applying "piny Hephaestus" to Thebes in the chorus' indignant description of Polyneices' attack at 123 underlines the impiety of that endeavor: see Benardete 3.162.

44. For the problems of interpreting 618–619, see H. Musurillo, "Firewalking in Sophocles' *Antigone*, 618–619," *TAPA* 94 (1963) 167–175, who believes that the reference is only to caution in walking over fire, not to a ritual ordeal of fire-walking.

45. The danger of rigidity reflected in Creon's simile here (473–476) is stressed by the recurrence of *enkratēs* to describe his own unyielding hardness later when Haemon applies to him the simile of a ship and its too tightly drawn sheets (*enkratē poda / teinas*, 715–716).

46. For the meaning of *ouranion achos*, see Jebb and particularly Kamerbeek, and for the significance of the celestial vocabulary see Benardete 2.3–4. Benardete takes the phrase to be indicative more of Antigone's unerring sense of direction in locating the body than of the gods' support, but the two views are not mutually incompatible. The guard, in any case, seems to lay his emphasis on the supernatural here (415–421). Hoey (above, note 21) 342 takes another view of the storm: as "earth flying in the face of heaven," it is another "inversion" which reflects the disrupted relation between gods and men, soon to be developed in the "bloody dust" which overcomes the light and mows down the living, if one reads *konis* at 601ff.

47. "The region meant is the furthest and highest part of the Theban plain (1197), where the body of Polyneices still lay," says Jebb on line 1110.

48. On the image of transgression in general, see Goheen 10–11. Some critics have tried to make the sense of 852ff. favorable to Antigone, but the characterization of the chorus is against this. For a survey of the discussions see Hester (above, note 25) 35 and nn1–2.

49. Gerhard Müller, "Überlegungen zum Chor der Antigone," *Hermes* 89 (1961) 405–406, notes the close parallel in both expression and meter between *hypsipolis/apolis* and *pantoporos/aporos,* denoting the equal capacity of man for civilization and savagery as for resourcefulness and helplessness in both Antigone and Creon. The true relation is temporarily hidden by the shifting between reality and illusion characteristic of the tragic situation in Sophocles, but death will finally reveal the true *apolis* and the true *hypsipolis* and separate the illusion from the reality. Kells (above, note 1) 58 views the terms as part of the chorus' value system which defines moral goodness exclusively in terms of the city. Bona (above, note 4) 144–148 suggests that the chorus is only raising the issue of who is the *hypsipolis,* who the *apolis,* but cannot yet tell.

50. On Antigone's devotion to honor and the problematical, harsher aspects of her character, see the survey of discussions in Hester (above, note 25) 21, 41ff., and 58–59; Kells (above, note 1) 53–57; Knox, *HT* 92 and also 29–30. The question of the balance of our sympathies between her and Creon has been much discussed, from Hegel on: there is a general agreement in recent scholarship that though Creon has nothing approaching equality of right on his side, he is not without sympathy: "The audience must feel that the issue is difficult, that there is much to be said on both sides . . . Without this the play will fail in dramatic and human interest" (Bowra 67). See also B. M. W. Knox, *Gnomon* 40 (1968) 748–749 (reviewing G. Müller's commentary on *Antigone*); J. C. Hogan, *Arethusa* 5 (1972) 93–100; Segal 62–64; Vickers 526–546; Suzanne Saïd, *La faute tragique* (Paris 1978) 119–132.

51. Benardete 2.41 suggests that Haemon is here deliberately exaggerating the city's unity behind Antigone, a view which, though possible, is hard to prove. In any case the lines suggest the fragmentation of the total unity of the city under his rule that Creon supposes and needs to suppose (see 289ff., 734ff.).

52. Martin Ostwald, *Nomos and the Beginnings of the Athenian Democracy* (Oxford 1969) chap. 2, distinguishes thirteen separate meanings for *nomos*.

53. Note also Antigone's complaint about the *nomoi* which cause her to be led to the living tomb, 847–848, I need not here go into the question of 905–920 which, with most recent critics, I regard as genuine. For recent discussion and bibliography, see Hester (above, note 25) 55–58, Kamerbeek, and Winnington-Ingram (above, note 25) 145 and n80 (rejecting the lines).

54. Jebb takes *gēn* with *pyrōsōn*, "to burn the land," whereas Kamerbeek prefers the zeugma with *diaskedōn* and translates, "in order to lay waste their land and to wreck their laws."

55. On 613–614 see Ostwald (above, note 52) 22–23.

56. Ibid. 31, n1; Müller (above, note 49) 421–422 finds in this relation to the "established laws" of 1113 a *Doppelsinn* which contrasts Antigone and Creon, the one having died to keep these laws, the other hesitatingly discovering what Antigone had known all along. Her fate is implicitly contrasted with that of a lesser figure and a smaller person who comes to her instinctive understanding only through coercion and ultimately destruction. For good observations on Creon's violation of *nomoi*, see R. Trousson, "La philosophie du pouvoir dans l'*Antigone* de Sophocle," *REG* 77 (1964) 31ff. ("L'erreur de Créon est de surestimer la parcelle d'ordre divin qu'il est chargé d'administrer").

57. See above, chapter 1, section III and notes 5–6; also below, chapter 9, note 1. *Antig.* 359–361 may contain an oblique reference to prophecy in the statement about man's coming "to nothing in the future without resource," but, if so, the phraseology is such as to leave the divine element wholly out of view. The context of 368–369 makes it unlikely that these lines referred to religious institutions, even if we accepted Pflugk's *perainōn*. Reiske's *gerairōn*, however, accepted by Jebb, still seems to me the more likely reading.

58. For Creon's ambiguous piety, see also 514, 730–731 and in general Segal 68–69; Knox, *H T* 101–102; Joachim Dalfen, "Gesetz ist nicht Gesetz und fromm ist nicht fromm. Die Sprache der Personen in der sophokleischen Antigone," *WS*, n.s. 11 (1977) 14–20; Rudolf Bultmann, "Polis und Hades in der Antigone des Sophokles" (1936) in Hans Diller, ed., *Sophokles,* Wege der Forschung 95 (Darmstadt 1967) 315ff. MacKay (above, note 30) 166ff. seems to me to take too positive a view of Creon and too mild a regard of his violence. With the paradox of this kind of piety we may compare Pelasgus' remark to the Egyptian herald in Aesch., *Suppl.* 921, "Addressing the gods, you show the gods no reverence."

59. See Gerhard Müller, ed., *Sophokles, Antigone* (Heidelberg 1967) *ad loc.* (p. 84), with the corrective of Knox's review (above, note 50) 751–752; Bona (above, note 4) 134; Benardete 1.189–192.

60. See U. von Wilamowitz-Moellendorff, *Der Glaube der Hellenen* (Berlin 1931) I, 210–211; Bona (above, note 4) 144 and n4; Hoey (above, note 21) 339; Benardete 1.191.

61. Note also Ismene's entrance at 527–528, with sisterly love, who drips tears down (*katō*) and has a cloud (*nephelē*) of grief above her brows (*hyper*).

62. With Jebb and Kamerbeek I follow the mss. reading, *konis*, "dust," instead of the emendation *kopis*, "knife" at 603. The occurrence of dust three times in connection

with the forbidden burial of Polyneices (246–247, 256, 429) also supports it. By the second stasimon we are prepared for the ominous significance of dust in connection with the family curse. For a not dissimilar use of "mowing," also in connection with a curse, cf. *Ajax* 1178. See also Hoey (above, note 21) 342–343; Benardete 2.27–28; N. B. Booth, *CQ* n.s. 9 (1959) 76–77, replying to H. Lloyd-Jones, *CQ*, n.s. 7 (1957) 17–19; P. E. Easterling, "The Second Stasimon of *Antigone*," *Dionysiaca. Nine Studies in Greek Poetry Presented to Sir Denys Page* (Oxford 1978) 146–149.

63. As Jebb notes on line 599, *nin* can have either *phaos* or *rhizan* as its antecedent. Jebb prefers *phaos*, as does Kamerbeek, but perhaps the two words really merge into one. With Pearson's OCT I prefer to read *etetato* with a stop after *domois*.

64. See Benardete 1.189–191 and 2.3.

65. For Creon's "earth" in the political sense, see 110, 187, 287, 736, 739, 1162.

66. Creon's claim to the *kratos* or royal power *kat' anchisteia* in 174 uses this technical term of Attic law: see Jebb and Kamerbeek.

67. This theme of destructive and ominous "doubling" is a leitmotif throughout the play and is especially prominent in the first part, particularly in connection with the curse on the house of Oedipus: 13–14, 51–55, 145–146. See in general Girard chap. 2 and above, chapter 3, note 17.

68. See MacKay (above, note 30) 168: "The dispute between Creon and Antigone is, in poetic and symbolic form, the dispute between citizenship as a functional status and as inherited, inalienable family status."

69. On Creon's use of Hades in threats, see Knox *H T* 100; Segal 82.

70. On the nature of these public and private altars and their pollution, see Jebb on lines 1016 and 1083. As Jebb points out on 1080–83, Sophocles may be alluding to the larger pollution in the refusal to bury warriors other than Polyneices, an action which resulted in the second expedition against Thebes and the subsequent destruction of the city.

71. See J.-P. Guépin, *The Tragic Paradox* (Amsterdam 1968) 104.

72. See Wilhelm Nestle, "Sophokles und die Sophistik," *CP* 5 (1910) 138–139.

73. For the relevance of the *pharmakos* pattern to the play, see R. Y. Hathorn, "Sophocles' *Antigone*: Eros in Politics," *CJ* 54 (1958–59) 113; Guépin (above, note 71) 89; Girard (above, note 67) 190–191. It is perhaps worth noting that the ritual in Athens involved two *pharmakoi*, a man and a woman.

74. See Jebb on line 1303 and Kamerbeek on line 995. The latter finds also in 993 and 995 allusions to "Megareus' sacrificial death on Teiresias' instigation" (p. 172). See also Coleman (above, note 25) 6 and n22 and pp. 24–25.

75. The schol. on line 1301 remarks on *bōmia* "slaughtered like a sacred victim (*hiereion*) at the altar."

76. See Kamerbeek, Introduction 26 and n2 and 31–32; Jebb on line 1111 rightly observes that Creon's "foremost thought is of saving Antigone," but he certainly does not act on that thought. See also Bowra 111.

77. Benardete 3.163 has interesting observations on the importance of burning rather than burying the body, though he interprets its significance rather differently from the view set forth here.

78. Kamerbeek on line 1202 remarks, "The Messenger is not sparing of gruesome details. Among the last things we hear of Polyneices is this phrase so awfully suggestive of Creon's cruelty."

79. On the Blabai (personified) as the Erinyes here, echoing 1075, see Kamerbeek on line 1104.

80. On Antigone's legal status as *epiklēra* and Creon's obligations in that regard under Athenian law, see P. Roussel, "Les fiançailles d'Haimon et d'Antigone," *REG* 25 (1922) 63–70.

81. One may wonder whether Pluto in 1200 (only here in the play) may be an ironical echo of the now cancelled "wealth"—*ploutos*—of Creon's house in the first part of the Messenger's speech some thirty lines before (1168). This play on the two words is not uncommon: cf. *OT* 30 and Gellie 269–270.

82. The actual details of the cave and Haemon's entrance into it, however, are left characteristically vague: cf. Tycho von Wilamowitz-Moellendorff, *Die dramatische Technik des Sophokles* (Berlin 1917) 11–14; Carl Robert, *Oidipus* (Berlin 1915) I, 372ff.

83. As Jebb points out, 1224 can mean (a) "the destruction of his bride (who is) below" or (b) "the destruction of his marriage-bed, which is to be (only) below." Recent editors prefer (a): so Jebb, Mazon, Kamerbeek; but it is not impossible that the phrase is meant to contain both possibilities, especially after all the emphasis on Antigone's marriage to Hades in the lower world (e.g. 817). For the fusion of marriage and death in the imagery of the play throughout, see Goheen 37–41.

84. For the harbor as an image of ambiguous enclosure, doubling with the enclosing hollows of the earth in death, see *OT* 1208; Aesch., *Pers.* 250. The "hollow bridal chamber of Hades" in 1205 is perhaps also relevant here and provides another link of difference-in-similarity between Creon and Antigone. Such hollow enclosures frequently fluctuate between sheltering womb and all-engulfing tomb: compare *OT* 1262, *Trach.* 692 (the box that holds the love-charm-poison) and 901 with *Ajax* 1165, 1403, *Phil.* 1081. On the symbolism see John Hay, *Oedipus Tyrannus: Lame Knowledge and the Homosporic Womb* (Washington, D.C., 1978) 87ff., 104ff.

85. *Orthos* is among Creon's first words in his confident *gnōmē* about the gods' righting the ship of state, 162–163, repeated at 190; cf. also 83, 635–636, 685, 706, and the related *euthynein* of 178 and 1164. The metaphor of sailing on an upright ship recurs in a very different sense when Teiresias tells him that he "steers this ship on an upright course" because of his obedience to the prophet (993–994). The reversal in Creon's confidence about control is then marked by the Messenger's opening announcement at the peripety, "Chance (*tychē*) sets upright (*orthoi*) and chance inclines again the man of good fortune and the man of ill, always" (1158–59).

86. See Guépin (above, note 71) 141 and n35. For Antigone as the bride of Hades and the connections with Persephone, see Jebb on 1204, Kamerbeek on 801–805; H. J. Rose, "Antigone and the Bride of Corinth," *CQ* 19 (1925) 147–150; Roussel (above, note 80) 71, who points out also the inversion of the nuptial to the funeral procession.

87. With Danae's gold of fertilization contrast too the harsh "clashing of gold" of Thebes' defeated attackers in 130, which leads to the sterility of Antigone's house.

88. For the cave and the "in-between state" of Antigone, see Reinhardt 90 ("Gleichnis ihres Zwischenzustands, ihres wurzellosen Schwebens"). This heavy emphasis on the cave may be Sophocles' invention. According to Ion of Chios (740 Page) she was burnt with Ismene by a son of Eteocles in a temple of Hera.

89. For the male-female conflict, see 525, 678–680, 741, 756 and also Ismene in 61–62 and Creon in 290. See in general Segal 69–70; Kamerbeek on lines 484–485; Goheen 88; Kells (above, note 1) 51–52.

90. Of *kratē* in 484 Jebb says "deeds of might and so prevalence, victory"; see also *El.* 689.

91. In Aesch., *Sept.* 1031–32 Antigone laments the doom of her house connected with the burial of Polyneices with the cry, "Terrible the common womb—*koinon splanch-*

non—from which we were born from our wretched mother and ill-fated father." *Homos-planchnos* is used at *Sept.* 889–890 also in connection with the curse of the incestuous house, but in a somewhat different sense, as referring to the double fratricide. For *splanchna* of the womb and birth, see also Pindar, *Ol.* 6.43 and *Nem.* 1.45.

92. See Froma I. Zeitlin, "The Dynamics of Misogyny: Myth and Mythmaking in the *Oresteia,*" *Arethusa* 11 (1978) 149–184.

93. See in general Émile Benveniste, *Le vocabulaire des institutions indo-européennes* (Paris 1969) I, 212–215, 217–222.

94. Ibid. I, 222. Also p. 213: "Effectivement, *phrātēr* ne désigne pas le frère de sang; il s'applique à ceux qui sont reliés par une parenté mystique et se considèrent comme les descendants d'un même père."

95. The relation of the phratry to the significant political unit of the deme under Cleisthenes is not entirely clear. There seems to have been some overlap, and the phratries had some political significance: see W. K. Lacey, *The Family in Classical Greece* (Ithaca, N.Y., 1968) 92, 95–97.

96. See Benveniste (above, note 93) I, 221–222, 212–214.

97. Ibid. 219.

98. See Lacey (above, note 95) 90–99.

99. For Greek views of filiation in the mid-fifth century and their relation to these issues, see Zeitlin (above, note 92) passim, especially 168–174 with the references in the notes on pp. 180–181.

100. For these contradictions in Creon's use of the family as a model of civic order (cf. 659ff.), see Benardete 2.32–35.

101. See Zeitlin (above, note 92) 160ff.

102. See Benardete 1.152, 176, 183.

103. See e.g. 51–52, 56–57, 146, 172 of the two brothers; 864–865 of Oedipus' incest. Compounds in *auto-* also mark Antigone's defiant burial of her brother: 503, 696 and also 821, 875, 900. Note Creon's use of *autocheir* in 306 to brand the criminal nature of the burial. Cf. also 700, 1175, 1315, and Benardete (above, note 11) 1.149; Kamerbeek (above, note 4) on lines 49–52 and 172; Knox, *HT* 79; W. H. Will, "*Autadelphos* in the *Antigone* and the *Eumenides,*" *Studies presented to D. M. Robinson* (St. Louis 1951) 553–558. For *koinos* of the family curse cf. 146. The word also describes Antigone's exclusive allegiance to kin ties in 539 and 546. Contrast Creon's political usage ("common decree," 162) and the larger sense of the word beyond the perspectives of both protagonists in 1024, 1049, 1120.

104. The two passages contain the only occurrences of *splanchna* in this sense in the extant Sophocles. The word occurs one other time, in a different sense, at *Ajax* 995.

105. Note also Creon's use of *physis* as a criterion of authority in 727; contrast Haemon in 721. Goheen 89 remarks Antigone's "instinctive identification of *physis* and *nomos* as part of her identification of herself with a final order of things that is partly natural and partly divine."

106. For the word play see Benardete 3.176; for ancient awareness see Apollodorus, *Bibl.* 1.16.3 with Frazer's note, *ad loc.* in the Loeb Classical Library edition.

107. Note that in 172 Creon had himself used *autocheir* of the *miasma* of fraternal bloodshed in Antigone's house. In 306 he applies it to the illicit burial of the corpse in defiance of his decree. Cf. also 900.

108. Note also the possible echo between *phanētō . . . ho kallist'. . . hameran agōn* in 1329–30 and *to kalliston . . . phanen . . . hameras blepharon* in 100ff. Sophocles could hardly have expected many in his audience to catch this *Fernverbindung,* and yet it seems

too organically related to the structure of the play and to the obvious reversals in the imagery of light to be merely accidental. Creon is also echoing Antigone's words of 809–810 as he echoes the road image there too (*tan neatan hodon,* 807; *dystychestatēn keleuthon . . . hodon,* 1212–13; *agriais hodois,* 1274). I now find some of the contrasts between the parode and fifth stasimon discussed in Vincent J. Rosivach, "The Two Worlds of The *Antigone,*" *Illinois Class. Studies* 4 (1979) 25: Dionysus' light is "a light which shines in the night but does not fully dispel its darkness . . . Thebes itself has now become a city of darkness, not the city of light promised by the parodos." We may also compare the flash over Parnassus in 1126–27 with the failure of the flash of fire in 1007. Rosivach 25 n29 points out that this Parnassian flash is itself smoky (*sterops lignys*), and we may compare the smoky fire of perverted sacrifice and failed man-god mediation in *Trach.* 794, discussed above, chapter 4, section II.

109. For the interaction of Creon's *atē* and Antigone's, see Saïd (above, note 50) 199ff., 364–365.

110. The attempt to soften the tone of Antigone's words to Ismene at the end of the prologue by Parodi, (above, note 19) 100–101, is not successful. She does not, for example, cite 86–87.

111. See Kamerbeek and Jebb, with Jebb's Appendix 258–263.

112. There is much fluidity in the myth, and the exact form prior to Sophocles is uncertain: See T. von Wilamowitz (above, note 82) 15ff.; Robert (above, note 82) I, 349 and cf. 375 and 445; Roussel (above, note 80) 76ff.; Kamerbeek, Introduction 1–5. See also the additional references in the following two notes.

113. Roscher, *Lexicon* I.1 (1884–90) 372–373, s.v. "Antigone"; Meuli, s.v. "Laodamas" *RE* XII.1 (1924) 696–697.

114. Schol. *Antig.* 1350 and *Hypoth. Antig.* 9; see Jebb, Introduction xxxviii and n1; E. Bethe, s.v., "Antigone," *RE* I.2 (1894) 2402–2403. In Hyginus, *Fab.* 72 Haemon kills her when their marriage is discovered. Roussel (above, note 80) 79–81 argued against Robert (above, note 82) I, 366–367 that the marriage to Haemon had already been introduced into the myth prior to Sophocles, but firm evidence is lacking.

115. I follow Jebb, Kamerbeek, Dain-Mazon, and others in keeping the mss. reading, against Pearson's OCT. On this "rawness" see Knox, *HT* 23, 65; Bowra 87–88; C. S. Levy, "Antigone's Motives. A Suggested Interpretation," *TAPA* 94 (1963) 142; Gilberte Ronnet, *Sophocle, poète tragique* (Paris 1969) 148, remarks that *ōmos* "ne peut évoquer autre chose qu'une idée de sauvagerie, de dureté inhumaine."

116. Note the emphasis on eating through the repetition of the root *bora* (117) in the verb *bebrōtes,* 1022. On the connotations of animality in *bora,* see above, note 18.

117. Benardete 3.13.

118. See Hannah Arendt, *The Human Condition* (Garden City, N.Y., 1959) 27–34.

119. For these attitudes of ambivalence toward woman in fifth-century tragedy, see Philip Slater, *The Glory of Hera* (Boston 1968) and "The Greek Family in History and Myth," *Arethusa* 7 (1974) 9–44; also Zeitlin (above, note 92) passim.

120. Kurt Von Fritz, "Haimons Liebe zu Antigone," *Philologus* 89 (1934) 18–33 = *Antike und Moderne Tragödie* (Berlin 1962) 227–240, has argued that the love motif is relatively unimportant (21–22, 28–30 = 228–229, 236–237). Yet its presence and role in the catastrophe cannot be denied given the third stasimon and the strong sexual imagery of Haemon's death. For qualification of Von Fritz's view, see now Kamerbeek, Introduction 2; Coleman (above, note 25) 15–16.

121. We may perhaps compare Freud's notion of the diffusion and sublimation of eros into friendships and the cooperative, "aim-inhibited" relationships that make society

possible; see *Civilization and Its Discontents,* trans. Joan Riviere (Garden City, N.Y., 1958) 49. On the shifting values of *philia* in the play, see Knox *H T* 80ff.; Dalfen (above, note 58) 23–26; Victor Ehrenberg, *Sophocles and Pericles* (Oxford 1954) 31; William Arrowsmith, "The Criticism of Greek Tragedy," *Tulane Drama Review,* 3.3 (1959) 42–43.

122. See Benardete 2.34.

123. Aesch., *PV* 90; Hom. Hymns 30.1 with the note of Sikes-Allen-Halliday (Oxford 1936) *ad loc.;* Meleager, *Anth. Pal.* 5.164.1; *Epigrammata Graeca* 823.4 Kaibel; *Orphica,* frag. 168.27 Kern. See in general Roscher, *Lexicon* I.2 (1886–90) 1570 s.v. "Gaia": Benardete 1.192. Only here does the epithet seem to be applied to a mortal woman.

124. See in general Eur., *Phoen.* 915–1018, 1090–92. In Aesch., *Sept.* 474, Creon's son, "seed of Creon, of the race of the Sown Men," is also called Megareus, but nothing is said of him except his assignment at the gates by Eteocles. For the myth and probable identification of Megareus and Menoeceus, see Francis Vian, *Les origines de Thèbes, Cadmos et les Spartes* (Paris 1963) 212–215; Jebb on line 1303; Kamerbeek on line 995; Benardete 2.30, 3.183–184. Doubts about the identification are raised by Robert (above, note 82) I, 356ff. and note 45 in vol. II, p. 125; Louis Méridier in *Euripide,* Budé ed., 5 (Paris 1950) 138.

125. Note, for example, the sinister significance of "earth-born" in *Trach.* 1058–59 and Eur., *Bacch.* 538ff. and 995–996, and see C. Segal, "Euripides' *Bacchae:* Conflict and Mediation," *Ramus* 6 (1977) 108–109, 115; Vernant, *MP* I, 27–28. For Creon's failure to consider the myth of the Spartoi in his conception of his city of Thebes, see Benardete 3.156, 183–184.

126. For the problems of text and interpretation of the difficult passage, 125–126, see Jebb and Kamerbeek.

127. Benardete 3.177.

128. See Ronnet (above, note 115) 27.

129. See Laszlo Versényi, *Man's Measure* (Albany, N.Y., 1974) 197–198, 209; K. Kerényi, "Dionysos und das Tragische in der Antigone," *Frankfurter Studien* 13 (1935) 8: "Ihr Kampf ist eine Erneuerung des alten Götterkampfes, in dem die titanischen Naturkräfte und die Götter des ungeistigen Lebensdienstes und der Blutsverbindung den neuen Göttern, den geistigen Mächten, die in der Welt der klassischen Schönheit herrschen, unterlagen."

130. Cf. also 178 and 203, where Creon emphasizes the solidarity of the whole city under his laws. Later, however, Haemon presents a different view of civic solidarity in relation to both Antigone (693, 733) and Creon (737–739).

131. See Schmid (above, note 2) 15, "Auf diese Anerkennung der Erfolge des Rationalismus fällt aber ein kalter Strahl durch die Worte *Haida.*" On the importance of the theme of death and Hades, see also Ehrenberg (above, note 121) 26–27; Kerényi (above, note 129) 9–10; also above, note 51.

132. Anonymus Iamblichi 7.3 and 7.5 in DK, vol. II, 403. For some of the issues discussed here, see Segal 83–85.

133. The discounting of the odes by A.J.A. Waldock, *Sophocles the Dramatist* (Cambridge 1951) 115ff. as mere "lyric interlude," "lyrical embroidery," "tangential" (115, 117, 121) is rightly criticized by I. Errandonea, "Das 4. Stasimon der Antigone von Sophokles,' *SO* 30 (1953) 17; see also Errandonea's remarks on the links between the third and fourth stasima, "Sophoclei Chori Persona Tragica," *Mnemosyne,* ser. II, 51 (1923) 183–185. See in general Goheen chap. 4. For further discussion of the relation among the odes of the play along the lines presented here, see C. Segal, "Sophocles'

Antigone: The House and the Cave," *Miscellanea di Studi in memoria di Marino Barchiesi* (Rome 1978 [1980]) 1181–87.

134. See Segal (above, note 4) passim.

135. On the imagery of alternating light and dark in the second stasimon, see especially Goheen 58ff.; also above, note 108. On the ode in general, see Easterling (above, note 62) 141–158.

136. For the theme of wedding death, see 654, 750, 804–805, 816, 891–892, 1205, 1240–41, 1224, 1303. See Errandonea, "Sophoclei Chori" (above, note 133) 193; Goheen 37–41, who remarks: "But it is just in this building of severe tension between different realms of essential life that the fused imagery of marriage and death has its fullest bearing within the play."

137. For the affinity of Hades and Eros in the main antitheses of the play, see Bultmann (above, note 58) 319: "Aber auch sie gehören als jenseitige, alles Menschliche begrenzende und relativierend Mächte zusammen." See also Albin Lesky, "Sophokles und das Humane" (1951) in H. Diller, A. Lesky. W. Schadewalt, *Gottheit und Mensch in der Tragödie des Sophokles* (Darmstadt 1963) 68.

138. On the third stasimon, see Von Fritz (above, note 120) 26ff. = 234ff. He also points out how Haemon becomes another instrument to punish Creon and another victim of the curse of the Labdacids (p. 28 = 236). See also Coleman (above, note 25) 15–16.

139. For the problems of the fourth stasimon, see Goheen 68ff.; Bowra 104–105; Errandonea's essays (above, note 133) 16ff. and 181ff. respectively, and also "Über Sophokles, Antigone 944–987," *Philol. Wochenschrift* 50 (1930) 1373–75; Müller (above, note 49) 414–415; Kitto, *Form* 171ff. Hester (above, note 25) 38–39 gives a useful brief review of previous scholarship, though I cannot accept his view of the ode as "a lyrical interlude to release the tension before the final battle" (39); if there is anything that this complicated and dark ode does *not* do, it is releasing tension. More to the point is Coleman (above, note 25) 20–22, who concludes (22): "This confession that suffering has no ultimate moral meaning, no sure justification, makes the fourth stasimon one of the most disturbing odes in Greek tragedy, and its bewildered pessimism is a grim farewell indeed to the abject princess."

140. Bengt Alexanderson, "Die Stellung des Chors in der Antigone," *Eranos* 64 (1966) 99–100, stresses the links between Creon and Lycurgus; cf. Lycurgus' "insulting tongue," *kertomiai glōssai* (961–962) and Creon's vehemence in passages like 1039–40. Alexanderson well observes that the myths here, though ostensibly relevant to Antigone, also have an application to Creon; and that fact would be in accordance with the ambiguity of *hypsipolis/apolis* in the first stasimon. See also Müller (above, note 49) 414.

141. Müller (preceding note) 416 n1: "Die wilde Landschaft am thrakischen Bosporos liefert den Hintergrund für das Blutvergiessen: hier gibt es keine Humanität."

142. Müller, ibid. 416 gives a good paraphrase: "Die beiden Augenhöhlen scheinen als Fluchgeister (*alastoroisin,* v. 974) nach Rache." Note also the recurrence of the verb *arattō,* in different forms, of the two acts of blinding, 52 and 975, another link between the fourth stasimon and the family curse of Antigone. For the importance of the motif of blinding in the tale of Phineus' children, see Goheen 71–72 who detects a further warning to Creon, even though the ode is offered, ostensibly, as a lesson to Antigone.

143. On this reversal see Benardete 1.167, who also points out the echo between 148 and 1115.

144. For the contrast between the two deaths of Antigone and Creon, fullness versus emptiness, see Reinhardt 102–103.

145. See above chapter 2, section I, and notes 13–14.

146. Kitto, *Form* 155; see also his further comments, p. 176.

147. The fifth stasimon has received surprisingly little attention. Kitto, *Form* and Müller (above, note 49) pass over it quickly, the latter calling attention to the similarities to hyporchemes like *Ajax* 693ff. or *OT* 1086ff. (p. 418). Bowra 110–111 confesses himself surprised by its "note of wild exultation" and interprets it didactically as a reflection of excessive confidence that holds "a lesson in store." Goheen 45 sees a link with the ode on Eros in the theme of crossing the sea (cf. 785 and 1117–19). Errandonea, "Sophoclei Chori," (above, note 133) 198–200 seems to me to tie the ode down too narrowly to specific characters. Kerényi (above, note 129) 10–14 has some suggestive but rather mystical remarks on the Dionysiac element in the tragedy. Paul Vicaire, "Place et figure de Dionysos dans la tragédie de Sophocle," *REG* 81 (1968) 358ff., stresses the bacchantic quality, but seems to me to lay too much emphasis on the positive, "integrated" nature of Dionysus in civic cult (p. 369). The ode, I believe, is meant to strike a note of dissonance in keeping with the movement of the action, reflecting the problematical mixture of beauty and violence, calm and passion, in the outside world as within man: nature, like man in stasimon I, moves now to evil, now to good. The contrast with the Dionysiac mood *within* Thebes in the parode is here particularly important: see Rosivach (above, note 108) 21.

148. For the local, Theban associations of Dionysus, see also 152–154, 1136–37: see Vicaire (preceding note) 360–365; Goheen 146 n34; Ehrenberg (above, note 121) 6, with good remarks on the problem of incorporating Dionysus into the city as a polis-god. On the other hand, Dionysus' relation to Thebes remains somewhat ambiguous, as Euripides' *Bacchae* makes clear. That relation to Thebes, after all, involves the violent death of his mother, Semele, alluded to in 1139, *matri . . . kerauniāi*. A variant legend also made Dionysus the sender of the Sphinx: schol. on Eur., *Phoen.* 1031.

149. See Vicaire (above, note 147) 361; Guépin (above, note 71) 269–270; Pindar, *Isth.* 7.3–5 with scholia *ad loc.* For the identification of Iacchus and Dionysus and its problems, see most recently Fritz Graf, *Eleusis und die orphische Dichtung Athens in vor-hellenistischer Zeit* (Berlin and New York 1974) 51ff.

150. See chapter 3, above, and notes 26–27.

151. For the theme of madness, see also 135, 765, 790, 959, 962 and cf. also 492 and 633. Jebb remarks on lines 135ff. that "this is the only place where Soph. connects *evil* frenzy with the name of a god whom this same Ode invokes (154)."

152. Compare Eur., *Ion* 1078ff. (the aether and the moon dancing with the chorus); there too, however, there are ominous overtones of perverted ritual: a beginning with Hecate and an ending with death (cf. 1048ff.). Cf. also *Helen* 1454–55, where the Phoenician ship that will save Helen is "chorus-leader of the lovely-dancing dolphins" (*chorage tōn kallichorōn / delphinōn*), a possible reminiscence of the *Antigone*. For Dionysus' astral associations, especially with the Hyades, termed "the Nurses of Dionysus," see Phyllis Ackerman, "Stars and Stories," in Henry A. Murray, ed., *Myth and Mythmaking* (New York, N.Y., 1960) 96–97.

153. For Dionysus' role as a fertility god, especially at Thebes, where he may have functioned as the young consort of the Great Mother in prehistoric times, see B. Moreux, *REG* 83 (1970) 1–14; H. Jeanmaire, *Dionysos* (Paris 1951) 211–214; E. R. Dodds, *Euripides, Bacchae*[2] (Oxford 1960) 76–77.

154. In Eur., *Phoen.* 1010 the human sacrifice involves leaping into the dragon's "precinct of dark depths" (*sēkon es melambathē*). This earlier threat to the polis, then, also has to do with a cave in the earth. Euripides does not call the dragon's den specifically a cave (cf. *thalamai, Phoen.* 931); but the dragon himself is closely associated with the earth

("earthborn," *Phoen*. 931, 935) and, as the guardian of Dirce's streams (932), is also connected with subterranean places. The victim sacrificed to him must give his blood "to the earth" (933).

155. In this connection we may also think of Lévi-Strauss's analysis of the Oedipus myth (see above, chapter 2, note 12) and his focus on the problem of born from earth or born from men. Our analysis would redirect the former element in the dichotomy from autochthony per se to the ambiguous relation to civilization, house and wild, reflected in the myth of Oedipus.

156. Max Scheler, "On the Tragic" (1923), in Lionel Abel, ed., *Moderns on Tragedy* (New York, N.Y., 1967) 254.

7 Oedipus Tyrannus

1. Marie Delcourt, *Oedipe ou la légende du conquérant* (Liège and Paris 1944) 3, points out that Oedipus and Paris are the only children exposed by their own parents (as opposed to an uncle, grandfather, stepfather).

2. Cf. Aristophanes, *Clouds* 1427–28; *Birds* 755ff. and 1343ff.; see K. J. Dover, *Aristophanes, Clouds* (Oxford 1968) on line 1427; J.-P. Vernant, "Ambiguïté et renversement: Sur la structure énigmatique d' 'Oedipe Roi,' " in *MT* 128–129; also Knox, *Oedipus* 43 and n79, citing Dio Chrys. 10.29–30. Cf. also Seneca, *Oedipus* 639–640, *quique vix mos est feris / fratres sibi ipse genuit,* and *Hippol.* 913–914, *ferae quoque ipsae Veneris evitant nefas / generisque leges inscius servat pudor.*

3. See Vernant, *MT* 117ff.; J. P. Guépin, *The Tragic Paradox* (Amsterdam 1968) 86ff. with the references there cited; Thalia Philies Howe [Feldman], "Taboo in the Oedipus Theme," *TAPA* 93 (1962) 139; Francis Fergusson, *The Idea of a Theater* (Princeton 1949) 26ff. For further discussion of the *pharmakos* ritual, see Ludwig Deubner, *Attische Feste* (Berlin 1932) 187ff.; Erwin Rohde, *Psyche*[8], trans. W. B. Hillis (London 1925) 296 and n87, 321 with the references there cited; Walter Burkert, *Griechische Religion der archaischen und klassischen Epoche,* Die Religionen der Menschheit 15 (Stuttgart, Berlin, Köln, Mainz 1977) 139–142.

4. *Odyssey* 11.275–276.

5. For the problems of this line and the meaning of *trophē*, see A. D. Fitton-Brown, "Oedipus and the Delegation," *CQ* n.s. 2 (1952) 2–4; Kamerbeek, *The Plays of Sophocles,* IV, *The Oedipus Tyrannus* (Leiden 1967) *ad loc.*, who aptly cites from Racine's *Esther,* "de l'antique Jacob jeune posterité." For a searching stylistic and thematic analysis of the line, see the excellent remarks of Gellie 264–266. H. F. Johansen, *Lustrum* 7 (1962) 235 rightly criticizes Fitton-Brown's doubts about "a beautiful and perfectly intelligible line." For *trophē* in the sense of "offspring," cf. also Eur., *Cyclops* 189.

6. Sky is also involved in Oedipus' "cloud of darkness . . . borne on ill-omened wind" at 1314–15. For the totality of the disease and its implications, see Marie Delcourt, *Stérilités mystérieuses et naissances maléfiques dans l'antiquité classique* (Liège and Paris 1938) 31ff., and see Gellie (above, note 5) 79–81.

7. On the ironic reversals in Oedipus' movement from *tyrannos* (ruler by usurpation) and *basileus* (inherited kingship), see Knox, *Oedipus* 55–57, also 32.

8. See Delcourt, (above, note 1) 4ff.; Otto Rank, *The Myth of the Birth of the Hero and Other Writings,* ed. Philip Freund (New York, N.Y. 1964); Lord Raglan, *The Hero* (London 1936).

9. See Aesch., *PV* 450; cf. also Eur., *Suppl.* 201–202; Hippocrates, *Ancient Medicine* c. 3.

10. Alister Cameron, *The Identity of Oedipus the King* (New York 1968) 68, points out that the gods in fact do save Thebes, but so does Oedipus: he reenacts 442–443 in the course of the play itself. On the role of *tychē*, see Knox, *Oedipus* 164–168, 176ff.; Bowra 198–199, 207–208; Victor Ehrenberg, *Sophocles and Pericles* (Oxford 1954) 69–70.

11. Pearson's reading, *kalon*, taken ironically, gives attractive sense, though it is found only in citations by Eustathius. The mss. (followed here) have *deinon*, "Terrible the insult . . . of my swaddling clothes," retained by R. C. Jebb, *Sophocles, the Plays and Fragments,* Part I, *Oedipus Tyrannus* (Cambridge, 1893).

12. See G. E. Dimock, Jr., "The Name of Odysseus," *Hudson Review* 9 (1956) 52–70; Norman Austin, "Name-Magic in the *Odyssey,*" *Calif. Studies in Class. Antiquity* 5 (1972) 1–19. The reverse process, the loss of a name, is a part of King Richard's loss of his crown and his kingship in Shakespeare, *Richard II,* IV.i.255–259: "I have no name, no title;/No, not that name was given me at the font,/But 'tis usurp'd. Alack the heavy day,/That I have worn so many winters out/And know not now what name to call myself!"

13. Schol. on Plato, *Theaetet.* 160e; Hesych. s.v. *Amphidromion ēmar.* For further discussion and references, see J.-P. Vernant, *MP* I, 161–164; N. J. Richardson, *The Homeric Hymn to Demeter* (Oxford 1974) 231ff. (on *h.Dem.* 231–255); Lise and Pierre Brind'Amour, "Le *dies lustricus,* les oiseaux de l'aurore et l'amphidromie," *Latomus* 34 (1975) 51ff.

14. For the play on *Plutos/Plouton* here, see Gellie 269–270. Note also Oedipus' vulnerable "wealth" in 380. It is in Hades, of course, not in the house, that Jocasta will rejoice in her rich family (*plousiōi genei,* 1070); and it is the knowledge of that reunion in Hades that Oedipus gives as his chief motive for his self-blinding (1369–74).

15. See Knox, *Oedipus* 147ff. and also his "Sophocles' Oedipus," in *Tragic Themes in Western Literature,* ed. Cleanth Brooks (New Haven 1955) 15ff. See in general F. D. Harvey, "Two Kinds of Equality," *C & M* 26 (1965) 101–146, with further bibliography.

16. On the symmetry between ostracism and the expulsion of the *pharmakos,* see Vernant, *MT* 125–126; Burkert (above, note 3) 140.

17. See Vernant, *MT* 108.

18. For 425 I follow the reading of the mss. and Jebb, ἅ σ' ἐξισώσει σοί τε καὶ τοῖς σοῖς τέκνοις. Wilamowitz, followed by Pearson in the OCT, reads ὅσ' ἐξισώσεις, "which you shall level equally on yourself and your children." With Jebb, I feel that the change, though easy, is unnecessary and weakens the sense. For this theme see also 1250, 1405ff., 1485, 1496–99.

19. See the schol. on line 16: "For they are there at the altars before the king's palace as if at the altars of the gods." See also Knox, *Oedipus* 159, 181–182; Vernant, *MT* 114; Whitman 126.

20. This opening of the Sphinx's riddle, reported by several ancient sources (cf. Eur., *Phoen.* Hypothesis and schol. on line 50; Athenaeus 10.456B) probably predates Sophocles' play; part of it appears on a famous red-figure vase of ca. 470 B.C. showing Oedipus and the Sphinx, now in the Vatican museum. See Carl Robert, *Oidipus* (Berlin 1915) I, 56 and II, 24 n21; Eduard Fraenkel, *Aeschylus, Agamemnon* (Oxford 1950) p. 581; Kamerbeek, Introduction 5. Cf. also the riddle in Eur., *Oidipous,* frag. II Austin = *P. Oxy.* 2459. 20ff.

21. For these counting patterns, see also 605–606, 715, 1062, 1275, 1280, 1398. Significant alternation of singular and plural occurs also at 60–69, 292–293, 750, 1097 (plurality of mothers and fathers). See in general Knox, *Oedipus* 151–154 and n147, p. 252; Kamerbeek, Introduction, 13; Vernant *MT* 105 and n12; W. C. Greene, "The

Murderers of Laius," *TAPA* 60 (1929) 75–86. On lines 122–124 W. B. Stanford, *Ambiguity in Greek Literature* (Oxford 1939) 166 remarks, "The use of the singular by Oedipus after Creon has emphasized the plural is significant and carefully phrased to be so by Sophocles." Most recently, Sandor Goodhart, "*Lē(i)stas ephaske:* Oedipus and Laius' Many Murderers," *Diacritics* 8.1 (Spring 1978) 55–71, focuses on the logical structure involved in the problem of numbers; and John Hay, *Oedipus Tyrannus: Lame Knowledge and the Homosporic Womb* (Washington, D.C., 1978) is concerned with the problem of "nondistinction and indiscriminate border-crossing" (p. 104) implied in the movements from oneness to plurality: "(Oedipus) has returned to a pre-ontogenic state, corresponding in turn to the pre-cosmogonic state of Chaos, a state of oneness, sameness, identity, total integration. Then, by an ordeal of initiation, he is reborn back into the world of differentiation and plurality, but being now, in some sense, in touch with the secrets of the world, of the scheme of things." See my review in *CW* 72 (1978–79) 432–433. Oedipus would seem to use the shelter of plurality to escape the terrible oneness of his identity, which is also synonymous with the fearful oneness of his incestuous marriage. Having come too soon and too fully to this oneness in this union with the origins of his life, he perpetually shapes strategies of delusion about numbers to conceal the plurality of names beneath the apparent oneness of his identity (son *and* husband, brother *and* father, legitimate heir *and* usurper). Conversely, the one thing he cannot confront and must evade is the awful oneness or sameness of that "homosporic womb" where he is both sown and sower. From a different point of view, where the normal path of the male's development is separation from the mother and the differentiation of the important female figure in his life into two, a mother and a wife, Oedipus counts only to one. Jocasta, by opposing the spirit of logical calculation with the optimism of inconsequentiality (cf. 977ff.), ironically only furthers calculation and its dread results. For a moment the two change places without realizing it: Oedipus uses analysis to keep away the only reasonable conclusion before him, while Jocasta dismisses that conclusion with her instinctive hold on life. To that hold on life she would gladly sacrifice logic, but in her ignorance she only furthers its inexorable march.

22. On the verbs of walking in 798ff., see Hay (preceding note) 83. Laius, of course, does not walk, but rides upon his chariot, *apēnēs embebōs* (803).

23. See Seth Benardete, "Sophocles' Oedipus Tyrannus," in Thomas Woodard, ed., *Sophocles. A Collection of Critical Essays* (Englewood Cliffs, N.J., 1966) 105–121, especially 111: "His defect, however, by placing him outside the species-characteristic of man, allowed him to see the species-characteristic."

24. Cf. 1292–93. Note, too, Hesiod's image of man as a tripod in winter, *Opera* 533–535. For Oedipus' reliving the riddle in his own life, see Lattimore, *Poetry* 91; Oliver Taplin, *Greek Tragedy in Action* (Berkeley and Los Angeles 1978) 152–153; Kamerbeek 25.

25. On the multiple meanings of the *skēptron*, see Benardete (above, note 23) 106; Taplin (preceding note) 110; Hay (above, note 21) 31–33.

26. Friedrich Nietzsche, *The Birth of Tragedy,* ix, in *The Birth of Tragedy and the Genealogy of Morals,* trans. Francis Golffing (Garden City, N.Y., 1956) 61.

27. Sigmund Freud, *Civilization and Its Discontents,* trans. Joan Riviere (Garden City, N.Y., 1958) 35; see also Gilberte Ronnet, "Le sentiment du tragique chez les Grecs," *REG* 76 (1963) 329.

28. For "yoking" as a sexual metaphor with bestial associations, see also *Trach.* 536, frag. 538.11N = 583.11P (*Tereus*). In Eur., *Phoen.* 25 the pierced ankles are also described in the beast metaphor of *kentra,* "iron goads."

29. See Gellie 267–268; also above, note 6.

30. See Howe (above, note 3) 127ff. with the further references there cited; Delcourt, (above, note 6) 31ff.; Benardete (above, note 23) 107, who cites Xenophon, *Mem.* 4.4.20–23.

31. Paul Vicaire, "Place et figure de Dionysos dans la tragédie de Sophocle," *REG* 81 (1968) 366, seems to miss the ambiguities and sinister overtones of Dionysus here when he insists on his protective and purificatory functions as a civic god.

32. There is a lacuna in the text of 214–215, but the precise word to be restored does not seriously affect our interpretation: see Kamerbeek (above, note 5).

33. Most translations miss the effect of this juxtaposition, blurring the sense of one of the key words. Knox, *Oedipus* 81 also calls attention to the political or juridical meaning, "What is investigated can bring capture and conviction . . . ; what is neglected allows escape and acquittal"; see also 111ff. and nn 6–8, 234.

34. Aesch., *Ch.* 752–760; cf. also Plato, *Timaeus* 44a–b; in general see above, chapter 2, section VI.

35. See Arnold Van Gennep, *The Rites of Passage* (1908; Engl. trans. Chicago 1960); P. Vidal-Naquet, "The Black Hunter and the Origin of the Athenian Ephebeia," *PCPS* n.s. 14 (1968) 49–64 and "Les jeunes: Le cru, l'enfant grec et le cuit," in J. Le Goff and P. Nora, eds., *Faire de l'histoire* (Paris 1974) 3, 137–168; H. Jeanmaire, *Couroi et Courètes* (Lille 1939); A. Brelich, *Paides e parthenoi,* Incunabula Graeca 36 (Rome 1969).

36. Contrast the version reported by Jocasta in Eur., *Phoen.* 39–41: the driver of Laius' chariot is quoted directly as asking Oedipus to stand out of the way of the king; Oedipus moves, "saying nothing, but thinking proud thoughts," and he strikes Laius down when the horses tread on his feet. See also the version of Nicolaus of Damascus discussed by Robert (above, note 20) I,81–82. In Eur., *Suppl.* 669–674 the absence of reply by a herald is considered a violation of civilized behavior.

37. Euripides makes the inversion of human and bestial in the scene even more explicit by having the blow that provokes the quarrel come not from Laius, but from the horses trampling and injuring Oedipus' feet (*Phoen.* 41–42), a symbolical reenactment of the father's ancient crime against his son's means of locomotion. In Peisander's version the "goad" of Sophocles is replaced by a whip (schol. on *Phoen.* 1760).

38. For the ambiguity of *physis* here, see H.D.F. Kitto, *Sophocles, Dramatist and Philosopher* (London 1958) 60.

39. Oedipus meets Laius at that crossroads because Oedipus has just come from consulting the oracle (787ff.) and has just been given the "fearful and unhappy" prophecies (790–793). We are not told why Laius is going to Delphi (see Kamerbeek, 9 and comment on line 114), but it is a good guess that he is consulting Apollo about the Sphinx (cf. 126ff.), much as Oedipus, at the beginning of the play, sends Creon to consult the oracle about the plague. We should note too the emphasis on the oracle given Laius in Jocasta's speech, 711ff. In Eur., *Phoen.* 36, Laius goes to Delphi to ask about his exposed son. Earlier versions of the myth placed the meeting at Potniae, on the road between Thebes and Plataea, with Laius going as *theōros* to Delphi and Oedipus going to Orchomenos to seek horses: cf. Aesch., frag. 173N, schol. on *OT* 733, and see Robert (above, note 20) I,82–83, 273, and 2.32 n49; Kamerbeek 6. The shift to Delphi has obvious dramatic and thematic advantages which Sophocles certainly discerned. Sophocles himself, however, may not have been the innovator of the change but may be reworking material which had already undergone revision under Delphic influence: see Jebb xviii–xix; Robert (above, note 20) I,102–104; Cameron (above, note 10) 10.

40. Note too a possible echo of the "double goad" of 809 in the "double grief" and "double woes" of 1320.

41. Note especially 924–926, "a fantastic conjugation of a verb 'to know where,' " remarks Knox, *Oedipus* 184 and see his discussion 182–184; Benardete (above, note 23) 112–113; Vernant *MT* 113–114; Philip Vellacott, *Sophocles and Oedipus: A Study of the Oedipus Tyrannus* (London 1971) 131–134. Note also the play in *empedon . . . pros podi* in 128–130 and the occurrence of *oida* or its compounds 5 times in 40 lines as the discovery becomes imminent (1008, 1014, 1038, 1041, 1048); other verbs of knowing occur six times in the next thirty lines (1054, 1065, 1066, 1068, 1078, 1085).

42. Oedipus' "knowing where" is also related to the Sophoclean hero's sense of being "in" a place: see Otfried Becker, *Das Bild des Weges,* Hermes Einzelschrift 4 (1937) 197–198.

43. The Shepherd's *dystēnos,* "unfortunate," in 1155 could be taken as a cry of lamentation for himself, but it can also easily be understood as an exclamation in the nominative for Oedipus; see Jebb. The latter is the more likely, in fact, because of the nominative participle *proschrē(i)zōn,* in the same line, which unambiguously refers to Oedipus.

44. For the connection with Herodotus, see J. T. Sheppard, *The Oedipus Tyrannus of Sophocles* (Cambridge 1920) on line 719 (p. 147).

45. For the inversions of inner and outer, see Thomas Hoey, "Introversion in the *Oedipus Rex,"* *CJ* 64 (1968/69) 296–299. In Homer strangers (*xenoi*) may also be "outlaws" who live with no fixed abode in a city, but "roam randomly over the sea" and wander "hazarding their lives, bringing trouble to men of other lands" (*Odyssey* 3.71–74). The heavy ironies of being both near and distant develops early in the play; see especially 137–138 and 264–265, with the scholia *ad loc.* See also Stanford (above, note 21) 167. In another perspective, this paradoxical state by which the alien is also the familiar and vice versa relates to the play's philosophical concern with the problem of illusion and reality.

46. See Hay (above, note 21) 113–114; also P. Rödström, *De Imaginibus Sophocleis a Rerum Natura Sumptis* (Stockholm 1883) 33. Cf. Theocr. *Idylls* 14.43, on the "bull in the woodland" which, once loosed, is not easily recaptured.

47. Compare the fifth stasimon of *Antigone.* On the setting see Vellacott (above, note 41) 233.

48. The reading *nomad(a)* in 1350 is not entirely certain; it is Elmsley's emendation for *nomados,* and is widely accepted. The word can probably have both meanings, "shepherd" and "wandering" (for the latter see Jebb). The meaning "wandering" will then stand in a kind of oxymoron with the "fetters" that bind fast in the preceding line.

49. For such "anagrammatic" devices see Pietro Pucci, "On the 'Eye' and the 'Phallos' and other Permutabilities in *Oedipus Rex,"* in *Arktouros, Hellenic Studies Presented to Bernard M.W. Knox on the Occasion of his 65th Birthday* (Berlin and New York 1979) 131–132. For the inversion of life and death, cf. also 1453–54. See P. W. Harsh, "Implicit and Explicit in the *Oedipus Tyrannus,"* *AJP* 79 (1958) 258.

50. For example, 793, 1007, 1012, 1404, 1514; cf. also 1482.

51. Both Jocasta and the Sphinx commit suicide by falling: cf. Vickers 183–184. For the ominous associations of falling and heights in the play, see also Lattimore (above, note 24) 96ff.; Musurillo 89–91.

52. Cf. also 380–381, where Oedipus accuses Teiresias in terms of envy excited by "skill that reaches above skill," *technē technēs hyperpherousa.* On the implicit reference to Oedipus in 876ff., see G. H. Gellie, "The Second Stasimon of the *Oedipus Tyrannus,"AJP* 85 (1964) 113–123.

53. See Vernant, *MT* 122.

54. Jacqueline de Romilly, *Time in Greek Tragedy* (Ithaca, N.Y., 1968) 107 and, on time in general in the *OT* 107–110; also Tom F. Driver, *The Sense of History in Greek and Shakespearean Drama* (New York, N.Y. 1960) 154–159, 161.

55. See also Homer, *Odyssey* 18.136–137; Soph., *Antig.* 788–789, and in general above, chapter 5, note 7.

56. The Greeks could, in fact, conceive of time as an active force: cf. Pindar, *Nem.* 1.46ff., *Ol.* 10.54ff.; see D. E. Gerber, "What Time Can Do," *TAPA* 93 (1962) 30–33; Paolo Vivante, "On Time in Pindar," *Arethusa* 5 (1972) 107–131.

57. For measuring and its ironies, see Knox, *Oedipus* 147–158.

58. With Jocasta's *algos* or "illness" in 638 contrast the exchange between her and Oedipus in 1066–67: "Understanding well, I am telling you what is best."—"That 'best' has been my illness (*algos*) now for a long time." Disease, of course, is a dominant image throughout the play, from the prologue on (10–11). Here in 638 the disease and its pain (*algos*) move dangerously from the public to the private realm, from the city to Oedipus himself, a reflection in microcosm of what happens in the plot as a whole.

59. Note too the "great eye," *megas ophthalmos*, of the death of Oedipus' supposed father in 986, with the word *megas* repeated in 987. On the theme of "greatness" in the play, see H.-J. Mette, "Der 'grosse Mensch,' " *Hermes* 89 (1961) 332–344.

60. Jocasta, trying to turn Oedipus away from the "old," *palai*, in this scene uses the word three times (916, 947, 973), until Oedipus, rejecting her good sense, throws it back at her in his determination to confront that old disease, his ignorance which has been paining him of old (*algynei palai*, 1067). In the closing section of the play too *palai* is a reminder of the distance which Oedipus has traversed to uncover the destructive force of what lies buried of old in his past: 1214, 1226, 1245, 1282, 1394–95.

61. Note "long time" in 1141; "young" in 1145; "old man" in 1153; "long ago" in 1161.

62. See Knox, *Oedipus* chap. 3, 116ff.; P. Vidal-Naquet, *Sophocle, Tragédies* (Paris 1973), Introduction 30.

63. Cf. the "fire-bearing god" in 27, 200, 206; the fire of the plague and Ares in 167, 174–178, 190–192; Apollo's fire in 469–470; Oedipus' wish to hide from the sun's "all-nourishing fire" when he is the revealed pollution in 1425.

64. See Delcourt (above, note 1) 105.

65. For the ironies of saving and loosing in the play, see the excellent remarks of Knox, *Oedipus* 137–138. For the sinister associations of loosing, see also 879–881, where the chorus, after singing the dangers of hybris, alludes to Oedipus in the "useful foot" of 878 and then goes on to pray that the "god may never *loose* the wrestling that benefits the city."

66. See Sheppard (above, note 44) 101, who aptly cites Aristotle, *Pol.* 3. 1284a3ff. apropos of 33–34 and the godlike citizen in the polis. In addition to the passages cited in the text, see also 515 and, if genuine, 1527, on the sinister connotation of *symphora;* in 1527 god-man boundaries are also in question: cf. 1528.

67. See U. von Wilamowitz-Moellendorff, *Griechische Tragödie übersetzt* I (Berlin 1899) 12–13 (Introduction to the translation of *OT*).

68. Kamerbeek points out the contrast between 38 and 396–398.

69. See Vellacott (above, note 41) 188.

70. See E. Schlesinger, "Erhaltung im Untergang," *Poetica* 3 (1970) 380–381.

71. See Girard chap. 3.

72. See Cameron (above, note 10) 67–68, esp. 68: "The Corinthian is certainly an odd figure as the answer to a prayer for 'cleansing deliverance,' but that is precisely what he is, and the irony of it, of course, belongs to the gods." For this ironical answer to a prayer compare also the Paedagogus' entrance in apparent answer to Clytaemnestra's prayer at *El.* 660.

73. Note also how the repetition of "honor" (*timiai, timai*) in 895 and 909 link together the two aspects of the chorus' concern, dance and oracles.

74. For the overlap between riddle and oracle, see also Sophocles, frag. 771P; also Kamerbeek, "Sophocle et Héraclite," *Studia Vollgraff* 88, citing Heraclitus 22B93DK. In Aesch., *Ag.* 1112–13 riddles and oracles are also associated; this is also a passage where communication with the gods and the divine *logos* to men are ambiguous: see Fraenkel's note (above, note 20) on *Ag.* 1112–13; also Taplin (above, note 24) 44 and 152–153.

75. Schol. on Eur., *Phoen.* 1760 and 45; see Delcourt (above, note 1) 135.

76. See Aesch., *Sept.* 541; Pindar, frag. 177 Snell; Eur., *Phoen.* 1025 and 1505, *El.* 471–472. For more details see Robert (above, note 20) I,517ff.; Lesky, s.v. "Sphinx," *RE* III A 2 (1929) 1712ff.; Höfer, s.v. "Oidipus (und die Sphinx)," Roscher, *Lexicon* III.1 (1897–1909) 715ff. Euripides' *Oedipus* contained a detailed description of the Sphinx in its monstrous form: *P. Oxy.* 2459 = Eurip., *Oidipous,* frag. I Austin. Cf. also Seneca, *Oedipus* 92ff.

77. Cf. Asclepiades, frag. 21, quoted by the scholiast on Eur., *Phoen.* 45. See Robert (above, note 20) II,52ff. and nn11–12, II,23–24; also the illustration of the pelike of Hermonax on p. 54, fig. 20. See too his *Die griechische Heldensage* = Preller-Robert, *Griechische Mythologie*⁴ II.3 (Berlin 1921) 892–893. The association of the Sphinx with the Sphinx Mountain, Phikeion Oros, is as old as Hesiod (*Theog.* 326).

78. Apollodorus 3.5.8.7; see Lesky (above, note 76) 1723.

79. Ibid. 1703, 1709, 1715; also Kamerbeek, Introduction 4.

80. For the "music" of the Sphinx, cf. Eur., *Phoen.* 808ff., 1028–29, 1505ff. For the Sphinx as "une ogresse musicienne" see Delcourt (above, note 1) 133, also 133–35 on her affinities with Harpies and Sirens; in "Tydée et Mélanippe," *SMSR* 37 (1966) 139–140, Delcourt compares her to other "personifications de la Mort dévoratrice." See also Lesky (above, note 76) 1705.

81. Eur., *Oidipous,* frag. II Austin, *surixasa* (= *P. Oxy.* 2459.4).

82. On Teiresias' ambiguous relation to truth, see Reinhardt, 116ff.

83. Geoffrey H. Hartman, "Language from the Point of View of Literature," *Beyond Formalism* (New Haven 1970) 348.

84. Ibid. 350.

85. Sheppard (above, note 44) on line 841 (p. 149) recognizes the link between 841 and 767–76 but interprets *perissos* only psychologically, in terms of "the state of mind of Jocasta."

86. The parallel is noted and discussed by Reinhardt 135. I do not, however, accept all of Reinhardt's conclusions, based as they are on a linear view of the evolution of Sophocles' tragic vision.

87. Note also the ambivalent "his wife the mother of his children" in this passage, with the close juxtaposition of *gynē* and *mētēr* (928). "Happy and with happy (kin) . . . , being his complete, fulfilled wife," *pantelēs damar,* is the Messenger's equally ambiguous reply (929–930).

88. I follow here the emendation of Brunk, with Pearson in the OCT. Heath's *legōn,* accepted by Jebb, gives a sense not far removed ("make trial in speaking"), but is less

pointed and to my mind less effective. Note how the emotional force of language replaces its cognitive, intellectual functions in this scene (especially 359–365), as speech rapidly degenerates into insult (*oneidos,* 372).

89. The herdsman's use of the verb *aikizein,* "outrage," marks this threat of torture as especially violent and brutal: cf. *Antig.* 206, 419 and above, chapter 6, note 20.

90. See W. B. Stanford, *Greek Metaphor* (Oxford 1936), 47ff., esp. 56; C. Segal, "Synaesthesia in Sophocles," *Illinois Class. Studies* 2 (1977) 89–91.

91. In the prologue smell is also present in the incense, *thymiamata,* 4. On the terms of perception, see Marjorie W. Champlin, "*Oedipus Tyrannus* and the Problem of Knowledge," *CJ* 64 (1968/69) 337–345.

92. On the importance of touch, see Taplin (above, note 24) 66–67. Gellie 102 observes that Oedipus' paternal concern at the begining reappears, much transformed, at the end when "his power to serve has shrunk to the tiny domestic circle of a ruined father and two girls born in incest."

93. See S. C. Humphreys, " 'Transcendence' and Intellectual Roles: the Ancient Greek Case," *Daedalus* 104. 2 (1975) 106: "It is characteristic of the difference between Aeschylus and Sophocles that the only extant tragedy that emphasizes this isolation of the suffering hero is the *Prometheus,* in which the hero knows his future destiny. Prometheus can contemplate his own sufferings with dignity because he knows how it will end. Sophocles' heroes—with the exception of the aged Oedipus—achieve the same dignity without the foreknowledge."

94. Cf. Eur., *HF* 1155ff., 1214ff., 1231ff., 1398ff. and *Suppl.* 764ff.; *OC* 1130ff. See in general Vickers 153–156.

95. See Peter Szondi, *Versuch über das Tragische*[2] (Frankfurt a.M. 1964) 70: "Der König erwartet das Unheil nicht als Fremden am Wegesrand, sondern am Ziel seiner eigenen Erkenntnis. So markieren die Orakel in den drei Schicksalen, die zugleich ein einziges bilden, eine tragische Steigerung, in der das Entgegengesetzte immer enger aneinandergebunden, die Zweiheit immer unerbittlicher zur Einheit getrieben wird." On the paradoxes of blindness and sight, see also W. C. Helmbold, "The Paradox of the *Oedipus,*" *AJP* 72 (1951) 293–300.

96. Rainer Maria Rilke, *Letters,* trans. J. B. Greene and M. D. Herter Norton (New York, N.Y., 1948) II,308 (to Lotti von Wedel, May 26, 1922).

97. E.g. Aristoph., *Frogs* 962; Gorgias, *Helen* 16 and *Palamedes* 4; cf. *Vita Aeschyli* 7 and 9.

98. In an unpublished essay John E. Erwin develops an interpretation of the *OT* as a paradigm of the experience of drama, Oedipus' loss of identity having an aesthetic and psychological equivalent in the spectator's loss of identity as he involves himself in the dramatic fiction. I am grateful to Professor Erwin for allowing me to ready his essay in advance of publication.

99. Knox, *Oedipus* 77.

100. Ibid. chap. 5, esp. 189 and 195–196; Cameron (above, note 10) 119–120; Kamerbeek, Introduction 25, sees the play "not only as an exemplification of human ignorance contrasted with divine omniscience, of the frailty and speciousness of human fortune and happiness contrasted with the grim realities of existence, but also of human greatness holding its own against all Fate can do." So too for E. R. Dodds, "On Misunderstanding the *Oedipus Rex,*" *G & R* 13 (1966) 48, the play is not only "about the blindness of man and the desperate insecurity of the human condition," but also "about

human greatness . . . , inner strength . . . to pursue the truth at any cost, and strength to accept and endure it when found."

101. See Howe (above, note 3) 134ff.; Gellie 101.

8 Electra

1. J. T. Sheppard, "The Tragedy of Electra, According to Sophocles," *CQ* 12 (1918) 80–88; "*Electra:* A Defense of Sophocles," *CR* 41 (1927) 2–9; "*Electra* Again," *CR* 41 (1927) 163–165 (henceforth cited as Sheppard I, II, III, respectively). Henceforth I shall cite works in this note and in notes 2 and 3 below by author's name or short title only.

2. For example, R. P. Winnington-Ingram, "The 'Electra' of Sophocles: Prolegomenon to an Interpretation," *PCPS* 183 (1954–55) 20–26, now much expanded in his *Sophocles: An Interpretation* (Cambridge 1980) chap. 10; Holger Friis Johansen, "Die Elektra des Sophokles, Versuch einer neuen Deutung," *C & M* 25 (1964) 8–32; C. P. Segal, "The *Electra* of Sophocles," *TAPA* 97 (1966) 473–545; Hans-Joachim Newiger, "Hofmannsthals *Elektra* und die griechische Tragödie," *Arcadia* 4 (1969) 138–163; G. H. Gellie, *Sophocles, A Reading* (Melbourne 1972) 106–130; J. H. Kells, ed. *Sophocles, Electra* (Cambridge 1973) 1–2 and passim.

3. The quotation is from T. M. Woodard, "*Electra* by Sophocles: the Dialectical Design," p. 2, *HSCP* 70 (1965) 233 n98, with a useful survey of recent discussions there; see also Segal, "Electra" 474–475. Among recent scholars who argue that the matricide is an uncomplicated, affirmative action are Adams 59; I. M. Linforth, "Electra's Day in the Tragedy of Sophocles," *UCPCP* 19.2 (1963) 119–121; Musurillo 100ff., with the references in 100 n1; A. S. Owen, "TA T'ONTA KAI MELLONTA, The End of Sophocles' *Electra,*" *CR* 41 (1927) 51–52; Vickers 572. For the opposite view see, in addition to the authors cited in note 2, A. Lesky, *TDH* 237–238; H. Lloyd-Jones "Tycho von Wilamowitz-Moellendorff on the Dramatic Technique of Sophocles," *CQ* 22 (1972) 225; Richard W. Minadeo, "Sophocles' *Electra:* Plot, Theme and Meaning," *C & M* 28 (1967) 114–142, especially 115–116, 133, 139–142 (henceforth cited as "Minadeo"). Wilamowitz' view, "Die beiden Elektren," *Hermes* 18 (1883) 237, that ending with Aegisthus' death and not Clytaemnestra's serves to play down the matricide, has been severely, and justly, criticized by a number of scholars, notably J. C. Kamerbeek, *The Plays of Sophocles, V, The Electra* (Leiden 1974) 17; J. de Romilly, *L'évolution du pathétique d'Eschyle à Euripide* (Paris 1961) 13–14; Kells 168–169 (on 957); see also Segal, "Electra" 523 and n64. The Erinyes too, though obviously far less important than in Aeschylus, are also much in evidence: 112, 276, 491, 1080, 1388, 1417. See Kamerbeek on lines 488–491, 784, 1417. The most recent attempt that I have seen to reassert the traditional view is P. T. Stevens, "Sophocles: *Electra,* Doom or Triumph," *G & R* 25 (1978) 111–119, but his discounting of 1424–25 (p. 113) or of 766–772 (p. 115) rests simply on assertion and produces no satisfactory view of the play as a whole.

4. Gellie 110; see now Winnington-Ingram, *Sophocles* (above, note 2) 218.

5. See Gellie 116, who stresses the play's "double bearing, outward to the act of vengeance, inward to Electra's spiritual conflict."

6. For this view of the play, see Gellie's chapter, 106ff., especially 122ff.; Johansen 31; Segal, "Electra" 540ff. Hofmannsthal seems also to have understood this aspect of the *Electra:* see Newiger 156–158, with the passages there cited.

7. See Kamerbeek on line 4.

8. On these antitheses see Woodard's essays, "*Electra* by *Sophocles:* the Dialectical

Design," *HSCP* 68 (1964) 163–205 and 70 (1965) 195–233, henceforth cited as Woodard I and II.

9. For the ending and its dark tone, including the isolation of Electra, see W. M. Calder, III, "The End of Sophocles' *Electra,*" *GRBS* 4 (1963) 213–216; Segal, "Electra" 529ff.; Newiger 145–146; Johansen 9–10 and 27–29; Wolf Steidle, *Studien zum Antiken Drama* (Munich 1968) 94–95 and n170. Vickers 573 finds "a moral vacuum at the end of the play." The optimistic view, recently reiterated by Bengt Alexanderson, "On Sophocles' Electra," *C & M* 27 (1966) 79–98, is rightly criticized by Hans Strohm, *Anz Alt* 24 (1971) 151. Woodard (II) 227 suggests that "Orestes and Electra both die and are reborn, like the yearly cycle of vegetation, or like the rotation of day and night." But as J. Carrière points out, "Sur l'essence et l'évolution du tragique chez les Grecs," *REG* 79 (1966) 19 and n45, even when Orestes is "reborn" it is as a kind of demon of Hades.

10. Cf. Sophocles, *Antigone,* 582–625.

11. See Kamerbeek on lines 417–419, 421–423; Segal, "Electra" 487ff. For the psychological implications of the dream, see George Devereux, *Dreams in Greek Tragedy* (Oxford 1976) 220–255.

12. For the ambiguities of Electra's relation to *dikē,* see Winnington-Ingram, 22ff.; Johansen, 18ff.; Segal, "Electra" 534–537; Newiger 148; Minadeo 133–134.

13. Commentators are divided on whether 610–611 refer to Electra or to Clytaemnestra. R. C. Jebb, *Sophocles, The Plays and Fragments,* Part VI, *Electra* (Cambridge 1894) *ad loc.,* argues for Electra, while Kamerbeek, Kells, and earlier G. Kaibel, *Sophokles Elektra* (Leipzig 1896), believe that the chorus means Clytaemnestra. The arguments for Clytaemnestra by D. B. Gregor, "Sophocles *Electra* 610–11," *CR* 64 (1950) 87–88, do not seem decisive: e.g. it is by no means clear that "Electra's speech was not a passionate utterance but a calm statement" (p. 87). It is perhaps true, as Kamerbeek suggests, that the chorus is unlikely to question Electra's concern for justice; yet they do criticize her excessive emotionality earlier (213–220, 369–371), though they also praise her *eusebeia* in the first stasimon, 1093ff. A gesture from Clytaemnestra expressing sudden loss of temper, as Kells suggests, is possible; on the other hand Electra has been the main focus of attention, and it is her mounting passion that we have been seeing and hearing for the fifty lines immediately preceding. See also Minadeo 123; Segal, "Electra" 536 and n83; N. B. Booth, "Sophocles, *Electra* 610–11," *CQ* n.s. 27 (1977) 466–467, who also argues for Electra as the point of reference. The lines are too calm and objective in tone to be included in Clytaemnestra's speech, as D. J. Lilley suggests, *CQ* n.s. 25 (1975) 309–311. See also A. D. Fitton-Brown, *CQ* n.s. 6 (1956) 38–39.

14. For example, Plato, *Protagoras* 324a–d; Democritus 68B181DK; Antiphon the Sophist 87B44, A and B DK, especially the latter fragment.

15. See Kells on 417ff. and Segal, "Electra" 487ff., 493–494. Note also the theme of the "uprooting" of a house in 510 and 764 and see *Antig.* 599.

16. See Richard Kannicht, *Euripides, Helena* (Heidelberg 1969) on *Hel.* 1055–56; Segal, "Electra" 491 and nn20–21. The scholiast suggests Pythagoras. The simile of the shining star, however, may also recall the murderous warrior of the *Iliad,* e.g. 5.4–8, 11.61–66, 22.26–32, 22.314–319.

17. On the contrast with the end of the *Oresteia,* see Winnington-Ingram 25; Segal, "Electra" 527–528; Minadeo 141–142.

18. The impossibility of raising up the dead, a *topos* of consolation to Electra in 137–139 and a rhetorical figure (an *adynaton*) in 940, is made good in a paradoxical way on stage when Orestes seems to return from the dead to Electra ("the living has no tomb," 1219), who has "died" for him (1152).

19. With Kaibel (above, note 13) and Jebb on line 841 I accept the second of the scholiast's three explanations of *pampsychos*, "he who has preserved all his own life" (*psychē*). LSJ, s.v., translate "with full life." Kell's version, "amid a throng of souls," seems less well-suited to the context. The ominous life of this *psychē* seems to answer Clytaemnestra's claims on Orestes' *psychē*, 770, and cf. Electra's "drinking her life's blood" (*psychē*) at 786. Cf. also 980.

20. Cf. *El.* 59–81 with *Phil.* 79ff. and 108ff. See also F. Solmsen, "Zur Gestaltung des Intrigenmotivs in den Tragödien des Sophokles und Euripides," (1932) in E.-R. Schwinge, ed., *Euripides,* Wege der Forschung 89 (Darmstadt 1968) 326–344.

21. E.g. Aesch., *Ag.* 11, 351, 1625–27.

22. For this *anagkē* in the play, see 221, 256, 308–309, 620, 1193, and cf. also 575. See also Sheppard (I) 87; Winnington-Ingram 23–24; Segal, "Electra" 508–509.

23. See Kells *ad loc.*, who cites *OT* 1463–65 for the theme of the daughter's nurture in the house. For *trophē* in the play, see also 603, 1058–62, 1147, 1183, 1190.

24. For the reversals in the normal patterns of male and female interiority and exteriority in the house, see the important essay of Jean-Pierre Vernant, "Hestia-Hermès: Sur l'expression religieuse de l'espace et du mouvement chez les Grecs," *MP* I,124–170, esp. 131ff., 134–138; also Vickers 396ff. For the sexual symbolism of scepter and hearth, see Devereux (above, note 11) 230ff., 238ff.

25. See Kamerbeek on line 784, citing Winnington-Ingram 5.

26. On the theme of "nature" and learning from a parent in the play, see Segal, "Electra" 498–500.

27. For these distinctions between wild and civilized in fifth-century anthropology, see above, chapter 1. See in particular Aristoph., *Birds* 1346–68 and *Clouds* 1409–29; Democritus 68B275–280DK; Antiphon the Sophist 87B49DK; also Segal, "Electra" 498.

28. Cf. Hom., *Il.* 6.345–348, 13.139; *Od.* 20.63. Also Segal, "Electra" 511–512.

29. For the spatial contrasts of Electra and Orestes, see Woodard (I) 167 and passim.

30. For the syntax of the dense expression of 155, (*achos) pros ho ti sy tōn endon perissa,* see Jebb and Kamerbeek; for the tone see Kells.

31. On these passages see also Steidle (above, note 9) 92 n161, who suggests that Electra increasingly is able to separate herself from the interior of the house, until at the end she stands before an empty house.

32. For *anchistos* as "next of kin," see, e.g. Eur., *Tro.* 48 and Hdt. 5.79; Kamerbeek on line 1105.

33. On the tragic ironies and ambiguities of 1367–74, see Kells and Kamerbeek.

34. On the ambiguity of 1424–25, see Kirkwood 240–241; Kells; and Kamerbeek ("a tone not of confidence . . . , but of anxiety"). Even Linforth (121, 124) and Alexandersson (above, note 9, 92–93), who take the more optimistic view of the play, acknowledge the sinister and ambiguous tone of these lines. See also Segal, "Electra" 534 and n79.

35. Steidle (above, note 9) 94 describes this passage as "diese—man darf wohl sagen—in ihrer Wirkung grandiose Szene der Toröffnung." For other ironies in this passage, see the commentaries *ad loc.*

36. Note also the theme of Clytaemnestra as the "mother/no-mother" in 273–274, 1154, 1194. For the negations and inversions of *philia*, see also Segal, "Electra" 501–504.

37. "Old" and "of old" (*palaios, palai*) are important in the play: 4, 484–485, 764–765, 1049, 1199, 1311, 1417–21, 1490.

38. See Jones 157; also Adams 72, especially on Clytaemnestra's reactions in 766–771.

39. See Ursula Parlavantza-Friedrich, *Täuschungsszenen in den Tragödien des Sophokles* (Berlin 1969) 35: "Das doppelte *teknon* ist wohl das eindringlichste Beispiel dafür, welche Kraft und Bedeutung einer Anrede innewohnen kann." Owen's remark, 52, that Clytaemnestra's "one touch of human feeling (770–1) is quickly forgotten," is disproven by 1410–11 if nothing else. On this sympathetic side of Clytaemnestra, see also Adams 72.

40. On the force of *deinon* in 770, see Jebb and Kamerbeek; Minadeo 138–139. Quoting 770, *deinon to tiktein estin,* Virginia Woolf remarks, " 'There is a strange power in motherhood.' It is no murderess, violent and unredeemed, whom Orestes kills within the house, and Electra bids him utterly destroy—'strike again.' No; the men and women standing out in the sunlight before the audience on the hillside were alive enough, subtle enough, not mere figures, or plaster casts of human beings": "On Not Knowing Greek," *The Common Reader,* First Series (1925; New York, N.Y., Harvest Books, n.d.) 28.

41. The play on the etymological significance of Electra's name may go back at least to the sixth century: see Xanthus, frag. 700 *PMG;* Kamerbeek's Introduction 2.

42. Kirkwood 140; also Newiger 147–149.

43. See De Romilly, *L'évolution du pathétique,* 14: "Electre a, chez Sophocle, toute l'ardeur d'une meurtrière; l'on comprend à peine qu'un mur sépare ainsi cette fille implacable de la victime à laquelle elle s'adresse."

44. On these echoes see Wilamowitz, "Die beiden Elektren," 246 n1; Johansen 28; Gellie 127; H.D.F. Kitto, *Sophocles, Dramatist and Philosopher* (London 1958) 52; Segal, "Electra" 501, 525; Minadeo 135.

45. For time in the Electra, see Woodard (II) 196ff.; Whitman 170–171; R. M. Torrance, "Sophocles: Some Bearings," *HSCP* 69 (1965) 307ff.; Kamerbeek on lines 781–782. For this way of speaking of time, see W.K.C. Guthrie, *Orpheus and Greek Religion,* rev. ed. (New York, N.Y., 1966) 85.

46. For a closer analysis of the passage see Segal, "Electra" 520–522 with the references there cited; also Kells on lines 1485–86.

47. See also Kamerbeek.

48. For the importance of *kerdos,* "profit," here see Segal, "Electra" 522 and n63.

49. Note also the image of mingling in the parable of the two jars (*ammeixas, Il.* 24.530; cf. *El.* 1485, *memeigmenōn*).

50. Cited by Newiger 156.

51. For the calculated emotional effects of this speech see Parlavantza-Friedrich (above, note 39) 36–37.

52. Sheppard (II) 7 notes a connection between the two passages and suggests that the foreshadowing is "not a good omen, since it links Orestes with the man who laid the curse upon the house." Wilamowitz' attempt (unsuccessful, in my opinion) to explain away the reference to the curse in 504–515 is in keeping with his view that Orestes' deed must be "durchaus löblich und Gott wohlgefällig" ("Die beiden Elektren," 217–218).

53. For the metaphor see Kamerbeek on line 838, who cites Aesch., *Ch.* 617. Gold in this connection may also recall the golden ram further back in the dark history of the house: cf. Eur., *El.* 698–746; Carl Robert, *Die griechische Heldensage⁴* (Berlin 1920) I,294–297; J. D. Denniston, *Euripides, Electra* (Oxford 1939) *ad loc.*

54. E.g. Aesch., *Ag.* 767–773, 939–940.

55. Note also the rich table at 361–362 and the empty table in her lament at 192;

cf. 450–458. In 1090–92 the chorus prays that Electra may live "lifted above (her) enemies in hand and wealth," a combination which has perhaps an ominous ring, for "hand" suggests the violence of kin against kin in the house (e.g. 296–297 with Kamerbeek's note, 476, 489, 1394, 1422), replacing the more innocent terms of Electra's struggle against Clytaemnestra in 326, 431, 458.

56. Some scholars (e.g. Adams 73, Linforth 102–103) have argued from 957 that Electra really intends to kill Aegisthus only and not her mother. But against this view stand her earlier virulent statements like 437, 582–583, 603–605, as well as the subsequent course of the action. For cogent arguments against Adams and Linforth, see Kells and Kamerbeek on line 957; Johansen 21–22; Gellie 119.

57. There is doubtless a certain ambiguity in the epithet Lykeios (cf. Pausanias 2.19.3), but the Paedagogus' etymology, "wolf-killing," *lykoktonos*, stresses the darker, vengeful side; cf. also Aesch., *Ag.* 1257 with Eduard Fraenkel's note *ad loc.* For further discussion see Segal, "Electra" 477 and n11; Wilamowitz, *Der Glaube der Hellenen* (Berlin 1930) I,147 and nn2–3; Nilsson, *Gesch.d. gr. Rel.* I,537–538.

58. See *nyn oun* 15; *ēdē* 17; *prin oun* 20; *ouketi* 22. It is tempting to think that scene-painting might have indicated these places, though of course a gesture and a bit of imagination on the part of the audience would suffice.

59. For the metaphor of 516, cf. 721 of horses; also *Antig.* 587 and frag. 401P; Hdt. 2.65; Xenophon, *Cyn.* 7.7. For drinking blood cf. *Antig.* 531–532. For dogs and barking with sinister overtones, cf. *OT* 391 (of the Sphinx) and also frag. 211P. See in general P. Rödström, *De Imaginibus Sophocleis a Rerum Natura Sumptis* (Stockholm 1883) 28–29. For other animal imagery, cf. 196, 567–568, 837, 1054.

60. For the interpretation of 1058ff., see Kells; Segal, "Electra" 488–489.

61. See Kells on lines 1384ff.; also Kamerbeek on line 1107 for *mateuein.*

62. The parallel is noted by Kamerbeek.

63. I now feel certain, with the scholiast, that Electra means "dogs and birds" by her "buriers" of 1488, though I would still maintain for the expression of this idea the nuances which I claimed for it in "Electra" 520–521 and n60. For recent discussion see Kamerbeek on lines 1487–88; Alexanderson (above, note 9) 94; Gellie 128 and n25, 291.

64. See Froma I. Zeitlin, "The Motif of the Corrupted Sacrifice in Aeschylus' Oresteia," *TAPA* 96 (1965) 463–508 with the "Postscript," *TAPA* 97 (1966) 645–653; also Vidal-Naquet, "Chasse et sacrifice dans l'Orestie d'Eschyle," *MT* 135–158; Walter Burkert, "Greek Tragedy and Sacrificial Ritual," *GRBS* 7 (1966) 119–120. The differences between the Sophoclean and Aeschylean treatments of the sacrificial theme are well discussed by Jones 157–158, although in my judgment he oversimplifies the Sophoclean version in taking Electra's defense of Agamemnon at face value as the poet's answer to the moral dilemma in Aeschylus. Sacrifice is also a central motif in the Euripidean *Electra* (cf. 774–843): see Froma Zeitlin, "The Argive Festival of Hera and Euripides' Electra," *TAPA* 101 (1970) 651ff. and esp. 658 n42 for a comparison with Sophocles.

65. Wilamowitz, "Die beiden Elektren," 249–250; cf. also 220.

66. Jebb *ad loc.* Cf. also V. di Benedetto, *Euripidis, Orestes* (Florence 1965) on *Or.* 191.

67. Cf. also Eur., *El.* 805–810, where Aegisthus and Orestes pray for different things at the sacrificial rite.

68. Musurillo 104 perversely argues (after citing 1419–21) that "the use of the sacrificial blood imagery" shows the matricide "as perfectly in accord with both human and divine justice, and demanded by private feeling and decency."

69. Kells on 1508ff.; cf. Aesch., *Ag.* 972–973. *Hormē*, "impulse," "attack," recalls the personified blow of the axe which "rushes forth" (*hōrmathē*, 196) like a beast of prey. Cf. also line 70 and Minadeo 137.

70. The *ololygmos* of 750, like the *sparagmos* in 748, can also be a term of sacrificial ritual: cf. Homer, *Od.* 3.450; Aesch., *Ag.* 594–597 and Fraenkel on *Ag.* 597; also Burkert (above, note 64) 108 n48 for further bibliography.

71. See above, note 16.

72. See Kells and also 86ff. On *archēgetein* in 83, see also Jebb ad loc. Kamerbeek's refutation of Jebb is not convincing. *OT* 751 does not really tell against Jebb's view.

73. The echo of Aesch., *Ch.* 140–141 in *El.* 307–309 is important here: Sophocles' Electra sees the virtues of moderation and piety as no longer accessible in her world. See in general Sheppard (I) 84 and (II) 6; Kamerbeek on lines 307–309; Segal, "Electra" 499–500 and n33. Cf. also 249–250, 589–590, 968–969.

74. Gilbert Murray, "Hamlet and Orestes," in *The Classical Tradition in Poetry*[2] (Cambridge, Mass., 1930) 220.

75. Gellie, 123, remarks, "Electra's feelings become the more poignant if they appear to be spent on an unloving object of her love." See also Solmsen, "Intrigenmotiv" (above, note 20) 339. For *lypē* see also 120, 355, 363, 533.

76. See Kells on lines 82ff., citing Eur., *Phoen.* 1667. Perhaps we are to think of the impossibility of washing that mutilated corpse and thereby achieving purification from the pollution of the murder.

77. Note concealment also in connection with the manipulation or perversion of ritual in 55 (Orestes' concealing the urn) and 638 (Clytaemnestra's concealed prayer).

78. See Kamerbeek on lines 437–438.

79. The parallel between the laughter at 277 and 807 is noted by Kamerbeek. The ritual aspect of this perversion in 277 is perhaps also present in the word *poioumena*, which can connote ritual acts: see LSJ s.v. A II 3. For other aspects of violation of ritual, see Kaibel *ad loc.* (pp. 112–113).

80. For the urn see Segal, "Electra" 515–517; Parlavantza-Friedrich (above, note 39) 40–48 has a good analysis of the tensions between recognition and deception in the urn scene, and so also Friedrich Solmsen, "Electra and Orestes, Three Recognitions in Greek Tragedy," *Meded. der Koninkl. Nederlandse Akad. van Wetenschappen,* Afd. Letter-kunde, n.s. 30. no. 2 (1967) 26–30 = 54–58.

81. In Hesiod's *Catalogue of Women* Electra "rivals in form (*eidos*) the immortal goddesses" (frag. 23a, line 16 M–W.). Electra *emprepousa algesi*, 1187, "conspicuous in her woes" (see Kamerbeek), may also be an ironic echo of the regal "appearance" (*prepei*) of Clytaemnestra in 663. It is also modelled on Aesch., *Ch.* 17–18. Cf. also Soph., *El.* 639.

82. I have borrowed some sentences in this paragraph from my "Electra" 516.

83. Solmsen, "Recognitions," (above, note 80) 33 = 61, contrasts the immediate joy of the Sophoclean recognition with its postponement in Euripides' *Electra*; yet he understates the grimness of the repeated interruptions of that joy (1236, 1238, 1243–44, 1251–52, 1259, 1292, 1309ff.). Gellie 123 is more to the point: "Electra's happiness now glows against the matt surface of Orestes as much as did her wretchedness." De Romilly *L'évolution du pathetique,* 46–47, observes how the direct emotional effects of Aeschylus become in Sophocles a complex intellectual matter of appearance and reality, truth and falsehood.

84. Parlavantza-Friedrich (above, note 39) 48.

85. Note the language of 903–905: ἐμπαίει τί μοι / ψυχῇ σύνηϑες ὄμμα, φιλτάτου

βροτῶν / πάντων Ὀρέστου τοῦθ' ὁρᾶν τεκμήριον ("At once, alas, the familiar form seizes my soul (as I thought) that I was seeing the token of Orestes, dearest of all mortals to me.") *Psychē* can go with both "seizes" (*empaiei*) or with "familiar" (*synēthes*). In characteristic manner, Sophocles' dense syntax creates an interlocking of words which suggests something of the inner life of the character, the special closeness between *psyche* and *psychē* and the thrill of emotion which moves from "eye" and "form" (both connoted by *omma*) to spirit and mood (*psychē*).

86. *Saphes,* "clear" in 1223 recalls the clear token of the urn in 1108 and 1115, but also harks back to Chrysothemis' token of the hair in 904. For the theme cf. also 774, 885ff., and Solmsen, "Recognitions," 21ff. = 49ff., and Parlavantza-Friedrich (above, note 39) 39.

87. See Kells on lines 1400–1401.

88. Those who can find the matricide a matter of "simple justice" will agree perhaps with Adams 59–60, "In this drama Apollo is very near," and take the statements about Apollo in the prologue at face value as does Owen 52. On the ambiguities see Sheppard (II) passim; Kells on lines 35ff.; Minadeo 116.

89. The traditional view (no complications about Apollo's commands) is reasserted by Alexanderson (above, note 9) 80ff. and maintained, although with some hesitation and qualification, by Parlavantza-Friedrich (above, note 39) 39 and Gellie 107. In defence of Sheppard see now Kells' Introduction 4ff. Minadeo, 131–132, also observes that Electra herself goes ahead with the matricide unaware of (and unconcerned with) Apollo's sanction or nonsanction.

90. Wilamowitz, "Die beiden Elektren," 214 n1.

91. Sheppard (II) 2.

92. See Soph., *OT* 203 with the commentaries of Jebb and Kamerbeek; see also above, note 57.

93. For Zeus and justice in the play, see A. Maddalena, *Sofocle* (Turin 1959) 188–190.

94. The tension between heroic style and unheroic plotting in the prologue (cf. 1–2, 49–50) already prepares for this contrast. Cf. also the Homeric similes at 66, 98, 1151, and the poetic language of the horse race, especially 698–722 and 736–756, and the commentaries on these lines. Particularly important are the epinician language of 692ff. and the parallels between 720–722 and Antilochus' victory in *Il.* 23.323 and 334ff.: see Kamerbeek on 693–695, 700–701, 712, 714, 718, 720–722, 729–730.

95. See Kamerbeek on 679: "It is clear that the poet is bent on reminding the audience of the deceit that is to follow."

96. See inter alia 469, 1011–12, 1033, 1251ff., 1288ff., 1322, 1335, 1372.

97. Gellie 112. For the question of Electra's evasiveness about the matricide here, see also above, note 56.

98. Cf. also the theme of madness in 135, 294, 473, 879, 941, 1153.

99. Even if line 610 refers to Clytaemnestra (see above, note 13), my point about the degeneration of logical debate into passion is still valid. The violence in Electra in 616ff. is contained like a coiled spring, in contrast to Clytaemnestra's overt outbursts at 622 and 626–627.

100. I follow Kells in taking *logōn* with both *poi* and *amēchanōn*. On the significance of the lines, see also Segal, "Electra" 514 and 531–534 on *logos/ergon* generally; also Woodard (I) 175ff., 191ff., and (II) 213.

101. See Woodard (I) 168: "The purpose of Electra as protagonist is in fact to play out, in all its grimness, the cleavage that we found externalized, as it were, in the Prologue,

in the separation of Electra from Orestes." See also Gellie 218. On *logos/ergon* generally see also Minadeo passim.

102. "A silent witness," remarks Sheppard (II) 8.

103. Sight: 422–425, 761–762, 878ff., 903–904, 1459–60, 1466–69, 1475; hearing: 884, 926, 1406ff.; *phaneros:* 833; *emphanēs:* 1108–1109, 1454; *saphēs:* 23, 885, 1115, 1223, 1366; *sēmeia:* 24, 886; *tekmērion:* 774, 904, 1108–1109; *kryptein:* 55, 436, 490–491, 638, 825, 1294; see Kamerbeek on 923.

104. See Kells on 1228–29.

105. See above, note 16.

106. See C. Segal, "The Two Worlds of Euripides' *Helen,"* *TAPA* 102 (1971) 553–614, esp. 600–604, 610–612.

107. See Jan Kott, "Theatre and Literature," *Papers in Dramatic Theory and Criticism Presented at the University of Iowa, April 7, 1967,* ed. David M. Knauf (Iowa City 1969) 37–45; also David Cole, *The Theatrical Event* (Middletown, Conn., 1975) chap. 1, on the notion of "imaginative presence" in the dramatic performance. For this aspect of the urn, see my "Visual Symbolism and Visual Effects in Sophocles," *CW* 74 (1980/81) 136.

108. Woodard (I) 196: "Clytaemnestra's body under the sheet plays the same part as Orestes' urn: both serve as pivots for a reversal from delusion to truth." Yet one must add that the essential dramatic function of both, fictitious ashes and real corpse, is to deceive.

109. For this interpretation see Segal, "Electra" 545.

110. Ibid. 544.

111. Virginia Woolf, "On Not Knowing Greek," (above, note 40) 27.

9 Philoctetes: The Myth and the Gods

1. E.g. Aesch., *PV* 484–499; Plato, *Protag.* 322a; Diodorus 1.16.1; Eur., *Suppl.* 211–213; Democritus 68A74–75DK; Prodicus 84B5DK; Critias 88B25.12ff.DK. See A. T. Cole, *Democritus and the Sources of Greek Anthropology,* APA Monographs 25 (1967), chaps. 2 and 3. In the Homeric *Hymn to Apollo* the Cretan sailors make an altar as soon as they land on a foreign shore (502–510). On Sophistic elements in the play, see Peter Rose, "Sophocles' *Philoctetes* and the Teachings of the Sophists," *HSCP* 80 (1976) 49–105, esp. 49–64 (henceforth cited as "Rose").

2. On Philoctetes' "savagery" see Vidal-Naquet, "Le 'Philoctète' de Sophocle et l'éphébie," *MT* 168–172; C. Segal, "Divino e umano nel *Filottete* di Sofocle," *QUCC* 23 (1976) 73 (henceforth cited as Segal, "Divino"); F. Turato, *La crisi della città e l'ideologia del selvaggio* (Rome 1979) 127–136.

3. Note the association of Demeter and Dionysus on the east frieze of the Parthenon (nos. 25–26) and also in Eur., *Ba.* 274–285, a passage usually connected with the influence of Prodicus.

4. See A. Lesky, *TDH* 173–174.

5. Edmund Wilson, *The Wound and the Bow* (Boston 1941) 272–295.

6. See Hans Diller, "Menschendarstellung und Handlungsführung bei Sophokles," *Antike u. Abendland* 6 (1957) 168–169; Jones chap. 1, esp. 16ff.; Charles Garton, "Characterization in Greek Tragedy," *JHS* 77 (1957) 247–254. Letters 283 has a balanced formulation: "In other words, though the drama, considered as a character play, works through the actions of the three conflicting personalities themselves, the divine superintendence, while giving them the rein, is seen throughout adroitly using every turn and

bias of the ground to guide their waywardness and bring them home abreast." See in general my chapter 1, above, section V, and nn 13–14.

7. See C. Segal, "Philoctetes and the Imperishable Piety," *Hermes* 105 (1977) 153 (henceforth cited as "Piety"). See also below, section IX.

8. For 1440ff. and their significance in the play as a whole, see my "Piety" (preceding note) 133–158 and the next chapter.

9. For this aspect of Philoctetes' Lemnos, see Rose 58–64.

10. *Antigone* 365. On the vocabulary of *technē* in the play, see Vidal-Naquet, *MT* 174 n80.

11. For these differences of response to Philoctetes' cave, see Jens-Uwe Schmidt, *Sophokles, Philoktet, Eine Strukturanalyse* (Heidelberg 1973) 24–25.

12. See Rose 59. The Hippocratic *Ancient Medicine* is, of course, the locus classicus.

13. See Aesch., *PV* 452–453; Democritus 68B5DK (vol. 2, p. 136, line 9 = Diodorus 1.8.7).

14. Plato, *Protag.* 322a-b; see also Rose (above, note 1) 64ff.

15. Jones 218; see also R. C. Jebb, *Sophocles, The Plays and Fragments,* Part IV, *The Philoctetes* (Cambridge 1898) on line 30. Note the recurrence of *monos* or *erēmos* in 172, 183, 470, 471, 487, 954, 1018, and so forth.

16. See Karin Alt, "Schicksal und *Physis* im Philoktet des Sophokles," *Hermes* 89 (1961) 173–174 on this "menschlichen Unzulänglichkeit."

17. For this primitive food-gathering before agriculture, cf. Th. 1.2.2, Hdt. 1.202.1, 1.216.3, Diodorus 1.8.5 (= Democr. 68 B5DK) and in general Cole (above, note 1) 29, 37. For the *aneres alphestai,* see also Vidal-Naquet, *MT* 169 n38.

18. E.g. 43–44, 162, 274, 308, 700, 706, 712, 956–957, 1108–1109. See also *Ajax* 1065 and *Antig.* 775.

19. For other aspects of this imagery of pastoral song, see C. Segal, "Synaesthesia in Sophocles," *Illinois Class. Studies* 2 (1976) 92–93.

20. On this aspect of Euripides' *Cyclops,* see most recently G. Serrao, *Museum Criticum* 4 (1969) 51–52; Turato (above, note 2) 69ff.

21. For the reading and phrasing in 534, *eisoikēsis,* see A. A. Long, *Language and Thought in Sophocles* (London 1968) 32 n16. D. Page, *PCPS* 186 (1960) 51 proposed *exoikēsis,* accepted by H. Lloyd-Jones, *Gnomon* 33 (1961) 545.

22. Jebb on line 30. See 19, 30, 152, 954, 1087, 1149. See also Vidal-Naquet, *MT* 170 n45.

23. For *oikouros* and its derivatives in this sense, see *Trach.* 542, *OC* 343, frag. 487.4P (447.1N).

24. See Apollodorus 2.4.11 and Diodorus 4.14.3; Jebb on lines 197–198. Also P. W. Harsh, "The Role of the Bow in the *Philoctetes* of Sophocles," *AJP* 81 (1960) 412; Knox, *HT* 140; Segal, "Piety" 152–153.

25. Cicero, *Ad Fam.* 7.33, Accius, frag. X Ribbeck: *pinnigero, non armigero in corpore* / *tela exercentur haec abiecta gloria* ("These arrows are used against a feathered, not an armored body, all glory cast away.").

26. For this initiatory aspect of the play, see especially Vidal-Naquet, *MT* 172ff.

27. A number of critics have stressed the warmer and more humane side of Philoctetes, e.g. H. C. Avery, "Heracles, Philoctetes, Neoptolemus," *Hermes* 93 (1965) 280ff. Yet this side of Philoctetes is potential only and is encased in the hatred from which it must be freed. Indeed, the presence of the capacity for warmth in the midst of his unsocial and bitter life is essential to make this isolation tragic. Philoctetes is, of course, entitled

to his bitterness, and his just anger is part of his greatness of spirit too: see Hartmut Erbse, "Neoptolemos and Philoktet bei Sophokles," *Hermes* 94 (1966) 196–197. G. Perrotta, *Sofocle* (Messina-Florence 1935) 471.

28. See Segal, "Piety" 133–158.

29. See e.g. Pierre Vidal-Naquet, "The Black Hunter and the Origin of the Athenian Ephebeia," *PCPS* 194 (1968) 49–64; Marcel Detienne, *Dionysos mis à mort* (Paris 1977) sect. 2, esp. 64–98.

30. E.g. M. I. Finley, *The Ancient Economy* (Berkeley and Los Angeles 1973) 123.

31. Cf. Homer, *Il.* 7.467–469, 23.749; Aristoph., *Peace* 1162, and the story of the rivalry of Hephaestus and Dionysus for Naxos or Lemnos, schol. on Theocr. 7.149. For discussion and further references, see L. Preller and Carl Robert, *Griechische Mythologie* (Berlin 1894–1924) I, 176–178; U. von Wilamowitz-Moellendorff, *Der Glaube der Hellenen* (Berlin 1931–32) II, 60 and n2; G. Dumézil, *Le crime des Lemniennes* (Paris 1924) 31–32; article "Thoas" (2), *RE* 6A (1936) 297–299.

32. See *Electra* 257ff. and *Trach.* 999; J. C. Kamerbeek, "Sophoclea, II," *Mnemosyne*, ser. 4, 1 (1948) 200 and 203. For another aspect of the metaphor of growth, see chapter 10, section VII.

33. For a full list of the hunting images, see M. H. Jameson, "Politics and the *Philoctetes*," *CP* 51 (1956) 225 and n22.

34. "Catching" the bow: 68, 81; "catching" the man: 14, 101, 103, 107. Note also the usage of *agein*, "leading" or "bringing," in 90 and 102. See David Seale, "The Element of Surprise in Sophocles' *Philoctetes*," *BICS* 19 (1972) 96.

35. E.g. *sophisma*: 14, 77, 119; *technē*, 80; *kerdos*, 111.

36. Philoctetes' verb, *hypelthein*, of "stalking a hunted prey" in 1007, recurs in Odysseus' mouth of his fear in 1231, "How some fear has crept stealthily (*hypēlthe*) upon me."

37. *Episigma* is Bergk's virtually certain emendation: see Long (above, note 21) 79.

38. For the disease as bestial, see also 265–266, 268, 520, 650, 743–744, 758–759, 791–792, 807–808; also Long (above, note 21) 77; Kamerbeek (above, note 32) 198–204; Musurillo 119.

39. Kamerbeek (above, note 32) 200 defines *enthēros* as "in quo bestia (i.e. morbus) imminet, insidiatur, latet."

40. For pity as the quality of a refined and humane soul, see Eur., *Electra*, 294–295: "Pity does not lie in rudeness (*amathia*), but in men who have wisdom" (*sophoi*). On the importance of pity see most recently Rose 66–68, 74–75.

41. For the pseudo-departure see also 461, 526ff., 1060–61, 1134–35, 1179–80, 1218–19. For another view of the theme of abortive sailing, see Seale (above, note 34) 98–100, who suggests that Sophocles deliberately creates a pattern to manipulate the audience's uncertainty.

42. For *kerdos* and the language of baseness, see most recently Rose 92.

43. This interpretation of *anakaloumenō(i)* follows Walter Burkert, "Jason, Hypsipyle, and New Fire at Lemnos. A Study of Myth and Ritual," *CQ* n.s. 20 (1970) 5.

44. See Jebb on 986; also the scholion on Nicander, *Theriaka* 472. Contrast Odysseus' use of civilizing fire against the Cyclops, *Od.* 9.328, 375–394.

45. Note also the collocation of fire and "device" (*mēchanasthai*), 295ff.

46. For some aspects of this significance of fire and civilization in the play, see Segal, "Divino" 74–75. It is true, as Marie Delcourt suggests, *Stérilités mystérieuses et naissances maléfiques dans l'antiquité classique* (Liège and Paris 1938) 29–30, that the fear of contagion was very strong among the Greeks and could lead to placing the sick outside the

house (see Plutarch, *De occulte vivendo* 3.3). Yet this motive does not fully account for the way and place in which Philoctetes was exposed.

47. Details and references in Lesky, *TDH* 172.

48. Wilamowitz, *Glaube der Hellenen* (above, note 31) II, 142, suggests that the cult of Hephaestus may have been brought to Athens under the Peisistratids, after Miltiades' subjection of Lemnos.

49. Sophocles also wrote a *Lemnian Women* (Frags. 384–389P = 353–357N), where Chryse is the name of a place and the island is inhabited (cf. frag. 353N, "O Lemnos and Chryse's nearby crags").

50. See Burkert (above, note 43) 1–16.

51. Scholion, Pindar, *Ol.* 13.74g.

52. For the problem of Mosychlos and the volcanic fires of Lemnos, see Dumézil (above, note 31) 26–27; C. Fredrich, "Lemnos," *MD(A)I* 31 (1906) 254–255.

53. Photius, s.v. Kabeiroi; Page, *PMG,* frag. adesp. 985; see Burkert (above, note 43) 10.

54. For Lemnos as the repository of Prometheus' fire, see Accius, *Philoct.,* frag. II, lines 532–6 Ribbeck (Cic., *TD* 2.10.23). Also Preller-Robert (above, note 31) I, 179 and n3.

55. Homer, *Il.* 14.230–231. For Hypnos' mythical abode, see Hesiod, *Theog.* 758–761. Leaf on *Il.* 14.230 remarks, "Why Lemnos should have been chosen as the spot at which Sleep was to be found we cannot even guess." The Homeric scholia *ad loc.* offer little real help.

56. According to *Athenian Tribute Lists* the assessment for Hephaestias, which may have represented the whole island, was 900 drachmas in 454/3, about a decade before Sophocles served as hellenotamias: see B. D. Meritt, H. T. Wade-Gery, M. F. McGregor, *ATL*[3], (Princeton, N.J., 1950) 23.

57. For the theological issue and Neoptolemus' relation to it, see Segal, "Piety" 142ff., 150–152.

58. For a review of previous interpretations of *theia tychē,* see Segal, "Piety" 150–152, with the references there cited.

59. Ludwig Radermacher, "Zur Philoktetssage," in *Pankarpeia: Mélanges Henri Grégoire* (Brussels 1949) 503–509.

60. References in Segal, "Piety" 152 and n49.

61. See Stephanos of Byzantium, s.v. Lemnos and s.v. Kabeiria; Dumézil (above, note 31) 40, 48.

62. For the sexual implications of lameness or a wounded foot, apropos of Hephaestus, see Richard Caldwell, "Hephaestus: A Psychological Study," *Helios* 6 (1978) 49ff. with the literature there cited. For comparative data see Géza Róheim, *The Eternal Ones of the Dream* (New York, N.Y., 1945; reprint 1971) 8ff.

63. See the scholia on *Phil.* 194 and 1326 and also on *OT* 188. Further references in "Chryse," *RE* III.2 (1899) 2488.30ff. and Frazer on Apollodorus 3.26. One may wonder if the title "Golden" is not a euphemism for darker qualities.

64. See Preller-Robert (above, note 31) I[4] (1894) 328 and n5.

65. See Von Sybel, s.v. "Chryse," Roscher, *Lexikon* I (1884–90) 901.

66. See the scholia on *Phil.* 194 and 270; Philostratus the Younger, *Imag.* 17.

67. Schol. on *Phil.* 270.

68. Schol. on *Phil.* 194; Hyginus, *Fab.* 102; Eustathius on *Il.* 2.723; Stephanus of Byzantium s.v. *Neai.* See also Türk, s.v. "Philoctetes," in Roscher, *Lexikon* III.2 (1902–9) 2318–19.

69. Appian, *Mithridates* 77.

70. For the Heracles myth and male anxieties about female (and especially maternally female) power, see Philip Slater, *The Glory of Hera* (Boston 1968) chap. 12.

71. See Preller-Robert (above, note 31) I⁴ (1894) 174–175; L. R. Farnell, *Cults of the Greek States* V (Oxford 1909) 393–394.

72. See above, note 54.

73. See Jebb on *Phil.* 986–987; Preller-Robert (above, note 31) I⁴ (1894) 179.

74. See Hellanicus, *FGrHist* 4F71c; F. G. Welcker, *Die Aeschylische Trilogie, Prometheus, und die Kabirenweihe zu Lemnos* (Darmstadt 1824) 206–207, observes the connection with the Homeric epithet *sintis* of lions and wolves and the dangerous Sinis of mythology.

75. Cf. C. A. Lobeck, *Aglaophamus* (Regensburg 1829) 1181ff.; U. von Wilamowitz-Moellendorff, "Hephaistos," *NGG* (1895) 243; H. Herter, s.v. "Telchinen," *RE* A IX (1934) 197–224; Caldwell (above, note 62) 47.

76. See Preller-Robert (above, note 31) I, 847–864; Burkert (above, note 43) 9ff. and for recent bibliography s.v. "Kabeiroi," *Kleine Pauly* 3 (1969) 34–38.

77. Hesychius, s.v. Kabeiroi; see Lobeck (above, note 75) 1249ff. On the ambiguous gait associated with smiths, see Marcel Detienne, "Le phoque, le crabe et le forgeron," *Hommages à Marie Delcourt, Coll. Latomus* 114 (1970) 219–233; Preller-Robert (above, note 31) 175 and n2; Farnell (above, note 71) 375; Frazer on Apollodorus 1.3.5 (vol. I, pp. 22f. of the Loeb Classical Lib. edn.).

78. See Wilamowitz (above, note 75) 231–232, 238ff., has some interesting speculations on Lemnian Hephaestus and a possibly indigenous, pre-Greek fire god of the Northeast Aegean.

79. For some of these parallels, see Friedrich Marx, "Philoktet-Hephaistos," *NJbb* 13 (1904) 685; Wilamowitz (above, note 75) 217ff., especially 219–223.

80. Philostratos, *Heroikos,* 2.171.28ff. Kayser; see also Türk (above, note 68) 2319–20.

81. Westermann, *Mythogr. Graeci,* 197.2.

82. Eustathius, on *Il.* 2.724; Philostratus, *Heroikos* 2.171–172; see Farnell (above, note 71) 386.

83. See above, note 78 and Marx (above, note 79) 673–685. The doubts of O. Gruppe, *Bursian's Jahresbericht* 137 (1908) 596–598, were dismissed by Fiehn. s.v. "Philoktetes," *RE* A XIX.2 (1938) 2505. See also Radermacher (above, note 59) 508–509.

84. See Myrsilus of Methymna, *FGrHist* 477F1a and b; schol. on Eur., *Hec.* 887 and Apollon. Rhod. 1.609. See in general Preller-Robert (above, note 31) II.⁴ 3, *Die griechische Heldensage* (Berlin 1924) 850–851; RE IX.1 (1914) 437–438, s.v. "Hypsipyle"; Dumézil (above, note 31) 13–14, 35ff.

85. Myrsilus *FGrHist* 477F1a = schol. on Apollon. Rhod. 1.609e.

86. Photius, s.v. Kabeiroi.

87. Philostratus, *Heroikos,* 2.207–208 Kayser. Burkert (above, note 43) brilliantly explores the connections between the myth of the Lemnian Women and the cults of Lemnos. See also Farnell (above, note 71) 381ff.; M. P. Nilsson, *Griechische Feste* (Berlin 1906) 470–471. For the idea of "regenerating time" in rites of renewal in general, see Mircea Eliade, *Patterns in Comparative Religion,* trans. R. Sheed (New York, N.Y., 1958; repr. 1963) 398ff.

88. See Burkert (above, note 43) 7–9; Welcker (above, note 74) 248.

89. Philostratos, *Heroikos* 2.172 Kayser; Fiehn (above, note 83) 2505. Some tradi-

tions even make Philoctetes one of the Argonauts despite the chronological difficulties: see Preller-Robert (above, note 31) II, 3.787 and nn2, 3.

90. Philostratus the Younger, *Imag.* 17.2. It is perhaps worth noting that Philoctetes, also like the Lemnian Women, runs afoul of Aphrodite: see Martial 2.84.

91. For the echo between 874–875 and 902–903 see Perrotta (above, note 27) 447 and nn1–2. Note also the echoes between *en eucherei* ("in ease") in 875 and *dyschereia*, "difficulty," in 473; *eucherēs*, "easy," 519.

92. Philostratus, *Heroikos* 2.171.29–32 Kayser. See above note 78.

93. Wilamowitz, *Glaube d. Hellenen* (above, note 31) I, 20, goes too far in saying that when Hephaestus is used by metonymy for fire "he is no Hellenic god." For the cosmic significance of the battle of Hephaestus and Scamander in *Il.* 21, see M. N. Nagler, *Spontaneity and Tradition* (Berkeley and Los Angeles 1974) 149–158. The saving of Hephaestus by Thetis in the sea (*Il.* 18.395ff.) reflects a very different relationship between the two elements, perhaps, as Preller-Robert suggest (above, note 31, I, 175), the association of volcanic fire and the sea.

94. Arrian in Stobaeus 1.246.18W. See Marx (above, note 79) 684.

95. See Burkert (above, note 43) passim; Dumézil (above, note 31) 20, 25, 35ff. See also Fredrich (above, note 52) 75. Dumézil lists the texts (chaps. 2 and 3) and also provides a useful survey of other lines of interpretation (chap. 4).

96. Dumézil (above, note 31) 30, 54–55; Fredrich (above, note 52) 77f.

97. Fredrich (above, note 52) 72ff. and 254f., citing Dioscurides, *Materia Medica* 5.113.

98. Hesiod 4B7DK.

99. Homer, *Odyssey* 8.280–282, 294.

100. On the interlocking of divine and human in the play, see N. T. Pratt, Jr., "Sophoclean 'Orthodoxy' in the *Philoctetes*," *AJP* 70 (1949) 273–289; Robert Muth, "Gottheit und Mensch im 'Philoktet' des Sophokles," *Studi in onore di Luigi Castiglioni* (Florence 1960) 2.641–658; Segal, "Piety" passim.

101. For Odysseus' relation to the gods, see Segal, "Piety" 138–142; for his relation to the oracles, see 140–141 and n19.

102. See also *Phil.* 254, 315–316, 446–452, 776–778, 992; Perrotta (above, note 27) 421–422; Segal, "Piety" 148–150 with the further literature there cited.

103. For the problem of the wound and divine justice, see Segal, "Piety" 150ff. with the bibliography there cited.

104. *Algos* is emotional pain in 66, 86, 368, 806, 1011, 1170; it is physical pain in 734, 792, 827, 1326, 1378–79; it is both in 339–340. See also Long (above, note 21) 132, who dismisses the metaphorical meaning of *algos* rather too lightly: the fact that the "bite" of anguish is a familiar image (*Il.* 5.493 and Hdt. 7.10) does not lessen its particular force and its renewed power in this play about physical pain and emotional as well as physical disease. For the symbolism of the wound as the inner bitterness of Philoctetes, see Penelope Biggs, "The Disease Theme in Sophocles' *Ajax, Philoctetes,* and *Trachiniae*," *CP* 61 (1966) 232–233; Segal, "Piety" 149–150.

105. Lessing, *Laocoon* chap. 4, sect. 1. See also Letters 278: "No snake-bite in the annals of science could have tormented a man ten years instead of killing him within a few hours." Perrotta (above, note 27) 437–438 criticizes earlier attempts to look for realism in Philoctetes' disease.

106. See the metrical hypothesis to *Phil.* and the scholion to 94. Also Hyginus, *Fab.* 102; Philostratus the Younger, *Imag.* 17; Dio Chrys. 59.9. For further discussion and bibliography see Segal, "Piety" 151–152 and n47.

107. John A. Moore, *Sophocles and Arete* (Cambridge 1938) 54–55.

108. See Kamerbeek (above, note 32) 200–201; L. Radermacher, *RhM* 85 (1936) 1–3.

109. For these aspects of the bow, see Segal, "Piety" 144–145.

110. For this word play, see David B. Robinson, "Topics in Sophocles' *Philoctetes,*" *CQ* n.s. 19 (1969) 43–44; "Philoctetes would seem to speak truer than he knew" (p. 44). See also J. C. Kamerbeek, "Sophocle et Héraclite," *Studia Vollgraff* (Amsterdam 1948) 84–98.

111. Another indication of this gap between heroic past and abject present is the contrast between the stately spondees of 262, *tōn Hērakleiōn onta despotēn hoplōn* ("master of the arms of Heracles") and the choppy tribrachs resulting from the resolutions in 932,

ἀπόδος, ἱκνοῦμαί σ᾽, ἀπόδος, ἱκετεύω, τέκνον·

Give back, I beseech you, give it back, I beg you, child.

112. See Whitman 183, 187 on the inner divinity of the hero and its relation to Heracles and the bow.

113. *ta tox' helōn,* 762 and 931.

114. Cf. the use of *kleinos,* "glorious," to describe both Philoctetes (575) and the bow (654).

115. See Diller (above, note 6) 166; Segal, "Piety" 153–154 with the literature cited in note 54.

116. Cf. especially the rocks in 160, 272, 296, 937, 952, 1081–82 and in general Segal, "Divino" 74; "Piety" 154.

117. For other aspects of the sea, cf. Segal, "Piety" 154–156.

118. Tycho von Wilamowitz-Moellendorff, *Die dramatische Technik des Sophokles* (Berlin 1917) 279, finds this ode to Ge particularly disturbing for the spectator. Reinhardt 182 suggests that it forms part of men's manipulative use of the divine for their intrigues. For the sacredness of Ge, see also *OC* 39–40, 1574, 1654, where Earth has much more solemn significance. For the worship of Ge in this period, see Wilamowitz, *Glaube der Hellenen* (above, note 31) I, 202–208; Gerhard Müller, *Sophokles, Antigone* (Heidelberg 1967) 83–84, apropos of *Antig.* 338.

119. Note also *bora* used of Philoctetes' food in 274 and 308, appropriate inasmuch as it carries associations with the harsh diet of the hunter or the food of animals: see C. Segal, "Euripides, *Hippolytus,* 108–112: Tragic Irony and Tragic Justice," *Hermes* 97 (1969) 297–298.

10 Philoctetes: Society, Language, Friendship

1. See Renata Scheliha, *Der Philoktet des Sophokles* (Amsterdam 1970) 15–16.

2. For a more detailed discussion of the limitations of the chorus' and of Odysseus' views of authority, human and divine, see C. Segal, "Philoctetes and the Imperishable Piety," *Hermes* 105 (1977) 137–142 (cited henceforth as "Piety").

3. One may compare Creon's tyrannical definition of civic government in *Antigone* 736–738 ("Is not the city regarded as belonging to its ruler?" 738).

4. Pierre Vidal-Naquet, "Le *Philoctète* de Sophocle et l'éphébie," *MT* 177–178, views the conflict of Odysseus and Neoptolemus differently: He sees Neoptolemus (with Philoctetes) choosing "familial values" over "civic values." Yet these "familial values" also imply a view of society, and the "civic values" of which Vidal-Naquet speaks here are

primarily those of Odysseus and not necessarily the only type of civic values envisaged in the play.

5. Werner Jaeger, *Paideia,* trans. G. Highet, II (New York, N.Y., 1944) 174. P. E. Easterling, "Philoctetes and Modern Criticism," *Illinois Classical Studies* 3 (1978) 37, also touches on this idea of a recreation of heroic society. For *philia* as the basis of society in Plato, see *Protag.* 322d and *Sympos.* 182c.

6. For this interlocking of divine and human in Philoctetes' "return," see Segal, "Piety" 133–158, esp. 149ff.

7. Knox, "Ajax," 1–37, and see above, chapter 5; A similar view of the *Philoctetes* is suggested by Charles R. Beye, "Sophocles' *Philoctetes* and the Homeric Embassy," *TAPA* 101 (1970) 63–75. For reasons that will appear below, I do not consider this formula entirely satisfactory for an interpretation of *Philoctetes.*

8. See Musurillo 127. Odysseus does the will of the gods, but for the wrong reasons: see on this point the good remarks of Gennaro Perrotta, *Sofocle* (Messina and Florence 1935) 459–461. Vickers 272 aptly applies to Odysseus Swift's analogy: "Is not religion a cloak . . . and conscience a pair of breeches, which, though a cover for lewdness as well as nastiness, is easily slipt down for the services of both?" Easterling (above, note 5) 38 is also right to view the "ambiguous figure" of Odysseus as representing "the ambiguity of the world of the Greek army."

9. Ivan M. Linforth, "Philoctetes: The Play and the Man," *UCPCP* 15.3 (1956) 106, observes of the chorus' little cry, *tlēmon,* "poor man," in 161, "Even so slight a hint of sympathy as this had not appeared in the whole conversation between Odysseus and Neoptolemus."

10. Unlike Aeschylus and Euripides, Sophocles never questions—at least in the *Philoctetes*—the essential validity, justice, and nobility of purpose in the Greek expedition against Troy.

11. Heracles' words in 1413, "I have left my abode in the heavens and come for your sake" (*sēn . . . charin*), might also mean, "I come out of kindness toward you," taking *charis* more emphatically.

12. See A. J. Podlecki, "The Power of the Word in Sophocles' *Philoctetes,*" *GRBS* 7 (1966) 233–250.

13. See Peter Rose, "Sophocles' *Philoctetes* and the Teachings of the Sophists," *HSCP* 80 (1976) 83.

14. See Knox, *HT* 130–132.

15. The lack of a human voice and human response figures also in Accius' version of the play, where the hero laments (frag. XI. 549–551 Ribbeck): *iaceo in tecto umido/quod eiulatu questu gemitu fremitibus/ resonando mutum flebilis voces refert,* lines which Cicero deemed worthy of citation on three separate occasions.

16. For the role of language in fifth-century culture histories, see Soph., *Antig.* 353–354; Plato, *Protag.* 322a; Diodorus 1.8.3 (= Democritus 68B5DK); see in general A. T. Cole, *Democritus and the Sources of Greek Anthropology,* A.P.A. Monographs 25 (Cleveland 1967) 33, 60ff.

17. See P. W. Harsh, "The Role of the Bow in the *Philoctetes* of Sophocles," *AJP* 81 (1960) 410–411.

18. Sophocles may here be criticizing Euripides' treatment of language and his characterization of Odysseus, who, according to Dio Chrysostom 52.14, possessed "an overmastering and wondrous power in speaking." Likewise in 52.11 Dio contrasts Aeschylus' rugged simplicity with Euripides' skill which is "most oriented toward politics and oratory" (*politikōtatē kai rhētorikōtatē*).

19. For this clash between the persuasion of the oracle and the force of Odysseus, see Oliver Taplin, "Significant Actions in Sophocles' *Philoctetes,*" *GRBS* 12 (1971) 38; D. B. Robinson, "Topics in Sophocles' *Philoctetes,*" *CQ* n.s. 19 (1969) 46ff.; Easterling (above, note 5) 28–29, 31–32; David Seale, "The Element of Surprise in Sophocles' *Philoctetes,*" *BICS* 19 (1972) 95–97. For further discussion and bibliography on the question of the oracles in general, see Segal, "Piety" 140 and n19.

20. For these ironies see Rose (above, note 13) 72 and 83.

21. For *physis* and *nomos* in language, see e.g. Democritus 68B26DK; Plato, *Cratyl.,* passim; see in general W. K. C. Guthrie, *A History of Greek Philosophy* II (Cambridge 1965) 474–476; Felix Heinimann, *Nomos und Physis* (Basel 1945) 156–162.

22. *Mythos:* 1410, 1417, 1447. See Podlecki (above, note 12) 244–245.

23. Note also the interplay between Philoctetes' *epoiktereite me* (1071) and Neoptolemus' *ephyn oiktou pleōs* (1074).

24. Adams 153; also Podlecki (above, note 12) 241; Reinhardt 191 and n1.

25. On these repetitions see Wolf Steidle, *Studien zum antiken Drama* (Munich 1968) 181; Perrotta (above, note 8) 451.

26. On the repeated *ti drasō,* see Knox, *HT* 132–133; Steidle (above, note 25) 181–184.

27. With Pearson's Oxford text, I keep the mss. reading at 1383: see T.B.L. Webster, *Sophocles' Philoctetes* (Cambridge 1970) *ad loc.* Linforth (above, note 9) 146 n27 takes the verb to refer to "the benefit which is promised by the gods in the prophecy of Helenos," a defensible view, though it need not be restricted quite so narrowly to benefit from the gods. Philoctetes' reply in 1384, "Do you mean benefit to the Atreids or to me" need not, as Jebb thinks, imply that the "help" in 1383 referred to the Atreids and therefore require emendation: R.C. Jebb, *Sophocles, The Plays and Fragments,* Part IV, *The Philoctetes* (Cambridge 1898) *ad loc.* Philoctetes has his hatred of the Atreids uppermost in his thoughts and therefore turns Neoptolemus' words, bitterly, in this direction.

28. On this "error" see Knox *HT* 136; also Suzanne Saïd, *La faute tragique* (Paris 1978) 379ff., who has well emphasized its deep moral significance and association with justice, honor, and nobility.

29. Thucydides 2.40.4. Sallust, under Thucydidean influence, describes the Athenians thus: *magis . . . dandis quam accipiundis beneficiis amicitias parabant, Catiline* 6.5.

30. On *eunoia* see E. A. Havelock, *The Liberal Temper in Greek Politics* (New Haven 1957) 232; also Rose (above, note 13) 56. In Hdt. 7.237 the despotic Xerxes cannot understand the relation of *eunoia* among citizens who are equals, and sees only envy and suspicion.

31. See Knox, *HT* 135–141; Vidal-Naquet, *MT* 166: "Le *Philoctète* nous offre l'exemple, unique dans l'oeuvre de Sophocle, d'une mutation d'un héros tragique."

32. A late scholion on 1402 is a very weak peg on which to hang the view that Neoptolemus is still unchanged in deceiving Philoctetes at the end, as does W. M. Calder, III., "Sophoclean Apologia: *Philoctetes,*" *GRBS* 12 (1971) 153–174. The chief objections are these: (1) how could an audience know that Neoptolemus is practicing deception in scenes like 895ff. or 1222ff.? (2) Neoptolemus is resistant to Odyssean trickery even when Philoctetes is not onstage or "hears nothing," in, for example, the prologue and 839–842; (3) the argument that the great repentance scene, 1222ff., is played for Philoctetes' benefit is weak, since Philoctetes (*pace* Calder, p. 116) is in his cave from 1217 on; (4) an oath like that of 1289 would be strange blasphemy for a character otherwise shown as reverent and sympathetic, and one would again have to ask how an audience could suspect that this oath is false.

33. See *Ajax* 125–126 and Knox, "Ajax" 22, 25–28. Compare Cyrus in Hdt. 1.86.6 and see my remarks in "Croesus on the Pyre: Herodotus and Bacchylides," *WS* 84 N.S. 5 (1971) 50–51.

34. See Hartmut Erbse, "Neoptolemos und Philoktet bei Sophokles," *Hermes* 94 (1966) 195 and n1; also Karin Alt, "Schicksal und *Physis* im Philoktet des Sophocles," *Hermes* 89 (1961) 147–148; H. C. Avery, "Heracles, Philoctetes, Neoptolemus," *Hermes* 93 (1965) 289.

35. See Beye (above, note 7) 72.

36. For the initiatory theme, see especially Vidal-Naquet (above, note 4) passim. The motif of the youth's search for a "father" and teacher has been much discussed, particularly with reference to the terms of address between the two protagonists: see Avery (above, note 34) 285ff.; Erbse (above, note 34) 180–182; Reinhardt 176ff. Kitto, *Form* 110, 114; U. Parlavantza-Friedrich, *Täuschungsszenen in den Tragödien des Sophokles* (Berlin 1969) 63–65.

37. Gilbert Norwood, *Greek Tragedy* (London 1920) 162, remarks, "Life after all is not a blaze of glorious war as his father Achilles found it, but a sordid affair of necessary compromises."

38. It is striking that at the end Neoptolemus does not speak of fame any longer but of avoiding blame or guilt among the Greeks (*aitia*, 1404). See Alt (above, note 34) 171. And yet by undergoing an inversion of aims analogous to the experience of Philoctetes, he attains a deeper, more authentic heroism than that which Odysseus offered him at Troy.

39. The theme of teaching is particularly marked also in 387–388, 971ff., 1010ff., 1359ff. See in general Knox, *HT* 122–124. On the reversal implied in 1387, see also Eilhard Schlesinger, "Die Intrige im Aufbau von Sophokles' Philoktet," *RhM* 111 (1968) 146, who speaks of Neoptolemus' "Höhe des *phronein* . . . , die es dem jungen Sohn des Achilles gestattet, zu dem Älteren im Ton väterlicher Ermahnung zu sprechen."

40. On the importance of the personal gesture of friendship here, see Linforth (above, note 9) 155; Bowra 302–303; Max Pohlenz, *Die griechische Tragödie*[2] (Göttingen 1954) I, 331.

41. For the echo see Podlecki (above, note 12) 245.

42. See Knox, "Ajax" passim; Beye (above, note 7) 69ff. For the significance of Ajax in *Phil.*, see also Schlesinger (above, note 39) 129–133 and Erbse (above, note 34) 198.

43. Jebb, Introduction xxviii, note, remarks that "Neoptolemus would naturally feel some fresh remorse and shame when he perceived (from v.1365) that the whole extent of his duplicity was not even then surmised by Philoctetes." Adams' view, 137, that Neoptolemus really had been deprived of Achilles' arms is well refuted by Knox, *HT* 137 and n30, 191. See also Calder (above, note 32) 150–151; Schlesinger (above, note 39) 129ff.; Perrotta (above, note 8) 419–420. Th. Zielinski, *Tragodoumenon Libri Tres* (Cracow 1925) 109; Jens-Uwe Schmidt, *Sophokles, Philoktet: Eine Strukturanalyse* (Heidelberg 1973) 84–85.

44. Schlesinger (above, note 39) 132 suggests viewing the lie about the arms as "ein dichterische Bild oder Symbol einer Realität." See also Whitman 177.

45. For the parallels between Philoctetes and Achilles, see Beye (above, note 7) passim; Schlesinger (above, note 39) 103–105, 129–130.

46. See Whitman 177; Schlesinger (above, note 39) 134.

47. On the pathos of this "perhaps" (*isōs*) in 261, see the sensitive comment of Reinhardt 261. For other functions of these lines, see Parlavantza-Friedrich (above, note 36) 62.

48. On this cathartic function of Heracles, see Albert Cook, *Enactment: Greek Tragedy* (Chicago 1971) 54–55.

49. Whitman 187, "[Heracles] is the archetype of Philoctetes' greater self, the pattern of his glory." See also Bowra 301. Vickers 278 views Heracles' appearance as "an indication of Philoctetes' stature. Only a hero and a god can win him over to a life which will free him from suffering and end in glory." Of Heracles Eugen Dönt, "Zur Deutung des Tragischen bei Sophokles," *A.u.A.* 17 (1971) 52, remarks, "Er selbst hat gezeigt, wie man im Tragen des Leidens sich dem Göttlichen so weit wie möglich nähern und die *eusebeia* verwirklichen kann . . . Der Mensch kann danach sein Dasein als notwendig schwach und vergänglich begreifen, sein Leid aber als einen Weg zur Erfüllung der ewigen göttlichen Ordnungen." For a different view of Philoctetes at the end, stressing the intransigence which only divine intervention can overcome, see Knox (above, note 14) 140–141; A. Spira, *Untersuchungen zum Deus ex Machina bei Sophokles und Euripides* (Kallmünz 1960) 28.

50. For the double function of Heracles at the end, see Segal, "Piety" passim, with the further literature cited there, esp. 135 n10.

51. For this triangular pattern, see Cook (above, note 48) 48.

52. For further discussion of this view of the ending, see Segal, "Piety" 158.

53. Such, by and large, is the view of Joe Park Poe, *Heroism and Divine Justice in Sophocles' Philoctetes, Mnemosyne* Supplement 34 (Leiden 1974) passim, esp. 49–51. On this view Heracles' appearance continues Philoctetes' "humiliation and his helpless ineffectuality" (49), and "Philoctetes' failure becomes a paradigm of the frustration and futility of mankind" (51). The tone of Heracles' speech and Philoctetes' own last lines, however, point in quite another direction and suggest that such a view of the outcome, though possible theoretically, is not the view which Sophocles means us to take.

54. See Penelope Biggs "The Disease Theme in Sophocles' *Ajax, Philoctetes,* and *Trachiniae,*" *CP* 61 (1966) 235; Segal, "Piety" 158.

55. For a diagrammatic synopsis of some of these relations, see my "Divino e umano nel *Filottete* di Sofocle," *QUCC* 23 (1976) 85–86.

56. Note also the compound epithet in *naus poikilostolos* 343 and the Homeric ring in *bia Odysseōs* (314, 321, 592), on which see A.A. Long, *Language and Thought in Sophocles* (London 1968) 102 and n138.

57. Compare the lion simile of Diomedes and Odysseus in *Iliad* 10.297 and see also 5.554. See in general P. Rödström, *De Imaginibus Sophocleis a Rerum Natura Sumptis* (Stockholm 1883) 40. The negative view taken of the simile by Avery (above, note 34) 296 seems hardly justified by the context. See *contra* Bowra 304–305. It is possible, however, that the twin lions of Eur., *Orestes* 1401–1402 and 1555 are a grim reply to our passage, with a darker view of epic heroism: see Charles Fuqua, "The World of Myth in Euripides' 'Orestes', "*Traditio* 34 (1978) 22.

58. For the importance of this pattern of coordinate pronouns throughout the play, see my brief remarks in "Divino e umano" (above, note 55) 79–80. Easterling (above, note 5) 35 and Steidle (above, note 25) 187 note the importance of the notion of reciprocity in 1436–37 but do not recognize its significance as a patterned sequence throughout the play. Steidle, 187 n72, however, sensitively observes the gestural configuration implied in Heracles' words in 1436–37: "Die Pronomina erfordern eine—wie immer gestaltete—Zeigegebärde, die die schon an sich nachdrückliche Formulierung unterstreicht."

59. See also Aesch., *Septem* 354 and Pindar, *Isth.* 3.17.

60. E.g. Kitto, *Form* 105, 128; Linforth (above, note 9) 150. See also Calder (above,

note 32) 169 and n89; Beye (above, note 7) 74–75. For a more positive view, see Cook (above, note 48) 54–55; Schmidt (above, note 43) 245.

61. Odysseus has a small glimmer of the reward due Philoctetes at the sacking of Troy when he calls him "equal to the best (*aristoi*), with whom you must (*dei*) take Troy and raze it by force" (997–998). Even so, Philoctetes is only one of several *aristoi*. Kitto, *Form* 122–123, gives undue weight to these lines and thereby puts Odysseus' stance here into far too favorable a light.

62. See Erbse (above, note 34) 178.

63. On this struggle between truth and appearance in the play and in Sophocles generally, see Reinhardt 202–203; Schlesinger (above, note 39) 154.

64. The importance of this dual aspect of Philoctetes' movement out of savagery is argued at length in my "Piety" passim.

65. See Schlesinger (above, note 39) 156: "Erst in der freien Annahme seines ihm bestimmten Schicksals vollendet sich das Heroentum der sophokleischen Menschen." See also H. Diller "Über das Selbstbewusstsein der sophokleischen Personen," *WS* 69 (1956) 78. We should note that this hero's 'destiny' includes a grace from the gods that is not necessarily a part of the fifth-century version of the myth: in Pindar, *Pyth.* 1. 52–55, Philoctetes goes to Troy and vanquishes the city, but is not cured of his disease.

66. For other aspects of nature in the closing scene see Vidal-Naquet, *MT* 179–180; C. Segal, "Nature and the World of Man in Greek Literature," *Arion* 2.1 (1963) 38–39.

67. For the reading of 533–534, see above, chapter 9, note 21.

68. For the landscape of Lemnos as a kind of "soulscape" of its inhabitant, see Beye (above, note 7) 67; Schlesinger (above, note 39) 147–148; Lilian Feder, "The Symbol of the Desert Island in Sophocles' *Philoctetes*," *Drama Survey* 3 (1963) 33–41; Segal, "Piety" (above, note 2) 153ff., with the further literature there cited. Jones 271–272 suggestively contrasts the distance between the hero and nature in Aeschylus, *PV* 88–91 and the association of nature with the quality of the hero's personality in Sophocles.

69. For Philoctetes' ambivalence toward Lemnos, "hated and loved, the barren island and the comforting haven," see Feder (above, note 68) 40; Segal, "Piety" (above, note 2) 155.

70. See schol. on Pindar, *Ol.* 13.74g; Preller-Robert, *Griechische Mythologie* I⁴ (Berlin 1894) 858, 856 and n4.

71. See 21, 292ff., 716–717, 1214 and above, chapter 9, section IX.

72. See Vidal-Naquet, *MT* 180: "C'est l'ordre divin qui permet aux hommes de redevenir les maîtres de la nature sauvage. Tel est le dernier renversement du *Philoctète*."

73. For the pathetic echo of 133–134 and the theme of *sōtēria* in the play generally, see M.H. Jameson, "Politics and the *Philoctetes*," *CP* 51 (1956) 227 and n51.

74. U. von Wilamowitz-Moellendorff, *Der Glaube der Hellenen* (Berlin 1931) 363 and n2, observes the significance of the fact that not Zeus directly, but the *daimōn* is mentioned here. He adds (pp. 363–364): "Zufall soll es nicht sein: ein göttlicher Wille steht hinter allem was geschieht, aber mehr erkennen wir nicht immer." Cf. also the destructive *moira* of Achilles in Neoptolemus' lie, 331. Already for Pindar Philoctetes exemplified the obscure workings of *moira:* The Greeks brought him back to Troy which he sacked, ending their toils, "going with weak foot, but it was destined" (*moiridion, Pyth.* 1.55).

75. For further discussion of Philoctetes' attitudes towards the gods and the change in his last speech, see Segal, "Piety" 148–150, 154–158.

76. See Dönt (above, note 49) 48; Spira (above, note 49) 32; Perrotta (above, note 8) 422.

77. See Reinhardt 202; Perrotta (above, note 8) citing *OC* 394, remarks, "In this dark atmosphere resound the desperate cries of Philoctetes, innocent and great of soul." (p. 471).

78. So Robinson (above, note 19) passim and Linforth (above, note 9) 151.

79. For this manifestation of divine justice, see Kitto, *Form* 134–136; Schlesinger (above, note 39) 142. On the other hand Bowra (above, note 40) 305–306 views the play too simplistically as the manifestation of divine justice ("The close of the play shows that Zeus' will is done.").

80. Schmidt (above, note 43) 247 notes the importance of 1426–27 but does not give the lines their due: "Wenn schliesslich gerade jenem, der dem *kakon* den äussersten Widerstand entgegengesetzt hat, die Aufgabe übertragen wird, den *aitios tōnde kakōn* (1426) zu töten, so scheint mir auch das nicht ohne Bedeutung in die Herakles-Eröffnungen hineingekommen."

81. See Reinhardt 202–203; Bowra 263–264.

82. On the deathlike state of Lemnos, see Knox, *HT* 129, apropos of 621ff.; in general, Segal, "Piety" 156.

83. The possibility that Neoptolemus may be lying about Thersites in 445 is suggested by George Huxley, "Thersites in Sophokles, *Philoktetes* 445," *GRBS* 8 (1967) 33–34, followed by Calder (above, note 32) 159. Even if Neoptolemus is being devious here, the pattern of the inversion of life and death remains unchanged. In fact, it would be even more poignant were the facts distorted into this pattern by Odyssean trickery and its manifestation, still, in Neoptolemus' acquiescence to it.

84. For possible connections between the play and current political events, see Jameson (above, note 43) and Calder (above, note 32).

85. On the phrase *es phōs* "into the light," in 1353, Jebb *ad loc.* comments "into the public gaze" and cites 581, which contrasts "dark" and "open" speech. But the phrase need not be restricted to that meaning, especially after the references to Hades and life just a few lines before (1348ff.). Return to the public world *and* to open speech (cf. 578–581) accompanies the return from death to life, from the Hades-like existence of the cave to the upper world, from obscurity and savagery to heroism and humanity. Physical life, figurative rebirth as a civilized man, and the renewal of language here all come together.

86. On the importance of the cave, see Robinson (above, note 19) 34–37; W. Jobst, *Die Höhle im griechischen Theater des 5. und 4. Jahrhunderts, SB Wien* Phil.-Hist. Klasse 268, no. 2 (1970) 41–43; A.M. Dale, "Seen and Unseen on the Greek Stage," *WS* 69 (1956) 104–106. Further bibliography in Segal, "Piety" 156 n64.

87. See Perrotta (above, note 8) 464: "E Filottete rientra nella sua grotta per chiudersi come in una tomba."

88. Reading *syneisei*, with Reiske and Pearson, against *synoisei*, "You will endure (with me") of the mss. and scholia.

89. See Jobst (above, note 86) 44.

90. For the significance of the cave of *Od.* 13, see C. Segal, "The Phaeacians and the Symbolism of Odysseus' Return," *Arion* 1.4 (1962) 48 and n34.

91. Dönt (above, note 49) 51–54.

11 Oedipus at Colonus: The End of a Vision

1. For the importance of friendship and personal ties in late fifth-century drama, see Bruno Snell, *Poetry and Society* (Bloomington, Ind., 1961) 88–90, with examples from the end of Euripides' *Heracles* and beginning of the *Iphigeneia at Aulis.*

2. See Knox, *HT* 148: "His opening speech shows us a man who seems to be at the end rather than the beginning." See also J. Carrière, "Sur l'essence et l'évolution du tragique chez les Grecs," *REG* 79 (1966) 22–23.

3. See E. Schlesinger, "Die Intrige im Aufbau von Sophokles Philoktet," *RhM* 111 (1968) 154.

4. See Knox, *HT* 174–175 n83; W. Pötscher, "Die Oedipus-Gestalt," *Eranos* 71 (1973) 42–43; David Grene, *Reality and the Heroic Pattern: Last Plays of Ibsen, Shakespeare, and Sophocles* (Chicago 1967) 157, 163; Peter Burian, "Suppliant and Savior: Oedipus at Colonus," *Phoenix* 28 (1974) 410ff., esp. 418.

5. For "profit" (*kerdos*) cf. 72, 92, 579, 1421; for "help" (*onēsis*) see 287–288; for "savior" (*sōtēr*) cf. 84ff., 457–460, 463, 487. Cf. also A. J. Festugière, "Tragédie et tombes sacrées," *Rev. de l'Histoire des Religions* 184 (1973) 16ff.

6. John Gould, "Hiketeia," *JHS* 93 (1973) 90.

7. For the importance of place in the *OC* in general, see Jones 214–235, esp. 223ff.

8. See also 744–745, 944ff.

9. E.g. 3, 50, 123–124, 165, 347ff., 444, 745–746, 949, 1096, 1363. See also Jones 218.

10. For the imagery of the road, see Otfried Becker, *Das Bild des Weges,* Hermes Einzelschrift 4 (1937) 210–212.

11. For the importance of nurture in the play, see P. E. Easterling, "Oedipus and Polyneices," *PCPS* 193 n.s. 13 (1967) 1–13.

12. The hunting motif in the play is briefly noted by M. G. Shields, "Sight and Blindness in the *Oedipus Coloneus,*" *Phoenix* 15 (1961) 70.

13. The legal basis for such a position does not, of course, correspond to Oedipus' understanding of the situation: see T. G. Rosenmeyer, "The Wrath of Oedipus," *Phoenix* 6 (1952) 102–103 and n42.

14. Homer, *Odyssey* 7.145ff., especially 7.165–181; 9.271.

15. J. Gould (above, note 6) 101.

16. Ibid. 100.

17. See Burian (above, note 4) 422ff.

18. Note the theme of the "seat" also in 1160, 1163, 1166, 1179; see in general Easterling (above, note 11) 5–6.

19. In 1373 Turnebus' emendation, *keinēn ereipseis,* for the mss. *kenēn erei tis,* is accepted by most editors: see R. C. Jebb, *Sophocles, The Plays and Fragments,* Part II, *The Oedipus Coloneus* (Cambridge 1885) *ad loc.*

20. See also 96, 163; also above, note 10.

21. See Bernd Seidensticker, "Beziehungen zwischen den beiden Oidipusdramen des Sophokles," *Hermes* 100 (1972) 274: "Als Jüngling führt ihn ein böser Daimon am Scheideweg den falschen Weg, jetzt geht er, von einem Gott geleitet, sicher dem Ziel entgegen."

22. See Easterling (above, note 11) 11.

23. See in general O. Gruppe, "Die eherne Schwelle und der Thorikische Stein," *Archiv f. Religionswissenschaft* 15 (1912) 361–363; Festugière (above, note 5) 11; Carl Robert, *Oidipus* (Berlin 1915) I, 24ff.; U. von Wilamowitz-Moellendorff in Tycho von Wilamowitz-Moellendorff, *Die dramatische Technik des Sophokles,* Philol. Untersuch. 22 (Berlin 1917) 320–325.

24. See J. G. Frazer, *Pausanias' Description of Greece* II (London 1913) 366–367 (on 1.28.7) and 395–396 (on 1.30.4); Festugière (above, note 5) 8 and 14. F. Jacoby, *FGrHist*

on 324F62, vol. IIIb, Supplement, pt. II (Leiden 1954) 154–155. For the grove as a place of *katabasis* to the Underworld, see also the scholion on *OC* 57.

25. For the Thorician Rock and the sacred pear tree, see Gruppe (above, note 23) 364ff., 357ff. The schol. to Lycophron 766 and to Pindar, *Pyth.* 4.246 establish a connection with the creation of the first horse through an ejaculation of Poseidon. Both the pear tree and the white stone are connected with the themes of new life, rebirth, the crossing between life and death. The Thorician Rock has also some similarities with the "White Rock" of the Second Nekyia of the *Odyssey* (*Od.* 24.11), on which see Gregory Nagy, *HSCP* 77 (1973) 137–177; also Eustath. on *Od.* 11.292 (p. 1685.33).

26. On this ambiguity of the tomb, see Wilamowitz (above, note 23) 327.

27. See Festugière (above, note 5) 11ff.; Robert (above, note 23) I, 33; Erwin Rohde, *Psyche,* trans. W. B. Hillis (London 1925) 430 and n112, 455. I. M. Linforth's secularizing view of the play, "Religion and Drama in *Oedipus at Colonus*," *UCPCP* 14.4 (1951) 75–192, esp. 75–82, is well criticized by H.-F. Johansen, *Lustrum* 7 (1962) 214.

28. For the chthonic role of Oedipus in his associations with Demeter and vegetation, see Robert (above, note 23) I, 21–22, 44–46. Pötscher's criticism of this view (above, note 4) 12–14 takes too spiritualizing an approach to the cult of heroes: see below, note 30.

29. See Kirkwood 197.

30. For the goddesses' double aspect, see Jebb (above, note 19) xxvii–xxviii; Knox (above, note 2) 194 and n12; R. P. Winnington-Ingram, "A Religious Function of Greek Tragedy: A Study in the *Oedipus Coloneus* and the *Oresteia*," *JHS* 74 (1954) 18. See also Linforth (above, note 27) 93–94; P. Sgroi, "Edipo a Colono," *Maia* 14 (1962) 288; Franz Stoessl, "Der Oedipus auf Kolonos des Sophokles," *Dioniso* 40 (1966) 14. Attempts to banish the goddesses as Erinyes from the play, like that of Adams 165, are not successful. For the double aspect of chthonic deities and heroes in their chthonic associations, see U. von Wilamowitz-Moellendorff, *Der Glaube der Hellenen* (Berlin 1931) I, 210ff.; H. J. Rose, "Chthonian Cattle," *Numen* 1 (1954) 216–217; A. D. Nock, "The Cult of Heroes," *HThR* 37 (1944) 159–161.

31. Although there is no sure evidence for the sacred grove of the Eumenides at Colonus prior to Sophocles' play, it is unlikely that Sophocles made the whole thing up, as is suggested by L. S. Colchester, "Justice and Death in Sophocles," *CQ* 36 (1942) 23. Existing evidence, analogies with other local legends like those of the Heraclidae and the body of Eurystheus, and the importance of the tomb of Oedipus elsewhere (e.g. Eur., *Phoen.* 1589ff., 1703ff.) point to existing traditions, possibly refurbished and made more lustrous by Sophocles, developing a local into a Pan-Athenian cult: see Festugière (above, note 5) passim, esp. 8ff., 20ff.; Robert (above, note 23) I, 33–41 and 44; Rosenmeyer (above, note 13) 99 n30. Still, we cannot be sure that the intimate linking of Oedipus' grave with the grove of the Eumenides antedates Sophocles. Androtion, *FGrHist* 324 F62 (p. 75, 19ff.), mentions the sanctuary of the Eumenides at Colonus without any reference to a tomb of Oedipus there; but again the argumentum ex silentio is not strong. See below, note 43.

32. See Winnington-Ingram (above, note 30) 18.

33. For the sinister association of the forbidden grove with Oedipus' incest, see B. Lefcowitz, "The Inviolate Grove," *Literature and Psychology* 17 (1967) 78–86; E. Lorenz, "Oidipus auf Kolonos," *Imago* 4 (1915) 22–40; Helen Bacon, "Women's Two Faces: Sophocles' View of the Tragedy of Oedipus and His Family," *Science and Psychoanalysis,* Decennial Memorial Volume (New York, N.Y., 1966) 10–27.

34. The sadness of the nightingale is a recurrent theme in Sophocles: *Ajax* 627;

Trach. 105, 963; *El.* 107, 147; also *Antig.* 423–425. See in general P. Rödström, *De Imaginibus Sophocleis a Rerum Natura Sumptis* (Stockholm 1883) 30–31; A. S. McDevitt, "The Nightingale and the Olive," *WS* Beiheft 5 = *Antidosis, Festschrift f. Walther Kraus* (Vienna 1972) 231.

35. On the narcissus and death here (in contrast to the life-giving olive of 698), see McDevitt (preceding note) 234–235; also Jebb on line 683; Robert (above, note 23) I, 23; Knox, *HT* 155; Ileana Chirassi, *Elementi di culture precereali nei miti e riti greci*, Incunabula Graeca 30 (Rome 1968) 143–155; Louise Vinge, *The Narcissus Theme in Western European Literature up to the Early 19th Century* (Lund 1967) 33–35. Note that *oinōpan*, "wine-faced," in 674 modifies "ivy," whereas the vine's fruit is referred to only obliquely in *myriokarpos*, 676. In 17, however, vine and olive, along with the laurel, are explicitly mentioned. See Jebb on lines 675–676. Sgroi (above, note 30) 284 takes too idealizing a view of the grove and its setting, "dove tutto è fresco e animato nella libera letizia del vivere."

36. For a somewhat different view of the connection between the sea and Theseus here, see McDevitt (above, note 34) 236.

37. P. Vicaire, *REG* 81 (1968) 366–367, tries unsuccessfully to play down the maenadic aspect of Dionysus and sees here only a "tableau idyllique" which shows "un Dionysos apaisé" (p. 367). The reference to the "divine nurses of Dionysus here in 678–680 certainly suggests his connection with maenads (cf. *Iliad* 6.132) and also with the seasonal cycles of a vegetational deity.

38. This meaning is supported by Pollux. Jebb prefers the more common meaning, "unvanquished," but allows the former meaning as possible. The olive which "springs up by itself" (*autopoion*) also recalls the living rock near the grove on which Oedipus sits: *autopetros* (192).

39. So Knox, *HT* 155–156.

40. *Ibid* 156: "The city of Sophocles' youth and manhood will put on immortality, like the old, blind man who has now become its citizen." See also Whitman 210.

41. See McDevitt (above, note 34) 237.

42. The meaning of *nēphōn* here goes beyond the sense of "not drinking wine" because of Oedipus' hard fare: see Linforth (above, note 27) 92–93 and n12.

43. See Frazer (above, note 24) *ad loc.;* Festugière (above, note 5) 6ff. Androtion, *FGrHist* 324F62 (= schol. *Od.* 11.271) locates Oedipus' death and tomb "in a sanctuary of Demeter and Athena Poliouchos" at Hippios Colonus; and thus some scholars have argued that the location of the tomb in the sanctuary of the Furies was Sophocles' invention: see Jacoby on the passage from Androtion, (above, note 24) 155; Robert (above, note 23) I, 39ff. and also his remarks in *Griechische Heldensage* (= Preller-Robert, *Griechische Mythologie* II.3⁴ [Berlin 1921]) 902 and n4. But there were probably several variant legends in Sophocles' time about Oedipus' place of burial: see *Odyssey* 11.275–276, *Iliad* 23.679, and schol. on *OC* 91. One of these may have included burial in the Furies' grove. If that is Sophocles' addition, it reveals again the boldness and rightness of his mythopoeic imagination.

44. Gellie 168 suggests, "Oedipus himself is a tamed Erinys in this play." For Oedipus as *alastōr* and its grim associations (cf. Aesch., *Ag.* 1501ff., and *Septem* 723–725; Eur., *Suppl.* 835–836 and *Phoen.* 1306 and 1556) see Festugière (above, note 5) 18–20.

45. There is a persistent danger in viewing Oedipus as a kind of precursor of a Christian saint, "comme auréolé par le malheur et dégagé de toute faute" (Festugière, above, note 5, p. 5; cf. Shields, above, note 12, p. 73). See the strong warnings of Linforth (above, note 27) 100ff., with his bibliography, p. 100 n19; also D. A. Hester, "To Help

One's Friends and Harm One's Enemies: A Study in the *Oedipus at Colonus*," *Antichthon* 11 (1977) 22–41. See also Rohde (above, note 27) 455–456 and n115; Kirkwood 272; Burian (above, note 4) 426–427. This is also the just emphasis of an unpublished essay by Philip Vellacott, "Oedipus at Colonus: An Alternative View."

46. See Rosenmeyer (above, note 13) 110 and n75. Stoessl (above, note 30) 22ff. effectively stresses Oedipus' separation from his past and views the action as a series of temptations of Oedipus back into "Diesseit," away from the call into the beyond; but his interpretation rather overstresses the otherworldliness at the cost of the real violence and hatred still strong in old Oedipus.

47. For the brilliance of Athens see Pindar, frag. 64 Bowra = 76 Snell; Eur., *Medea* 824–845. In tragedy, however, such places, transfigured as sacred groves or enclosed gardens of the Muses, also embody the vulnerability, fragility, and unreality of art or other idealizing visions of life. Cf. *Trach.* 144–160 and *Ajax* 558–561 discussed above in chapters 4 and 5. Hence here at *OC* 720 we should keep in mind still the sinister associations of the grove in the Colonus ode as well as the later qualifications in the third stasimon. For a stimulating discussion of the ambiguity of the holy garden, see Pietro Pucci, *The Violence of Pity in Euripides' "Medea,"* Cornell Studies in Classical Philology 41 (Ithaca, N.Y., 1980) 116–127.

48. Sgroi (above, note 30) 287–288, "il canto della fondamentale e totale tristezza della vita umana" (287). He points out the contrast between this ode and the first stasimon, the Colonus ode. On this ode and its grim tone, see also Hester (above, note 45) 29, with his bibliography, p. 41.

49. Cf. lines 260, 279–280, 287, 1006–1007, 1125–27. Reinhardt 210 suggests that the reference to "Athens most god-revering" in 260 functions almost as a reference to this "genus" of encomiastic poetry; see also 204–206, 216.

50. On time here and its possible reference to the earlier Oedipus play, see Whitman 198–199; also Knox, *HT* 146.

51. For the contrast see Reinhardt (above, note 49)221–222; Letters 304; F. M. Wasserman, "Man and God in the *Bacchae* and in the *Oedipus at Colonus*," *Studies Presented to David Moore Robinson,* II (St. Louis 1953) 565. On the idealization of Theseus here and his relation to the idealized Theseus of Euripides, see Albin Lesky "Zwei Sophokles-Interpretationen," *Hermes* 80 (1952) 103–105.

52. For *empolis* here see Burian (above, note 4) 416–417.

53. Note also Theseus' sea image in his assurances to Oedipus, 663; see above, note 36.

54. The importance of *charis* for the *OC* is noted also by Kirkwood 244–245 and Burian (above, note 4) passim.

55. For Creon's *bia*, "violence," see also 867, 874, 903, 922.

56. For the interplay between the "fulfilling *charis*" of 1489 and the "just *charis*" of 1498, see also Burian (above, note 4) 428.

57. I follow here the reading of the mss., accepted by Jebb *ad loc.* At 1751–52 Pearson in the *OCT* prints Martin's emendation, *charis hē chthonia nyx apokeitai,* "where the night under the earth lies as a blessing," or possibly, "lies as a blessing under the earth." Though lovely in its way, this statement seems more commonplace and less appropriate to the ambiguous, mysterious quality of Oedipus' end, where hatred is as strong as peace. For further discussion see Jebb's Appendix, 295 and also Kirkwood 244 n24.

58. The contrast between the *charis* of 1106 and 1183 is characteristic of the contrast in Oedipus' relation toward his daughters and toward his sons: see Easterling (above,

note 11) 10–11; Rosenmeyer (above, note 13) 109 n71; Marie Delcourt, *Oedipe ou la légende du conquérant* (Paris 1944) chap. 2; U. von Wilamowitz-Moellendorff, *Griechische Tragödie übersetzt* I (Berlin 1899) 8.

59. On these reversals see Burian (above, note 4) 410ff., 422–424.

60. See Burian (above, note 4) 424.

61. Burian, 408–429; Vickers 472.

62. Compare e.g. 48–49 with 285–286, 428 with 1273–74 and 1278–79, and see in general Easterling (above, note 11) 7.

63. See Wilamowitz (above, note 23) 358–359, who points out how the speech reveals "den ehrgeizigen, rücksichtlosen Mann, der seine Pläne zu verfolgen weiss und an der Spitze seines stolzen Heeres des Erfolges sicher zu sein glaubt; nur den Vater muss er gewinnen, sonst ist alles verloren." Max Imhof, "Euripides' Ion und Sophokles' Oedipus auf Kolonos," *MH* 27 (1970) 83, sees here "einen Prunkstück episch-archaischer Schilderung," after the manner of the teichoskopia of *Iliad* 3.

64. For this echo of the *OT,* see B.M.W. Knox, "Sophokles' Oedipus," in *Tragic Themes in Western Literature,* ed. Cleanth Brooks (New Haven 1955) 28 and *HT* 147; also Burian (above, note 4) 429 n1; R. D. Murray, "Thought and Structure in Sophoclean Tragedy," in Thomas Woodard, ed., *Sophocles: A Collection of Critical Essays* (Englewood Cliffs, N.J., 1966) 23–28.

65. See Seidensticker (above, note 21) 268–269, comparing *OT* 300–462 and *OC* 1254–1446; Adams (above, note 30) 164; Umberto Albini, "L'ultimo atto dell' Edipo a Colono," in *Interpretazioni teatrali da Eschilo ad Aristofane* II (Florence 1976) 65 (originally published in *PP* 157, 1974, 225–231). On the danger of insisting too strongly on the links between the two Oedipus plays, however, see the cautionary remarks of Hans Strohm, Griechische Tragödie, . . . Sophokles," *AnzAlt* 26 (1973) 4–5.

66. For discussion and full bibliography, see Hester (above, note 45) 29–30 and 40; also Burian (above, note 4) 421ff.; Whitman 196–197; Letters 301–302.

67. See Rosenmeyer (above, note 13) 96.

68. See Arnold Van Gennep, *The Rites of Passage,* (1908; English trans. Chicago 1960) passim, esp. 10ff.; also Gould's essay (above, note 6).

69. Verbal self-defense: 258ff., 521ff., 960ff., and cf. 466 and 548. Ritual acts: 465ff. and 1598ff. Seidensticker (above, note 21) 263 stresses the contrast with the deep pollution of Oedipus in the *OT* See also Rosenmeyer (above, note 13) 97 (on the anti-conservative spirit of this cleansing); Reinhardt 203–204; Thomas Gould, "The Innocence of Oedipus" pt. 3, *Arion* 5 (1966) 491–494. Linforth (above, note 27) 104–109 is unconvincing in trying to view the pollution as appearing "only in residual form" (109).

70. Wilamowitz (above, note 23) 356 calls attention to the parallel with *OT* 1413–14. See also Thalia Phillies Howe, "Taboo in the Oedipus Theme," *TAPA* 93 (1962) 141; Lesky (above, note 51) 104.

71. Easterling (above, note 11) 8 has good remarks on how the plea of Polyneices has an ironical undertone which subverts his own position, recalling the wrongs of Oedipus, though she believes that he retains our sympathies. See also Knox, *HT* 159–160; Adams 173–174; Reinhardt 224–228; Vickers 473–475. A harsher view of Oedipus' curses is taken by Linforth (above, note 27) passim; Rosenmeyer (above, note 13) 97ff.; A.J.A. Waldock, *Sophocles the Dramatist* (London 1957) 226; Hester (above, note 45) passim.

72. On the importance of "throne" and "scepter," see Easterling (above, note 11) 7–10.

73. On this echo see Easterling (above, note 11) 10; Winnington-Ingram (above, note 30) 24 and his "Tragedy and Greek Archaic Thought," *Classical Drama, Essays for H.D.F. Kitto* (London 1965) 43.

74. For *patrōon* see Jebb on line 1390, who notes among the word's possible associations here the darkness "which hides Laius" and the darkness of Oedipus' blindness.

75. Easterling (above, note 11) 6, though sympathetic to Polyneices, observes the "extraordinary tastelessness and artificiality" of language, which she explains as "a kind of awkward frigidity rather than hypocrisy."

76. Antigone's *ō pai*, "O child," in this line (1420) stresses the theme of kinship.

77. On this pattern in Sophocles see Knox, *HT* chap. 1.

78. See Burian (above, note 4) 427: "Oedipus' curse stands outside the boundaries of ordinary moral judgment"; also Winnington-Ingram (above, note 30) 24.

79. Gellie 176 suggests that the function of this bleak ode is to put Oedipus into a more favorable light in the next scene, showing the sufferings of old men. An effort along these lines is also made by Hester (above, note 45) 29, with further bibliography, p. 41. The ode, however, may also suggest that point of remote contact with the absolutes of human existence, "being and nonbeing," where Oedipus stands. From that perspective, he will have little patience with quarrels for power. Still involved in family strife, he at least stands at the edge of things where these issues receive the harshest and strictest, least humane judgment.

80. See Whitman 201: "Now Oedipus comes to Athens, and there is no yelping of 'insatiable bronze-footed bloodhounds,' but only the music of the birds, as if all the past evil of the house were transformed by the mysterious forces of time and suffering into a present of tranquil beauty and a prospect of hope." See also Bacon (above, note 33) 18. From a different perspective, Lefcowitz (above, note 33) 80 sees in the return to the grove "symbolically a repetition of an earlier tabooed act or an example of what Freud calls 'repetition compulsion.' "

81. See Festugière (above, note 5) 16. The particular connotation of Oedipus' holiness is relevant here: *hieros*, unlike *hagios*, carries the connotations of strength, vitality, energy emanating from the divine rather than the notion of the fearful barrier separating the sacred from the profane, which is the sense of *hagios*: see Émile Benveniste, *Le vocabulaire des institutions indo-européennes* (Paris 1969) II, 174–207, esp. 192ff., 202ff.

82. See Knox, *Tragic Themes* (above, note 64) 29.

83. The *logos* as healing incantation is deeply rooted in Greek literature: see in general P. Laín Entralgo, *The Therapy of the Word in Classical Antiquity,* trans. L. J. Rather and J. Sharp (New Haven and London 1970) chaps. 1 and 2, esp. 47–48. See Hom., *Odyssey* 19.457–458; Pindar, *Pyth.* 3.51, *Nem.* 4.1–5; Aesch., *PV* 172; Soph., *Ajax* 581–582 and *Trach.* 1001ff.

84. On the oracles in general, see Linforth (above, note 27) 82ff. and on Oedipus' increasing oracular power see Knox, *HT* 153–154, 156, 159–160. Hester (above, note 45) 30 (also 31 n101) is right to warn against endowing Oedipus with "a quasi-divine power of justice," but is far too skeptical of his "supernatural powers of prophecy," which are clearly in the text.

85. See my "Synaesthesia in Sophocles," *Illinois Classical Studies* 2 (1977) 95–96.

86. Cf. the cries of Ajax, Heracles (in *Trachiniae*), Philoctetes; for tragedy and the limits of speech in general, see above, chapter 10, section II.

87. See Jebb on line 1271, who calls attention to the similar broken lines, 315–318. The whole passage dwells on the themes of speech and silence. See also Reinhardt 225–226.

88. The form of set speeches in this scene underlines the lack of real communication between father and son. We may contrast the *antilabai* in the discourse between brother and sister soon after: see Imhof (above, note 63) 83–84: "Unfähigkeit, auf den anderen einzugehen, ist hier die besondere Form der Einsamkeit des sophokleischen Helden" (p. 83).

89. See 815, 817, 854, 861, 867, 873, 883, 892, 960.

90. For the theme of the "small word," see Kirkwood (above, note 29) 245; also J. W. MacKail, "Sophocles," in *Lectures on Greek Poetry* (London 1910).

91. Note also the contrast between Oedipus' curse by "Tartarus' paternal darkness" in 1389–90 and the Athenian chorus' concern for their "mother earth" in 1480. For the contrasts of chthonic and Olympian, compare 1462–71 with 1556–78 and 1463–64 with 1606. For more detail see my "Synaesthesia in Sophocles" (above, note 85) 95–96; Reinhardt 234 ("eine Konzert göttlicher Stimmen, die durch Zeitalter und Religionen vom Himmel herab zu gottbegnadeten Sterblichen geredet haben"); Lesky, *TDH* 249 and 255; Albini (above, note 65) 58, 62–63; Festugière (above, note 5) 15.

92. With Jebb I follow the mss. reading at 1662, *alypēton,* "without pain," against the poorly supported *alampeton,* "without flash of light," printed by Pearson in the *OCT.*

93. E.g. Homer, *Odyssey* 1.241, 14.371; 20.77–78; in general see Rohde (above, note 27) 56–57.

94. So Wilamowitz (above, note 23) 367 and also 363.

95. So Kirkwood 272; Linforth (above, note 27) 115ff.

96. Albin Lesky, "Oidipus auf Kolonos v. 1627f.," *RhM* 103 (1960) 377–378, calls attention to the deliberate vagueness, as also in 1623. Does the first person plural, *mellomen,* "Why do we delay to go?" in 1627 imply a possible union or identification of Oedipus with these undefined supernatural powers?

97. Oliver Taplin, *Greek Tragedy in Action* (Berkeley and Los Angeles 1978) 56 (apropos of Euripides' *Bacchae*).

98. See Albini (above, note 65) 64–65.

99. Here I would severely qualify Albini's view (above, note 65) 65, that Sophocles "has pardoned the gods and sees, after their wrath, their clemency . . . The old victim receives the embrace of his persecutors, becomes one of their brothers. Sophocles has offered to his gods the opportunity to be merciful."

100. For this "religious function" of tragedy in putting the polis in touch with both its chthonic and its Olympian deities, see Winnington-Ingram (above, note 30) passim, esp. 21–22.

101. See Reinhardt 217, 229.

102. For these local appeals at the end, see Albini (above, note 65) 63.

103. For some connections between the *OC* and the *Oresteia* in their concern with Zeus and the chthonic powers, see Winnington-Ingram (above, note 30) 21–24.

104. See Reinhardt 227: "Er flucht nicht so sehr als menschliches Gefäss der allwaltenden Mächte als Kraft seines bitteren und verletzten Herzens."

105. W. W. Jaeger, *Paideia,* trans. G. Highet (New York, N.Y., 1939) I,281. For Oedipus as the essence of the tragic hero, see Aristophanes, *Frogs* 1182ff.; also Howe (above, note 70) 134.

106. Becker (above, note 10) 212 would see in the exit of Oedipus the ultimate image of the hero's tragic road of life "in seiner letzten Berechtigung und Heilung, in einer Apotheose des Tragischen."

107. See above, chapter 3.

108. "Could Sophocles have failed to see in this Oedipus an image of his own

glorious close and poetic deification?": Letters 296; see also Stoessl (above, note 30) 26: "Kaum je ist antike Tragödie zu so ergreifender Selbstaussage des Dichters geworden wie hier." See also Reinhardt 202–203. Sophocles' own involvement with the cult of heroes perhaps strengthens the possibility of the more or less conscious identification of poet and his tragic character: see Wilamowitz, *Glaube der Hellenen* (above, note 30) II,224–225, and his remarks in Tycho's *Dramatische Technik* (above, note 23) 371–372; Knox, *HT* 54–55.

109. For this paradox see Knox, *HT* 155–156.

110. W. B. Yeats, "Sailing to Byzantium." Yeats, we may recall, translated the Colonus ode.

Selected Bibliography

Myth, Ritual, Society

Benveniste, Émile. *Le vocabulaire des institutions indo-européennes* (Paris 1969), 2 vols.

Brelich, Angelo. *Paides e parthenoi,* Incunabula Graeca 36 (Rome 1969).

Burkert, Walter. "Greek Tragedy and Sacrificial Ritual." *GRBS* 7 (1966) 87–121.

———*Griechische Religion der archaischen und klassischen Epoch,* Die Religionen der Menschheit 15 (Stuttgart 1977).

———*Homo Necans: Interpretationen altgriechischen Opferriten und Mythen,* Religions-geschichtliche Versuche und Vorarbeiten 32 (Berlin 1972).

———"Jason, Hypsipyle, and New Fire at Lemnos: A Study of Myth and Ritual." *CQ* n.s. 20 (1970) 1–16.

Caldwell, Richard. "Hephaestus: A Psychological Study." *Helios* 6.1 (1978) 43–59.

———"Psychoanalysis, Structuralism, and Greek Mythology." In H. R. Garvin, ed., *Phenomenology, Structuralism, Semiology, Bucknell Review* April 1976 (Lewisburg, Pa., 1976) 209–230.

Cook, Albert. "Lévi-Strauss and Myth: A Review of *Mythologiques.*" *MLN* 91 (1976) 1099–1116.

———*Myth and Language* (Bloomington, Ind., 1980).

Delcourt, Marie. *Oedipe, ou la légende du conquérant,* Bibliothèque de la Faculté de Philosophie et de Lettres de l'Université de Liège (Liège and Paris 1944)

———*Stérilités mystérieuses et naissances maléfiques dans l'antiquité classique,* Bibliothèque de la Faculté de Philosophie et de Lettres de l'Université de Liège, fasc. 83 (Liège and Paris 1938).

———"Tydée et Mélanippe." *SMSR* 37 (1966) 139–188.

Detienne, Marcel, Jean-Pierre Vernant, et al. *La cuisine du sacrifice en pays grec* (Paris 1979).

———*Dionysos mis à mort* (Paris 1977); Eng. ed., *Dionysos Slain,* trans. M. and L. Muellner (Baltimore 1979).

———*Les jardins d'Adonis: La mythologie des aromates en Grèce* (Paris 1972); Eng. ed., *The Gardens of Adonis. Spices in Greek Mythology,* trans. J. Lloyd (London 1977).

———"La mythologie scandaleuse." *Traverses* 12 (Sept. 1978) 3–18.

Dodds, E. R. *The Greeks and the Irrational,* Sather Classical Lectures 25 (Berkeley and Los Angeles 1951).

duBois, Page. "On Horse/Men, Amazons, and Endogamy." *Arethusa* 12 (1979) 35–49.

Dumézil, Georges. *Le Crime des Lemniennes: Rites et Légendes du monde égéen* (Paris 1924).

———*Le problème des Centaures: Étude de mythologie comparée indo-européenne,* Annales du Musée Guimet, Bibliothèque d'études 41 (Paris 1929).

Eckert, Charles W. "The Festival Structure of the Orestes-Hamlet Tradition." *Comparative Literature* 15 (1963) 321–337.

Selected Bibliography

Edmunds, Lowell. "The Oedipus Myth and African Sacred Kingship." *Comparative Civilizations Review* 3 (fall 1979) 1–12.

Eliade, Mircea. *Patterns in Comparative Religion* (Cleveland and New York 1963).

Entralgo, P. Laín. *The Therapy of the Word in Classical Antiquity,* trans. L. J. Rather and J. Sharp (New Haven and London 1970).

Foucault, Michel. *Madness and Civilization,* trans. Richard Howard (1965; reprint New York, N.Y., 1973).

Freud, Sigmund. *Civilization and Its Discontents,* trans. Joan Riviere (Garden City, N.Y., 1958).

Frye, Northrop. *Anatomy of Criticism* (Princeton 1957).

Girard, René. *La violence et le sacré* (Paris 1972); Eng. ed. *Violence and the Sacred,* trans. P. Gregory (Baltimore 1977).

Gould, John. "Hiketeia." *JHS* 93 (1973) 74–103.

Guthrie, W. K. C. *A History of Greek Philosophy* II (Cambridge 1965) and III (1969).

———*In the Beginning* (Ithaca, N.Y., 1957).

Havelock, E. A. *The Liberal Temper in Greek Politics* (New Haven 1957).

Heinimann, Felix. *Nomos und Physis: Herkunft und Bedeutung einer Antithese im griechischen Denken des 5. Jahrhunderts* (Basel 1945).

Hubert, Henri and Marcel Mauss. *Sacrifice: Its Nature and Function* (1898), trans. W. D. Halls (London 1964).

Jaeger, Werner, *Paideia*², trans. Gilbert Highet (New York, N.Y., 1943–47), 3 vols.

Kirk, G. S. *Myth, Its Meaning and Function,* Sather Classical Lectures 40 (Berkeley and Los Angeles 1970).

———*The Nature of Greek Myths* (Harmondsworth 1974).

Lacey, W. K. *The Family in Classical Greece* (Ithaca, N.Y., 1968).

Leach, Edmund. *Culture and Communication* (Cambridge 1976).

Lévi-Strauss, Claude. *The Raw and the Cooked: Introduction to a Science of Mythology* I, trans. J. and D. Weightman (New York 1970).

———"The Structural Study of Myth." in *Structural Anthropology,* trans. C. Jacobson and B. G. Schoepf (Garden City, N.Y., 1967) 202–228.

Mattes, Josef. *Der Wahnsinn im griechischen Mythos und in der Dichtung bis zum Drama des fünften Jahrhunderts* (Heidelberg 1970).

Nagy, Gregory. "Phaethon, Sappho's Phaon, and the White Rock of Leukas." *HSCP* 77 (1973) 137–178.

———"Six Studies of Sacral Vocabulary Relating to the Fireplace." *HSCP* 78 (1974) 71–106.

Pachet, Pierre. "Le bâtard monstrueux." *Poétique* 12 (1972) 531–543.

Preller, L. and Carl Robert. *Griechische Mythologie*⁴ (Berlin 1894–1924).

Radermacher, Ludwig. "Zur Philoktetssage." In *Pankarpeia: Mélanges Henri Grégoire* (Brussels 1949) 503–509.

Redfield, James. *Nature and Culture in the Iliad: The Tragedy of Hector* (Chicago 1975).

Robert, Carl. *Oidipus* (Berlin 1915), 2 vols.

Rohde, Erwin. *Psyche*⁸, trans. W. B. Hillis (London 1925).

Rosellini, Michèle and Suzanne Saïd. "Usages des femmes et autres *nomoi* chez les 'sauvages' d'Hérodote: Essai de lecture structurale." *Annali della Scuola Normale Superiore di Pisa,* Classe di Lett. e Filos. 8.3 (1978) 949–1005.

Rudhardt, Jean. *Notions fondamentales de la pensée religieuse et actes constitutifs du culte dans la Grèce classique* (Geneva 1958).

——"Les mythes grecs relatifs à l'instauration du sacrifice: les rôles corrélatifs de Prométhée et de son fils Deucalion." *MH* 27 (1970) 1–15.

Scarpi, Paolo. *Letture sulla religione classica: L'inno omerico a Demeter* (Florence 1976).

Segal, Charles. "The Homeric Hymn to Aphrodite: A Structuralist Approach." *CW* 67 (1973/74) 205–212.

——"Nature and the World of Man in Greek Literature." *Arion* 2.1 (1963) 19–53.

——"The Raw and the Cooked in Greek Literature: Structure, Values, Metaphor." *CJ* (1973/74) 289–308.

——"Tragic Heroism and Sacral Kingship in Five Oedipus Plays and *Hamlet.*" *Helios* 5.1 (1977) 1–10.

Slater, Philip. *The Glory of Hera: Greek Mythology and the Greek Family* (Boston 1968).

——"The Greek Family in History and Myth." *Arethusa* 7 (1974) 9–44.

Stoessl, Franz. *Der Tod des Herakles* (Zürich 1945).

Szondi, Peter. *Versuch über das Tragische*² (Frankfurt a.M. 1964).

Turato, Fabio. *La crisi della città e l'ideologia del selvaggio nell'Atene del V secolo a.C.* (Rome 1979).

Turner, Victor. *Dramas, Fields, and Metaphors* (Ithaca, N.Y., 1974).

——*The Forest of Symbols* (Ithaca, N.Y., and London 1973).

——"Metaphors of Anti-Structure in Religious Culture." In Allan W. Eister, ed., *Changing Perspectives in the Scientific Study of Religion* (New York 1974) 63–84.

——*The Ritual Process* (1969; reprint Harmondsworth 1974).

Van Gennep, Arnold. *The Rites of Passage* (1908), trans. M. B. Vizedom and G. L. Caffee (Chicago 1960).

Vernant, J.-P. *Mythe et pensée chez les Grecs*² (Paris 1969), reissued in two volumes by Maspero (Paris 1974).

——*Mythe et société en Grèce ancienne* (Paris 1974).

——and Pierre Vidal-Naquet. *Mythe et tragédie* (Paris 1972).

——"Sacrifice et l'alimentation humaine à propos du *Prométhée* d'Hésiode." *Annali della Scuola Normale Superiore di Pisa,* Classe di Lettere e Filosofia 7 (1977) 905–940.

Vidal-Naquet, Pierre. "The Black Hunter and the Origin of the Athenian Ephebeia." *PCPS* n.s. 14 (1968) 49–64.

——"Les jeunes: Le cru, l'enfant grec et le cuit." In J. Le Goff and P. Nora, eds., *Faire de l'histoire* 3 (Paris 1974) 137–168.

——"Valeurs religieuses et mythiques de la terre et du sacrifice dans l'Odyssée." *Annales. Economies, Sociétés, Civilisation* 25 (1970) 1278–1297.

Wilamowitz-Moellendorff, U. von. *Der Glaube der Hellenen* (Berlin 1931) 2 vols.

Yamaguchi, Masao. "Kingship as a System of Myth: An Essay in Synthesis." *Diogenes* 77 (1972) 43–70.

Zeitlin, Froma I. "The Dynamics of Misogyny: Myth and Mythmaking in the *Oresteia.*" *Arethusa* 11 (1978) 149–184.

——"The Motif of the Corrupted Sacrifice in Aeschylus' *Oresteia.*" *TAPA* 96 (1965) 463–508.

——"Postscript to Sacrificial Imagery in the *Oresteia, Ag.* 1235–1237." *TAPA* 97 (1966) 645–653.

Greek Tragedy, Aeschylus, Euripides

Arrowsmith, William. "The Criticism of Greek Tragedy." *Tulane Drama Review* 3.3 (1959) 31–57.

Selected Bibliography

Becker, Otfried. *Das Bild des Weges und verwandte Vorstellung im frühgriechischen Denken,* Hermes Einzelschrift 4 (Wiesbaden 1937).

Burnett, Anne P. *Catastrophe Survived: Euripides' Plays of Mixed Reversal* (Oxford 1971).

Carrière, Jean. "Sur l'essence et l'évolution du tragique chez les Grecs." *REG* 79 (1966) 6–37.

Cook, Albert. *Enactment: Greek Tragedy* (Chicago 1971).

Festugière, A. J. "Tragédie et tombes sacrées." *Rev. de l'Histoire des Religions* 184 (1973) 3–24.

Finley, John H., Jr. "Politics and Early Attic Tragedy." *HSCP* 71 (1966) 1–13.

Goheen, R. F. "Aspects of Dramatic Symbolism: Three Studies in the *Oresteia.*" *AJP* 76 (1955) 113–137.

Guépin, Jean-Pierre. *The Tragic Paradox: Myth and Ritual in Greek Tragedy* (Amsterdam 1968).

Jones, John. *On Aristotle and Greek Tragedy* (London 1962).

Kitto, H. D. F. *Form and Meaning in Drama* (London 1956).

Knox, B. M. W. "Aeschylus and the Third Actor." *AJP* 93 (1972) 104–124.

Lattimore, Richmond. *The Poetry of Greek Tragedy* (Baltimore 1958).

Lebeck, Anne. *The Oresteia: A Study in Language and Structure* (Washington, D.C., 1971).

Lesky, Albin. *Die tragische Dichtung der Hellenen*[3] (Göttingen 1972).

Peradotto, John J. "Cledonomancy in the *Oresteia.*" *AJP* 90 (1969) 1–21.

Romilly, Jaqueline de. *L'évolution du pathétique d'Eschyle à Euripide* (Paris 1961).

———*Time in Greek Tragedy* (Ithaca, N.Y., 1968).

Ronnet, Gilberte. "Le sentiment du tragique chez les Grecs." *REG* 76 (1963) 327–336.

Saïd, Suzanne. *La faute tragique* (Paris 1978).

Schlesinger, A. C. *The Boundaries of Dionysus,* Martin Classical Lectures 17 (Cambridge, Mass., 1963).

Segal, Charles. "Pentheus and Hippolytus on the Couch and on the Grid: Psychoanalytic and Structuralist Readings of Greek Tragedy." *CW* 72 (1978/79) 129–148.

Stanford, W. B. *Ambiguity in Greek Literature* (Oxford 1939).

———*Greek Metaphor: Studies in Theory and Practice* (Oxford 1936).

Taplin, Oliver. *Greek Tragedy in Action* (Berkeley and Los Angeles 1978).

Versényi, Laszlo. *Man's Measure; A Study of the Greek Image of Man from Homer to Sophocles* (Albany, N.Y., 1974).

Vickers, Brian. *Towards Greek Tragedy* (London 1973).

Winnington-Ingram, R. P. *Euripides and Dionysus: An Interpretation of the Bacchae* (Cambridge 1948).

———"Tragedy and Greek Archaic Thought." In M. J. Anderson, ed., *Classical Drama and Its Influence, Studies Presented to H.D.F. Kitto* (New York and London 1965) 31–50.

Sophocles

Adams, S. M. "The *Ajax* of Sophocles." *Phoenix* 9 (1955) 93–110.

———*Sophocles the Playwright, Phoenix* suppl. 3 (Toronto 1957).

Albini, Umberto. "L'ultimo atto dell' Edipo a Colono." *PP* 157 (1974) 225–231; reprinted in *Interpretazioni teatrali da Eschilo ad Aristofane* II (Florence 1976) 56–65.

Alexanderson, Bengt. "On Sophocles' *Electra.*" *C & M* 27 (1966) 79–98.

————"Die Stellung des Chors in der Antigone." *Eranos* 64 (1966) 85–105.

Alt, Karin. "Schicksal und *Physis* im Philoktet des Sophokles." *Hermes* 89 (1961) 141–174.

Avery, H. C. "Heracles, Philoctetes, Neoptolemus." *Hermes* 93 (1965) 279–297.

Bacon, Helen. "Women's Two Faces: Sophocles' View of the Tragedy of Oedipus and His Family." *Science and Psychoanalysis,* Decennial Memorial Volume (New York, N.Y., 1966) 10–24, with a discussion by S. H. Fisher, 24–27.

Benardete, Seth. "A Reading of Sophocles' *Antigone." Interpretation: A Journal of Political Philosophy* 4.3 (1975) 148–196; 5.1 (1975) 1–55; 5.2 (1975) 148–184.

Beye, Charles R. "Sophocles' *Philoctetes* and the Homeric Embassy." *TAPA* 101 (1970) 63–75.

Biggs, Penelope. "The Disease Theme in Sophocles' *Ajax, Philoctetes,* and *Trachiniae." CP* 61 (1966) 223–235.

Bona, Giacomo. "*Hypsipolis* e *Apolis* nel primo stasimo dell' Antigone." *RFIC* 99 (1971) 129–148.

Bowra, C. M. *Sophoclean Tragedy* (Oxford 1944).

————"Sophocles on His Own Development." AJP 61 (1940) 385–401 = *Problems in Greek Poetry* (Oxford 1953) 108–125.

Burian, Peter. "Suppliant and Savior: Oedipus at Colonus." *Phoenix* 28 (1974) 408–429.

————"Supplication and Hero Cult in Sophocles' *Ajax,"* GRBS 13 (1972) 151–156.

Calder, W. M., III. "The End of Sophocles' *Electra." GRBS* 4 (1963) 213–216.

Camerer, Ruth. "Zu Sophokles' Aias." *Gymnasium* 60 (1953) 289–327.

Cameron, Alister. *The Identity of Oedipus the King: Five Essays on the Oedipus Tyrannus* (New York, N.Y. 1968).

Cohen, David. "The Imagery of Sophocles: A Study of Ajax's Suicide." *G & R* 25 (1978) 24–36.

Coleman, Robert. "The Role of the Chorus in Sophocles' *Antigone." PCPS* 198 (1972) 4–27.

Dalfen, Joachim. "Gesetz ist nicht Gesetz und fromm ist nicht fromm: Die Sprache der Personen in der sophokleischen Antigone." *WS* n.s. 11 (1977) 5–26.

Diller, Hans. "Göttliches und menschliches Wissen bei Sophokles." (1950) In Hans Diller, W. Schadewaldt, A. Lesky, *Gottheit und Mensch in der Tragödie des Sophokles* (Darmstadt 1963).

————"Menschendarstellung und Handlungsführung bei Sophokles." *Antike u. Abendland* 6 (1957) 157–169.

————, ed. *Sophokles,* Wege der Forschung 95 (Darmstadt 1967).

————"Über das Selbstbewusstsein der sophokleischen Personen." *WS* 69 (1956) 70–85.

Dimock, G. E., Jr. "The Name of Odysseus." *Hudson Review* 9.1 (1956) 52–70.

Dodds, E. R. "On Misunderstanding the *Oedipus Rex." G & R* 13 (1966) 37–49.

Dönt, Eugen. "Zur Deutung des Tragischen bei Sophokles." *A.u.A.* 17 (1971) 45–55.

Dugas, Charles. "La Mort du Centaure Nessos." *REA* 45 (1943) 18–26.

Easterling, P. E. "Character in Sophocles." *G & R,* ser. 2, 24 (1977) 121–129.

————"Oedipus and Polyneices." *PCPS* 193 (n.s. 13) (1967) 1–13.

————"Philoctetes and Modern Criticism." *Illinois Classical Studies* 3 (1978) 27–39.

————"Sophocles, *Trachiniae." BICS* 15 (1968) 58–69.

Ehrenberg, Victor. *Sophocles and Pericles* (Oxford 1954).

Erbse, Hartmut. "Neoptolemos und Philoktet bei Sophokles." *Hermes* 94 (1966) 177–201.

Errandonea, Ignacio. "Les quatre monologues d'*Ajax* et leur signification dramatique." *LEC* 36 (1958) 21–40.

————"Sophoclei Chori Persona Tragica." *Mnemosyne* n.s. 50.4 (1922) 369–422; 51.2 (1923) 180–201.

Feder, Lilian. "The Symbol of the Desert Island in Sophocles' *Philoctetes.*" *Drama Survey* 3 (1963) 33–41.

Ferguson, John. "Ambiguity in *Ajax.*" *Dioniso* 44 (1970) 12–29.

Fraenkel, Eduard. "Zwei Aias-Szenen hinter der Bühne," *MH* 24 (1967) 78–86.

Friedländer, Paul. "*Polla ta deina.*" *Hermes* 59 (1934) 54–63.

Fritz, Kurt von. "Haimons Liebe zu Antigone." *Philologus* 89 (1934) 18-33 = *Antike und Moderne Tragödie* (Berlin 1962) 227–240.

————"Zur Interpretation des Aias." *RhM* 83 (1934) 113–128.

Gellie, George. "The Second Stasimon of the *Oedipus Tyrannus.*"*AJP* 85 (1964) 113–123.

————*Sophocles: A Reading* (Melbourne 1972).

Goheen, R. F. *The Imagery of Sophocles' Antigone* (Princeton 1951).

Gould, Thomas. "The Innocence of Oedipus: The Philosophers on *Oedipus the King.*" *Arion* 4 (1965) 363–386; 582–611; 5 (1966) 478–525.

Grossmann, Gustav. "Das Lachen des Aias." *MH* 25 (1968) 65–85.

Harsh, P. W. "The Role of the Bow in the *Philoctetes* of Sophocles." *AJP* 81 (1960) 408–414.

Hathorn, R. Y. "Sophocles' *Antigone*: Eros in Politics." *CJ* 54 (1958–59) 109–115; reprinted in *Tragedy, Myth, and Mystery* (Bloomington, Ind., 1966) 62–78.

Hay, John. *Oedipus Tyrannus: Lame Knowledge and the Homosporic Womb* (Washington, D.C., 1978).

Hester. D. A. "Sophocles the Unphilosophical: A Study in the *Antigone.*" *Mnemosyne*, ser. 4, 24 (1971) 11–59.

————"To Help One's Friends and Harm One's Enemies: A Study in the *Oedipus at Colonus.*" *Antichthon* 11 (1977) 22–41.

Hoey, Thomas F. "The Date of the *Trachiniae.*" *Phoenix* 33 (1979) 210–232.

————"Inversion in the *Antigone*, A Note." *Arion* 9 (1970) 337–345.

————"On the Theme of Introversion in the *Oedipus Rex.*" *CJ* 64 (1968–69) 296–299.

————"Sun Symbolism in the Parodos of the *Trachiniae.*" *Arethusa* 5 (1972) 133–154.

————"The *Trachiniae* and the Unity of Hero." *Arethusa* 3 (1970) 1–22.

Howe [Feldman], Thalia Philies. "Taboo in the Oedipus Theme." *TAPA* 93 (1962) 124–143.

Imhof, Max. "Euripides' Ion und Sophokles' Oedipus auf Kolonos." *MH* 27 (1970) 65–89.

Jameson, M. H. "Politics and the *Philoctetes.*" *CP* 51 (1956) 217–227.

Johansen, Holger Friis. "Die Elektra des Sophokles: Versuch einer neuen Deutung." *C & M* 25 (1964) 8–32.

————"Sophocles, 1939–1959." *Lustrum* 7 (1962) 94–288.

Kamerbeek, J. C. "Sophocle et Héraclite." *Studia Vollgraff* (Amsterdam 1948) 84–98.

Kapsomenos, S. G. *Sophokles' Trachinierinnen und ihr Vorbild* (Athens 1963).

Kells, J. H. "Problems of Interpretation in the *Antigone.*" *BICS* 10 (1963) 47–64.

————, ed. *Sophocles, Electra* (Cambridge 1973).

Kirkwood, Gordon M. "The Dramatic Unity of Sophocles' *Trachiniae.*" *TAPA* 72 (1941) 203–211.

————"Homer and Sophocles' *Ajax.*" in M. J. Anderson, ed., *Classical Drama and Its Influence, Studies Presented to H.D.F. Kitto* (New York and London 1965) 51–70.

————*A Study of Sophoclean Drama,* Cornell Studies in Class. Philol. 31 (Ithaca, N.Y., 1958).

Kitto, H. D. F. *Poesis: Structure and Thought,* Sather Classical Lectures 36 (Berkeley and Los Angeles 1966).

———*Sophocles: Dramatist and Philosopher* (London 1958).

Knox, B. M. W. "The *Ajax* of Sophocles." *HSCP* 65 (1961) 1–37.

———*The Heroic Temper: Studies in Sophoclean Tragedy,* Sather Classical Lectures 35 (Berkeley and Los Angeles 1964).

———*Oedipus at Thebes* (New Haven 1957).

———"Sophocles' Oedipus." In *Tragic Themes in Western Literature,* ed. Cleanth Brooks (New Haven 1955) 7–29.

Lacarrière, Jacques. *Sophocle dramaturge* (Paris 1960).

Lefcowitz, B. "The Inviolate Grove." *Literature and Psychology* 17 (1967) 78–86.

Lesky, Albin. "Sophokles und das Humane." (1951) In Hans Diller, Wolfgang Schadewaldt, Albin Lesky, *Gottheit und Mensch in der Tragödie des Sophokles* (Darmstadt 1963).

Letters, F. J. H. *The Life and Work of Sophocles* (London and New York 1953).

Linforth, I. M. "Antigone and Creon." *UCPCP* 15. 5 (1961) 183–260.

———"Electra's Day in the Tragedy of Sophocles." *UCPCP* 19.2 (1963) 89–126.

———"Philoctetes: The Play and the Man." *UCPCP* 15.3 (1956) 95–156.

———"Religion and Drama in *Oedipus at Colonus.*" *UCPCP* 14.4 (1951) 75–192.

———"Three Scenes in Sophocles' *Ajax.*" *UCPCP* 15.1 (1954).

Lloyd-Jones, H. "Notes on Sophocles' *Trachiniae.*" *YCS* 22 (1972) 263–270.

———"Tycho von Wilamowitz-Moellendorff on the Dramatic Technique of Sophocles." *CQ* n.s. 22 (1972) 214–228.

Long, A. A. *Language and Thought in Sophocles: A Study in Abstract Nouns and Poetic Technique* (London 1968).

———"Poisonous Growths in *Trachiniae.*" *GRBS* 8 (1967) 275–278.

McCall, Marsh. "Divine and Human Action in Sophocles: The Two Burials of the *Antigone.*" *YCS* 22 (1972) 103–117.

McDevitt, A. S., "The Nightingale and the Olive." *WS,* Beiheft 5 = *Antidosis, Festschrift für Walther Kraus* (Vienna 1972) 227–237.

MacKay, L. A. "Antigone, Coriolanus, and Hegel." *TAPA* 93 (1962) 166–174.

MacKinnon, J. K. "Heracles' Intention in His Second Request of Hyllus: *Trach.* 1216–51." *CQ* n.s. 21 (1971) 33–41.

Minadeo, Richard W. "Plot, Theme and Meaning in Sophocles' *Electra.*" *C & M* 28 (1967) 114–142.

Moore, John. "The Dissembling-speech of Ajax." *YCS* 25 (1977) 47–66.

———*Sophocles and Arete* (Cambridge, Mass., 1938).

Müller, Gerhard. *Sophokles, Antigone* (Heidelberg 1967).

———"Überlegungen zum Chor der Antigone." *Hermes* 89 (1961) 398–422.

Musurillo, Herbert. *The Light and the Darkness: Studies in the Dramatic Poetry of Sophocles* (Leiden 1967).

Nestle, Wilhelm. "Sophokles und die Sophistik." *CP* 5 (1910) 129–157.

Newiger, Hans-Joachim. "Hofmannsthals *Elektra* und die griechische Tragödie." *Arcadia* 4 (1969) 138–163.

Parlavantza-Friederich, Ursula. *Täuschungsszenen in den Tragödien des Sophokles* (Berlin 1969).

Perrotta, G. *Sofocle* (Messina-Florence 1935).

Podlecki, A. J. "The Power of the Word in Sophocles' *Philoctetes.*" *GRBS* 7 (1966) 233–250.

Pötscher, W. "Die Oidipus-Gestalt." *Eranos* 71 (1973) 12–44.

Reinhardt, Karl. *Sophokles*[3] (Frankfurt a.M. 1947); Eng. ed., trans. H. and D. Harvey (Oxford 1979).

Robinson, D. B. "Topics in Sophocles' *Philoctetes.*" *CQ* n.s. 19 (1969) 34–56.

Rödström, P. *De Imaginibus Sophocleis a Rerum Natura Sumptis,* Diss. Uppsala (Stockholm 1883).

Ronnet, Gilberte. *Sophocle: poète tragique* (Paris 1969).

———"Sur le premier stasimon d'*Antigone,*" *REG* 80 (1967) 100–105.

Rose, H. J. "Antigone and the Bride of Corinth." *CQ* 19 (1925) 147–151.

Rose, Peter. "Sophocles' *Philoctetes* and the Teachings of the Sophists." *HSCP* 80 (1976) 49–105.

Rosenmeyer, Thomas G. *The Masks of Tragedy: Essays on Six Greek Dramas* (Austin 1963).

———"The Wrath of Oedipus." *Phoenix* 6 (1952) 92–112.

Schiassi, G. *Sofocle, Le Trachinie* (Florence 1953).

Schlesinger, Eilhard. "*Deinotēs.*" *Philologus* 91 (1936–37) 59–66.

———"Erhaltung im Untergang: Sophokles' Aias als 'pathetische' Tragödie." *Poetica* 3 (1970) 359–387.

———"Die Intrige im Aufbau von Sophokles' Philoktet." *RhM* 111 (1968) 97–156.

Schmid, Wilhelm. "Problem aus der sophokleischen Antigone." *Philologus* 62 (1903) 1–34.

Schmidt, Jens-Uwe. *Sophokles, Philoktet: Eine Strukturanalyse* (Heidelberg 1973).

Schwinge, E. R. *Die Stellung der Trachinierinnen im Werk des Sophokles,* Hypomnemata 1 (Göttingen 1962).

Seale, David. "The Element of Surprise in Sophocles' *Philoctetes.*" *BICS* 19 (1972) 94–102.

Segal, Charles. "Divino e umano nel *Filottete* di Sofocle." *QUCC* 23 (1976) 67–89.

———"The *Electra* of Sophocles." *TAPA* 97 (1966) 473–545.

———"The Hydra's Nurseling: Image and Action in the *Trachiniae.*" *AC* 44 (1975) 612–617.

———"Mariage et sacrifice dans les *Trachiniennes* de Sophocle." *AC* 44 (1975) 30–53.

———"Philoctetes and the Imperishable Piety." *Hermes* 105 (1977) 133–158.

———"Sophocles' *Antigone:* The House and the Cave." *Miscellanea di Studi in memoria di Marino Barchiesi* (Rome 1978 [publ. 1980]) 1171–88.

———"Sophocles' Praise of Man and the Conflicts of the *Antigone.*" (1964) in Thomas Woodard, ed., *Sophocles* (see infra) 62–85.

———"Sophocles' *Trachiniae:* Myth, Poetry, and Heroic Values." *YCS* 25 (1977) 99–158.

———"Synaesthesia in Sophocles." *Illinois Class. Studies* 2 (1977) 88–96.

———Visual Symbolism and Visual Effects in Sophocles." *CW* 74 (1980/81) 125–142.

Seidensticker, Bernd. "Beziehungen zwischen den beiden Oidipusdramen des Sophokles." *Hermes* 100 (1972) 255–274.

Sgroi, P. "Edipo a Colono." *Maia* 14 (1962) 283–298.

Sheppard, J. T. "*Electra:* A Defense of Sophocles." *CR* 41 (1927) 2–9.

———"*Electra* Again." *CR* 41 (1927) 163–165.

———*The Oedipus Tyrannus of Sophocles* (Cambridge 1920).

———"The Tragedy of Electra, According to Sophocles." *CQ* 12 (1918) 80–88.

Shields, M. G. "Sight and Blindness in the *Oedipus Coloneus.*" *Phoenix* 15 (1961) 63–73.

Selected Bibliography

Sicherl, Martin. "Die Tragik des Aias." *Hermes* 98 (1970) 14–37; Eng. trans., "The Tragic Issue in Sophocles' *Ajax.*" *YCS* 25 (1977) 67–98.

Simpson, Michael. "Sophocles' Ajax: His Madness and Transformation." *Arethusa* 2 (1969) 88–103.

Solmsen, Friedrich. "Electra and Orestes: Three Recognitions in Greek Tragedy." *Meded. der Konikl. Nederlandse Akad. van Wetenschappen,* Afd. Letterkunde n.s. 30.2 (1967) 31–62.

————"Zur Gestaltung des Intrigenmotivs in den Tragödien des Sophokles und Euripides." (1932) in E.-R. Schwinge, ed., *Euripides,* Wege der Forschung 89 (Darmstadt 1968) 326–344.

Spira, A. *Untersuchungen zum Deus ex Machina bei Sophokles und Euripides* (Kallmünz 1960).

Stanford, W. B. "Light and Darkness in Sophocles' *Ajax.*" *GRBS* 19 (1978) 189–197.

Steidle, Wolf. *Studien zum Antiken Drama* (Munich 1968).

Stoessl, Franz. "Der Oidipus auf Kolonos des Sophokles." *Dioniso* 40 (1966) 5–26.

Strohm, Hans. "Griechische Tragödie, 9. Fortsetzung: Sophokles." *AnzAlt* 24 (1971) 129–162.

————"Griechische Tragödie, 10. Fortsetzung: Sophokles (Nachtrag)." *AnzAlt* 26 (1973) 1–5.

Taplin, Oliver. "Significant Actions in Sophocles' *Philoctetes.*" *GRBS* 12 (1971) 25–44.

Trousson, R. "La philosophie du pouvoir dans l'*Antigone* de Sophocle." *REG* 77 (1964) 23–33.

Vellacott, Philip. *Sophocles and Oedipus: A Study of the Oedipus Tyrannus* (London 1971).

Vicaire, Paul. "Place et figure de Dionysos dans la tragédie de Sophocle." *REG* 81 (1968) 351–373.

Waldock, A.J.A. *Sophocles the Dramatist* (Cambridge 1951).

Welcker, F. G. "Über den Aias des Sophokles." *RhM* 3 (1829) 43–92, 229–364 = *Kleine Schriften* II (Bonn 1845) 264–340.

Wender, Dorothea. "The Will of the Beast: Sexual Imagery in the *Trachiniae.*" *Ramus* 3 (1974) 1–17.

Whitman, Cedric H. *Sophocles: A Study of Heroic Humanism* (Cambridge, Mass., 1951).

Wigodsky, Michael. "The 'Salvation' of Ajax." *Hermes* 90 (1962) 149–158.

Wilamowitz-Moellendorff, Tycho von. *Die Dramatische Technik des Sophokles,* Philol. Untersuch. 22 (Berlin 1917).

Wilamowitz-Moellendorff, Ulrich von. "Die beiden Elektren." *Hermes* 18 (1883) 214–263.

Winnington-Ingram, R. P. "The 'Electra' of Sophocles: Prolegomenon to an Interpretation." *PCPS* 183 (1954–55) 20–26.

————"A Religious Function of Greek Tragedy: A Study in the *Oedipus Coloneus* and the *Oresteia.*" *JHS* 74 (1954) 16–24.

————*Sophocles: An Interpretation* (Cambridge 1980).

Woodard, Thomas M. "*Electra* by Sophocles: the Dialectical Design." *HSCP* 68 (1964) 163–205 and 70 (1965) 195–233.

————ed., *Sophocles: A Collection of Critical Essays* (Englewood Cliffs, N.J., 1966).

Index Locorum

Aeschylus
Agam. 914–925: 56
Agam. 1072, 1202ff.: 58
Agam. 1343–44: 285
Agam. 1344–45: 262
Agam. 1382: 72
Agam. 1387: 16
Agam. 1388–93: 41, 261
Agam. 1392: 16
Agam. 1415ff.: 16, 194
Agam. 1447: 16
Agam. 1580–81: 72, 270
Agam. 1611: 270
Agam. 1654ff.: 262
Choeph. 433ff.: 273
Choeph. 470–474: 34
Choeph. 585–638: 57
Choeph. 629ff.: 307
Choeph. 753–762: 31
Eum. 13–14: 33
Eum. 131–133: 57
Eum. 191–197, 803, 911: 33
Eum. 968–975: 57
Persians 181–196: 29
PV 484–500: 158
PV 593ff.: 54
Septem 531ff.: 31
Antimachus of Colophon
46Wyss = 44Kinkel: 305
Aristophanes
Frogs 1080–86: 53
Aristotle
EN 7.1145a 15ff.: 13
Pol. 1.1253a 2–7, 25–29: 13
Pol. 3.1284a 3–12: 13

Bacchylides
11: 36–37
16.17ff.: 62

Democritus
68B5 DK: 33
68B70 DK: 31
68B117 DK: 56
Demosthenes
Against Neaera 122: 64

Dio Chrysostom
59.5: 296
59.11: 299
Diodorus
1.8.5: 33

Euripides
Bacchae 699–702: 32, 49
Bacchae 726–727: 49
Bacchae 1104: 91
Bacchae 1197: 54
Bacchae 1206: 91
Cyc. 113–124: 90–91, 297, 298, 300
Cyc. 297ff.: 305
Cyc. 369–373: 271
Helen 1049–52: 286
HF: 38
HF 869–870, 892, 897, 996–1000: 37
HF 1210–12: 35
Hipp. 1423–30: 50
Ion 10–11: 75
Iph. Taur. 285–300: 141
Iph. Taur. 670–671: 44
Medea 819: 54
Medea 824–845: 5
Medea 1342–43, 1358: 50
Orestes 226, 387: 35
Phoenissae 807: 238
Phoenissae 1760: 238
Supp. 211–213: 158
Troades 44: 75
Troades 436: 34
Eustathius
on Iliad 2.723: 326

Hellanicus
FGrHist 4F 71a: 311
FGrHist 4F 187b: 29–30
Heraclitus
B119 DK: 8
Herodotus
1.110–111: 224
1.207: 44
3.99–100, 101: 29
4.184: 212
6.87: 327
8.115.2: 33

499

Index Locorum

Seneca
  Thyestes 772–775: 71
Servius
  on *Aen.* 3.402: 313, 327
Soph.
  Frag. 24P = 872N: 65
  Frag. 384P = 353N: 309
  Frag. 432P = 399N: 4
  Frag. 479P = 438N: 4
  Frag. 799P = 731N; 34, 39

Theognis
  1290–94, 31
Thucydides
  3.36.4: 34
  3.81–82: 5, 6, 34
  3.82–83: 95

Virgil
  Aen. 8.290–291: 61

General Index

Achilles, 32
Acrisius, 36
Adonis, 31
Aeneas, 23–24, 31; and Dido, 79
Aeschylus, 7; *Agamemnon*, 11, 45;
    Eumenides, 33; *Oresteia*, 12, 15, 19,
    28; *Persians*, 29; *Septem*, 31
Agamemnon, 16; *Trach.*, 75
Agave, 28
agriculture, 9, 25, 27, 29, 31, 33, 36;
    Antig., 172–173, 197–198; *Phil.*,
    300–301, 324–325; *Trach.*, 62–63,
    75, 83, 90–91
Agrios, 1, 32–33, 315
Ajax: and Electra, 266; *Iliad*, 112–113,
    148
Alcestis, 28
Alcman, cosmogony of, 441n10
Amazons, 30
Anaxagoras, 5
Anchises, 22–23, 31
Antigone, and Electra, 266
Antiphon the Sophist, 5–6
Aphrodite, 22–23
Apollo, 26–27, 33, 218, 281;
    Epikourios, 1; *Trach.*, 75
apotheosis: *Trach.*, 99–102
Ares, 218
Aristophanes, 51–52; *Frogs*, 53
Aristotle: and tragedy, 8; *Ethics*, 13;
    Politics, 13
Artemis, 32, 218, 281, 309
Atalante, 31
Athena, 26–27, 33, 218; *Phil.*, 309
auto-compounds, 448n103
autochthony, 453n155

Bacchylides, 18, 239; *Ode XI*, 35–36
Bassae, 1
beast: *Ajax*, 129–131, 139; *Antig.*,
    157–158; *Elec.*, 269–270; *OT*, 211,
    216–217, 223–224; *Trach.*, 95–98,
    104–105
beast-man, 87–88
Bellerophon, 3
Bendis: *Phil.*, 309
bestiality: *Trach.*, 77–79

birth: *Trach.*, 74
boundary: *OC*, 369–376
bow: *Phil.*, 298–300, 318–322,
    345–346, 349
burial: *Ajax*, 143–146, 149–151; *Antig.*,
    157–161, 173–176; double b. in
    Antig., 159–160, 442n25; *Elec.*,
    270–271, 272–278

Cabiri: *Phil.*, 301, 310, 311, 314
Cabirus, 308; *Phil.*, 314
cannibalism, 29–30, 32, 34–35, 39–40
Cassandra: *Trach.*, 75
cave: *Phil.*, 358–360
Centaurs, 2–3, 30, 33, 87–88; *Trach.*,
    91–92
Cephalus, 31
change: *Phil.*, 340–344
character, 8–9, 479n65; *Phil.*, 294, 318
charis: *Ajax*, 136–137; *OC*, 380–382,
    401, 402–403
child, 31; *OT*, 221
Choephoroe, and *Elec.*, 273
choral lyric, 10
Chryse: *Phil.*, 308–312
Circe, 61; and Deianeira, 92; and
    Odysseus, 79
civilization, 61–62; *Ajax*, 111, 127,
    131–133, 145–148, 150; *Antig.*,
    152–155, 158, 160–161, 167, 168,
    170, 190, 192, 196, 201–202, 204;
    definition of, 2–4, 60–61; *Elec.*,
    249–250, 257, 267, 291; and *eros*,
    449n121; Greek theories of, 4–5,
    29–30, 39; *OC*, 376–378, 379–380,
    405, 406–407; *OT*, 207, 218–219,
    221–223, 232; *Phil.*, 293–294,
    297–299, 303–307; relation to
    violence, 6–7, 42; *Trach.*, 89–92,
    102–104
Clytaemnestra, 16; and Antigone, 195;
    and Deianeira, 88; and family, 82;
    Trach., 73
Cocteau, Jean, 11
code, 14–16, 19, 56
Colonus, grove of, 371–376, 391–392,
    482n31, 483n43, 484n47

Martin Classical Lectures